The Scramble for China

ROBERT BICKERS

The Scramble for China

Foreign Devils in the Qing Empire,
1832–1914

ALLEN LANE
an imprint of
PENGUIN BOOKS

ALLEN LANE

Published by the Penguin Group
Penguin Books Ltd, 80 Strand, London WC2R ORL, England
Penguin Group (USA) Inc., 375 Hudson Street, New York, New York 10014, USA
Penguin Group (Canada), 90 Eglinton Avenue East, Suite 700, Toronto, Ontario,
Canada M4P 2Y3 (a division of Pearson Canada Inc.)
Penguin Ireland, 25 St Stephen's Green, Dublin 2, Ireland (a division of Penguin Books Ltd)
Penguin Group (Australia), 250 Camberwell Road, Camberwell, Victoria 3124,
Australia (a division of Pearson Australia Group Pty Ltd)
Penguin Books India Pvt Ltd, 11 Community Centre,
Panchsheel Park, New Dehli – 110 017, India
Penguin Group (NZ), 67 Apollo Drive, Auckland 0632, New Zealand
(a division of Pearson New Zealand Ltd)
Penguin Books (South Africa) (Pty) Ltd, 24 Sturdee Avenue,
Rosebank 2196, South Africa

Penguin Books Ltd, Registered Offices: 80 Strand, London WC2R ORL, England

www.penguin.com

First published 2011
2

Set in 10.5/14 pt Linotype Sabon
Typeset by Ellipsis Books Limited, Glasgow
Printed in England by Clays Ltd, St Ives plc

ISBN: 978-0-713-99749-1

www.greenpenguin.co.uk

Mixed Sources
Product group from well-managed
forests and other controlled sources
www.fsc.org Cert no. SA-COC-1592
© 1996 Forest Stewardship Council

Penguin Books is committed to a sustainable future
for our business, our readers and our planet.
The book in your hands is made from paper
certified by the Forest Stewardship Council.

For Kate, Lily and Arthur

Empire Day, when we try to remember the names of all those ... who so gallantly gave their lives to keep China British.

Monty Python, *The Meaning of Life*, Part II

Contents

List of Illustrations

Images 3, 16, 18, 19, 26, 27 and 29 can also be viewed with similar photographs and additional information at the *Historical Photographs of China* website: http://chp.ish-lyon.cnrs.fr

List of Maps and Figures

Introduction

Lester Little was the last man out. The fifth foreign inspector-general of the Chinese Maritime Customs Service announced his resignation on 10 December 1949, to take effect after six months' leave that would start on 1 January 1950. By the time he handed over his office there were no other foreign employees left in the service.[1] Over ninety years of involvement in this Chinese state agency by a total of 11,000 foreign nationals drew to a close at a refugee headquarters on the island of Taiwan. Little, an American, posed for a final photograph with his senior Chinese colleagues, and sailed out on a Jardine, Matheson & Co. steamer to Hong Kong; from there he shipped across the Pacific back to the United States. Little and his British private secretary who stood there in the group with him, Elsie Danson, had the option of leaving and making their way home or onwards, a choice denied to most of his Chinese colleagues. As the confident armies of the Communist Party grew in strength after 1945, the exhausted Chinese Nationalist state had begun to collapse. Its own forces were defeated in battle, or slunk off and aligned themselves with their former enemies. In the Customs headquarters in Shanghai a secret Communist cell was formed to prepare to take over the organization. While they did so Customs vessels shipped tremendous cargoes of bullion to Taiwan to fund the refugee government and the expected future reconquest of the mainland. After evacuating Shanghai in April 1949, and moving to Canton in the south, Little had been instructed to move on himself to Taiwan in October 1949, following his Chinese superiors and their gold. Weeks later, his patience exhausted, most of his men now stationed in areas under Communist control, and all of his foreign employees paid off, Little concluded that he was superfluous and sent his resignation to the Minister of Finance. For the foreign actors in China's drama it was time to go.

Some of that paragraph seems surreal today: a foreign national in charge of a Chinese government agency which in fact was often the single biggest source of state revenue – and he was the fifth to hold the post over a ninety-year period. Eleven thousand others served at one time or another. How had this come about, and why? Answering that question is one of the aims of this book, and it requires an understanding of the world foreigners created in China. Assessing that world's impact and legacy are other aims, both its impact in China today and its legacy for that country's foreign relations. Its thousands of private legacies need remembering too. Almost sixty years after 1949, in a quiet lane in Greenwich, Connecticut, the accoutrements and mementoes of Little's China career were spread out on a polished table for me to examine. Two miniature flags which had once graced his service desk, the standard of the Chinese republic and the ensign of the inspector-general – the 'IG', as he was known – were brought down from an upstairs windowsill. A small shrine to an official Chinese life was assembled in this American dining room, one already decorated with knick-knacks and curios brought back from the country. There were photographs and testimonials, there were Little's letters and his books; and his diaries lay there also, a private and personal record of forty years' service under Chinese flags. Little's daughter prepared all this for me, and we talked over lunch about the foreign life in China, of the Customs Service world, of her childhood and of her own adult life in Shanghai in the later 1940s, when her husband worked for an American bank and they lived in the inspector-general's large mansion. Scrapbooks documenting the varied minutiae of a childhood in Shanghai lined her office wall. Here were bus and concert tickets, invitations and keepsakes, documents from the Shanghai American School, which she attended, records of a world that was destroyed by the Japanese war and the Communist revolution, and which was then forgotten by most. Little himself kept an advisorship for a few more years, but then retired from the active China fray. Even then, however, and later in the 1960s and 1970s, he turned his attention to keeping alive a better memory of the impact and character of his old service than that which was broadcast from China. He wrote to the press, talked to historians and aided research into the Maritime Customs and its role in China's modern history. He died in 1981.

The IG's house still stands, and the offices and other installations of the Customs Service too, dotted across the changed city. On the riverfront Bund the magnificent 1927 Shanghai Customs House, topped with its striking clock tower, no longer dominates the skyline. Five large bells shipped from England still rest in the upper reaches of the building, but modern loudspeakers instead shout over the city traffic, a futile contribution to the modern Shanghai symphony. Across the Huangpu river the towers of the Pudong district now soar high above the once fêted Bund, where all bar one of the old array of buildings which moulded the vision of the city in Chinese and foreign eyes still stand. Once they headquartered businesses which dominated the city – Jardines, Hongkong and Shanghai Bank, Butterfield & Swire – and whose foreign managers also ran its Municipal Council in their spare time. Now they mostly house high-end shops and expensive restaurants.[2] The Customs House is still home to the Shanghai Customs, however. The staff who work there still pass underneath the gleaming mosaics that decorate the entrance hall, pictures of an array of Chinese junks that testify to one of the more appealing obsessions of Little's predecessor, Ulsterman Sir Frederick Maze (who also commissioned large wooden models of junk types still to be found in European and American museums). The bells no longer strike the Westminster chimes once heard across this Chinese city, and the statue of the greatest of the inspector-generals, Maze's uncle Sir Robert Hart, was carefully winched off its plinth in 1943 and eventually consumed in the metals shortage at the close of the war. But the Customs functions efficiently, the present-day successor to the old Commissioner occupying the exact same office as his pre-revolutionary predecessors, although the view outside has changed and a massive new building houses the bulk of the service's operations across the river. The service traces its family history back through Little, Maze and Hart, and those 11,000 foreign nationals who served at some point between 1854 and Little's departure – these foreign-dominated years are an accepted part of its history. The China that so robustly re-emerged into international society after the closed decade that followed the outbreak of the Cultural Revolution in 1966, was partly made by men like Hart and Little, who tried to shape it according to their own visions of its future and place, and by the ordinary men and women who served under them.

In homes all over North America, and in Europe, Australia and New Zealand, indeed anywhere across the global diaspora of the Europeans, you can find these little collections, remnants of foreign lives lived in China. Most who worked as adults in that era have passed away, but many of their children still thrive, and many more of their families store the paraphernalia and memorabilia of their life in that other Chinese world, the internationalized country that was lost sight of during the early decades of the new People's Republic led by Mao Zedong. In what was termed 'New China' after 1949, the 'old' was bad, and those foreigners who had not left when the Communists triumphed were slowly but steadily manoeuvred towards departure. The big companies surrendered their assets, their buildings and plants, and recalled their foreign staff. Banks became party headquarters; race clubs were turned into museums. The corruptions and decadence of the past were rectified in the new society. So Party cadres sat where managers once lounged, wholesome folk music replaced nightclub jazz, and socialist realism graced the walls of the members' boxes.[3] Even the dead were disturbed – cemeteries were relocated, or simply turned into parks. Cultural Revolution 'Red Guards', Mao Zedong's revolutionary shock troops, smashed those remaining during the upheaval he championed. Not much else was actually destroyed, though, at least not until the urban redevelopment of the 1990s and after, when China's cities were levelled by the demolition gangs. And even though the foreign company names incised in stone on facades and foundation stones were often scraped away, you could still spot them, and the buildings themselves were granite testament to another world. As China's building boom continues you can find still standing some of the buildings which testify to the pervasive reach, achievement and ambition of the foreign establishment that was built up in China after the wars of the mid nineteenth century. They are dwarfed by the glass and steel towers of resurgent China, but they once stood tall and had their say.

This book revisits that world. It is not the first to do so. On Chinese bookshop and library shelves you can find its history recounted in books with titles like *A Century of National Humiliation*. There is even a *Dictionary of National Humiliation*, a handy catalogue of infamy. Putting your finger on that massacre, this treaty, or those 'incidents' takes but moments. But while the finer details might need looking up, all China knows the grand narrative off by heart. In academic and popular texts, in museums and in schools, in conversation and blog, the story continues to be told. It goes like this: unequal treaties were forced on China at gunpoint by foreign imperialists, and accepted by their craven collaborators, the decadent, feudal Manchu emperors, warlords and deracinated bureaucratic capitalists. The country's modern development was skewed by such impositions. Territory was seized, and sovereignty elsewhere was almost fatally impaired. The Customs IG, Robert Hart, was an imperialist agent, running the service to further British ambitions in China. Foreign residents of treaty-signing powers enjoyed the benefits of extraterritoriality – they were outside Chinese legal jurisdiction, subject only to the laws of their homelands and the authority of their consuls and diplomats – and abused their status with gusto. A score of mini statelets under foreign control grew in Chinese coastal cities and deep inland. Imperialists strutted these Chinese streets or lounged along them in rickshaws. Their enterprises and the comforts of their daily lives were based on exploiting and humiliating the Chinese – exploiting their poor, starving rickshaw pullers – and corrupting China's leaders. Foreign missionaries turned Chinese converts against their own culture and communities. Hundreds of thousands of people across the vast mass of China lost their lives through war and invasion, and in their grim, hungry aftermaths. The catalogue of conflict is crowded: the Anglo-Chinese opium wars (1839–42, 1857–60), the Sino-French (1884–5) and Sino-Japanese wars (1894–5); the Boxer uprising and war (1900–1901), when troops from eight foreign states invaded north China; the subsequent Russian occupation of Manchuria and the bloody Allied 'punishment' expeditions. And then, above all, there was the Japanese invasion of the northeast from 1931, and of China more widely from 1937. Russia and Japan fought on and over Chinese territory in 1904–5, and again at Nomonhan in 1939. Britain, Japan and Germany fought in Qingdao in 1914. People suffered, and culture suffered. Priceless treasures and relics were looted or destroyed; libraries were burned. The glorious Summer Palace of the ruling Manchus was vindictively and systematically destroyed in 1860, to 'punish' the defeated court. Caravans of plunder made their way to the coast and then to Europe and America. The absolute centre of power and authority, the imperial palace in Peking, was seized and occupied in 1900. Foreign soldiers marched in victory through the gates; their officers snapped themselves posing on thrones. Almost four decades later Japanese soldiers marched again through a Chinese capital, this time the bestially traumatized city of Nanjing in December 1937. What cruelty could be inflicted, was inflicted on China and its suffering people, and where technology and science innovated, tragedy in China followed: aerial bombing of undefended cities, even biological warfare experiments. The country was weakened; its very existence seemed threatened. At the turn of the twentieth century many feared the extinction of the Chinese state, and feared that China, like an Asian Poland, would cease to exist as European predators and Japan carved away slices of the 'Chinese melon'. The *Dictionary of National Humiliation* is no slim volume: it is one and a half inches thick.

The foreign residents of China had their own version to tell, however, and did so in their memorials and ceremonies, in public gatherings and sharply worded private notes to diplomats. There is no matching dictionary, but they celebrated and surveyed their achievements and spoke of their famous men in print, and they designed their buildings to tell of their power and of their success.[4] They found, they recorded, a closed and hostile society, which walled them out of its cities and stoned them on its streets. In desultory compliance with the letter of the treaties it allotted these unwelcome foreign guests sterile mudflats to build on, a 'wilderness of marshes' which they made good. They constructed roads, drains and jetties, smart banks, busy business '*hongs*' (offices) and 'godowns' (warehouses), churches, schools and clubs. They developed efficient and democratic municipal councils to order the streets and oversee the police, the public health officers and schools, and in time most of the functions of good local government. They made, they like to recall, excellent harbours, 'bunding' the water fronts, dredging the silt, constructing lighting systems, and devising rational procedures for the arrival and despatch of goods and people. They built railways, made maps and charts, and ordered all that they saw. They brought regularity and rationality, sanitation and salvation, science, revelation, and culture. They found, they said, a once fine civilization in decline, the 'sick man of Asia', and they raised him up. Men like Hart and his staff had China's best interests at heart, but official obstructionism and populist xenophobia sometimes collided in anti-foreign outbreaks, which had to be managed by foreign marines and gunboats. They did not want to fight, recalled the foreigners, but by jingo when they had to they fought firmly and fairly. They were there to help China, to bring it out into the world, and while they had every sympathy for the good people of Cathay, they often had little for their corrupt rulers. The men from the West had their rights under treaty, and they wrote, lobbied and sometimes demonstrated to preserve them. They knew and spoke for China, they said, and they knew the Chinese, knew the Chinese better even than they really knew themselves. They dominated reporting on the country, advised its presidents and warlords, reformed its currency, saved its souls, and healed its sick. They were proud of what they had done. They made Shanghai, they claimed; they built up great cities from those stinking mudflats, constructed hospitals and universities, brought employment, and aided what they saw as the reform and the modernization of China's government, society and culture. They saved China from itself, and they helped it save itself from its enemies. Why, they ask, does no one thank them?

Reconciling these accounts of modern China's entangled history might seem an impossible, if not a pointless exercise.[5] Even with its uncompromising language stripped away, there is enough in the *Dictionary*'s roll-call of shame to cause even the most sceptical observers to pause, for much of what it records is incontestable fact, however alienating we might find the approach. And if pungently anti-imperialist accounts fail to convince, there is often very much in the archives and all the various documents of the foreign enterprise in pre–1949 China that can shock, even material lodged in otherwise harmless looking papers. There is evidence enough of racism, rape, murder, brutality on the field of battle and off it, harsh justice and harsh judgement. But more insidiously, perhaps, the daily round on the China coast was clearly infected with the routine violence of everyday colonialism and its blunt thinking, its blunt talk, and its blunt and often bloody action. The bars and clubrooms, the swimming baths, parks, gardens, Bund-side lawns and ships' cabins they built and celebrated were very often segregated. It is most unlikely that anybody ever put up a sign that read 'No dogs or Chinese' in the public gardens on Shanghai's waterfront, but everybody knew, even the illiterate, that that was what the signs really hissed in between the neutrally phrased regulations that ordered the use of city parks. 'Gentlemen' and 'Chinese' said the notices outside the doors of the Sassoon Building's toilets in downtown Shanghai in 1933.[6] In private, in their houses, the 'missee' might battle with the cook, and the master hit the servant. Most of their interaction was a converse of confusion as usually neither spoke the other's language. It could be out of Africa, or out of India. We are vaguely aware of the Chinese stage of imperialist play, but the detail mostly escapes us. The sorry tale of opium is lodged in the popular mind, although it found a firm grip too in representations of Chinese as the source of narcotic evil, not its victims.[7] Only the Japanese assault on China strikes a readily persistent note, but that is because it chimes with European and US experiences of the lightning Japanese strikes in 1941–2 and the atrocities and captivities of the Pacific War which affected Europeans and Americans. Solidarity in wartime against a common enemy obscured the tensions and conflicts that marked China's relations with its new allies, and Chinese relations with their foreign guests.

But now that we are all post-imperialists, we think, now that we have sufficient distance from the time, and old wounds have healed, perhaps (some might, and do, suggest) we can see past the celebratory language of the old China hands, which we can all agree overstates its case, and find kernels of truth in some of what they said. Perhaps we can think about agreeing that, given the different standards and contexts of their times, they were just doing their jobs, and all things taken into consideration we should not judge them by twenty-first century standards. They did build; they did bring to China new ideas and new things, new practices and new opportunities, and they helped make modern China what it became. Even some in China have adopted this approach. As post-Cultural Revolution, if not post-Socialist, China reintegrates itself fully back into the global economy, all sorts of institutions and enterprises reclaim a foreign heritage that was once suppressed or traduced. 'New China' has reclaimed some of the terrain of the old. And it has done so in English as well as in Chinese. Tsingtao Beer – China's leading brand – commemorated its centenary in 2003, its local and its global marketing stressing with pride its origins as the

8

product of the Anglo-Germania Brauerie Company. The Shanghai Symphony Orchestra laid out its 120-year history in 2001, with a survey that fully integrated its 60-year history as the 'Town' and 'Public Band', and then 'Municipal Orchestra', the cultural flagship of the foreign-controlled Shanghai Municipal Council. Cosmopolitan credentials might thereby be secured for beer and brass alike.[8] There are no denunciations here, no settling of the anti-imperialist scores, just the plain facts that the old China hands might have laid out themselves. See, the latter might add, due acknowledgement of our contribution is now forthcoming. We are thanked at last.

They might add that surely no one thinks about any of this any more in that old way, and overseas who really thinks about it at all, except the historians who dredge it up again and again, pedants that they are. In Britain the return of the Crown Colony of Hong Kong in 1997 perhaps marked a high point in public memory of the inequities of – or at least the broad shape of – the past relationship with China (and how anodyne the word 'relationship' itself can seem). But the handover was a largely ephemeral moment, and the early and even the more recent colonial history of Hong Kong were only vaguely understood. The sight of the last British governor's departure on the last royal yacht from one of the last colonies was a quaint anachronism in 1990s Britain, and quickly forgotten. And on the whole the British picture of the imperial past is dominated by India or Africa, or, less clearly for many, by the Anglophone world – the former Dominion territories: Australia, Canada and New Zealand. Continental European memories have even less space for China. German Qingdao, Frenchtown Shanghai, the Belgian and Italian concessions at Tianjin are mostly forgotten outside universities or are only just being revisited. The Cold War largely defined the shape of US representations of the recent Chinese past, although there Protestant missionaries and their supporters had a bigger influence than elsewhere.[9] As China resumes its central place in the global economy, as a global China fever takes hold, then all of this surely becomes simply history, done and dusted in foreign eyes. China now and China next provide the preferred focus, not China then. We want to understand how China works, how it thinks, where it is going and where it is taking us all. We need to think about how global politics will change as China grows stronger and wealthier.

Disagreements over Burma and Sudan, Tibet or Taiwan, already herald a significant new variable in the post-Cold war world. The present is the key thing, then, not this half-remembered, barely thought-of past. China's historic humiliations do not matter.

But in fact we cannot understand the resurgence of China now, and its sometimes quiet, sometimes raucous and foul-mouthed anger at the world, unless we understand the traumatic century which followed the first opium war, however much it might seem mere history. For mere history matters in modern China, and the past is unfinished business. The Tsingtao Brewery and the Shanghai Symphony Orchestra remember the past, but so does the state. The preamble to the country's constitution outlines this vision of a country reduced gradually to a state of what was termed 'semi-colonial' weakness from which it was saved by the Chinese people who overthrew imperialism and its Chinese allies 'through hard, protracted and tortuous struggle, armed and otherwise'. The memory of the era of National Humiliation is embedded then in the state's very articulation of itself, and its *raison d'être*. It is also present in the way its diplomats react to foreign criticisms of China's foreign or domestic policies, and in the way individual citizens debate their sense of their country's place in the world and in the inflamed world of the chatrooms and blogs. It is embedded in the country's teaching of its young as a key part of a nationwide 'patriotic education' campaign, consolidated over years of instruction into a roll-call of foreign wrong and Chinese humiliation.[10] Certainly the sites of the old foreign establishment that remain seem harmless enough, mostly either unimpressive – except that they seem unusual sights to be found where a visitor might expect something 'Chinese-looking' – or else pompous, overblown statements of importance echoing down to the present from this otherwise dismembered past. Their inhabitants, the Lester Littles and Elsie Dansons amongst them, hardly seem to fit the parts allotted them in the grim tale of national disaster and foreign aggression. And indeed, much of the story of China's open century bears other interpretations. While some – many – of those involved in and with the country were idealists aiming one way or another to aid China and its peoples (albeit aid it in their terms), for most of them being in China was a sort of accident of global history. As the foreign establishment grew it became a normal part of the global networks that developed in the nineteenth century, and a perfectly ordinary place to find work as a nurse, teacher, typist, Customs officer, policeman, salesman or clerk. There were spasms of an earlier China fever, when fortunes were thought to be waiting for any who could get there and graft a while, but it was more often than not a more ordered and predictable world. Did Elsie Danson, stenographer and PA, really inflict such harm on modern China as is recorded in the thick annals of humiliation? In some eyes, yes; and bridging these versions of modern China's experience – the ordinary, the accidental and the traumatic – is essential if we want to get inside the country's modern mind, and if we want to understand the course of its modern history.

This book charts a century of Sino-foreign interaction, confrontation and confusion, from 1832, a year of augury, when British ships sailed north into forbidden Chinese waters from the Canton delta, carrying pamphlets, textiles and opium, through decades of change that unfolded thereafter. Three of those ships belonged to the same firm that carried Little out of his China service in 1950; Jardine, Matheson & Co., still active today in China and occupying a suite of offices in the heart of the City of London. This was a connected world, and the continuities are important, but there was no grand scheme, design or plot. There was no imperial 'project' at the heart of this story, unless European and American history in the nineteenth century can itself be accounted a project. There were certainly some consistent inclinations and responses amongst the actors in this story, and sufficient repetition in their actions and statements to demand notice, but contingent event, opportunity, and even defeat, gave equally as much shape to the world that developed. My narrative follows the course of events of the untidy, unplanned scramble for China. The chase was joined by missionaries, merchants and mercenaries, by Britons, Americans, Russians, Parsees, and Malacca-born Chinese, by all comers from all corners. The Qing empire which ruled China had not been closed to foreign intercourse before 1832, but it regulated it tightly, and restricted it to one point on its coastal periphery. After 1842 those controls were sharply degraded, and communities of foreigners and their Chinese allies and partners developed in major coastal cities, eventually as far north as Tianjin, the coastal gateway to the imperial capital at Peking. The growth of these settlements, their travails and their impact on

Sino-foreign relations is the subject of this book, which seeks to explain how and why this slice of Chinese and of world history still matters. How was it, for example, that such a post as Customs inspector-general came to be held by a foreign national, indeed held until 1943 by a Briton through bilateral diplomatic agreement. What had happened? This is a report from the inside, and from the belly of a strange-looking beast. This was not the terrain of formal British or French empire, but it was not 'not-empire'. The Qing and their successors ruled independent states, and yet they were not wholly so. This new world they hosted within their borders was intimately tied to and fed off a growing chain of foreign empires. Chinese possessions were accounted in the swag bags of imperial powers and marked as such on maps of empire in French, English, Russian, Japanese and other scripts. But at the same time this was also a plural enterprise, multinational and multilingual, though English, or rather Englishes, outspoke the rest and outshouted them too. It was global in its connections, but usually parochial in its vision. It peaked in influence and power as a multinational enterprise in the summer of 1913, when more than ever before foreign actors controlled Chinese government finances, but when the evolving shape of local and national politics was at the same time countering effectively the assumptions and ambitions of the foreign presence. We shall follow the course of events from a decisive moment in 1832, through to that moment of greatest foreign ascendancy and the beginning of the end of this dark, complex phase in modern China's history.

Lester Little himself certainly arrived more or less by accident, and he had no sense that he would stay for the best part of four decades. He joined the Customs in October 1914 when it was at the peak of its power and influence. That same month six other Americans, nine Britons, four Danes, a Finn, an Italian, two Norwegians and a Swede also joined, alongside five Chinese. This was a pretty representative random sample, skewed only by the absence of German recruits. A good number of those had joined every year instead of returning home from the German naval colony at Qingdao after completion of their military service, but their numbers were down as the war bit, although Briton and German worked side by side in the Customs until China declared war on Germany in 1917. Little was a Dartmouth College graduate, and a chance encounter had brought notice of the Customs his way. Even so, 'Going to China in those days,' he later joked, 'was like going to the moon.'[11] It seemed an outlandish place to choose to work in, made all the odder for an American by the intense Britishness of the world he found himself in once he got there. This was unfamiliar and uncomfortable at first, but Little got used to it. His path to that photograph in Taibei took him via language study in Nanjing, postings to Xiamen (Amoy), Peking, Tianjin, Shanghai, a coveted Commissionership at Canton in 1934, and then the tricky business of running the service from 1943 onwards. Little outlasted all of those who joined that October. One Tidewaiter stayed less than a month, but other recruits lasted over thirty years. By contrast to Little, Elsie Danson, one of a handful of foreign women on the Customs books, was Shanghai-born, and Shanghai-rooted. She began working for the Customs in March 1931 as a stenographer, and her sister joined her two years later. Their father George, son of a colliery manager, had been a policeman working for the foreign-run Municipal Council at Shanghai for about fifteen years until his dismissal in 1905, and he then worked for the Harbour Conservancy Board, dying in Shanghai in 1937.[12] Elsie's departure from the Customs in 1949 marked the departure of the family from a sixty year residence in China.

These different paths to China, and to the entrance to Taipei's Customs House, tell us something about the varied shape of the world the foreigners had made and that they moved within. The English-woman's route began through lower-class service in the Shanghai police. George Danson had married a mariner's nursery governess; their children seized local opportunities to fend for themselves in Shanghai, the only world they had properly known. Britain was a place they had rarely visited. They were overseas Britons, one family amongst many, part of the largest and most widespread of global diasporas after that of the Chinese and Indians. Lester Little was more firmly placed. A university graduate, he was initially trying out his luck for a few years in a new and different place. He remained very much tied to family and his Rhode Island hometown, Pawtucket, throughout his China years, and his first wife was a neighbour from home, whom he brought out to China in 1917. Little was also very much involved in the American establishment in China which grew in size and confidence in the 1930s and 1940s. So the Customs brought Elsie Danson, the

China-born 'Shanghailander' together with Little, this university-educated, cosmopolitan but rooted American, before the Chinese civil war forced them both out, Little back to his native place, Elsie on to an England she barely knew. The foreign establishment that was built up in China after 1842 brought Little, the Dansons and thousands like them to China, gave them employment, built the churches in which they married, or were baptized, and laid out the cemeteries in which thousands were interred.

This book explores the world which created that final photograph and its many sites and fields of action. It has left its records in stone and brick *in situ*, or recorded now only in photographs, plans or maps, sometimes in oil or watercolour – in formulaic scenes of waterside buildings painted by Chinese artists and sold to foreign residents. It is pictured in family albums and described in print. Its ephemera is sold on eBay, where Shanghai medals and old photographs trade for high prices. China's new rich, and Hong Kong's settled wealth, covet and collect some of these relics of the old China coast. Chinese city governments commodify China coast sites and sights; overseas collectors have made a market for its documentation. The two meet on the city 'old streets', tourist spots sometimes built in brand-new shopping malls, where replicas adorn retro restaurants and bars. The reconstructed past seems to be everywhere in ferociously modern China.[13] But it is also well and securely preserved in archives, many scattered like the old China hands across the globe, but others close to where they were created, in Chinese libraries. Missionary records, the Customs files, court reports and consular correspondence, all these documents track its high drama and its routine, the law-abiding and the crooked, its arguments and its statistics. It can be explored through diaries dull or scandalous, in memoirs worthy or utterly fantastical, in *romans à clef*, in light verse or hunting journals, and through the surviving ephemera, the tickets and invitations pasted in scrapbooks, the dance cards and the menus, incidental traces of otherwise lost moments in another realm. I want to use this material not to locate collaborators and select crimes for indictment, for that has been one use of the archives left behind in China, but to try to explain why and how it happened, how a half-floating, half-land-perched world of traders in the Canton delta in 1832 moved more firmly onshore, talked and fought their way into Chinese cities, and there built roads and bunds, and arrayed along those all the infrastructure of settlement. To join them came all sorts, high church and low-life, idealistic and greedy. They did not simply build trading posts, but little states within a state, each with a constitution and its own peculiarities and history; and combined together these formed a system that stretched across China, deep inland from the port cities, reaching along roads and rivers to mission stations far from the sea.

I begin with an account of the landmark reconnaissance along the Chinese coast made at the cusp of change in 1832, and in two chapters explore the contrasting yet tightly connected worlds of the foreign traders and of the Qing empire in the early 1830s. Then I narrate the multifaceted growth of new communities established on the Chinese coast and the recurring wars and treaties which gave rise to them and underpinned their development. Traders, consuls and missionaries leapt into China, and others followed on their coat-tails. A frontier zone was carved out of parts of a sovereign state: in its coastal cities, outside the walls of river towns, in time in villages across the countryside. Disorder followed also, but then there came new structures for order such as Robert Hart's Customs Service. Why conflict recurred nonetheless, and why enmity seemed latent, is a theme the book pursues. Mutual incomprehension and deliberate misrepresentation alike infected relations between the Qing and the Western world. Honour matters in this story, dignity too. The Sino-foreign conundrum seemed partly to derive from the simple impossibility of each side according the other sufficient dignity, or understanding when the other felt wronged, or else in perceiving slight when none was offered. Much changed very swiftly in China, but did so globally too: rapid change flavoured the entire nineteenth century. Change in the empire of the Qing was driven by and in turn helped shape that century's globalizing energies. New technologies were crucial: steamships, weapons, telegraphy, new mass media, all shaped the course of the international scramble for China. Flows of people, ideas, goods and information coursed through China as they circulated globally. The book shows how the Chinese conundrum was constantly reshaped by the evolving global context and affected that too, but also how deeply influenced it was by the particularities of the new settlements established, and the treaties which framed them, and of the meeting of Chinese and European cultures.

As a multinational enterprise, the scramble for China started to unravel after 1913. That year one set of foreign interests – a consortium of foreign banks – secured a massive loan to the Chinese government underpinned by the imposition of foreign controls over domestic administration greater than any ever before seen. At the same time, another set of interests – of foreign businessmen administering the International Settlement at Shanghai – was thwarted in a long-running bid to expand the area they controlled. The story of China's twentieth century is not the subject of this book, except insofar as that story has been influenced by understandings of the story of the long nineteenth century, and the paths to 1913, to victory and defeat.

Foreign residents in China were always themselves conscious of their history, for there lay justification underpinning the status quo they sought to preserve, as well as conclusive proof, as they saw it, of this or that unchanging Chinese trait. Events of the 1830s and earlier were routinely used to justify this or that policy, or resistance to this or that reform. A vision of an immutable unchanging Chinese 'character' reinforced this.[14] A sense of history unfinished also drove action and shaped predispositions: we gave up too early last time, they would say; we settled for too little. We must see things through fully, firmly, when we have the opportunity. Communities cohere through their histories, or a particular narrative of that history, for it does not need to be a history that scholars snuffling around the archive would find or write. The communities that developed after the 1830s made their histories, and in time were also confronted with other histories, their versions supplanted by other narratives. Celebration was rewritten by others as condemnation. History was ever a public act, but it was also ever a private passion. As Lester Little made his way out of the country in the winter of 1949–50 he mulled over his own thirty-five years in China, and the way its buildings and sites echoed his own past. The temporary Canton headquarters of the Customs were in the city's Customs House on the former concession island of Shamian (Shameen), which had been his home when Commissioner from 1934 to 1942. 'Memories, memories, happy and sad, cling about this old house, this old island and this older city,' he mused. He had been married and widowed here, and interned for five months – 'lonely days' when he was restricted to his home after Pearl Harbor.[15] But in amongst private sadness he was very much conscious of the 'old island' and all it stood for, the 'historic old Church of England in the Protestant cemetery', the attractive camphor-tree lined streets of the concession itself. Canton was almost where it all began, the first step into China after Macao for the Westerners itching to get in as the nineteenth century dawned. In September 1949 in Hong Kong he found himself in the company of members of foreign families who had long served in China – four generations in one, five in two more, one of those linked to 'Chinese' Gordon's 'Ever Victorious Army' of the 1860s, which fought the Taiping rebels on behalf of the Manchus in the countryside around Shanghai, and the other to Little's first predecessor, Horatio Nelson Lay, and through him three generations of Customs men.[16] As the story seemed to be closing Little talked history, and carried some with him too, for safely stowed in his luggage when he left Shanghai were extensive transcripts of Robert Hart's forty-year correspondence with his London-based agent, which form a key record of the history of the Customs, and of Sino-foreign relations more widely. Little had read these in Canton as China collapsed, and corresponded with the daughter of one of Hart's lieutenants about her efforts to find a publisher for her father's memoirs.[17] And on the first day after stepping aside from the Inspector-Generalship, Little was called on by Dr George Mackay, son of a Taiwanese mother and the first Protestant missionary to Taiwan, Canadian George Leslie Mackay, who had arrived in 1871. George junior had, he told Little, a 'vivid recollection' of Taiwan before the Japanese arrived in 1895, and remembered seeing the then Commissioner of Customs, American H. B. Morse, 'being carried in his sedan chair, by four white-uniformed bearers' from his house to his office.[18] So, as the Chinese Communist Party was turning their world upside down, and was preparing to rewrite their history in it, two ageing men sat on a drizzly New Year's Day and talked about the sedan-chair past. How had this come to pass, where lay the roots of the world that brought them together that day, and in that place?

2

Unwelcome Guests

They shouldered their way in. At Mr Lindsay's order, Mr Simpson and Midshipman Stephens put their shoulders against the barred entrance to the Daotai's quarters and heaved, twice. The doors fell to the ground 'with a great clatter', and the first British visitors to Shanghai barged their way into this regional administrator's compound, scattering all before them. As they had approached, winding through the narrow streets of the walled city, the Daotai's staff had hurriedly tried and failed to bar the outer doors in time. But the gatemen thought they had at least safely secured the entrance to the inner office until the doors were torn off their hinges.[1] Historians often discuss China's fraught opening to foreign intercourse with metaphors of open and closed doors; but metaphor met its perfect match in Shanghai as Hugh Hamilton Lindsay of the East India Company and his colleagues stood inside the Daotai's sanctum and, as the dust rose up around them, demanded to be seen and demanded to be heard. Bewildered, the staff inside the office offered them 'tea and pipes' and waited for the return of their chief.

The Britons certainly knew they were not welcome. As their ship, the *Lord Amherst*, had sailed east and then north from its anchorage near the tiny old Portuguese colony at Macao, the local authorities in each port had informed the court at Peking of their progress, and had done all they could to prevent entrance at each of the cities visited. All Chinese ports bar one were closed to foreign trade, and to any foreign visitors, and had been since 1757. Only at Canton, eighty miles from the sea at the mouth of the Pearl river were foreigners allowed to reside and trade, and then only during the October to January trading season, under the close supervision of the local authorities, the Canton

Governor, and the Chinese Customs superintendent, known to them as the 'Hoppo'. At other times the British and other foreigners lived at Macao. But at Xiamen, Fuzhou and Ningbo, the British ship had entered nonetheless, warily evading the war junks that had tried to intimidate them, and the squads of soldiers lined up ashore to demonstrate the military might of the Manchu empire. Local officials had delivered stern warnings to the interlopers, and pasted up declarations on city walls fiercely forbidding the populace to trade with them. Some inquisitive local inhabitants had been whipped with bamboos and paraded through the streets in the *cangue* (a portable stocks) for trying to contact the foreign vessel. But even so, in every port – and hardly on the sly – the same officials had usually tried to cut deals to purchase some of the great store of goods the *Lord Amherst* carried. They were, to a man, puzzled beyond measure that the vessel shipped no opium. For what was a British ship doing on the coast, if it was not shipping opium?

What, indeed. It was the early summer of 1832. The 29-year-old Lindsay had received his instructions in early January. A Supercargo (commercial agent) who had worked for the East India Company at Canton since 1820, he was the well-placed son of a former chairman and director of the Company. Tall, droll Lindsay, nephew of the Earl of Balcarras, was ordered to sail north 'to ascertain how far the northern ports of this empire may gradually be opened to British commerce'.[2] Theirs was a reconnaissance. They were to examine which ports might be best for foreign trade, to find out if some cities were more amenable than others to dealing with foreigners, to test the market and gauge prices, and especially to explore the potential for a direct trade in tea. They carried bales of calicoes, yarns and Indian cotton. To protect themselves, they took on assumed names that could not be traced back to them in Canton, where they could easily have been identified from amongst the barely four score British residents, and they concocted a story at each port to explain their unexpected arrival – they had come from Bengal, were heading to Japan, had been blown off course, had been becalmed and were short of water. They were not much believed, but their bluster and imprecision made officials rightly wary. They did not disguise the fact that they were British. On the contrary, they aimed to explain who the British really were and what they really wanted.

To do this they took copies of a small pamphlet, a translation into Chinese by a missionary, Robert Morrison, of *A Brief Account of the English Character* penned by Charles Marjoribanks, formerly in charge of East India Company operations in Canton, and soon to enter the British Parliament. Marjoribanks had first conceived of the voyage and had given formal instructions to Lindsay, and privately schemed with him and others to effect a change. They also took a draughtsman, who was to survey the harbours; and their captain, Thomas Rees, had participated in surveying operations in the 1820s and had sailed north before with the British embassy of 1817. They compared their soundings with those already known (including Marco Polo's account), and where it took their fancy they christened the islands and coastal passages with their own stout English names – Gutzlaff Island, Amherst Passage, Marjoribanks Harbour. So as they sailed they wiped the British map of China clean and recast it afresh on more useful anglophone lines.

It had taken them over a month to get to Xiamen, and then three more to Shanghai, with leisurely stops at Fuzhou and Ningbo. 'How pleasantly I have passed my time,' wrote Lindsay to his mother from Xiamen: 'this kind of life is delightful to me.'[3] Despite fierce rows, they had often, where they landed, been the subject of cordial interest from poor country folk and officials alike. The pamphlet itself was popular, if puzzling, for it was written in very indifferent Chinese, 'pidgin-Chinese' concluded one scholar.[4] But what really fascinated and perplexed people was the fluent Chinese spoken by one of the foreigners, the mission's translator Karl Gützlaff.[5] 'I know you to be a native of this district traitorously serving barbarians in disguise', barked one hostile official to him at Xiamen, and others shared their disbelief that a foreigner could speak and read Chinese so well.[6] But Gützlaff, a Lutheran missionary from Pomerania, had not only learnt Chinese in the six years he had been in Asia, studying first in Java and then in Bangkok; he had also sailed up the Chinese coast before, shipping on a trading junk. He had travelled in somewhat uncomfortable disguise at times, especially given the crew's predilection for prostitutes, wine and opium in each port. It was not a large vessel, and Gützlaff remained onboard this floating 'Sodom' for his own safety during at least one of these salty bacchanals.[7] 'Fully' persuading himself that he was 'not prompted by self-interest and vain glory' in making this journey, a conclusion not shared by most later commentators, Gützlaff had been taken as far north as Tianjin. This was barely seventy miles from the imperial capital Peking, though he had dared progress no closer than the port city at the mouth of the Hai river, which reminded him strongly of Liverpool, and whose inhabitants spoke a dialect that reminded him very much of Swiss.[8] Thus was exotic China prosaically rendered for his readers. Gützlaff had arrived back south in Macao barely two months before the *Amherst* sailed, and his reports, if not his lobbying to be able to return, had clearly encouraged those planning the expedition.

The 'famed emporium of Shanghae' impressed the *Lord Amherst*'s leader. Indeed, noted Lindsay, 'fame had not magnified its commercial importance'.[9] Now they sipped tea and waited for the Daotai Wu Qitai in his *yamen*, his official residence. First along though, came the Zhixian, or county magistrate, a lesser official, apoplectic with rage, who brusquely ordered them to return to Canton. If they had anything to say they could only say it there, by imperial decree. There could be no questioning this. They must agree. They must depart. Lindsay, however, instantly resumed a pointed game of protocol and precedence, one that had coloured the two unsuccessful British embassies to the Qing court, those of Lords Macartney and Amherst, in 1793 and in 1817. This 'audience question', as it was later known, was to colour foreign relations with China for decades to come.[10] British and Chinese, Britain and the Great Qing Empire, were not equals in Chinese eyes, and all relations and interactions between them needed to demonstrate this fact clearly. In addition, the foreigners had no right to be in Shanghai: they could not be recognized; they could not be accorded even the elementary courtesies of formal interaction that might thereby accord them any status. So the magistrate would not countenance their sitting in his presence; officials scribbled notes instead of proper letters, and refused to accept correspondence from Lindsay; they deliberately neglected all customary politeness and tried to leave no formal trail of their frustrating interaction with the stubborn trespassers. It could cost them their jobs, and it was not proper: the British were not equals and they were not to be treated as such.

At Canton the officials refused direct contact with the foreigners, even with the East India Company which officially represented the

British state, and which held a legal monopoly on the tea trade with China. All communication in either direction was addressed to and channelled through a group of Chinese traders (who alone could trade with the foreigners) known as the *cohong*, or *hong* merchants. The *cohong* was held responsible for the actions of the foreigners, the insecurities of whose position were balanced by the profits of their business. The British could not speak for themselves.

Lindsay knew that these Chinese assumptions would flavour his meetings with officials, and was ready to perceive slight and note omission in any and every part of his exchanges with them. He was forward, and aggressive, in demanding courtesy and due protocol as he saw it. He was determined to speak for himself and to be heard. He was determined to speak for himself in Chinese, too, to rebut any attempt to speak to him in 'Canton-English', in pidgin. He knew how to talk for himself in the language of the country. Lindsay also acted on a reflection that he had made 'several distinct errors' earlier in the voyage in encounters at Xiamen: he should not stand if officials sat, he should not even meet without first securing an 'understanding that we were to be treated with due civility and courtesy', he should not have accepted any of their prohibitions. 'Less submission on our part would have met with greater readiness to meet our wishes on theirs,' he concluded.[11] The hypersensitivity of this young Scot was to be echoed by foreign consuls and ministers, missionaries and traders, all through the nineteenth century and beyond. Honour was at stake: British honour and Lindsay's honour. Here in the Daotai's office it began with a silent game of musical chairs, as the magistrate and Lindsay alternately stood, sat and stood, the one denying equality, the other demanding it. It concluded when the magistrate stalked silently out of the room.

If he is to be believed, a Lindsay had shouldered down doors in China before, and had also refused to pay due obeisance, to 'knocky head' to Chinese authority – as beseeched by the senior *hong* merchant – that is, to kowtow to the Canton Hoppo. This recusant was the young man's father, Hugh Lindsay, Commodore (senior commander) of the East India Company ships anchored at Canton in 1811, who had by his own account learnt the value of an obstinate insistence on rights and redress which perhaps helped inform his son's attitude.[12] The Chinese authorities were refusing to allow the Company fleet to sail until they had settled the case of the death of a Chinese man involving three British seamen. In British eyes this had been an accident – manslaughter – but the Qing legal code did not, they thought, distinguish murder from manslaughter in its punishments. Even to hand a man over for questioning in such a case was deemed by the British to be 'a provisional sentence of death', and it was clearly an acknowledgement of their own precarious position in relation to Chinese authority and power.[13] They thought also of the gunner of the ship the *Lady Hughes*, judicially killed in 1785 after being handed over for examination in the accidental killing of two Chinese boatmen. More recently, they considered the American sailor Francis Terranova, whose culpability in the death of a Chinese boatwoman in 1821 was far greater, but whose trial and execution by the Canton authorities appalled the foreigners. Unless there was clear evidence of wilful murder they were disinclined to cooperate. As the *hong* merchants refused to transmit their protest at the Hoppo's action (fearful of the consequences for the messenger of such a rebellious message), the Company's Canton Committee took the 'less regular and usual mode of effecting the object in view', bypassed the *hong* merchants and despatched a delegation led by Lindsay and the Committee's junior member to deliver it in person. 'Finding no material obstruction on entering' the Canton Governor's offices, continued the final report, the document was delivered. For Lindsay senior, writing four decades afterwards, there was no 'obstruction' because, at the head of a sixty-strong column of Company marine officers he had yelled 'Hurrah to the gate!' as it was being blocked, and then 'we in a body sprang forward and luckily reached it at the instant the gates were shut . . . with one consent we put our shoulders to them, and the gate flew open before us, throwing all those inside to the right and left.' 'A steady and temperate resistance' to Chinese demands 'had never failed,' he asserted, 'in obtaining redress.'[14] Perhaps the father's account was coloured by the son's, but the predisposition to a forceful demonstration of intent certainly ran in the family.

The fact that the younger Lindsay sailed in a vessel named after that last hapless envoy to China also struck an appropriately challenging note, one just right for changing times and for a man who demanded to sit as an equal, as he felt his country was equal. When it became clear to Qing courtiers in July 1817 that Lord Amherst, like Earl

Macartney before him, was not going to accord the Son of Heaven (the Emperor) proper courtesy and refused to undertake Chinese ceremonial, then he and his retinue had been denied audience and kicked out of the Summer Palace north of Peking without ceremony. They had passed not a single night there. 'Your King is respectful and obedient,' announced the messenger sent to order them to depart, 'the Ambassador is not.'[15] Amherst had refused to *ketou* or kowtow, to kneel and bow his head to the ground three times. The ambassador's bowels were so disordered 'from the use of a Chinese diet', noted one of his retinue, that he could actually barely stand. But he had refused the firm entreaties of the officials even to rehearse the gesture. So off he was packed back down south and away to wherever he came from, somewhere over the oceans, far from civilization. Now Lindsay was sailing north without invitation, and with even less tact than the ambassador. But the choice of vessel was actually an accident.

It marked a more momentous change in another way. Lindsay was ordered on his trip to the north by the president of the East India Company's 'Select Committee' at Canton. The Canton British, the Company men and the private traders, were angry as never before. The previous year had seen them struggle hard to make their anger heard, and to make their precarious position on the fringe of the Chinese empire understood by their superiors in India and England, their government in London, and even by the people of Canton. They wrote letters and sent petitions; they circulated far overseas their newly minted newspapers, the *Canton Register* and the *Canton Courier*, whose articles were picked up and reprinted verbatim in the imperial press. They had these new and powerful tools to make Britain's Canton voice heard globally, and they used them. They were angrier than usual because they felt under threat. Eleven months earlier, during the off-season, while their premises were unstaffed, the Governor of Canton had ordered the demolition of some building work at the East India Company 'factory' (its premises); had restated various irritating restrictions on foreign traders; arbitrarily – it seemed – punished some of their Chinese associates; and deliberately – it seemed – insulted the King of England, whose full-length portrait by Sir Thomas Lawrence graced the shut-up dining room of the Company.[16] The Governor had yanked open the curtains which protected it, and deliberately sat himself with his back to the painting. On learning of this, the British had flailed about in angry protest, suspending trade, demanding that Calcutta send them warships, and on 31 May they had pasted up on Canton walls and circulated in Canton shops a remarkable appeal in Chinese to the people of the city. 'The English,' it began, 'came to China for the purposes of Commerce. They wish to be friends of the Chinese people, but their Canton Factory has been attacked, and their property destroyed ... The English,' it concluded, 'can never submit to oppression.'[17] But submit to the Governor they had had to in the end, if not to oppression – at least in acknowledgement of their powerlessness in the face of imperial decree. This heightened their anger. Lindsay himself had been sent personally to deliver their boycott notice to the Governor, and with it the keys to the factory that he had shockingly made himself so comfortable in. But the notice and keys had been rejected to his face, and he had been ordered to return to Macao. So personal, public humiliation had been added to the grievances Lindsay carried north.

Lindsay had written three years earlier of discussions about trying to 'open a trade' through the coast, about sending a ship 'north with a message'. A congeries of disputes with the authorities had led the Company to keep its fleet out of Canton waters at the start of the 1829–30 season. Lindsay had been assigned to stay with it at the Cumsingmoon anchorage north of Macao, to make contact with coastal trading junks and encourage them to trade directly with the fleet, and to 'conciliate' local villagers and persuade them to provision the fleet. He tramped around, speaking to assemblies of villagers ('to the best of my ability'; but he fancied himself a linguist), and he had a Chinese document explaining the Company position that was circulated and posted in public. As many times before, the Company eventually capitulated and resumed normal trading in February. There was no support for their position from Calcutta, let alone from London. There was also no agreement at Canton, where the then Company President, William Plowden, had resolutely opposed the more confrontational plans of his younger colleagues. Tension among the Company men in China persisted thereafter, aggravated by the growth in numbers of non-Company British traders with whom they groused, connived and conspired.[18] This episode taught Lindsay to hate such conciliatory predispositions, to believe that greater familiarity with 'our characters' – with the British character – would win over ordinary Chinese people, and that once 'we had given the Mandarins a few good beatings' a proper set of relations could be established.[19]

Calcutta at last listened to them in 1831, and sent ships. One of these, the cruiser *Clive*, carried a letter of protest from the Governor General in India. Gleeful indeed that they now had use, even temporarily, of a warship, the Canton committee decided to send the *Clive* along the coast, and now Lindsay got his first chance to ship north. They wished to overleap the Canton administration that hemmed them in, and aimed to get their complaints heard elsewhere along the coast and transmitted thereby to Peking. They also hoped to test the potential of a wider market. To the frustration and anger of the Canton British in 1832 was now added the certainty of change in the near future. The end of monopoly was in sight. The East India Company's directors in London had already been told three years previously that the monopoly on the tea trade with China would not be renewed in 1833. Its demise would see the end of Company authority and its formal presence in Canton, and so new opportunities for its competitors, and for men like Lindsay, who were looking to a future outside the Company and, they hoped, elsewhere in China. This was a moment to seize, to stake a forward claim. But the *Clive*'s captain had baulked at the extent of the cargo that was shipped onto his vessel. His was a cruiser, he declared, not a merchantman, and he refused to proceed. The *Clive* left for Bombay instead.[20]

Quickly to the Company's aid came instead other parties and volunteers, for a reconnaissance of the coast suited both the Company men and the 'country' traders, the private British merchants who now dominated the intra-Asian shipping routes and who also looked forward to a future free from monopoly. The *Lord Amherst*, a six-year-old teak 350-tonner, belonged to Cruttenden & Co. It had arrived from Bengal in late August, and it was just fresh from a trip to Singapore, a British trading post formally established as a colony eight years earlier. The cargo of sample goods was transhipped. Additional European crew members were found to augment the thirty-four Indian sailors (as 'the Chinese in general hold natives of India in little estimation'), and to provide additional security, not least to man the four brass cannon added to the vessel.[21] A Scottish free trader, William Jardine, was closely involved, 'I had made up my mind to Mr Gützlaff being engaged' he had written in January. 'He may collect useful information for future purposes' – useful for Jardine's purposes that is.[22] Lindsay was issued his instructions, and a contingency of 2,000 dollars, and reminded that this foray 'had no political object whatever, but that of enquiry as to the native and Government character, and their disposition to commercial intercourse'. He was to exercise 'strict reserve' as to the 'origin and the objects of his mission'.[23] It was hardly that clandestine, though. It was widely gossiped about, and even the *Canton Register* and the *Chinese Repository* noted the ship's absence on voyage as well as its destination. The *Canton Register* recorded the *Lord Amherst*'s departure on 27 February, passengers H. H. Lindsay, Esq., and the Revd C. Gützlaff, on an 'experimental voyage' to the east coast.[24] Whereas the official British were learning Chinese and publishing in the language, official Chinese were not then able to learn of British feelings and actions from such open sources. Their later frantic, frequent queries about the mysterious English ships on their coast might have been swiftly and definitively answered by reading Canton's English press.

There was more to this than reconnaissance, for the Company men were keen again to try out their new weapon, their Chinese printing press. In November 1831 they reported to London that they had printed up copies of Marjoribanks's pamphlet in Chinese. This 'may be regarded,' they claimed, 'as forming a new era in our connections with China'. The single copy of the pamphlet which survives in Britain – handed out at Ningbo, and presumably sent accompanying a despatch from there to the Canton authorities and sent on by them for an explanation to the Company's Select Committee at Macao in July – seems innocuous enough, a flimsy, seven-page document. But print was the new agent of action, and propaganda was the aim. 'We have the means if we have the inclination,' they claimed, 'to throw off in a few hours, any number of copies of any document in the Chinese language,' and they confidently expected to be able in this way to state their case to Peking: 'it would be extraordinary if one copy among hundreds should not find its way within the walls of the Imperial Palace.'[25] The *Canton Register* had sight of a transcript that same month (sent, it was claimed, to Chinese from Ningbo via Suzhou) and – tongue somewhat in cheek – published a 'translation' of this 'rather *florid*' and 'curious' paper being distributed by 'three foreign ships' that were attempting to trade at Ningbo, backed up, it was claimed, by twenty British warships.[26] As the *Amherst* wandered by itself up the coast, panicked report inflated the single barque into a fleet of hostile vessels.

The pamphlet claimed that the British had no desire for territory and wanted only to trade, and had done so in China for two centuries, to mutual benefit. But it complained that the authorities in Canton were corrupt, capricious and cruel, and through their actions impeded amicable commerce and contradicted the 'imperial benevolence of mind' – the emperor's wishes – which had allowed the British to come to China. There were some economies with the truth within its tale of recent British imperial expansion in Asia, and its idea that the British wanted no territory in China. Macartney's embassy had gone with a list of requests that included the setting aside of a British base, away from the Portuguese restrictions at Macao. The pamphlet was an oddity, for it was 'perfectly unintelligible' in many parts remarked one official Chinese account published in the *Jingbao*, the 'Peking Gazette' (a periodic compilation of court and government news), setting aside the fact that it was 'highly rebellious and full of falsehoods'.[27] But copies were snapped up with alacrity, by those offered them, although the longer-lasting impressions on the spot were more likely to have been made by the Chinese-speaking Prussian, Gützlaff, and the pushy Company men. The robust reporting network of the Qing state clearly scooped up the pamphlet and sent it on to Peking, just as its originators had hoped. The court also received plenty of accounts of their progress, copies of which were widely disseminated and were also patiently assembled back in Canton by the East India Company officers who disclaimed all knowledge of this Englishman Hu Xiami (Hoo Hea-me/ Hamilton) and this fluent Chinese speaker Jia Li (Kea Le/Gützlaff).[28] Lindsay defended the pamphlet in his later account of the voyage, and after all it did manage as planned to lay British complaints before the emperor's eyes, however much its rotten Chinese strained them. Others were less convinced. Propaganda in English ran the risk of embarrassing, and how much more so that propaganda translated into a language still only shakily mastered by British scholars. But an account of the English character, however partial, however 'bombastical' (as Jardine thought it) – English here used for British, as Chinese does not ordinarily distinguish – was outlined on paper and widely circulated, and it was fleshed out in the beefy shape of Lindsay and his swaggering, door-heaving colleagues.[29]

That Lindsay was offered tea at the Daotai's *yamen* in Shanghai was an act of appropriate courtesy, but it was tea that had brought the British to China in the first place. The galloping demand from British consumers, which had so grown apace since Samuel Pepys first tasted the novel 'China drink' in September 1660, and the thirst of the British treasury, had led the Company to Canton. One tenth of British government revenue came from tea duties, remarked one scholar, as did 100 per cent of the Company's profits.[30] To pay for the shipments west from India, the British had continued to probe the Chinese market with cottons and woollens, but for decades the only thing they could take that found a Chinese market was bullion pure and simple. There was no sustained or substantive demand for Manchester cottons, or English clocks, or woollens, which might support growing tea purchases. So the British traded silver at Canton for tea, and silver flowed to China until 1808.[31] But after Bengal came into East India Company hands in 1757 a new commodity, opium, was gradually added to that stock of goods that could be tried out on the Chinese market. The drug took. Opium was already long-embedded in Chinese elite leisure culture – the British hardly needed to create the market that bought prodigiously when it could – and it was spreading further through different circles in society, combining to generate a powerful demand.[32] From 1808 the flow of silver reversed direction. While the Company held a monopoly on the sale of opium produced in its Indian territories, it did not ship it east itself, as its import had been proscribed by the Qing in 1729 and later edicts had clearly targeted maritime imports.[33] The Company left that task instead to the country traders, Indian and British – very often in partnership – who had grown to dominate intra-Asian commerce after the end of the Company's wider monopoly in 1813. In brief, a classic triangular trade had developed, with Indian fortunes flowing to the British isles via China. The principal elements were the two drugs: the Company sold opium to the country traders, who shipped it east. The cash they realized was converted into Company bills payable in London or

Calcutta, while the Company bought tea (and alone could do so), shipping it back to Britain.

But men like William Jardine and his partner James Matheson, who worked closely with Parsee trader Jamsetjee Jejeebhoy in Bombay, chafed at the restrictions placed on trading at Canton and Macao. They went to meet their market directly. In 1823 the Scots traders, then styled as Magniac & Co., had for the first time traded with Chinese buyers at Xiamen, sending a vessel to make contact with potential buyers, who would ship the chests to shore on what became known as 'smug-boats'. Others had followed, but the resistance of local authorities had led to a falling off in this enterprise for everyone. So their own close interest in the *Lord Amherst* mission, and in Gützlaff, was linked to their desire to renew and develop the trade, which they did spectacularly. The looming end of the monopoly concentrated trading minds. It would bring greater competition to the China trade, including the clandestine commerce in opium. 'It can hardly be worth pursuing on the old plan,' mused Jardine, speculating a year earlier on the need to innovate, to seek intelligence and to use their own ships on the coast to take the goods to the market.[34] This was a commercially brilliant move, which raised the stakes all round. The *Amherst* voyage was a key part of the new plan. The Jardine ships *Sylph* and *Jamesina* were soon after despatched in sequence along the coast, with Gützlaff barely stepping back ashore in Canton before boarding the former, and two more vessels would sail in the autumn of 1832. The missionary was vital: 'I would give a thousand [Mexican silver] dollars for three days of Gützlaff,' wrote the independent trader James Innes (the Canton Committee had paid him 1,500 for the *Lord Amherst* voyage). Gützlaff neglected to mention opium in his widely published accounts of the voyages he made on Jardine, Matheson ships. Jardine 'has exempted me from every duty with the nefarious drug' he claimed to Lindsay, although few believed him.[35] He was paid handsomely for his work interpreting on the ships smuggling the drug north, cajoling and stonewalling officials: getting them out of the way. By 1838 the firm controlled a dozen vessels: clippers that whisked the opium from Bengal, and the coasters that took their goods up north to discreet anchorages where Chinese traders could come directly to them. This way the Chinese could undercut the prices locally of those who sourced from Canton, while Jardines could evade price-fixing amongst Chinese buyers at the port.[36] The new trade, and the Jardine, Matheson fleet, expanded rapidly. It was met on the coast by a complex indigenous smuggling network, which rendezvoused with the vessels in quiet anchorages, purchased stocks, and shipped them far inland by river and along country paths.[37] 'Smuggling' was often a relative term for a trade intermittently carried out in full view of authority, both Chinese and British. Jardines were not the only firm on the coast, of course: Dent & Co, their great Canton rivals, also expanded, acquiring the *Lord Amherst* on the way. We find Thomas Rees and his ship in Chinchew Bay north of Xiamen in 1836, fixing a deal with Jardines not to queer each other's sales locally. A year later we have a passing reference to its striking a 'small junk' with its cannon fire.[38] In fact, the vessel was to spend the rest of its career on this coast.

It must have been a true relief to Lindsay to stretch his legs in 1832, to roam abroad, away from the physical and social confines of the Canton delta. 'I never saw a spirit of *roving* and adventure more strongly developed than in him,' declared an acquaintance.[39] And the foreign China life was an enclosed life. They were shut up in Macao, precariously lodged in a Catholic enclave subject to 'unprovoked acts of annoyance' from their hosts; they were shut up still more claustro-phobically at Canton, squeezed into the factories, the combined ware-houses and residences that stood on a small patch of the Canton shore; and they were shut up in their ships.[40] As well as the strict limitations on their freedom to trade, they were also forbidden to enter the city of Canton, forbidden from residing in the factories outside the trading season, and forbidden from bringing women with them to the city. They were effectively forbidden from even learning Chinese, through the simple fact of it being a capital offence for Chinese to teach them. They could barely stretch their legs in the factories, living life in a 'pinhole', one commentator noted,[41] allowed six times a month to visit the Fati (Huadi) gardens a few miles along the river to walk.[42] That was some relief from the factory compound, which itself contained two small gardens, one of them barely sixty paces wide. That a man counted his paces suggests how confined a world it was. Two hundred and seventy steps took a man from one end of the factories to the other, and he had to jostle each one forward. He was never alone. Chinese

REFERENCE.

A. Pwanting Qua Street.
B. New China Street.
C. Old China Street.
X Guard House.
D. Hog Lane.
E. The Creek.
F. Jack Ass Point.
L. Old Clothes Street
N. Old Tom. Linguist.
O. Carpenters Square.
P. Bridge over Creek.
G.H.J. Custom House.
K. King Qua's Hong.
M. Man Qua's Hong.
X. Hou Qua's Hong.
X. Honam Joss House.
Y. Hou Qua's House.
Z. Pwanting Qua's House
C.H. Conseo House.

THIRTEEN FACTORY STREET

SQUARE

Danish Factory
Spanish Factory
French Factory
Chun Qua Factory
American Factory
Paou Shun Factory
Imperial Factory
Swedish Factory
E.J. Co Old Factory
Chow Chow Factory
E.I.Co.New. Factory
Dutch Factory
Creek Factory

Lane

Suburbs

Suburbs

Pearl River

To Whampoa

Island of Honam.

To Hwa-Te Gardens

Sha Ming.

To Macao

1. The Canton factories in the 1830s

hawkers and idlers crowded the grounds fronting the *hongs*, come to look at the foreigners, come to provision those visitors, come to fleece them, cut their hair, or tell their fortune. Still, the residents ate and drank well, and they drank hard. But William Hickey, who knew how to find fun, found it a limiting world nonetheless, and tired quickly of the 'repetition of the same round'.[43] That round in March 1832 encompassed about seventy resident Britons, half of them company men, twenty Americans, and a handful of Dutch, Spanish, French, Swedish and Danish traders. Portuguese and the Parsee traders added to the total.

There were thirteen factories at Canton, rented from the *hong* merchants and located on a bare fifteen acres of riverside, most of it reclaimed land. They were long, narrow two-storey buildings, arrayed along the north side of what was really too cramped a space to justify its description as a square. Business rooms took up the lower floors, with kitchens and servants quartered at the rear, while upstairs were rooms for the traders, with a dining room facing the square and the river opening onto a verandah, to tease some coolness in. They were divided into four blocks by New China Street, Old China Street ('distinguished for its breadth', at twelve foot wide), and Hog Lane (distinguished for its filth). These were lined with small shops and stalls selling trinkets and curios ('adapted for the European market' remarked one buyer),[44] with Hog Lane in addition the source of the cheapest 'samshu', rough rice wine sold to foreign sailors up from the moorings at Whampoa. There was 'Old Jemmy Apoo', 'Old Good Tom', and 'Young Tom seller of wines of all kinds and prices'.[45] 'Fine day, Jack', 'How you do, old boy', called out the shopkeepers, eager for custom from seamen all too eager to drink.[46] Better fare, and better wine, were served to their betters at the factory tables, on a 'satisfactory scale of abundance', remarked American Augustine Heard, seeing a bottle of wine being set beside each place.[47] The Company men in particular lived well, their large dining room graced by that full-length portrait of George IV.[48] It was faced by one of Lord Amherst, who had eaten well and thankfully in the room on his departure from China in January 1817. Their factory was twice the width of the others. There was a chapel set out in one of the rooms and another was organized as a library, which in 1832 held 4,000 volumes, so there were quieter moments even during the season.[49] A fanciful porticoed entrance fronted the Company *hong*, and the Union flag flew from its staff in front of the building.

The factory residents spent much of their time off duty on the water, idling or exercising, holding occasional races and regattas. Local boatmen learned to build the craft needed. With less choice in the matter, the crews of the merchantmen, which had brought cargoes from India and Europe, and would sail with the tea and silks purchased from the *hong* merchants, were confined to life on the water at Whampoa, eleven miles south outside the fortified river mouth, the Bogue, Bocca Tigris, or 'Tiger's Mouth'. Local people and river people provisioned them, supplying them food, fuel, drink and sex (at 'Lob Lob Creek' in Hickey's time, courtesy of women he knew as 'Lob Lob ladies'), and scavenging their refuse.[50] Toogood Downing, a surgeon based at Whampoa for some months in 1836 recalled the cries of the washermen, whose 'character in some points will not bear too severe an examination', as they solicited for trade as ships arrived: 'Ah, you missee chiefee matee, how you dooa? I saavey you long tim, when you catchee Whampo last tim.'[51] Pretended familiarity added to the real familiarity of interaction at the anchorage. Crews were well served then, so were their ships. There were well-established suppliers holding, as a later account put it, 'every thing that a ship can require, from spare spars down to India pale ale'.[52] Further south off Lintin island, the traders moored their receiving ships, floating opium warehouses, nominally out of sight in the sheltered anchorage there, and very well armed. The commanders often had their families with them, and there was here as well an established relationship with the population of this small island. It might be 'rather barren', but it was a secure enough community for Harriet Low, a young American living with her merchant uncle in Macao, to visit the barque *Lintin* for a month in October 1832, exchanging calls with the wives of the captains, picnicking on the island, dancing – for all the world as if this was a small town ashore. There were some twenty ships at anchor, and to the *Lintin* came the Chinese smuggling boats to fetch the cargoes, to speed them to shore and into the inland supply routes.[53]

For all its claustrophobia, and its hindrances and irritations, this was actually a settled, well-ordered world, based on now long-established

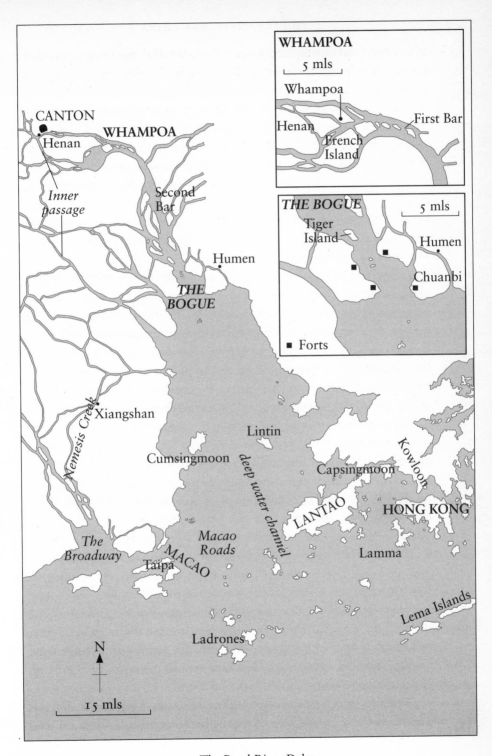

WHAMPOA

5 mls

Whampoa

Henan

French
Island

First Bar

THE BOGUE

5 mls

Tiger
Island

Humen

Chuanbi

■ Forts

CANTON

Henan

*Inner
passage*

WHAMPOA

Second
Bar

Humen

*THE
BOGUE*

Nemesis Creek

Xiangshan

Lintin

Cumsingmoon

deep water channel

Capsingmoon

Kowloon

LANTAO

HONG KONG

*The
Broadway*

*Macao
Roads*

MACAO

Taipa

Lamma

Lema Islands

N

Ladrones

15 mls

2. The Pearl River Delta

practices, clearly understood, which ensured the smooth delivery from Canton of Chinese tea, taken directly by the East India Company, and by European and American ships. In the 1831–2 season 93 British, 41 American, 34 Spanish, 19 Portuguese and 24 other Dutch, Danish, French and Prussian vessels arrived to trade. They brought textiles, iron and lead, watches, locks, pearls, elephants' teeth, shark fins, ivory and 20,580 skins. They also brought opium, 14,225 chests of it that season in the third of British and American shipping that sailed no closer than Lintin. While Lindsay sailed, 5,578 chests were lodged in the receiving ships at the anchorage.[54] The predictable regularity of this internationalized trading world was periodically upset, as in any port city, by human failing and misadventure, by the drunken or frustrated tar, the misfired cannon salute, by events. Then that seemingly unbridgeable gulf between aspects of Qing and foreign legal theory could be exposed, and an act of manslaughter could be punished as murder. Such episodes were rare, but they were remembered, even when the Canton good life mostly ambled on smoothly enough. At least, tea was shipped, trade accomplished, fortunes made or lost.

The little foreign world in Canton, with all its irritations, was much described in contemporary travel accounts, and later in memoirs. The window on China that it offered was a small one, but effective none-theless. It was not isolated, and where visiting or resident foreigners had the interest they were able to learn more about the country they were in, and events which were taking place there. The *Canton Register*, *Canton Courier* and the more ambitious and scholarly *Chinese Repository*, edited by Elijah Bridgman, the first American missionary to China, all conveyed up-to-date news, description and opinion across the seas.[55] China was hardly unknown. Jesuit and Franciscan Catholic missionaries had long been active at the Ming and Qing courts. Following the pioneering Matteo Ricci's example, the Jesuits had carved out a role for themselves as astronomers and mathematicians.[56] They introduced the court to European music, and they designed a number of the buildings at the Qing summer palace, the Yuanmingyuan. Their letters to Europe were widely circulated and served to encourage the Sino-philia that infused eighteenth-century European culture. Enlightenment political thought, interior design, the visual arts and garden landscaping were equally inflected by the Chinese craze. Leibniz and Voltaire contrasted the reason and rationality they saw in Confucian ideals and practice, as they understood them, with the superstitious irrationalities of Christianity, as they saw them.[57] The eighteenth century was the heyday of chinoiserie, encouraging the growth of a British, European and American world of imported Chinese goods: porcelain, wallpaper, tea, medicinal rhubarb. Orders placed for dinner services in Derbyshire were channelled to Canton, and back two years later came the goods, decorated with the designs sent out east. More recently the unsuccessful embassies had resulted in a glut of publications from participants, while the base at Canton did allow some greater capacity in foreign knowledge about Chinese culture and conditions, and its natural history, to be built up.[58]

All such crazes pass, and the irony was that growing familiarity in fact directly fed a growing contempt. The reports published by participants in the two British embassies had authoritatively confirmed the growing shift in foreign popular and informed opinion away from a Sinophile tendency to a Sinophobic one. It was also unfortunate that perceptions of China were intertwined with Protestant Britain's awkward relationship with Roman Catholicism, and the conflict with France. The picture recorded in Jesuit letters, extrapolated and idealized in Enlightenment authors, was flatly contradicted by the reports issuing out of the more phlegmatic British embassies. 'The empire of China,' concluded Lord Macartney in a famous phrase, 'is an old, crazy First rate man-of-war . . . She may perhaps not sink outright; she may drift some time as a wreck, and will then be dashed to pieces on the shore.'[59] China was viewed close up by Macartney and his companions, and deemed wanting. Jesuit reports were now seen as Jesuitical ones. The forging of a firmer 'British' identity during the long war with France exacerbated distrust and disdain for a China once wholly refracted through Catholic and French Catholic reports. Chinese religion seemed anyway Romanish, with its 'idol-worship', its monks and nuns and its foggy mystification. So behind the immediate anger of the Canton British, irritated beyond words by what they saw and felt as capricious and demeaning restriction, was a wider falling off in cultural sympathy. But they were there, nonetheless, and they rifled their Canton window for all that it was worth.

We know well what this world actually looked like. Not only do we have many rich travelogues – such a small, cloistered world perhaps invited the retention of even minor detail – we have many visual records: portraits of personalities, views of the thirteen *hongs*, of the ships off shore and their anchorages. Visitors and residents commissioned paintings from Chinese artists working in a European style. A bankrupt British artist, affable but ugly George Chinnery, lived at Macao from 1825 until his death in 1852, at a good distance from his creditors and from his wife. His rival, perhaps sometime pupil, Lam Qua (Lin Guan) provided work from a studio on New China Street (next to Polly the Hat-maker's shop) which complemented Chinnery's record of the trading world they worked within. Their paintings of the *hong* merchants, the foreign traders, of Gützlaff – Chinnery's portrait of whom was exhibited at the Royal Academy in the spring of 1835 (the early sketch for this had been hand-drawn for Lindsay in 1832)[60] – and of the simpler sights and scenes of the delta form a powerfully evocative record of the foreign Canton life. Lesser artists beavered away too, and amateurs, including William Prinsep, who sketched Lindsay in one of the comfortable 'fastboats' which ferried men to and from Macao. In fact we have a far better pictorial record of the Canton enclosure and Macao than we do of the early years of the settlements which were to follow, established east and north along the coast. There were other records, including the scores of paintings of tumour patients which Lam Qua produced for American medical missionary and diplomat Peter Parker.[61] Less disturbingly, the Canton botany was well known too: the south of China had been 'ransacked' by botanists, reported the naturalist Robert Fortune later.[62] Ship's captains found fame when they brought back new plants; East India Company staff corresponded with botanist Joseph Banks, President of the Royal Society and a man who saw clearly how science and British empire could serve each other nicely. Back they sent to Britain seeds, specimens and information gleaned from their Chinese contacts, and they helped the men Banks and his successor sent out to Canton to collect specimens.[63]

There was still much to learn, and new skills to develop, so they could make better sense of the new and ever-growing market and its commodities, and make better deals. Hemmed in at Canton, prevented by law from visiting the districts producing the products they were purchasing, and prevented by their linguistic and cultural shortcomings from understanding the context of the things they bought or the proper quality of them, the foreign traders had to teach themselves as best they could. They had to learn to assess the right colour, taste and texture of the goods brought to them. They had to learn afresh to smell. Understanding tea saw the development of the profession of 'cha-see', the tea taster, who sniffed the leaf and tasted brews and blends before confirming or rejecting purchase. There were other products. In December 1830 William Jardine wrote from Canton to London describing his attempts to identify good quality musk, the extremely expensive perfume which came from a gland of the musk deer, known as a 'pod'.[64] Too many shipments had been adulterated, or were rotten. Coloured clay was being mixed into the pods, and lead was hidden inside to add weight. 'A handsome profit' could be made on Chinese musk, if deception could be avoided and quality sustained. Jardine had his reputation to protect as shipper, but also as buyer, and clearly something needed to be done. He secured various samples and taught himself to identify by sight, taste and smell good-quality pods. Ultimately, he was so confident that he declared himself better able to do so than the Chinese merchants. Such confidence in the foreign ability to know China better than the Chinese themselves was to be oft rehearsed. And such determined and assiduous attention to detail, to securing a grasp of the facts so as to be able to meet Chinese dealers on their own terms, marked Jardine's approach to all aspects of his company's business. In the future foreign firms would establish collaborations with Chinese agents, called compradors, who they could trust to provide such fundamental market information to them, but in 1830 this Calvinist Scot had no option but to train himself to appreciate the smothering sensual purities of one of nature's most powerful perfumes.

Other things were being learnt. Accompanying the Amherst embassy on its fruitless, uncomfortable journey north in 1817 had been Robert Morrison, the first British Protestant missionary to China, making his first journey out of the confined world of the Pearl river. The pidgin Chinese of the Marjoribanks pamphlet was a poor standard-bearer for the tiny, but growing, school of men studying Chinese. The odds and Chinese edicts were against them, but in Morrison they had their pioneer and teacher. The 25-year-old Northumbrian had arrived in

Canton already equipped with a good knowledge of Chinese learnt from a Cantonese living in Britain. Lindsay bemoaned the fact that the foreigner's inability to speak and understand Chinese other than the rough pidgin usually used meant that they were 'very generally spoken of in the most contemptuous terms before their face, of which they remain in perfect ignorance'.[65] Gützlaff's ability to engage with high officials and ordinary people impressed Lindsay, as it did the traders, who were to employ him for most of the rest of the decade. Morrison laboured for years on a massive dictionary, whose publication was eventually sponsored by the East India Company, which retained him as its official translator from 1808 onwards. Their patronage was vital for the Protestant missionary in securing him a billet in Canton, just as Jardine's sponsorship (and cash) was vital for Gützlaff. Their pioneering work was supported from Malacca by an Anglo-Chinese College, established at Morrison's prompting in 1818, and run by William Milne. It trained Chinese converts sent there, such as Liang Fa, a printer who had worked with Morrison in Canton, who became a minister for the London Missionary Society (LMS) back in the city after being ordained in 1821. It helped prepare missionaries for the hoped-for days to come when China was opened to them.[66] These early missionaries, 'exempted' like Gützlaff, at least in their own minds, from the 'nefarious drug', were in fact wholly embedded and implicated in the China trade, and that trade revolved increasingly around opium, first, and pungently foremost.

But on 21 June 1832 China was still mostly closed, the missionaries waited at Malacca, and at Shanghai Lindsay, Simpson, Sinclair and Gützlaff waited and sipped their tea. Outside it rained. The angry magistrate eventually returned, announcing that Daotai Wu would indeed meet them, but not here in his now besmirched and trespassed quarters. Instead they should go back outside the walled city to the Tianhou Gong, the Temple of the Queen of Heaven close by where they had first landed. They bid him farewell, which 'usual Chinese salutation' he ignored. 'In my country the government officials are civil to strangers,' retorted Lindsay, eliciting eventually a return salute which the magistrate delivered 'with very bad grace'. At the temple such sullen exchanges continued. Now Lindsay withdrew, now the Daotai refused to keep his petition, now the document was passed from room to room

a half-dozen times, now the Daotai sent an order, lacking any formal stamps, witheringly throwing back the petition and ordering the
'barbarian' ship to depart. 'The English nation are not barbarians,'
wrote Lindsay, again rejecting the return of his document, 'but foreigners, nor is there in the world any nation superior to them in power,
dignity, and extent of dominions.'[67] They argued, as scholars still argue
today, about the meaning of the term '*yi*', which the British interpreted
as 'barbarian', and which the Daotai and others in writing and in person
assured them carried no negative connotation.[68]

They spent the following two weeks at their mooring at Wusong,
close by the mouth of the Huangpu river, walking into the local
countryside where they found, Lindsay reports, 'Company' (*gongsi*) a
prominent mark of quality in shops. They sailed to Chongming island
in the wide mouth of the Yangzi. There were also near daily deliberations
with representatives from the Shanghai authorities, but as the foreigners
clearly would not move on, the higher officials arranged to talk again
face to face back in the city. Lindsay returned to Shanghai on 5 July,
and had what proved this time to be a friendly talk with the magistrate.
Afterwards they were permitted to make private purchases of Suzhou
silks and crepe from city shops, 'which may be considered,' Lindsay
noted, 'the first European traffic ever carried on in Shanghai'.[69] But the
success of the reverse trade was on plain view; many of the city shops,
reported Lindsay, sold European goods. The following day they returned
to the temple for a formal meeting with a higher official, Bao by name,
from the Governor General's staff.[70] 'With much urbanity' he parleyed
with the Britons. All understood the law, he averred, and all wanted
friendly and fruitful relations, but the law was only going to change
through proper process, regardless of how far it was being ignored in
practice. If their king petitioned the emperor for a widening of trade,
he told Lindsay, and if the emperor consented, then 'we shall be
delighted to see you' in Shanghai. But until then they should return to
Canton, without delay. They left that afternoon with a promise that a
polite and properly formal response to their petition would follow next
day. Only when the officials were shown a similar document received
earlier at Ningbo, duly stamped with official seals, would they stamp
this one, but at last it was done, and personal and national honour was
defended. As it 'abstains from the use of all offensive terms, particularly

that of barbarian' and as 'It being now evident that no advantage is derivable from any further stay at this place', they weighed anchor and left.[71]

For the *Canton Register* the voyage exposed the military weakness of the Chinese state and highlighted the friendliness of the people, and the readiness of merchants to buy British goods. It brought back useful intelligence.[72] But the *Register* was after all Jardine's paper. In London the members of the Court of Directors of the East India Company were to prove distinctly unimpressed, as some of Lindsay's acquaintances predicted they would be, when they read the manuscript report.[73] The Court thought it all a very sorry show, censured the Canton Committee and Lindsay himself, and expressed their 'pain and regret' at the manner in which the mission had been handled. The subterfuge was unfitting, contradicted established policy, and must eventually come to light and discredit the Company. They might also have noted wryly that Gützlaff also distributed a 'Tract against Lying' wherever he so lyingly went.[74] There were minor acts of violence: a 'trifling fracas' at Fuzhou saw four of Lindsay's men board a war junk and cut its cable to force it to move away from them; at Ningbo two Chinese officials were knocked overboard with sticks when trying to board the *Amherst*'s longboat while it was surveying.[75] The criticisms of the Canton authorities outlined in the Majoribanks pamphlet and rehearsed repeatedly by Lindsay in his talks with all officials who would listen were improper. Lindsay had far exceeded his brief, and indeed it turned out that he had been ordered not to take the pamphlet at all by Marjoribanks's successor, John Davis, but had secreted 500 copies aboard regardless, after making a feint of surrendering a crate of them to his superior. How could Lindsay, they asked, complain about Chinese faithlessness when he adopted such clandestine methods and had lied his way along the Chinese coast? Why should he think it reasonable to seek privileges that no Chinese vessel would ever be allowed to secure in British waters? How could he record in such triumphant tones that the civility received was often engendered by the fear that the arrival of the *Lord Amherst* instilled amongst officials and people?

'Go smoothly and calmly,' Marjoribanks had advised Lindsay privately, recognizing the impatience and principled stubbornness in his protégé that might endanger his career, as well as Company and national interests. While Lindsay prowled the coast, Marjoribanks talked up the voyage in the City of London on his arrival there in May 1832. It was 'much approved of out of India House,' he wrote, meaning the headquarters of the East India Company, and predictably condemned within it, but what did that matter, was the implication: it was done and India House would soon lose its China powers.[76] Not for the last time, the men on the spot had far exceeded their brief. Distance meant that the representatives of the Company, and later of the British military or diplomatic establishment, had great liberty to take action. They might be damned for it later, but perhaps the immediate consequences would see the achieving of a desired end that would eclipse their overreaching. And they felt that they knew, with utter confidence, what needed to be said and to be done, and when it was right to do it. The view from Canton, from the deck of the *Lord Amherst*, might not accord with the view from London. Company servants lived within the small world of the Canton and Macao British, in the thick of it together. These were the men they talked with, an incessant daily chatter and complaint about the problems they faced: the Canton authorities, the lack of understanding at home, the insults to honour and dignity, the need for action. There was little talk of anything else. They were constantly lobbied. Marjoribanks and Davis had taken advantage of their autonomy to send the vessel on its journey north. But they in their turn had been at the mercy of Lindsay and Gützlaff, sent off north and spending three months longer than ordered on their expedition. Davis was sharply critical in print, pointing to the violence of their actions, their glorying in the 'terror' they had raised.[77] But the man on the spot – on the deck of the *Lord Amherst*, in the Daotai's sanctum – hated the desk-wallah back home, or back along the coast. He lived, he felt, with the realities of the situation, and would act as he saw those. He might display 'some degree of bravado, that was not strictly justified', as Lindsay admitted of Rees's actions at Ningbo, but he had the freedom to make a 'slight experiment' from time to time, as Lindsay summed up his provocative actions at Fuzhou. That is, of course, a 'slight experiment' in violence.[78] Nobody in London, Macao or Canton could stop him, and hang the consequences. And anyway, such minor acts of violence brought, they argued, respect: standing up for themselves, 'carrying your point at all risks', 'increased the estimation they held us in':[79] 'Nothing but practical experience can convince one of the truth of it,' he wrote.[80] Hugh Hamilton Lindsay conflated his own personal honour with that of his nation. Every personal slight was a national question. Such understandings and predispositions were to be the subject of much conflict to come. Every foreigner in China seemed to be clothed in his flag. Every contact with Chinese officials was an occasion for slight. Every minor difficulty was to become a matter of principle. In his physical, verbal and written interaction, Lindsay was on his guard: swift to react, and to chastise. And he was ready to go further. He was ready to turn to violence, to shoulder down the door, and to rehearse and repeat his coarse vandalism in verbal threats. He will have shrugged off the criticisms, for he was not interested in the East India Company past, but in an open future: 'I feel,' he wrote to his mother from Xiamen, 'that the period of our degradation here cannot last much longer.'[81]

Lindsay thought that fifty British soldiers would easily defeat the massed war junks at Wusong. Half a dozen ships could take care of Fuzhou. Four men, he boasted, were able to seize a vessel there, and they carried only two axes between them. This was another recurring idea, a constant in the foreign mind: that either through superior arms, superior discipline, or superior morale and determination, Chinese forces of far greater numbers could be defeated by British troops. Their forts were decrepit and crumbling into dust, their ships were under-gunned and small, their men were cowards, mere umbrella soldiers. The Britons surveyed each port, and examined the forts and other defences, blustering their way close to them even when warned off with shows of force.

Perhaps the most striking thing is what did not happen in Shanghai, nor in Fuzhou or Xiamen, nor later in Weihaiwei. They were not seized. They were not imprisoned. They were not attacked. However much they were – in their own eyes – rudely treated, these violently spoken, violently acting foreign nonentities were granted audience with the most senior of local officials: Daotai Wu, supervisor of the administration of southern Jiangsu province (one of five officials running the province under its governor); the Zhixian (magistrate or governor) of the county of Shanghai. They were met by a more senior official than either of these from the provincial governor's staff at Suzhou. These interlopers, with few manners and less right to be in Shanghai, were to be persuaded, not forced, to leave. Some of these palavers were tense. The situation was often brittle; the injunctions to leave were terse and imperative, but brusque passages were usually followed by smoother ones, and curiosity about the world these men came from very often surfaced. They were treated with almost excessive tolerance and patience. There was no clearly uttered threat of force: that was instead voiced by British lips, and was rehearsed by British guns, axes, sticks and stones.

In 1833 the East India Company monopoly was abolished, and the British state moved to establish a successor institutional presence in Macao and Canton to replace the select committee and its president. A chief superintendent of trade was appointed, Lord Napier, a man who crowed to his diary that 'the empire of China is my own', and that (echoing Lindsay – perhaps through reading Lindsay) a few warships could open up China's ports: 'I should like to be the medium of such a change,' he wrote.[82] So began the 'Napier fizzle', whereby the Scots naval veteran, who had fought at Trafalgar and at close quarters throughout the war with France, arrived in Canton on 25 July 1834, two years after Lindsay's appearance at Shanghai. His duties were to represent British mercantile interests on behalf of the British government, to press (if there was an opportunity) for a relaxation on trade restrictions, and to oversee a survey of the coast. Despite instructions to 'observe all possible moderation', Napier courted confrontation, and he broke all the rules, believing like others before him, that if he pushed the Chinese would give, that the old man-of-war needed boarding and mastering.[83] His arrival in Canton without securing permission first at Macao was prohibited; taking up residence in the factories in Canton was prohibited; presenting his credentials directly to the governor general of Canton and Guangxi provinces was prohibited. Napier followed Company precedent and published proclamations on Canton walls presenting a true account of the history and state of relations between Britain and China, and accusing the governor general of lying. Give me 'three or four frigates or brigs,' he wrote to the Foreign Secretary, Lord Palmerston, 'with a few steady British troops,' and he would settle things 'in a space of time inconceivably short'. Order a small force from India, he pleaded in despatches, which got more and more hectic as his predicament worsened.[84] He was cheered by most of the foreign merchants, warned by worried Chinese ones, and put rhetorically and physically in his place by the local authorities. They simply shut down trade, ordered Chinese staff to vacate the factories, and sealed them off. Napier they put under house arrest, surrounding his residence with soldiers, withdrawing his Chinese servants and denying him fresh provisions, which had instead to be smuggled in to him. They let him stew, and insulted him in public counter-proclamation.

Napier stewed, and he fell ill. He ordered two British navy frigates to come up to Canton, but they failed to make it through the blockade. So much for the impact of just a handful of British ships. Starting out, however, they had fired the first real hostile shots in Chinese waters, when fusilladed by the forts guarding the entrance to the Pearl river, a passage so narrow it was like 'a second Dardanelles' remarked one participant.[85] Two British lives were lost. All this fury and posture came to nought, and worse than that for Napier, for it all proved fatal. Isolated, harried, ill, he withdrew from Canton after two months, dying in Macao of a fever within a further fortnight. He had not been able to leave without written permission, and that was not granted until he had ordered the warships to leave the river. It was the 'last time he put pen to paper'.[86] Broken in spirit, wounded in health, Napier was not permitted to leave down that same river, but was made to travel slowly down inland waters under a large Chinese military escort. On the way the vessel carrying his party halted for thirty-six hours, 'amidst noise, confusion and the beating of gongs, such that his Lordship could barely support'.[87] The bells in Macao were quieted at the request of his physicians, but it all proved to no avail. James Matheson, like others, was disappointed, but 'we cannot but think that in shelling the Chinese forts, he has placed us in a better position than if he had quietly yielded to them in the first instance,' he concluded.[88] Napier fizzled, but guns had spoken clearly to the China British and their supporters, and the rough music which had accompanied his disgraced departure down to Macao was never forgotten.

There followed the first of the British China funerals – not the first burial of the dead, hardly that, for the Protestant cemetery at Macao was already well inhabited, and Robert Morrison had been interred there only two months earlier. But it was the first political funeral, an event marking communal grief and political anger amongst the China British. There would be more of these. Salutes were fired from the *Andromanche*, which had last fired at the Bogue forts, and from British merchant vessels. Portuguese troops fired three volleys over the grave to which the bier was escorted in grave procession with the full honours due a representative of the British crown. Those honours denied him in Canton in life by the Chinese, were performed in Macao, at his death, by the Europeans. The Napier episode was instantly the stuff of legend, and the hapless envoy immediately a martyr, 'driven to death by Chinese official barbarities',[89] conducted to Macao 'as though he were a prisoner, with almost a constant beating of gongs and tomtoms' to torment him.[90] His supporters at Canton (a minority opposed his actions) set to work through the press, pamphlets and private letters, to argue the rightness of the course he took. It was well recognized in time that his pugnacity had occasioned his downfall, that he had ignored the real spirit of his instructions, and their reiteration from London – the Duke of Wellington wrote to insist that it was 'not by force and violence' that British policy would develop – and that a softer course would have worked a solution. But that he had died, his family at his side in Macao, and as a result of treachery and cruelty – setting his fever aside, as his hagiographers did – was to be rehearsed again and again by those who supported his policy and shared his views. Forget the 'ostentation' practised by Macartney and Amherst, he had urged Palmerston; 'leave all presents behind, all musicians and idle amateur gentlemen, literary and scientific'. 'Go to work in a manner determined to carry what you mean.'[91] One of those escorting the coffin was Captain Charles Elliot, the junior member of his staff, who would succeed to the position of superintendent in 1836, and who would direct the drift to war between Britain and China in 1839.

Those in the community who supported Napier, led by William Jardine and James Matheson, opened a subscription for a memorial, and an appropriate monument duly arrived in 1839, 'erected by the British community of China'.[92] Matheson held off directing its erection in the Macao cemetery, as 'we may,' he reported to Lady Napier, 'ere long have a British settlement in this part of the world, in which the monument will be more appropriately placed.'[93] The measured tone of the inscription – 'His valuable life was sacrificed to the way which he endeavoured to discharge the arduous duties of his situation' – contrasted very strikingly with the violent hate talk that had started to become commonplace. Napier's own reports were full of harsh words.

Lindsay was back in England before the Napier affair. 'Always ready, for adventure of any kind', he had travelled back via steamer from Bombay to Egypt, and then overland by camel to the Pyramids. Buy a carpet for your tent, he advised future travellers; make sure there are enough camel drivers, and take at least eighteen quart bottles of mineral water.[94] Passenger steam travel from India was new, and was intimately associated with the Lindsay name – the first and most famous of the steamers, which had pioneered the Red Sea route in 1830, was named after his father (ironically so – the Company under his chairmanship had opposed the initiative) and on this he travelled west to Suez.[95] In 1836 he prepared to travel back to China to trade on his own account as a private merchant, but prefaced his return with the first of several belligerent forays into public debate through a series of pamphlets and later through speeches in Parliament, to which he was elected in 1840. Lindsay was to become, declared one scholar, the foremost of the 'war hawks'.[96] Perhaps a violent (and humiliating) assault that he had barely survived in Macao in December 1832 while on a hunting trip did not further help his humour, but the *Amherst* report shows that the even tenor of his views was already well set, and that Majoribanks's concerns were well judged.[97] 'The Chinese,' Lindsay announced in 1836, 'were predetermined to insult' Napier, their conduct was 'treacherous', his experience 'humiliating', and were 'the strongest grounds for resentment which the Chinese have ever given'. The British had two options, he wrote: to withdraw from trade with China altogether, or 'by direct armed interference . . . demand redress for past injuries, and security for the future'. Dismissing the former, he presented a blueprint for war grounded in his observations from the *Lord Amherst*: twelve ships (including three armed steamers) and 3,000 men could blockade the major ports, take the fleets of Chinese coasting junks hostage, and force concessions from the Qing. The aim was a 'commercial treaty on terms of equality' – equality in language and status, to escape the 'barbarian' taint – and the end of monopoly and petty restriction, and the major restriction of trade to Canton. But this would also be a war of words:

the flag ship was to carry a Chinese printing press. Chinese ports were to be papered with pamphlets outlining the causes of British anger, the objectives of British arms, and the desire of the British for peaceful relations with the people of China.[98]

Lindsay was not alone. The war of words (and over words) was joined by others. William Jardine's partner, James Matheson had also resorted to print, publishing in pamphlet form in England what their newspaper shouted about from far Canton. But they were answered by milder voices: 'recourse to arms to teach the Chinese ettiquette' was not universally admired as an argument, and better translators than Lindsay disputed the translation as 'barbarian' of the term commonly used of foreigners by the Chinese.[99] Sir George Staunton, who as a boy had accompanied Marcartney's embassy to China, learning Chinese on the way, and who had established a good reputation as a scholar, took up his pen to try to forestall an unprovoked conflict.[100] Lindsay had happily fired his salvo, an open letter to Lord Palmerston, and sailed back east in the late spring of 1836, taking a lead in organizing an international General Chamber of Commerce in Canton, which body he chaired and so was its formal spokesman, ready to cry grievance and demand his armed steamers.[101] Nobody was happy with the state of relations with China, or with the insecurities and situation of the China British, but still they stayed and still the trade grew, legitimate and contraband, intertwined and inseparable.

People commingle even when laws forbid, and amongst all the bellicosity and diatribes of the frustrated merchants you can find echoes of friendship and intimacy. Shortly after Lindsay sailed north in 1832, James Matheson wrote to John White in Calcutta, responding to the sad news from India that White's brother William had died. Matheson outlines the winding up of William White's Canton financial affairs.[102] He had previously kept a house in Macao before leaving about three years earlier, and had left evidently intending at least initially to return, but had then directed that the house be given up. He had left, reported Matheson, a standing desk and a chest of drawers containing some old accounts and letters, and there was also his 'pensioner', his Chinese mistress. When White had returned to Bengal he had left his house, property and servants in the care of this 'superior class' of woman, who was educated, literate and also able to speak Portuguese. She had come originally from Canton, and was now 'outcast' from her family. When White decided to delay his return, or not return at all, he had asked Matheson to locate and rent a suitable house for her. Matheson was concerned that John White made no mention of her; was she to receive no pension from his brother's will? If not, then might he ask 'with some earnestness' that something be arranged. It would 'be extremely distressing to the deceased's friends who respect his memory' if she was to sink into penury. 'I have not seen the woman since the melancholy news reached me,' concluded Matheson, 'and I believe she is still ignorant of her loss.' This had been no perfunctory, mercenary arrangement, and that real emotional ties had started to thread people and communities together across the apparent gulfs of language and culture was outlined here by the importuning Scot. There is plenty of hate in this narrative, but there was also always somewhere, at the same time, affection, amity and love.

3

On a Chinese Stage

Was it a dream? Were his eyes deceiving him? He pressed forward through the crowd, the report goes, to get a better sight of the strangers, and 'immediately began rubbing his eyes'. But they were still there when he looked again, he could not rub them away, they would not go. One of the two men he came to stare at thought him a comic sight, and comic too the reactions of hundreds of others, who poured out of their buildings and leaned out of windows as a cry went up, that there were foreigners on the riverside walk at Shanghai.[1] The curious crowds who had mobbed Lindsay and Gützlaff, and who together with this man mobbed missionaries Walter Medhurst and Edwin Stevens on their sudden irruption out of the rain and the river onto the same Shanghai waterfront three years later, were affable. They were too affable for the liking of officials, too inquisitive, too boisterous, too eager to grab one of the booklets the foreigners handed out (Protestant tracts only this latter time; no accounts of the English character), and they needed marshalling, and restraining. Placards were soon posted up wherever the men and their ship anchored off shore, forbidding trade and promising stern punishment; and when the foreign backs were turned the books were seized and burnt there on the embankment where they had been handed out.

The missionaries clambered ashore opposite the Tianhou temple, the Temple of the Queen of Heaven, 'spoken of by Gützlaff and Lindsay' they recalled, and made their way towards it with a sullen Yankee sailor and their bag of books, and prepared to dole them out. They had sailed north on a small brig, the *Huron*, loaned them by American Canton trader David Olyphant, who wanted good news about God shipped north along the coast, not foul advice about opium. With their cargo of 20,000 books and tracts they had already stopped at Weihaiwei on the coast of Shandong, and had spent three weeks visiting small bays on the north and south coasts of that peninsular, doling out their literature. The ship was now moored at Wusong and they had been rowed the last stretch on a ship's boat by five sailors, whose language darkened with the weather and appalled the clerics. Now, as they were getting their bearings on shore, they were quickly interrupted by the sound of bamboo staves being drummed on flagstones and whipped out at bystanders obstructing passage: local officers and their attendants had rushed to the scene. Medhurst, a Londoner, was an eighteen-year veteran of London Missionary Society work amongst the Chinese of southeast Asia, and was perfectly able to converse with these officials, and to accept their invitation to enter the temple for a quiet discussion (and tea and cakes) in a private room. And so, yet again, the Tianhou temple at Shanghai played host to parley, and the crude theatrics of private diplomacy, as Medhurst in particular stood, or rather aimed to sit, on his dignity as yet higher officials, the Customs superintendent (with a foreign cloak, he noted) and the district magistrate, came along in turn to sort things out, and found the foreign intruders rudely rebuffing the requirements of propriety when meeting officials of the Great Qing. 'I am determined not to stand,' said Medhurst, if the magistrate was going to sit. 'He is the greatest Chinese in Shang-hae,' argued the officials. You must stand, as we do. Well then, said Medhurst, you see here 'the greatest Englishman in Shang-hae', who does not 'choose to compromise the honour of his country'.[2]

But meanwhile, as all this went tediously, tendentiously, predictably on, we can, I think, assume that the performance on stage resumed. For the second time in its recent history, foreigners had also interrupted a show: an opera was in progress at the temple, and shows were special events. Probably it continued with a somewhat distracted air, as a flowing hubbub marked the course around the audience, musicians and performers of discussion about the newcomers. Perhaps some of the crowd drifted away, to wait for another look at these curiosities, to follow Stevens back out into the street, where he soon went to distribute his books while his colleague conversed and argued with the officials. The sailor sat mutely and watched the palaver. Medhurst and Stevens, like Lindsay and Gützlaff three years before them, had walked in in mid-performance, diverting all eyes to themselves from the actors, as they made their way with the officials to private quarters. 'Every one's attention was turned to us,' Lindsay had written (Gützlaff does not mention the incident), and 'our appearance immediately stopped' proceedings on stage (at least, of course, as he reports it, placing themselves centre-stage in that day's drama).[3] And if we wearily respond that all these foreigners place themselves centre-Chinese-stage, then we might remember that this is always the privilege of the reporter, even when it is always the self-important habit of the European interloper. How dramatic an entrance they made, then, all eyes turning, all falling mum. It is worth noting though that Medhust, like Gützlaff, had no eye for what he had interrupted, although as we shall see later he was a man of great curiosity about the China (and the Shanghai) that he was to find himself living in. It is only from the account by Stevens, a Connecticut man, almost three years now in Asia, that we learn that there was anything going on at the temple when the three men approached it, and that there were many people already assembled there.

Understanding what they were congregating for on this dreary October day in 1835, and had been watching that wet June morning in 1832, and why at a temple, will help us develop a fuller picture of the China that first Lindsay and Gütlzaff, and then Medhurst and Stevens, were so intent on interrupting with their presence. Indeed it will help if we understand more about the temple itself, which so stood out on the Shanghai waterfront close by the Customs House and under the highest point on the city wall, and which so stands out in these two landmark accounts of foreign visits to the city. And we need to understand, too, who these men were who rushed along to challenge the two sets of truculent foreigners, and also their superiors who then came along to rebuff them, as well as the organization they brought to bear on the barbarian merchants. This way we can better understand the China of the early 1830s outside the narrow confines of the factories, the roads, Macao, that narrow semi-foreignized sliver of the Canton delta that so overfills accounts of the early Sino-foreign encounters. So this chapter explores the world of the Qing of the early 1830s, tracing it from the Tianhou temple stage to the court at Peking, an empire that was pestered by these vexatious visitors with their pamphlets and demands. They were not of great concern to it – as we shall see, there seemed to be issues of more moment to the administrators of the Qing and to the peoples of the empire – but even so, and even if slowly, the minor incidents, the little disturbances in Shanghai at the Tianhou gong and nearby, presaged new problems which came to demand the attention of Peking.

Medhurst was to publish a potted history of the Tianhou temple fifteen years later, when he translated a selection of entries from an official history of the city into English as a *General Description of Shanghae and its Environs* (1850), although by that time it was not the sight foreigners tended to note when they rounded the final bend in the Huangpu river and looked on the city ahead of them on the west bank, south of the confluence with the smaller Wusong river, for new developments were then to catch their eyes.[4] Founded originally in the late thirteenth century, during the last years of the Song dynasty, the temple lay north of the Customs House between the city and the river, and was dedicated to the 'Queen' (as they then had it, we would more accurately now say 'Empress') 'of Heaven'. This deity, based like many on a historical figure, was the focus of a bundle of popular religious practices and beliefs along the south and eastern coasts of China, and in Taiwan (where she is still known more commonly and colloquially as Mazu, 'ancestral mother') and amongst emigrant communities from these regions, but she had also become the centre of an officially sanctioned cult.[5] Medhurst and Gützlaff will have known the Empress of Heaven, who protected seafarers, fishermen, sailors and rich merchants who travelled the maritime highways along the coast and out to the southeast. She was the object of the 'disgusting' 'idolatry' practised by the sailors who carried Gützlaff north from Bangkok to Tianjin in 1832 – his words, his visceral reaction. She sailed in all ships and was propitiated every day. Emigrants from Fujian, who had long sojourned in the city, had brought her with them to Shanghai from the south, although symbolically the temple was never brought within the walled city – Tianhou stayed by the water over which she had dominion. The city god, the Chenghuang (at Shanghai a virtuous official, Qin Yubo, thus ordained by the first emperor of the Ming), held sway inside the wall and held court at his own temple. Handily, the Tianhou temple being next to the Customs House, the two formalities of voyaging could be dealt with on the same errand, the rendering of dues to this world and to its yet more powerful shadow. This cult generally, and as a result its temple, like many others along the coasts, had been sanctioned by a decree of the Qianlong emperor in 1737.[6] Such official support, which involved the formal promotion of the goddess to 'Empress', has much to do with the Qing dynasty's long and difficult pacification of the Chinese coast after its invasion and defeat of Ming China in 1644, and it brought it under the supervision of the 'Li Bu', the Board of Rites, one of the six boards which formed the administrative heart of the dynasty at Peking. The cult was therefore formally recognized and approved, and as a result local officials at Shanghai were required to participate periodically in formal ceremonies at the temple. At some cities one Tianhou temple might be the preserve of these official rites, and another the haunt of the people, but at Shanghai there was no such effective distinction, although there were numerous Tianhou altars in the city.

This was not the furthest north of the Tianhou temples, but it suggests powerfully how closely connected Shanghai was to the coastal trading routes which the foreigners followed north, and at the same time suggests how far the reach of the state extended into Chinese life. As scholars have observed, such official sanction – making an empress out of Mazu – involved no laying down of the law about the content of such approved religious belief, no Thirty-Nine Articles or Tridentine catechism, but regulated its outward forms, standardizing these as orthodox practices. These the state tolerated, and recorded. The officially unrecognized and heterodox, however, it could and did smash when it saw a need or an opportunity, and when it had the force. Such official practices have shaped recent scholarly debates about processes of cultural integration, which seek to understand how a dizzying array of local cultures and languages (and the legions of gods in thousands of villages) were patchworked into a visibly and apparently homogeneous 'Chinese' culture, one equally recognizable amongst the emigrants in Singapore and at the heart of the empire, and carried on the ships in between.[7] Sanctioned thus by the government, listed in official histories, temples were funded by donations from their communities of worshippers. Sailors and travelling traders will have worshipped there on safe arrival with gratitude, and prior to departure with expectation, leaving offerings, lighting incense, praying. Wealthy Fujian traders in the city, in particular, will have patronized Tianhou more regularly, as a fixed spatial point in Shanghai that came within their Fujian Shanghai world, and they will have borne the costs of the temple's periodic renovations. This way they demonstrated their own wealth and status, and banked a little useful credit with the gods. Close by the temple they also established a guildhall, and so had a little slice of Fujian in this foreign northern city.

A temple was not a church. It had no priest. Physically it was a complex of halls and courtyards which opened out from a main gateway. These housed altars, sometimes a permanent stage and galleries, a bell tower and drum tower in large temples, inscribed large stones – stele – on which were written details of key events in the temple's history or similar texts. The courts and halls might be erected one behind the other along a single axis from the entrance, with smaller halls and other buildings at the sides, but there was no rigid pattern, and shape and splendour, or dowdiness and dilapidation, reflected their fortunes. A temple was as grand as the funds available at its foundation or last renovation, and as the coins of visitors allowed, and the largest were generally the largest buildings within a community. There were Buddhist and Daoist temples (and some were both), with monks or nuns, but most were neither. They were instead manifestations of the ordinary religious and communal life of the Chinese. Different gods in their different temples, or on their different altars within a single temple, or at altars elsewhere, served different functions: communal protection, moral order, health, fertility, commerce, wealth. Shanghai had temples for gods of plague, pestilence, drought, agriculture, literature, fire, water, and many more; above all for the earth god, the god of war and the city god. (The Confucian temple does not quite fit within this taxonomy, as it was not a site of any popular religious practice, but solely of state ritual.) The vibrancy of a temple might rise and fall with the perceived interest of the deity in answering the calls made on him or her, on the efficacy of prayer, of offerings, obeisance, vows and on the usefulness of the gods. Useless gods got short shrift, as well they might. The Europeans often called the temples joss-houses, and the writhing, lingering smoke of incense burned in great jars or from masses of small sticks always struck them, always obscured in their minds and eyes much else that went on; it suffocated their toleration. They usually hated them, seeing in them corruption, superstition, decrepitude. Gods were offered incense, food and drink. They were offered operas: the stage would be placed where they could watch the proceedings. Their birthdays were celebrated, they were processed about, placated, sometimes punished. Gods and people were busy with each other. A popular temple was also a commercial and economic site, selling goods for worship, or hosting markets and fairs in their precincts or at their gates at times of religious festivals. They were embedded in the daily public space of the city, casually used for recreation as much as for any religious purpose. They shaped rural and urban life, and they shaped cities.

They also shaped the year, and communal lives. At the Tianhou temple Fujian merchants will have patronized the periodic ritual operas that took place, and which both sets of interlopers interrupted.[8] The biggest event of the year was the god's birthday, on the 23rd day of the 3rd lunar month. There were processions, and celebrations at the temple, and also at the various guildhalls which had Tianhou altars (there was more than one Fujian guild). The temple quarter was shrouded in a fog of incense: lanterns bloomed, boats congregated by the waterside, and 'cymbals and drums assault the ear' reported one spectator.[9] Shopkeepers vied for attention and custom. The opera performances that took place were ritual religious acts, but not overtly so; they were not glossed with active, solemn devotion. They were communal acts, whereby Fujian sojourners came together and showed off their cultural wares, the richer providing for their less wealthy compatriots. And they were clearly also simply entertainment, for fellow provincials, for connoisseurs, for the curious. Medhurst, who certainly understood Fujianese (he had published a dictionary of it), might have found the performance familiar, if ever in the various Chinese communities he had lived and worked amongst in southeast Asia he had seen a Fujianese opera at a guildhall or a temple. There is nothing in his writings to suggest that he had, but missionaries often sought out crowds and set up a stall to preach to them, and theatre always attracted masses of people. Medhurst earlier boasted about how he liked to shove his way into temples, assailing devotees with the 'folly and madness' of their actions.[10] It is not immediately clear that he saw anything as he did so, other than misguided souls. He did not look to the stage. Gützlaff had experienced Chinese drama 'such as it is', dismissing its 'unnatural representations' and the 'jarring sounds of the music'.[11] The interrupted performances would have been in that same recognizable style, but Europeans who ventured into Chinese theatrical performances generally loathed what they saw and what they heard, and found the experience wholly bewildering.

This was unfortunate. Drama, as ritual and entertainment, was a pre-eminent part of Qing culture, and was patronized across society, from the imperial household with its private theatres to rural communities which could stretch to hiring a ramshackle troupe for an annual festival. Styles, forms and content moved from urban theatres to rural stages with troupes of travelling actors, and around the country with merchant and official patronage. Its vibrancy meant that it needed policing. Originally actors had had low status, but by 1800 could be stars in any modern sense of the term. Eighteenth-century emperors worried about the infection of Manchu soldiers with the lust for theatre. By the 1830s all were infected, the imperial household too.[12] There was a rich and extensive corpus of dramas, and a variety of styles and traditions ranging from folk dramas crudely presented on simple temporary stages to glitzy productions staged at Peking's theatres by professional troupes. Chinese drama differed from European in important ways – it dispensed with scenery and was accompanied by music, and so seemed closer to opera than theatre, and in some styles acrobatics featured very heavily. Although Shanghai supported an urban entertainment culture that included brothels and teahouses, there was no dedicated theatre there before 1842. Peripatetic companies performed in private houses, at the guildhall and temple, or on temporary stages. In richer cities an individual merchant might support a company. At Yangzhou, Suzhou and Peking permanent theatres were by 1832 long established, but for decades after the growth of theatres in Shanghai, dramas continued to be performed at guildhalls and temples.[13]

Whether marking one of the calendar festivals, a day marked out for a particular deity, a private celebration (an individual's birthday, success, return from afar), a commercial venture (its launch, an anniversary, thanks for protection from disaster), a theatrical performance was invariably also a public affair. Hundreds of people could crowd in to watch, hear, experience. The well-heeled and the lowly would all be there, though they would find their different stations and contrasting comforts inside, and entertainers, acrobats and snack-sellers, as well as pickpockets and sharpers, would congregate in the temple grounds and outside. Food, tea and conversation were the stuff of the event too, and the more *renao* (hot and noisy) the atmosphere, the better by far. There was bustle and chat outside, inside, before, during and after – about the quality of the performance; about these strangely dressed, sodden, foreigners perhaps; about nothing much in particular. These were all part of the event, adding spice and flavour. On stage the actors, accompanied by musicians, would perform dramas taken from episodes in the classic pantheon of popular novels, such as *Water Margin*, a saga of righteous outlaws, and *Journey to the West*, the retelling as legend of the monk Xuanzang's journey to India to procure Buddhist scriptures with, among other companions, the acrobatic, crafty Monkey King. There were martial themes, history plays and love stories. Most in the audience would be familiar with the plots, and with their stagings. There was a wide range of styles across China, and regional opera styles were in the ascendant, learning from each other, shaping each other and changing; the most influential was the one we now call Peking Opera (*jingju*). The performance at the Tianhou temple might have been a popular drama in the Minnan canon of dramas in the Fujian style, which was not ornate in its costume or headdresses like the increasingly popular Peking Opera. It is likely that a temple performance would have featured acrobatics, for the gods were well entertained by tumblers. But what was being staged depended on the occasion, and who was paying – the temple, a guild or a private patron. We cannot know, but we do know that the temple and the gathering so rudely interrupted by these bumptious foreign travellers were part of the fabric of Shanghai life and culture, in which were tightly interwoven the sojourning communities of commercial China, men from afar, whose trading activities were a key component of its wealth and importance. Shanghai was not a large city, and it was no cultural powerhouse. It was not famous for its culture as were the nearby cities of Yangzhou or Suzhou. But such performances were part of Shanghai's life nonetheless.

The year at Shanghai, at Xiamen, and at all the ports visited, was marked by calendar events that gave shape to Chinese lives, and which occasioned celebration, ritual and opera performances.[14] The different festivals had a focus on family, on community or on both, but all gave rhythm to the year. The *Lord Amherst* had set sail three weeks into the lunar new year, a time of family celebration, feasting, gambling, the paying off of debts, new clothes, and exchanging visits. Shops closed, trade came to a standstill, the mahjong sets came out and fireworks and the clicking of gaming tiles punctuated the holiday. The end of the celebrations and the reopening of trade was marked on the fifteenth day by a festival of lanterns, which sprouted up on buildings and were paraded through the streets. In each locale these festivals had their own minor variations, their own regional, provincial or micro-local flavourings: different ingredients in the seasonal dumplings or cakes, the pleasantries exchanged, the rituals undertaken in household, temple or street. All were different, but all were the same: all were Chinese. As Lindsay and Gützlaff arrived at Xiamen, the Qingming ('tomb sweeping') festival was about to be celebrated, family graves were tidied up, and offerings made to ancestors. As their ship lay in harbour at Ningbo, a celebration for Guandi, the god of war was held. As they sailed north towards the Yangzi, Shanghai and other cities celebrated the Duanwu festival (the summer solstice). At Fuzhou, as at other coastal cities, thirty or forty 'dragon boats', organized by temples or guilds, would race each other, while city inhabitants picnicked and watched.[15] The ship's boat from the *Huron* arrived at Shanghai with the 1835 autumn high tides, and at a city *en fête*. It was the 18th day of the eighth moon, three days after the mid-autumn or moon festival. At this autumn equinox families came together, sweet or savoury *yuebing* (moon-cakes) were eaten, and the sight of the full moon savoured. As the celebration drew to a close a local one took place, for the precise day that Medhurst and Stevens arrived was the Birthday of the God of the Tides, the day of the autumn high tide. People travelled to Haining, outside Hangzhou south along the coast, to watch the sometimes thirty-foot tidal bore move up the Qiantang river, and at Shanghai people came to the east of the city to look at the high tide on the Huangpu. The Danfeng tower, on the city wall behind the Tianhou temple, was the highest spot available for this. So the customs of the ritual year will have drawn more people to the river bank, to watch the drama, and to watch the high-tide peak on the river early in the afternoon on that grey, damp day.

Some of these religious festivals stretched the limits of official tolerance. Like many of the educated elite, officials often had little time intellectually for popular religious practice. As guardians of order and peace they saw such large gatherings as attended temple processions as repeated causes of conflict between groups (as devotees of one deity or immigrants from one place clashed with others); as sites of transgressions of moral order (prostitutes, for example, parading in the city god's annual procession); and they were clearly magnets for thieves and loafers. An orderly city was one which placated the demands and energies of popular religious culture as well as the intellectual scepticism and sensitivities of the educated, and kept order on the streets. Potentially the most unruly of the festivals took place over three days in the seventh month, and was celebrated in particular by the sojourner merchant communities in Shanghai. During this time hungry ghosts were fed. Buddhist in origin, but adopted far beyond Buddhist practices, it involved opera performances, processions and bonfires in the street where people made offerings of paper clothes and money to pacify ghosts who had been released from the underworld for the duration. Charitable acts associated with the festival further enhanced its popularity, and so made it a source of greater official unease and a flashpoint for crime and disorder.[16]

There were traders from Fujian in the city, enough of them to support the temple and two guildhalls, and to support such communal festivals and sprees. There was a community from Canton and from relatively close-by Ningbo. These three groups were the most powerful of the Shanghai sojourners, with the Ningbo men ascendant. Shipping and traders also came from Tianjin and from Manchuria in the north. Junks sailed in from Canton, Taiwan and southeast Asia to the south. Lindsay claimed that 400 vessels were counted by his crew in one week alone, all heading to the city past Wusong. He had his reasons for stressing the commercial importance of the port, of course, but we have no reason to doubt, and plenty of evidence to support, the view that the city was a thriving commercial centre.[17] Geographically it was close to the southern point of the Grand Canal, the main artery of supply for the imperial capital in the north, and in its hinterland were the great cities of the Jiangnan delta – Suzhou, Yangzhou, Nanjing – and the richly productive farmlands that surrounded them. Shanghai could not be better placed for maritime trade: fifteen miles from the mouth of the Yangzi, up the sheltered Huangpu river. Its administrative position reflected its commercial importance, for the Daotai, one of five in the province, was based there. It was not a large city – its population of roughly 200,000 was about equal to that of Xiamen or Tianjin, and was dwarfed by Fuzhou's half a million – but it was a trading city which attracted all comers from the Chinese world.[18] And sojourners and settlers prefer familiarity to adaptation where possible; as with the British in Canton, so with the merchants from Ningbo, Fujian or Canton in Shanghai. They preferred their own speech, their own food and, when they could have them, their own prostitutes. So they combined in provincial associations (*huiguan*, 'guilds' in English) which established buildings whose size and sophistication represented their own relative wealth as a community, and which provided a point of call, a place for fellow countrymen to meet. They also preferred to mediate intra-communal disputes themselves, aided fellow provincials down on their luck, and shipped the dead home to rest in more comfortable and familiar soil. The authorities expected them to regulate themselves in this way too, as they did the British at Canton, and as a body the *huiguan* represented the community to the local administration, and to other societies. The city of Shanghai was thus formed of a complex set of communities and institutions, and this complexity, in a small city on the coast, might alert us to the wider complexities across the great empire of the Qing in all of its glory.

Scholars have begun in recent decades to look beyond the rhetoric of some schools of Chinese statecraft, particularly insofar as it articulated hostility to commerce and placed the merchant in a lowly social position. For China – Ming China, and after 1644 Qing China – was a bustlingly busy and complex commercial realm, one strongly bound into trade networks extending far beyond its borders. Indeed, scholars of the later Ming have been placing China at the centre of the global economy, rather than oblique to it, which helps a better understanding of global economic history, let alone the cosmopolitan Ming.[19] Trade brought the state increasing revenues in the eighteenth and nineteenth centuries.[20] With commerce grew the wealth and through that the status and ambitions of merchants, who lived like their gentry betters where they could, sponsoring the scholastic endeavours of their kin, patronizing the literati, enhancing their status by purchasing degrees, works of art, and the services of teachers and scholars.[21] While most commerce was regional at its greatest extent – and scholarship has worked with an understanding of eight basic macro-economic regions within China – there was significant long-distance trade across a far wider, empire-wide economy. Porcelains circulated from Jingdezhen, tea from Zhejiang and Jiangsu provinces, textiles from Suzhou – all carried on a transportation network that moved goods and people along waterways and overland routes. The 'primacy of commerce' shaped the cityscape of Hankou. Salt merchant wealth was the rock of Yangzhou's ebullient culture. In addition, provisioning Peking, remitting the annual grain tax (in kind) north to the capital, was an enormous logistical undertaking: 6,000 junks were used to ship the produce along the Grand Canal.[22] And as goods and merchants flowed, so too did ideas, books, styles, fashions, students, officials, exiles, gods even, backwards and forwards, all circulating within the realms of the Qing.

They circulated beyond it too. Commerce was clearly also international in scope, and Japan, southeast Asia, Europe and South America (via Manila) were key components. As the *Lord Amherst* dropped anchor at Wusong, two Shanghai junks were preparing to return from British Singapore with the southeast monsoon. Canton boats arrived there with goods for the emigrant Chinese – fireworks for their festivals, dried foods, tea, medicines – the necessary, soul-affirming stuff of home. The Shanghai junks carried silks, and these were bartered for pepper, birds' nests, sharks' fins, camphor, luxury foreign goods for Xiamen, Canton and Shanghai. Gützlaff's junk had sailed its well-travelled route from Bangkok to Tianjin with its cargo of pepper, wood, sugar and tin.[23] From Zhapu in Hangzhou Bay ships sailed to and from Japan. Silver had flowed into Ming and Qing China to pay for the tea, silks and porcelains purchased by the Japanese. Spanish American dollars had become the silver coinage of preference in the realm, arriving via Manila or Europe.[24] From 1757 onwards maritime trade with the Europeans had been restricted by fiat to Canton, and the traders forced to deal only with a handful of Chinese firms, the *cohong*, who were granted monopoly trading rights and who were required to supervise and control the foreigners. The riches that could accrue to *cohong* merchants were also reflected in the direct financial returns this system provided for the imperial household in Peking. For it appointed from its own staff there the Hoppo at Canton, who was required to remit funds annually to the palace.[25] In this way funds from foreign trade were channelled straight to the palace at the heart of the empire. Aside from Canton there was also a small Russian outpost at Peking itself, and a legitimate overland trade to Russia in tea was coordinated from Hankou while a vast smuggling trade took place across the inner Asian Russo-Qing borders.[26] So foreign goods, like foreign silver, were far from unknown by Chinese consumers, who might have as little knowledge of their origins as British tea drinkers had of the hills their leaf came from (or of the fact that black and green tea were not products of different plants, as was thought). And as Lindsay noted, shops advertised that they sold foreign goods, and the East India Company's Chinese name was recognized and used in a way that resembles a trademark.

The views from the deck of the *Lord Amherst* or the *Huron* of the cities they visited provided enough anecdotal evidence of the scale of commerce across the realm to whet foreign appetites, and what they learned from their pestering of merchants and seamen is reinforced by modern scholarly studies.[27] There were Xiamen's 'wealthy and enterprising' merchants, great numbers of them, with strong ties to southeast Asia – forty junks a year sent to Bangkok; boats sailing to Manila, Batavia and Singapore. Xiamen traded rice to Taiwan, sugar to Ningbo, Shanghai, Tianjin and Manchuria. They shipped soybeans south. Fuzhou was tied closely to trade with neighbouring Zhejiang province, and its approaches were crowded with coastal vessels readying to ship timber and tobacco. At Ningbo there were 'handsomer' shops than any Lindsay had seen before.[28] Beyond their coastal ken, we have a fragmentary but increasingly detailed picture of the world of commerce of the early nineteenth century and its limits. Although most people lived on small family farms (the rural population was an estimated 93 per cent of the total), and most of these were subsistence farms, participation in a wider economy beyond the fields was a vital strategy for survival.[29] Farmers engaged in handicraft production – and some regions specialized in particular processes and products – or

worked as porters or peddlers. The rural landscape was pocked with
market sites, and a farmer was rarely more than half a day's walk from
one. The family, local and wider economies were inextricably tied
together through such markets. The cross-regional grain market meant
that farmers in Jiangsu province could grow mulberries for silk
production. Tea was distributed across the empire, and to its neighbours.
Merchants from the northern Shanxi and Shaanxi provinces travelled
to the south to procure tea that was shipped north and onwards to
Mongolia and towards Russia. They also travelled to Sichuan, home
to a highly industrialized salt industry, which supplied the market in
neighbouring Hunan and Hubei provinces, and attracted capital and
merchants from as far away as Jiangsu province.[30] The involvement
of the state in all of this was in fact minimal, but as its administrators
routinely enforced written contracts it thereby greatly facilitated this
complex world of commerce. And it retained some key monopolies
which delivered important revenues, salt in particular, and the trade
with the Europeans at Canton which so vexed and frustrated Lindsay
and his ilk. They knew so well many of the possibilities that lay beyond
their reach by imperial order, and engaged in shrewd estimate and
wild conjecture – so many customers for British cotton goods, so
much coastal traffic for more efficient foreign vessels, perhaps for the
new steamers. And the elusiveness of these possibilities enraged and
offended them.

Ordering all this was an emperor, a state, codes of law and imperial
decrees, and a tight mesh of regulation and precedence: the empire of
the Da Qing, the 'Great Brightness'. The year 1832 was the twelfth
year of the reign of the fifty-year-old Daoguang emperor, Qianlong's
grandson. He had become in 1821 the sixth of the Manchu rulers of
China since their armies had swept south in 1644 and shattered the
reeling empire of the Ming, whose last emperor had committed suicide
as soldiers of a great peasant rebellion stormed his capital. In the later
seventeenth and eighteenth centuries the great Manchu emperors had
consolidated their hold over the country, finally extirpating rebellion
and the Ming-loyalist forces that held Taiwan for almost forty more
years, and then they had marched into the west, conquering the Muslim
areas they subsequently termed Xinjiang, the 'new frontier'.[31] From
the palace complex at the heart of Peking the Manchus ruled a massive

multi-ethnic and multinational empire, of which subdued Ming China was one part, albeit the largest by far, stretching from the Himalayas to the mouth of the Amur river in Siberia, and from central Asia to the island of Taiwan. Beyond the formal Qing realms the rulers of neighbouring kingdoms, such as those in what are now Vietnam and Korea, acknowledged in symbolic form the power of their neighbour, sending gifts and ambassadors in periodic recognition of the overarching sovereignty of the Son of Heaven. The Daoguang reign saw no new colonizing ventures, and although military expeditions were sent to suppress rebellion in the Muslim west in 1825–8, the colonial consolidation and expansion of the emperor's predecessors was largely foresworn as Daoguang and his bureaucracy dealt with the conundrums of ruling some 400 million people, a task no other state in human history had ever had to face. And that population was growing, putting pressure on natural resources. They had to find a way to deal with incipient revolts, a treasury greatly reduced by the costs of suppressing rebellion during his father's reign, and in 1824–6 by a major logistical crisis caused by the silting up of the Grand Canal and the stranding of the capital's grain supply. As a younger man the emperor had proved his own martial prowess when, in 1813, rebels attacked and entered the imperial palace. This was part of a wider 'Eight Trigrams' uprising in north China, when members of a number of religious sects became convinced that a new era was imminent, that it needed midwifing, and that the midwifery duty fell to them. They aimed to overthrow the Qing, and so punch their way into their new world. One group attacked the palace in a bid to assassinate Daoguang's father, the Jiaqing emperor. In the ensuing mêlée at the gates and on the walls, the prince had personally killed two of them with a musket, putting into effective deadly practice the military training that was part of the education the Manchu princes received. The armies of the Qing eventually dealt with the rest.[32] Those captured were interrogated, their confessions minutely recorded, and then they were sliced to death.

Daoguang has been under-served by history. His latter reign is well known, the last dozen years especially, but assessments have focused mostly on his handling of the Canton question, the growing opium crisis and its fallout, and on exploring the roots of the cataclysmic revolt that broke out shortly after his death. Bizarrely, the only biography of this emperor which has been published in any European language was written by Gützlaff, appearing in 1852, the year after the Pomeranian's death. Assessments of his reign have not strayed far from the bare essentials outlined by this contemporary account, although they have been stripped of their evangelical hostility.[33] We now know more about Daoguang's real private world, however, thanks to recent work on the imperial household. We know he had a taste for plain, northern Chinese foods; spent thirty years, man and boy, in the palace classrooms; had twenty consorts and nineteen children; and, uniquely for a Qing emperor, was actually the son of an empress. All the others were sons of consorts, sometimes women of relatively low birth.[34] We also now know a little more about Daoguang as ruler, as he appeared off the record when interrogating his officials. He comes across as informed about issues, unsure about the reliability of the detail provided by his officials (with good cause as we shall see), and a 'professional and dedicated ruler'. He was not the stuff of hostile European fancies, all quixotic vice and harem. He was no oriental despot. Nor was he the despised feudal archaism of the Marxist history of communist-era China, which castigated the failures of the late Qing monarchs to combat imperialism's assault. Daoguang was the emperor, a diligent and concerned administrator, and emperors mattered. They were not simple figureheads, ruled by their officials.[35]

And he was a Manchu. The ethnic identity of the Manchus was a serious matter, and we now also have a much better sense of the way in which they regarded themselves as such. This might seem an odd statement, but the fact is that for a long time the Manchu-ness of the Qing was occluded, largely by assumptions that they had been thoroughly 'sinicized'. This was the argument that to rule China, they had had to become Chinese, that China had eventually conquered them. This was not just a nice conceit for the conquered, but an attempt to explain how a relatively tiny conquest elite kept control for 250 years. But one mechanism for doing so was in fact the keeping of very clear ethnic distinctions. Being Manchu was vitally important to them: it was transmitted from generation to generation, articulated, regulated, displayed and protected.[36] The Manchus remained acutely conscious of themselves as such throughout their long rule over China, and conscious too of the ethnicity of their subjects. They were conquerors, and they ruled the conquered. They extracted total acquiescence and fealty, and they shredded any sign, any hint, any inadvertent echo of treason, or of disrespect. They conquered Chinese bodies, by ordering that all men shave their foreheads as an outward sign of submission, and grow their remaining hair long, keeping it braided in a queue. The Qing emperors certainly faced real revolt, as the young Daoguang had learnt, from millenarians, underground Ming-loyalist secret societies, Muslim subjects, and tribal groups. But the merciless campaigns against literary 'crimes' directed by his grandfather Qianlong, which had peaked in the early 1780s, were driven more by suspicion of treason, by apparent anti-Manchu comments or hints, and by the zeal of lower officials, rather than by a real threat of rebellion.[37] Anti-Manchu comments were hunted down because of this continuing strong ethnic identity, in which important components included the Manchu language, dress and food (Manchus were meat-eaters, and hunters). But this was not simple carnivorous despotism, as the contemporaneous British state – which suppressed the radical press, Jacobin supporters, and the crowd at Peterloo – was not simply a police state. Qing rule was grounded ideologically. They did not rule simply 'on horseback', as a martial tyranny through the right of conquest, but instead through the granting of the 'Mandate of Heaven', which they argued had been withdrawn from the Ming as their dynasty collapsed, and which had passed to them in 1644. In practical terms they ruled through a multiracial bureaucracy coordinated from Peking, which ran on lines directly inherited from the Ming. Most of their administrators were Han – that is, ethnically Chinese. This was no wildly unrestrained despotism, for at times that bureaucracy could and did temper the actions and judgements of the emperors, who also had to bear Confucian propriety in mind, a body of thought and practice that was greater by far than they were or could ever hope to be. The bureaucracy conducted lively and considered debates about policy formulation. Ultimately, however, decisions lay wholly in the hands of the emperor.[38]

The Qing did not rule their empire through a single unitary state system. Like the British, theirs was a multinational empire and they had different relationships with different territories and different groups of subjects. China proper was mostly ruled through the central bureaucracy from Peking via the provincial governors and governors general.

But in the southwest, administration of significant non-Han groups was in the hands of hereditary 'native chieftains' whose status was conferred on them by the Qing in return for their ensuring stability and fealty. Conquered Xinjiang in the west was under a military administration. Tibet was the most autonomous of the regions, and its relations with the Qing complex, but its spiritual and temporal leader, the Dalai Lama, acknowledged (in Qing eyes) the supremacy of the Qing, and a Manchu official, an Amban, represented the emperor in Lhasa. In both regions, as in Mongolia, administration was in the hands of local elites, and not the Chinese bureaucracy. But more importantly, Qing rulers embedded themselves into the religious life of the Buddhist sects which predominated in Mongolia and Tibet, presenting themselves as reincarnations of the *bodhisattva* Manjusri. They had themselves painted in this guise, and sponsored the construction of important and symbolically located temples at the heart of the empire. The Qing presented themselves as rulers of five peoples, whose languages (Chinese, Manchu, Tibetan, Mongolian and Uyghur) were accorded equal status, at least symbolically, in the life of the empire. This was an empire that was adept at dealing with different peoples, their customs, beliefs and languages. It administered each in the way which seemed best, or most pragmatic at the time, and given considerations of resource and capability. It was well used to dealing with sojourning foreigners from outside its formal domains, like the British at Canton. But such pragmatism also had to coexist with the fact that Qing rule was predicated on an assumption of universal empire. The emperor was lord of all under heaven, and all other rulers owed him at the least a symbolic acknowledgement of their subservience. Neighbouring rulers in Korea or Vietnam, whose cultures were strongly shaped by Chinese patterns and beliefs, were conspicuous in their ritual periodic demonstrations of subordination, the sending of what were termed in English 'tribute missions'. More distant rulers were expected to be less active in their demonstration of subordination, but were at least expected to acknowledge the supreme overlordship of the emperor at Peking.

The bureaucrats that Lindsay knew from Canton, and their peers that he met in Shanghai and in other ports, were part of the nationwide system of administrators, few in number in real terms but powerful, who ran the Chinese heart of the Qing system. Six boards, one of which, the Board of Rites, oversaw officially sanctioned temples, coordinated the bureaucracy at and from Peking, and their members formed part of the Grand Council, which advised the emperor. The eighteen provinces of China were administered by governors (Xunfu), although in most cases a governor general (Zongdu) was responsible above them for two provinces, while below each governor authority was vested in the intendants, the Daotais, of whom there were eighty-four across China in the later nineteenth century, and under them prefects and some 1,400 district (or county) magistrates (Zhixian).[39] At each of these levels was a set of subordinate officials who oversaw particular activities, and each official was supported by a local establishment as well as his own entourage, a personal private office, and servants. There was a parallel military structure. At Shanghai the 'Su-Song-Tai' Daotai supervised the prefects at Suzhou and Songjiang, a sub-prefect, and twenty magistrates. The Shanghai magistrate reported to the prefect at Songjiang, but the Daotai, based in the city, was much closer to hand.[40] The magistrate was the key representative of the central state in the administration of Qing society: appointed by the Board of Civil Office at Peking, forbidden from serving in his home province, bound into a tight and swift reporting and supervisory system up through the provincial hierarchy to the centre. Magistrates' posts might be of lesser or greater importance administratively, but each was nonetheless the centre of daily administration and justice, and oversaw orthodox religious practice, for the tens of thousands of people who lived in the counties they controlled.[41] The magistrate also oversaw supervision of the lowest levels of the empire-wide examination system, which channelled candidates to the biennial provincial, and from there to the triennial national examination held at Peking, when between three and four thousand candidates travelled from all over the country to the capital. Around 300 of those would proceed to the very apex of this system, the Palace Examination, overseen (sometimes in practice, but at least nominally) by the emperor himself, from which the highest officials were selected. From a vast pool of candidates, some two million strong at the lowest levels, this vast and carefully supervised system winnowed out all but some few hundred holders of the metropolitan and provincial degrees to staff the administration of the Qing.[42] Centuries now of anglophone hostility to imperial officialdom in China, and twentieth-century Chinese judgements on the failures of the Qing, routinely castigate the examination system and its graduates as hidebound, useless literati, skilled in penning highly formulaic texts – the famous 'eight-legged essay' – but no good for active governance. To call an official a 'mandarin' is no compliment: the word itself derives from caustic descriptions of the Chinese system. But that system worked. It regularly refreshed the administration with new personnel, brought talent out of the provinces into the centre, and was probably much more successful at that than anything that could be found in Hugh Hamilton Lindsay's Europe.

A comprehensive and well-regulated communication network bound this system together. Senior administrators, such as the governor generals, could write memorials to the throne directly, and would secure a speedy response – replies were despatched the day after a memorial was received by the emperor. The speed and circulation of the reporting of the *Lord Amherst*'s progress along the Chinese coast shows how robust this system was (and at Shanghai three years later they already knew that the *Huron* had probably come from Shandong). But the evasions, silences and exaggerations that show up when contrasted with the British accounts and the correspondence with officials that Lindsay kept, show how theory met practice. Reports were submitted up the chain to Peking, carried by riders covering some sixty miles a day along the routes of the state's extensive official postal network.[43] (And if they were too slow, or the mail was damaged or tampered with, they were punished.) Reports were also carried to neighbouring provinces, warning that a ship was on the coast, sharing the information that could be gleaned from the dissembling foreigners. As many of these were published in the court gazette, and as copies circulated to Canton, the East India Company men and the foreign traders were able to see how the bureaucracy dealt with the issue – in fact, it was their only source of news for the progress of the ship before its return.

One of those writing was Lin Zexu, governor of Jiangsu province, who was stationed at Suzhou some fifty miles west of Shanghai, and who would come to figure prominently in Sino-foreign relations. The son of a teacher, Lin was a native of Fujian, and after early examination success – he was a high-ranking candidate in the 1811 Palace examination – was appointed to his first substantive post, as supervisor of the Yunnan provincial examination, in 1819 at the age of thirty-four. Thereafter he held an intendant post in Zhejiang on the east coast, and then became successively judicial commissioner in Jiangsu and Shaanxi provinces, financial commissioner at Nanjing, and then in Hubei and Henan provinces, before becoming governor in Jiangsu in 1832. There were other commissions on the way in this spectacular rise through the bureaucracy, and Lin was already famed for his justness and honesty. We shall meet him again in this story, but in 1832 he was cosignatory with his superior, the governor general at Nanjing, Tao Chu, of a number of memorials about the *Lord Amherst*. Lindsay had refused to leave Shanghai unless permitted to interview or communicate with Tao. At first the Daotai had refused to even forward such an improper request: he knew the law, and he knew his job. But as the foreigners showed no signs of leaving, evidently something was arranged to break this peculiar impasse. A Fuxiang, a lieutenant general from Lin Zexu's staff at Suzhou – Bao – eventually came to investigate and meet them at the Tianhou temple. Bao restated all the arguments they had already heard, and heard all along the coast, and made it very clear that they could not expect anything else.[44] But he did so with, in their eyes, civility and grace. It was with this meeting that Lindsay concluded that honour was satisfied (as satisfied as it was going to be) and that it was time to move on. But in the formal Chinese record outlined in the despatches carried north by the post riders, the meeting never happened. In fact, as Bao's superiors, Lin Zexu and Tao Chu had it, the foreigners had had no meetings at all, and nor could they have had, for the *Lord Amherst* had never arrived in the city nor had it even entered the mouth of the Yangzi. What ship? What foreigners? Hu Xiami had never interrupted the play, never stomped about the temple, or strolled through the city. Instead, as a result of preparations by the local military, alerted by earlier memorials, the ship was thwarted in its attempt to reach shore, was ordered to depart, and after waiting a night for good weather had sailed south, escorted part of the way by the local military. A potential rupture in the normal ordering of Qing Shanghai was thereby efficiently and effectively thwarted, on paper.

Interesting, noted the emperor, who saw all such correspondence and commented on it, but how, he next wrote, could this actually be so when the ship was now reported on the coast of Shandong? Caught out this way, 'reporting with ambiguity' as Daoguang put it, the officers tried to evade the obvious charge by fussily proposing courses of action for dealing with the ship, but their neglect of duty earned them an investigation by the Board of Civil Office.[45] At the very least the governor general and the governor themselves had not been informed of the unorthodox local management of the foreign vessel, and did not know that their subordinate staff had acted warily to forestall any potential conflict which might rebound to their detriment (but the arrival of Bao suggests that Lin Zexu at least was aware of the real situation). A quieter life is always an official's preferred life. Getting the problem to sail away was always going to be the main aim of those who first came into contact, but the truculence of the intruders, and their persistence, their refusal to sail, their insistence not just on being met and heard, but also their tiresome concern with proprieties (as they saw them) and their sensitivity about language tangled everything up, and for days and days they would not go. Instead they indulged in recondite debates about terms and texts. As far as we can see the officials at Shanghai and at Suzhou aimed to sort it out locally, and then report it as done and dusted. So the swift and efficient reporting network of the Qing, which laid the facts of the nation in front of the emperor every morning in Peking, was only ever as good as the information submitted to it. In this of course, as we shall see, there was no Chinese monopoly. And while officials lied, dissembled or evaded at their deathly peril, they clearly did not always have a vested interest in communicating the facts fully and frankly. Allowing the *Lord Amherst* to sojourn for eighteen days at Shanghai so contravened the standing instructions of officials that it had to be tidied up into a neat account of the forthright and efficient dismissal of the foreign ship before it could even enter provincial waters.

The administrators of the Qing had bigger worries in the spring and summer of 1832 than the bizarre voyages along the ever troublesome coast of the strangely shaped foreign ship. Three weeks before Lindsay slipped out of the Macao roads, a major rebellion had erupted on the northwest borders of Guangdong province, in the highlands where the province bordered Hunan and Guangxi. This was a revolt of a non-Han people, the Yao, who, in anger at the depredations of neighbouring Han communities who competed with them for scarce resources, rose and struck out at the Qing. The state lacked any routine effective presence in such areas, and so there was nobody to prevent Han communities preying on their aboriginal neighbours through secret organizations. Yao anger turned to revolt, led by a 'Golden Dragon King', as he termed himself, Zhao Jinlong, who wore imperial yellow, and led what proved to be an intractable rebellion. The Jiaqing reign had been mired in such revolt, of the Miao aboriginal people in 1795–1806, and of the millenarian Buddhist 'White Lotus' sect in 1796–1805, decade-long uprisings which had shattered the provincial status quo, drained the imperial treasury, and exposed serious weaknesses in the Qing military systems. Now there was tribal revolt again, and the news from the south was for too long worryingly bad. Government forces were defeated in the field. The military commander of Hunan province was killed in an ambush. And all this by people regarded as uncivilized savages, 'stupid and violent' as one official put it later, even though he was sympathetic to the roots of their discontent.[46] When the rebels in Hunan were defeated, and Zhao killed amongst them, a related revolt exploded further south across the provincial border. The governor general at Canton was cashiered for failing to suppress the uprising. Hundreds of the troops from Canton were found to be useless because addicted to opium. The emperor's brother-in-law was ordered to investigate and to lead a final campaign to suppress the rebels, and, as he reported it, succeeded. The Yao were bribed into submission.[47] But there was also rebellion in Taiwan, and there were bad harvests. There was spirited debate about the Yao rising after it was suppressed, and the uselessness of some of the Canton troops came into the foreground as evidence of a problem far greater than that of the troublesome tribesmen, who could eventually if enough force or resource was brought to bear be wiped out or bought off. The regiments were incapacitated by opium, and so must have had easy access to the drug; and so, as opium was illegal, and its trade illegal, and as the governor general had only the previous year been ordered to crack down on the covert trade, they must be themselves complicit in its circulation. The very guardians at the gate were addicted. The governor general could not, or would not control them or the trade, or bring himself to report his failure. Something was wrong: Canton was rotten. This was the real worry in 1832, a problem of the heart, the seeming ineffectiveness of administration and military in the south, and their poisoning by the foreign drug.

This then was the wider Chinese stage. The language of drama often pervades contemporary reports, and historical accounts. This is not a peculiarity of writing about China, it is a more common affectation. The historian lists the dramatis personae at the front of the narrative, and then sets the scene. Enter the actors, the decks of the *Lord Amherst* and the *Huron*, and the Tianhou temple their platform. Offstage the ships at Lintin shifted their illicit cargoes to the busy smug boats, and Canton soldiers smoked the drug and could not fight. The language of drama can of course belittle. But the foreigners took China seriously, and yet they didn't. Gützlaff took Daoguang seriously, and yet he didn't; Medhurst took Chinese culture seriously, it was the key to his success, and yet in temple or in shrine he could not help but interrupt and denounce the futility of it, the grand emptiness of all of this learning and belief. As each of these and others reported, they placed themselves calmly at the centre of the mandarin storm, ineffably unflustered by the crude theatrics of their interlocutors, the choreographed fancy dances of the warships at each port, the seemingly forbidding forts and defences. The gaudiness of it all, as they saw it, kept striking them. There seemed to be no divide between the temple stages and the diplomatic and military spectacle prepared for Lindsay and Medhurst – all highly stylized, all rigidly conventional in movement and effect. They thought it all play-acting, all acting out of the required script (with room for a little improvisation sometimes, when the ship was out of sight and a man might trade). Those forts, they concluded, were flimsy painted slats, signifying nothing. Lindsay was ever deadly serious, of course, and Medhurst too. But readers of their reports found support enough there for their own ever-contradictory prejudices and convic-tions: that the China trade should be opened and that the laws of China should be respected; that the dual monopoly of *cohong* and Company was evil and that the seemingly anarchic country trade was anathema; that violence was abhorrent and that a little force in the right place could solve the problem easily. Look, some said, there was no adequate coastal defence. Lindsay had shown that we have simply 'fancied forts, armies, and navies to repel every intruder from the coast'. We have 'fancied' that the people were hostile to trade, 'fancied' that they were hostile to foreign goods, but now 'these prejudices must vanish'.[48] So it was serious for all readers, and yet Hugh Hamilton Lindsay, stage name Hu Xiami, acted out his petulant, needy Britishness on stages all the way from Xiamen to Korea, before his bewildered but patient audience of officials and hapless passers-by. The whole thing – the tenor and hysteria of it, all that honour, those dramatic exits, the refusal to return to the set – the whole thing, it has to be said, was as ridiculous as it was deadly serious. John Crawfurd, formerly governor at Singapore and commissioner in Burma, a persistent critic of the Company monopoly (and on a handsome Bombay retainer to be so), thought there was much serious stuff in Lindsay's book. But, oh, if 'it was printed by the dealers in cheap publications' it 'would be almost as entertaining as *Robinson Crusoe*', and if 'introduced on the stage', well, he concluded, it would make a fine pantomime.[49]

4

Lindsay's War and Peace

Some pantomime. Hugh Hamilton Lindsay got his war, his *'leviathan'*, he called it. Those Napier-ordered bombardments of the Canton forts were simply 'minnows' compared with the just desserts of Chinese obstruction and insult that were to be meted out by British warships.[1] The illegal coastal trade greatly expanded after the Napier debacle, and the Qing authorities had decided to act decisively to deal with the disorder and corruptions that the opium boom gave rise to. Officials knew that the imbalance in trade – the rapidly increasing outflow of silver from China – was destabilizing regional economies and the imperial Treasury. They knew that the impact of opium addiction on individuals and their families and communities, and of the disorder engendered by the smuggling rings on society and authority, was widespread, sustained, and intense. Moral and practical considerations were tightly intertwined, but the practical issues were far more pressing for officials.[2] There was a problem at Canton, but that problem leeched far and wide. Imperial decrees prohibiting the drug were being flouted; it was time to act. The course of events that followed is well known.[3] How Lin Zexu was sent as a special commissioner to investigate the problem in Canton and to put a stop to the trade, how he made his way overland to the city and set about making his mark: all of this has been much narrated. Lin certainly made an impression, and earned his place in Madam Tussaud's waxworks, in *Punch* magazine, and at the heart of early Victorian British popular culture. No other Chinese bureaucrat ever became so globally known: an actor playing this oriental bogeyman for the anglophone world even joined 'Napoleon', 'Henry VIII' and 'Queen Elizabeth' on stage in London in 1842.[4]

Of this worldwide life to come, of course, there was no inkling when

Lin arrived in Canton on 10 March 1839 with lists of prominent Chinese and foreign participants in the illegal trade. As a governor general in Hunan and Hubei, to which post he had been appointed in 1837, Lin had already piloted a strategy aiming to strike hard at Chinese consumers of the drug and smugglers. Advocates of this policy were in the ascendant in the Qing bureaucracy, and a campaign at Canton would visibly demonstrate resolve to the foreigners and, it was expected, force the official British to check the illegal trade.[5] Lin set to work with vigour. He issued decrees ordering smokers to hand in their pipes; ordered officials to attend properly to their responsibilities, and not to subvert the law, and ordered Queen Victoria to do so as well. A letter to her was printed and circulated to foreign ships and beyond, on the same principle that the British had in mind earlier with their pamphlet, that out of so many at least one copy would somehow find its way to the addressee.[6] And then Lin ordered the foreigners to surrender their opium, and he had the factories cordoned to focus their minds on the issue. The streets leading into them were blocked off, with a thousand guards preventing any traffic, and no supplies were allowed in. The foreign traders, all of them, were to be held hostage for the drug, without fresh food, without their servants, worried that the commissioner's little list – headed by Lancelot Dent, closely followed by James Matheson – presaged individual arrests and possibly torture or other Chinese punishment.

Charles Elliott, by now the British superintendent of trade, rushed to Canton from Macao in cocked-hatted full dress uniform, evading the blockade and thereby deliberately adding himself to the hostaged fray, and the British Crown to the roster of injured and insulted parties. Backtracking rapidly on his initial defiance ('a firm tone and attitude' would settle Lin he thought),[7] Elliott broke the deadlock on 27 March when he ordered all the stocks of opium formally to be surrendered to him, on the promise of future compensation from the British government, and then to be handed over by him to Lin's officers. It was a bold move, one that took away the breath of every Canton trader, not least because Elliot acted entirely on his own initiative, committing the Crown, in the end, to a deal worth £2m (about £135m at 2009 prices). What commercial bliss it was that hot Canton spring, tarnished only by the boredom and privations in the factories. Never had the trade been so easy, so profitable, so secure as it was when Her Majesty purchased, sight unseen, 20,291 chests of the finest Patna and Madras; never were the ships that rushed to discharge their loads at Lintin so assured of a good deal, a gilt-edged deal; never were they so hurried – Elliott had promised Lin 20,000 chests, but this was more than the stocks in hand, and shipments afloat were called to make their way swiftly onwards. And Elliott had saved them all that clandestine labour and risk, the transhipment of these cargoes along the coast, the extra costs of subterfuge and time involved in taking them to market. It was, declared James Matheson, whose firm surrendered 7,000 chests, 'far more advantageous than if we had to work off so large a stock in an overburdened and persecuted market'.[8] And what was eventually left over, why, when the hullabaloo was over, and when Lin's officers had spent three weeks in April and May overseeing the smashing of the balls of opium and their flushing out to sea at Humen, close by the Lintin anchorage, then what a market there was for it, and what prices it could now fetch if discreetly, much more discreetly, sold along the coast to the friends disappointed by the diversion of the spring stock.

Somebody was going to have to pay for all of this. As soon as they could, the Canton British sent back representatives to lobby for proper action this time, to avoid an Elliott fizzle, and to make sure that their interests were heard, all two million pounds worth of them. Lindsay scurried home, skipping the Pyramids. So did Matheson's nephew, while William Jardine, now retired and living in London, was also to join the fray. Matheson noted the need in addition to 'secure . . . the services of some leading newspaper to advocate the cause'.[9] Pamphlets poured off British presses. The China trade lobby met ministers and sent them petitions and suggestions, for after all they knew China, knew Canton, and knew better than anyone what it might take to prosecute a war. They took their maps along to Palmerston, and showed him where to strike. 'Is the war with China a just one?' asked one of Lindsay's pamphlets; well, yes, of course it was, he concluded. Would we expect otherwise? There was all that recent history of insult and injury, of Napier, and Lord Amherst, of yearly irritation and capricious decision, all that insecurity of factory life to avenge. But more importantly, there was the insult at Canton, the confinement of the entire foreign community, Britons, Parsees, Americans, those complicit in the drug trade and those opposed to it, as some were, and of Elliott by Lin. They were kept confined until 5 May, and sixteen of the more prominent were ordered to stay until 24 May after all the opium had been handed over. Conditions had been successively eased at each significant stage of the surrender of the 20,000 chests – supplies of food let through, their laundry seen to, their servants allowed back – but the insult remained to be righted. They had scrubbed their own floors, cooked their own meals, milked the cows, played ball in the square, sang old songs and composed topical new ones, drunk – there was never any shortage of wine or beer – and all the while excoriated 'this scoundrel of a commissioner' who had held them all hostage, whether or not they were opium traders.[10] And to cap it all Commissioner Lin introduced a new bond that all must sign who arrived at Canton, forswearing any involvement in opium trading on pain of death. But so all-encompassing did the wording seem that the foreigners assumed that it meant that all involved with a vessel would suffer for any offence committed by any individual on board. They were wrong, but they were not going to take any chances at the hands of Chinese justice.

The sullen moves began that mark the onset of a war. The British community evacuated Canton on Elliott's orders in May 1839, moving to Macao, but the fallout from yet another routine and routinely squalid encounter between British seamen and Chinese villagers, this time on the Kowloon peninsular, opposite Hong Kong island, forced them to move again. A villager died at the hand of a seaman; the handover of the culprit was demanded by the Chinese authorities; the request was refused by Elliott. It had happened before, many times, but now Commissioner Lin, buoyed by the spring's success, was in no mood to compromise, and moved to threaten the British at Macao en masse. So they decamped to Hong Kong, where some seventy British vessels were concentrated, a refugee community awaiting action. The contraband traffic along the coast had resumed smoothly, if much more secretly than ever before, and was now coordinated and resupplied at Manila, further internationalizing the trade. And during all this, as successive reports made their way back to Britain, and as the lobbyists worked their words, the pressure on the British Cabinet to vote for war grew. On 1 October 1839 the decision was taken, and it was decided moreover that the Chinese would pay for Elliott's 20,000 chests. The war decision was taken not to enforce an illegal trade, and not to secure that £2 million, but to secure redress for insult – the holding of the Canton British hostage for their opium stocks, and the holding of the Crown's representative. Lord Palmerston's Ministry needed to act; any Ministry would have needed to act. The immorality of the contraband trade, the economic consequences of a restricted China trade, the potential of the commerce that could be grown with the end of the Canton restrictions were all debated and discussed. But for the Cabinet, China was one issue among many, and the issue that stood out so clearly was that which had animated angry Hugh Lindsay in the Daotai's *yamen* in 1832: honour, and the consequences of failing to maintain it; insult, and the consequences of failing to redress it.[11] Orders were shipped east. An expeditionary force was assembled in India, and it arrived in the Canton delta in June 1840 spoiling for a fight.

An episodic conflict followed. Bouts of fighting were interspersed with parleys and negotiations, and with defence of insecure occupations of Chinese islands that steadily drew a popular resistance. Disease laid waste the British forces and crews. Straggling ships were captured by the Chinese and their crews imprisoned. The war tested the easy blockade proposals of Lindsay and his like-minded warmongers, and found them wanting. First the fleet sailed for the north, bombarding defences at Xiamen, seizing the island of Zhoushan, east of Ningbo, and then moving north to the mouth of the Beihe, and the approaches to Peking. It had a letter to deliver, Palmerston's 20 February 1840 demands 'to the Minister of the Emperor of China', which outlined the problems, and sought 'satisfaction and redress for injuries inflicted by the Chinese Authorities upon British Subjects resident in China', and those inflicted on the British Crown, in the person of Elliott.[12] Delivery proved difficult under the circumstances, but contact was finally made at Beihe. Formal discussion was promised at Canton, so the British sailed back south – they could barely even actually see the coast at Beihe, as the shallows forced them to moor far from land, and they could not be seen. There was nothing but mud to fight there. Even so, the court knew they had come so far north, and this was clear, multi-masted evidence of Commissioner Lin's abject failure to solve or contain the British problem, and so he was dismissed. Back at Canton the British gave notice of what they could do in the first days of 1841, bombarding, seizing and disabling the first line of defences across the mouth of the Pearl river. Elliott's violence secured an agreement, the Chuenpi (Chuanbi) Convention, but when it seemed to be unravelling, his forces finished the job in February. And if the British forces were disabled by disease, the Chinese defences were rendered obsolete by the most significant of the new additions to the British naval armoury. Lindsay had called for armed steamers in his 1836 pamphlet, and the China expedition had come east with them. Most significant of these was the *Nemesis*, which had sailed from Portsmouth around the Cape to join the force being assembled, arriving in Macao in November 1840.[13] In the Canton delta she came into her own, roving at will in all weather, free from reliance on the wind, steaming along the narrowest of inlets, her guns raking the Chinese defences with seeming impunity. And she could tow behind her ships full of soldiers ready to land after her bombardments. In 1793 when Lord Marcartney and his entourage had left China, the Qianlong emperor had ordered his officials to make sure that the military might of the Qing empire was on view at all times. So as the embassy had sailed south their journey had been lined with soldiers. They found them, so they wrote, decorous and were not much inclined to be impressed, but there is no doubting that that year neither British nor Chinese had any military advantage over the other. The *Nemesis* changed all that, and that change won the war.

Elliott led his forces from the delta up to Canton itself in early spring, smashing all remaining defences and savaging Chinese forces wherever they were found. The city was his to master, but he was rightly disinclined to attempt to actually seize it, and instead made it pay – cash, 6 million silver dollars on the nail, to a six-day ultimatum – to be spared an assault. At Zhoushan and around Canton the conflict was vicious on both sides. The British and Sepoy troops cared little for taking prisoners; and almost 300 British and Indian survivors (mostly the latter) from the wrecked ships *Ann* and *Nerbudda* were murdered in captivity in Taiwan. In the late summer of 1841 a reinforced and resupplied fleet sailed north again, led by Sir Henry Pottinger who was to replace Elliott, bombarding and seizing coastal ports as it went. What Queen Victoria labelled the 'unaccountably strange conduct of

Charles Elliot' in settling for the Chuenpi Convention – the barren rock of Hong Kong most of all – had 'mortified' Palmerston and outraged much of British opinion. It secured too little, and ignored instructions.[14] There was no British honour regained by Elliot's peace, and the superintendent was recalled. The Qing too repudiated the agreement that their envoy Qishan had signed, cashiered and banished him, and prepared for more conflict. Pottinger was charged with prosecuting the war to a proper finish. And this he did. In the spring of 1842 the British captured Shanghai. Their troops lodged themselves in the City God temple, looted pawnshops, dressed themselves up in the gorgeous fineries they found in them, and burned Shanghai libraries in their cooking fires or used them as toilet paper. Then the seventy-five vessels of what *The Times*, which opposed the war, labelled this 'engine of evil' sailed up the Yangzi, heading to seize the southern end of Peking's main supply artery, the Grand Canal.[15] In Zhenjiang's Jiaoshan park today you can still see the site of the forts which failed to stem the assault on that city on a horrendously hot 21 July. The twelve guns of the Jiaoshan battery had been pounded into silence a week earlier by two of the armed steamers, and were then seized and destroyed on 17 July. 'Here,' read the signs, 'was spilled the hot blood of the patriotic Chinese people.' It flowed profusely on the 21st, staining Zhenjiang's streets. In nearby Beigu park you can buy a pamphlet commemorating the furious but ultimately unsuccessful defence of the city. Its illustrations show British soldiers spitted two at a time on the spears of the defenders, or cowering as swordsmen made ready to despatch them, or looting in the aftermath of the battle. Over thirty died (and sunstroke rather than spears took more than a few), but thirty British dead did not sway the day. At 'the prettiest Chinese town I had seen', as one of its attackers described it, Manchu troops fought stubbornly and surprisingly hard, would not surrender, and did not decamp. The commander immolated himself when the day was lost. Over a thousand of his soldiers died and survivors were reported to have killed their families and then themselves rather than fall into British hands. The suburbs burned; the pretty city was a 'monument of death and desolation'. The slaughter and self-slaughter sickened the British on the spot (and garnered a wretched press back home) – 'Women and children in dozens hanging from beams,' one reported, 'or lying on the ground with their throats cut, or drowned in deep wells.' The British were impressed by the tough resistance, which they had also met at Zhapu southwest of Shanghai on the north shore of Hangzhou Bay, but they were bewildered by the wider private massacres their victory unleashed.[16]

At Nanjing – and at 'the cannon's mouth' as one commentator put it, with British forces ready to strike there and at Yangzhou – the Chinese parleyed, Gützlaff interpreting.[17] The fall of Zhenjiang left the Grand Canal open for the British, whose fleet now controlled the lower Yangzi. On 29 August four copies of the peace treaty, bound in yellow silk, were signed aboard the fleet flagship, the *Cornwallis*, and thereafter despatched to London (where they were one of the first ever such documents to be copied through photography). Palmerston's list was embedded in the new 'Nanjing Treaty': Hong Kong island and its harbour, which had sheltered the refugee British, was transferred to British sovereignty 'in perpetuity'; five ports were to be opened to British trade and residence (all of them bar Fuzhou had been occupied or attacked by the British during the campaign); British consuls under a superintendent of trade at Hong Kong were to be stationed in each port to oversee the British residents, who were to be exempted from Chinese law and subject only to the jurisdiction of the new officers; communication between British and Chinese officials was to be under-taken in forms and with terms indicating 'a footing of perfect equality', and a suitable, in their eyes non-demeaning, mode of correspondence was proposed for the non-official British. They were to be 'barbarians' no longer. The *cohong* was abolished; a 'fair and regular' customs tariff was to be introduced; and the Chinese agreed to pay an indemnity of 21 million dollars – 6 million to reimburse the confiscated opium, 3 million to pay off various *cohong* debts, and 12 million to pay for the cost of the war. Ransoms already extracted from cities such as Yangzhou and Canton were to be credited to the indemnity, but the British were to hold on to Zhoushan, and to Gulangyu island opposite Xiamen, until the full sum was handed over. The news reached London on 22 November, accompanying better news from the ongoing disaster of the first Afghan war. There were 'mixed feelings' from *The Times*, at the conclusion of a 'miserable war', and the 'ill-gotten gains' therefrom. But at least it was over, and British soldiers were no longer to be

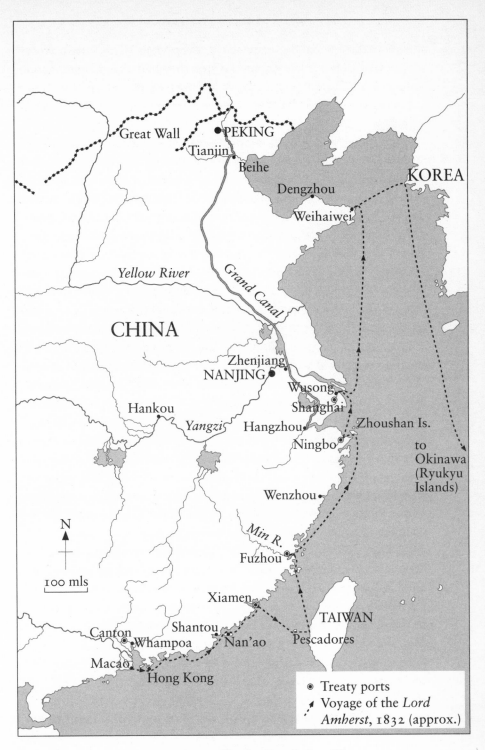

3. Treaty Ports after the First Opium War

slaughtering 'crowds of pig-tailed animals' in a grossly unequal contest on the battlefield.[18] *The Times* was not swayed by the Canton lobby and opposed the war as grotesque, but it saw virtue in the peace.

It had been an odd sort of war, and it ushered in an odd sort of peace. It was very clear to the British that they had won. At home letter writers called for public celebration and thanksgiving. The expedition had stormed up the coast and along the Yangzi. Even where the defenders had fought well – more than well enough to earn the respect of their typically contemptuous attackers – they had nonetheless been overwhelmed. If the coast had not been effectively blockaded as Lindsay and the lobbyists had proposed, the lower Yangzi had certainly fallen into British hands. They had secured their objective – a treaty that accepted all their demands – and the overall aim, a free trade with China, and a trade free of caprice, was now seemingly guaranteed. But even so, even with a signed and sealed treaty, even as the British hastily set about appointing men to staff their new consular establishments, even as Walter Medhurst and the missionaries in Malacca got ready to sail (and to bring their printing press with them), and as speculators, plant hunters and men of science made ready, and even as the trading firms planned their moves into the new ports and bought land in Hong Kong, it was also clear that the Chinese did not seem to recognize that they had been defeated. This is not to say that overt hostilities continued, although occupation and bombardment left bitter legacies that made life difficult for most of the early residents in the new 'treaty' ports, and Canton was a particularly bitter city. Rather, it was that the Qing state, and its bureaucracy, did not much appear to recognize that the Nanjing Treaty and defeat in the field really meant very much in the great scheme of things. We know that differing perceptions in particular of the importance of Canton to the British helped inform this comedy of error. Lin Zexu and his allies assumed it was the key war target of the British, and the fact that it did not fall was taken (and trumpeted by them) as a signal victory. But the British saw no military value in storming angry Canton, knew the cost in lives would be high, and so were content with the ransom they received and with the fact that they had neutralized its defences and threat. They looked north instead, and aimed to hit the state hard, not the provinces. There was the further fact that in a much-celebrated incident, 10,000 village militiamen were marshalled to confront a much smaller British column north of the besieged city at Sanyuanli on 30–31 May 1841, which sensibly withdrew, with but a single casualty, and this gave heart to factions within the bureaucracy that saw in such mobilization a tool for victory. The myth of victory at Sanyuanli was also much lauded in Communist-era China, as a victory of popular peasant resistance against imperialism.[19] The trouble was that the British seemed entirely unaware that there had been an engagement, let alone a defeat (let alone scores killed as the story had it). But they soon recognized the potency of myth. There was a 'rabble multitude assembled on the heights against our forces' that they should have dealt with, one officer later reported, because not doing so meant the Cantonese 'have always imagined themselves capable of contending with foreign soldiers'.[20]

However unsettled (and however obscure understandings of the war), peace was a fact, and the British advantage needed to be pressed. Hong Kong, taken into a sort of possession from 1840, when the refugee British moved there from Macao, and formally taken over under the terms of the abortive Chuenpi Convention in January 1841, was already springing up a makeshift city, Victoria. War brings all sorts of opportunities, and the transfer to British title of the island sparked a bout of speculative land purchasing and building, a 'sort of hallucination' one critic, Robert Montgomery Martin, labelled it, the first of many such bouts that were to characterize a major part of the new business world of the new possessions: 'They thought Hong Kong would "rapidly out-rival Singapore, and become the Tyre or Carthage of the Eastern hemisphere,"', he continued.[21] And first among the builders: Hugh Lindsay's firm, Lindsay & Co., which constructed the Albany Godowns in what became the Wanchai district. The senior partner was now based in London, and had been one of a number of the Canton lobby who had entered Parliament in 1840 determined to have their say (Jardine was another; Matheson followed in 1843). Not content with their pamphlets and their print, their meetings with politicians at home, and their lobbying of Elliott in the delta, they had taken themselves into the House to represent their China concerns and their demands at the heart of the country and of the empire. This was hardly an unusual trajectory for merchants on the make socially, but the prime motive was the need to influence at a pivotal moment, rather than the need for status alone. So there was no longer anything peripheral or offshore about the men from Canton and their interests. Nominally Lindsay spoke for Sandwich, in Kent; hostile constituents shouted that he spoke for 'gold' (that he had bribed his way in, a charge he denied); clearly he spoke for Canton, and for free trade.[22]

Others started to speak for 'China'. In the aftermath of the war – indeed, before it was over – its participants published their memoirs and reflections. The early British embassies had seen two waves of interest, and now there were new books; the warmongers (and their opponents) had churned out new pamphlets; Parliamentary committees sat and took evidence. There was much, much more available to help the reworking of the Jesuit-flavoured fantasy of a strong and enlightened Cathay, not least as it was now defeated. The thirst for China knowledge was met in other ways, not least as edifying public entertainment. Nathan Dunn, a Quaker from Philadelphia, had amassed a large collection of Chinese objects while resident in Canton between 1818 and 1831. When he retired he built a chinoiserie 'cottage', and a new public philanthropic reputation back home.[23] This collection, the largest of any it was boasted, he put on display in Philadelphia in 1838 to great acclaim, and it was accompanied by a printed descriptive catalogue which fleshed out the world introduced by this 'China in miniature', and gave some shape and context to Dunn's amorphous and random mass of material. In December 1841 Dunn and his things sailed to London, where the exhibition opened for public view the following May at a Chinese-fronted address in Knightsbridge, proclaimed to the street outside with Chinese script (a London first, perhaps), and was the toast of the season. This exhibition of porcelains, clay statues of Chinese officials, women and craftsmen; draperies, weapons and paintings – a higgledy-piggledy collation of things Chinese – was a sensational success, visited by royalty and seamlessly incorporated into metropolitan culture (the recently established *Punch* magazine issued its own sarcastic guide). It inspired catcalls and copycats as well as successors, and in addition to all of these material objects – including six years later a real junk to join the model ones, the *Keying*, which was sailed to London and moored in the East India Dock for three years, where Charles Dickens thought it a 'ridiculous abortion' – Chinese people were also brought for show: the crew of the *Keying*, a Chinese family brought and paraded to society and royalty in 1851, and others. The *Keying*'s captain even gatecrashed the royal opening of the Great Exhibition that year.[24] These shows, for shows they were, far more than exhibitions as we would now think of them, brought curious orientals to accompany the oriental curiosities on display in London. The impact of all of this is debateable, but China was in this way being normalized as an object for such display and ethnographic and other curiosity. Stronger still would be the accumulating body of printed and private report from, as one writer put it, 'the country where the quaint figures that are familiar to us on porcelain have a real existence'.[25]

The British had been waiting for China, and now it was ready for them and their allies and business partners (the Parsee traders in particular were soon on the spot), and for others too. American and French warships had shadowed the British expedition, and soon after the British peace their deputations arrived – Caleb Cushing for the United States, Théodore de Lagrené for France – and treaties were signed according them the same new concessions as those embedded in the Nanjing Treaty and the October 1843 Supplementary Treaty of the Bogue. The benefit of this for the Qing was that it brought possibly countervailing powers into the new arrangements, established direct relations with them, and ensured that the British had no advantages over the other powers. The Sino-British Bogue Treaty included much of the finer detail of British residence and trade, and Chinese agreement to the most-favoured nation principle, that is that any rights and privileges subsequently allowed other nations should apply also to the British. The newcomers also adopted this key proviso, and so foreign nationals of recognized 'treaty nations' found themselves all on an equal footing in Chinese eyes, all with similar rights and subject to similar restrictions. So were established the foundations of what became a common ethos, one crossing nationality and language, if not in fact a common identity. They were foreigners with 'treaty rights', and that shared community of interest – in protecting those rights, and acting on them – vied with and often outweighed national jealousies and imperial rivalries, and came to infuriate diplomats and consuls. The one outstanding feature of the French and American treaties was that the French secured a commitment to re-legalize Christianity in

China (Catholicism in practice), which had been proscribed in 1724, and assumed for themselves the mantle of responsibility for Chinese Catholics. Thus from the start, the 'opening' of China was quickly about very much more than simple free trade. The Anglo-Chinese College at Malacca, and its printing press, were swiftly transplanted to the new colony by the London Missionary Society (LMS), now able to train Chinese converts on China's doorstep.

But for all the reconnaissance, for all the practical preparation, there was now the problem of how to press home the initiative. The British China establishment had found the Canton factories a tight squeeze, but there were not trained, experienced (Chinese-speaking) personnel enough to populate five ports and a colony.[26] Soldiers aside, there were hardly enough to staff the war: missionaries like Gützlaff and John Robert Morrison had been drafted in as official interpreters and civil officials – Gützlaff, of all people, found himself a magistrate during the British occupation of Zhoushan and Ningbo. The war had brought men east, and there were traders at Singapore and other southeast Asian parts of what was already a Sino-British world who would come north. There was a scramble to find suitable officials (and funds to pay them), a scramble to find assistants for the new branches of the merchant houses, a scramble to find men ready to serve the Protestant cause: 'Oh Protestants! Where is your zeal?' cried out the Shanghai pioneers of the LMS, desperate for more to join them, to replenish their ranks (Morrison gone, Stevens had died in 1837 after another voyage), and to increase them.[27] There was much, much to learn, and the foreign scramble could only advance with Chinese collaboration, in cahoots with in and partnership with the interests at Canton – high and, as it turned out, low – which had made the trade there work. The Canton system, or at least its participants, spilled out up and along the coast, but the 'Canton-ization' of the new system, while unavoidable, was to bring all sort of problems in its wake.

There was a scramble to build. West of Lindsay's Albany Godowns in Hong Kong, described in 1847 as a 'double row of substantial stone buildings', costing 15–20,000 dollars to erect, grew the new British city, one of over a dozen Victorias across the British world, straggling along the sides of Queen's Road.[28] Jardines built large, so large and self-sufficient and standing outside the heart of the new city that a later, laconic American visitor, William Maxwell Wood, thought it 'somewhat an independent though allied sovereignty of Hong Kong', which was not far from the truth, at least in company thinking.[29] The cost of all of this was immense. The funds required for the new infrastructure needed, the new establishment that needed staffing (and salaries and housing for those men – the governor's salary alone was £7,000 p.a.) – all this far outpaced the immediate returns, or in many eyes any prospect of future returns. Most land purchasers had not even paid for the plots they had been assigned, in an early deal of Elliott's designed to encourage development (and given that some of his major purchasers had their funds tied up in the assets Commissioner Lin had had flushed into the Pearl river). Robert Montgomery Martin, briefly treasurer, estimated that only two members of the colonial government had had absolutely no involvement in land or building, and one was himself.[30] Martin was not short of praise for the new officials in the face of the challenges involved in building a colony from scratch, and at speed, but the new colony seemed to have embedded corruption within the administration, or at least an opaque relationship between government and speculation. Martin also rehearsed a litany of complaint before a Parliamentary Select Committee in 1847 to underscore his argument that the colony was 'the most unfortunate step that has been taken with regard to our position in China': it was too small, too barren, the harbour was only half in British hands – for only the Kowloon peninsular on the mainland was acquired – it was surrounded by Chinese-controlled islands, it was too far from Canton to help trade there, and too far from the tea and silk centres north along the coast. It had attracted thousands of new Chinese residents in no short time, as they were needed to build it (and, he added, act as servants to the Europeans), but they were, with but one single respectable exception (and he had died of disease), vagabonds, pirates, smugglers and robbers. Their presence and power damned the place in Chinese official eyes, and forced Europeans to 'sleep with loaded pistols under their pillows'.[31] And the place itself slaughtered people: regiments lost a third of their men to disease, ships great swathes of their crews. There was no more dangerous station in China than Hong Kong. The British had fought so hard, and their prize was this enormous expensive hospice, where they sent their soldiers to die in an appalling, stinking heat. But others saw a future for it, and some discovered causes of affection early. Plant hunter Robert Fortune agreed with all of this and more besides, but he still thought the scene of the harbour by moonlight in 1848 'one of the grandest and most beautiful that can be imagined'.[32]

On top of all this, for Martin and others, the new colony had turned itself into 'a smoking shop for the empire' of China. In 1844 it permitted, under licence, the selling and smoking of opium. Martin was opposed on moral grounds, but also thought it hampered legitimate trade, as it alienated Chinese officialdom. Henry Sirr, sometime vice consul at Hong Kong used his 1849 study *China and the Chinese* to draw attention to the evils of the British traffic there. Others argued that it diverted commercial attention – its returns making Chinese merchants unwilling to experiment with other products (and so stimulate a demand for them) – and lowered the purchasing power of the Chinese. Anti-opium petitions flowed towards the British Parliament in this light from men who had no truck with moralizing about the drug (which was, after all, widely in use in various forms across British society).[33] It was a simple practical issue. Martin also argued that China should be treated as 'France, America or Russia' would be, if they enforced such a prohibition and if Britain held an island like Hong Kong off their coast. An oddity of the Nanjing Treaty, of course, was that opium was barely mentioned (barring under the indemnity article). Pottinger had tried to have the trade discussed, but its illegality prevented the Chinese negotiators from so doing. There was no stopping the drug itself though: 'demand is brisk,' reported Matheson's nephew Alexander a year after the peace.[34] A fairly normal, if more cautious, covert trade had continued throughout the conflict, but now here in the heart of the capital of British China – for Hong Kong was planned (if anything was planned) as the headquarters of the wider China enterprise – the British Crown was recognizing and legalizing it, in effect aligning itself formally, openly, wholly, with the drug. Worse, the monopoly established was very quickly purchased by Lo–aqui, pirate, gangster, vice-king; Canton friend of, supplier to and briber of the British.[35] So setting the moral problem aside, legitimizing opium in Hong Kong greatly compromised the new colony's security and prospects for growth. Arrogant opium swaggered its way along to the newly opened ports. Jardines had fourteen receiving ships by 1845, and usually ten thereafter, served fortnightly from Hong Kong.[36] 'Sir Henry Pottinger,' noted Alexander Matheson, 'will do nothing adverse to the trade so long as it is not forced on his notice at the five ports'. In a proclamation in February 1843 the superintendent of trade (and now governor of Hong Kong) had warned opium traders that they could not expect any British government support or protection in China.[37] But every one of the open ports acquired its own Lintin, its receiving and transhipment station, and they were now more visible. Hulks were moored just outside the recognized harbour boundaries, and so just outside consular jurisdiction and 'notice'. There the drug brought along the coast was stored, and there were established new sites for conflict and the low-level disorderliness that filled the consulate letter books.

It took time for the British to prepare their new China establishment, and the regulatory framework which would underpin it, but meanwhile the traders were already pushing forwards and the consequent legal haziness of their operations generated much correspondence and dispute.[38] The opium receiving stations were always involved in legitimate trade as well, for the one continued to fund the other, and months before the treaty ports were finally opened, British and other foreign vessels were trading as close as they dared to them. Consuls began to ship into their new stations at the end of 1843. George Balfour, a Royal Artillery officer who had served in the China campaign, arrived at Shanghai on 8 November, delivered his credentials, located a house in the city, and formally opened the port for British trade from 17 November, the first vessel arriving two days later. Within a week he had his first consular case to deal with: a young boy had been wounded by men hunting game. He had already requested that British subjects not come ashore with weapons, but 'my endeavours have not met with that ready assistance which I anticipated.'[39] Thus was set, from the very start, one of the continuing features of the working of the new official China establishment the British built up – British subjects were not much minded to respect or obey it, if they could get away with not doing so. They had cried for official support for decades, but they did not really want to swap one set of officials regulating their activities – limiting their opportunities – for another. Robert Thom arrived at Ningbo on 19 November, opening the port from 1 January 1844. Thom had been in China ten years, and had acquired a good command of

Chinese (his mistress was a useful teacher).[40] But even that did not make it any easier for him to secure accommodation, as he later wrote: 'For several days [after arriving] did I continue to trudge up and down the streets of Ningbo, endeavouring to rent any kind of house but without success.'[41] Balfour had had a similar (though shorter) experience, and aside from the difficulty of locating suitable lodgings (and lodgings suitable for Her Majesty's representative) both found the new British presence faced a widespread passive resistance from the Chinese. The previous year's conquerors had returned all smiles and affability, but the war left real sores.

George Tradescant Lay had a thoroughly, and maddeningly, miserable time at Fuzhou. By training and inclination a naturalist, by prior occupation a missionary, he had served on the 1825–8 expedition of HMS *Blossom* through the Pacific to north-west Alaska. In 1836 he was appointed to Macao as an agent of the British and Foreign Bible Society; he had attempted to scout out Brunei in 1836, and with a number of the Macao missionaries had attempted to land in Japan in 1837. He had learnt, he announced in 1836, within but a few months of arriving in Macao, that the Chinese were motivated only by avarice, or by fear; that all practical policy should be based on that understanding, but that they were 'friendly to good order', and could 'rank with the most quiet, most happy, and best conducted subjects of the British Empire' should fate ordain.[42] Like most of the early missionary community in China, he secured a post with the British official establishment during the war, and turned it into a secure position thereafter, arriving in Fuzhou on 1 July 1844. But Fuzhou did not want him. Chinese officials refused him accommodation within the city, they 'tampered with my linguists and servants, and so hedged me round with their emissaries'; and they told him there was no potential for foreign trade. It took eight months for Lay to establish himself and open an office, by which point there was clearly something awry in his despatches to Hong Kong, let alone his behaviour in Fuzhou: 'people come from all quarters, in thousands, merely to get a sight of the foreign Officer, and as they will not leave without being gratified,' he announced, 'I am obliged daily to take a seat in some elevated part of the grounds, to be gazed at by the multitudes that throng the place.' To complete the pantomime, he had had two enormous flagstaffs erected, flew the Union flag from one, and from the other 'a red flag with Chinese characters, displaying at once the independence of the British Nation and the regal dignity of our gracious sovereign'.[43] 'He thinks the people adore him,' reported the consulate interpreter, Harry Parkes.[44] The Fuzhou authorities justified their own unwillingness to allow the British into the city by the fact that no access was granted at Canton, which was a reasonable point, not least as Lay had himself formally established the new British presence at that port in July 1843 on that basis. Lay was transferred to Xiamen, and died within a year, but his sons and descendants formed one of the earlier and most prominent of the new China dynasties that emerged amongst British families; a hundred years later they were still working in China.

The accommodation problem was more than an inconvenience and cause of madness in consuls, and it was to have far-reaching consequences. The British at Shanghai could not secure lodgings or offices in the city, despite repeated requests to the Daotai to issue proclamations reminding people that it was quite legal to do so. The walled city closed itself against the foreigners. Balfour had spied out the lie of the land in October 1842, on his way back from the Yangzi campaign, and he now proposed a formal setting aside of space for British use. Aiming to combine 'utility with ornament' he laid out a small grid of seven streets at right angles to the river, and fashioned a riverside road and one west and parallel to it (it became 'Bridge Street') on which, in agreement with the Daotai, 'the mass of the Chinese people are to move', so keeping them off the river road (not yet by 1846 given its more famous name, the Bund), and so 'effectually guarding against crowds'.[45] So, early on, segregation and exclusion were enmeshed with the fabric of the new settlement. This 'scantily occupied' tract reaching 1,200 yards northeast along the Huangpu river from the walled city was then bought up by British merchants as they began to arrive and establish themselves, and the lots were registered with the British Consulate. Jardine, Matheson secured lot 1, a three-acre parcel of land fronting the riverside next to the massive consulate site that was laid out at the confluence of the Wusong river (which foreigners came to call the Soochow Creek, as it was in fact the trade route to the city of Suzhou) and the Huangpu. Dent took lot 8. Lindsay & Co. took lot 24 – two acres of land on Bridge Street – and so Lindsay got a little parcel of Shanghai, though he never was to return to see the site. (His company's opium hulk was moored, with all the others, outside the harbour limits at Wusong.) As all land in China belonged to the emperor it could not be sold to the foreigners, so a procedural fiction was inaugurated, and the land was rented in perpetuity from its owners. There was greediness for the plots as speculation sailed in alongside more legitimate needs for space: 'your firm has been well taken care of,' begins one rebuff from the Consulate, 'we cannot countenance the buying up of large quantities of land.' Balfour recommended the British government do just that, and noted that 'I might have made a large fortune had I jobbed at this port in land.'[46] Within a couple of years, half the river frontage was already occupied. A new Customs House was built on the waterfront in amongst the British merchant lots. A cemetery was laid out, the site of a jail established, and the small British community lodged a demand for the government to build a church.

It had the look of a proper little colony. Lot number 1 was a prime spot, far from the northern suburbs of the city and their inhabitants (people of 'quiet habits', but nonetheless inquisitive), and from the eastern gate to the city, where Cantonese and Fujianese lived, a rougher group.[47] It was convenient for the Consulate, and it was here that Jardines kept their Shanghai headquarters until forced to leave 110 years later. The missionaries set themselves a little apart from their confreres, occupying plots to the southwest where they built a chapel and installed their printing press, which they relocated from Batavia (Jakarta). The earliest British arrivals had roughed it. Robert Fortune, on commission from the Royal Horticultural Society, arrived on his first visit before the end of 1843. Rain and then snow blew through the windows of his 'cheerless and fireless' lodging, meals were make-shift, and 'Whenever we moved out of the house hundreds of people crowded the streets, and followed in our wake.' People gazed 'as if we had been inhabitants of the moon'.[48] (Londoners likewise gaped at Chinese visitors, at the Chinese children at Nathan Dunn's exhibition in London, and at its sixty clay statues of Chinese figures, and at the waxwork of Lin.) But the excitement of being there, of the newness of everything, of finally making straight progress after the mires of Canton 'kept us,' he reported, 'in good health and in excellent spirits'. That was not going to last, and nor would the foreigners last in such rough and readiness. The comforts of the Canton British life, and the excesses of the Canton British lifestyle, would very quickly find their way to the north. Robert Fortune returned to Shanghai in 1848, struck immediately by the number of foreign vessels in port, and by the appearance of 'a new town, of very considerable size' which had sprung up. There was a 'pretty English church', a plain cemetery (more trees needed, he argued) which was already populated (a missionary bride, 22-year-old Elizabeth Fairbrother, was the first British burial in Shanghai), and there were good foreign gardens. As a botanist, Fortune was particular about gardens and the horticultural experiments of the British. It was no go with the potato, but the first apple tree had already fruited in Mackenzie, Brothers & Co.'s grounds. Boatloads of plants for sale were moored along the river banks to stock these foreign gardens.[49] 'What they call the Bund', noted one new arrival in 1851, 'is quite a Promenade of an afternoon, a regular Rotten Row also', as ponies and horses were brought to Shanghai and stabled in the *hong* compounds. A racecourse was laid out, and business shut down for the days of the spring and autumn races, and 'really, the sport was good'.[50] There was a leisureliness to the new uncrowded townscape, remembered one old resident later. It looked, he thought, like leafy St John's Wood in London, 'the houses stood each in its compound, surrounded by a wall, with trees and shrubs between it and the road.'[51] This was certainly the case with Lindsay & Co.'s property, 'Quanloong', as we know from an 1860 painting: it was a large two-storey porticoed building, with an extensive garden which also housed two aviaries.[52] The garden alone was bigger than the miserable crowded plot down south that Lindsay himself had walked. What a change from the fifteen acres of the Canton factories: space, greenery, privacy, freedom. Robert Fortune hymned the horticultural exchange he saw, on the one hand the foreign plants imported by the British and Americans – out of nostalgia, a desire for the familiar, to eat – and on the other the great loads of Chinese shrubs he shipped off to London, the 'finest plants' he had collected.[53]

Fortune was a self-publicist, and his books recounting his travels in China and his successes in securing seeds and young plants helped him secure new commissions, but he had a new suggestion to solve the continuing problem of the British and other foreigners. This was their desire to earn respect from the Chinese for their civilization and attainments, and not simply impose respect through the armed steamers. 'Nothing, I believe, can give the Chinese a higher idea of our civilization and attainments,' he wrote, 'than our love for flowers'.[54] It was in fact less the flowers and shrubs than the buildings, and in time the wider roads, the streetlamps and policed orderliness of the Settlement that attracted Chinese attention and curiosity. Already by 1848 Thomas Beale's fine two-storey house, across the road from Lindsay & Co. on one side and from the church on the other, was the destination of many curious visitors, who asked to see inside.[55] We know that as the Settlement grew people travelled from all over the region to try out the foreign doctors' cures: 8,000 had presented themselves to William Lockhart by September 1844, not a few of them workmen injured building the new settlement's houses. Some came from as far as Zhenjiang and Nanjing, and they also came to look at the new foreign town that contrasted so completely with the norms of Chinese urban landscapes.[56] Early paintings and photographs of the houses, white-painted, two-storeyed, shaded by verandahs, and situated off wide roads, show distinctly how alien this was. The men from the moon had brought their lunar landscape with them, reconstructing it in precise detail on the banks of the Huangpu, in Fuzhou, in Xiamen, and in Hong Kong. Architecturally it was in fact more a southeast colonial vernacular, a style that stretched from India through to China, but over the decades it brought more of the domestic with it, and British, French, German and other architectures were to compete and show off in Chinese streets. The cruel irony that was to dash Fortune's hope for horticultural understanding was that the tendency to segregation, to keeping the prying multitude out, logically led to more and more spatial segregation, and in time to by-laws preventing Chinese entrance into parks in the Settlement. There were to be no public flowers on un-restricted view for Shanghai's Chinese until 1928.

James Dow arrived as a 'Cha-see', a tea taster, in September 1851 after some months in Canton, and was to work for Blenkin, Rawson & Co. until their failure in 1858, when he struck out on his own.[57] Like others he noted the gardens, and the scale of the new houses and *hongs*. Labour was cheap, he wrote, so a sedan chair to get around in was affordable, as well as 'indispensable' in hot weather, and it would keep your clothes clean on wet days and nights. The firm did itself proud with two houses and godowns on a lot adjoining Jardines, but the recently completed Jardines pile was 'magnificent: a 70–80 foot first floor drawing/dining room, divided by columns, opened out through a row of windows onto a verandah overlooking the Bund and river, and how pleasant to see the river and the shipping'. Jardines dined and drank well there too, 'but such is always the case in China': 'very good soup & fish, two or three joints, fowls and pheasants ... the pastry also was abundant, fruits and four or five sorts of wine'. They all dined well, these gentleman traders, though game was rare in Hong Kong, and Shanghai residents sent birds down for their friends there. Some, like Lindsay's, or the American firm Augustine Heard, were clearly more extravagant than others, but it was a relative difference.[58] Dow joined a typical establishment, a firm dealing in tea, opium – whatever sold. Their front house opened onto the Bund: up some steps you went, he wrote, into the hall, with offices to the left, one housing a lithographic press to print off circulars, some private rooms, his tea-tasting room out back, and upstairs a large dining/drawing room, and more private sets of rooms. Across the rear garden, behind the go-downs, was another even larger house. Such display – display at table, architectural display – announced probity and confidence (to each other, to Chinese merchants), but it also spoke of vulgarity and extravagance. Of course, the profits of China trading could be very good: over five years of tea trading at Canton after 1848, William Melrose cleared £5,833 in personal profit, equivalent to £4,000,000 in 2007 terms. Hong Kong lawyer Henry Kingsmill was reported to be heading home in 1865, 'having made his £20,000'.[59] So rich were the returns, so cheap was the labour, that firms lived well because they could, because a man could aim to make his twenty thousand pretty quickly anyway, and so why, he felt, shouldn't he live well on the way?

Balfour had chosen his Shanghai site with defence very much in mind. Two sides fronted by rivers, the third facing the city by a creek. There was access for reinforcement, and natural advantages to be incorporated into defence works if needed. The tendency to think in these terms would long remain, but it was also reinforced by provisions in the Supplementary Bogue Treaty forbidding the British to visit any non-treaty ports. Further clauses, the detail of which was to be agreed locally, restricted them to travel only short distances from these cities. The diplomats and consuls wanted no upcountry incidents, nothing out of their sight that could inflame relations. Balfour had had to labour hard to dampen down the affair of the young boy shot in November 1843, who was permanently blinded, and he wanted no more such incidents. The usual restriction was that travellers had to be able to return to the city that same day. But the foreigners were curious; they wanted to look, to wander, to hunt, and so the rules were often ignored. Missionaries were also driven to proselytize. Balfour's successor thought that the murder of an American missionary, Walter Lowrie in late 1847, was salutary: perhaps such deaths would focus minds on the issue when regulation and consular authority were failing to.[60] Robert Fortune's mind was wholly focused, though, and he cheerfully ignored the regulations. He had virgin territory to romp through and no regulation was going to stop him. He disguised himself in Chinese clothes, shaved off his hair, and set off out of the city accompanied by a servant to seek out botanical specimens. Such flagrant – and globally publicized – exploits exasperated consuls, but the reality was that many foreigners, if not most, saw the new treaty network as but a provisional arrangement, heralding an expected wider opening up of the country to foreign enterprise. Walter Medhurst published his own account of such a journey in 1849, which commenced with a lengthy guide to donning Chinese disguise, not least a lesson in using chopsticks and a reminder to wear dark spectacles if the traveller had light-coloured eyes. 'Of beef and beer' you must take your leave, he noted. Fortune donned his disguise perfectly, but he forgot about the chopsticks, and went hungry for days until he learnt how to use them.[61]

Article IX of the Treaty of Nanjing explicitly addressed the often perilous position of those Chinese, mainly Cantonese, who worked with or for the British. An amnesty was agreed that would cover all of those who had collaborated with them, and also aimed to spare from retribution those who had lived under British rule during the conflict and its aftermath. As well as the wartime suppliers and helpers of the British, this partly addressed a long-term problem: the insecurity of the position of the 'linguists' in particular. Seemingly random punishment, often execution, had been meted out to those of them who had (in Chinese eyes) too well or too closely served the foreigners. And recall that Gützlaff had more than once been mistaken for a 'traitor' during the *Lord Amherst*'s voyage. 'Real' Chinese traitors (labelled as such) had found themselves targets during the war and especially during the occupation of Zhoushan. Moreover, the servants of the foreigners had often been the first to be threatened when officials moved against their foreign problem, and Canton restrictions had more than once forbidden foreigners to have Chinese servants entirely, or else restricted the numbers sharply. But the Canton trade – at the factories, at Lintin and Macao – had required or involved great numbers of Chinese participants: *cohong* merchants, linguists, the compradors who provisioned the merchantmen, boatbuilders, washerwomen, watchmen.[62] The war had required a vast expansion of this community, which evolved into a wider community of mutual interest. The British China trade always needed its Chinese partners – their expertise, connections, information, and language. It needed Chinese labour, and Chinese skills. It came to rely on Chinese investment and it needed its Chinese markets. It needed its Cantonese in particular, for all the continuing hostility of Canton that was to keep the British penned in to the factories there for years to come – in December 1842, for a start, a riot spiralled out of a brawl between local men and Indian seamen and led to the destruction of the New British Factory, and two others. The 'calmness of the evening' made the sight of the burning buildings 'a beautiful one' reported the *Canton Repository* somewhat laconically, but it also presaged some more years yet of violent Canton problems.[63] The city remained closed and hostile.

Along the coast with the British Cantonese went nonetheless, or followed soon after. There had always been movement along the coast, but now it acquired a new density, a different form and a new, international flavour. It was also essentially unscripted. The treaties were incapable of addressing the multifarious situations that would arise. Consular case law would see to that in time. Meanwhile everything was new, local Chinese authority was on the defensive, British administrators were in offensive mode, and so everything and anything might be tested. Just about every issue caused by the migrant Cantonese was potentially a treaty issue, an international affair, because of that British protection, because their British employers or partners offered them the shade of the treaty, an ongoing amnesty, a semi-treaty status, or else they claimed (or bought) the same, and bullied local power brokers and others with it, threatening them with British vengeance for treaty infractions. The potential for trouble was further heightened by the fact that there was both a new, legitimate trade network and presence in the open ports and, intertwined with it, the illegitimate shadow presence in the hulks and shanty villages that sprung up by them outside port limits. The Cantonese went north as middlemen, interpreters, servants, prostitutes (the 'salt-water sisters'), and as suppliers of the new legitimate establishment. They knew what the merchant needed, and what Jack Tar drank. They went north for the opium traders as part of their rougher littoral world.[64] They went north also because the opening of the additional ports and of Hong Kong was an undoubted blow to the Canton economy: so there was a push, as well as the pull of the uncharted opportunities offered by the treaty system.

Cantonese migrants and sojourners were quick to see additional value in association with the British, and equally quick to protect their long monopoly of the foreign trade, even though it had moved. Local officials at Xiamen and at Shanghai had attempted to hem the British into new local monopolies, but these were brushed aside by the consuls. Others tried less official means to seek advantage through monopoly or preferred agency, hastening along the coast to do so. 'Canton Agents,' claimed Lay at Fuzhou in 1845, were 'ready to execute any species of fraud and iniquity, in order to keep the trade in the[ir] hands.'[65] Forty men there were causing trouble in 1847, 'under the pretext of being in the employ of British Subjects', assuming 'an arrogant and disorderly bearing towards Natives of the place, and even those of their own countrymen [that is, fellow Cantonese] not belonging to their association'. The consul thought they had some connection with British opium traders, and instructed all British captains to identify Chinese employees ashore and make them register with him.[66] Such informal British recognition of the bona fide Chinese employee was a pragmatic response to a troublesome situation, but served to extend the notion, in Chinese and British eyes, of who was actually protected by the treaties. In fact the Treaty of Nanjing had paved the way, when it secured amnesty for Britons' Chinese associates. The Chinese partners and servants of the British came in under the treaty umbrella. British consuls paid much attention to securing the safety of their servants and staff, 'as persons forming part of the Establishment of British subjects', sometimes explicitly using the Nanjing Treaty provisions.[67] Legitimate traders followed this lead; and so did the men of the offshore opium establishment. And almost as soon as the practice began there were also Britons ready to properly rent out their formal patronage to Chinese who needed it, and in this way the para-British community grew and grew.

Chinese movement encompassed territory far greater in scale than the domestic coasts. The British empire already had Chinese subjects, and soon they came north as well, from Singapore, Penang and Malacca. The Ningbo Daotai was not alone in being puzzled at what to do with them. These were Chinese who had defied Qing laws forbidding emigration. They must be punished. He moved in July 1844 to arrest one such merchant, but the man was Malacca-born, and so a British subject, and so secured consular protection. It was just a ploy by the Daotai to extort money from him, claimed the consul, wholly misunderstanding how the arrival in Chinese ports of men with new papers, new identities and new patrons was disrupting the official landscape of Chinese governance. Dealing with foreigners was surely simple enough, but dealing with this uncharted hinterland of Chinese people was unexpected, and it was profoundly unsettling. Here were Chinese, here at the heart of Chinese cities, who were shrugging off imperial authority, putting themselves beyond reach of the accepted order of things, because of their papers and protectors.[68] The British consular system was to find much of its time taken up with the empire Chinese (who were quick to register at the consulates), whose activities are interwoven in the archives with the metropolitan British, their marriages and deaths recorded in the registers alongside their land ownership, mortgages, and all the normal travails of their lives in the treaty ports. In an attempt to clarify their position they were ordered to wear foreign clothes in China if they wished to secure protection, but foreign dress was a haphazard marker, not least as it could then quickly be adopted by Cantonese and others who had no right to British protection.[69]

As the Straits Chinese came in, emigrants in turn left for other parts of the world. The manner of their leaving raised consular difficulties of an entirely different order. The 'coolie trade' carried out by British entrepreneurs, who organized the emigration of indentured labourers from Hong Kong and Xiamen, and later unopened Shantou, was a source of local tensions, diplomatic conundrums and global colonial scandal. Even if Chinese men had voluntarily agreed to ship out to Cuba, Peru, California and Australia – and thousands did during the gold rushes – the conditions under which they often laboured, and often died, were a source of diplomatic concern and moral outrage. 'Common humanity forbids the looking with indifference on what is taking place,' recorded Pottinger's successor Dr John Bowring. At Xiamen, Britons James Tait, 'who has all the advantages and influence which his being Spanish, Dutch and Portuguese Consul gives him' – that is, freedom from the direction of his own British consul – and Francis Syme had erected 'barracoons' – holding sheds – in one of which hundreds of emigrants, 'stripped naked, and stamped or painted with the letter C (California), P (Peru), or S (Sandwich Islands), on their breasts' were marshalled before embarkation.[70] They were prevented from leaving Syme's 'shed' into which many claimed they were tricked or pushed, and testified to being beaten when they asked or tried to leave. The mortality on some of the voyages was very high. Maltreatment on the American vessel *Robert Browne* in 1852 prompted a murderous mutiny. The captain had his crew cut off the emigrants' queues, and 'had their bodies washed with hard brooms'.[71] Chinese 'brokers' – for Tait's firm, and Syme's – were a source of local conflict. Charges of press-ganging men for the emigrant ships were not always unfounded. Syme's man Lu Guanghong was a 'Canton traitor' one petitioner remarked; he was a purchaser of human beings claimed another.[72] When the man was arrested and Syme attempted to force his release from the Xiamen magistrate in December 1852 events spiralled into a riot that provoked the landing of a British force that killed or wounded a dozen Chinese. Syme was urged to pull down his shed. Consul Rutherford Alcock at Shanghai had earlier refused permission for one to be built, but rumour spread there nonetheless after the Syme debacle that Chinese agents were kidnapping children to be shipped overseas for foreigners.[73]

The treaty system was quickly integrating coastal China in new ways with Spanish Cuba, the British West Indies, the Pacific, North and South America, and Australia, as it sparked the mass transit of labour or provided opportunities for voluntary emigration. It forced the British for the first time to hold cross-empire discussions to discuss the global context and management of the Chinese emigration issue.[74] But for them the Indian connection remained one of the strongest. And it was also of course an Anglo-Indian world, as it was at Canton. In many ways, the treaty ports were a Chinese offshoot of Britain's Indian empire, and the new ports were like many of the other sites of British power around the Indian Ocean. The East India Company, East India regiments, East India merchants, shipping, seamen, officials, capital, produce (opium not least of all) made up the new worlds built up in the suburbs of the open ports. Company men like Lindsay turned private China traders. Some consuls and governors were drawn from the Anglo-Indian establishment. Dhunjeebhoy Rustomjee held lot 19a in Shanghai in 1848; Parsee firms vied in number with British ones in the earliest days in Hong Kong, and Elias David Sassoon sailed into the colony from Bombay in 1843, establishing offices there and later in Shanghai, and pioneering the modern Jewish presence in China.[75] Sepoys had undertaken much of the war; lascars – south Asian seamen – manned many of the ships. A destitute Madrasi, suspected to be a Sepoy deserter, was one of the earliest 'distressed British subjects' to be deported by the consulate.[76] Lascar deaths prompted Balfour's purchase of a burial ground in 1844. Tindal Meer Basha was murdered at sea by fellow seaman Poono in 1844, the victim of Shanghai's first British murder case. The killer was sent to Hong Kong for trial.[77] Lascar deserters, Manilamen (Filipinos), Cantonese and 'even' European seamen populated at Wusong a shadow 'colony of the most disreputable character'. The opium anchorage was effectively outside British and Chinese law, and although the hulk captains were well paid, and had 'everything very comfortable & fitted up like dwelling houses', it was a monotonous life, and chancers and crooks found it fertile ground. And when things grew too hot, the coolie traders also shifted offshore to the opium anchorages.[78] The British Indian state itself formally sought to take advantage of China as it was opened. It corresponded with the China consuls seeking tea seeds or young plants.[79] Robert Fortune's second sojourn in China was under commission from the Court of Directors of the East India Company, and the aim was to secure what was necessary to develop a tea industry in Assam – long an aspiration, and the motivation behind the earlier sending of agents to China, such as George Gordon in 1834. In April 1851 Fortune arrived in Saharunpur with 13,000 tea plants ('as green and vigorous as if they had been all the while growing on the Chinese hills') and eight Chinese tea-growers and their tools from Huizhou. They were 'first-rate green-tea makers', willing to teach their trade to Indians (and in time to leave government employ for the growing private tea sector).[80] The ties that bound the British Indian and China enterprises were many, and were reinforced by language, by the casual importation of the empire's other *lingua franca*: Anglo-Indian slang. At each new treaty port a bund was built, firms employed a shroff (who counted specie in lakhs), clubs provided tiffin, members signed chits, houses needed a verandah. These were soon joined by Anglo-Chinese or Pidgin-Chinese neologisms aplenty, but the Anglo-Indian character of the British presence in China was to persist until the very last days of the treaty port world.

British power attracted all comers. It was far safer, and far more convenient, to sail with British papers. It might conceivably make pirates think twice, but this could be double-edged. His foreign nationality seems to have cost Walter Lowrie his life: those who had captured and ransacked the Chinese boat he was a passenger on evidently thought his survival too great a risk. But the sight of a foreigner or foreign papers would generally make Chinese officials hesitate, if not back off entirely from acting in many situations. Consuls quickly reported a systematic pattern of abuses, especially as piracy increased after the mid-decade. Jackson outlined in January 1848 how Portuguese *lorchas* – vessels with a European-style hull but Chinese rigging –were convoying with British colours Chinese trading junks from Fuzhou north to Ningbo and Xiamen. This was little short of extortion – such escorts were often themselves the pirates (and acted as such at times), but in this way they rationalized their operations somewhat.[81] Regardless of this, their aggressive behaviour – firing on all and sundry to force them to keep their distance – tarnished the British name yet further. The only foreigners the coastal people come across, Jackson lamented, were smugglers, or these quasi pirates, men such as the Portuguese master and crew of the *Victoria*, owned by an Indian living in Hong Kong, which 'hoisted British colours and passed for an English vessel ... during the whole passage the Master was constantly firing upon every Native craft, without distinction'.[82] Ships flying Danish, Dutch and Portuguese colours joined in this convoy trade.

Conversely the British took foreign papers if they could, as they long had in old Canton, but now instead of a basic right to trade, they sought a canny means to evade, that is to place themselves just far enough outside British jurisdiction to shrug off inconvenient trading regulations. Lindsay's man in Shanghai, William Hogg, was Consul for Hamburg in 1854; D. O. King spoke for Prussia. British merchants were reportedly eager to represent the Netherlands or Belgium. Even the Portuguese, close by in Macao, gave papers to Thomas Beale in Shanghai and John Dent at Canton. Tait at Xiamen showed the consequences of this internationalizing of national authority. As Spanish consul he signed off his own business activities as compliant with Spanish law. Such consular conveniences, compounded by confusions or obfuscations of ownership, proprietorship, staffing and more, proved fertile ground for fraud and evasion of authority into the 1930s. When nominal participants in the treaty system neglected to provide effective representation on the ground, their foreign agents were free to innovate as best profited them. It was some decades before a truly effective US consular system was established, and American merchants such as John Griswold at Shanghai filled such posts initially. As the wayward perks of consulships were threatened or superseded by formal representation, others could be sought. Panama and Mexico in time found nominal registration in China, the scale of the activity of the consul inversely proportionate to the size of the Panamanian population there, and to Sino-Panamanian trade.

Balfour resigned in 1846. His successor, Rutherford Alcock, presented a comprehensive picture in 1848 of the five-year progress of the 'little town' which had developed at Shanghai, and which looked like a 'British colony rather than a settlement of foreigners in China'. This 'just born' city grew faster even than towns 'in our new West' remarked an American visitor.[83] Twenty-four firms had established themselves; there were five shops now; twenty-five private houses; the cemetery and church; and now a hotel, club and racecourse. Balfour had laid things out, but the land-renters were expected themselves to develop the public works without which the Settlement could not function effectively. A Committee of Roads and Jetties was formed at a public meeting, and in a lackadaisical and under-resourced fashion oversaw work on the development of those facilities, as well as bridges, and a rudimentary watch system. But interest in the public good was often far outweighed by interest in private profit and enjoyment. The racecourse rather than the roadways consumed attention, and it could do so while the Settlement was still modest in size. But Alcock looked ahead 'on the supposition that sooner or later Shanghae must become the great centre of our trade with China', and lobbied for funds to purchase more ground, and that ground 'unembarrassed' by a Chinese population, which was already growing up in a 'dense suburb' around the Settlement.[84] Even within the existing boundaries, the mixture of nationalities and jurisdictions already offered much scope for conflicts and disputes, but as it promised to grow, it promised greater complications by far.

Within two more years the Shanghai community had a newspaper which could report on, stir up and pronounce upon these complications. New Hong Kong had gained a press from the start. The *Canton Register* had been moved there in 1843 from Macao, to which it had fled along with the British community, becoming the *Hong Kong Register*; the *Friend of China* started publishing in the colony in 1842; and there were others. For a relatively small community there was a lively press, one which reflected the turbulent, unsettled new world of the 1840s. Now it was Shanghai's turn. The *North China Herald* appeared for the first time on 3 August 1850, with a souvenir first edition printed on silk. Editor Harry Shearman had come from Canada as an auctioneer, and was a man of strong Protestant conviction, which gave the paper a different flavour from the start (the *Dismal Jenny* as Dow and his circle labelled it). But Shanghai was already tired of being spoken for, and the *Herald* opened another front in the global war of words over China. Shearman's opening 'Address to the Public' mocked the 'wild exaggerations of a Gützlaff; the ill-digested statements, and crudities of a Montgomery Martin, the amusing twaddle of a Fortune, and the malignant inventions of a Sirr'. Shanghai could now speak for itself and it wanted a 'fair and open field' of British and foreign merchants that could only lead to 'a far wider spread of civilization – refinement, science, arts and true religion'. British authority was challenged to push for this; Chinese authority was assailed for obstructing it; and these *soi disant* China experts were avidly lapped up by readers back home. Meanwhile the *Herald* listed in its inaugural issue all foreign residents in the city, and carried classifieds that pitted the bread and biscuits sold by Edward Hall against those offered by P. F. Richards and Co. Two cottages were for let just west of the British consulate, plus a plot of land close by the bridge leading from the north gate of the city. The London Mission Society press offered 'reasonable terms' for book-binding; J. Miller was set to auction a billiard table; catastrophe for the foreign churchgoing community had been narrowly averted on 24 June: after a heavy night's downpour the roof of Holy Trinity Church had collapsed at 5.30 on a Sunday morning, crushing to pieces the pews below.[85] A certain ordinariness seemed to be beginning to creep into the new China life of the British: ordinary commerce, ordinary structures of trade, even ordinary disaster; but this was a diversion from the continuing essential unordinariness of the post-Canton China compromise, and its unsettled state. The *Herald* aimed to argue, and to lobby, to push things forward from Shanghai in 'the true interests of mankind' to make the city 'the permanent emporium of trade between [China] and all the nations of the world'.

As the British and the Qing each interpreted the war in different ways, so they held different understandings of the peace. For the Qing the basic shape of the original Canton system had been extended to the other ports. In each the communities of Britons administered their own affairs, and such an arrangement was simply a variant of the long-established practice of allowing sojourning communities to organize their own affairs. The foreigners were given what they wanted – trade – where they wanted it, and their presence was then to be based solely there and was to be hedged around with restrictions, both those embedded in the treaties and those which were agreed at local level. That system was more routinely a feature of the Asian land frontiers of the Qing than its maritime world, and it was thereby far less peculiar in its overall shape and in the practice of the empire than it might have seemed, and than it has often seemed to observers. It was certainly extorted by British violence, but it was standard Qing practice none-theless. Even the new British base on Hong Kong had a precedent in

Macao, which had been in Portuguese hands since 1557. For good measure Canton was to remain the key, for the Canton governor general was to be concurrently the imperial commissioner who dealt with the chief Briton – the governor at Hong Kong and superintendent of trade. This entire understanding, however, was at variance with that of the British. Ideologically, free trade ideas dominated their understandings of political economy and underpinned the actions of statesmen, administrators and businessmen.[86] They had an infrastructure established across the five China ports, headquartered from Hong Kong. They had acquired other ports and settlements in southeast Asia, and these new possessions were part of that world. And for them the treaties with China also echoed the capitulations and extraterritorial privileges long enjoyed by foreigners in the Ottoman Empire. So rather than being simply a Qing practice, the arrangement was in their eyes an internationally intelligible one. Furthermore many, including officials, saw the new treaty ports as bridgeheads – jumping-off points – not reservations, and they had no intention of staying put. They aimed to push hard, as they had pushed hard from Canton, and go further. And while for the Qing communication was to be channelled through a southern governor, the British expected to talk to the central state. The Qing saw restrictions modified, access still controlled and commerce still regulated; many of the British saw China opened and trade freed.

They had by 1852 built bunds and barracoons, corralling the river at Shanghai, and corralling the emigrants at Xiamen. Holy Trinity at Shanghai was re-roofed. There were mission chapels and dispensaries. They were there. An itinerant daguerreotypist, Herman Husband, arrived from Peru via Hawaii and offered to take portraits of the new settlers in 1852, to fix them and their buildings and their views in Shanghai and in Hong Kong.[87] They had brought new sights; they brought new sounds. Just in time for New Year's Day 1853, a bell was raised in Holy Trinity's tower to toll the hours and quarters at Shanghai. The 'sound of its music at a distance and in the silence of the night', the Shanghai night, tolling nostalgia, disturbed Chinese slumber with its strangeness, just as the hours and minutes on the clock face slowly began to alter the pace and shape of the Chinese day.[88] There were hymns in the chapels, strange words set to strange music; obscure new abstractions and terms in the language of scripture preached in temple grounds and narrow city streets (in Chinese strangely, haltingly, spoken) offered new worlds of sound and thought for Chinese audiences. Missionaries were disturbed at what they saw as the seeming lack of 'reverence and propriety' in their congregations, although perhaps that is too strong a term for their early audiences, who came to watch these performing wonders, the Chinese-speaking foreigners. Rare it was that 'the preacher commences and ends his discourse without a single interruption'.[89] As well as their chapels and forays into the public spaces of the cities they also ventured further out, 'itinerating', visiting other towns and villages, handing out tracts where it was safe so to do. It was not always safe to do so – Medhurst, Lockhart and a colleague were nearly killed at Qingpu in March 1848 when out and about on one such trip.[90]

Most of the new arrivals were keen to push onwards, not content with their urban bridgeheads. They pushed at the treaties and local regulations. They went in disguise deep into the countryside in search of economic advantage; they journeyed in plain view out of curiosity to the closed cities neighbouring the treaty ports; they built themselves makeshift stations at Wusong, at Namoa island (Nan'ao), outside effective legal supervision. Syme was unrepentant about the violence of his brokers, or his own. Tait simply moved his own operations to Nan'ao, where British officials feared a 'catastrophe'.[91] Xiamen residents attacked Canton brokers in the streets, securing in that way an effective rough justice.

As they fixed themselves in, they also wanted to fix their history. The 200-year China traffic was constantly in British minds as they argued and pamphleted. Lindsay had interrogated people in Ningbo in 1832 for news of any 'signs or remnants' of old foreign residences there – the East India Company factory of 1755–7.[92] History – the Terranova case, the gunner of the *Lady Hughes*, Lord Macartney, Lord Amherst, Lord Napier – was a rooted factor in their expanded China life. Their aim was never to forget their history of humiliation and insecurity, and never to allow their compatriots and representatives to forget the lessons of their Anglo-Chinese history. It was a double-faced source of legitimacy: that conferred by a once more open trade, and that conferred by sacrifice and shame. In fact they often talked, wrote and taught, as the Chinese came to talk, write and teach about the lessons of history, and the importance of remembering national humiliation. The histories of China and the China trade that were published with the war narratives contributed to the formation of a kind of discursive museum, presaging the concrete ones later created by the Chinese at Sanyuanli, at Humen (where the confiscated opium was destroyed in 1839), and elsewhere – one built on the descriptions of the insults and privations suffered by the China British. Foreign memorials and cemeteries from the first acquired the reverence due their legitimizing power. It helped a little that they were populated so quickly as disease culled the garrison regiments. Fortune reported the makeshift British cemetery at Gulangyu 'already nearly full' in 1843, 'and the earth was red and fresh with recent interments'. The British also remembered in stone, and where there were earlier traces of the British China dead, those were also incorporated into the new story. Fortune noted that early eighteenth-century gravestones found on Gulangyu island were repaired or replaced by the newly confident victors, carving afresh the names of their China dead. Non-commissioned officers of the 35th Regiment erected a monument at Zhoushan (restored in 1853) to the 431 men of the regiment who died there or who were killed in action.[93] Lord Napier's memorial languished at Macau, however, for his friends and supporters were either dead or back in Britain when conditions provided a site in Hong Kong, and his stone was not shipped onwards from Macao to the new colony. But as the new roads and buildings grew up in the treaty ports they were to acquire new memorials, and new sites for commemoration and celebration. And as the brittle and unsatisfactory peace meandered on, there was to be new cause for commemoration, and for adding to the competing sagas of humiliation and injury.

5

Model Settlements

'Shanghae is not China,' noted Harry Shearman in his opening address to readers in 1850. Nor was the Settlement or its sister colonies enough of China for many: for those keen to trade, learn, take, preach or give. Shearman complained of the only 'very partial application' of free trade in China, and wanted an end to the 'miserable red tapeism' of the consuls and treaties that bound people to the open ports, and hedged around with dense thickets of local agreement their freedom to profit from the new China order. This was a point of view. There were others. Governor Bowring believed that at Hong Kong he 'carried out the principles of Free Trade to the fullest'. The policy of the foreign treaty powers of turning a blind official eye to the ever-growing coastal opium trade was hardly 'red-tapeism'.[1] But there was much left still unsettled by the first treaties, and much had emerged for potential dispute as consuls and Daotais set to work implementing the details and informing their people, guiding their respective charges towards understanding what was now allowed, and what was not permitted, and smoothing out the inevitable tensions and bother that people encountered and created. Balfour's first incident, the blinded boy, was not his last; the riot in Xiamen was not the most serious. Open in principle, the city at Canton was to be kept closed by the local authorities until, they said, popular hostility to the British had abated. But abate it they could not, or abate it they would not – as the foreigners believed, with some justification. Six Britons were murdered near Canton in December 1847. Governor Davis's 'raid' in April that year – three steamers and 900 men had broken the city defences and occupied the factories to reinforce his demands for entry – had somehow failed to soften popular hostility. An agreement to permit entry in two years' time was brokered, although the Chinese had no intention of honouring it.[2]

Canton extremes aside, however, this mostly seemed trivial stuff. Consuls found themselves intervening to restrain the behaviour of foreigners towards their Chinese servants (or being exhorted to aid the disciplining of servants), and settling neighbourly disputes, as often as they tried to guide communities through the wider issues of principle and practice that confronted them. One Chinese delegation arrived at the Shanghai consulate in 1848 with their British neighbour's goat, which offending animal was apparently damaging their property. Wearily the consulate ticked off its charge to better control the beast.[3] But domestic crisis was no small matter when rumour swept around, when many harboured attitudes of contempt towards the Chinese, and when that contempt was flavoured with ignorance and with the inability to communicate in a consistently intelligible way. A beaten servant, a cook dismissed without pay, arguments over a grazing goat or at a market stall: all such minor disturbances of men and women could presage consular grief, and sometimes spiral into something worse.

Communication was a continuing problem. Nearly all foreigners could or would still only talk a pidgin English which strung English words together in Chinese sentence patterns. It was equalled in its seemingly ridiculous cadences and rhythms only by its clear disavowal of the importance of the real Chinese tongue. 'I find great difficulty in understanding their broken English,' noted James Dow. 'If you want a man to come, you say "show so & so come here one wantee talkee him". Then in dealing with them you say, "After I have makee tastee I will talkee with you."'[4] But he would have got used to it, they all did, and he would have got a better sense of its vocabulary and conventions. Some whiled away their Asian hours translating English poetry into pidgin doggerel (Longfellow's 'Excelsior' was a favourite, 'Topside Galan!' the translated refrain). But as a means of communication it did actually work, and it was certainly seriously used (and if you don't like it, suggested the *Chinese Commercial Guide*, then you had better learn Chinese). Handbooks for Chinese users were actually published in Shanghai and Canton matching Shanghainese and Cantonese transliterations to pidgin English words and phrases.[5] But it also clearly spoke equal parts contempt and convenience, and it did to China's spoken tongues what British soldiers did to Shanghai books in 1842. The *Herald* printed useful phrases in Shanghai dialect – 'What are you doing? Bring me a cigar. Now bring me the newspaper' – but pidgin triumphed.[6] Even so, as they built, so some – a very few – learned nonetheless. They learned to speak local dialects, learned to read even, and some also learned more.

If Shanghai was not China, then what precisely was it, and what was its history? The British had long known it as an important port, its junks arriving in their colonial harbours in southeast Asia. The Lindsay mission and other coast voyages had brought first-hand accounts of its vibrant crowded harbour, and of stores filled with imported goods. Even in Canton, where the long British presence gave them some purchase on that city's history, and a window through which to learn about China – from the *Peking Gazette*, from books and conversations – they had barely scratched the surface. Elijah Bridgman's *Chinese Repository* had since 1832 outlined in its essays and reviews attempts at understanding the warp and weft of Chinese life and culture. It lay great emphasis on testing new and long-trusted Western-language accounts against 'the most approved native authorities', as these could now easily be found and by 1832 there was more expertise available to read and interpret them.[7] At Shanghai Walter Medhust took a similar course, publishing at the London Mission press in August 1850 a *General Description of Shanghae* and its neighbourhood. This was a translation and précis of local histories and compilations usually now known in English as local gazetteers, but, thought Medhust, previously unknown to foreign scholars. They were voluminous, even for Shanghai, and it was, he claimed, possible to use these to render China 'as much known as any given section of the Western world'.[8] Even though it was shortly thereafter excerpted in the *North China Herald,* this was hardly a popular rambler's guide, but it filled in the great blank space of Shanghai in foreign eyes, giving it a long and vibrant history, and explaining its structure, economy, government and topography. There seemed little excuse now for ignorance about what Bridgman had termed 'the stupendous *anomaly*' of a closed and inaccessible China.[9] With increasing knowledge of the language, and with the acquisition of such tools as the local gazetteers, then it could be known just as well as the 'Western world'. As collections slowly grew in Europe – Robert Morrison's collection of Chinese books was donated to the new University College in London in 1837, and his son's was deposited in the British Library in 1847 – then China could also be studied from afar in Europe and in America.[10] Still more people saw 'China' through Nathan Dunn's show, its less authentic imitators, or through the junk *Keying* and its crew and artefacts, than through serious collection and scholarship.[11]

Even so, most of the China British and the other new foreign residents in the treaty ports were not very interested in knowing much about where they were. They were not there for long, and so aimed to make themselves comfortable by recreating the familiar. China was a business inconvenience which they endured. It was interesting – novel, perhaps – but it was not their European or North American reality. To this end they installed their church bells, planted their apple trees, shipped in sherry and port (sold in 'cases of three dozen, quarts' by Sykes, Schwabe & Co.), and subscribed for a guinea a year to the Art Union of London, that way receiving once a month a large fine print to hang on their walls, such as *The Death of Nelson*: good British fare for good British homes. A subscription library was established in 1849, and provided good solid reading – *The Art of Dining, Rambles in North & South America, The Flower Garden, The Story of Nell Gwyn, Deeds of Naval Daring* and *Uncle Tom's Cabin*. More books arrived about Egypt than China in one early batch. Children's books were for sale from the *Herald* office.[12] China was all around, suffocatingly so for some, so other vistas were desired: views and words of worlds far away from the daily business of being in China. All of this was hardly unexceptional for empire subjects or commercial migrants. They were not cosmopolitan travellers: they were not seeking new experiences, new cultures or new ideas. They were not interested in Chinese antiques or decorative arts, but might pick up in desultory fashion a few curios from time to time, and 'curios' they called them.[13] There was no successor to Nathan Dunn, whose collection in part or in whole remained on show in London and New York until it was finally sold off in 1851.[14] Certainly they commissioned or bought the same type of export art that they had acquired in Canton – paintings of their new bunds and *hongs* – but on the whole they wanted and recreated the familiar. They wanted their cigar brought, and then their newspaper. So they made themselves at home on the Huangpu, the Min, Gulangyu island, the slopes of Hong Kong, as snug as they could manage, and read weeks-old news about the real world over the ocean in a fug of finest Havana.

They were sojourners, mostly: that is, they intended to stay to conduct their business for as long as it took them to secure their futures, and would then move on. So it was comfort they sought, and while some comforts could be found locally – servants and sex not least – most of what they sought as comfort, that is the stuff of daily lives that brings respite, had to be imported or recreated. Servants had to be taught to cook in a Western style. Furnishings had to be shipped in or local craftsmen trained to approximate them. Even as a world of ersatz goods developed, they still wrote home for shoes, clothes, glasses, sheet music and paper. Their sojourns were not short. They were measured in years and not months, and so they were certainly not content with the makeshift life of the pioneers. And when they had achieved their aims, then mostly they would move back to Britain or America, where lay opportunities for real fulfilment and real social preferment – Parliament or Congress for some, charitable work, local estates, local politics and local standing for others. Some took longer to achieve this, but the turnover of names in the various registers, directories and almanacs was steady, and this pattern long continued. Thirty of the 168 residents and their families listed in the first edition of the *North China Herald* in August 1850 were not listed two years later. By 1861 only twenty-three of the 168 remained, and many of these were missionary or lower level consular staff. Others included an auctioneer, provision merchants, and men who had been mercantile assistants in 1850 and were now managing firms. Some had died and were buried in the cemeteries, their goods auctioned off, with imported items securing premium prices; some had gone back broken in health. Others had moved to other China ports, and five were in newly opened Japan. Many surnames persist, as networks of family ties provided openings, not least in a business culture where trust remained important and China remained so distant: it took fifty-one days for the London mail to arrive in Shanghai in 1850. Missionary Robert Nelson and his family took 145 days to sail there from Boston the following year.[15] Increasingly there were individuals and families who stayed on longer and longer. The tea and silk men could sell up and pull out when satisfied or broken, but the growing body of service providers – the bakers, ships' chandlers, tailors – were all tied more firmly to their Shanghai or Hong Kong livelihoods. Their children found openings, their daughters married newer arrivals. And some were disinclined to move, perhaps feeling too distant and their experiences too different to easily move home. Or perhaps they were just too comfortable where they were.

But then enter the younger brother of Jesus Christ, who came to discomfort all these lives, and to convulse all of China for fourteen years of rebellion and war. This was no small surprise, but it was a direct if accidental consequence of the new foreign presence in the empire of the Qing. Under the treaty dispensation the missionaries were able to talk, to print and to circulate their tracts. At Shanghai the London Missionary Society had printed 370,000 pages of various sermons, a catechism, and a commentary on the Ten Commandments by October 1844. They handed out around 200 copies of the text of their weekly sermons every Sunday. At Canton in the bad old days they had imported their material from the same press, then in Batavia, and their distribution was often covert, and their distributors chased and harried. But, as Lindsay and Gützlaff had found, people were instinctively curious about books, and took them when they were offered. In 1836 outside the examination hall at Canton a 23-year-old student, Hong Xiuquan, took one such tract from a foreign missionary, probably Edwin Stevens. This Protestant work, *Good Words to Admonish the Age,* had been written by the Christian convert Liang Fa, and combined excerpts from the Old and New Testaments with commentaries and exhortatory essays. It roundly condemned China's decadence, the failings of Buddhism and Daoism, and the failings of the Chinese. It proclaimed that salvation lay through the Christian God, and through adherence to the Ten Commandments.[16] Hong Xiuquan eventually failed the examinations five times (and so failed his family and his community five times, for it looked for preferment and protection through his success), pursued in 1847 the vision of Chinese reformation offered by Liang by presenting himself along with a relative at the Baptist chapel in Canton run by Tennessee-born missionary Issachar Roberts, and asking to be formally baptized.[17] By this time Hong had in fact been building a Christian community in Huaxian, north of Canton, for three years, and finding a striking success in securing acolytes, drawing in his family, neighbours and marginal people like himself, members of China's Hakka minority. Medhurst, Stronach, Roberts and all the foreign brethren could but dream of such rapid success, and such attentive and focused audiences. Dreaming was in fact the key. A year after receiving Liang Fa's book Hong had been ill, and in his illness had had a number of visions, from which it became clear to him on later studying Liang's work that he was in fact the Christian God's younger son, and had been charged by his father and by his brother with the solemn duty of saving China and her people by purging it of sin, idolatry, and of demons and devils – that is of the Manchus. He studied with Roberts for two months, but on the point of baptism, Roberts suspected him of being driven more by want of employment than of salvation.[18] The ceremony was postponed. Hong returned to his village, and then continued on northwest across the provincial border into Guangxi to join a distant relative and early convert who had established a 'God Worshipping Society' in an inaccessible mountain area, preaching to larger and larger gatherings. In his visions Hong had been handed a sword. Now he used it. In the face of official persecution, Hong raised his standard of defiance, and within three years of doing so his followers had burst out of the Guangxi highlands. Rechristened as the armies of the *Taiping tianguo* – the Heavenly Kingdom of Great Peace – and three-quarters of a million strong, they marched northeast a thousand miles and captured the city of Nanjing on 19 March 1853, slaughtering its Manchu garrison. There the failed scholar Hong Xiuquan, now the *Tian Wang* – the 'Heavenly King' – and his motley, fanatical followers, flush with remarkable victory, established the heavenly capital of a heavenly kingdom. For good measure, Hong instituted a Taiping civil service examination: now he could set the questions himself.

The fourteen-year Taiping rebellion was as much a consequence of the new order and disorder in China as were the new settlements at Hong Kong and Shanghai. It was as rooted in the roiling disturbances of the new foreign presence as the treaty ports were shaped by Chinese authority, local compromise and Chinese collaboration. It was a Chinese revolt, and so it was a revolt informed by the new intellectual currents from over the oceans which were at work in Chinese cities and in the networks of people, goods and ideas that flowed through them as much as it was informed by indigenous currents and trends.[19] The Taiping were Liang Fa's bastard converts. They were autodidact Christians. They baptized themselves without missionary permission and without Southern Baptist intercession. They heard the Christian message on their terms, and created a theocratic Christian state. And they communalized property, preached equality for women, and forbade opium smoking, prostitution and slavery. So this was revolution, not simple rebellion, and as revolution it is lauded still today in China. The revolt was also shaped by the destabilizing economic impact of the new order on the China coast. Commissioner Lin's suppression of the opium trade and the assault on Qing power by the British forced a redrawing of the economic maps locally. The new arrangements of peace, the shift of the focus of foreign operations east and north from the old 'cradle' of China commerce had dislocated the regional economy, widely damaging local employment in the tea and opium trade networks. Peace had also made soldiers redundant. So they floated towards violent solutions and the easy pickings violence offered. Into the harsh highland world of Guangxi, where in the absence of an effective state communities united to defend themselves against banditry and against their neighbours (often the same), came all these new refugees from changes in the delta as well as groups seeking the spoils of the dislocated covert trade. Foreign warships had by now suppressed the scandals of privateer convoy protection and struck hard against piracy, dislodging many bands from the coast into the hinterlands.[20] Hong's core supporters remained the Hakka, the 'guest people', a linguistically distinct minority with some key cultural differences from Han Chinese, not least that they did not practise footbinding of women. There was endemic conflict between them and other communities over land and access to water. Han Chinese secret societies, many of them anti-Manchu, were present too. Into this mix Hong Xiuquan and his associates and followers brought a Christian fundamentalism, tightly organizing military units that recited the Ten Commandments every day and fought fanatically and fiercely. Theirs was hardly the first religious revolt against the Qing; but it was the first Christian one. Their faith made them formidable warriors; the act of uprising – daring to stand and daring to fight – also meant that they had nothing to lose. They had to win. Hatred – of the Manchus, and of sin – focused their minds. Their military organization brought them victory after victory. Success cowed doubters, and many were swept up through *force majeure*, but the Hakka poor and their allies found power in Taiping ideology, and its interlinked military organization and tactics, and that power brought them to Nanjing and through its walls.

Rumour of rebellion some way off from the restricted haunts of the foreign traders was nothing new. East India Company correspondence and the *Canton Register* noted news of revolt as it came to them in Canton. The first record of disturbances in Guangxi seems to have come in April 1849 from Bowring, then consul at Canton. From 1850 a steady stream of reports issued from the consulate, usually penned by Thomas Taylor Meadows, interpreter there and, unusually, a man who had come to China through love of the language.[21] Keeping abreast of developments which could overwhelm Canton, and which could affect trade there, was one incentive behind this steadily growing interest in the 'Kwangsi rebellion'. As its Christian character began to be hinted at in reports, debate began. Once the Heavenly Kingdom of Great Peace was established at Nanjing, something had to be done to understand it, and to communicate with it as soon as possible. So to Shanghai and then up the Yangzi went the British superintendent of trade and governor of Hong Kong, Sir George Bonham, in late April 1853, within a month of the Taiping capture of the city. Meadows, now based at Shanghai, had already tried and failed to get through alone; nevertheless he returned with astounding intelligence confirming the Christian doctrines and practices of the 'long-haired rebels'.[22] The conflict had already been further internationalized – the Shanghai authorities had recruited a fleet of partly foreign-manned *lorchas* as well as foreign ships to aid the defence of the lower Yangzi east of Zhenjiang and to try to recapture that unlucky city. Good wages and the chance of plunder occasioned a wave of desertions from foreign naval shipping at Shanghai to join the makeshift Sino-foreign fleet. The British consul, Rutherford Alcock, had been eager to help suppress the rebellion, calling for formal intervention. But Bonham decided on strict neutrality, and as the foreign mercenaries already recruited could be confused with formal support for the beleaguered Qing authorities, issued strict instructions forbidding such ventures.[23]

Bonham's journey on the *Hermes*, with Meadows again paving the way and interpreting, was one of the stranger official forays of the British representatives in China. He was followed in December that year by the French Minister, and then the newly arrived US Minister in late May 1854. (An attempt to pre-empt the British expedition by his predecessor, the bumptious but shrewd US Commissioner to China, Colonel Humphrey Marshall, had ingloriously run aground with his steamer the *Susquehanna*, only a few miles from the mouth of the Huangpu.)[24] Whilst they grew increasingly sceptical of the long-term chances of the Taiping, they were also far less impressed with the longer-term probability of Qing survival. Bonham aimed to assess Taiping intentions, understand their motives and stress British neutrality. Instead, the British found themselves subjected by all and sundry, high-ranking and low-ranking, to enthusiastic theological discussion and interrogation, and they were showered with books and pamphlets outlining Taiping theology. So, for once, Britons were receiving tracts, not distributing them. Their Taiping interrogators, the Northern and Assistant Kings (the Taiping leaders were all of them Kings), were keen to find out: were their Ten Commandments the same as those of the new Kingdom? Yes. Was the Taiping God the foreigners' God? Yes, of course: His Lordship was universal. 'They spread all kinds of lies about us,' one told the visitors, 'they say we employ the magical arts: the only kind of magic we employ is prayer to God.'[25] All of this was electrifying. The news of the Chinese Christian rebels shot around the Christian world, and took away Christian breaths. The account of the magic of prayer was reprinted in *The Times*. 'The huge balloon,' it announced flippantly – that is, the Manchu state – 'has collapsed at the prick of a needle.' Hitherto 'the very type of all that was unchangeable, formal and slavish', stagnant China was revolutionized at an instant. 'The deep recesses of ancient empire are opened to light, we enter, and China becomes part of the world.'[26] The Christian and mission press chattered frantically, poring over the scraps emerging. Was this Gützlaff's doing? Bonham assumed so. Although from 1843 until his death in 1851 Gützlaff was Chinese Secretary to the colonial government in Hong Kong, he continued his missionary activities with unwavering vigour, albeit to inconclusive (if not chimerical) effect. A new network of adepts and converts, the Christian Union, had proselytized in the area the God worshippers had emerged from, and although there was much fraud and dissimulation amongst those working for the Union, there were genuine converts.[27] Two of its members had invited Hong to Canton for that encounter with Issachar Roberts. The Taiping used Gützlaff's translation of the Bible, indeed they used it as the basis of the official Taiping Bible printed at Nanjing in late 1853. Others thought it Catholic in origin, but it was also noted that the Catholic Chinese term for God – *tianzhu*, lord of heaven – was not used. The Taiping worshipped *shangdi* – the sovereign on high – the Protestant God.[28] The missionaries and others began to debate. Bonham's voyage furnished all the documents they needed. The elder Medhurst set to work translating and précising, agog and enthusiastic at what he read and heard: it was 'a moral revolution – it is the wonder of the age'.[29] Certainly there were errors and oddities, and Hong's vision and interpretation of it worried some – his own account was quickly published in full – but in 1853 it truly seemed that all was changing.

'China becomes part of the world': such was the fancy, and the early hope, for the new Settlement in south China. But for the British even here, even in the heart of a rebel camp, with its surfeit of kings and Christian revelation, the Lindsay tic persisted and was irritated, and the visiting British insisted on appropriate treatment, and on equal treatment, on paper and in person.[30] As with Qing officials, so with rebel kings. They explained the Nanjing Treaty to the Taipings, and sent them a copy, and they insisted on being accorded the respect their diplomatic status warranted. They sent back without ceremony and with harsh criticism the first missive from the Taiping leadership that had been sent on their arrival. While the Taiping leaders wanted to discuss the universal saviour, Meadows tried to instruct them in universal diplomacy. Bonham attached translations of key texts in his despatches to London, and was clearly convinced of the sincerity of the beliefs of many, but he suspected that anti-Manchu politics and more venal ambition were actually in command.[31] Bonham, like Lindsay the son of an East India Company mariner, had long served the Company, and from 1837 to 1843 was governor of the Straits Settlements. By all accounts an easygoing man, famous for his plum puddings, he had presided over Chinese populations there, and at Hong Kong since 1848, but nothing could have prepared this able British public servant for Taiping enthusiasm. He was not amused. Others were struck by the otherwise open-minded affability of the Taipings, who crowded enquiringly onto the *Hermes* when permitted, examining everything they could. The vessel's commander, Edmund Fishbourne, evangelical himself, was most impressed. He thought them 'practically a different race', 'quite un-Chinese'.[32] And they talked back as frankly as they were talked to and at. The best hit came from a Taiping general at Zhenjiang, in discussion with Meadows: 'he then introduced the subject of opium, saying we ought not to sell it'.[33]

Along the coast, there was uproar. Qing power seemed in the balance. Canton was threatened. Anti-Manchu secret society rebels rose and captured Xiamen in May 1853. This bloody six-month episode, which culminated in a siege and the slaughter of insurgents and innocents, was led by returnees from Singapore, all Chinese British subjects, and members of a group founded by one of their number four years earlier, a Jardine, Matheson employee. The official British preserved their neutrality (until the final massacre proved just too distasteful and they intervened to stop it), but the 'coolie' traders Syme and Tait, and the other unofficial British, profited hugely from supplying the rebels with munitions. As the British consulate was evacuated in the face of the rebel advance, its archives and treasury were moved for a while (until Bonham objected) onto Dent & Co.'s receiving ship, that old stager the *Lord Amherst*, long pensioned off from active service, and now moored outside the port confines and stuffed with opium. For security's sake she was brought into the harbour, and then during the ambiguous siege of the rebel-held city which began in late August she fired again four times in anger at the imperial fleet, some twenty-one years after Captain Rees's first 'experiments' in British violence at Ningbo and Fuzhou.[34] Order restored, trade resumed, and indeed boomed at Xiamen once the rebels had been cleared out, and once the speculative stockpiles of gunpowder bought in by the British firms had been dispersed.

Hong Kong was little affected by rebellion and revolt, although large numbers of Canton residents moved to the apparent security of the colony, fearing an attack on their city. This did the real estate market no harm. And the markets and stores hummed with the opportunities that disorder provided, while rebellion itself actually strolled the streets, quietly learnt from what it saw and heard, and then took it to Nanjing.

The *Tian Wang*'s relative, Hong Rengan, who had studied with him under Roberts, and who was known to the Qing authorities, had fled to the apparent safety of 'foreign countries', as he later put it, to Hong Kong, in 1852.[35] This was possibly one of the first times that the foreign-controlled city had provided a safe haven for a political refugee from China, and one of the first times that such a refugee took care to see what there might be to learn, and went back emboldened to teach.

The Taiping rebel had lived and worked with the colony's missionaries and enthralled them. He was 'the most genial and versatile Chinese I have ever met', remembered James Legge, who directed the LMS Theological Seminar in Hong Kong – the old Anglo-Chinese College. 'I liked to listen to his animated narratives,' remembered Theodore Hamberg. Hong Rengan provided Taiping texts, not least the account of the Taiping visionary's spiritual journey, which was swiftly translated by Hamberg and published to raise funds.[36] He met Roberts again, and he met Bridgman. Foiled in an attempt to reach Nanjing through Shanghai in 1853, Hong Rengan returned by steamer and settled in the colony for four years, studying astronomy and working as a catechist for the LMS. The missionaries aimed to mould him – he was formally baptized, and when he went north in 1853 he went with Bridgman (and lodged with Medhurst), and he was equipped with tools to teach the Taipings – maps of the world in Chinese, a map of China and one of Palestine, a telescope, a compass, a thermometer, models of Western printing equipment. They wanted Christian and Western knowledge to shape and aid the Taiping challenge. In 1858, with funds in his pocket provided by the LMS, Hong Rengan travelled overland to the Heavenly Capital where he took over direction of important elements of the struggling Taiping government and reinvigorated the movement. Ultimately the disappointment of sponsors like Legge was 'great', as Hong Rengan seemed too often to sacrifice principle for expediency, but he brought to the Kingdom a far firmer grasp of orthodox Christianity, strong links to foreigners, and an appreciation of the merits of the Western technology he had seen, lived with and travelled on.[37] And then Roberts came to join him in Nanjing.

Shanghai itself fell on 7 September 1853 to a sojourner coup. The Daotai, Wu Jianzhang, was himself Cantonese; he also had more than a smattering of English, and had been a successful merchant closely connected to the American firm Russell & Co. Foreign officials were none too happy about his appointment in 1852, seeing it as a deliberate move to implement a 'retrograde policy', aiming to 'Cantonize the whole of our relations' with the Chinese.[38] He was aiming to set the foreigners against each other, claimed the consol, Alcock, and he surrounded himself with his fellow provincials who aimed to monopolize trade in a new *cohong*. But with the eruption of the Taiping, Wu acquired additional worries, hired his makeshift fleet to hold the rebels at Zhenjiang, strove to ensure a sound flow of treasure from the Customs collection at Shanghai, and with the aid of his fellow provincials organized a militia to defend the city from attack. Doing so with the local leading light of a Cantonese secret society would not have had the effect that it did, if Wu had been able properly to pay the militia thereby raised. But he could not, or would not, pay them. Although negotiations to regularize their standing led to a proclamation putting them on an official footing, it did not prevent an uprising two days later. To the utter exasperation of the foreign authorities, who did not want a problem so close at hand when the whole region was aflame with rebellion, the city fell without resistance into the hands of a coalition of Cantonese and Fujianese groups usually referred to by the name of one of their number, the Small Sword Society (*Xiaodaohui*). Wu was lucky that the ties that bound him to his fellow provincials were so strong. Even though he refused to head their government, they allowed him to flee and his American contacts provided him with safe quarters.[39]

For the British, this was all just too much. It was a 'very disgraceful' affair, griped Alcock, and the arrival a month later of a force attempting to recapture the city did not improve his temper. He could think of nothing 'more futile or more incredibly puerile' than the tactics used by the attackers – 'miserable mountebanks' – whose only effect was to impoverish and threaten the lives of Chinese residents not caught in the city.[40] It was quite a spectacle though. It lasted for months and the foreigners had grandstand seats. The church tower came into its own, providing 'a complete bird's-eye view of the country for miles' reported Thomas Hanbury, a Quaker silk merchant who had just arrived in the city. So many crowded up there to watch the fighting that the *Herald* urged people to desist, fearing a catastrophe – the tower was but 'slightly built' it reported.[41] This illusion of security, of safe distance even when conflict raged yards from Settlement boundaries, of the inviolability of the foreign concessions, grew and grew. It was a recurring feature of Settlement life and thought for decades to come: that from the top of the church tower, and later from other, higher vantage points, events out there – over there – in China, could be safely watched (as long as too many did not crowd up the rickety staircase). If stray shots passed over there would be formal complaint, and stern rebuke. So, having struggled for so long to break out of the confines of factory Canton, they then re-imagined themselves back inside closed safe havens, from whence they could observe China with detachment, and often with refreshments.

But the dangers to Shanghai were clearly real, and focused minds. They brought some fine minds to the port, seeking pragmatic solutions for the problems of the moment – the flight of Chinese authority, the cessation of trade, an influx into the Settlement of Chinese refugees and foreign seamen, the danger posed by the Short Swords, by the imperial forces (the 'imps' some termed them, part-punning along Taiping lines), and by deserters, robbers, and the defeated in flight. Foreign officials needed some temporary structure for trade, one which would allow them to meet their treaty obligations in the absence of Qing authority. They also needed better administration for the settlements, a police force, better defence: in short, a stronger voice and a firmer hand. So there was a customs compromise – the consuls of Britain, France and the US, after much wrangling, agreed with Daotai Wu an arrangement whereby he employed foreign inspectors of customs to assess duties at Shanghai, which would be paid to the Chinese authorities – altogether a far cry from the days of the Hoppo. There was an administrative compromise – the Committee of Roads and Jetties became a fully fledged Municipal Council with new powers and expectations. It advertised for a clerk and a police force, and twenty-nine men led by Samuel Clifton arrived from Hong Kong where they had been recruited from the force there, and by September 1854 had begun to patrol the Settlement. And out onto the fields west of the Settlement, on 4 April 1854, trooped the merchant ranks of the new Shanghai Volunteer Corps. The odd thing – perhaps not so odd – was that this action, taken to 'chastise an inroad upon the settlement', was

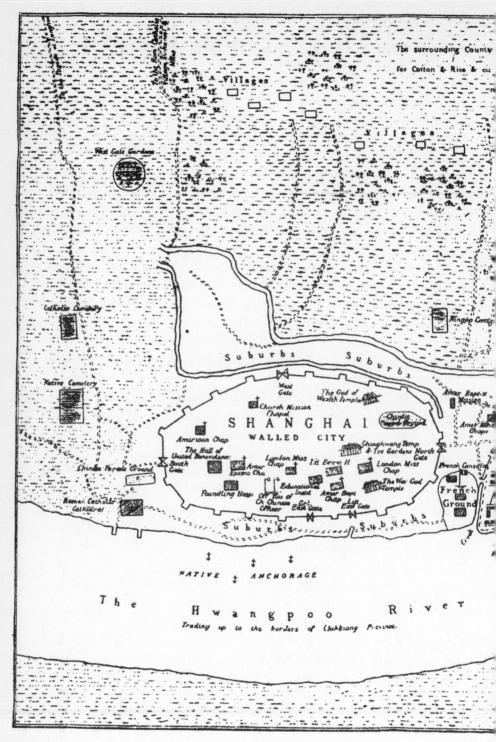

4. Contemporary map of Shanghai and its suburbs in 1853

directed against Qing troops, and not against the rebels. But there was a long-standing suspicion that the Daotai was trying to seize the Settlement as he regained the city.[42] The engagement was also the culmination of a growing belief that the Settlement should not only be neutral, but absolutely inviolate. It also grew from a growing sense among the China Britons that they should themselves be ready to meet violence with violence. They had already been 'accustoming themselves to military drilling' in Canton by 1847. They had agreed to form a Volunteer Corps in Shanghai in 1853.[43] They were ready for a scrap, to deliver a few good beatings to the mandarins, or whoever.

Qing forces besieging the rebel-held city camped too close, and drew rebel fire over and into the foreign enclave. Moreover, residents had been assaulted, including Walter Medhurst. A lady had been fired on. So, after an ultimatum to withdraw was ignored, 300 men – 'gentleman volunteers', and British and American sailors and marines – marched west from the church, 'with drums beating and flags flying', and attacked the camps, driving away the defenders after a sharp engagement that left fifty defenders and four attackers dead. Consul Alcock, who had accompanied the column, reported his satisfaction that a lesson in 'respect' had been taught. Hanbury was shocked at the way the foreign fighters looted and burned the camp, and the sorry state it presented when they had finished with it. Back marched the victors, 'decked with strings of cash and other spoils which they had secured'. Gentleman volunteer John Brine, a 24-year-old auctioneer, was buried in the Shantung Road cemetery, accompanied to his grave by foreign consuls, ships' officers and a guard of sailors, marines and volunteers, who fired three volleys as the service ended. A picture of his gravestone was given pride of place in a later history of the volunteers.[44] Brine had likely as not been shot by his own side, one American participant later mused, as there had been 'no clear understanding between the English and American commanders as to the plan of operations'.[45] But such inconvenient facts were not allowed to obscure the essential lesson of victory: that the application of a little force could sort things out to foreign satisfaction.

War made Shanghai. The ground had already been prepared – literally so. Balfour's streets and his land purchasing arrangements had delivered an orderly and ordered space, and one which could be defended with a stockade if needed (one was erected on the western boundary in late 1854). Foreign residents (for it was never solely a British settlement) had accepted the need to pay for communal goods – the roads and jetties and removal of nuisances. Although it cannot be said that they were ever happy to pay their dues, they had become accustomed to so doing, and to devoting time in turn to municipal affairs as councillors. This was part growing public-spiritedness, and part protection of their own interests, and some firms grew accustomed to seeing little difference between their interests and those of the Settlement. There was the Council, whose existence and functions were underpinned by a constitution of sorts, based on the initial land regulations issued by the Daotai in 1845, and variously revised, to which a growing body of by-laws were appended. They had signboards made up for the roads announcing their 'wholesome, intelligible names', and employed a Chinese writer to fix numbers (in English and Chinese) on all the Settlement's Chinese houses, and to compile a list of them.[46] There was a police force. There was local defence, and foreign warships were anchored in the Huangpu. Hong Kong was close by, close enough to send up reinforcements from the garrison, or arms and ammunition. With the region in turmoil it was hardly surprising that the Chinese, who had so effectively kept foreigners out of their city, now flocked to the policed and armed security of the foreign settlement. And while many foreigners moaned, or stridently shouted that their residence within it was contrary to the treaties, Chinese tenants spoke with their purses the language loved by foreign landlords.

Up flew new houses, gimcrack in quality and design, but serving the purpose during the emergency, and lining foreign pockets. There was a side to this that was welcomed (if, after debate, it could be properly managed), and a side that was seen as threatening danger. Some 10,000 'squatters', and Chinese of 'the lowest class' had 'overflowed the banks of the Creek [the Yangjingbang]', announced Alcock in November 1854; the population had grown in two years from 500 to 20,000. They had 'infested the whole settlement, forming a dense and filthy suburb' of houses, 'eating houses, gambling shops and brothels'. Others crowded onto boats moored off the Bund. It seemed that the city had turned itself out and removed to the settlements. The new police ferried indigent beggars across the Huangpu to leave them in Pudong as fast as they could round them up.[47] This disorderly population grew in the interstices of foreign control, between the tiny French concession in the south (little more in practice than the signboard which announced it to the world, thought William Maxwell Wood)[48] and the British settlement. Finally, patience exhausted, the foreign consuls, with the support of the magistrate, sanctioned the forcible removal and demolition of the Yangjingbang suburb. The land was sold off, and the inhabitants recompensed with the proceeds, but there was now a new principle accepted, that 'respectable' Chinese could be allowed to stay but their less respectable kin would be cleared out.[49] Municipal government was never going to prove quite so simple, and the process by which the nominally exclusive British settlement, a base for the British China trade, had started to become an object of great value in and of itself, for the security its alienated status offered Chinese residents, was now well in train. The number of Chinese residents never returned to its pre-Small Swords level, and it steadily increased. The Taiping disorder lasted another ten years, driving many more refugees to the Settlement. At Shanghai, the British found themselves governing a growing population of Settlement Chinese, and Hong Kong likewise profited from the insecurities of war.

Order, compromise, reform: this was certainly not to everybody's taste. For all the gentility and growing pomposity of the new establishments, the scale of potential returns and sheer bloody-mindedness encouraged sharp practice with regard to regulation, even though trust between merchants themselves was crucial. They hated the new Customs system – assailed, assaulted and sued its employees, and simply resorted to smuggling when it suited them. Horatio Nelson Lay, a British vice-consul who became the British representative to the new Customs system in 1855, and from 1859 its formal inspector-general in Chinese employ, listed a sample of infractions by prominent firms in the later 1850s. None were excluded: Russell & Co. (smuggling rice, whose export was prohibited by Chinese law, as well as resisting Customs officials with violence); Gilman & Co (false manifests); Lindsay & Co. (smuggling copper coins 'dexterously concealed' in coal barrels); Blenkin, Rawson & Co. (smuggling specie); Jardine, Matheson & Co. (transhipping outside port limits to evade duties; smuggling along the Yangzi). Firms and chambers of commerce were loud in their complaints about the alleged inefficiencies and inconsistencies of the Customs and the 'most despotic nature' of its regulation of trade, but as Lay rightly and roundly rejoined, they were in fact simply angry at regulation: 'the merchant prince found himself on the same footing with the storekeeper' under the new system, and 'he who had had Admirals and Ambassadors as guests in his house, who asked his opinion and sometimes acted on it, naturally chafed at having to conform to any rules of regulations whatever.'[50] And so Lindsays had their coal and cash confiscated, and Jardines their ships seized.

Still, the disorder in the city needed even firmer action. Rebellion provided profit for those supplying arms and other necessities to the rebels. The US consul, unlike the British officials a merchant consul, profited from various services provided to his firm's old business partner, Daotai Wu, for he was manager of Russell & Co.[51] Neutrality remained British policy, despite the depredations that the siege occasioned. It was the French who finally decided that they had had enough. In December 1854 they began operations against the city, launching an unsuccessful assault on it in January 1855 that was repulsed partly through the involvement of foreign mercenaries fighting on the rebel side, such as thirty-year-old Londoner George Roberts, one of a group of such men who helped kidnap richer Chinese and imperialists from the Settlement and surroundings. Captured and jailed by the British consul, he simply crowbarred his way out and rejoined the fight.[52] On 17 February a combined French and Qing operation opened up the city, the rebels started to flee, and Qing forces regained control and killed those they found there. Only two foreign fighters were captured, a Dane and an American. Roberts, recaptured later in the year, was sent to Hong Kong for trial and jailed for twenty-four months, hard labour, in the somewhat more secure accommodation provided there.[53] Order was restored to Shanghai, but was absent outside it. Ningbo letters were all about piracy, noted the British consul in 1855. One of its subjects was old Captain Rees, ex-*Lord Amherst*, who sailed his newly purchased fifty-ton Ningbo barque *Psyche* from Wusong to Changzhou on the Yangzi, to ship a cargo of rice. One observer thought he had paid too dearly for the vessel, bought from his employers, Dent & Co., and that he was probably drunk when he agreed to buy it, 'which is frequently the case'. At Changzhou the

Singapore-born mate was seized and thrown overboard by the Chinese crew. As he surfaced and before making his way to shore, he saw Rees stabbed on deck, and his body dumped into the river down which it floated, his blood leaking steadily out into Chinese waters.[54]

Those international tensions and suspicions at Shanghai highlight the ways in which the increasingly common identity of foreign treaty port residents was also affected by the shifting rivalries and alliances, local and global, of the foreign powers represented in the beleaguered city and along the open coast. There had been long-standing tension with American residents at Shanghai, not least over issues of jurisdiction and land registration in the 'British' Settlement. US merchant consuls were not content to bow to British supremacy there. A semi-separate American settlement developed north of the Suzhou Creek around the American Episcopal Mission's church, and was given clearer form when the first professional consul arrived in February 1854, raising his flag over it. The French had marked out their concession in 1849. At Canton, consulate interpreter Harry Parkes had clashed with the French over the erection of a French flagstaff on the public ground. An almighty squabble ensued: the French landed sentries to guard the flagstaff while 'several foolish young [British] men paraded the garden with pistols in their pockets'. Parkes demanded and secured apologies for insults to national honour and consular authority.[55] But when Roberts and other British deserters took pot shots at the French in January 1853, the United Kingdom and Louis Napoleon's Second Empire had been allied in the war against Russia for nearly a year, so this was an even greater embarrassment. The 1853–6 Crimean War was not so very far distant, and had its Pacific theatre too. Alcock worried that the contraband, but still British-owned, opium stocks on the coast provided a tempting target for the Russian Pacific fleet. What was a consul to do about such tempting British treasure?[56] Hong Kong seemed vulnerable – with insufficient naval protection – to either a Russian or even a pirate assault, and moreover 'the peculiar composition of the Chinese population of the place' provided a further danger. British inhabitants were requested to join a hastily formed volunteer corps.[57] At Shanghai, as at Hong Kong, and in every foreign community, such sentiments as were later expressed by Consul Robertson on behalf of the British and French residents of Shanghai were to be rehearsed again and again –

'although sixteen thousand miles of Land and Sea separated them from home, by sixteen thousand times the more was their love for their country increased.'[58]

So the European campaign was followed and marked in China. Naval ships in Shanghai's harbour had fired salutes on receipt of the news of the fall of Alma; the Shanghai British raised funds for dependants of servicemen; they celebrated the fall of Sebastopol with a grand public dinner.[59] They clearly saw lessons in the victory over 'an irresponsible Despot', as Robertson labelled the Tsar, and of the triumph of what the *Herald*'s editor called the 'love of liberty' – for were they not themselves together challenging a similar 'gigantic despotism'?[60] Empires in the Pacific had fashioned other changes as well. The *Susquehanna*, which had failed to reach the Taiping, had proved more successful on the mission which had actually brought it to Shanghai: as part of the flotilla of 'black ships' commanded by Matthew Perry, it had arrived in Edo Bay in July 1853, and set in motion the process which led to the signing of treaties between the US and Japan, and later in the year the Anglo-Japanese Friendship Treaty. These were given teeth and detail in new treaties in 1858 which prompted the re-creation in the opened Japanese cities of the China coast system – formally, as institutions and practices were copied from the existing models such as Shanghai, and informally, as China coast firms set up Japanese branches and their personnel were transferred, together with their assumptions about the right ordering of relations with their nominal hosts. Bowring was sent to Siam to negotiate a trade treaty with the Kingdom. Asia was opening up.

China, meanwhile, seemed still not open enough, but now a new opportunity arose to redress Harry Shearman's 'partial application' of free trade principles. The Taiping challenge to the status quo did not fade. But their expeditions to the north failed, although the first and most successful got to within seventy miles of Peking in October 1853. So they remained firmly entrenched in Nanjing and their central China kingdom. The Qing state was too weak to regain and press home the initiative, and to add to its woes it faced a further and seemingly intractable rebellion, of the 'Nian'. These were well-entrenched bandit groups, rooted in a longer history of anti-dynastic activity. They came to the forefront after cataclysmic flooding and drought caused by the shifting after 1851 of the course of the Yellow River from one that led it to the sea on the southern side of Shandong province to a new route on the northern side. An estimated 7 million people were affected by the floods and dyke-failures that presaged the great change.[61] The Taiping march north through the region further inflamed and militarized this battered countryside, and by 1855 the state was facing a second determined onslaught. The Nian had no ideological drive, but they fought well, trained and hardened through years of banditry, undermining management of the Taiping crisis and outlasting it. On top of all of this the Canton question – the still-closed city – and its attendant complications exploded again, furiously. The Qing faced a third threat, and a second war with the British, and a first war with the French. These foreign armies went where their envoys had been denied access since 1842: they went into Canton, and they went to the north, to Tianjin and to Peking, to the seat of imperial power. The fight was hard in all these places, occupation was bloodier and the terms imposed more unpalatable. They left an indelible mark on China – literally, they left standing ruins you can see today. They finished what had been started in 1840, and imposed a new set of treaties, and a new framework for relations with the reeling Qing. But by doing so they at last also acknowledged their support for the dynasty. They were going to keep Macartney's 'old man of war' afloat. They had seen the Taiping up close. For a moment, just a moment, they had paused, and wondered if this Chinese rebellion was not the answer to their Manchu problems; but then that moment had passed. They were dissuaded by the unshakeable absorption of the rebels in their own disturbing version of Christianity. No missionary visitors to the Heavenly Capital, not even Issachar Roberts himself, who stayed for two years as 'foreign secretary', could bring the Taiping into line and encourage a more palatable, manageable, orthodox Christianity. No one could shake them from their faith in the Hong Xiuquan's visions and his divinity. Taiping talents were recognized, but a fratricidal civil war, and the fact that the movement seemed to have lost the initiative – to have reached its high tide with without actually dislodging the Qing – sealed the business. So the foreigners placed their faith in the Qing, once they had warred with them, beaten them, and humiliated them.

Again, it all began in Canton. The crew of a *lorcha*, one of those difficult, cosmopolitan vessels, this one named the *Arrow*, Hong Kong register no. 27, was seized in the harbour early in the morning of 8 October 1856 by officers of the local police. The very type of ship was a Sino-foreign compromise, a good working condominium form, with Chinese rigging on a foreign hull making it swifter at sea than the standard coastal junk. As a type it was associated with the Portuguese colony at Macao. This one had been built in 1854, had been registered at Hong Kong on 27 September 1855, and had been in the habour at Canton for five days, having arrived with a cargo of rice from Macao. It was due to sail on the day of the incident. Registration of these vessels was no easier matter than registration of Chinese from British colonies in Xiamen or Fuzhou, or more seemingly *bona fide* British subjects, who played the system, parlaying their foreign consulships into trade advantages, but remembering to be British subjects when it suited them. Bowring's free trade haven at Hong Kong exacerbated the problems. 'Vessels came from every quarter and from every nation,' he recalled. 'They entered, they departed, and no official interfered, except to record whence they came and whither they went.'[62] This is not quite right, for in 1855 the authorities introduced an Ordinance registering the colony's own ships. Chinese residents who rented Crown land and who posted a security could register vessels. After querying, this had been approved by London 'in the peculiar circumstances of Hong Kong', in which there were 'hardly ... ten Chinese who can legally be called British subjects'.[63] The *Arrow* was registered by one Fong Ah-ming, and captained – fairly nominally in practice – by Ulsterman Thomas Kennedy. It was crewed by twelve Chinese. It may or it may not have been smuggling. It may or it may not have been involved in piracy in some form. As its very type and ownership and registration were multifaceted, so probably were its activities and those of its crew. From the deck of another vessel moored 150 yards away, where he was breakfasting with associates, Kennedy observed the arrival of two 'Mandarin boats' at the *Arrow*. By the time he hurried over to his ship her Chinese ownership had been established, the crew had been bound and removed to the boats, and, he and others alleged, the British flag had been pulled down by the officials who had decided it was merely masquerading as foreign. Securing the release of two of them to help him man the vessel, Kennedy then hurried to find the consul, to get the other men released, and this mistake rectified.

No little discussion has since ensued about the role and the subsequent actions of the man Kennedy alerted. Harry Parkes was twenty-eight, an orphaned cousin of Karl Gützlaff's third wife Mary Wanstall, who had followed his sisters to join her in China in 1841 when he was thirteen. (One of those sisters then married William Lockhart and went to live with him in newly opened Shanghai in 1844.) Parkes had grown up as British China had grown up. He had grown with conflict and he had grown accustomed to conflict. China was his adult life, his only life, but it was China on his terms, and so on British terms. In October 1841 there were clearly opportunities lying ahead for a young English-man who studied his Chinese books, so Parkes was set to learn the language by such family missionary friends in Macao as John Robert Morrison. Many – most – of these men were employed by the British war establishment as interpreters. Parkes clerked for Morrison, learnt Chinese, and greatly amused and impressed his seniors, who petted him, and took him with them to Nanjing during the Yangzi campaign. There Parkes had walked through the aftermath of the Zhenjiang slaughter, had been introduced to the Chinese negotiators at Nanjing, and had been present when the treaty was signed. His education, remarked his biographer, guilelessly, 'really opened up on the decks of men-of-war, in the council chambers of plenipotentiaries, and on the field of battle'.[64] And this was the education he later brought to bear on Thomas Kennedy's little problem on 8 October 1855. After the war Parkes had worked for Gützlaff for a year when the sometime mission-ary served as British magistrate on occupied Zhoushan island, and then in 1843, aged fifteen, he arrived for the first time at Canton as an assistant in the consulate, and Harry Parkes arrived there in a *lorcha*.

The first British consuls had come from all walks of life. Alcock was a surgeon, Balfour came from the Royal Artillery and service in India, Lay was a missionary, Bowring had been a Member of Parliament (his initial consulship rescued him from bankruptcy). They all brought experience, and made up for their general lack of any understanding of China or of Chinese by bringing to the new China establishment a wider knowledge of the world. But Parkes knew only China. He knew only the early struggles as the ports were opened, knew the importance of show, and knew the continuing privations of closed Canton, where in 1852 his daily routine began as days had begun in the factories of

Lindsay's day: '[I] pound round "the garden" for an hour', its circumference 'exactly one mile', and this ground was still the only resort residents had other than the river.[65] He knew direct insult, and he knew direct assault too, having been stoned at Fuzhou in 1845 when out riding ('My blood boils'). He had more than once before in other ports insisted on proper redress – and visible, acknowledged redress – for perceived insult; and on proper apologies, as he understood them. He had demanded an apology from the French, and he had demanded an apology from the Chinese. As a consul in Canton he represented the Crown, but he also clearly represented family. British China was that family. Family was to respond in time: they put him up in bronze effigy, with a statue unveiled in 1890 on the Bund at Shanghai opposite the entrance to Nanjing Road, the Settlement's prime thoroughfare – erected, the inscription read, 'by the foreign merchants in China in memory of his great services'. He 'did noble service to his country', declared Queen Victoria's third son, the Duke of Connaught, who unveiled the statue on 8 April that year, 'and, I hope we may say, to the world; certainly to the civilized world at large'.[66]

On 8 October 1856 Parkes fired off a note to Governor General Ye Mingchen (Yeh Ming-ch'en) from the civilized world at large, as he would think it, and then made his way to where Kennedy's crew were held, still in the boats, and demanded their release until the issue of jurisdiction was resolved. Ye had no right, he stated, to seize men from a British vessel, even to board it. He claimed in a private letter to have been 'struck one blow' by the guards as they fended off his attempt physically to assert his right to 'claim the men' until the matter of jurisdiction was settled.[67] Anyway, even if true – and some think him a liar – a man who asserts himself, alone, physically, against a crowd of soldiers is liable to receive a physical rebuff, however minor. The crew of the *Arrow* had been arrested on a charge of piracy on the evidence of a victim of an attack the previous month, and this was held to stick to two of them at least. The governor general released and handed over all but these men, but dismissed Parkes' points of principle, dismissed them out of hand with little ceremony. And no flag, he wrote, had been flying. The vessel was owned by a Chinese, he wrote, so it was not a foreign *lorcha*. It was useless to debate or dispute the point. Parkes had met his match with Ye Mingchen, who was to become as well known in Britain for a time as Commissioner Lin. The position of the governor general of the two provinces of Guangdong and Guangxi was complicated by that fact that the Qing had decided to keep the foreigners at a distance by making the post-holder concurrently the imperial commissioner responsible for dealing with them. They had therefore to direct their attentions to him, and while the fact that the British establishment was headquartered at Hong Kong, where the governors were themselves concurrently superintendents of trade, made this superficially a logical arrangement, it was also designed to restrict official contact and communication to Canton. While Qiying (Kiying) held the post relations with Sir Henry Pottinger had been reasonably affable – he had negotiated the Nanjing Treaty, and noted the young boy Parkes on the *Cornwallis*. He visited Hong Kong and was fêted there. But Hong Kong Governor Davis proved less amenable as unresolved issues festered, not least the local question of entrance to the city of Canton. Qiying's successors were themselves less amenable, and Ye Mingchen, who succeeded to the post in 1852, was no friend of the foreigners. A 'stubborn diehard xenophobe' he had, with his predecessor Xu Guangjin, defeated the British in 1849 over the Canton city issue, forcing Bonham to climb down from his demands for enforcement of the 1847 agreement. The actions of Xu and Ye perfectly accorded with elite and popular sentiment locally, which feared British designs, and assumed that a second war was in the making over the issue in 1849. They raised a popular militia, men in their thousands rallying to the call, prompting the despatch of British and American ships and marines, and then they forged an edict from the emperor forbidding entry while the people opposed it. Faced with this refusal, Bonham left the matter 'in abeyance'. He was not going to go to war over it, and any action along the lines of Davis's raid was out of the question given the popular mobilization that was ready to meet any attack. The apparent collapse of British policy was therefore a victory for those officials who were hostile to compromise and negotiation. 'All show and no force,' declared Ye of the British.[68]

Fractious relations did not prevent local collaboration against piracy. Royal Navy activities were often undertaken in collaboration with, sometimes at the request of, local Chinese authorities. The British had drawn the line at aiding Ye when he faced a massive secret-society, anti-Qing uprising in 1854 (the 'Red Turban revolt'), despite the piratical consequences in the Canton delta, so he had himself overseen the defence of the province and by January 1855 the destruction of the rebels. Governor General Ye was not a man ready to bow to Harry Parkes. So the *Arrow* incident escalated surely, swiftly, smoothly into catastrophic, ghastly violence. Parkes had immediately sent for a naval ship, that way 'materially strengthening' his position and the threats in his notes to Ye.[69] He refused to accept the return of nine members of the crew, as his demand that they be handed over in his presence, on the *Arrow*, was ignored, and he lobbied Bowring for an appropriate act of reprisal – an easy local action say against Chinese warships in the harbour – that would be free of 'danger or prejudice', that is, which would demonstrate the 'inviolability of the British flag' and which could be contained. Ye ignored the issues of principle which Parkes raised and focused on. Were the Chinese to decide what was British and what was not? Surely not, Parkes wrote, and so they must be swiftly disabused of the notion that they could. Bowring was clearly happy to oblige, a co-conspirator in violence, hoping (as he noted privately to Parkes) to write 'a bright page in our history' using the *Arrow* as a 'stepping stone from which with good management we may move on to important sequences', that is, to open the city to British officials, and perhaps more.[70] Parkes later wrote of a divine hand 'clearly traceable in the whole affair', and that 'it was the cause of the West against the East, of Paganism against Christendom'. But the clearly traceable hands were his and Bowring's.[71]

Bowring had authorized the seizure of a Chinese warship if no apology was forthcoming, and no guarantee given to respect the British flag in future. An ultimatum was sent, no satisfaction received, and so a junk was seized (by mistake an innocent trading vessel). Another ultimatum was sent, no satisfaction gained, no reply even, so the Barrier forts were seized and disarmed. Another ultimatum was sent, no satisfaction gained, again no reply, and so forts at Canton were seized and disarmed. A large detachment of marines landed at the factories and garrisoned them while Canton's foreign inhabitants found themselves 'beginning to experience many inconveniences', as Mrs Parkes put it. Servants departed; shops were ordered to stop supplying the foreigners. Shades of 1839: having 'no fancy for cooking their own dinner' most merchants left for Hong Kong with their archives and treasure.[72] But this was 1856 and Parkes was not Elliott: the Royal Navy shelled the city, and parts of it burned. They fired a shot every ten minutes for four hours into Ye's headquarters, his *yamen*, on 27 October. And now Ye replied, placarding Canton with notices offering $30 for each Briton killed, and informing the United States consul that a state of war with the British now existed. The British raided (and looted) Ye's *yamen*, but buoyed up by such actions though they were, they were clearly getting nowhere. They bombarded government buildings in the city. Within three months the factories had been burned to the ground, neighbouring Chinese houses and large parts of the city laid waste, and numerous minor engagements steadily increased the death toll far beyond the 'slight effusion of blood' Parkes thought would be needed.[73] Private Charles Bennett's was the first head delivered up for reward; it brought the village where he died total destruction at the hands of the British.

Parkes enjoyed all of this. He was often at the front of these actions, literally singeing his whiskers at one explosive point, and he stamped with 'gratification' and his own boots his contribution to Ye's 'humiliation', by surveying the governor general's desecrated, looted *yamen* on 29 October. 'True,' he remarked to his sister, 'I am up to my neck in hot water, but I hope to use it in washing an immense amount of Canton filth that has accumulated during years past.'[74] Communications which did come from Ye reiterated the facts of the *Arrow* case as he saw them, consistently rejected any impropriety in his actions, and expressed surprise at the belligerence of the British (even, he pointed out, fighting on their Sabbath day), which he had ordered his own forces not to respond to. And, he pointed out, he knew full well that the issue was not the *Arrow*, but the city question, which of course it now was; and that, he announced was closed. A bloody stalemate was reached. The British were powerful enough to inflict damage on the city and its inhabitants at will, but could not take it with the small forces at hand. For a month after the total destruction of the factories they entrenched themselves in those same well-walked factory gardens, now all they could effectively hold. Parkes sketched the site, his 'consulate' now a boat moored behind the church in a scum of 'dead cats and various luxuries', the whole emplacement opposite a range of ruins: the

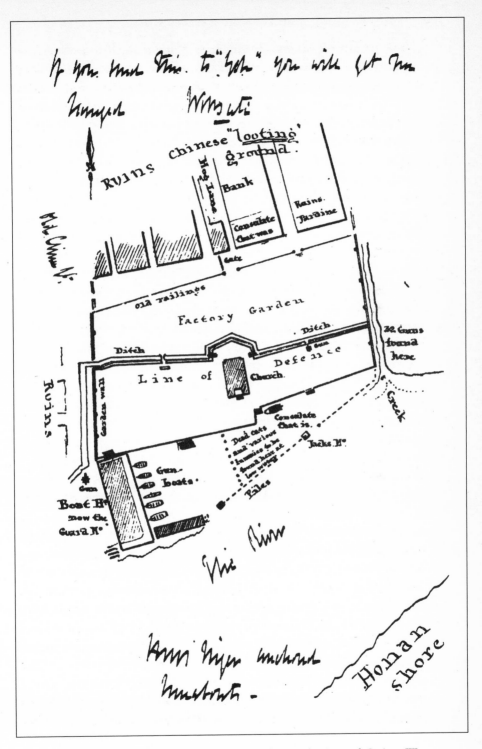

5. Sketch map of Canton after fighting during the Second Opium War

consulate, Jardine's *hong*, the rubble stepping stones from which 'the opening of China' could result, as Parkes hoped it would.[75] This perch too perilous, they withdrew. The escalating conflict had seen United States forces exact reprisals from the Chinese for the bombardment of one of their ships. Taiping rebels in Hong Kong and in the delta vainly offered their services and the remains of a fleet that had sailed from Singapore. A Bavarian was beheaded. An elderly man, William Cowper, was kidnapped from his vessel at Whampoa. The entire crew of a British postal steamer, and a Spanish diplomat on board, were seized and decapitated by men who had come aboard as passengers. Their headless bodies were found in the burnt-out remains of the hull. In February 1857 a Chinese bakery in Hong Kong sent out poisoned loaves to its customers. If less arsenic had been used, some 400 people might have died (instead, most vomited it up), but as it was there were few immediate fatalities, though one who died as a result was Lady Bowring. As no culprit could be identified, the baker and his staff were acquitted after a trial. At least they were given a trial. Many voices, including the colonial secretary in Hong Kong, called for their summary execution and for the imposition of martial law, so as to impress upon the colony's Chinese population the inadvisability of challenging British rule. Meanwhile some made their Chinese cooks taste everything in their presence, just in case.[76]

The *Arrow*, with its expired registration, and a poor record of abiding by the processes laid down in the Ordinance, was a sorry subject for such a lesson, a 'scandal to us', remarked the newly appointed British ambassador extraordinary, Lord Elgin, in private.[77] But the 'great and stirring news' from Canton 'fairly elecrified' the British at Shanghai, for whom developments unfolded in fits and starts as the *Lady Mary Wood* steamed up the Huangpu fortnightly carrying the latest batch of papers from the south. There was some dissent, but speaking probably for the majority, the *North China Herald* announced that 'to feel the sense of satisfaction which the occasion warrants, one should be an old resident in China', one long exposed to the 'insults and contumely' hurled at foreigners in Canton.[78] But in Britain, in public, in Parliament, and in the press, the *Arrow* confrontation was not so well received. The minor acts of violent retribution over the *lorcha* had hardly proved free from 'danger or prejudice', certainly not to Private

1. Karl Gützlaf in
Chinese clothes, 1832

2. The only known image of Hugh Hamilton Lindsay

3. The Tianhou Gong, Ningbo

4. Harry Parkes

5. Caricature of Ye Mingchen

6. Ye Mingchen in captivity, 1858

7. View of Shanghai, *c.* 1860. The Lindsay & Co. *hong* to the right (with aviary)

8. Sacred space: the British graves in the Russian cemetery, Peking, *c.* 1863

9. Royalty and the drug: the Duke of Edinburgh arrives at Hong Kong, 22 November 1869, flanked by opium hulks

10. Robert Hart, *c.* 1866

11. Hart's band, 'the only thing I am interested in apart from work', *c.* 1900s

12. The arsenal at Nanjing, 1871

13. 'The path of duty was the path of glory': The Margary memorial, Shanghai, *c.* 1886

14. Fan commemorating the Tianjin massacre, *c.* 1870

15. Ruins of the Catholic cathedral, Tianjin, 1871

Bennett, or William Cowper, or to the hundreds of Canton residents caught as the British guns devastated the city, or to the soldiers and militia who clashed with the Anglo-French force. Those who had hoped and planned for treaty revision were satisfied; that the opportunity was manufactured out of an incident that might have been resolved by a simple exchange of letters was politically awkward, but Lord Palmerston's government survived its 'Chinese election'. In Parliament in a lengthy debate in March 1857 he was attacked on the inconvenient details laid out so very clearly in the published correspondence from Canton, not least the 'shifting issue', as W. E. Gladstone put it, that underpinned the dispute, and on the descriptions of British naval violence being sent back officially and privately. 'You have turned a consul into a diplomatist,' charged Gladstone, 'and that metamorphosed consul is forsooth to be at liberty to direct the whole might of England against the lives of a defenceless people.'[79] It was an unjust and immoral war. But Palmerston counter-attacked *ad hominem*: his radical opponents displayed 'an anti-English feeling', he claimed, they rejected 'all those ties which bind men to their country and to their fellow-countrymen' – those ties, we might note, that had bound the Shanghai British and the Shanghai French to the Crimean War across those 16,000 miles of land and sea. Critics of Bowring and Parkes thought that 'Everything that was English was wrong, and everything that was hostile to England was right,' charged the prime minister.[80] He narrowly lost the vote, but he won the resulting election, in which China was by no means the substantive issue. The mood of imperial affairs then darkened, due to the Sepoy Mutiny in India.[81] Chinese events were subsumed within a wider sense of imperial crisis, and a need to unleash definitive violence to extract revenge for insult, and to punish opposition, disobedience and obduracy. Representations to the United States and to Russia to join the assault on China were rebuffed, but the French acquiesced, presenting as their *casus belli* the judicial killing of a Catholic priest, Auguste Chapdelaine, in Guangxi province in February 1856. Most-favoured-nation clauses in all the treaties meant that even those who stood to one side for now would benefit from any new gains.

James Bruce, eighth Lord Elgin, former governor of Jamaica and of British North America, was hardly caught up in the general bellicose mood. 'I never felt so ashamed of myself in my life,' he wrote to his wife, looking at the war machine assembled in front of the ruins of the Canton factories, ready to add fire to his final ultimatum to the governor general on 14 December 1857. Ye's 'twaddling' replies were no help. 'I hate the whole thing so much,' Elgin reported when the attack began; but later wrote that 'on the whole, the results have been successful'.[82] The British had, as before, waged war in Chinese print as well, posting notices, darting into shore to hand out leaflets (Parkes as ever at the front) castigating Ye, explaining their own position, professing their hopes for peace with the people of Canton. Then they let loose the guns of their warships. In 1859 a note in *The Times* pointed out that by then Canton had 'been bombarded both in real and mimic warfare'. Elgin's 'horrid bombardment' was portrayed in Charles Wirgman's numerous swiftly printed sketches in the *Illustrated London News*, and immediately replayed as grand metropolitan spectacle. Astley's Amphitheatre, on the south side of Westminster Bridge in London, was 'filled to overflowing' in April 1858 as audiences crammed in to watch and celebrate *The Bombardment and Capture of Canton* and enjoy 'the pomp and circumstance of glorious war' while at that moment in the streets of that city Canton irregulars began a steady guerrilla assault on its occupiers, and reprisals for killings saw streets burned and bystanders slaughtered in their dozens.[83] Secure by the Thames, Astley's had long specialized in equestrian spectaculars, and the 'picturesque confusion' of the show's Chinese procession and a promised 500 participants, including real soldiers, was augmented with live horses, and somewhat less authentic Chinese dancing girls in and around which was weaved a silly *chinoiserie* love story. Ye Mingchen, demonized in the press internationally as the butcher of Canton, a man who had had 70,000 beheaded as he suppressed the Red Turban rebellion, was shown presiding over a 'feast of 10,000 flowers' before British bluejackets came hunting him, cornering the governor general to 'the strongly expressed satisfaction of the spectators'. Then the walls of Canton were revealed, bombarded, and scaled by British and French forces who raised their flags above them, and so the evening finished as 'Canton is won'.[84] Canton was won. And here we are again at the closed gates of the city and at the closed doors of the *yamen*. Lindsay and company had shouldered them down in Shanghai. Parkes and co. fired six shots an hour at them from a warship. Then on 5 January 1858, the city in their hands, its loot in the rucksacks of French sailors and British soldiers (who 'presented a most grotesque appearance ... waving Chinese banners, their heads covered with mandarin caps'),[85] a party of a hundred marines, led by Parkes, hunted for Ye. He 'was my *game*' Parkes wrote later that month. They coursed through the twisting streets of Canton for hours, finally forcing the doors of a nondescript compound after a tip-off. Here were the governor general's archives, and there, in mid-flight towards the rear of the compound, was Ye. They knew him; they had his likeness. A British sailor, reported the *Times* correspondent, 'twisted the august tail of the imperial commissioner round his fist' while Captain Key of the *Sanspareil* claimed the prize. The party 'tossed up their hats and gave three rattling cheers'.[86] They had him. So Harry Parkes had entered the city at last, and there he had secured his audience with the governor general.

At Shanghai, at Xiamen and at Ningpo there was no war. The 'anomalous state of things' they found themselves in, with 'war at one port and peace at another' was difficult, but 'neutrality' was aimed at. Consuls discussed the practical implications for local relations of sourcing supplies for the Anglo-French expedition from Shanghai, but mostly, certainly at Shanghai, they had other worries – the growing burden of police cases involving the steadily growing Chinese population (they abandoned dealing with them in 1857); increasingly thorny questions about jurisdiction; the intense dislocation caused by the rebellion.[87] The Taiping kingdom was still entrenched and the lower Yangzi disturbed. So meanwhile the British at Shanghai panicked about the Russians. The Russians were buying land at Zhoushan island, the Russians were buying a strip at Pudong opposite the Settlement Bund in Shanghai – the Russians were coming, they were marching on China, they were muscling in on British gains. The Russians were everywhere in the febrile imagination of the mid-Victorian British. They must have helped the Chinese design the forts at Dagu, which guarded the Beihe river and the route to Tianjin and Peking. They must have been in those forts on 25 June 1859: 'Some of our fellows solemnly swear they saw Russians quite distinctly,' wrote one participant in the failed British assault on the forts that day. 'They must have been Russians; no Chinaman ever fought like those fellows did yesterday.' They were not, but the Russians had indeed offered arms and advisors, men who could train Chinese soldiers to fight the British or design fortifications.[88] The Anglo-French expedition had carried the war north in 1858, having failed to secure satisfaction either at Shanghai from contacts there or at Suzhou in discussion with high-ranking officials. Go back to Canton they were told (again); talk there. But they went north, and in May 1858 had walked over the forts, whose defenders had fled, and into the city of Tianjin. A treaty was signed there. Elgin had been canvassing opinion since his arrival in China. The China British told him what they wanted, and he had his own instructions from London: it all seemed to have been settled. But when the new British minister, Elgin's younger brother, Frederick Bruce, went north again in June 1859 to secure ratification of the Tianjin Treaty before establishing himself in Shanghai, he was determined to do so in grand style. Unfortunately, the grand style and the route chosen looked like war, and so his flotilla was received this time by the Dagu fort guns with precise and deadly fire, and their marines drowned helplessly in the mud under the walls of the forts on 25 June. They lost four ships, over 400 men, and gained in their eyes a stinging, humiliating defeat. Galvanized by the un-expected clash and victory, those in the Manchu court who opposed concessions abrogated key elements of the Tianjin Treaty, and so the British and French went back to war.[89] They went back to China, to the Beihe: Elgin, Parkes, almost 18,000 troops, 200 ships, and a 2,000-strong Cantonese labour corps; and they took the forts from the landward side in August 1860, then marched on Peking, bouts of negotiation interspersed with bloody clashes. The British had new rifles, the Enfield .577, twenty times better than its predecessor, its range and accuracy heightened by a new army training regime.[90] Their firing was rapid and deadly. And as they had been designed to do, their new artillery, Armstrong guns – 'wonderful' instruments – lacerated the Chinese forces. The fight was hard, and was brought to the walls of the capital on 6 October, and to a close with new French and British conventions with the Qing, which confirmed the Tianjin Treaties and extracted additional concessions from the Chinese. Photographers travelled with the armies, most famously Felice Beato, framing the warships in Hong Kong, arranging the corpses of the Chinese dead at Dagu to best effect, even poking their cameras into the treaty ceremony.[91]

In the fog of war, Parkes and a party under a flag of truce had been seized, held captive and treated poorly. Half of them died. Parkes was by his own admission an abuser of the flag of truce, but the rage of the British and French at the incident, which compounded the bloodiness of the Canton conflict, the Hong Kong poisons, Ye's blood-money rewards, and the humiliation of the Dagu slaughter in 1859, found vent on 18 October.[92] In a gesture designed as a personal punishment of the emperor, who had fled across the Great Wall to Chengde, and outlined as such in proclamations pasted up in Peking by the British, Elgin decreed that the Summer Palace, the Yuanming-yuan, an enormous, beautiful complex of gardens and buildings northwest of the city, whose beauty had left Lord Macartney speechless, should be destroyed. The French demurred, and thought it more appropriate to destroy the imperial palace in Peking, the Forbidden City. But Elgin persisted and the French stood to one side, their troops having already run riot through the complex. Dating to the eighteenth century and including palaces, very well known in Europe, that were designed by Jesuit missionaries, the 850 acre site was systematically burned and looted. 'The clouds of smoke, driven by the wind, hung like a vast black pall over Pekin.'[93] 'A pang of sorrow seizes upon you,' recalled one involved in the destruction, 'you cannot help it, no eye will ever again gaze upon those buildings which have been doubtless the admiration of ages.' But then he remembered the relics of the captive foreign dead, some of which had been found there, and turned to 'gaze with satisfaction on the ruin'.[94] They did not try to photograph their handiwork that day: hard work, reported Colonel Charles Gordon, 'wretchedly demoralizing work' for troops 'wild for plunder', who had little time for pillage, and burned knowing they were turning treasure into smoke.[95] Surveying the imperial palace a week later from Coal Hill, north of the Forbidden City, Elgin thought it a claustrophobic place: 'I don't wonder that the Emperor preferred Yuenming-yuen', he mused.[96] The man who so anguished over the war machine assembled to bombard Canton, would and did argue that he had found a solution to the question of appropriate punishment which spared Chinese lives and livelihoods. So Elgin did not burn the city. And so he did not impose an additional punitive indemnity that the people of China would have to pay. But he was inured now to the sullen violence of the conflict, and converted to its awful metallic logic. So the destruction of the palace hangs 'like a vast black pall' over Elgin's reputation, and over the history of British and French relations with China.

6

China El Dorado

What do you want? Elgin asked the China British. What do we not want, was their reply. The envoy had his formal instructions – reparations, the proper opening of Canton and all the existing ports, compensation for material loss, and then proper representation at Peking and direct communication there, with new open ports and freedom for Chinese vessels to sail for Hong Kong. The accompanying finer detail attached much importance to the need to secure 'unrestricted access' for British merchants – and missionaries – to the interior, to build on the success of the alienated site at Shanghai, to regularize, and so to legalize, the opium trade, as well as Chinese emigration. All the inadequacies and evasions of the first peace were to be redressed. The traders and the missionaries lobbied hard in London, at Hong Kong, and at Shanghai. They had their chambers of commerce, and they wrote as individuals. They wanted an extension of the Shanghai Customs compromise, the foreign-supervised inspectorate system that had kept things moving during the Small Swords emergency. They wanted the covert trades regularized – the coastal shipping trade, opium. They wanted Shantou (Swatow) formally opened – the port was actually already fixed into coastal shipping networks: 120 foreign ships came and went in 1857. Missionaries, drug merchants and coolie shippers were all active there. The merchants lobbied for an open Tianjin, and for Penglai (Dengzhou) on the north coast of Shandong. Consuls worried about all the treaty grey areas, about the pernicious impact of unregulated foreign adventurers – the 'offscum of the European nations' Alcock termed them, still smarting from the difficult year of rebellion in Shanghai – and the weakness of their own control over opportunist British freebooters and Chinese claiming to work for foreigners, all of

151

whom cloaked themselves in British power and bullied their way along the coast. It was a 'national reproach as well as a public calamity,' Alcock wrote. Many Chinese had met no other foreigners than the violent bullies at the end of the illicit trade routes. Whether it was individual insult (which foreigners felt they received daily in return) or armed assault, the corrosive impact on perceptions of the foreigner was sustained. When a combined force from four opium ships belonging to Dent's and Jardines attacked the village of Yamtaya (Yancheng), near Dagou (Takow) on Taiwan's western coast in January 1860 in 'revenge' for the murder of a Prussian mariner, wrecked nearby ('a gentle hint that European life must count' recorded one narrative), and when those opium gangsters marched through the town nearby and berated the 'headman', they represented both no country and all of them. The white face of free-trade violence besmirched and endangered all those trading in China.[1] The 'first-fruit' of extraterritoriality was lawless licence: the Nanjing Treaty system had failed. Alcock, at home on leave when Elgin sailed, was also particular to include missionaries and Chinese Christians within this picture. They were no more innocent than others when it came to obeying the letter and spirit of the existing treaties, and no less able to provide flashpoints for conflict, and Elgin put the same point to missionary petitioners in Shanghai.[2]

The new treaties delivered all of this, and more, and to British and French gains were added American and Russian ones. To the five ports were added new coastal cities, and the great Yangzi was thrown open. Zhenjiang and two more Yangzi ports were to be opened, as were Tianjin, Niuzhuang (Newchwang), Penglai and Shantou. Taiwan was brought into the system with the opening of Danshui; Hainan in the south with Qiongzhou. So from the south central and southeastern littoral the treaty system was pushed far north into Manchuria, far inland along the great river, east along the coast and onto Taiwan. The British Minister now acquired the long-sought right to reside at Peking, and to secure a site there. Having marched into the city once, the British retained a right to return or stay and to be heard at their demand, and not at provincial whim in Canton. They were allotted a mansion in the capital, and prepared it as a legation. The French did too, and in addition they secured a different kind of site, deliberately and symbolically obliterating the Canton source of foreign troubles: Ye's *yamen*

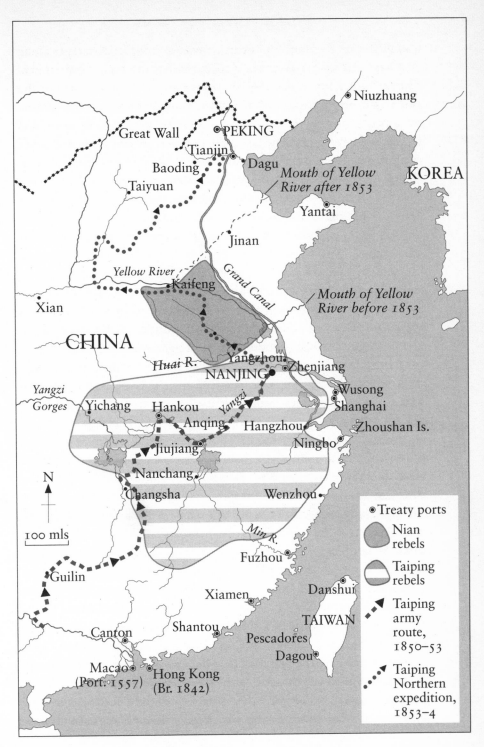

Map legend:

- Treaty ports
- Nian rebels
- Taiping rebels
- Taiping army route, 1850–53
- Taiping Northern expedition, 1853–4

Labels on map:

Niuzhuang

Great Wall
PEKING
Tianjin
Baoding
Dagu
Taiyuan
Mouth of Yellow River after 1853
KOREA

Yantai

Jinan

Yellow River
Kaifeng
Grand Canal
Mouth of Yellow River before 1853

Xian

CHINA

Huai R.
Yangzhou
NANJING
Zhenjiang

Yangzi Gorges
Yichang
Hankou
Yangzi
Wusong
Shanghai
Anqing
Hangzhou
Zhoushan Is.

Jiujiang
Ningbo

Nanchang

N

Changsha
Wenzhou

100 mls

Min R.

Fuzhou

Guilin

Xiamen
Danshui

Shantou
TAIWAN

Canton
Pescadores
Dagou

Macao
(Port. 1557)
Hong Kong
(Br. 1842)

6. Treaty Ports after the Second Opium War

was chosen by the French minister, Gros as the spot for the construction of a new Catholic cathedral. More generally the French treaty paid additional attention to religion, providing protection for converts and requiring restitution of historic Christian properties. Symbolism remained important to the treaty drafters: the Americans required that signed treaties be kept and 'sacredly guarded' at the court in Peking, not left – as those of the 1840s had been – in the provincial archive at Canton (they had been found there by the victorious British in 1857). The British forbade official use of the vexatious term '*yi*', which they had long interpreted as 'barbarian' – the stuff of Lindsay and Gützlaff's debate at Shanghai in 1832, protocol vying in importance with the Yangzi.

Russian diplomacy was blunter. Operating deftly in the fog of confusion and panic caused by war and rebellions, their envoys secured a rich territorial prize: the transfer to Russian sovereignty of vast tracts of land in Manchuria north of the Amur river and east of the Ussuri, and in Xinjiang. Aside from tiny Hong Kong, the permanent alienation of territory had not featured in European treaty demands, but China's northern neighbour had long been pushing to acquire northeastern Manchuria and maritime Siberia. Russians acquired the same rights in the open ports as their rivals, too, but the slicing off of thousands of square miles of territory controlled by the Qing – territory that was the ancestral heartland of the dynasty – was a portent of greater losses to come. The Russians dubbed the new Maritime Province's city showcase 'Vladivostok': 'Lord of the East'. Yearning and ambition were in this way marked in future on all the maps of the region. The British were thoroughly outmanoeuvred by this. The Russian advance worried them. Would it stop there, fretted commentators, were the Russians now in a position to take all of Manchuria from a weaker Qing?[3] But practically realizing their own new treaty gains consumed their immediate attention. Parkes was sent with a British naval force in the spring of 1861 to reconnoitre suitable ports beyond Zhenjiang (where he marked out ground for a British concession and raised the Union Jack), turning down this one, selecting that (he chose Hankou and Jiujiang), gazing with horror at the cities and towns wasted by the rebellion, this one 'obliterated', while this one's suburbs 'can only now be traced by brick heaps'. 'Heaps of melancholy ruins' were all that could be seen, one participant reported.[4] The re-energized Taiping still held their capital and their kingdom, but the China British were ready to move inland regardless.

In they leapt. They knew now what they could make of the new concessions, and their steamers were ready to go straight up to the central China tea marts. They went before treaty ratification, relentlessly seeking advantage (after all, a single good season could make a man a fortune). James Dow sent an agent up to Hankou in July 1861, and set off himself as soon as he could thereafter, his man having secured a good riverside plot for the tea firm, one of forty laid out by the new British consul. At Jiujiang and Zhenjiang, Dow found he was too late to add to his bag of new properties, not that anybody actually had possession yet. It was a postwar moment of uncertainty, and potentially of local conflict. Diplomatic agreements needed to be translated into practical arrangements, and this often involved displacement, and consequently dispossession. There was violence when the land surrendered by officials had to be turned over by its Chinese owners by spring 1862. None had yet been handed over at Hankou, where the traders pestered officials and rented land or properties meanwhile or worked from hulks. 'Men always carry revolvers,' noted Dow of the foreign pioneers at Hankou and Zhenjiang, and a 'thick stick' too.[5] Peace had been proclaimed and placarded on Hankou walls, but the Peking peace which so casually traded names of cities and towns would wrenchingly dispossess some at the far away, newly opened ports. The foreign warships were ready, though, and the foreign soldiers could, and did land, to enforce the new provisions and to demonstrate their power to those who had not yet tasted the bitter violence of the Europeans.

Soon the Shanghai model was being adopted on the British side as they steamed into the new ports, and populated their concessions along the banks of the Yangzi and on the Beihe at Tianjin. Versions of Shanghai precedents – all the now established forms of local self-administration, fifteen years' worth of precedent and practice, regulation and by-law – advanced with them to get things organized: bunds, roads, wharves, the necessary infrastructure for a Europeanized trade. Staff were recruited from Shanghai in particular to fill positions in the new administrations, and in the new branch *hongs*. Younger men like Archibald Little struck out on their own. He left his position with a

German firm in Shanghai, two years after arriving in China, and seized the opportunity to establish his own firm at Jiujiang, funded in significant part by Chinese partners, designing a new house flag ('rather pretty'), securing a lot (disappointingly located at the back of the concession), and summoning his brother Robert from England to join him.[6] 'The energy of Europeans is seen at a glance,' wrote Dow, surveying buildings already constructed at Hankou by Dent & Co., and the bunding work, and new godowns 'rearing their solid walls rapidly'.[7] It was Chinese capital that actually funded most of this: European initiative needed Chinese resource.

The opening of the river was the greatest excitement. It seemed to offer the complete surrender of shut-off China to foreign trade, to foreign exploration, to all that 'energy'. With Parkes up the wide Yangzi in 1861 went a delegation from the Shanghai chamber of commerce, and a small party of explorers led by Lt Col Sarel of the 17th Lancers, aiming to trek overland to India. China opened now meant new routes across its borders could be traversed, and surveyed. Papers in learned journals narrated these early forays, and these new opportunities to take China beyond the realm of geographical imaginings. A man could now hike overland from Peking through Russia on to Britain – previously as likely a route as travelling back from China 'by way of the moon' remarked Alexander Michie, who made the journey home this way via St Petersburg. He could sail up the Yangzi from Hankou, try to reach the great river from Burma, travel overland from the imperial capital to Manchuria, or bring back new knowledge from Taiwan.[8]

The swiftness of the incorporation after 1860 of the new sites of treaty port China into these far wider networks in fact shows just how interconnected it already was, but also how much more powerful China's foreign adversaries now were, and how hungry they were for more knowledge, for more access, for more licence. We might pause to consider the new global circuits with which China increasingly intersected. For all the parochial wants and vision of the China British and their allies, the pressures facing China and the developments that swept it were more than simply the consequence of the belligerence of Harry Parkes. Globalization, international migration, the growth of British and other European empires and the networks that cut across and through them, all had a bearing on developments in China. All helped shape and were in turn shaped by developments in the realm of the Qing and we ought now to explore some of these. We can start by thinking about some of the captives of the late war, their origins, and their experiences: Governor General Ye and his entourage, Parkes and the truce party. By 24 October 1860, when allied troops paraded into the heart of the imperial capital escorting Elgin and Gros, two bands in the vanguard heralding their intrusion and the imminent treaty ceremony, China was already being fashioned steadily into new networks – of communications, of people, and of ideas. This happened on European and American terms. But with the new treaties, and with the subsequent ascendance of a robust reform faction at court, the 'self-strengthening' movement, this process was accelerated and diversified. China was never, of course, 'closed', it never was the 'stupendous' global anomaly that Bridgman and others liked to characterize it as. Its existing internationalized trade networks had lured Europeans, Americans and South Asians to it for centuries, in many cases following backwards the routes pioneered by Chinese traders. And as colonial power crept closer the British, the Dutch, the Spanish (and decades later the Americans), all found themselves governing Chinese populations and benefiting from Chinese commerce. At Canton before 1839 foreign trade had been contained, and teas and silks were routed through the city out to London, Boston, Paris. But that containment, as we have seen, was too tight, too restrictive, too contrary to emerging European interests and practices, and free trade beliefs, and in its daily details too contrary to notions of personal and national honour to survive unchallenged. And the grittily and violently pragmatic foreign and Chinese opium traders blew holes in the Canton system from all sides, all along the coast and deep inland. By the time Ye and then Parkes and his companions were taken captive, China was already deeply embedded in new-fashioned networks, and these brought to Canton and to the North China Plain the men, goods and ideas which populate this story.

The British took Ye to Calcutta and lodged him on Captives Row, in a villa opposite that of the exiled King of Oudh, the Nawab Wajid Ali Shah. Anti-imperialism would in time form alliances across the battlefields of empire – but empire's enemies were already being confined together. It had been a dreary journey. First they reassured Ye that he was not to be killed, and then he was taken in his chair to a naval steamer, *Inflexible*, on the way passing his nemesis, Elgin, who later authorized his dispatch from the city to Hong Kong, with a view to removing any focus for popular resistance. But Ye was in the process of being disowned by the populace who had suffered heavily for his intransigence, and by his superiors, who cashiered him in absentia. Absent he became, because on 23 February 1858 the *Inflexible* steamed out of Hong Kong harbour towards Calcutta. The act 'will make a salutary impression on the Chinese mind,' thought the British Foreign Secretary Lord Malmsebury, 'a proof that cannot be gainsaid of the power of foreign nations'. It was a demonstration indeed of the British power to reshape utterly the terms of the encounter, or at least the confident belief that British power was so absolute that it could do this, that it could remove kings and governor generals and so reorder relations in its own way. In the chess game of nations it changed its opponents' pieces when fancy or need arose.

In fact the former governor general was now an irrelevance to all but the British, and no salutary impression was enacted. Immediate practical considerations on the ground induced Elgin, heavily lobbied by Parkes, to remove Ye, so as to convince Chinese officials in the city that they could act with the British to restore order without fear of incurring their former chief's displeasure. Hong Kong was too close, and too vulnerable, and the Straits Settlements had too large a Chinese population, so he was transported to Calcutta, where he might be adequately housed according to his station, and with him went his assistant, two servants, a cook and a barber, a Chinese-speaking consul, Chaloner Alabaster, and 'great stores' of Chinese food. With him too sailed George Wingrove Cooke, the special correspondent of *The Times*, a barrister and writer who had accepted a commission to report on the Elgin mission on the strength of earlier reportage on the Crimean War, and who was now heading home. So a celebrity journalist accompanied the seasick celebrity prisoner on the weary way to India. Cooke watched and pestered Ye, generating more copy for *The Times* (and in time his own book), and so for the English press internationally, which reused its articles. Elgin hated it all, glibly exaggerated as it was for effect. *The Times* always needed a 'telling letter'; facts alone could not suffice.[9] Story needed villainy, and not since Lin Zexu had a Chinese administrator become such a figure of global debate, and of global scorn. Nor were any ever so shown to the world. Ye's likeness was sketched immediately after his capture, copied and lithographed in Hong Kong, and parcelled into letters home. Later portraits derived from a photograph taken in Calcutta were also widely circulated. For a season Ye's was the international face of China, crudely, and nastily, drawn from life by a British army officer.[10]

Cooke taunted Ye with the reach of British power (while Ye had taken solace earlier in news of the British crisis in India). The *Inflexible* might sail all the way to Britain, the journalist told him, and 'at every spot where the ship cast anchor he would find a British governor, British soldiers, and the British flag'.[11] That the British had a choice, and the means, to swiftly remove Ye does in fact demonstrate the sinews of the power that they could now exercise on Chinese matters. The ramshackle journeys of the first steamers, such as the old *Hugh Lindsay*, lurching slowly along loaded down with coal and plastered with coal dust, had now been superseded by faster, more reliable ships, and a network of coaling stations that fuelled these maritime highways. And India, even an India still recovering from the catastrophic Mutiny and uprising, was a base which could be drawn on. It had sucked in Elgin's forces in the spring of 1857 as the uprising unfolded there, but it was yet able to provide troops for the China war, who arrived at Hong Kong just as Ye was transported out. Britain's was an empire that controlled and directed movement. Transported is the appropriate word: Ye was not the only, but he was certainly the most high-profile Chinese captive transported out from Hong Kong, and he was one of the last to be shipped overseas.

British power had included the Chinese within its worldwide networks of punishment fifteen years earlier. Between 1844 and 1859 just over 550 Chinese men were sent by the Hong Kong courts to penal stations in Van Diemen's Land (Tasmania), the Straits Settlements, Borneo and Sind (now part of Pakistan). Six men, convicted of robbery, were dispatched from the still-young colony in November 1844 on the *Osprey*, arriving in Tasmania two months later. The authorities took them, but unwillingly, and although thirty-two were sent to India in December 1846, most thereafter were sent to Penang, Singapore or Labuan. There was disagreement and discussion about where such men should be sent, but for fifteen years the colony routinely tipped its prisoners into the global convict network developed by the British.[12] Even with the ending of transportation (which meant at Hong Kong that they had to build a new jail), the disposition to control the flows and presence of Chinese on the foreign spaces carved out at Hong Kong or in the suburbs of the open cities remained and grew. As the concessions and settlements merged spatially with the rest of these developing cities, their autonomous judicial systems and practice routinely returned to deportation as a legal punishment, or even as simply an administrative process – to clear, for example, Shanghai streets of beggars or paupers by taking them to the Settlement boundaries and decanting them on to Chinese-administered territory. 'Returning from deportation' or from 'expulsion' was itself still an offence into the 1920s in the International Settlement at Shanghai. The land and property booms of the 1850s and after left the policy of exclusion of Chinese from residence in the British settlements in tatters, but still consuls and councils wished to demarcate, and to demonstrate at least the principle that (once they had removed the original owners) Chinese had no automatic right to reside in these foreign enclaves, but did so on sufferance. Without gates, walls or other barriers (although these were habitually erected during times of crisis), it was difficult to police deportation when a man might simply stroll across a street and leave one jurisdiction for another, but it nonetheless remained vital to the idea of what these settlements were, and who they served.

The empire of movement was otherwise unrestricted. Chinese were on the move, and the foreign establishment profited from this, encouraged it, and channelled it. The convict labourers were greatly outnumbered by those voluntarily crowding onto ships heading to the Californian or Australian goldfields, whose dispatchers – Boyd & Co., Syme, Muir & Co. – earned good rates from the passage monies. The emigrants were pushed by circumstance, by the disorder on the coast, or they were lured by visions of fortune over the water. They went to what they called 'Old Gold Mountain' (San Francisco) and to 'New Gold Mountain' (Melbourne). Between 1849 and the shutting of the gate in 1882, there were 300,000 Chinese arrivals in the United States.[13] Almost 12,500 arrived in Australia in 1856, the last year of peace. There were almost 40,000 Chinese in Australia by 1861. Most returned –

some in coffins as ships carried the dead home to ancestral lands – but increasing numbers stayed on. Half of the 100,000 who arrived before 1900 were, by farming, labouring and shop-keeping, creating the nucleus of a Chinese-Australian community.[14] The recruitment of indentured labour intensified. Chinese bodies were a global resource, as long as they could be mastered. The second China war itself saw for the first time substantial recruitment of Chinese labour to support the allied armies. Given the paranoia that swept through Hong Kong as the bread was poisoned and as Europeans fell victim to Ye's head-hunters; and especially given the very wide suspicions about the level of allegiance of Chinese in the colony – not a servant, it was felt, was to be trusted – recruitment of Chinese for the British war effort was contentious.[15] There was some cause, for we know that Ye had a network of informants in Hong Kong who were sending him inform-ation, while others organized guerrilla attacks. But the fears of early 1857 were outmatched by the desperate need for labour.[16] So the British recruited a tatterdemalion corps for the Canton attack, the prominent subject of a number of Charles Wirgman's sketches for the *Illustrated London News*. Over 2,000 men, mostly Hakkas, were then recruited to support the northern expedition in 1860 (each 'of more general value than any three baggage animals', thought one officer). This 'Canton Coolie Corps' – 'mostly thieves and pirates' claimed one participant – was certainly useful, if not vital, and it was as wild for loot as all participants in the Peking campaign.[17]

But Elgin had thought so much of them at Canton that he proposed they be thought of as a wider colonial asset. He saw in them potentially 'a means of raising troops capable of enduring the trials of a tropical climate, and available, therefore, if the necessity should arise, for service in India'.[18] The British and others were thinking afresh about the place of Chinese in their colonial worlds, and they thought, as ever, globally. The Chinese had technical expertise – in tea cultivation for example, so India recruited cultivators from tea districts, as the Dutch tried to. Perhaps inevitably, naïve, reductionist assumptions about the ability of all Chinese to grow tea – because tea came from China – saw shoemakers from Calcutta's small Chinese quarter, or hapless labourers from Singapore hired for such work. This was not a success, but there was later a debate that rumbled on for decades about recruitment of

Chinese as agricultural settlers for the 'tropics', notably Australia.[19] Chinese were mainly seen as labour, although they were to be recruited as policemen, first in the makeshift force in occupied Canton (not returned to full Chinese administration until 1861), and then a very short time later in the concessions and settlements. They were never to serve in colonial police or military functions elsewhere as Elgin proposed. India and Indians provided such empire-wide police reserves, and Sikhs were to be recruited for British-led police forces in Hong Kong, Shanghai, Tianjin, Xiamen and Hankou. But Chinese soldiers were destined to fight and die for the British, and to fight against their own countrymen, before the century was out.

Hitching China further into Indian circuits was naturally a key British ambition. And Indians were of course fighting in China. Even as Anglo-China, that Anglo-Indian offshoot, refined further its own patois, and invented its own traditions, the China script for the performance of British power and identity in the treaty ports was borrowed from the Subcontinent, as were many of the performers. This was the case elsewhere in the British colonial orbit, and just as Messrs Hall and Holtz advertised in the *North China Herald* their stocks of Bombay chutney, mango pickles and curry powder for the kitchens of the Shanghai British, so public ceremonial and private behaviour likewise developed a familiar Indian taste, and crisis called for the Indian legions to be despatched.[20] The juxtaposition of nations the British engineered was a subject for amusement and condescension – the novel sight of Sepoys being shaved by Chinese barbers at Canton was a fit one for sketches in the *Illustrated London News* – but the men were there to fight and fought there well.[21] Of the thirty-eight men captured with Parkes on 18 September 1860, eighteen were Sikhs, troopers in Fane's or Probyn's Horse, volunteer units raised specifically for the China campaign. Bound tightly, then manacled with irons, and roughly treated, Prem Singh, Ramdem Singh, Jawalla Singh and six others did not survive. Indian troops had of course fought in the first China war, and now they were again there, four regiments of Punjab infantry, Madras Sappers, the 21st Madras Infantry regiment, the Sikh Loodianah (Ludhiana) regiment, and the cavalry irregulars, over 4,000 men, including the main body of the allied cavalry – 'fine handsome men . . . becomingly dressed, well mounted'.[22] Admiration for the appearance of the Sikhs, the 'colour' they were felt and said to have brought to China, and to British display in China, and their fighting skills, were to be recurrent reflections in the private and public writings of foreigners in China. But they went hand in hand with more ambivalent and hostile images, of 'darkies' running wild in the frenzy of loot, of alleged cowardice in the face of the ultimate test: 'Let dusky Indians whine and kneel' runs one line in the China campaign's most widely known image, Sir Francis Doyle's much anthologized verse, 'The Private of the Buffs', which reports the purported tale of a British soldier and some Sikhs, captured and ordered to kowtow. For Doyle, a school friend of Elgin's, the Sikhs complied, the Briton refused and so the Briton died. Whatever the facts, it captures the ambiguities of the British relationship with Indians in the post-Mutiny era. The reality was something else entirely: those accompanying Private John Moyse, the 'Private of the Buffs' whose death lies at the heart of this imperial myth, were actually men of the Chinese Coolie Corps; his British companion had kowtowed merrily, by his own account; and Moyse had probably drunk himself to death.[23]

News, rumour, myth – all now travelled faster and faster, and farther and wider. This Moyse story was spread through a report on the capture of the Dagu forts published in *The Times* on 3 November 1860. It was the work of Thomas Bowlby, the paper's second special correspondent of the war, who had sailed out with Elgin earlier in the year (and been shipwrecked with him at Ceylon). Having been unhappy about Cooke's reporting, Elgin had hoped that having a well-regarded journalist with him would see the British public 'correctly informed' about the China issue, and British interests there.[24] Bowlby's long-lasting contribution to British understandings of China was unhappily rather different. He had sent his long dispatch on 25 August 1860. It shipped south and then west by sea and eventually by telegraph, the news arriving in Marseilles and Moscow on 1 November, and in London the following day. The story was reinforced by editorial comment and in discussion by letter writers, and was picked up by provincial and overseas newspapers. The poem was written swiftly, and was published in time for the December 1860 issue of *Macmillan's Magazine*, accompanied there, and in numerous anthologies since, by a snippet of Bowlby's dispatch. But by the time the news arrived in London the *Times* correspondent had been captured with Parkes and was long dead. The journalist became the story not least because Bowlby was already well known. Like Cooke, he had successfully reported for the paper before, in his case on the 1848 revolutions in Europe. The speed with which news was now circulating and being responded to, and was entering as fact or myth a wider culture, read at school speech days, lodged in didactic anthologies, and in British memories, as well as the arrival in China of dedicated correspondents, shows how far the China enterprise and responses to it had changed. Gone were the days of the homespun Canton press, run off on poor machines in the fetid Canton *hongs*. British foreign secretary Lord Malmesbury had heard of Ye's transportation by news telegrams, and so diplomatic correspondence also now entered a two-speed era, sometimes keeping up with the news wires, sometimes falling far behind them. Starting in 1850 submarine telegraph cables had begun to link Britain and continental Europe, but it still took sixty-nine days from 25 August for Bowlby's report, and Elgin's official dispatch, to get to London in 1860. Communication was, remarked Harry Parkes in 1862, an issue of 'vital interest' to all concerned.[25] Telegraph lines snaked their way thereafter to China. Cross-Mediterranean lines were soon laid; Malta and Alexandria had by 1861 become forward points for sending onwards news received by steamer from India. A land route through Turkey was built in 1864, speeding up communications further, although they were expensive and at the mercy of the English-language skills of Turkish staff, so for a while a new uncertainty entered the markets. A route via Russia was established in 1869. By 1873 average times from India to London on this route reached 3 hours 9 minutes. Strategic defence considerations dictated the laying of a wholly British controlled submarine cable from England to Alexandria, and then from Suez to Bombay, by 1870; and Singapore was linked to Madras and to Hong Kong by 1871.[26] In 1860 Britain waited for fifteen days to hear the outcome of the attack on the Dagu forts, news of the launch of which had arrived back on 16 October, having been sent with a steamer that had left north China on 13 August. By 1873 news (and rumour and myth) from Hong Kong was being published in London two days after dispatch.

Information greased the system, and was itself a precious commodity. The speed of the mails and just as importantly the speed of their

distribution on arrival, obsessed merchants, who might scoop the
market with advance information, and knew that their competitors,
like Jardines, who often carried the mails for free up the China coast
on their own clippers, would hold back others' mails while they bought
or sold on their own intelligences. The official mails were slow, but
they were generally predictable and reliable, and got steadily faster.
Amongst Lord Napier's first actions on arriving at Canton in 1834 had
been the establishment of a post office.[27] This office outlasted the
hapless superintendent, but most mail travelled privately until the
formal establishment of a Post Office in Hong Kong in 1842. Each
consulate in the open ports acted as a postal agent, with staff responsible for mail heading out to the other ports or to Hong Kong and
from then on to Europe. The Crown Colony was formally hooked into
the imperial postal network in 1845 when the Peninsular and Oriental
Steam Navigation Company (P&O), secured a heavily subsidized
contract to ship mails there from Southampton via Alexandria, Suez
and Ceylon; and in 1850 the service was extended to Shanghai.[28] The
mail travelled faster and faster – 84 days on average from Hong Kong
in 1844, 57 days on the P&O's new steamer *Lady Mary Wood* in 1845,
and a record-breaking run of 48 days in 1851. It took 43 to 46 days
in 1860. It sailed more frequently, twice a month, from 1853 onwards.
It sailed from India, from Bombay at least after 1847, with large and
profitable cargoes of opium as well, which perfumed the ships (we
'soon get used to it' remarked Dow, who assumed it was its permeating
scent that had helped him sleep so well on the final leg of the journey
out).[29] This developing and interconnected infrastructure prompted
one China merchant, Frederick Angier, to start new papers in London
in 1858, the *London and China Telegraph* dedicated to publishing the
news from China as soon as it arrived, and the *London and China
Express* full of European news for the China audience on the day the
outward mails sailed east. China was getting clearer and clearer, better
known, and more swiftly reacted to.

The information that circulated was not confined to market reports
or war stories. The growing presence, and relative ease of transmission
of goods and people, locked China more and more closely into knowledge networks, not least geographical and scientific ones. Charles
Grant and Alexander Michie presented accounts of their overland

travels to a Royal Geographical Society meeting in London, and the pages of its journal (and newspaper reports) disseminated them more widely still. Men back on leave from China came along to add their thoughts to the discussion. What quickly and formally became the North China Branch of the Royal Asiatic Society was formed in 1857 in Shanghai. Colonel Sarel's expedition brought back geological samples, ferns, new maps and meteorological data.[30] Private individuals corresponded with learned society journals, sending back reports and samples. Thomas Hanbury sent back to London seeds, crickets and goldfish, as well as a mass of data and materials purchased from medicine shops in Shanghai to his pharmacologist brother, Daniel, whose work partly explored the chemical properties of Chinese medical preparations. The Horticultural Society of London and private nurseries sent more collectors.[31] The Acclimatisation Society of Victoria advertised in Shanghai its willingness to buy examples of new species to see if they could be useful in any way in Australia, as those seeking to shape the colonized landscape there looked to newly opened China for resources.[32] The utilitarian impulse aside, a clearer understanding of China's botany, geology and pharmacopoeia was developing rapidly. Further institutional changes, notably the evolution of the network of Maritime Customs stations under Robert Hart in the 1860s, saw a vast expansion of the business of dissecting and cataloguing China, and making it known overseas through print and exhibition.

Things travelled in both directions of course: opium one way, tea and opium revenues the other. There were other goods traded into China – the cloth, brass buttons, telescopes and pistols that reached closed Chongqing from Canton, and exported – the Summer Palace loot that washed up in auction houses and state collections on the return of the expeditionary forces (and the fake loot, the theatrical costumes sold in Hong Kong as 'vestments warranted imperial').[33] The expedition to Hankou found the market already served with foreign goods via Canton. Traders experimented, trying out the readiness of Chinese markets for new products, to add to those already profitable. Unexpected objects found a Chinese life. The *Illustrated London News* correspondent might be expected to note that 'the Chinese are very fond of decorating their walls and junks' with his newspaper, but other writers noted incidentally the eagerness with which people snapped up stray copies of this journal, and how they used it.[34] Photographs too found a ready audience. Jules Itier was the earliest photographer of China whose images survive, but he lost several of his daguerreotypes to his sitters, who snatched them away once shown them.[35] Portraits were soon popular, so were other genres: the North China Herald in 1863 drew the attention of its readers to the swiftness with which 'filthy' European photographs penetrated China: at Qianmen in Peking, a stereoscope stand entertained viewers with pornographic photographs, which were known to be circulating widely in both China and Japan.[36] Debates and concerns about such awkward circulations of images of European women would persist for decades to come.

Foreign life in China was still an individual trauma, of separation and often of loss, and however insular it got the community was always desperate for news from home. At Hong Kong residents flocked on board arriving ships, buttonholing passengers for news or newspapers, while mail boats were readied to race on with business letters and packets to Canton.[37] An otherwise languid account of British life in Shanghai published in 1860 highlighted the sojourner craving for news, the excitement of the mail days, as men looked out to Wusong through spyglasses to see the flags of the ships there. Was there a red ensign with yellow anchor flying? Then the mails were in, and now in the hands of 'wild looking China boys on wilder ponies' and soon to arrive at the settlement:

A packet is flung in my face. In a moment I am surrounded by anxious, enquiring faces . . .

1st Querist: A Straits Times?
2nd do.: Silk up or down?
3rd do.: Down 6d, I'll bet – isn't it?
4th do.: How about the teas?
5th do.: What is France doing?[38]

And on and on: issues of note, opportunities and disappointments were talked about in Shanghai as the news came in, and the North China Herald as it circulated further beyond the Settlement carried 'home' and 'foreign' news to readers increasingly located after 1860 far across China. But the telegraph relocated events in China for Europeans and North Americans, accelerating the speed with which reports of events were received, bringing them much closer to home. They could afford to get nonchalant now, as Bob Little remarked in 1865: 'We have the telegraphic news now at least three weeks in advance of the mail, so that the fortnightly papers cease to interest. . . . I am getting an old enough resident to care little for European news.'[39] The sojourner was mentally relocating, settling in, his sense of where he formally belonged shifting.

Shipping was still of course the key to speed, and to this newly feigned ennui. The steamers were getting more reliable, more powerful and faster. They presented new opportunities to break into the coastal trade, but there was also the new business of fuelling them – of locating, mining and transporting coal. Hugh Hamilton Lindsay invested heavily – too heavily by far – in the Eastern Archipelago Company, which received in 1847 exclusive rights under charter to mine coal at Labuan, Borneo, with the aim of supplying P&O, the Royal Navy, Singapore and Hong Kong. The 1850s and 1860s saw the glory days of the China clippers. These tea ships, the fastest sailing cargo vessels ever built, were designed to whisk the first crop to London and the highest prices on the market. They outperformed (and undercut) the steamers on the China route until the opening of the Suez Canal in 1869. Lindsay was no less eager to innovate than ever. Aiming to compete with the American clippers which had been able to carry the new seasons' crops to Britain direct with the repeal of the Navigation Acts in 1849, he commissioned a new 700-ton vessel from a London dockyard. He based its design on a swift American ship, the *Oriental*, which they had dry-docked in 1850 after a 97-day journey west. The *Challenger*, launched in December 1851, made its maiden journey out to Shanghai in 111 days and took but 112 to return with its cargo, and was consistently faster – and so could charge higher freight rates – than most other British ships over the next decade, making the journey back in 101 days in 1856.[40] The clippers added glamour to the China trade, glamour sorely lacking in a commerce otherwise wreathed in poppies. Alexander Michie, who sailed out to work for Lindsay's in Hong Kong in 1853, recalled the excitement on board as *Challenger's* 'shapely back hull and white sails reflecting the morning sun' were spotted in the Strait of Malacca.[41] Lindsay's pride and other British-built ships beat the Americans out of this trade. Britain was not the only destination – in 1854 ships sailed from Shanghai to Australia, the United States, Hamburg and Canada – but overwhelmingly tea was shipped to Britain, and until 1869 shipped in clippers around the Cape. In his warmongering in 1840, Lindsay had laid great stress on the 'fragrant herb' and the ties which bound Britain and China through the 'indispensable' British habit, tea drinking, the province of 'the sovereign in her palace' and 'the peasant in his cottage'. And then there was the tenth-part of British and Indian revenues derived from tea duties.[42] The romance of the tea clippers, a maritime romance which endures in Britain and is accorded a central place in the story of sail, symbolized not least in the survival of the *Cutty Sark* at Greenwich, is nonetheless a conscious obfuscation. It is a displacement romance for the clippers which dare not speak their name, those that raced in the other direction out of India eastwards, weighted down with case upon case of fragrant, indispensable poppy.

Underpinning all of this movement was a fitful programme of surveying and mapmaking, and assembling of meteorological data. China needed mapping and the ways to China needed mapping. It was fitful as with most things, because desires to note, record and create archives of useful data were always circumscribed by financial parsimony, and by the availability of other resources – not least expertise. But the war fleets in 1858, 1859 and 1860 knew well enough where they were heading and the topographical snares and challenges ahead (even if they hideously underestimated the power of the Chinese guns at Dagu). The East India Company until 1779 had mostly relied on the experience of its commanders to get its sailing fleet, some thirty vessels annually, out and back to Britain. Only that year did it start to support the hydrographic work of William Dalrymple, but this work then fed into a more systematic compilation of data from ships' logbooks and new surveying operations. The Royal Navy took this over (and after 1844 had an official 'China Station' headquartered at Hong Kong). On a number of voyages between 1806 and 1820 Daniel Ross directed a series of official surveys of China seas, taking advantage of the Amherst embassy in 1817 to survey harbours and coastlines in north China as well. This information was used extensively in what became the standard pilot book for vessels heading to India and China from Britain, James Horsburgh's *India Directory*. New work fed into this. The Canton delta was thoroughly surveyed; the new Canton press published meteorological tables. Midshipman Stephens and Captain Rees on the *Lord Amherst* kept themselves busy in 1832 producing charts of each harbour the ship blustered into (and received handsome bonuses for these). Rees later supplied data for Horsburgh on typhoons. Lord Napier was instructed in 1834 to explore the possibility of conducting a more systematic new coastal survey. It was the Royal Navy that consolidated and expanded this work, and war was the driver. Prominent figures in British naval hydrography cut their teeth on the China coast. Richard Collinson was appointed 'surveying officer' to the fleet assembled at Canton in 1841 (itself an innovation), and was joined by Henry Kellett. In advance of operations their parties took soundings and marked channels, but once the conflict was over Collinson led a three-year survey of China Sea coasts, islands, reefs, and of Taiwan, that produced over ninety published Admiralty charts. The work was hardly complete, but it served war well, and combined with work on the Indian Ocean, Red Sea and the Atlantic, vastly improved understandings of the coast and maritime highways for commercial vessels. The Royal Engineers established a meteorological station at Hong Kong in 1853.[43] China's coasts and rivers were integrated steadily into routine bodies of knowledge, and they were this way rendered comparatively safer, and so more predictable for a growing traffic. The process of actually getting to the better charted straits and coasts was vastly aided by new understandings of ocean currents and prevailing winds, collated in charts and after 1851 in a guide by US Naval hydrographer Matthew Maury, which enabled shipping to make its way more predictably and swiftly.[44] Problems remained, notably understanding of typhoons, which continued to wreak regular havoc on shipping and ports. Foreigners adopted the Chinese word (derived from the Chinese for 'great wind', *taifeng*) for these tropical cyclones whose intensity was exacerbated by the size of the warm Pacific Ocean, and whose danger was heightened by their caprice, for there was no observable indication that they were imminent. There was a slowly developing understanding that changes in barometric pressure could warn of their arrival, and there was intense scientific debate about the formulation of a 'law of storms', but meanwhile the holy rage of the typhoon left observers in China floundering, wrecked ships and buildings, and mocked the power of the Europeans.[45]

People moved more swiftly nonetheless, and more of them moved. It was still an expensive business. Michie recalled that it cost about £150 to land a man in Hong Kong, and almost as much again to kit him out properly. A man needed kitting out properly if he was to arrive socially credible in the eyes of a still relatively small society where gentlemanliness was vital for mercantile interaction. The P&O passage rate in 1867 was £125 London to Hong Kong for a single passenger, and £10 more to head on to Shanghai. When James Dow sailed east in 1851 there was champagne twice a week, a 'very tolerable' five-piece band playing at meal times, a dozen stewards for thirty-two passengers, and an 'abundance . . . almost approaching an extravagance' of food. The long journey was itself important, an extension of, or an introduction to, the China coast world, fostering acquaintanceships and connections that were to prove vital. Dow's companions included Russell & Co.'s William Hunter who could, and did, regale him throughout with his tales of Canton in the brittle 1830s (such accounts presumably as those he later published in The 'Fan Kwae' at Canton Before Treaty Days and Bits of Old China). There was a fellow 'griffin' (another Anglo-Indian term naturalized by the China British, meaning newcomer), young Aspinall, heading out to join Gibb, Livingston, with whom he would privately speculate in tea purchases.[46] On arrival they formally made and received calls, properly announcing their arrival to the ladies of the settlement. Nine calls sufficed, 'society' being so small, but it was vital for reputation and recognition.

Society was growing and diversifying. The China establishment began to need professionals too: lawyers, physicians and engineers. Hong Kong was fixed into the circuits of official colonial employment. Its governors started to come from further afield than India, and brought their experience of running other colonies with them. Discharges from the army and navy, and from merchant vessels, further populated the settlements, with men far less likely to present their name cards to the consul's wife. The rebellions at the coastal cities, the Arrow war and then the Taiping surge towards Shanghai in 1860 brought many more ships and troops to the coast, and many stayed on: ninety-one men were recruited straight from the British army into the municipal police in 1863 alone. The Foreign Inspectorate of Customs, now placed on a permanent footing, needed foreign 'outdoor' staff – tidewaiters and coast watchers – hiring almost a thousand men mostly of this class between 1859 and 1865 as its operations commenced at the newly opened ports. They might not stay long, but some did, in the same service, or finding useful niches outside, running a hotel, a tavern, a brewery, or becoming overseer at a dock. Commercial directories show how steadily the foreign communities grew, as firms established new branches, new hopefuls arrived, and as the increasing size and complexity of the China establishment itself drew towards it more and more people. The Hong Kong census in 1853 listed almost 500 resident Europeans and Americans (who employed almost four times that number of servants), 350 Indians, Malays and Filipinos, and 460 Portuguese (Macanese in fact). Another 200 discharged foreign seamen were also in port. Three years later, the foreign establishment had doubled: there were 1,100 Europeans and Americans (including 200 children), and 74,000 Chinese. At Shanghai in March 1851 there were 256 Britons, mostly single adult men, and, seamen aside, mostly merchants or their assistants. By December 1859 there were 569 foreigners, and by 1865 2,800 foreign residents, around half of them British, listed in the first census of the concessions (bolstered yet further in numbers by almost 3,000 soldiers and seamen).[47] Directories listed seventy foreign firms and stores in the port in 1854, around 110 in 1861, and over three times that number in 1877. Foreign residents came from Europe and America directly, like Dow or Little, but they also came from other ports of empire, particularly from southeast Asia. Still an overwhelmingly male society, nine-tenths so in Shanghai in 1865, the established ports began to lose their pioneer feel, with families starting to settle.

As its social composition evolved, social and other attitudes evolved too, and another set of connections arose, more rhetorical in form, with precise and deliberate consequences. For Rutherford Alcock the marauders who operated under any or no flag, and often just under the simple flag of whiteness, undermined the lawful business of the governments and subjects of 'the great European family'. The free-booters took advantage of whiteness. The legitimate agents of the states of the West needed to think along similar lines, to act in concert to protect their common interests. Most tellingly, during the slaughter at the Dagu forts in 1859, as the British forces floundered, the American naval observer on the spot, Commodore Josiah Tatnall, abandoned neutrality, using his steamer to transport reinforcements and the wounded from ship to shore, while his men 'like true sailors, amused themselves by taking a turn at the [British] guns': they 'amused' themselves by trying to kill Chinese. A veteran of the 1812–13 war with Britain, Tatnall reportedly excused himself with the simple statement that, after all, 'Blood is thicker than water.' It was 'impolitic from the viewpoint of diplomacy', noted one later observer, but it was taken as symbolizing the routine practical fact of, and for many the continuing practical need for, Anglo-American – and 'white' – solidarity in China. 'Never were men more unwillingly neutral' reported one participant.[48] British newspapers linked this episode with what they saw as a wider picture of American diplomatic frustration, and of exasperation with Chinese evasions and humiliations. The US mission to ratify the treaty travelled on donkeys to Peking: how the British laughed, and later pointed to evidence they found of it being treated as a 'tribute mission'. There were plenty of Anglophobic American officials and traders in China, and no shortage of Britons who thought little of Americans.[49] But overriding such national rivalries and frictions was a growing community of whiteness, of interests that converged, encouraged by evolving discourses of race, and by the fact that under the most-favoured nation clauses that were affixed to each treaty, subjects of a foreign treaty nation had no advantages over those of any other. Certainly the diplomats were to continue to represent their own national and imperial interests, and the games of nations were played out as readily in China as elsewhere. Chinese diplomats worked adroitly at times to exploit differences and rivalries, as did for different ends shysters and crooks. Spats, rows and insults fill files in the archives. But the formal structures of the treaty framework channelled many basic interests along at least parallel lines. The 'Consular Body' in this port or that one, or the 'Diplomatic Body' at Peking, often acted in concert. They were all 'foreigners' in China, and they needed to remember that, and Tatnall's actions were pointed to by writers over and over again during the decades of the treaty-port world. Communities of interest transcended nationality as often as they were shaped or hindered by it. And very often the consciousness of whiteness shaped actions and attitudes, not least to those not 'white': Indians, Japanese, Eurasians and Chinese.

Newspapers helped generate and reinforce this consciousness. The early China press had aimed to represent specific interests (and represent them as 'British' interests), but it also created a British China community, and it helped create a community of foreign interests, even when those conflicted, for now they could conflict in public letters or editorials. The newspapers helped bind this scattered set of interests together, and helped shape the evolving British community in China in particular, for at this stage they were all British-owned or -edited newspapers. Once the 'British community in China' was the sum of its numbers in Macao and Canton, but now it was thousands strong, and stretched from Macao to Niuzhuang. Even as they developed their local tics and differences, they were conscious of themselves forming one wider community. The press helped give shape to this, and spread a sense of community wider yet. Up and down the coast went the *North China Herald*, or the *China Mail* from Hong Kong. Australian newspapers reprinted news gleaned from these two, as did others internationally. The press made a British China, and it made and worshipped Harry Parkes, the British China celebrity. Returning to Britain in February 1862, a country he had only visited once as an adult, Parkes' progress through an adoring society was marked by deputations, honours and opportunities. His was the China voice of the year. Received at Dover by the mayor, lauded at London and provincial banquets, listened to intently at the Royal Geographical Society, Parkes was 'the lion of the season'. Two ships were named for him and a KCB awarded to him. His China actions were parlayed into metropolitan prestige, and social advancement, the fruit of twenty-five years' hard work overseas for an orphaned nonentity.

There was prestige to gain then, with China no longer necessarily a dead end for ambition, and there were riches too. China wealth, like India wealth, had long been converted into domestic social and political capital. Men bought estates, played squire, and bought or smoothed their way into Parliament, playing politician. Wealth in China itself meant nothing: any clerk in any reputable firm lived in luxury. Lindsay's allegedly spent £12,000 a year in Shanghai on living expenses for its eight employees, excluding wine and rent.[50] The point of wealth was what it purchased on repatriation and what new paths it smoothed. Lindsay had taken himself into Parliament; he invested in new ventures, such as coal mining in Borneo. His nephew would take himself from the Municipal Council at Shanghai onto the London County Council. With his earnings from a by now huge Shanghai property portfolio, Thomas Hanbury bought in 1865 a large estate on the fashionable 'English Riviera' on the Franco-Italian border, creating a highly regarded and much visited botanic garden, La Mortola. It received in time the royal seal of approval, a visit from Queen Victoria, and recognition and honours from the Royal Horticultural Society.[51] Tighter communications meant that some could retire from the fray, like Hanbury, yet entrust their business to local agents. La Mortola was also a business venture, part of a parcel of investments in the region, and the insecurities of China trading saw others direct their gains elsewhere overseas. The profits of the Forbes family went into railway investment in the United States. Meanwhile, the second China war and the surge against the Taiping sparked a China gold rush. The new trading opportunities, soldiering against the Taiping – the pursuit of gold or glory – promised fame or fortune or both for a man in the right place: friends said 'my fortune was as good as made' Charles Dyce recalled after his appointment to a China firm in 1863.[52] 'The present El Dorado of commercial men', editorialized The Times in September 1864, 'seems to be China'. Go to Shanghai, it advised, where 'a merchant could easily afford to attach a deer park to his house and warehouse in the best part of the settlement'. It was 'the great opportunity of the day for the youth of the commercial classes'. This idea of Shanghai was no creation of The Times: E. C. M. Bowra used the same phrase in the spring of 1863, sailing to Shanghai, 'an Eldorado of wealth of hope and fortune'.[53] The ships docking in Hong Kong and Shanghai disgorged eager volunteers for the China fray.

If the Dagu forts debacle had provided a false start for the new treaties, the traders were already prowling around as the marines floundered. 'Time must be taken by the forelock,' noted Alexander Michie: 'how was one to take advantage of the opening and be first in the field' when so little was really known about north China? His employer, Lindsay and Co., like its senior partner almost three decades earlier as the end of the Company monopoly loomed, was forward in heading into the commercial unknown. Michie was one of those who 'with the utmost secrecy' went on exploratory forays to the Bohai Sea in April 1859, scouting out which of the north Shandong coastal harbours would best serve the soon-to-be-opened city of Dengzhou. They arrived at Yantai (Chefoo) with cargoes of merchandise, introduced themselves to the merchant community, and 'pegged out mentally the site of the future settlement'. Michie raised the Lindsay flag, enjoyed the change of scene, and then set out across the sea to Niuzhuang, raising the Union flag on the Liao river. They shot off back down south when they learnt about the mauling of the British expedition and the resumption of hostilities.[54] It was the closest most outside Canton and Hong Kong actually got to the conflict, or at least the conflict with the Qing. At Shanghai the defeat of the Small Swords had brought a return to normality, which meant a return to rapid change and development. In 1855 a new city was 'rising on the ruins of the old one as rapidly as wood can be obtained'. As the British Settlement was filled with new houses a bridge was built over the Creek northwards, and property and land values rose. The Chinese population again rose. War was certainly a worry – foreigners worried about increasing numbers of Cantonese arriving during the early phase of the conflict – but most of the problems were the now routine ones of trying to find a steady way to keep order with insufficient police, poor jail facilities, and hundreds of ships visiting every year – 434 in 1855, 2,812 by 1862. That 'anomalous state of things', with 'war at one port and peace at another' was difficult, but 'neutrality' was aimed at. Consul Alcock considered that Shanghai should as far as possible stay outside the China war, and ought not to be considered even as a source of supplies for the expedition.[55]

War did come to Shanghai again, but not the expected conflict. In May 1860 Taiping forces wiped out the government army that had been besieging their capital, and then they decided to grab the richest prize, the city of resource, of steamers and weapons: the city of Shanghai. They did not aim to seize the foreign settlements, and planned to purchase their fleet, but their fellow, foreign, God worshippers had had enough. As the Taiping armies marched easily east, taking Suzhou, moving on Songjiang and Wusong, the British landed troops and promised the Shanghai authorities that they would support them in the defence of the city. On 18 August the rebels took the French Jesuit college and church at Zikawei (Xujiahui), south of the city, and moved on the gates, but found them defended by British Enfield rifles and artillery. They moved north through the river suburbs, getting as far as the Tianhou temple, from which their flags were seen flying. In response, and to clear their lines of fire, the French laid waste the temple and the suburb around it (and all the warehouses of Chinese merchants therein). When Army Surgeon Charles Gordon arrived there in December only a single large incense urn remained on the site of the temple.[56] Foreign volunteers manned barricades around the settlement, and being spared attack themselves had an altogether jolly time of it, eating and drinking well at their posts. Four days of assaults inflicted great damage on the suburbs, and no little damage and great bewilderment on the attacking forces. They had aimed by arriving at Shanghai to open formal relations with the foreign powers, but found themselves instead repulsed by foreign force, with prohibitions then put in place to properly suppress the supply of arms and supplies by foreigners to the Taiping. The missionaries were still parlaying with them, not least Roberts, trying to browbeat them into orthodox Protestantism. Li Xiucheng, the leader of the Shanghai expedition, submitted an astonished plea for the foreigners to remain neutral and to believe and act on Taiping offers to talk. But that time was now passing. That same summer, the Heavenly King restated his own divinity to a recently arrived Southern Baptist missionary, Landrum Holmes, dismaying the missionary community. Holmes thought it 'revolting idolatry', and found that they would not be 'instructed' by those like himself 'competent to expound' biblical truths.[57] The appointment of Issachar Roberts as 'Foreign Secretary' of the Heavenly Kingdom of Great Peace was laughed at. The 'dirtiest, greasiest white man I saw', sneered one fellow Baptist. Roberts was poorly educated, and his Chinese was execrable.[58] The abject state of Nanjing was taken as evidence of Taiping misgovernment rather than its recent long siege; the destruction caused by the lower Yangzi fighting was seen as proof that the rebels had no rationale but pillage. The human cost was now judged too high, and too close. Neutrality could now only be maintained by force, by 'chastisement' as Bruce put it, to keep the Taiping out of foreigners' way. Formal neutrality remained for two more years, but for many the time for ambivalence about the rebellion was past.

The new peace in the north would bring no benefits while rebellion swept the south. Recruitment of an ad hoc force of foreign volunteers had already been approved by the foreign consuls in 1860, who still at first preferred to keep a formal distance from the new policy of support for the Qing. The Taiping always retained some supporters – Augustus Lindley published his romanticized account of his work for their 'wonderful revolution' in 1866 – but their numbers dwindled.[59] The expedition to the Yangzi had also served to change minds. The banks of the Grand Canal were 'literally white with human bones' noted the Commander of HMS *Centaur*; 'human remains were lying about in all directions' reported Consul Forrest: 'Devastation marked our journey.'[60] While a modus vivendi was reached with the Taiping at Nanjing to allow foreign shipping equipped with passes to head up the river to the new ports, the rebels were no longer being seen as China's solution, but instead as China's problem. They were still, however, in command at Nanjing, and agreed to further British demands, most importantly not to attack Shanghai nor to move troops within thirty miles of it.[61] But the arrangement was only to last for the year, and with the new year came a new assault. The Heavenly Kingdom was now under great pressure, having lost the city of Anqing, southwest along the Yangzi from Nanjing, in September, which fatally imperilled their capital. They struck towards the wealthy east again, seized Hangzhou and Ningbo, and marched on Shanghai in January 1862. But now the foreigners came back at them, defending the treaty port, sending troops into the surrounding districts to enforce a thirty-mile exclusion zone, and actively supporting newly formed foreign-officered Chinese battalions of what became the 'Ever Victorious Army' and the 'Ever Triumphant Army' which campaigned against the Taiping in the cities of Jiangnan.

This was a wild year for Shanghai – of Taiping attack, Anglo-French intervention, mercenary opportunity, and cholera. Refugees poured into the Settlement, camping out on the Bund. House prices spiralled even as speculators threw up new ones as quickly as they could. High wages sucked foreign men off their ships and out of the Municipal Police into the mercenary units. Americans Frederick Ward and (after his death from wounds) Henry Burgevine led one corps, foreign involvement in which was permitted by changes in neutrality regulations.[62] Their Chinese troops fought well, and looted well, but Burgevine swaggered like a bandit and was dismissed (he took his services off to the rebels instead). The British commander-in-chief in Shanghai recommended his brother-in-law as a replacement, and out of this nepotistic move was created an enduring British empire legend. Captain Charles George 'Chinese' Gordon led the force until its dissolution after the final victory. Fresh from Tianjin, where he had marked out the new British concession, placing boundary stones, and assessing values, Gordon found fame through military victories against the rebels. He also found it through moral victories over his employers (in his eyes, and in British eyes). His good treatment of his troops, and most importantly his good treatment of Taiping captives, was widely contrasted with the apparent poor leadership of the Qing forces, and their alleged cruelties. Clearing Jiangnan of the Taiping was a 'service to humanity', claimed newspaper editorials, and Gordon's role deserved the 'admiration' of observers.[63] But many of his foreign troops happily served the rebels in Fuzhou after the disbanding of the Ever Victorious Army. This was the foreign establishment at its freebooting worst, but also doing what it seemed to do best: using its resources and technologically advanced violence – its Enfield rifles and its Armstrong guns – in the service of its political aims, or in the service of the highest bidders. The opium gang which attacked Yamtaya in Taiwan and the Ever Victorious Army were not all that far apart.

The lessons of defeat were being learnt. The Taiping wanted steamers; the government wanted steamers. It commissioned a fleet of them from the British, and seven gunboats were built or bought and sailed out to China.[64] The newly strengthened Foreign Inspectorate of Customs was to pay for the ships and their operations. Sanctioned if not actively encouraged by the British government, the newly designated inspector-general of the Customs, Horatio Nelson Lay, organized the initiative, and appointed a British naval officer, Sherard Osborn, to command it. They were harassed by applications from volunteers eager to sail. At a Royal Geographical Society meeting in London they were blessed by Gladstone, who was sure that Osborn would come back 'with a great accession to his personal fame and celebrity', adding to the 'character of England in that distant quarter'. Osborn offered to rely on humanity rather than his guns, and Lay was widely understood to have proposed shipping the Taipings to Borneo to solve the problem.[65] The initiative was interpreted by the China British (and others) as heralding a first step towards 'India over again', and so towards a protectorate. 'How fast we are bringing China into English hands,' crowed Bob Little.[66] 'When they have put down the pirates they will probably have to put down the Mandarins also,' purred Alexander Michie. The 'vampire fleet', as some knew it, arrived safely by September 1863, but the initiative foundered after weeks of argument in Peking. Questions of command and *lèse majesté* led to Lay's sacking – he had arrogated to himself the command of the fleet and proposed himself as the sole conduit of orders to Osborn. The fleet shipped homewards, and was sold, the ships in time ending up in Japan, Zanzibar, Egypt and India.[67]

Seamen, soldiers and refugees packed Shanghai nonetheless. In mid-July 1862, 171 vessels were in the harbour; two months later the total peaked at 268.[68] Seamen deserted in droves to join the mercenary bands, or simply to take advantage of the opportunities for plunder provided by rich refugees and inadequate policing. The Council admitted its deficiencies. Almost a 'reign of terror' existed north of the Soochow creek in the informal American settlement at Hongkew, as gangs roamed unchecked, robbing and looting. The first (and public) execution of a foreigner for murder in April 1864 was one solution. John Buckley went to a makeshift gallows at the US Consulate, trying to play the game of nationalities on the way – appealing to the British consul as a Guernsey-or-Ireland-born Briton, and not the US citizen he had previously claimed to be, had been tried as, and had argued as, in a fatal dispute about the American Civil War. Buckley was not believed, and was anyway found guilty of murder. He went quietly to his death, the site guarded by twenty-four policemen in case an attempt was made to rescue him, and he was not thereafter missed. As the US Minister Burlingame dryly noted, 'there has been a regular exodus of foreigners from China since.' David Williams had cut his own throat to avoid a similar fate a month earlier. James White broke out of jail and fled.[69] Large numbers of new police were recruited, but they quickly clogged up the consular court-sheets with their drunkenness, violence and desertions. Buckley had been one such deserter.[70] The jail filled up. So did the cemetery. Sixteen hundred foreigners died at Shanghai in 1862 and 1863 as cholera clawed its way through the city, denuding ships of their crews and regiments of their soldiers. And almost that number of Chinese were dying there daily from the disease in July 1863.[71] Except at the Dagu forts in 1859, disease had always accounted for more foreign military casualties than battle, in China as elsewhere.[72] A new little cemetery just outside the city wall saw a burial of a British soldier at least every two days between 1862 and 1864. A second new cemetery had to be built by the Settlement authorities, and the epidemic was hardly restricted to the lower foreign classes. A Shanghai career might last decades, but it might last only seventeen days. Such caprice added dire urgency to the money-making spirit. A man 'has to snatch a fortune from the jaws of death' wrote Rutherford Alcock, and so he had even less truck than ever before with rule, regulation and community.[73] Municipal inadequacies hardly helped. It was easier to secure funds for wharves, jetties and roads – cemeteries, even – than for dull, effective work on water supplies and drainage.

The Taiping reeled from new attacks. Nanjing finally fell in July 1864, shortly after the Heavenly King died, and so the Kingdom of Heavenly Peace melted away. Some of his supporters harried Qing forces for another year, but the rebellion was now effectively over. The Gordon myth often gives all credit to the foreign-led regiments, but the rebellion was beaten through its own weaknesses, and through the steady building up of fiscal and then military resources by a new generation of Qing officials. Chief amongst these was Zeng Guofan, governor of Jiangsu and Jiangxi provinces, and his protégé Li Hong-zhang. Zeng had created what became known as the Xiang Army, which had driven the Taiping back from his own home districts and had grown into a major new fighting force, outside the existing Qing military system and funded by new taxes on trade. Li created the Huai Army, and between them these new-style officials undertook the hard work of victory. They were wary of Western ambitions, but keen to build up arsenals and navy yards, to train troops on Western lines, and to use steamers, the new rifles, the new artillery – whatever it would take to exterminate rebellion, and to protect the dynasty from its internal and foreign threats. By 1868 the Nian rebels were beaten too. Muslim revolts had broken out in the southwest in 1855 and in the northwest in 1862, both sparked by the Taiping crisis, and peace was not restored until 1873. But with the fall of Nanjing the field had become clear, the threat to the Yangzi was lifted, and the foreign gains of 1860 could be more fully realized.

But the first impact of the new peace was utter debilitating crisis. The refugees went home, and the Shanghai boom turned to a Shanghai bust. Not only had the traders of Shanghai poured their money into new housing, but so large had been the returns that they had set about investing in machine shops, clubs, a gas works and new docks. But as people returned to the reconquered cities of Jiangnan the new houses fell empty – well over a quarter were vacant by the end of 1864 – and the crisis hit many foreign firms very badly. Historical legacies further weakened established firms: their property in China was often actually owned by retired or now 'home-side' partners in Britain or the US, who were receiving rents from these in advance at the prevailing 'fabulous' rates.[74] The local crisis was further compounded by the ending of the Civil War in the United States, which affected cotton exports, and by business failures in London. The vision of a Shanghai El Dorado vanished. The great Dent & Co., the second pillar of the British China coast firms, as 'sure as the Bank of England' in one sailor's eyes – was badly burned and had to retrench in 1865.[75] It survived two more years but then failed spectacularly in 1867. Less lucky, in early 1865, was Lindsay & Co. The company's fall shocked other merchants. 'When houses like Lindsays' fail & Dents' retrench, nobody can consider himself safe,' wrote Bob Little, whose own firm's circulars were filled with sentences about 'gloomy advices', 'disturbing letters' and the 'depressed state of the market'.[76] Lindsay's firm had hardly appeared spent as a business, and had been positioning itself to secure its share of the new dispensation right away. Lindsay's nephew, Robert Antrobus was its chief, based at Shanghai, 'the great Chinese merchant' one fellow passenger labelled him in 1863.[77] It had lots at Hankou, Shanghai and Fuzhou. It was just opening up in Japan. Its huge new steamer *Fire Queen* had been built for the Hankou run, arriving in China in October 1864. Michie had scouted for the firm at Yantai and Niuzhuang, and had been sent on the Shanghai Chamber of Commerce expedition along the Yangzi. Antrobus had been chairman of the Chamber, sometime commander of the Volunteer Corps, and sat on all the committees: church, recreation ground, Chinese hospital; and up to just before the firm's failure sat on the Municipal Council.[78] Pious, prim Thomas Hanbury was easily shocked by Shanghai extravagance, but the firm's reputed £12,000 a year housekeeping expenses at Shanghai staggered him: he thought a couple of hundred a year enough for a youngster. But Lindsay and Co. was not unusual: others lived just as opulently, and did so too in other treaty ports. The firm lived in this grand style right up to the crash and this 'total ruin of our fortunes', as Lindsay put it (he had to fire servants and sell his racehorses).[79] Hugh Hamilton Lindsay's three decades of China trading came to a sudden end. Lindsay's had been one of the upstarts crowding in at the end of the East India Company monopoly, positioning itself for a more open China trade, and pushing and hectoring relentlessly for an end to restrictions, even at the cost of war. Now it also faced a new generation of upstart firms, such as Bob and Archie Little's, and it came tumbling down.

But if some firms failed, even such giants, the outlook overall for the foreign enterprise was very good. Elgin, the Armstrong gun and the Enfield rifle (or, if you thought like Parkes, God) had delivered all that had been asked for (and prayed for). The river was open, the north was open, and the Qing now seemed open for advice, reform and persuasion. Walter Medhurst, the missionary's son, had sailed in with Balfour on a navy steamer to open Shanghai in 1843, and was consul at Hankou in 1864 – imagine the absurdity of that in 1832: a British consul in Hankou – when he reflected on the coming of age of the first among treaty ports, the 'model' Settlement at Shanghai. They had transported one merchant on that voyage, and now there were over 2,000 foreign residents at Shanghai. The consul reeled off statistics as a consul will: the volume of imports and exports, property values, the rise in population. What a contrast it all was to 1843. 'Then' it was a Chinese city; 'then' the surrounding countryside was 'charming' ('almost'); 'then' the 'mandarins cared not for foreign nations or appliances', and 'the people were contented to live and plod as their forefathers had done'. But now, he concluded, now 'what a change', for

the foreigner is present and prominent everywhere; he is regarded, and with reason, as the depository and source of all wealth, influence, and power.

Foreigners own the most magnificent houses, and conduct the most wealthy banks and firms; foreigners own and command the finest ships and steamers; foreigners are the most powerful and efficient mandarins; foreigners have the biggest guns and bravest soldiers; foreigners, somehow or other, collect successfully the most abundant revenue, and without the appropriation of a cent for themselves; foreigners are honest, reliable, rich and strong; in fact, foreigners are everything.[80]

This was the consul's view: 'foreigners are everything'. We can examine the detail of Sino-foreign mercantile cooperation for as long as we like, we can outline the ways in which the new generation of Chinese officials savvily adapted themselves, and their thinking, to take advantage of changing realities, of technology, of the opportunities provided by treaty system, of the Customs' revenues, of the rich interconnectedness of the enterprises that developed in China, the ambiguities of nationality, of capital, and the porosity of many boundaries and identities. All of this needs study, and all of it is germane. We can cast doubt on and indeed disprove the 'foreign character' of many 'foreign firms', reliant as they were on Chinese capital, expertise, informants and brokers. Diplomats and consuls needed their Chinese linguists too. It was a condominium enterprise.[81] All of this is true, and all of this is absolutely irrelevant, insofar as we also need to understand the triumphalism of the 1860s. For Medhurst, like Lindsay and many others, China was now smashed open; it was now almost an irrelevance to the new treaty world and to foreign China. The government was licked. The rebels were licked. Canton had been punished, the old system obliterated there, its governor gone, his archives seized, and his offices razed. A cathedral slowly rose where his dominating *yamen* once sat. Foreigners were not 'everything' – for most of China they were a dark rumour from the coast, a pirate raid, a vicious interruption to daily life – but many of the foreign China hands believed that they were now supreme, that they were in fact everything. This self-belief, this blithe confidence, was stamped into nearly all relationships with, and interactions between Chinese and Europeans and Americans. It was present like that thick stick a man kept to hand in Hankou, as master talked with servant, trader negotiated with trader, consul with Daotai, minister with minister. It was there in their writings and musings, in between the lines and writ large in plain English. The revolver was always kept to hand as well, just out of sight, mostly, but always there.

Hugh Hamilton Lindsay had lived this thick-stick life through the decades since his arrival in China in 1821. The ambitious young East India Company writer had seized his turns of luck, his moments of opportunity to sail north, smash down doors, barge in, hector, harangue. He had harassed officials in China and British politicians; he had harassed his business partners and his EIC superiors. He had lectured village headmen in the Canton delta, distributed Morrison's pidgin Chinese tract at the closed ports in 1832, and published his own broadsides in London. 'I have now set my mind so completely on Chinese affairs and politics,' he announced in 1829, 'and am now conceited enough to fancy that some day or other I may play a part therein which may gain me some little credit.' He shipped back east in 1836 with trunks of Chinese books, but those ambitions moved beyond China, which he left to the firm that grew in his name under his nephew's charge.[82] He was already rich when the Nanjing Treaty was signed – three seasons at Canton from 1836 had evidently served him very well indeed. For almost a quarter of a century thereafter the firm grew and diversified, exploiting, as Lindsay had himself always exploited, the opportunities that arose at the interaction of law and practical realities. Lindsay & Co. traded tea, opium, soy beans, pepper, coal, rice. They smuggled when they saw fit; they expanded to Japan and to the Yangzi as opportunity widened; they were a fixture of the new China coast world. Struggle and greed had coarsened the ambitious young Scot. The Eastern Archipelago Company venture had almost broken him, but his firm and its reputation had survived, and his own fortunes recovered through it until 1865. James Dow's firm fell that same year. But others survived, and the buccaneering spirit of the Lindsay era persisted, even as the foreign establishment was fleshed out and came of age. And the man himself? No credit perhaps, for this bullying life, not at least as he wished for it, but no little contribution ought to be recognized from the leader of the *Lord Amherst* expedition towards bringing into being this fractious, complex new world of treaty port China. Lindsay had chafed, fumed and spat in anger during 'the period of our degradation', and acted to bring that era to an end at Shanghai, Ningbo and Fuzhou; always experimenting, always acting out himself the role he had in mind for Britain and the British character in an opened China.

7

At the Heart of the Heart
of the Empire

Peking was now the formal heart of the presences of the treaty powers. Its walls within walls came to host settled embassies – not the transient establishments of the past, but diplomacy set in stone, advertising its presence on gateways and flagstaffs; and with it came other presences, such as missionaries, and the foreign Customs. This was victory indeed: for the Europeans, something marvellous to reflect on. Canton was to be reworked by foreign hands: this was a 'reality beyond one's imaginative dreams', as Gideon Nye, an old Canton hand put it. But the Canton problem had always been, remember, that it was never a Peking problem: it could never make itself noticed at the capital. Lindsay had doled out pamphlets on the Fujian coast hoping that one would find its way to Peking. Before 1859 envoys and armies had turned back at the Beihe. Then in 1860 they had gone all the way; and then they returned to stay. Gideon Nye put it pithily in retrospect. Peking was 'the Goal; – the Sole Hope of Peace'. He meant it as metaphor – religious metaphor, for it was 'Spes Unica', the 'sole hope', as was the Cross – and he meant it literally. Diplomatic audience and residence at the centre: these would surely end 'the assumption of supremacy' by the Qing. This was 'the arch of the superstructure of peaceful relations'.[1] This yearning had been met. At Peking, in a new bureau called the *Zongli geguo shiwu yamen* (General Office for Administering the Affairs of Various Countries), in the Customs Inspectorate-General, in legation, hospital and church, the gains of the war were consolidated and contested; the details of peace were thrashed out, and the gritty implications of peace unfolded. And Peking itself now assumed a central place in the story of the scramble for China.

But first they wiped Gideon Nye's Canton clear and started afresh.

An 1865 account reports how 'only a few broken slabs of granite here and there, and vestiges of concrete pathways' marked the former location of the hated Canton factories, which were otherwise covered in grass, not a trace of a ruin remaining. A new Franco-British concession area had been laid out, west from the old site, on the island of Shameen (Shamian), half of it raised from the Pearl river mud, the rest displacing a 'populous suburb' and two forts. It was separated from the city by a 100-foot-wide canal, and gated bridges. Harry Parkes had overseen the making of this, the 'most picturesque', the 'coolest' foreign settlement in China, with a spacious consular compound at the centre, and a public garden.[2] It was four times larger than the factories, but the Westeners did not confine themselves to the island, nor to Canton or their previous compromises with Chinese requirements. China was theirs, it seemed. Now they really had freedom to spread out, and to build. They built new mission stations and churches, new consulates and legations, bunds, wharves and jetties. New *hongs* were constructed, new godowns, cemeteries, race tracks and clubs. They could build lighthouses, moor lightships, dredge harbours. The Customs network greatly expanded, needing more staff, a more sophisticated structure, up-to-the-minute accounting systems, experienced technicians. New hotels were needed, masonic lodges, chapels, up-country agents, compradors, linguists, servants, converts, consorts and customers. They fashioned new networks – steamer lines, businesses, mission circuits – and they recorded and debated all of this in freshly established newspapers, learned journals, reports, guides and handbooks. They commissioned new maps and charts, established new systems to collect more data, organized in Shanghai a proper census, and commissioned a fresh professional survey of the International Settlement, now boasting over 12,000 houses and 93,000 residents (90,000 of them Chinese).[3] They built in stone, and they fashioned new structures of knowledge. And there was now even greater opportunity for the grey world, for foreigners to rent out their names, nationality and muscle to Chinese gambling houses, or to Chinese firms ('lie *hongs*', the British called these: Chinese companies fronted by Britons), for cheats and for scammers. But it was all a grey world to some extent, and the forms and structures of respectable society and respectable business were often simply different in degree, rather than in any absolute fashion.

A pukka company in hock to its comprador was all but a lie *hong* writ large: well dressed, mannered, gentlemanly, and mixing appropriately. As they built, they settled in, and some of the frontier wildness had to go: after seeing to a new consulate at Shameen, Parkes laid out a church. Of course, it had never been entirely makeshift, however fast the turnover of personnel and interests – the short-term mentality, making your twenty thousand and heading home. Success depended on some investment in a concrete infrastructure, and the Taiping boom had created a wholly new interest: the property-owning oligarchs. Meek Thomas Hanbury and his ilk were wedded to their interests in the Settlement at Shanghai even in their physical absence, looking for returns on similar lines in the new fields of play in the north and on the river. The property boom generated new sources of revenue, particularly from the Chinese tenants whose rents paid for Hanbury's Italian garden, and whose rates paid for the Shanghai jetties, roads and order that underpinned foreign trade. It was a very neat and accidental solution to the problem of who precisely was to pay for the treaty port world: the Chinese were. And so, the Council at Shanghai must, demanded Councillor Hanbury, exercise 'the utmost vigilance for the protection of Chinese in the settlement'.[4] It must protect his investment.

And, looked at the other way, from inside the Qing bureaucracy, it was a time for building too, but now it really needed to rebuild and strengthen. Daoguang's heir, the Xianfeng emperor, had died in August 1861 in beautiful Chengde, the mountain resort of the imperial family, where the Qing empire was represented in symbolic miniature some 200 miles northeast of the capital. There he had fled as the Anglo-French forces neared Peking. He had appointed his five-year-old son as his heir. After a tussle which cost his chief counsellor Sushun his head on the common execution ground – for he was an advocate of a continuing anti-foreign stance – effective power came into the hands of a triumvirate: Xianfeng's brother, Yixin (Prince Gong), his widow Xiaojin, rather better known in English as Yehonala, or Cixi, or simply as the Empress Dowager, and his senior consort. The late emperor had failed to return to his defiled capital, remaining instead in a lost land of symbolic Qing supremacy, surrounded at Chengde with advisors eager to pursue a hardline policy, however now discredited, for it was easy to talk war at a safe distance from the Lee Enfields. But foreign

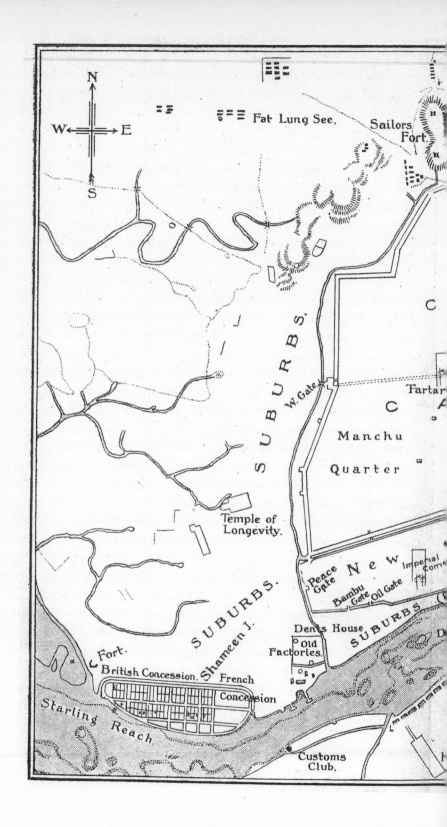

N

W ← → E

S

Fat Lung See.

Sailors Fort.

SUBURBS.

W. Gate.

Tartar

C A

Manchu

Quarter

Temple of Longevity.

Peace Gate

N e w

Imperial Com

Bambu Gate Oil Gate

SUBURBS.

Dent's House

SUBURBS

Old Factories.

Fort.

British Concession.

Shameen I.

French Concession

Starling Reach

Customs Club.

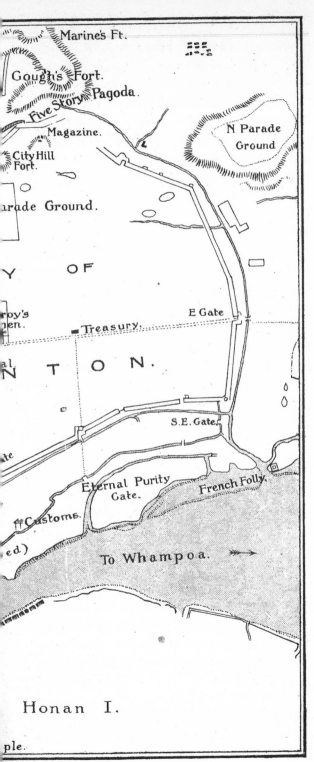

Marine's Ft.

Gough's Fort.

Five Story Pagoda.

Magazine.

City Hill
Fort.

N Parade
Ground

arade Ground.

Y   OF

roy's
en.

Treasury

N T O N.

al.

E Gate

S.E. Gate.

Eternal Purity
Gate.

French Folly.

Customs.

ed)

To Whampoa.   ⟶

Honan I.

7. Old Canton

ple.

diplomats were now resident at the heart of the empire. It was this triumphant, fragile alliance instead which turned the state towards confronting the new order imposed upon it in the name of the child emperor, Zaichun, whose reign title Qixiang ('good fortune') was changed to 'Tongzhi' ('return to order').[5] They needed to build armies, and a navy. They needed arsenals to turn out modern weapons, and shipyards to build steamers and warships. They needed training colleges to build a cadre of interpreters – loyal men and not traitor-'linguists' or comprador types, or Canton collaborators with the foreigners – and men who could understand the new rules and international law, Western science and foreign technology. They needed to contain the energy of the Europeans as far as they could, to hedge these conniving, duplicitous diplomats into place, to build institutional arrangements that could accommodate the strangers within the gates of Peking – physically, and procedurally within the ordering of the state. They needed to restore order with new tools and institutional innovations; with new knowledge. They needed to understand how to use the language of law that was always being quoted at them, or at least to have some men about them that were capable of understanding and using this language. The barbarians had discoursed interminably, tellingly, quoting eminent authorities back at them, trying to wrong-foot them with their own learning. (Remember Lindsay and Gützlaff deflecting the pronouncements of the scholar-administrators.) This was not a view born entirely from consensus, and debate would rumble on for decades to come. It was not based on any rejection of Chinese values and beliefs – far from it, for in fact both the enthusiasts for adopting foreign technology, and their opponents saw salvation as lying in a greater adherence to existing values and philosophies. Such terms as 'salvation' and all it implied about the proximity of cataclysm slowly started to become a normal part of Chinese debates. This was a revival, not a revolution: it was a 'restoration' of the dynasty, and labelled as such. The reform faction, headed by Daoguang's son, Prince Gong, aimed to turn to foreign learning and foreign tools, to use them to constrain and order the foreigners who had stomped their way into the capital. This was what became known as the 'self-strengthening movement', the practical heart of the 'Tongzhi restoration'.

The spatial heart of restoration was Peking. It is 6 June 1863, and

Horatio Nelson Lay, inspector-general of the Chinese Imperial Maritime Customs and his effective deputy, a 28-year-old Ulsterman, Robert Hart, repair to the 'Zongli Yamen' in the east of the capital. This was a new central government office, established officially in March 1861, charged with overseeing foreign matters.[6] It was inserted into the existing structure, sitting oddly there, but it took from the Court of Dependencies the handling of Russian affairs, and from the Board of Rites the management of affairs with other countries. It was not a foreign affairs department in the European diplomatic sense, although the foreigners called it the 'Foreign Office', but a general bureau for managing relations with the 'ferocious' British, the 'unfathomable' Russians, and what were seen as the more pliant French and Americans, who simply followed in Qing eyes in the wake of the former (and they did so in British eyes, too).[7] It was responsible for foreign matters in a wider sense, for the Inspectorate General of Customs came under its jurisdiction, as did a new Foreign Interpreters' College, the Tongwenguan, as well as military reforms. The college was now vital, for the foreign treaties had dictated the primacy of foreign-language correspondence, and foreign texts. The Qing were now dictated to on foreign terms, and needed to catch up swiftly. Canton–English primers were all very well for provincial merchants and shopkeepers, but the centre needed linguists. The business of restoration fell to the 'Yamen', which term stood both for the office and for its site, in a disused mint. It was never really meant as a permanent measure, and was partly designed as a practical obfuscation. It was practical in that it coordinated various foreign affairs initiatives, and the relationships with the diplomats in the ways that were imposed on the Qing by the treaties. But it was an obfuscation as it was not truly intended to admit any real equality of status. China was not like other countries, the Qing thought. In that, of course it was precisely like all other countries.

In the plain, unfussy, draughty halls of the Zongli Yamen the business of post-war China was now discussed this day in June 1863, a day like many others to come. Robert Hart had been there before, in 1861 the first time, deputizing for Lay, who had received his formal appointment in January that year, and responded to it by leaving China for Britain, on grounds of ill-health. Now Lay was back, and had finally come to meet his employers, travelling by two extremes of China transport:

steamer and bullock cart.[8] In this early afternoon meeting with Wenxiang, a Manchu, who had with Yixin and Guiliang proposed the new office, and who was now one of its assistant secretaries, as well as a member of the Board of War and the Board of Punishments, Lay ran through a little list he had brought, outlining what he wanted for his service and for himself. His wants were simple, far-reaching, and from the Chinese perspective simply appalling. Lay wanted freedom from the authority of provincial governors. He would, he averred, remit funds only to the Yamen, not to grubby, needy provincial pockets, and he wanted 'respect from all', for he was 'not a Chinese official', but a 'middle man, a *Yingguo ren* [a Briton], a *bangren* [helper] who was asked by China to *taipan* [undertake] a certain business'. And he was equal in status to a governor general. The Yamen must, he argued, 'take his advice on all foreign questions, no matter concerning whom, and consult with him in all cases before acting'. Oh, and he wanted a garden. In fact he wanted a *fu* – a palace – at his disposal as a residence. Robert Hart noted all this in his journal. A month earlier at Shanghai, meeting Lay just back from England, Hart had worried that his superior was 'greatly changed', that he was 'anglicized to a degree that I fear his task with the Chinese will be very uphill work'. 'He'll not meet their views,' he predicted, 'and he will insist on his own.' And so he did, and a year later published many of these very same views in his own defence – and more – after such bombastic vainglory led to his dismissal. 'The notion of a gentleman acting *under* an Asiatic barbarian is preposterous,' Lay wrote, although this he left unsaid on 6 June 1863, even if his meaning was clear. There 'is no such thing, at present, as equality between the European and the Asiatic,' he would argue. 'One or the other is the master of the situation'.[9] Well, responded the 'exceedingly shrewd, intelligent' Wenxiang to the only slightly less offensive tirade delivered that hot afternoon in the Yamen: to effect authority the inspector-general must hold formal office, and that 'would involve certain relations in point of rank, and modes of address, etc.' You must accept that you are indeed a Chinese official, he said, affably. And we have no palace to spare.[10]

So the Yamen paid him off, being in fact the masters of Lay's situation at least, and no one was sorry to see him leave. He made £14,000 for five months of this (and was widely reputed to have a substantial income from Shanghai property), more than enough by far to pay for the house and fifty-acre estate he leased in Surrey on his return, so Lay got his garden.[11] If China was to be advised, it could not be advised like this. Robert Hart, now appointed in his stead, took note, and built a fifty-year career out of principles and a demeanour entirely at variance with Lay's. '*Women di Hede*' – our Hart – the Chinese already called him.[12] This gentleman, the deeply religious son of a well-to-do County Armagh grocer, served his Asiatic masters for over fifty years more, and turned the Customs almost into the executive arm of the Zongli Yamen, so that the Customs, this accidental Shanghai innovation, became a chief coordinating body for foreign matters. His work helped to strengthen the state, and helped lock the realms of the Qing deeper into global networks, of trade, communications, diplomacy and knowledge. Here in Peking, on hand (for Hart was soon asked to base himself permanently in the city, rather than in Shanghai, the centre of the China trade), he functioned as both head of a revenue service, and coordinator of a number of intertwined initiatives at the heart of the self-strengthening enterprise. As the Qing state refashioned itself in the wake of defeat, its leaders marshalled new resources, allowing the governors and governors general fighting the Taiping to impose a new tax, the *lijin*, a levy on goods in transit, and this funded the new armies that stamped out the rebellion. They had new and rising revenues coming in from the Foreign Inspectorate, which moved to establish new Customs Houses at all the new ports, and they took on foreign advisors and agents: Ward, Gordon, Prosper Giquel, Lay, Hart. This was a matter of pragmatic need, if a bitter pill, for as even Wenxiang noted, it was 'a disgrace to have to make use of the assistance of foreigners'. Well, Lay had said to him, 'if a man was sick, he must have a doctor', and 'China coming into contact with foreigners, and not understanding the habits, modes of thought, or nature of the foreigners', mishaps were liable to occur, without foreign advice. 'Yes,' countered Wenxiang, 'but if the doctor, not understanding the sick man's constitution, gives him medicines, which, while they prevent death, deprive him of strength, and spoil his countenance, what then?'[13]

What then: for his part Robert Hart had already seen the worst of mishaps up close, at Canton, as secretary for a year to the Allied Commission that governed the occupied city with the local administration from 1858 to 1860, in the face initially of bitter popular resistance – the dry-mouth horror of violence in the sullen city in 1858. Canton streets were booby-trapped with explosives, solitary British or French troops picked off by militia. Terrible vengeance was unleashed against the population by way of reprisal, bystanders seized and shot in their scores.[14] Revenge was swift, orderly, and callous. So Robert Hart had had his fill of life in the foothills of a China apocalypse, had seen how vacuum would follow and violence ensue if the Qing could not hold, and foreign power, for all its professed good intentions, was too makeshift and weak, as it always would be, to effect replacement. So Hart worked to prevent this. It was an odd position for a man to find himself in, for an Irishman – 'a Paddy in heart & soul' – to be adopted like this by Manchus. Britons had served many foreign masters and causes, and would serve many more. They served revolution in South America, and the administration in Siam. They did so as mercenaries, serving themselves; and as formal or informal agents of their own governments, serving empire.[15] But few would secure such power and serve in such an anomalous position. He was a happenstance actor on the Chinese stage, and it suited him well, and he, it. Nominated by Queen's University Belfast to the British China consular service, Hart had arrived in the summer of 1854, an academic success, a reflective spirit, nineteen years old, soul and body in constant, strongly Methodist-flavoured contention. He was sent to Ningbo, passing first through rebellion-shattered Shanghai ('very melancholy in the extreme'), evading a pirate attack, arriving at Ningbo to be met by the consul, John Meadows, and at the consulate by Robert Fortune, passing through seeking yet more plants and yet more copy for his interminable books. He found also, that first night, 'a couple of China women', alerted to the fact that a new foreigner had arrived, 'peeping through my windows'. After all, John Meadows had his local paramour, his wife as he was to formally present her in later life, so presumably the student interpreter would need his. The going rate for 'absolute possession' was about a month's salary for a young student interpreter. But 'I hope,' Hart confided to his diary, that 'I may be able to control myself properly here.' So at Ningbo he learned his trade and the answers to essays set him by way of training by Sir John Bowring: 'The Street Literature of China', 'Signs and Aphorisms To Be Seen in Chinese Shops', 'The Peculiar Manufactories of Ningpo'.[16] He learned his Chinese in the ad hoc, unsystematic way that most men did; and was courted by the missionary community, who thought they could tempt him over, still short as they were of personnel. And, as we shall see later, he failed entirely to control himself 'properly', for he was in truth 'mad upon the pleasures of the couch'.[17] But Hart impressed his superiors and observers with his ready grasp of the language, and with his ability to work with Chinese officials, and to work hard.

Hart impressed Lay, who in 1859 offered him the post of deputy commissioner at the newly established Canton Customs, part of the expanding inspectorate system. On 1 July 1859 he transferred from British to Chinese service, and was soon effective deputy for Lay, making his mark in 1861, and displaying a masterly restraint in November 1863 on receipt at Shanghai, where he was commissioner of Customs, of a dispatch addressed to him as inspector-general. First he breakfasted, then he read from his Bible, and then he prayed. And then, and only then, did he open the letters appointing him to replace Lay. The restraint was entirely characteristic, and so was the work that followed: hard, relentless work. Hart planned, proposed, lobbied and ordered. He schemed grand visions, and he looked to minute detail. He had fits of energy which he applied to individual projects, moving on if these were premature, returning to them when the time was better. He kept his Bible close, but it was a secular project, secular in spirit and tone, for there was no Parkesian divine hand in all this, although there was a secular deity, 'progress', to which he subscribed, and in which he found China wanting as a civilization. Five years later Hart summarized some of what he and the Customs had by then already achieved, in a letter carefully batting away a bemusing offer from Lay – ever self-unaware – of renewed service to the Zongli Yamen. 'China', Hart wrote, has been 'gradually got *to run smoothly in the international groove*'. This was the foundation for any practical, 'productive' developments, for 'physical changes and practical results'. China had to become part of the world – the world as shaped by the West – this was Hart's aim, and there had been real progress. He worked with the Chinese 'progressionists'. They interrogated him about the world, and called upon him to interpret it. He furnished a translation of a standard textbook of international law, he advised the creation of the interpreters' college, the Tongwenguan, and helped secure staff for it. He is to be found checking the Chinese texts of treaties, proposing a paragraph here in the Portuguese treaty, suggesting they yield on this point in the Belgian. Remember also, he told Wenxiang, what Europeans think of you, that China is 'an uncivilized country', and this is why they dictate and fulminate, they have 'mistaken ideas', they are *wuzhi* (ignorant).[18] In 1865 Hart submitted a long memorandum (in Chinese, of course), known as the 'Bystander's View', outlining what he saw as the new dangers the Qing faced unless they enacted fundamental reform of the bureaucracy, the military and state fiscal policies, and unless they embraced cooperative, Sino-foreign development initiatives. But while the memorandum was too much for a still-divided bureaucracy to stomach, Hart and his patrons were effectively undertaking much of the work outlined, and others were too. As he wrote when deflecting Lay, 'shipbuilding has commenced. [John] Meadows' godown at Tientsin has half a mile of rail (small as it is: but from it will spring the Peking Railway!)' and coal mining 'with foreign aid & after a foreign fashion' had commenced. We have but to 'work and wait', he concluded.[19]

Work and wait, and 'be Chinese': this was his conclusion, his 'true policy, "*to be Chinese*"'.[20] Hart was in a unique position: he was the bystander, the middleman, and he was a zealot. He had ideas and ambition, and he had funds: a rare combination. He had patrons in the Yamen eager for him to initiate work and receptive to his practical proposals. He had the ear of the new legations – called there, listened, deflected, manoeuvred; and he had the ear of the Qing reformers. He was one of them, in fact. Rhetorically he was that neutral observer, but practical politics made him part of the bureaucratic faction now in the ascendance, the first European to find himself in such a position, and not simply a mercenary, and not as Lay saw himself, as proconsul, dictating terms from a vice-regal palace.[21] Hart sat and chatted and chatted with the men of the Zongli Yamen over cups of tea and plates of fruit, building up strong bonds of fond amity. But he also built up hard credit with Customs cash. The Customs delivered increasing resource as foreign trade grew, and as the network of Customs stations developed. And as total revenues grew the proportion directed by the Yamen to support its own projects grew, from an average of two thirds of expenditure in the 1860s, to over 80 per cent in the following decade.[22] Loans could also be raised on the security of the growing revenues. And the Customs Service, to the growing if still sullen resignation of foreign traders, could not be evaded or barracked away, even if some of the official British still thought him a traitor.[23] The Customs grew in size, sophistication and confidence. It built its stations at the centre of the new bunds and settlements. Its staff were schooled by Hart in careful detail about their place and role as Chinese civil servants. You must remember, he told them in a memorandum on 'the spirit that ought to animate' the Customs Service, that you are 'the paid agent of the Chinese government for the performance of specified work'.[24] So the merchants mostly paid their dues. And those dues were remitted not as target quotas, as had been standard practice, so leaving any excess for the pockets of officials, but in their entirety. A good year for trade meant a good year's revenues. The Zongli *yamen* spent its cash on the Tongwenguan, hiring through Hart foreign teachers of English, French, Russian, mathematics and chemistry, under the direction of American missionary W. A. P. Martin.[25] Two branch schools were established at Canton and Shanghai. Funds went to a growing network of arsenals, at Suzhou, Anqing and elsewhere; to feeding the armies that smashed the Taiping; supporting the provincial reform leaders, such as Zeng Guofan and Li Hongzhang; leading the development of the Jiangnan arsenal and shipyard at Shanghai; to Zuo Zongtang, and then Shen Paozhen at Fuzhou, who oversaw the creation of the naval shipyard under the direction of Griquel, who had organized the Ever Triumphant Army. Educational and translation projects were integrated into these two latter establishments, with particularly influential results at Shanghai where British missionary John Fryer oversaw from 1868 an important programme of translations of scientific works.[26] The fruits of the manufacturing industry by the end of the decade were impressive. Ships were being launched, tens of thousands of weapons being produced to the highest standards: a new world of military technology was at the direct call of the Qing. Customs funds underpinned all of this.

Robert Hart built his service and fashioned it into a mirror of the balance of foreign powers and interests in China, in time staffing it with Russians, French, Germans and Americans, in addition to the British. And as new interests emerged he recruited Italians, Danes, Austrians and Belgians. There were Dutch and Spaniards, Swedes and Norwegians. It was 'an awful drag on a coach', this political cosmopolitanism; it slowed everything down, but ministers and interests (who lobbied him) needed to be placated, needed heading off from diplomatic umbrage and sulky formal notes if they did not get their nation's share of the Chinese Customs pie, and the advantages that might accrue from this, or at least not accrue to others.[27] It could not be, overtly, a 'British' service – its British core must be diplomatically diluted – but British systems and norms mostly pervaded its work and culture. It was a multinational, but not a polyglot, institution. Hart fashioned systems to make it all work, prescriptions flowing from his own and copyists' pens and brushes about the precise forms of communication, and their precise contents. He recruited an experienced man from the British civil service, James Duncan Campbell, to come and institute an effective finance system for the Service. Uniforms, pennants, standards of behaviour (and of Chinese language ability) were all outlined. There was an amalgam of British and Qing practices in all of this, as systems were devised that could make sense to Hart's superiors (in forms that they would recognize), but which were obvious enough for foreign staff to adapt to with little discomfort. As his staff were recruited and dispatched to stations, and as they impressed their authority on the new trading communities, he impressed his own authority over his commissioners and the system. He was in charge. He hired, and he fired. He transferred and promoted. He acquired more power over the internal management of the Service than was actually usual in either the Qing bureaucracy, or in any comparable British body. And his power stretched well beyond this. He was in charge of new infrastructure initiatives. The Customs was never going to be able to build a railway, but it could start to establish a network of lighthouses, the logical next step onwards from the foreign charting of the Chinese coasts. A scheme for this was formally broadcast in 1868, and within seven years over sixty lights were built, including nine large coastal lighthouses. He needed to appoint or recruit medical officers to attend his staff, and so he could expect to extract from them annual reports, and publish these as a contribution to scientific knowledge. He could aim to use the lighthouses as they were established to collect meteorological data.[28] The Customs could serve its masters, providing the hard cash sinews of reform and self-strengthening, and it could serve foreign and Chinese trading interests by making China's coasts and harbours safer to navigate, and so also more predictable and therefore efficient. He could serve science, knowledge and humanity: that was his credo, that the Customs did, as he later put it, 'good work for China in every possible direction'.[29]

The Service assessed Customs dues, established a Marine Department to oversee the building of that new infrastructure, and it published, published and published. A printing office was established at Shanghai in 1865, becoming from 1873 the heart of a Statistical Department, which fashioned a wholly new, objective vision of China in print. Hart sucked information into his headquarters in Peking, read it standing up at a specially designed desk, and fired back his replies and instructions. His circulars outlined the data that needed to be submitted, and the frequency with which it must be sent. The clerks totted up the figures and laid them out clearly as directed – or they were told off and instructed to resubmit them – and sent them north. And then the data was collated and published. But the Service published more than just annual reports on trade, and data recording the same. They published medical reports, dictionaries, travelogues, trade guides, an account of Chinese music, even language primers. China was laid bare for the foreign gaze, and to counter that foreign ignorance more objectively and comprehensively than ever before possible, for now instead of scraping around for information and informants, the resources of a branch of the Chinese state were part-focused on generating it. The Service marshalled data, and to do so it had to help the fixing of terms and translations, identifying produce so that staff knew precisely what they were counting and assessing, laying out translations of names – always a two-way process – making the world of Chinese commerce more legible for foreign traders, and the imports of foreigners more legible for the Chinese. Decades of the Canton trade and of the open ports trade after 1842 had seen a good body of such work done, but as trade widened, as the steamers shipped in and out, greater volumes of a wider and wider range of produce and products were exchanged.

And Hart wanted to know more than just the details of trade: he wanted to know simply everything. His commissioners were required to write to him directly, fortnightly, 'semi-officially', on any subject of local note that they felt he should be apprised of. So they told him everything, everything that would not fit into a formal dispatch: rumours, panics, problems bubbling under the surface, information on personalities, on local scandals and disputes – all of it flowed into Peking, to the inspectorate compound in Goulan hutong close to the Chaoyang gate in the east of the city, to Hart's desk. He saw everything, certainly in the early years, for he later noted that he was delegating a little to the senior staff – the secretaries – who came to run different branches at the Inspectorate General. Official and semi-official, published and lodged in the growing collection of Inspectorate files, it all formed a vast Chinese archive of useful China knowledge.

From the Inspectorate General, and in his frequent parleys at the Zongli Yamen, and in the offices of Ministers, Hart talked all of this into existence. Three hours talk on 10 January 1867, for example, covered amongst other things: changes at the Tongwenguan, Prosper Giquel's work establishing a naval shipyard at Fuzhou, issues about rice exports, inland steamship navigation, a proposal about telegraphs, military reform, rifle sales by the French, beacons, and yet more – all to be supported, and Hart's prestige enhanced by, continuing increases in revenue.[30] Always Wenxiang and his colleagues deliberated and raised on all sides first principles. 'You must give us time,' they said, 'and we are poor.' (Not so poor as you were, Hart would probably reply, decorously, thanks to me.) Do not threaten us, Wenxiang continued, and also just think, 'in fifty years time ... you foreigners will be as anxious to stop our learning as you now hurry us into it!' Think, said the Manchu, think what will happen when all of this has succeeded: is that quite what you really want – China strong, resurgent, restored? Meanwhile they aimed to secure young boys from all over the country for the Tongwenguan, who, as they graduated and secured positions, provided a cadre of diplomats for the Qing trained in Western knowledge, speaking Western tongues. 'Just imagine,' wrote Hart to himself, 'men who had gone through the whole course going out into the provinces as Officials: China is *changed*, once & for all by such a measure.'[31] Sometimes he was despondent, seeing obstruction and danger, fearing that 'they have been treated kindly, & fed on "lollypops" too long', and that a bit of '*you must*' was needed. And he had to remind himself as he basked in their approbation, and as he and they nattered affably on about 'life, death, immortality', as they professed surprise that he was actually a Christian – that a man of learning would subscribe to superstition – that 'we are just the very people on whom the Chinese ought to look with the greatest dislike, the strongest hatred', for the British 'had dragged them into two wars, burnt their palace, & played the mischief everywhere: we have been the leaders in all acts of violence, & the loudest talkers about humanity, etc.!'[32] But he could do his bit, not least in remembering that while he might have 'always taken it for granted . . . made it a law of thought' that since the British were 'doing the work for China more honestly & more efficiently than others' they were 'trusted and liked' by the Qing, that the violences of the very recent past, the wounds of the city he worked in, were far from forgotten.

The Customs not only represented China in print, circulated globally, advertising the 'good work' it undertook, but was charged with representing China at international exhibitions. Other opportunities were also seized: an international geographical congress in Paris? We must be represented. Commissioners of Customs, directed one circular, please propose papers.[33] The random exhibitions of Nathan Dunn's things, of Summer Palace loot, of the *Keying*, were succeeded by a systematic programme, whereby the Customs solicited material from its network of Customs houses, shipped it to Vienna (1873), Philadelphia (1876), Paris (1878), Berlin (1880) and London (1883), worked it into catalogues and guides, and laid China out for international view. As well as manufactured products – ceramics, silks, cloisonné, furniture – botanical and geological material was displayed, and more: all China was put on show, to encourage trade and to contribute to the sum of European and American knowledge. Of course, the Customs itself acquired prestige and visibility, and deliberately did so, and was commended and awarded prizes for its achievements. At Vienna the Service had organized and shipped to Europe samples of products from all of its stations, and compiled a statistical epitome to demonstrate just how trade was developing and what opportunities there were. They made China visible – normal – in foreign eyes. We might think it odd that observers initially thought it a revolutionary move, arguing in reviews of the 1873 Vienna exhibition that it was 'something extraordinary in the history' of the Manchu empire, but of course it actually was.[34] The later nineteenth century saw a rash of exhibitions, the fashioning of massive 'dreamlike cities' which were visited by millions – all made easier by steam navigation and railways; driven by intra-imperial rivalry; coalescing national and imperial identities and self-assertion.[35] And here was China, officially representing itself (through its foreign agents) systematically and comprehensively, at an exhibition designed to promote industry and the arts. It was not gatecrashing, as He Xing from the *Keying* had gatecrashed the royal opening of the Great Exhibition at Hyde Park in 1851. It was being represented through foreign nationals in state employ, certainly, but here nonetheless was an integration of China – of Chinese things and Chinese opportunity – into the global encyclopaedia, on display in the capitals of Europe and in the United States. It might be exoticized and orientalized still, might offer meat – even then – for criticism and bolster foreign ignorance in some ways, but the intention was very much the opposite. The aim was to highlight the trading worlds and knowledge worlds of China. What became the routine display of China at such forums was a key strand in the project that Hart was leading. And of course he wanted his good work recognized: it helped things with the diplomats, politicians and the international press, it satisfied vanity, and earned him and the service an exhibition medal or two. But more than this, the routinely exoticized China, the weird China of Dunn's statues, was now joined by a formally organized, formally ordered China, one which bore more of a resemblance – as much as a representation at an exhibition could – to the place itself; or to places there, things there, people there, even fish from its rivers, lakes and coasts (an odd thought that – the worlds of Chinese fish laid out on view in London – but Hart's ambitions were nothing if not all-encompassing); a display which was organized by agents of the Qing state, who basically knew what they had and what they were doing.

So the Inspectorate General became the centre of its own network of stations, as well as a node in wider networks – regional meteorology, the international round of display and representation – and it drew to China more and more men, many of whom went on to different careers in the treaty port world, in newspapers, as diplomats, scholars, educators. It was also a centre of power, an odd, in-between one, one of a triumvirate in postwar Peking: Yamen, Inspectorate, British Legation. Her Britannic Majesty's Legation, the seat of formal British power, was established close by the old Russian church, southeast of the Forbidden City. The Qing had hoped that the foreigners would be content with a right of residence that they would not permanently use; after all, they were after trade, and trade took place down south, so they ought to be content to sit with it down there and talk with their merchants. But that was missing Gideon Nye's point, missing the fact that the diplomats had been seeking entry, ever since Napier blustered his way to disaster in old Canton. The Minister was allotted a *fu*, the Lianggongfu, the Palace of the Dukes of Liang, a 'fitting residence' for a British minister, thought Fortune.[36] It was an immense, rambling site consisting, as one resident described it, of two parallel sets of four courts, the eastern part formerly the palace, the western less 'showy'. It was 'very handsome', he wrote, gorgeously colourful, 'the ceilings of the state apartments being beautifully decorated with gold dragons, within circles on a blue ground, which again are in the centres of small squares of green, separated by intersecting bars in relief of green and gold'. It was also part wild. In the shadows slunk 'foxes, scorpions, polecats, weasels', noted another early resident, but it was grand nonetheless, and two giant stone lions guarded the main buildings.[37] It grew in size to encompass seven acres of courts and grounds by 1898, half the size of the old Canton factories, housing a large staff of diplomats, consular language students, constables to keep order (who drank hard, and were difficult to keep orderly). The diplomats liked it there, and they proved in time hard to shift, growing attached to its comforts and style, and attaching prestige to it, hitching their sense of diplomatic self to the palatial grandeur of the Lianggongfu. But before all that, of course, as we might have come to expect by now, while it was still dilapidated, and foxes prowled, they moved the Queen in, unpacking her portrait in June 1861. It might seem odd that we can find so much insistent quiet emphasis on the symbolic ordering of foreign space. Partly this was a response to understandings of Chinese conceptions, a breaking out of spaces and sites allotted them for reasons they interpreted (rightly sometimes) as intentionally demeaning. But they had their own such practices already, and two of them were immediately striking in new Peking: the placing of their sovereign and the place of their dead.

The young Victoria, regally framed, sceptre in hand, crown on head, was copied from a lifesize portrait by Sir George Hayter. Was this a religious icon, queried some of the Chinese workmen renovating the site. Almost, at times, would be an honest answer, given the holy rage expressed and umbrage taken at 'insult' to her uncle's portrait at Canton. At the Legation she was to oversee the reception of visiting Chinese officials, oddly situated in these Chinese surroundings, her new dominion of gold dragons (and polecats). What Chinese observers made of the giving of pride of place to – in their eyes – a partly naked woman, even if Queen, is another matter. At the same time a potent, and more visible, more public statement was made by the placing of the British dead. The first tract of land occupied by Britons in Peking was not the Lianggongfu, but five plots in the Russian cemetery occupied by the four bodies of the kidnapped dead that had been recovered in 1860, and an army doctor who had died of natural causes before the army withdrew to Tianjin. Theirs was an aggressive repose. Blue-painted concrete covered five mounds, and over them a white granite stone uttered a bellicose reminder of their fate. They had been 'treacherously seized in violation of a flag of truce, on the 18th of September, 1860, and sank under the inhuman treatment to which they were subjected by the Chinese Government during their captivity'. All this was not very diplomatic, thought one observer, now that we are at peace. It was a site of pilgrimage. A young consular recruit records riding out there one late spring morning in 1862 and copying the inscription memorializing 'the victims of Chinese treachery'.[38] Later in the decade they were moved to a newly established British cemetery outside the west wall of the city. The doctor was separated from those killed through treachery, who were placed at the heart of the cemetery, which was organized around a new memorial to them, simply listing under a white stone cross their names, and that 'The blood of Christ cleanseth us from all sin.'[39] Bowlby was also remembered in marble in England, but at the heart of this Peking cemetery, and at the official heart of the British China enterprise, were laid the martyred imperial dead.[40] An 1897 guide also noted that the handwriting of Parkes and of Loch could still be seen on the walls of the temple where they were imprisoned. Peking was inscribed with texts of English suffering.[41] Foreign observers chuckled at Chinese geomancy, at *fengshui*, even as they fashioned symbolic landscapes themselves, sacralizing space, creating sites for pilgrimage, reflection and remembrance.

A legation, for all its fitting grandeur, was only as powerful as its incumbents, and the force which lay just out of sight to back them up. Over the first two decades from its establishment there were three British ministers: Frederick Bruce, Rutherford Alcock and Thomas Wade. Bruce had spent two years as colonial secretary in youthful Hong Kong, then served at posts in South America and Egypt, and later hitched himself to his brother's staff during the *Arrow* war. From Peking he moved in 1865 to the United States as minister. He detested Peking, and the 'monotony and anxieties' of the work, but he steered British policy away from active military coercion towards an engagement aimed at encouraging 'cooperation' (the word of the decade), supporting Hart in particular. By this was meant cooperation with China, as well as cooperation amongst the interested foreign powers. The two were entirely intertwined. A restoration China, which abided by the treaties in theory and in provincial practice, would be good for British interests because it would involve no drain on the British treasury, through war, and no drain on diplomatic energies through dispute. Having the Zongli Yamen in place, he sought to bolster its power to discipline local officials, making a national state issue out of local disputes. There could be no hiding away at ports from the agreements monitored at the capital.[42] Parkes thought Bruce indolent – which was characteristic of him: everybody else was indolent – others hated the very idea of 'cooperation', when local disputes persisted, and when total victory had seemed to have been achieved in 1860. Alcock's aim was the deepening of this policy. Arriving back in China from Japan in late 1865, he told Hart that 'the system is still on trial yet'. He 'ruffled' his fellow ministers, assuming his own pre-eminence amongst them, basing this on the importance of British power and trade, flavoured with his own vanity. The diplomats had begun to club together, to try to speak with a single voice on common matters. Vanity notwithstanding, Alcock at least deferred greatly to Hart, whose interlocutory role was nowhere more evident than in the palavers which took place during

Alcock's term over the timing of the scheduled revision of the 1858 treaty. The Zongli Yamen indicated that Hart would be dealing with seven eighths of the negotiations, and both sides parried with and through him before meeting face to face. Wade rose firstly because of his language skills, and was Chinese secretary at the British Legation from 1861 onwards. He is 'the best friend in thought that China has got' wrote Hart in 1864, and he submitted his own proposals for dynastic reform in 1866: this and Hart's 'Bystander' memorandum were the subject of intense internal debate amongst senior Qing officials. This was not least because they seemed explicitly threatening, especially Wade's, for both sketched out possible scenarios for China's future should there be no greater reform, which were read as explicit threats. Wade was a scholar, but he was not a diplomat.[43]

Alcock and Wade, and their successor, Parkes, were China men, but the diplomatic establishment was increasingly being joined by career diplomats, who came from other posts, and went on to them as part of the normal diplomatic round. But they were also still building up their cadre of professional China consuls. The British consular establishment remained underserved by its recruits. China might be incorporated into a normal realm of colonial service and imperial opportunity, Queen's University Belfast might be invited to nominate a recruit, but the consular service was not high up the lists. Home service, India service and other ports of empire called first and caught the best. So they were not the most talented of their generation, nor was language proficiency factored into appointments until the twentieth century. And then those appointed were not well served by ramshackle arrangements for learning the languages that they would still need to master. The Tongwenguan offered much more by way of structured programmes. Ernest Satow arrived in China in January 1862, nineteen years old, heading for the Japanese service but first instructed to study Chinese at Shanghai, and then at Peking. His diary shows him trying to make the best of this tall order, taller indeed because so very few in the foreign communities were studying Chinese: calling on the Shanghai missionaries for textbooks, and practising with a succession of teachers in a manner that became standard for the student interpreters. They were assigned a teacher, who spoke no English. He pronounced, they parroted – for dreary Peking days on end.[44] It was entirely a hit-or-miss process, and attainment was thereby routinely low, although the assiduous, like Hart – indeed like Satow – would eventually secure a firm grasp of the language. It wasn't half a lark though, at times, for the young men at Peking, before their exile to Chinese ports. They had immunity, youth, energy, and the capital of the Qing to roam around in. Few observers were as nastily carping as Sir Edmund Hornby, fresh from Constantinople to establish the British Supreme Court for China, a man who thought the Legation a 'species of prison', and Peking more widely very little better. But in general they enjoyed themselves, rode small Mongolian ponies, bullied gatekeepers, bribed them, beat them, trespassed, and vandalized, Peking their playground. So difficult was their behaviour that foreign access was forbidden to many sites by 1865.[45]

Despite this frankly unpromising material, the official British created from their legation an information network to rival Hart's. With thirteen consulates established by 1867, they started to build up an archive of reports and correspondence as consuls and their assistants furnished periodic surveys of trade, sought instructions, and sent reports on their actions. In flowed this material, copies kept at consulates, sent on to London, with annual trade reports published by the government printers in London. Such systems, of course, are only ever as effective as the quality of the data actually collected, dispatched and interpreted, and as the finance available to keep archiving up to date, to deal with the flow of paper cascading in. At some ports the work was voluminous: 4,000 Britons at Shanghai on census day in 1865 (three hairdressers, three photographers, nine musicians amongst them) generated such fodder for consular work that they could barely keep up. But they were at least better served than the Americans, so understaffed that they could not handle the paperwork involved.[46] But at quieter ports, the more disappointing spoils of 1860, there was far less to do. The business of consular life was arid at Niuzhuang, where in 1865 Thomas Taylor Meadows whiled away his time and talents, overseeing a tiny British community: a couple of merchants, a storekeeper, a doctor, some outdoor staff in the Customs, and some pilots. No wonder then that he succumbed to the now established tradition of brittle consular oddity, and prosecuted ferocious personal vendettas.[47] But if some went mad, as some did, others hitched their hopes for escape from the Niuzhuangs of China to scholarship and publication, filling their off-duty time – and probably their over-ample office hours – with the compilation of guides, histories, primers, anything to get themselves noticed, using knowledge to stake a claim for professional preferment, using their books to participate in wider worlds of science and literature. So the growing consular establishment generated contributions to the understandings of China (of varying degrees of quality) both on and off duty. Customs staff were the same, and had an in-house publication programme to pitch their manuscripts to. We sometimes forget how the production of knowledge was also intertwined with attempts at personal betterment, and rooted also sometimes in dreary, dismal, profound boredom.

Knowledge work was hardly simply a foreign enterprise. The Zongli Yamen also built up its own activities, impressed by the way foreigners marshalled data and precedent. The Yamen took archives seriously.[48] The treaties of the 1840s had been sequestered in splendid provincial isolation at Canton, but even though the US Tianjin Treaty required documents to be kept at the capital, the Yamen of its own volition positively clawed to itself banks of documentation. Knowledge is power, they clearly believed, securing copies of correspondence from the archives of other bureaus, establishing elaborate systems of reporting and filing of materials, ordering copies of foreign-language newspapers from Shanghai, commissioning their new translations of foreign texts. Records of diplomatic envoys sent abroad were published, and keeping a journal was in fact one of their duties; other accounts of foreign matters were printed in a journal edited by W. A. P. Martin and in other volumes. They then had on hand records of precedents; these they could use to inform their responses to unfolding events, to match the banks of information deployed by the foreign diplomats as everyday encounters in a more widely accessible China generated more conflicts, disputes, incidents and cases, the stuff of the diplomatic round. They rightly never trusted that a superficially simple issue would remain simple, that an advantage might not be taken of the opportunity provided to 'clarify' something, to 'resolve' unrelated topics, to seize a moment to fix something seemingly left vague by the second round of treaties. There were some unresolved questions, the most vital in some foreign eyes being the perceived lack of formal observance of state to state equality: the fact that the diplomats had not, as they would expect elsewhere in the world of new Western diplomacy, been formally introduced to the monarch. The 'audience' question – a question of honour, national honour, personal *amour propre* – might remain in abeyance while the Tongzhi emperor was still a child, but always it hovered in the background to other discussions. So the Zongli Yamen was attentive to precedent, in a bid to fend off the danger of minor incident being used to secure wider advantage and change.

The Yamen acquired a novel piece of decoration in October 1867, when the American minister, Anson Burlingame, who was very shortly to retire after five years' service, presented a copy of the Lansdowne portrait of George Washington to Xu Jiyu, a member of the board, who had eulogized Washington in an 1849 book.[49] As they 'crammed' Burlingame's fifteen-year-old son with food ('I ate, and ate, and ate until I felt awfully full'), an affable exchange of pleasantries and restatement of cooperative hopes took place in the Yamen meeting hall. This was one of a number of parleys which led to the oddest cooperative enterprise of them all, the mission to the United States and Europe of Anson Burlingame as an official Chinese envoy. This seems to have been Robert Hart's idea. Hart had frequently noted how pro-Chinese Burlingame was (and the minister likewise consistently spoke well of Hart). The inspector-general found that Burlingame 'really wishes China well', 'talks up the cause of independence', supported Hart's policies, and found the British awkward and aggressive, and Alcock too full of himself.[50] The Hart precedent also emboldened the Zongli Yamen, while the coming tenth anniversary of the 1858 treaties dictated a need for a response, for all had built into them a mechanism for revision at that point. Like Hart, Burlingame seemed to be a man they could trust, although unlike Hart he spoke no Chinese, and was not fluent in Chinese cultural norms. But off round the world the new envoy was packed. He left with an entourage of over two dozen Chinese, some Yamen officials, some Tongwenguan students, and one British and one French Customs employee. This was of course funded entirely by the Customs. Burlingame was politically ambitious, and was looking to his own future. He genuinely seems to have believed that he could consolidate the gains of the postwar peace, but he was clearly very often carried away by his own flights of Sinophile rhetoric in the public speeches he gave as the mission travelled. 'Studied Buncombe & high talking' Hart called it, and the mission seemed to go awry fairly swiftly. Then Burlingame unilaterally assumed additional status and negotiating rights for himself in Washington and before anyone knew it 'he has made a *Treaty with the U.S.!!*', as Hart noted in his journal, which, as Wenxiang put it to him, 'surprises them very much'.[51] He had no right to sign anything.

Little harm came of this, for the 'Washington Treaty' was fairly anodyne, and was therefore ratified. It restated US non-intervention in Chinese affairs, heralded the principle of 'free emigration' between the two countries, which was not long to last, and it also pledged each to protect cemeteries, a clause likely to have arisen out of American protests at damage inflicted on an American missionary cemetery in Shandong.[52] Having evaded a bandit attack before they had even reached Tianjin, the Burlingame caravan meandered slowly through the United States, Britain and continental Europe, spending eight pleasant months in Paris (eased by Hart's bank drafts, one for a tidy £12,000 in August 1868) before reaching St Petersburg, where the envoy took ill with pneumonia and died. All in all it was probably the most convenient conclusion. It was a queer affair, the extension of Tongzhi restoration practice to overseas diplomacy, an attempt to smooth the way to treaty renegotiation, and to bide for time, to get the message across through a man who might have more credibility, as a foreign diplomat, that China was indeed getting into the '*international groove*', and doing so as fast as it realistically could. If that message could be got out then perhaps foreign impatience, belligerence and violence could be averted. It was also designed to evade any commitment to adopting international diplomatic practices, for Burlingame was carefully and explicitly instructed not to follow practices which might prompt reciprocal demands on Peking, such as the diplomatic right of audience. But he blithely ignored this, securing formal audiences or private meetings with President Andrew Johnson, Queen Victoria, Emperor Louis Napoleon, Bismarck and Tsar Alexander II. Not much harm was actively done, except in part to Burlingame's own reputation, which was excoriated by the treaty port communities.[53] The Burlingame 'buncombe' enraged them. In fact this was not the first Chinese mission overseas. Hart had arranged a year earlier for three

Tongwenguan students to accompany him when he went home on leave. They were led by a well-connected but not high-ranking Manchu official, Pin Chun, and this became an informal fact-finding mission that set a precedent on which Hart placed great hope for future developments in Zongli Yamen thinking about sending representatives overseas. It was the 'finis which . . . ends my first period in China', he wrote as sailed from Singapore westwards, '& it will form the starting point for the second'.[54] The circuses of Europe attracted a fair bit of the group's attention; so did some of its brothels. They visited foundries and the Crystal Palace, were introduced to Queen Victoria, and sang to the Mayor and Aldermen of Birmingham at the conclusion of an official dinner there, and caused much popular excitement, although they vied for British public attention with Chang, the eight-foot tall 'Chinese Giant', who was on public display in the Egyptian Hall in Piccadilly.[55] There were vicious attacks from the China merchant establishment on Hart, and on the mission, which ranged from criticisms of the dowdiness of their clothing on formal occasions, to complaints that a gullible European public was making itself a Chinese laughing stock by treating as important an insultingly low-grade envoy. 'We cannot,' complained the *China Mail* in Hong Kong, 'conceive of anything more injurious to our interests in the eyes of the Chinese than this vice regal reception to Mr Hart's protogés.' It was the old story, of China coast savviness about Chinese duplicity, about the need for real action, not for freak-show diplomacy.[56] Victory had hardly satisfied the hardliners, and they were most of them hardliners. 'How bitter the China press is,' noted Burlingame.[57]

The centres of power in Peking were nonetheless reaching out beyond China itself, slowly, haltingly establishing precedents, themselves important. There were more envoys, visits to shipyards and factories – and feasts with aldermen – to come. Peking was off-limits to foreign trade by the terms of the Tientsin treaties, but another community came in under the diplomatic shadow, for shortly after the diplomatic ministers came the missionary ones. They scrambled in as soon as it was safe to do so. William Lockhart arrived in September 1861, under diplomatic cover – officially he was the British Legation's doctor, and lodged in the Lianggongfu. Before the month was out he had witnessed the execution of the anti-foreign counsellor Sushun and had opened a hospital, treating over 3,000 patients before the end of the year. As they were counted by a young boy placing a bean in a bowl as each was treated, the figures might be a little optimistic, but clearly there were patients, and no shortage of them. First there were two or three a day, then a dozen, then twenty or thirty.[58] Lockhart, by now a seasoned pioneer, knew from his early Shanghai days that this would work: it would bring people in, establish a name, contact, trust, and an audience for talks and for handing out scripture and tracts to as they waited. They came from all ranks of society, and included heads of the Boards of Punishment and Revenue, and destitute street people. By the time he published his first report fourteen months later he had seen over 22,000 people, and Chinese apothecaries were advertising in nearby streets, having surreptitiously taken smallpox vaccine from his patients. (Smallpox vaccination had been enthusiastically taken up by Chinese residents of Macao and Canton in the early 1800s, not least helped by George Staunton's translation into Chinese of East India Company surgeon Alexander Pearson's account of the process).[59] Fake copies of foreign eye medicines were on sale within another year. 'I rejoice in being in Peking,' Lockhart wrote, as well he might, after two decades of China mission work. And the arrival in the capital of a publicly open institution like the London Missionary Society hospital (where treatment was free), was certainly a different facet of the evolving foreign presence. If the diplomats found themselves hemmed in, mingling only with officials, servants, their teachers and curio-sellers, the growing mission presence was engaging with a far wider spectrum of Peking society. When the Legation establishment grew too big to continue to host the hospital in 1865, they rented part of a Buddhist temple on a very busy thoroughfare. They had the gods removed under cover of night, to the consternation of local residents, but, it was smugly reported, with no sign of visible harm. Removing gods, as we shall see, literally or metaphorically, was not always to be quite so simple. The growing Protestant presence in Peking – there were ten missionaries by January 1864, from five different societies – made manifest in the capital the full implications of the new treaties, and missions grew steadily more prominent in Sino-foreign interactions, in cultural and intellectual exchange, but also in tricky diplomatic disputes.[60]

China saw more and more missionaries arrive, and fan out. They came by steamer or sail across the Pacific and east from Europe. And then by boat, chair, cart and mule they made their way to establish new hospitals (at Zhenjiang and at Hankou, for example, in 1864) and stations wherever they could secure a foothold. They took with them off the ships their furniture, their manners, modes, expectations, bibles, hymn books, instruments, and their litigiousness, doctrinal disputes and strategy conflicts. Lockhart was criticized for too much attending medical work, for example, at the expense of evangelical efforts. This was a great dispersal of the foreign mundane – at times simply, surreally European and American suburban – to China's heartlands, a presence that eventually staked physical claims of one sort or another in all but a handful of China's counties. The Catholic Church had more converts and workers by far, but a first general conference of Protestant missionaries held in Shanghai in 1890 brought together 445 men and women, working for thirty-six different societies or independently across China.[61] They were often a nuisance, but for many people clearly a medical godsend. And theirs was an autonomous imperative. The very foundations of Protestant theology drove their evangelizing mission. They were certainly not the shock troops of foreign governments, and they were not actively supported by them. But diplomat and missionary were at times useful for each other, and many missionaries would eventually apply too readily and too frequently for diplomatic support. And we must assume that the foreigners were mostly practising Protestants or Catholics. Bruce donated the good offices of the British Legation to secure the first LMS hospital site, as well as a good sum of cash from his own pocket. And the China coast world intermarried, very markedly in its early years, even if missionaries often frowned on the levity of the secular – refusing, it was publicly noted, to join in Legation theatricals. Harry Parkes was full of praise for his brother-in-law William Lockhart's Peking venture: 'The political good which your proceedings must have will be very great, and your mission will achieve more than the Diplomatic in impressing the masses of Peking in our favour.' With the hospital at Peking, Parkes concluded, 'we may say that China is really opened to the missionary': Peking, that 'Sole Hope'.[62]

Peking, resolutely, was different to all the other sites of the foreign presence, different in scale, meanings, history, experience and climate.

It was in effect three cities in one. At its core was the 'imperial city', an extensive complex of buildings, parks and lakes, but nonetheless a garrisoned redoubt with the palace – the 'Forbidden City' – at its heart. Around this was the square-shaped 'inner' Manchu, or as foreigners termed it 'Tartar' city, reserved initially for the Manchu nobility, and south of that was the rectangular 'Chinese' or 'outer' city.[63] It was a city on a grid of east–west and north–south streets, intersected by scores of alleyways – *hutongs* – of closed *fu* and massive temple sites, the Tiantan (Temple of Heaven) in the south, and the Ditan (Temple of Agriculture), the Yonghegong, (Lama Temple) and the Wenmiao (Confucius Temple) to the northeast, the central sites of official ritual observance for the empire of the Qing. To the northwest, outside the fourteen miles of 50 foot high and 40 foot wide walls, with their sixteen towering gates (closed at sunset, opened at dawn) was the Summer Palace and the ruined Yuanmingyuan. Peking was a city of dust and mud. This was always the first impression, for Chinese and for foreign visitors, and an abiding one: that it was a city of bad roads in a country of bad roads. Dust choked throats, mud clogged the wheels of the springless Peking carts, the only wheeled conveyances, which travellers hated as 'exquisite torture'. Even getting to the capital was no easy journey. It was a slog from Tianjin even if you took enough beer and champagne to make bearable the two-day cart ride.[64] The legations were established in the inner city, inside the Qianmen, the 'front gate', close by the southern wall. This was close to the offices of the various government boards, and the Zongli Yamen was established not too far distant. It was close to the entertainment quarter outside the gate, to its theatres, restaurants and brothels, so it was close by a bustling section of the city. This was not a reserved settlement, not space marked out for exclusive use as at the treaty ports, for Peking was not a treaty port. Outside the small diplomatic and missionary establishments, the Customs, and the reopened Catholic churches, there were few foreign residents, although the quarter supported four hotels and stores by 1877. They wandered at will. The Chinese city was more commercial than the inner city, but the Forbidden City was impenetrable ('short of a general sack and plunder' noted an 1867 guide, not necessarily ruling out the future possibility) as were many other sites, although this did not stop people attempting entrance.[65]

For all his frustrations, Lord Macartney had thought Peking a city 'justly to be admired', the scale and 'magnificence' of its streets, walls, gates and palaces all impressed themselves upon him. In William Alexander's drawings and paintings, the walls and towers soar up, rather more than in fact they actually did – the comparative lack of monumental architecture, the fact that it was a mostly one-storey city, depressed others.[66] While the writings of the two British embassies had shattered many Sinophile reveries, the city itself remained intriguing, largely because inaccessible, viewed only in print. In reality Peking had grandeur, but it also had squalor, and it was a perplexing experience. What you needed to do was to get up on to the walls or gate towers, for here were good sights and cleaner air. But the legations were so large, or large enough, and so unmastered was the city, that the foreign community made itself at home within them, sometimes closing themselves away within their ordered walls. The Peking dust and mud encouraged this, and encouraged too the resort to rented temples outside the city. There in season was a cooler life, but this was also in a small way the start of another type of colonial pretension to add to the imperial pomp that was got up amongst the Legation walls. For a hill resort, a hill station, was increasingly a fixed point in colonial life. Simla, the newly official summer capital of the government of India, was the best known; and now in China the foreigners began habitually to resort to little Simlas of their own, which were to develop near Shanghai, Jiujiang, Fuzhou, and in the Western hills near Peking. Other practical measures were taken to secure comfort. Robert Hart had a coal-gas plant built, and from 17 May 1869 there were gaslights in the Inspectorate. Within weeks, Li Shanlan, lecturer in mathematics at the Tongwenguan, was proposing to write a book on this new technology.[67] Everything was watched; all that they did was meat for Chinese innovation.

Peking was the centre of another change, for an odd by-product of victory, of the slow growth of this foreign official community in the capital of the Qing, was the rediscovery of a romance of China. There was, it seemed in foreign eyes, no romance in the south – nothing at Canton or Shanghai which could stimulate reflection or affection, or aesthetic sympathy. People hated the cities they had so struggled to enter, thought them rancid, dark and dank; routinely claimed that they offered nothing for a visitor. They settled instead, physically and mentally, snugly into their new Victorias, building up from differences in urban design a moral superiority. Their towns demonstrated space, light and cleanliness, and offered a stark contrast to what they claimed was Chinese Asiatic darkness: fetid streets and fetid minds. They read difference as inferiority. Now they had their entrance they spurned it, declaring it worthless. But the development of official banks of information and report by consul and commissioner was slowly augmented by a new stream of writing, and of photography, which built up a picture of the capital, developing greatly the glimpses offered by Jesuit or Russian residents, or the brief snapshots of the British embassies. Here was the Peking John Thomson and John Dudgeon photographed; here was Robert Fortune's positive account of this park-like city. Robert Hart's resident gas plant engineer from 1870 to 1887 was Thomas Child, coincidentally a very talented photographer, whose images of Peking sights are often the very earliest we have.[68] There was at first that ambivalence in responses. The cityscape was monotonous, in some eyes, unrelieved by monument or landmark. This in itself became a part of its charm: the closedness of the city; and in addition certain talismanic sites – the Yonghegong, the Tiantan – garnered more and more attention and approbation, and criticism too, for being allowed to be run down. But there was also a romance of ruin. Having destroyed the Yuanmingyuan, they now recast its ruins as sublime romance. 'Civility and bribes' would still secure you access to the open parts of it.[69] Some of those bribing their way in were photographers, and it was in large part recast through photography.[70] What was a war scar became a symbol of romance, an integral part of a landscape of ruins and dilapidation, rather than evidence of recent conflict, of British violence – although the scorch marks could be seen and were photographed.

So off to it they went. Satow and his teenage chums rode off to picnic there. John Thomson went with all the cumbersome bother carried by photographers. The wet collodion process that he used involved preparation and development on site of the glass plates, so a tent was humped along with the plates and chemicals, and pitched close by so that the photographer could work immediately. This was no discreet process. Thomson was a professional photographer, who spent ten years living in east and southeast Asia, and who had moved from Singapore to open a studio in Hong Kong in 1868.[71] His first published work on Chinese subjects was a set of photographs to accompany an account of the Ever Victorious Army; the second was a record of the Duke of Edinburgh's visit to Hong Kong in 1869, seven visions of a colony in royal fête. This was a British China: mercenary warfare, a Duke on the Praya, and studio portraits of the Hong Kong community. But he also travelled along the open coast in 1870–72, up the Yangzi, and through Peking to the Great Wall, publishing the results first via woodcut reproduction in the *Illustrated London News* or *The Graphic*, and then in four beautiful volumes, *Illustrations of China and its people* (1873–4). These are beautiful even despite the predictably tart and ignorant text. This was an 'accurate impression of the country', reported Thomson; it was a 'pictorial encyclopaedia' wrote one later editor; it was a 'colonizer's handbook' claimed another. There is something in all these, and the text is inseparable from the images. A photographer and his caravan were also, of course, foreigners, and their presence beyond the safe confines of the treaty ports was still capable of mis-interpretation, and of sparking an incident which fed its way into the text. The plate of Thomson's 'Chao-chow Bridge' was broken in the making, for it was 'taken at the point of the tripod', which he had used to beat off a hostile crowd as he escaped to a boat.[72] But allowance must be made for the imaginative power of these 200 images in projecting a new idea of China, one whose impact builds slowly through the books as Thomson reached Peking. There was an inter-ventionist aesthetic at work, for Thompson was not interested in anybody's handbooks, in 'lifeless charts' of the mechanical proportions of nature'. Rather than 'agglomerations of intricate detail' he aimed to produce 'poems', 'poems speaking not only to our senses but to our souls'.[73] Poetry is a nice luxury for power, but we lose our sense of the evolving meanings of China in foreign minds if we read every image or word as functional colonialism. And photography was not simply now a foreign science or art, and already had Chinese lives. Professional Chinese photographers were already active in Hong Kong and Shanghai, taking portraits and securing images of well-known sights for treaty port residents; but they were also innovating and experimenting themselves, fashioning photography as a Chinese science.[74] Missionary doctor John Dudgeon, one of Thomson's hosts in Peking, who took a number of photographs himself of the capital's ruins and sights, provided an article on photography for a Tongwenguan journal, and in 1873 published a textbook on photography in Chinese. Science, art and poetry spilled over.

Here it was, in Thomson's images: old China, scarred China, restoration China – Li Shanlan, Prince Gong, Li Hongzhang, Wenxiang – fresh caught by photograph, open to view wherever the books were seen. Thomson's aesthetic allowed for the importing of Chinese sights into the world of European sensibilities, of romantic ruins, and of sacred landscape. Two of his photographs, of 'Chinese Bronzes' and 'Ancient Chinese Porcelain Ware' show another way in which attitudes to China were fast changing in the 1860s, and how the small foreign colony at Peking was in the vanguard of this development. Loot had whetted appetites for Chinese decorative arts, for 'curios'. 'Like all foreigners who visit Peking,' Thomson wrote, 'I had been but one night in the metropolis when I found myself waited upon by half a dozen dealers in curiosities'.[75] The Legation is 'daily infested' with dealers, reported Rennie, its first doctor, in July 1861, and foreigners now habitually bought from them, snuff bottles being an amateur favourite. It became part of the little culture developing at the legations: Satow dabbled from the start – everybody did as part of the daily round.[76] There was an intense ad hoc trade, fuelled by the tremendous quantity of looted material in global circulation. Rennie reports John Dent arriving at the British Legation with pearls in his pocket purchased from a French sailor who had seized them in Peking, looking out intently for more.[77] Others started to act as agents of buyers overseas, building up contacts and relationships with Chinese dealers or owners, who sold or sourced items. The descriptive notes for Thomson's curio plates were supplied by the British Legation doctor, Stephen Bushell, who had taken the post on Lockhart's recommendation in 1868. Bushell spent thirty-one years in China, developing an international reputation as an expert on Chinese art, collecting on behalf of private and institutional buyers in Europe and the United States, forming collections that were to enter the British Museum and the Victoria and Albert Museum. He bought for 'Gilded Age' collectors, rich businessmen such as W. T. Walters in Boston and Heber Bishop in New York. He was to publish landmark catalogues and studies of porcelains.[78] So Chinese decorative arts gained in currency, for the amateur, for the collector and scholar, for institutions, and for European and American homes. They did so authentically, and they did so through a growing new wave of less authentic chinoiserie. For Osbert Lancaster, grandson of Hong Kong shipping owner Alfred Lapraik, Victorian tastes and Qing style combined to produce 'objects of transcendental monstrosity' which overwhelmed European interiors with a fussy feast of writhing 'Chinese' detail.[79] But in both cases, European and American culture was more than ever before infused with Chinese aesthetic, the fruit of victory, of the onward march into China's cities and towns, and into the imperial capital.

This new Peking, the object of romantic contemplation, suggested a China that might be appreciated rather than caricatured, and savoured rather than savaged. This view would slowly build in momentum, and it would take another war, and another dreadful peace, to lodge it firmly – by lodging the foreign presence firmly, securely, in the heart of the empire. But even in its early years there was nothing innocent about the romance of Old Peking, and it was driven by the fact of victory. There was that yobbish flavour too, as young foreign boys yahooed their way around the closed and crumbling sites of the city. For this turn to antique China also presaged the opening of another front in the foreign campaign. As China 'modernized', as it adopted some of the reforms long insisted on, foreign observers changed the rules. The old was glorified, and romanticized. New China was losing its soul. What was once a symbol of decay and stasis mutated into something wholesome. The old had integrity and soul, and reform came to be seen as something deracinating, un-Chinese, vapid. None of this was unique to China: it was the routine trajectory of the victorious colonial mind, shifting languages, keeping the subject of its talk always in the wrong, and always inferior. The discovery of Chinese art was part of this turn.

There was less art, or talk of art, at the open ports, although all had their curio hunters. While the high politics of imperial diplomacy were accompanied by the high jinks of the consular cubs, at the treaty ports the grand plans and speculations were buffeted by the 1865 crash, and tempered by the growing complexities of the little worlds that still grew apace. The rowdy and the awkward, violent sailors and violent gentlemen, threw up problems. The British and American Settlement at Shanghai alone housed more residents in more houses than in the whole of Hong Kong, but lacked its Colonial Office personnel and support. The minutes of the meetings of the Municipal Council grew in length and detail, its business needing more professional staff, and better systems. Standing out amongst its concerns, politically, is a systematic policy of rebutting attempts, or apparent attempts, by the Shanghai Zhixian or Daotai to exercise authority over Chinese in the settlement. Attempts to levy funds or taxes were rebuffed if the Council got wind of them – and get wind of them it did, because it evolved very markedly into a property-protecting institution, the tool of a 'real-estate oligarchy'. The Settlement housed scores of brothels, gambling houses and theatres. Legitimate attempts by the Chinese authorities, as well as apparently illegitimate attempts at extortion, routinely lumped together by the Settlement authority, struck at the heart of the accidental genius of the Settlement. For all those brothels, gambling houses and theatres were tenants of foreign landlords, men like Hanbury, who got himself onto the Municipal Council in a bid to rein in expenditure, and thereby property taxes, and to protect Chinese interests. The theatres displayed their foreignness, adding 'British' or 'American' to their signboards. Police beats were redesigned in 1865 to maximize the 'security of substantial Chinamen' living in the Settlement, and to stop the drift of the refugee rich back to post-rebellion Yangzhou or Suzhou.[80] So the foreign China enterprise at Shanghai was actually truly a real-estate imperialism, a working out in bricks and mortar of that Sino-foreign collaboration which had always underpinned the China trade. In smaller ways the other settlements mirrored Shanghai developments, notably at Tianjin and Hankou, and this privileging of the accidental off-shoot of rebellion as the heart of foreign interests in these zones set aside solely for foreign residence, ought to be seen for what it practically was. The treaty ports have been discussed as 'bridgeheads', as the advance guard of imperialist penetration of China, jumping-off points for invasion. But by 1865 they were profitable real-estate kingdoms, protected by treaty, consular and diplomatic interventions, warships and garrisons – and Thomas Hanbury, at Shanghai at least, was king.

So the business of Shanghai was the business of land: a tiny plot, intensely valuable. The business of the treaty ports was also the business of waste. Offal, faeces, garbage, ash, corpses, the detritus of shoddy building work, all of it unceasingly generated, day in day out: the stuff of human life. And there was mud and dust, and water, and vermin feeding off garbage. All that talk at the capital, all that chatter in press and pamphlet, all the work of the divine hand in Sino-foreign relations, led to this ongoing practical problem of urban waste, and the impact and by-products of waste; of drinking water unfit for consumption, noisome stenches in quagmired streets, hygiene dangers. Councillors needed to frame regulations, and they needed to build an infrastructure, to do something to manage and order their makeshift cities. So they needed to use the police to prevent public urination or defecation on Shanghai streets, and to stop residents throwing offal into the creeks or the Huangpu, while the Public Works Department installed urinals, and cleared 'nuisances'. There was also the business of dealing with chaos, numbering houses and sampans, and licensing (in 1864) 270 brothels, 200 opium shops and 73 gambling houses.[81] The Taiping threat had habituated the Settlement to restricting Chinese movement after dark, requiring passes and lamps. The Council periodically swept beggars from the settlement, shipping them over the Huangpu into Pudong, or into the Chinese city. It tried to order noise, to allow perhaps the bells of the church to ring clear, by prohibiting the cries of street vendors, issuing orders against the 'monotonous chaunt of the water coolies'. Foreign residents wanted to control movement across the landscape, and the tenor of the soundscape. An early Chinese account highlighted the restrictions imposed within the Settlement, warning visitors and residents to watch themselves, for the police would collar them and haul them to a new Mixed Court, which tried cases involving Chinese, and found itself dealing with dozens of petty 'nuisance' cases.[82] Police activities and by-laws aimed to educate Chinese visitors about the proper use of foreign public space, but the drive to document and regulate went further, into the houses of the Settlement. In late 1865 the Council established a (voluntary) Registration Office for Chinese servants, opening a file on each one registered, with a photograph and character references from employers.[83] A thousand were soon registered by their employers. It served to provide some order for the hiring of servants, but was also aimed at winnowing out the inefficient or allegedly dishonest. And the use of a still modern technology, photography, at the heart of the system, is worth noting. It suggests an aim for a modern, scientific surveillance, but it was also rooted in an age-old conceit, that Chinese all looked alike in foreign eyes. So at Shanghai they ordered space, responding as quickly as they were able to the breathtaking speed with which opportunities were seized, innovations latched onto, loopholes explored. They also ordered the Chinese use of public space, imposing new norms of behaviour, turning urination into a minor criminal category. They also attempted to order aspects of private space: the gambling house, the brothel, the household (trying to order the world of Chinese servants).

So there were different spheres of interaction. There was the connivance of Hart in the self-strengthening project, and the services provided by the other foreign experts in Chinese employ, the translators, teachers and engineers. There was the practical collaboration of the traders and merchants, the multifaceted activities of the Settlement at Shanghai, succouring the Chinese rich, protecting its tenants, and ordering the public behaviour of residents and visitors. There were private interactions too, of course, as there had ever been. These cut across the class lines that stratified the foreign communities, separating sailor from gentleman. One such gentleman, Hart, had married in 1866 in London, having explained his need to take leave, to his superiors, as his duty to look after his mother, which demonstrated entirely in their eyes his proper sincerity and sense of personal responsibilities. Hart returned to Peking with Hestor Bredon – and she gamely studied her Chinese characters, and gamely gave birth to their first, but in fact his fourth child, the others being the offspring of his relationship with a Cantonese woman, Ayaou. 'I found,' he later recorded, 'that any acquaintance I made kept his China girl', and he took her with him as he moved postings, eventually settling her in Macao, presenting her in 1866 with $3,000 by way of *finis*, and sending the children to Britain.[84] She was not his only such purchase, it seems. This was entirely routine. It became a cliché of the colonial novel; the young wife is brought back from Britain, and finds in her new husband's house, or compound, clear evidence of his earlier 'left-handed' makeshift. '*Quand on n'a pas ce qu'on aime, il faut aimer ce qu'on a*' (When one does not have what one loves, one must love what one has), reflected J. O. P. Bland in a later memoir. 'There were generally one or two' Chinese mistresses 'on the strength of the Customs Mess' at Hankou, and children often followed.[85] Shanghai surgeon Edward Henderson reported 'considerable numbers' of 'native mistresses of foreign residents' in 1871, mostly but not exclusively living in houses of their own, kept by their 'owners', as he put it, who had 'hired' or 'bought' them. Henderson was not disposed to believe that many had any 'real affection' for their foreign masters. We must not, like Henderson, simply reduce all relations between Chinese women and foreign men to prostitution, but certainly many of these relationships were temporary conveniences and involved payments. There will have been love and affection. But prostitution there certainly was – in Shanghai, for example, there were twenty-seven houses of Chinese (mostly Cantonese) women receiving only foreign men, and thirty-five receiving Chinese and foreign, and those mostly the lower-class foreign.[86] Thomas Hanbury was another who, like Hart, did right by his charge, conscience leading them to have their offspring taught and raised in European fashion, albeit out of their sight, and away from China, where the Eurasian was tainted. Hanbury's son Ahsu – Charlie – was sent to school in Paris. William Hunter's two sons were sent to college in Kentucky, from where they joined the Confederate army, one of them dying in service in 1864. But the more common attitude was perhaps that voiced by a character in a later novel of treaty port life and mores: 'I don't know where we shall all be if men are to bring up their children just as if they'd been properly married and all.'[87]

We know very little in fact about the Eurasians, and about the extent of the world of liaisons and relationships between Chinese and foreigners. At the rougher commercial end of sex and intimacy – male and female, male and male – we have glimpses enough, and know how visible in the streets the former could be. In 1866 Shanghai councillors rejected a proposal to create new wharves on the Settlement Bund partly because ships' crews would attract 'disreputable followers'.[88] Mostly this intimate world, of settled companionship and relationship, is not described or recorded because increasingly it was not approved of. Edmund Hornby claimed that in the mid-1860s a concerted effort was made to stamp out the practice of junior foreign staff keeping Chinese women in company messes. As he relates it, however, the practical result was an upsurge in the numbers of better class foreign prostitutes and courtesans: Henderson counted eighteen in 1871. Others hint that there had been a sea-change in public behaviour by the 1870s.[89] Open concubinage, long tolerated, was increasingly seen as inappropriate in a respectable society. But overt racism also hardened attitudes against even legitimate unions. Formal marriage with Chinese women was in some places prohibited by service regulation (in the police at Shanghai, later) or elsewhere more insidiously by informal, but no less rigid, practice. A man might lose his job, he might certainly lose all hope of preferment, if he contracted such a marriage.[90] An exception was Canadian missionary George Leslie Mackay, who married a Taiwanese woman, but he was a forceful and independent character who had few colleagues and recognized fewer established rules.[91] Marriage with indigenous women was a common feature on some colonial frontiers and in some settled societies, serving to demonstrate elite alliances, but this was not the case in China. A man might do what he liked in private, as long as it was without scandal, but marriage was out of bounds. This was also increasingly a matter of class discipline. Gentlemen would find an appropriate local partner for the duration, but could then travel home on furlough, like Hart, and find a wife. Such opportunities for lower-class men were much more restricted, so disciplining their potential for embarrassing society became more important. But some did marry Chinese, even in church and not simply quietly at the Consulate. Henry Dibdin, a policeman, married Xu Zhuxie at Holy Trinity, Shanghai in 1866; pilot Joseph Vaughan married 'Kung You' in 1867. Baptism registers add to the picture, with some Eurasian children brought by their parents, or en masse – from the Hanbury School, for example – the children of 'Nie Sue', 'Ah Ling', 'Chang Taicsun': little Annie and Ellen Hadley, Lillian Tregillus, Catherine Brown.[92] Wills sometimes obliquely made provision for 'housekeepers' and the children of such euphemistically described women. So there is evidence for intimate interaction. Hanbury squared his conscience in a further way, by endowing a home and school for those less supported by their fathers than was young Charlie. This opened in 1872, and had places for eighty-four children by 1891. Such a boarding school had first been proposed in 1869, and one had first opened in 1870. A similar school at Hankou was established in 1888.[93]

Provision for Eurasian children seemed in fact something vital for the new communities. The foreigners arrived, the windows were peeped through, temptation offered and accepted, purchases agreed, and children very often followed. Perhaps, wrote Hanbury, Eurasians 'might form a good link to promote a more kindly feeling between European and Chinese'.[94] But in fact they were routinely caricatured and hated, and there was no Eurasian bridge.

We know a lot about Hart's private worlds, although much is lost with the journals from late 1858 to June 1863, which he later destroyed. We know from what survives, and from his letters, of another realm in which he led the way. Hart's working method enabled him to wade through the reams of paper that arrived at the Inspectorate, but it also allowed him an hour a day for playing the cello, and another hour for the violin.[95] We base our histories on paper, on books and documents, often forgetting how much we live through other senses, unattuned to the copious hints we have of the music and song in people's lives. Music came to consume Hart's private life. The Inspectorate General was the site in time of an entirely novel private experiment of Hart's: in 1888 he created a brass band of Chinese players. Bands and orchestras had accompanied passengers out on P&O, and bands accompanied armies. Music offered a counterpoint to the roar of the foreign war machine, but it was intimately tied to conflict. The band of the *Susquehanna* enlivened the Shanghai round in 1853, bringing familiar and novel sounds to the sojourning foreigners, and their public and private Chinese worlds were full of music. James Dow had noted of the church in Shanghai that the 'singing at times is first rate, all amateur', and his friend 'the organist, is also amateur', but it did the job. Hong Kong advertised for a professional organist in 1854. A Thursday evening in December 1851 sees Dow at a 'Kind of Musical soiree', an out-of-tune piano not stopping the gentlemen from demonstrating the vocal talent of the Shanghai British, and coming 'out very strong'. But having got your piano to China, itself no minor feat of shipping, how were you to keep it in tune? From the private soiree to the amateur public performance was an easy step, and the newspapers report these in great detail.[96] But there was a thirst for more, and we can safely assume that the lower-class taverns of Shanghai rang to the sounds of different tunes. Travelling musicians started to add Hong Kong and even

Shanghai to their circuits, opera troupes travelling into the city from the mid-1870s onwards.[97] Hart's correspondence is full of requests for sheet music, instruments, and all the things needed by his band. 'It is the only thing I am interested in apart from work,' he noted. They became a fixture in the Peking foreign world, these young Chinese boys trained up to play their instruments, led by a Portuguese bandmaster listed on the strength as a postal clerk, dressed up in their uniforms and playing the tunes to which the diplomats danced or promenaded once a week in the Inspectorate gardens, or at Legation balls.[98]

Slowly there were other sources of public music. At Shanghai the Municipal Council sent to London for music and instruments in 1863 and told off six foreign policemen to form a band, later advertising for a bandmaster.[99] They played in public on the Bund, but we can also expect that they played as the police paraded, since music was the appropriate accompaniment to organized formations of uniformed men. So, naturally, the new model armies of the Taiping victory and the postwar decades that were drilled by Westerners needed trumpets and trumpeters, bands and bandmasters. Western music seeped into China through the private worlds of expatriate social life, the public world of military drill and the military bands, and also through missions. The band moved into Chinese public life, notably finding a role in Chinese funerals. And as the goddess Tianhou's image was processed around Shanghai in 1886, she was preceded by a brass band.[100] It served too to mark space in new ways. At Shanghai a wreck off the Bund at the mouth of the Soochow creek opposite the British Consulate had led to the growth of a mudbank which by 1862 had presented an opportunity for adding a plot of land to the Settlement as a public garden.[101] A park was laid out by 1868, and already by summer 1874 an amateur band performed there once a week in summer. A bandstand was built, and this little ritual – the band playing while the community congregated to listen or gossip – became a public icon of the wholesomeness of the new community in Shanghai. Music was ever also a private pleasure, a private relief, a source of succour: two hours of Hart's day free from paper and people. In the darkest days of his captivity, Henry Loch planned to seek out the whereabouts of his fellow captive Harry Parkes by singing 'God Save the Queen', or 'Rule Britannia'. To keep his spirits up a decade later, free but confined in

Peking exile, a young student interpreter, Augustus Raymond Margary, also resorted to song. Born in India, educated in France and England from the age of nine, three times failing the consular exams before succeeding in 1867, he arrived in China aged twenty-one. Dealing with the pain of separation was a fact of life across the British colonial world. Everyone had his or her own strategy. This young man's was rooted in the music of his home. 'Retiring as far as possible out of hearing of his species,' recalled Rutherford Alcock in a memoir, Margary 'sang all his old songs at the top of his voice, winding up with "God Save the Queen"'.[102] Always in Peking, I think, someone will in fact have heard him. Always someone will have heard the young foreigner belting out song in the capital's dry air, hoping through the sounds of England to exorcize the demon homesickness.

8

Inland Dreams

He was insistent, as insistent as only a man could be when his nine-year-old brother, Wu'er, had gone missing a week previously. So Zhang Zhixi had walked the ninety-five dusty miles from his home at Luanzhou, east of the capital, a town famous for its shadow puppetry. He had walked patiently, because he knew for a fact – as all China knew – that foreigners were paying Chinese agents to kidnap children. So Zhang had made his way to the capital, in which direction people had told him the young boy had been taken, and where he was told foreigners lived. Arriving late in the morning of 20 August 1870, he came through the Chaoyang Gate, close by the Customs Inspectorate, and asked where the foreigners might be found. People directed him southwest, to the streets behind the Qianmen gate. So Zhang made his way to the Lianggongfu, and at a back entrance to the British Legation, the first he had come to, he begged admittance and presented his case, armed with a 'rude, blunt spear'. If they would release his brother, Zhang said, he would find a replacement. It was a perfectly reasonable request. But what, you may well ask, would the foreigners want with the child, what would they do to it? Well, Zhang would have told you that they would gouge out his eyes. This is what the foreigners did, everybody knew this: they gouged out Chinese eyes and used them to make medicine with; they used Chinese hearts for the same purpose. So they needed Chinese bodies with which to make their medicines, and established orphanages and children's homes, tricking people into placing children in their care, and there in those homes the children were killed. Or they paid kidnappers to seize children from the streets, children like Wu'er, and they killed them. Even at Luanzhou, at a distance from any place of foreign residence, people knew about these things, and so they told Zhang, who did what he had to do, and went to rescue his younger brother, carrying his spear for protection.

Zhang Zhixi received eighty strokes of the bamboo cane for his action, having been seized by the Legation guards and handed over to the Zongli Yamen, who sent him to the judicial authorities. He was, wrote the British Minister, a 'common labourer', a 'simpleton' duped by 'designing persons', and he was sent back to his home.[1] Feng 'the lame', Wang Liu, Ma Hongliang, Zhang Li and Zhang Guoquan suffered far worse punishment, for they were executed in Tianjin on 19 October. Feng's spear was sharper than Zhang Zhixi's, and so was Wang Liu's, and more effective too were the swords and other weapons used by these and other men in Tianjin on 21 June 1870, two months prior to poor Zhang's honest enquiry at the Legation back gate. Twenty-one Europeans were killed that day and by those weapons, mostly French nationals, but also three Russians, an Italian, a Belgian, and an Irishwoman – the last three, and seven of the French, all nuns. The newly consecrated French cathedral was sacked and burned, the neighbouring French consulate was destroyed, the orphanage newly established just outside the city's east gate by the Sisters of St Vincent de Paul, who undertook in China the work of the Holy Childhood Association, was destroyed; the ten sisters were seized, stripped, muti-lated and murdered.[2] Tianjin had for weeks been gripped by fear, and by hostility to the French Catholic mission, and to the French. The summer was dry: a season of drought and fear. Kidnappers had been caught, had confessed, and had been executed. (Kidnapping, of course, undoubtedly happened, as it did elsewhere – for ransom, and for other purposes.) The Sisters had been paying parents who surrendered children to their home, as had become the custom for Catholic religious establishments, but their cemetery was full of newly buried bodies, bodies lacking eyes and hearts, people said. A local man, Wu Lanzhen, seized after a kidnapping attempt, deposed that he had been employed by Chinese staff at the cathedral and that he had gone out each day in a drug-induced trance armed with a 'red powder' that stupefied his victims, allowing him to bring them back to the mission. Official notices about kidnapping, the weird rounds of rumour, and the debilitatingly uncertain tensions of a dry time, all combined with a wider reaction across China against foreign missionaries. This was a movement to refute their teachings, ridicule their beliefs and practices, and repel their intrusions into towns and cities, like Yangzhou, far from the treaty ports, where they were trying to establish new sites, or the chains of small rural establishments being set up close by the treaty ports. Years of growing tensions across China, and weeks of fear across Tianjin, exploded on 21 June, and thousands of people found refuge from fear in collective violence.

It ought not to have happened. Growing accustomed by now to public disquiet about foreign mission activities, and knowing how these could escalate into riot, and so into diplomatic problems, the Zongli Yamen and some local officials were getting effective at meeting the suspicions of the people with calm, logical action. At Tianjin, as reports piled up about growing fear, and prophecies of violence, as foreigners found people increasingly hostile, the Commissioner of Trade for the Northern Treaty Ports, Chong Hou, had taken matters in hand. He worked with the Daotai and Zhixian to have an open investigation of the orphanage in order to categorically refute popular charges. This was a sensible act of public theatre, for these educated men clearly did not believe in such rumours, even if some of their peers elsewhere stoked them, as indeed 'designing persons' certainly did through literary attacks on missions. The Daotai and the Zhixian were responsible to their superiors for maintaining public order, and were responsible to the people too, and needed to respond to their fears and disquiet. They needed to do so in ways that would help them retain public trust, deflecting charges that they were simply tools of the foreigners, for such a charge was now being levelled at men like them. So it was an excruciatingly difficult path for officials to tread. On the morning of 21 June the local officials formally visited the cathedral, taking Wu Lanzhen with them. It quickly became clear that he had never been there before, knew nobody, and had lied about everything. Now they could settle this, and so they talked with the priest, Father Chevrier, about measures that could be taken to settle people's fears. Death rates in Catholic orphanages and foundling homes were notoriously high, but the cemetery was full of little coffins because of an epidemic, it transpired. The Sisters paid off parents by way of requiring them to surrender their rights over the children, so that the ties of the children to Chinese family, society, culture – all of it so antithetical to Christian living – could be fully sundered.

Chevrier and Chong Hou talked about this, about these chronic misunderstandings and what fed them, and agreed to take public measures to make it clear what the Catholics were doing, and why, and what they were not doing. They talked about how they might be more open about occurrences such as the epidemic, even at the cost of frightening people from bringing children forward. It now only remained for proclamations to be drafted and posted, and for public pronouncements to be made by the officials. Always the canker, fear, would remain, but if it could be proved groundless, if suspicion could be allayed, and if its extreme expressions could be quelled, then there would be no public outbursts. There would be no conflicts, no diplomatic crises, denunciations or demands, and the ten Sisters could continue their work in Tianjin, dressed in their blue-grey habits and their striking white-starched cornets.

The French consul, Henri Fontanier, wrote to his minister that same morning about the disquiet in 'Notre petite ville de Tien-tsin', penning his letter from the 'picturesque and striking' consulate building, lodged in a complex of former state apartments seized in 1860 by the French, over the river northwest of the walled city.[3] As diplomats do, he reported how well he was handling things, about how well he had handled the Daotai, who had come to him with Wu's deposition, and so too the Zhixian, who had been angry, and threatening, clearly feeling pressurized by public opinion. Fontanier recorded how things had been smoothed over, firmly smoothed over; how he had stood his ground, and reminded the Zhixian that public peace was that official's responsibility. It is a little self-satisfied, a little bumptious even, hinting at choler, though this was standard consular bluff. Fontanier had handled things well, in his eyes. So today the incident seemed 'à peu près terminé', almost concluded, for as he wrote the investigation at the cathedral was just taking place. But then in the early afternoon he heard of – probably actually heard – a fracas at the cathedral next to the consulate, built on the site of a Buddhist temple, some altercation between a watching crowd and Chinese converts. By the accounts we have this enraged him. Perhaps he thought it a double-cross, that all that smoothing over was a mandarin feint, and that the officials would not or could not control the mob, the mob which for some few days past had been shouting in the streets for vengeance. Having written too, to Peking, to the Minister – the letter was already in transit – he now faced a reporting difficulty, if not embarrassment, in the undoing of the promised calm. Fontanier then did what consuls typically did: he made his way swiftly to the highest authority he could find, to Chong Hou at his *yamen*, to demand action; he would have no truck with the lesser administrators now. This was becoming the China pattern. Consuls were expected to entreat, cajole or bully their Chinese counterparts, to make them act according to the stipulations of treaty – as the foreign diplomats saw them. While consuls made their demands, stomping their way to the *yamen*, or processing there in all their pomp and feathered finery – demanding entrance; demanding action or redress; urinating on the closed door in one case when it was shut against them; barging their way in, in that surely by now familiar China-side style – then at the centre ministers would hector the Zongli Yamen. So Fontanier did what a consul should do, and one account said that he kicked open the *yamen* door as he did so.

But he took a weapon – two pistols in fact – and with him came his assistant, M. Simon, sword unsheathed. Chong Hou had come out to meet him as they approached, having heard Fontanier was coming, to be met with a stream of invective hurled at him by the Frenchman, who, drunk with rage, reported one observer, then took a pistol and fired at the Superintendent. Chong Hou, unscathed, withdrew into an inner apartment, and the consul was seized, but in the *yamen* he started to smash up the room, uttering 'an incessant stream of abuse' as he did so. Then the Zhixian was said to be coming, to try to stay the crowd which had followed the Frenchmen, and which was growing, so Fontanier left in order to accost him. Chong Hou reports that he came out to entreat the consul to stay within, for his own safety, but out he went, and all agree that he then fired again at the Zhixian, fatally wounding one of the magistrate's subordinates. And so the crowd then washed over Henri Fontanier and Simon, and then washed over the cathedral, the consulate, the orphanage. They moved through the streets hunting out foreigners and converts, exorcizing their fear and hatred, bludgeoning or stabbing to death any Frenchman or Frenchwoman they caught, for they interrogated the foreigners they found, demanding to know if they were French, and the three Russians failed to convince them and were killed.

There were acts of kindness, and shelter offered from the storm, but over sixty people died in a three-hour fury, and Protestant chapels were also ransacked before quiet returned. Three days later Fontanier was pulled from the river 'fearfully mutilated', naked save his shoes and socks. The river yielded other European and Chinese corpses as it flowed past the British Settlement two miles downstream, for about forty converts were killed as well, no less hated than the foreigners. Very little remained of the Sisters, a few bones only, for their wrecked bodies were burned with their mission. The next few days were ghastly, with the foreigners in the concessions watching night and day, weapons to hand, fearfully waiting for gunboats summoned from the south. For a moment those in Peking wondered if the violence would come their way; servants at the French Legation vanished, and collective breath was held. Even two months later they worried, and so poor Zhang Zhixi angered and unsettled them. But that dark day's night at Tianjin, on 21 June, the heavens opened and rain poured down, ending the dry spell, and washing away the stench of death in the streets.

The missionaries knew it was coming. Of course, they always half expected martyrdom, and half wanted it, for the blood of martyrs sanctified the mission soil. More immediately, they expected it because they had faced some years now of opposition, opposition that was turning from sullen disbelief at the weirdness of Christianity, so at variance in its practices to civilized norms, to overt, violent hostility. Educated Chinese thought its teachings bizarre, objectionable and heterodox, and ordinary communities found missionaries demanding their converts cut themselves off from communal life, from their families, and especially from their ancestors. So there was already by 1861 what one scholar has described as a 'rabid and prolific anti-Christian tradition in China'. That year had seen the first appearance of *Bixie zhishi* ('A record of facts to ward off heterodoxy'), a violent denunciation of Christian beliefs and religious practices in a book that was reprinted, abridged and otherwise circulated for decades to come.[4] This was also intertwined with reactions against the Taiping rebellion, the rebel Christian kingdom which had so laid waste to central China, and which had been met initially with such missionary hopes. One longer term impact of the rebellion was a vicious, scatological pamphlet campaign waged against Christianity, which was rooted in horror at the Taiping harrowing of the lower Yangzi and designed to mobilize support against the rebels. Opposition to the missionaries came as a complicated, heady mix. There was this intellectual opposition, and there was the shock of communities at the way in which converts withdrew themselves, from 'pagan' or 'heathen' life, as the missionaries would have it; from community, as their neighbours, family members would have it. There were mixed-sex congregations, encouraging immorality, and it was thought, much more: priests seduced women, sodomy was encouraged, eyes gouged out, and worse – all of this people like Zhang Zhixi knew for fact. There were practical operating problems (scarce funds, over-ambition), which caused tensions. Orphanage death rates were high, as they were in similar institutions in Europe in the nineteenth century, but practical measures to address this lagged behind the reforms back home. Moreover, many inmates were not orphans, for the existence of orphanages expanded 'the market for otherwise unsaleable children', especially the disabled or already very sick offspring of the poor, and intimately intertwined these institutions with their host communities.[5] There was practical opposition to the spread of the missionary presence beyond the open ports: issues over property, the practical facts of a new foreign presence in wary communities, and the growing recourse by missionaries to consular and diplomatic redress when they encountered difficulties. There was the fact that in practical terms Christianity looked like a heterodox sect and seemed closely to resemble something like the Buddhist White Lotus sect. This was in fact one reason why certain more fundamentalist Protestant practices fared quite well in Chinese rural settings, for example speaking in tongues, for they resembled some of the practices of existing religious sects.[6] Overall, the problem was that Christianity touched too closely too much of the stuff of ordinary Chinese life to be anything but unsettling, and this, of course, was precisely the missionary aim.

Missionaries all worked in the shadow of foreign power, though there were crucial public differences here. The French state had nailed its colours firmly to the Catholic Church's mast by assuming a protectorate role over it in China, by insisting through treaty on ending the prohibition of 1724 and on the missionary right of residence in the interior, by going to war in 1857 over the killing of Father Auguste

Chapdelaine, and by securing through treaty the transfer of sites to the Church for new cathedrals at Canton and Tianjin, and the reopening of old ones, at Peking and Shanghai. The exercise of French power in China had little commercial logic: it was strategic in imperative, an imperial gesture – simply keeping up with the British – and so it adopted Catholicism as its particular and defining cause. It might indeed have helped a diffusion of wider French influence and secure information, for French Catholic missionaries naturally remained Frenchmen, and may have had their sense of Frenchness enhanced by the fact of being abroad, and being abroad in an Anglophone-dominated foreign society in China. For its part the state made visible its association with the Church. Fontanier had of course been there on 16 May 1869 when the cathedral was consecrated, and it was built on ground seized by the French and occupied by them. The British and others were much more diffident in their relationship with missionaries, and agonized over the right posture to adopt. Bruce had helped Lockhart with the LMS hospital, but Alcock was less amenable, either privately or publicly, for missionary cases were building up, and missionaries simply would not stay where they were clearly allowed to live. They followed their patients home, networking through patients' families and working back to patients' native places, following up the slightest sign of interest. The creeping pace of progress was marked in the pages of the new mission chronicle, the monthly *Chinese Recorder*, after it began publication in 1867: a convert here, five baptisms there – these were the stuff of reports in its pages. So slender, minuscule, the actual results – barely 3,000 Protestant converts by 1866 – that any and every small expression of interest was followed up – followed home – wherever it came from, wherever the trail led. They were driven too by the relatively greater success of the Catholic Church – a third of a million converts in 1850, almost half a million in 1881 (but even this was still painfully slow progress). Ningbo had eleven Protestant outstations by 1869, one of them 300 miles from the city. Fuzhou missions had sixteen. Even the London Mission in Peking had a 'chain of little stations' south of Peking by 1871, as its activities crept out of the established base there, as they did all over. The pattern here was a classic one: ad hoc itinerations became a more routine circuit, and a routine circuit needed a local venue, a base – a room was hired, and so a little mission outstation came into being, a new addition to the missionary 'machinery'. It would be visited, enquirers examined, catechized, formally baptized if deemed sincere, and then their new Christian life would be watched and tended by regular visits.[7] Elsewhere there were bolder moves. Thomas Hanbury recorded the arrival in Shanghai in March 1854 of a 'mere boy', James Hudson Taylor, ill-educated, unprepared, rushed out by Gützlaff's 'Chinese Evangelisation Society' at that moment of missionary excitement and Taiping enthusiasm, and 'found' wandering near their missionary village.[8] Taylor had been taken in by Medhurst the elder, had eventually worked independently of any mission at Ningbo, before returning to England in 1860 for six years. In 1866 he returned as director of a new provocatively self-styled 'China Inland Mission', with twenty-one fellow missionaries, an enormous party by existing standards, augmenting the entire Protestant presence by one tenth.[9] And they were going inland. This was to be nondenominational and a 'faith mission', free of the homeside bureaucracy of the LMS or other boards, and its members intended to work, in Chinese clothing, to 'bring the Chinese to a saving knowledge of the love of God in Christ, by means of itinerant and localised work throughout the whole of the interior of China'. Theirs was an uncompromising, urgent, evangelical Protestantism, and 'the whole of the interior of China' was their chosen field, for in their eyes this was a land in darkness, in which a million souls were lost every month as the pagan 400 million Chinese died.

On 1 June 1868 the China Inland Mission party moved to Yangzhou, and two months later a crowd several thousand strong, whipped up by the usual stories of dead infants, gathered and attacked them. 'I came here to propagate religion in accordance with the will of the Emperor as given in the Treaty of Commerce and Amity,' a desperate Taylor had written to the Prefect (the Zhifu, who administered the city and district) a few days before the attack. 'I request you to refer to the Articles of the Treaty, which state that British subjects are permitted to buy ground and build chapels in the interior.'[10] Taylor talked the talk of treaty, and had properly registered his intentions and his property with the consul at Zhenjiang, but on the street and at his very gate the retort was talk of 'Jesus venom', and of driving out the missionaries who were 'eating the brains and marrows of infants'. Pamphlets were being circulated and pasted on Yangzhou walls, and meetings were alleged to have been held, with the gentry swearing to eject the missionaries from the city. Taylor had stood his ground as a British subject with treaty rights, and the consular machinery moved to protect him. All the party survived the attack, although it was a close-run thing, and the local authorities were not swift to offer protection or quiet the mob. Things having blown over, their prime concern was to get the missionaries out of the city as soon as it was safe to do so, and to get them to state their formal claim for redress. This Taylor did, not omitting to express the hope that 'your Excellency will quickly take these prisoners and beat them, and make them wear the *cangue* before our house, as a warning to the multitude'. The Zhenjiang consul was on the spot quickly, meeting the party as they retreated under Chinese guard to the treaty port. Three weeks later Consul Medhurst from Shanghai was marching through the city with ninety men from HMS *Rinaldo*, berating the prefect, inspecting the damaged property and issuing demands – for reparations, repairs, release of Chinese associates of the mission from jail; a proclamation to be issued stating that the guilty would be punished, that British subjects could live at Yangzhou by treaty right, and those trying to prevent this would also be punished. And for good measure he demanded that the proclamation be also inscribed on a stone tablet to be erected at the mission property, and later drafted a text for this himself. One thing led to another and soon a much larger British force arrived in Nanjing, to encourage active negotiation of a settlement. On 15 November 300 men arrived at Yangzhou's Xuning gate, having marched overnight to meet two gunboats that had carried Medhurst, Taylor and other members of his party up the shallow Grand Canal. All was settled: local officials were dismissed, the property returned, and the proclamation issued. Taylor proved unhelpfully vague about some of his earlier charges, not least when it came to identifying gentry ringleaders, but perhaps this was diplomatic on his part. The force found the city, Medhurst reported, in a 'wretched condition', half-ruined, still broken – the legacy of the Taiping, the Christian Taiping, he did not add.

All of this was in its way very proper, noted the British Foreign Secretary, but it was also a most dangerous overreaction. The Zongli Yamen should have been the point to press for reparation and for pressure to have been applied locally. This was the system that Bruce and Alcock, the *yamen*, and the other diplomats, had all been endeavouring to get to work smoothly for the last eight years. And here, instead, the Shanghai consul himself had gone fulminating up the Yangzi to the very site of the riot, even though the missionaries were safe back in Zhenjiang; he had called for one gunboat and then returned again with an entire fleet. What disasters might have befallen them, and might have befallen British relations with China, as thousands gathered at Yangzhou to watch them arrive? This, we might think, was the precipitate haste of a Parkes, of a consular provocateur. The second big problem was that there was no sound treaty right of missionary residence in the interior. What right there was, relating to French missions, was founded on the Chinese text of the French Peking Convention of 1860. Most-favoured-nation clauses would extend that to British missionaries, certainly, but there was no equivalent clause in the French text of the Convention, and the Chinese clause was actually there by sleight of (probably) missionary hand, for missionaries had interpreted for the French, and looked closely to their own interests.[11] And the French text was actually the definitive one, so the treaty right was far from solid – far too weak a claim for gunboats to enforce. British public opinion was no less concerned at the handling of the episode. It was a quarrel, editorialized *The Times*, 'as disgraceful as it may prove costly'. It was shaming that British might, which could extract anything it wanted from China, was being used in this way. The dangers were multiple if British officials took the chastisement of local officials into their own hands: the Zongli Yamen would stop bothering to do so itself, British subjects would get too readily in the habit of calling for a little display of steam from the gunboats; and how could any of this endear Chinese communities and Chinese officials to the foreigners? 'The fact is,' said the former First Lord of the Admiralty, now the Duke of Somerset, 'we are propagating Christianity with gunboats.' What right do we have, he thundered in the House of Lords, 'to send missionaries to the interior of China', and who were these people? They are 'always provoking men of the world', claimed *The Times*, they are 'commonplace persons, not very well-educated, not quite gentlemen'. They are 'imprudent ... wrong-headed'; they have 'gone out with not much learning and still less knowledge of mankind'. Somerset had his critics in the House. Did missionaries forego their citizenship and treaty rights with their calling? Were British guns only to protect opium traders and grog dealers, and not men driven by the highest of motives, by the most fundamental of Christian imperatives?[12] The directors of the London Missionary Society asked the Foreign Secretary, the Earl of Clarendon, for clarification. We do not wish to embarrass you: where precisely might we reside? Be circumspect, was the response, do not live beyond consular reach. You will 'do well to follow in the wake of trade', for otherwise you run the risk of paralysing it.[13]

The missionaries were furious; furious: with Somerset, who blamed the LMS above all, furious with Alcock, and furious with Clarendon. Here they were, wrote Edkins, with their hospitals and their books building up immense credit for the foreign enterprise more widely. And yet they were to withdraw from the interior to save British trade.[14] They were not like the Catholics, who they routinely thought, like the British diplomats, acted insensitively and provocatively. And they were growing: there were eighty-six Protestant men and women in the field in July 1855, and 204 in June 1866. There were stations that month in all the open ports, as well as at Peking, the most recently (the year previously) established at Dagou (Takao) in Taiwan, and Jiujiang. They were British, American, German, Swiss and from all denominations: Methodists, Baptists, Anglicans, Presbyterians, Congregationalists.[15] Many had died – some violently, most through disease, some of old age. The toll on the lives of their families was also high, with wives and infants joining them in the improvised cemeteries of their small outposts. But the living were still not ready to give up their work, to kowtow to Sir Rutherford Alcock because he found them an inconvenience. Nor were they ready to bow to the London Missionary Society's directors, who at one point instructed their members to withdraw from the inland stations. The British Protestant missions took this dispute public, firing off at Alcock in July 1869 a lengthy defence of the mission enterprise, and rebuttal of the various charges they found laid against them. They had a perfect treaty right to reside in the interior. They did not ask for gunboats or force, but support, and they would through their influence bring greater amity between the Chinese and the European nations. Had they not published 100 works of learned translations into Chinese? Did they not 'know the language, mix with the people, and throw their influence all on the side of morality, peace, and good-will'? Were they not respectable and educated – gentlemanly – members of the treaty port world, which relied on them for its dictionaries, textbooks and the body of learning in the *Chinese Repository*? They had been no more enthusiastic for the Taiping than anybody in 1853. Yes, Christianity was revolutionary, and would unsettle society. But in fact it was 'the Anglo-Saxon' who was the real revolutionary, not the Anglo-Saxon missionary. The fact was they were opposed by the Chinese because they were foreign, not because they were missionaries. Taylor and his party were opposed because they were foreign. And how could that be otherwise, they argued, for what was this trade they were inconveniencing but the opium trade; what did Alcock represent at Peking, lodged in his Legation there 'at the point of the bayonet', but a vast, foreign – worse, vast British – opium combine. The Chinese 'look on missionaries as representatives of all foreigners, and all foreigners they believe to be encroachers on the rights of others, seekers after money and territory, or opium sellers'. They aimed to sting, but they got short shrift from Alcock. He was no anti-clericalist, indeed far from it. But he thought history entirely on his side, barring some 'miraculous intervention' in their favour. The chances of success were small, the pace of change would be minute, and meanwhile British commerce, and all 'the material elements of civilization which follow in its train' were too important to risk on Yangzhou questions: trade was the motor of change in China, not God. He would not risk war for missionary dreams and pretensions, to allow them to 'take possession' of any part of China 'in the name of Christ'.[16]

For all that they proposed a missionary alternative, it was the treaties – their treaty position, and their treaty rights as foreigners – that now drove them. Taylor thanked Alcock for 'the measures your Excellency has taken, which have so successfully issued in our reinstatement in Yangchow', for the indemnity and proclamations. This would 'facilitate . . . Christian missions generally throughout the interior of China', and, he promised, you will see 'great and permanent advantage accrue to British interests from the important and decisive action taken'.[17] But for all his caution and dismay, Alcock had been trapped by the Yangzhou episode, and by the precipitate actions of the man on the spot, Medhurst. It would be difficult to tread a fine line between non-interference and reacting when British subjects were in danger, accosted or attacked. This was not so unexpected, for missionaries had been putting themselves in the way of trouble since they first disembarked in open China, and well before China was opened. It was not as unexpected as the wider change in the missionary weather that followed, the new bellicosity of the China-based spokesmen for the Church Missionary Society (CMS) and the LMS. Where they had before been relatively discreet, now they entered the political fray. The Tianjin massacre was to prove a political gift. Before 1869–70, on the whole, the warmongers and hardliners had been the men of commerce, all free trade and Armstrong guns, pestering the consuls and diplomats, expecting good things of Osborn's fleet, unrolling their maps before ministers, and pointing to where they knew the expeditions could best effect entry. But in the later 1860s the missionaries had grown more vocal, and unhappy. They combined with commercial interests to lobby against what they saw as the inadequacies of Alcock's treaty revision priorities, and lobbied for wider residency rights. They were under attack on the ground in China, placarded against in Shanghai, Canton, Yangzhou, Taiwan; attacked by the British diplomatic establishment in China and in London; and slandered as they saw it in the House of Lords. These calumnies were swiftly spread globally via *The Times* and other newspapers. Others in China had joined in, castigating them in the treaty port press. But after Tianjin, the forward party amongst the foreign merchant community could but sit back and watch with bemused satisfaction, as the call for muscular intervention was taken up from a wholly unexpected quarter. The Tianjin massacre enraged the Protestant missions. It was not that their own chapels in Tianjin had been wrecked, which they had been in the general mêlée, but that this seemed the culmination of a murderous two-year campaign against all missions across China. We are anxious to know who the next British Minister will be, reported Joseph Edkins in a letter to the LMS Secretary in London in August 1870: 'everyone hopes it will be Sir Harry Parkes'.[18] Edkins did not hope for peace in China: he wanted a man of war.

War seemed possible, even probable in the wake of the massacre at Tianjin. 'The Yamen had *better not give the French an opening!*' Hart had written over a year earlier, after a French priest and forty converts had been killed in Yuyang, Sichuan, and a Chinese priest had led an even more bloody revenge attack. What was soon to distinguish Catholic missions and communities from Protestant ones was their preparedness to arm and stoutly to defend themselves.[19] After weeks of diplomatic discussion and the establishment of a common diplomatic front, the French chargé d'affaires took everyone aback by demanding the execution of the Daotai and the Zhixian, and threatening war. The death of the consular staff, and the murder of the religious: what, thought Robert Hart, 'more hideously successful combination' of insults could be devised for the French.[20] A general rising against the foreigner seemed threatened, and a panic swept the China coast communities. At Shanghai the Council reformed the late-disbanded Shanghai Volunteer Corps, ordered 500 rifles and two howitzers, secured a drill sergeant from the British garrison at Hong Kong, and kitted out its 400 part-time merchant soldiers with Tyrolean caps. Practice-range negligence added two unlucky Chinese casualties to 1870's victims.[21] Alcock had left China at the end of 1869, and Thomas Wade was now in charge. His former chief had outraged the missionaries; Wade now outraged everybody else. This was not, he cautioned, simply a murderous outbreak of xenophobia. He wrote as a scholar. There were firmly rooted grounds in Chinese society, and in Chinese medicine, for the types of charge levelled at the Sisters in Tianjin. They were not outlandish in Chinese eyes: they must be taken seriously as grounds for fear. The Chinese materia medica certainly included preparations involving human ingredients – such as skin, bones, flesh, hair, nails, blood, tears, bile and more – and popular practices added to this. So there was no logical reason why foreign medicine should not also be thought to use such materials.[22] (People elsewhere were to represent missionaries in similar ways, as vampires and kidnapping flesh-eaters.)[23] And kidnapping happened, as it could anywhere; and people believed in the bewitching power of potions and powders. The Sisters had not helped themselves by such common but still ambiguous practices as paying parents who surrendered children to them. Merchant John Meadows, who doubled as American consul in the city, adopted a similar pro-Chinese line. Yes, there had also been failures by the local officials, but the wider context was mission and its potential for disruption. To the missionaries, such caution seemed craven. The reports of Fontanier's mad violence at the *yamen* were widely disbelieved. Scholarly discourses on Chinese materia medica were deemed out of place. Meadows and Wade were lambasted in treaty port press and pamphlet; and Hart too, who had supported Burlingame's mad rolling circus: the light from the fires of Tianjin had exposed them all clearly as frauds and traitors.[24] Missionary and merchant alike charged that Chinese actions were simple xenophobia, at best not suppressed by officials, at worst actively sponsored by them to drive back the foreign presence. This was part of a wider plan, indeed a national plan. They proffered proofs. American missionaries in Shandong rushed to press in August a partial translation of a version of the *Bixie zhishi* as *Death Blow to Corrupt Doctrines*, a text 'secretly used', they claimed, 'as a powerful engine against us'; a 'true insight into the Chinese mind', 'directed against foreigners generally', for it proved that 'Religion is the point of attack'.[25] Did they not see a near-simultaneous outbreak of attacks on missions and disputes with missions across the country? Was this not proof of conspiracy? Only 'the Gracious care of God', claimed Jonathan Lees of the LMS and William Hall of the CMS in Tianjin, 'has prevented Tien-tsin from becoming a second Cawnpore'.[26]

The problem of Christianity, its impact and responses to it, was a complex one. It was not a simple question of 'Cawnpore', of dark fantasies of betrayal and slaughter, and violent heathen reaction. Christianity meant to disturb, and it did; but in China, as elsewhere, it had a life of its own beyond missionary intention and beyond effective missionary control, a life that magnified its impact and potential for trouble.[27] Above all, Christianity took root in Chinese villages, rather than in the towns and cities. The Yangzhou and Tianjin problems, while they demanded attention, were not to be the most intractable or far-echoing of conflicts. Setting aside the fact that missionaries were not Chinese, and came in under treaty, and so were obviously part of the new dispensation forced onto China, why was this so inflammatory? Why did missions find themselves 'the point of attack', a great political question of the day in Sino-foreign relations? Although it is not easy to precisely distinguish, it helps to understand what becoming and being a Christian meant both for personal relations, and for social relations in Chinese societies, for that will start to show how disturbing missionary activity was. Primarily, it recognized and respected no accepted conventions. It challenged the family. It challenged the community. As we saw earlier, missions followed their first stray converts home, working through family and wider kin networks, sometimes following these back from the overseas Chinese communities, from Batavia, Singapore or Bangkok. This sometimes led to situations where only a few members of a family would show interest and convert. Conversion required rejection of practices deemed 'pagan': of concubinage, due reverence for ancestors (considered 'ancestor worship' by missionaries) – and so it seemed of the filial respect on which was constructed the entire structure of Chinese society and culture. The Reverend Matthew Yates was not out of the mainstream when he declared in the *Chinese Recorder* in 1868 that 'ancestral worship' lay at the root of many of China's 'social and political evils'; that the Chinese were 'chained to the tombs'.[28] The usurpation of the Chinese soil by tombs was long a fixed image in foreign minds and reporting. Those chains needed breaking, and converts needed to withdraw from and reject heathen customs – from community opera, to the payment of temple dues. And as the family was the economic unit this rejection could lead to family fracture, property disputes, charges that missionaries were stealing people from their parents, husbands, wives, children, and their kinship responsibilities and duties. 'Westerners,' observed a hostile Chinese critic from London a few years later, 'do not understand what it means to have parents'.[29]

But why did people convert? What sense could they make of this alien cosmology haltingly interpreted into terms still often freshly coined, or loaded with existing meanings, delivered by men and women often not yet fluent in the use of Chinese languages, or through their Chinese workers, themselves not yet perhaps fully fluent in Christianity? Church rituals and practices seemed ill-adapted for Chinese society: their congregations, for example, mingled the sexes in a society where women were not seen in public. The topsy-turvy status of women in Christian activity was a point routinely highlighted by anti-Christian polemics, but it was an obvious point of contrast for any observer. Certainly there were those who converted for purely religious reasons. For many Christianity was a body of doctrine that seemed perfectly compatible with significant elements in Chinese thought and culture; it was nowhere near as alien to some as the raucous world of temple life and popular religion. And conversion could, like Hong Xiuquan's, take place far beyond the reach of the foreigner, for Christian books and tracts had lives of their own in Chinese society, even if some thought they might end up as wrapping paper in shops – all those tracts peddled by Gützlaff merely 'seed sown by the wayside'.[30] Moreover, conversion could take place through Chinese members of missions. The foreign missionary was hardly the sole agent of change.

For many we also know that conversion was a logical survival strategy in troubled times and troubled places. A family group might see virtue in conversion. It could bring enhanced status locally, and the ability to call on external influence to intervene in pre-existing resource disputes, for missionaries directly or indirectly protected their converts. This strategy could be reactive: it might seem the only route to success in an ongoing conflict or it might be known that it had worked for others nearby. It might be proactive, acting as insurance against future problems. Conversion could offer employment, income – rent from a room given over as a chapel, a moiety for a caretaker, a salary for a colporteur – a free education or free medicine. The extraordinary social mobility of groups of Protestant converts is well documented.[31] Missions needed trained staff, and English or French were key tools. Mission education in English particularly proved a great boon. Its graduates entered the Maritime Customs, for example, and treaty port commerce, where bilinguality was vital.

But far from the more sophisticated urban world of opportunity, Christianity could still destabilize villages. A marginal group could find itself greatly enhanced in status. A marginal man could suddenly become a community leader, upsetting an existing power structure and social relations, and displeasing local officials, gentry and power-holders. So a village might find a new grouping starting to operate. The Christians would refuse to pay temple or opera dues, damaging the fabric of local society, imperilling the common good, and insulting the gods. What had been communal enterprises were now recast as voluntary ones from which converts withdrew.[32] Chinese preachers were certainly heard to argue that it 'is cheaper to be a Christian than a heathen', a savvy appeal to the universal bottom line.[33] Christians might open a chapel, which could cause property disputes, for some of an extended kin network who owned the site were bound to object. Or they might seek to use communal property. Converts could cry religious persecution at every point they were thwarted in land, water or customary dispute, and missionaries, though they found they had to get wise to the real roots of dispute, would often as not be used to press points home legally. Sometimes missionaries were simply very happy to demonstrate their power this way, for it could help cement conversion. The 'restoration' of historic Catholic properties after 1860 under the French Peking Convention was also problematic, as many of the properties 'returned' to Catholic ownership had long had new functions, often religious or official ones. But the problem was far wider, as local groups and individuals found a new force in the land. It unsettled Chinese society and reached out far beyond the open ports into families and villages far from bunds, consulates and legations.

The missionary was no innocent in all of this, neither as agent or catalyst of change, nor very often as active intervener in local affairs. For if conversion enabled Chinese to assert new power, most foreign priests and missionaries were emboldened by the new dispensation after 1860. They were themselves possessed of treaty rights, and could at least call on the support of the consuls, and like Taylor, were not backward in communicating directly with local authority and stating their case and status. But they also often used their status directly or indirectly in dealings with local authorities on behalf of converts. The shadow of the consul and the gunboat followed them into magistrates' *yamens* and discussions with village power-holders, and was with them as they made cases for action or pleas for decisions. Always they might bring more power to bear; always a local administrator would have to balance the competing implications of any decision. It was never in his interest to allow a case to be escalated upwards, by missionary to consul, by consul to legation, from legation to Zongli Yamen, and then down again to him. That would draw too much attention to him, and was unlikely to bring a happy ending. But he was also responsible for maintaining local order, and had to keep the community or the powerful within it on his side: a wrong decision might lead to dissent, clamour – even to violence, and that complicated everything. Many missionaries played at the local level the China game of compensation for injury and damage, property restitution and repair, and symbolic gesture – judgement and proclamation set in stone, or transfer of communally important sites as punishment. They played Parkes. Some did so to show how powerful Church and mission were, how actively they could help; to reassure and protect existing converts, and to tempt others. Such action could also provide a stage for the rehearsal of the national honour script, the dignity of the nation residing in the person of the missionary and in his flock. Missionary men and women were also only human. They were Europeans and Americans in a different land, and their reactions to China and the Chinese covered much the same range as their secular fellow nationals. Tipperary-born Alice O'Sullivan, killed at Tianjin, was not alone in finding China and the Chinese utterly repugnant.[34] Individual missionary behaviour could be affected as much by such inability to sympathize, as by any more routinely assumed greater empathy and understanding.

Always there were exceptions, men and women horrified by this new world of local conflict and dispute that could unfold as people converted. But the mission enterprise was nonetheless mired from the start in such local dispute, at the same time as it was enmeshed with the wider foreign world in China through nationality, affinity, language, marriage, and wider kin networks. Taylor and his adepts might reject the overt foreignness of that world, and offend its mores by foreswearing Western clothing and headwear for Chinese, but they levered their way into Yangzhou through the consuls and treaties. And 'the warmest thanks of all who wish to see the relations of foreigners and Chinese established on a proper basis' were due to Consul Medhurst, announced even the *Chinese Recorder*, for 'never has a case been more promptly or successfully treated'.[35] The alacrity with which some accepted, encouraged or demanded such support from their consuls; the trickiness of many converts; the dull inevitability of dispute and conflict wherever convert communities were to be found, tarnished mission and convert reputations in the eyes of many Chinese officials (and not a few foreign ones). And they also seemed to fall into the category of Chinese 'traitors', like those Cantonese who had allied themselves with the enemy in wartime and acted under his shadow, with his connivance, in the postwar years. They acquired a vulgar type of extraterritoriality, a semi-extraterritorial status, for their relationship with the law was now always inflected by access to foreign power and influence: to the missionary who could call on the Zongli Yamen, the bishop, the consul, or the minister. The growing reputation of converts as ambiguously situated or low-status outsiders – scallywags at best, proto-rebels at worst – could not easily be countered, however much the evidence showed that men and women from all walks of life were among the converts, and that many could hardly be thought to be enemies of their communities. This slowly developed as a fixed image, pregnant with hideous danger. Converts ceased to be wholly Chinese, were set apart in official minds and in the eyes of their communities, just as they set themselves apart to become Christians.

War over a crusade against converts and missionaries was averted through France's battering by Prussia in Europe in 1870–71. French prestige was shaken by defeat at the battle of Sedan, and by the collapse of the Bonapartist state, and compromise was reached: reparations, heads of rioters (though not of officials) rolling in the Tianjin streets, the despatch of a mission of apology to Europe. Poor Chong Hou found himself ordered overseas to apologize in person in Paris, as if he had fired at Fontanier, and not the other way around. Two French employees of the Customs accompanied him. A bellicose war party emerged at the Qing court, furious at the French minister's demands, and talk of war persisted for months. Concern over the resolution of the case prompted a rebalancing of interests within the bureaucracy that allowed greater weight for wider discussion of foreign affairs.[36] One practical result was a significant impairing of the Zongli Yamen's ability to act swiftly. Another was that Li Hongzhang replaced Chong Hou as Commissioner for the Northern Ports, and for the next quarter-century Li worked from his base at Tianjin, establishing a powerful and internationally prominent role in China's foreign relations. Meanwhile, Chong Hou, travelling west through the Suez Canal (opened a year earlier), found the French government too preoccupied with the aftermath of the war to focus on Chinese issues when he arrived. He was eventually able to meet the president of the embattled new republic, who was keen to talk peace and accept his apology, not wanting a China problem when he had a shattered and divided country to rebuild. But China's inland problems were growing yet. The missionary establishment snuck further out from its bases, to outstations that became stations, establishing chapels that became churches, moving into Yangzhou, Hangzhou, Sichuan, Guizhou. Inland dreams moved others too, and the practical resources of a growing Church network, Catholic and Protestant, aided their attempts at realization. Christians accompanied explorers as interpreters and guides, and mission stations provided hospitality for secular travellers. It was impossible to disentangle missions from the increasing pattern of incursions into China outside the treaty ports.

The Tianjin massacre terminated any final hopes that Alcock's long-heralded treaty revision proposals, or Burlingame's long-winded sino-phile platitudes, could placate the intransigent interests in the treaty ports and overseas that demanded wider access and rights of residence. Alcock had secured a 'Convention' in 1869 that now bears his name, an agreement on a number of measures reforming the 1858–60 treaties, but this was then rejected in Britain after commercial and mission interests lobbied against it.[37] It actually entrenched many British privileges which were quite at variance with trading conditions in any other independent state, and so in principle might have been expected to please the aggressive men of commerce, but it codified these and it did not extend them. And its opponents often preferred the opportunities of the undefined, or underdefined world, while others also hated the very fact of implicit equality in the negotiations. They did not want China treated as a negotiating equal. They did not believe in it, and thought it treason to act as if China was 'civilized'. The minister's greatest triumph actually lay in the manner of the convention's making, for it was not the product of war. Its making seemed to signal the establishment in China of the 'normal' diplomatic round of discussion, of hard bargaining and tough negotiation. Its rejection was hardly likely to aid the Zongli Yamen progressives. They had also assumed that its signing in Peking was the making of the agreement, so its failure in London was a puzzle. So what, they might be asked by their opponents, was the point of all that palaver, all those interminable sessions with Alcock and Hart? Foreigners talk of the need for standard diplomatic practice, but when it does not get them what they want they reject it. They do not want to talk; they want to win.

Clearly they did want to win. They wanted possession. Merchant and missionary wanted wider, protected access and the stamp of legitimacy on their informal occupation. But encroachment took other forms, and was becoming intertwined with the Great Game imperialism of Anglo-Russian rivalries, the unfolding search for international status by Japan, and the growth of French empire in southeast Asia. The empire of the Qing was assaulted on all sides, as well as from within. There was Russian pressure in the northwest, with the 'Yili crisis' of 1871–81, whereby Muslim rebellion in Xinjiang provided a pretext for Russian occupation of a strategically important area, the Yili valley, and Anglo-Russian competition for influence with the rebel kingdom of Ya'qūb Beg in Kashgar.[38] French influence in Indo-China coalesced in a protectorate of Cochin China (around Saigon), established in 1862. There too, French force had been wielded in support of Catholic missions and converts in a four-year campaign. By 1874 France had moved north, effectively turning Annam too into a protectorate, and was asserting various privileges in Tonkin, while Qing sovereignty in Taiwan (also known as Formosa) and the tutelary status of the Ryukyu islands (Okinawa) was challenged by Japan. Even Chosŏn Korea, tied most closely to the suzerainty of the Qing, was threatened by newly assertive Meiji Japan.[39] The repertoire of relations between the Qing and these various infringed territories and their rulers had always been wide-ranging and complex. But the changing order in east Asia impinged at every turn on the established place of the Qing, and its view of the world. On its borders, and then at home, foreign power was endeavouring changes to the place of the Qing and its reach.

Perhaps the most compelling evidence of the perverted order of things from the point of view of the Qing, was the role of Japan. When the European and American diplomats in Peking had finally pressed their demands for an audience on the coming of age of the young emperor in 1873, their fleeting sense of triumph had been undermined. They were convinced, with very good reason, that a sleight of hand had masked the diplomatic audience in tributary trappings, for amongst other small but deliberate points, it had been held in a building outside the palace precincts which was customarily used to receive tribute missions.[40] But oddest of all was the fact that the foreign envoy who had preceded the assembled diplomats into the audience on 29 June 1873 was the Japanese Foreign Minister, Soejima Taneoni, who had come as Ambassador especially to participate in the ceremony, and whose status made him the most senior of the envoys present. Although initially this pre-eminence had been opposed by the other ministers in Peking, who also resented the intrusion of a non-Westerner into their midst, Soejima adeptly used accepted international practice to assert

his place, and he had actually learnt this from Tongwenguan translations into Chinese. He was received first, and alone, dressed in formal
Western-style diplomatic uniform, itself symbolic of the new Japan
moving into the east Asian international arena. Soejima had been
escorted to China by two Japanese-crewed vessels of the Japanese navy,
and although an American former diplomat was also accredited to the
mission, this was Soejima's show, for he was adept in the Chinese
cultural forms required, as well as in the new foreign diplomatic
protocols and assumptions. The Meiji restoration of 1868 marked the
start of a process of accelerated and deliberate Westernization of
significant sectors of Japanese society, economy and culture, and the
reorganization of government, the military and education. As Soejima
sailed, half of the senior members of the Japanese government were
on a global tour of inquiry, the 'Iwakura Mission' to Europe and the
United States, sent to seek out information about how these societies
worked and were governed, and to place on display Japan's commitment to change.[41] This intense spasm of reform also led to a new and
assertive foreign policy, a deliberate recasting of existing relations with
the Qing, and a slowly coalescing forward policy towards Korea and
Taiwan. Soejima had not come to Peking merely to secure his diplomatic
coup, but to start a conversation about Qing assumptions underpinning
relations with Korea and the Ryukyus, and the nature and extent of
its sovereignty in Taiwan. The killing of fifty-four shipwrecked Ryukyun
sailors by Paiwan aboriginal people on Taiwan's southeastern coast in
1872 provided an opportunity for Japan to assert its sovereignty over
Ryukyu, by pressing claims for reparation and punishment in the
European manner with the Qing, and to test out Qing preparedness
to assert its control over all of Taiwan and its peoples. Soejima, in his
eyes, secured statements from the Zongli Yamen that the aboriginal
population of Taiwan was not wholly under Qing control, and this
underpinned Japan's dispatch in 1874 of a mission to 'punish' people
in the area of the incident, and, more covertly, to establish a colonial
bridgehead.

Here at the heart of the Qing empire on 23 June was made plain the
ambition of this new Japan, once the tributary state, to be a formal
equal. And as Soejima's interlocutors at the Zongli Yamen, and Li
Hongzhang in Tianjin, all pointedly remarked, he did so in his Western

clothing, seemingly divested of his own culture.[42] The ambassador gently pointed out how even the clothes were useful; how his navy escort was entirely Japanese-crewed; and in short he turned teacher on his cultural mentors. But more than simple equality in international diplomatic terms, Soejima and many in Meiji Japan wanted their slice of the Chinese pie. Only eleven years earlier, the first modern official mission to China had set out from Nagasaki for Shanghai, on board a formerly British owned (and still British-crewed) steamer, renamed the *Senzaimaru*.[43] By the end of the decade a community of Japanese traders, painters and courtesans was growing there. In 1870 Shinagawa Tadamichi opened a proto-consulate in the International Settlement, and enquired at the Municipal Council offices if Japanese residents, of samurai status, might be permitted to wear swords in public.[44] At Japan's initiative a commercial treaty was signed in 1871, a concession made in part so as not to antagonize a near neighbour. But as 3,000 troops and labourers disembarked at Langqiao Bay in May 1874, a more routine script was being rehearsed. Taiwan's coasts had long offered a hostile reception to broken foreign ships. Dent and Co.'s freelance assault on Yamtaya in 1860, or foreign naval reprisals by British or Prussian ships, and most recently by US vessels in 1867 following the *Rover* shipwreck, were not unusual. Landing over 3,000 troops with Gatling guns was a different order of punishment expedition, and was more akin in scale to the early stages of the *Arrow* war, although it was on a literal periphery: Taiwan's southeast coast. While Japanese troops raided local villages in four weeks of fighting, and died in scores from disease, Japanese diplomats lobbied hard for a settlement, Chinese forces were mobilized for war, and Chinese civilians fled Taiwan and Xiamen ahead of the expected conflict. And it was, declared the Shanghai correspondent of *The Times*, 'one thing to let the Japanese into Formosa; it is quite another to get them out'. Many of those directly involved were not averse to a longer-term occupation of what was described as 'unclaimed' territory and people. The expedition was ready for this, and its base by early 1875 was almost a semi-settlement with shops, making a 'pleasant village'.[45] Freelance and well-paid foreign advisors, notably the former US Xiamen Consul General Charles LeGendre, encouraged the putative Taiwan grab, and American nationals accompanied the expedition until ordered away by their diplomats on pain of arrest. A British surgeon with the

Maritime Customs in Xiamen, Patrick Manson, was contracted to accompany it, arranging for the purchase at that port of boats, cattle and
horses, but then British diplomats too forbade their nationals from any
involvement.[46] The venture forced the Qing to rethink its administrative
practices in Taiwan, which was governed from the mainland as part of
Fujian province, and to more deliberately and ostentatiously incorporate
Taiwan into its mainstream systems. Moreover, as the crisis unfolded
approval was hastily given for the first time for the laying of a telegraph
cable and a line to link Taiwan's capital with Fuzhou.[47] The Japanese
withdrew by the end of the year, leaving a landscape littered with broken
beer bottles, still a menace fifteen years later.[48] In the aftermath new
roads were built, garrisons established, and surveys undertaken. The
Qing needed to look to its borders.

British mediation at Peking played a role in the negotiation of a
settlement, but at the same time not dissimilar British interests were
themselves being actively advanced.[49] The British threat now came
from the west and southwest, from India and its dependency in Burma.
As the British fleet assembled at the entrance to the Yangzi in November
1868, to send Consul Medhurst's second expedition up the Grand
Canal to turbulent Yangzhou, it was passed by a steamer coming down
from Hankou carrying T. T. Cooper, a self-styled 'pioneer of commerce'
who was on his way back from the Burmese border, and professed
himself bemused at the sight that met his eyes after months of tramping
overland.[50] Cooper had just been thwarted in an attempt to trek
overland from China to India, to open a direct trade route to Calcutta
for foreign commerce, the latest of a growing number of such exploratory forays. An otherwise undistinguished solicitor's clerk in
Shanghai, having arrived in 1863 at the height of the Shanghai gold
rush, he had in late 1867 secured support from members of the
Chamber of Commerce for a journey to the west. Equipped with a
copy of Blakiston's account of the 1861 Yangzi mission, and accompanied by two Hankou men – a Catholic interpreter, who had trained
for the priesthood in Macao but instead turned to trade, and who spoke
English, French and Latin, and a guide whose usual role was accompanying novice priests to their new posts – Cooper donned Chinese
clothing, had his head shaved, and set out in January 1868.[51] 'Good
Cavendish tobacco' and a small dog also accompanied him west

towards Tibet. But even this was hardly territory untraversed by foreigners, foreign ideas, or foreign things. Cooper stayed with missionary priests (a glass or two of port from a Chinese father trained in Rome was very welcome), met many converts, and visited missions and churches. Foreign piece goods preceded him to Chongqing, where 'cheap foreign watches and American clocks' filled shop windows; a Chinese print of a foreign steamer at Hankou greeted him on the road to Chengdu; a print of Don Quixote at a house on the Tibetan borders. At Bathang he sold his photographs of friends from Shanghai as there was great demand for them: the best-looking woman secured him 'three fowls and a bundle of hay'.[52]

Cooper's was a private enterprise adventure, viewed sarcastically by many in Shanghai, who were satisfied enough with their trade and their rents. Others had grander imperial visions, and from India official efforts were also being directed, not least because of the French prowling around from Indo-China. Francis Garnier's Mekong expedition of 1866–8 prompted official British perturbation, even though it concluded that there was no viable river route to Yunnan. So Burma was thought the key to the western road, and a route up the Irrawaddy river to Bhamo and then into Yunnan province was the way most closely surveyed and explored. There were well-established trading corridors in the region. The issue was how to refashion at least one of these for European purposes.[53] As Cooper was himself diverted from his westward foray south onto a route towards Bhamo in Burma, an official party led by Colonel Edward Sladen arrived there, and went on to Tengyue at the Chinese border. Both the British expedition and the pioneer of commerce encountered difficulties caused by rebellion in Yunnan, the self-styled Pingnan Kingdom ('Panthay' to the British), which grew out of local state violence against Hui (Chinese Muslim) communities in the province in 1856. Cooper survived imprisonment as a spy before heading back northeast to Hankou, and sailed out of Shanghai in January 1869, with free passage courtesy of the American firm Augustine Heard, to try again from Assam – Shanghai sarcasm having turned into real interest. He was again defeated, but his accounts of these forays were written up in populist Robert Fortune mode and gained a wide readership, stirring up further interest in the overland route and Upper Yangzi opportunity. Cooper had called on Wade before he voyaged. The Legation dispatched consul Robert Swinhoe in 1869 on an official foray west with two navy surveyors to explore the potential for trade and steam navigation should Alcock's convention bear fruit. As usual, Alexander Michie accompanied the party on behalf of the Shanghai Chamber of Commerce; Jardine's donated the services of a steamer.[54] Local Chinese officials' suspicion of these ventures dogged all of them. Who they were, and what they were doing heading towards rebel territory (where it was rumoured that foreign technicians were helping the rebels cast guns): these were both vexed issues. British parleys with the Panthay would hardly have helped if they were known about, for an unofficial embassy from the kingdom to Britain was even received in London in 1872 (Cooper accompanied it back to Calcutta, living rather better on Foreign Office funds than he had on his highland treks). The situation on the ground, far from the cosy map tables of London, Calcutta and Peking, and far from the meeting rooms of the learned societies, was complex and dangerous for dreaming explorers scouting out the so-called 'great highway to China' from Burma.[55]

Appetite was whetted nonetheless, and with Qing suppression of the Panthay rebellion in 1873, British exploration resumed. From the Indian government's point of view it offered a secure route to China which was not dependant on sea routes, access to new markets, and a counterweight to growing French power in Indo-China, which could potentially extend to southwest China. Diplomats and other observers fretted over 'influence' and 'interests'. Such scheming was a kind of cartographic sickness, a morbid, obsessive fantasizing over maps even though they were incomplete, and lacked precise detail – needed routes sketching out, data adding, place-names too. The ponderous weighing up of 'our' or 'their' 'influence' and 'interests' and how to effect, protect or demonstrate these, marks the last quarter of the nineteenth century and the beginning of the twentieth much more strongly than had been the case previously. An expedition here, a survey there, a Frenchman holding this post, a Russian mission lodged in that place, Japanese surveyors landing here: these became the moves in the China game. The legation ministers played it at Peking, over the dining table, at the Zongli Yamen over tea and fruit, via informal tête à tête, public note and gesture. Consuls too played it at ports. Newspaper correspondents and private letter writers talked the same game. A new British mission was despatched on the overland route to Bhamo in 1874, led by Colonel Horace Browne, who took a naturalist, a map-maker and an armed Sikh guard. Augustus Margary, that maudlin, singing student interpreter, was sent from Shanghai to meet them at the border, carrying passports to enable them to travel into China. Margary was enjoined to strict secrecy about his mission, and there was obfuscation generally about the expedition, as Wade had not informed the Zongli Yamen about its real government-sponsored nature or purpose, nor therefore was it equipped with precisely appropriate official passports from the Chinese. The mission had been represented as travellers, an informal party, not a formal expedition. There was no mention of soldiers. Margary seemed a good choice, as he had previously served in Taiwan and Yantai, and was thought promising. He worked hard at his Chinese, studying his textbooks with his Chinese Christian teacher-cum-official writer all the way west, when well enough. He had a mostly rotten journey, as he was often sick and needing to be carried. As he sailed up river he met drafts of Chinese troops heading east for the expected war with Japan over Taiwan. In January 1875 he duly arrived at Bhamo from Hankou, the first Briton to make the crossing from China. He had joked to his parents that they should look at the map and imagine him 'standing alone on the heights . . . on the Burmese frontier . . . anxiously scanning the country beyond for the first glimpse of Indian helmets approaching from the West'. But it was he who had surprised Browne's party. Picture 'China and India', he continued, 'grasping hands', not thinking to add that it would be British China and British India which would intrude into this complex frontier area.[56] China service had shown Margary the world. He had sailed east and back on leave, and had travelled west from Britain and across America on its uncomfortable trains in 1873. He had seen Japan too on the way. At Shanghai Margary had encountered the excitement of a riot in 1874, which erupted over French mishandling of the Ningbo guild property in the concession, had travelled in a newfangled invention, a rickshaw – a 'funny little vehicle, just introduced from Japan', you guided the puller with your stick – and he had waxed lyrical about the gaslit Bund-side public garden, its 'lawns and flower beds . . . kept up to a high state of perfection', the band playing once a week, the community strolling there. His journey in one sense was to end there at the Bund, for they would place his memorial close by the gardens, in hearing distance, a mock-Gothic monument for, as he noted to his parents, a 'massive opportunity of distinguishing myself has just been opened to me', and so indeed his name is remembered in diplomatic history and was cast in stone. For, trekking ahead of Browne's party back into China, he was ambushed, probably by tribesmen, and speared to death on 21 February 1875. The expedition was attacked the same day by a large irregular force, probably of Karen people, and retreated back to Burma. Margery's head was lopped off and displayed by the walls of a nearby town.

'As the years roll on', wrote the editor of Margary's posthumously published journal, England's

special work in the world comes out more and more clearly. In spite of herself – often against her will – she has task after task set her in the wild neglected places of the earth, amongst savage or half-civilised races. . . . The call comes, now from the oldest haunts and homes of men – from India, from China, from Arabia, from the Malay peninsula – now from the wondrous islands of the Pacific – now from the vast unexplored regions of central or southern Africa. . . . whatever the cause or form of the summons it is sure to have *'vestigia nulla retrorsum'* [no steps back] written over it. And the call, however urgent, however exacting, has rarely failed to bring out the right man, whether it were for missionary, or soldier, or merchant, or traveller, ready to spend himself for his country and his country's work; simply, cheerily, unreservedly doing deeds the reading and hearing of which here in England make our pulses bound and our eyes moisten

A new imperialism was coalescing in Britain, and more widely in Europe too. It used much of the older language, images, ideas and facts – the 'facts' that underpinned the need for empire, that helped a calculation of its British human costs: all these we are now familiar with. But it refashioned them into a much more coherent and activist imperialism. Queen Victoria was in 1876 made 'Empress of India' by Prime Minister Disraeli. Possession was refashioned into empire, and into destiny. And the servants of the British state overseas, the 'right' men, became agents of empire. Their deaths in service were imperial martyrdoms, no less martyrdom for being secular than the half-wished-for deaths of Taylor's disciples, or the religious at Tianjin. Margary was but the latest in the roll-call of those moistening English eyes, setting pulses a-racing and fists thumping on tables. As he travelled to Hankou on an American steamer – a 'river palace' he thought it – he reflected on British progress in China, how 'wonderful' it was that the river had been opened by 'our fleet of mighty men of war', and he could 'picture Colonel Gordon' on the heights around Nanjing.[57] Margary called on local officials, demanded they restrain and educate the curious crowds who appeared wherever he went, and stated calmly that when such aid was not close to hand, 'A kick and a few words in his own tongue telling him he is an ignorant boor will make a common China-man worship you.'[58] His death was incorporated into the same empire script that he rehearsed as he travelled, and at Shanghai they acted out their part too, with monument and ceremony. And it also set in motion that nasty old routine, the one that Alcock's convention seemed to have shown foresworn, of diplomatic huffing and puffing, excessive demand and brinkmanship, leading to gainful opportunity. Wade was never more obtuse and hardnosed than in the dispute over this affair. Poor Margary's slaughter presaged another round in China's despoliation, for it was a gift to the British hardliners. But it was also seen as a challenge, for there could be no 'acquiescence in a defeat', in the death of Margary and the failure of the expedition – even for Alcock, now in retirement, however cynical he was about the prospects of this overland trade.[59] There could be no turning back.

The French chargé d'affaire's demand for official Tianjin heads to roll had exasperated his peers in Peking. But the British now held the Yunnan provincial authorities entirely and fully accountable for the killings, and for the attack on Browne's party. Above all, Wade de-manded, in addition to financial reparation, the trial and punishment of the Yunnan governor. 'Nothing else he could ask would be more thoroughly distasteful to the government of China,' lamented Robert Hart, 'and why? Nothing else would force it to step out to the same extent before all China and say that the foreigner is a personage to be respected.' Hart could see this from both sides. 'As an *Englishman*', he wrote, 'I don't think he could devise a better demand, . . . but as I.G. of Customs, I know that China would rather do anything else, and that the Dynasty will go to pot rather than consent to this without war.' Yet again Hart played a crucial mediating role, for he thought war exactly what they might get. Wade was threatening. His counsellor, Mayers, was 'bellicose' and reportedly 'more Parkes-ian than Sir Harry himself'.[60] Exactly who killed Margary or attacked Browne's party was quite irrelevant. Wade in fact had not needed to wait for facts, and his first response on hearing the news was that 'the antecedent history of foreign intercourse with China' was such that it could only be an officially sanctioned outrage. A covert and roundabout directive to local officials and gentry must have gone to Yunnan ordering the repulse of the expedition. But even if it hadn't, the Chinese were 'an accessory after the fact at least, if nothing more'.[61] Regardless, he held the government responsible, and struck for satisfaction: his, and Britain's.

The Chefoo Convention, signed in September 1876 at that port, to which Wade had belligerently withdrawn, with threats of war and of seizing Dalian and Zhenjiang very clearly aired, piggybacked a host of new concessions for British and foreign trade onto a resolution of the Margary affair.[62] Compensation was extracted, a mission of apology instructed to proceed to England, and a British-approved proclamation was issued announcing the conclusion of the affair and instructing provincial officials to protect passport holders. The British gained a right to travel to see that this proclamation was being made public, as demanded. This was by now routine enough, but Margary's headless corpse was then used to extract four new treaty ports (Yichang on the Yangzi, Wuhu, Wenzhou and Beihai (Pakhoi)), revisions to Customs regulations, and a new code of etiquette to structure relations between foreign diplomats and consuls, and Chinese officials. So the usual cry, the need for proper, honour-serving ceremony and recognition was interpolated into the resolution. And all of this came about because the British had invited the inevitable, provoked an incident of some sort, by sending what seemed to local officials and gentry like the spearhead of an invading force: an armed party, surveying, recording, scouting out paths for entry; a party that was inadequately and dis-ingenuously documented and that had gone into frontier territory only recently re-conquered after a twenty-year rebellion. And even though there was British merchant dissatisfaction with the convention – 'we do not want a new treaty: we want the old treaty observed' claimed one,[63] and unanimous hostility to it from the other foreign powers, most of the provisions of the convention were effected and the size of the treaty port system grew, reaching yet further into China's provinces and along its coasts.

If the 'charred relics' of Alice O'Sullivan were deemed to 'consecrate the ungrateful soil of China', China was also yet more fully incorporated this way into notions of Britain's 'special work in the world'.[64] At Shanghai on 13 June 1880, the Settlement and its Bund were more fully integrated into the web of symbols that spoke that 'special work'. A locally designed 37-foot-high memorial was unveiled that day, one that had been carved in London by Farmer and Brindley, pre-eminent ornamental stonemasons, who had worked on the Albert Memorial (to which Margary's was clearly indebted) and the Natural History Museum in London, Manchester Town Hall and Glasgow University. Shanghai's public face was slowly losing its improvised feel as this process of calling on the orthodox, prestigious resources of British empire and the British world grew apace. Sited at the northern end of the Bund, close by the British consulate and the Suzhou creek bridge, Margary's monument was unveiled with due reverent ceremony, Legation secretary in attendance, Cathedral dean opening the proceedings. Bob Little, now chairman of the Council, accepted the privately subscribed memorial on its behalf, Margary's death 'another proof' that – and Tennyson was here brought in, to 'prolonged applause' –

> Not once nor twice, in our rough island story
> The path of duty was the path of glory.

In private, shortly after the death, Little had articulated another common response: 'In such a case, better 50 innocent people suffer, than one guilty escape! The white skin there must be protected by Fear.'[65] That same summer Colonel Gordon himself was back in Shanghai on an abortive mission of advice to the Qing court about its response to the continuing Yili question and the threat of war with Russia.[66] He took time to take offence at the poor condition of Shanghai's older monument, a stubby obelisk commemorating the forty-eight dead foreign officers of the Ever Victorious Army, first situated on the Bund opposite the junction with Peking Road. New gilt was applied.[67] It was not much of a memorial: it resembles 'a better class milestone' thought the North China Herald, and local wags had painted it red one night in 1866, but its meanings and associations – the application of force in Chinese affairs, the sometime necessity of foreign intervention, the developing association with British imperial celebrity in the shape of Gordon, the path of glory – these were far richer than the simple listing of names it carried. The French concession had seen the unveiling in 1870 in the consulate grounds of a statue of Admiral August Protet, who had died in 1862 in an action with the Taiping, and this stood too for all the French forces killed in action in 1855–62. A private British monument to two of the Peking captives lay in the British consulate grounds.[68] The public face of Shanghai was being written over with these monuments to foreign violence and foreign sacrifice, all humming together the insidious, insistent refrain of 'no turning back'.

9

Coastwise

It was beautiful, Kwaliang Bay: clear water eight fathoms deep, a strip of sandy beach fringed with virgin forest teeming with wildlife, and cliffs of white coral limestone. It stretched eight miles from point to point, from the South Cape (Eluanbi) to the South West Point, the far southern extremities of the mountainous island of Taiwan. Beyond the shoreline a single peak rose a thousand feet, north beyond that two peaks climbed, visible sixty miles off on a clear day. But the days were not always clear and the waters hid reefs. Not for nothing was Taiwan *'ilha formosa'*, beautiful island, to the Portuguese, but this stunning beauty was ever-tempered by its deadly reputation. It was a wrecker of ships, and worse; for beyond the Chinese towns and settlements of the western plain, that verdant, mountainous forest hid 'savages', semi-naked 'wild men', who killed off – killed off and, it was widely claimed, consumed – those who staggered ashore from their broken ships. Onto that same brilliant, shining beach, which stood out so strikingly against the darker forest, had struggled the survivors of the wreck of the *Rover* in 1867, to be cut down, their blood smirching the pristine coral sand. Surveying parties were attacked in the 1860s, narrowly escaping to their boats.[1] The initial foreign response was two-fold. First, foreigners sent private or public expeditions to wreak some kind of vengeance on the communities held responsible, dispatching columns that flailed around, led weary dances by the aborigines, and often reduced to firing blind into the dense foliage, for it seemed near-impossible to confront the inhabitants in such awkward, mountainous terrain. Instead, they shot the trees and bombarded the forest. Second, more damagingly, perhaps, they wrote the natives up and off in books, reports and articles as aborigine savages. 'CAUTION', noted the Admiralty's *China Sea*

Directory: 'little or no hope of life can attend the misfortune of ship-wreck' – and it was a shoreline fringed with drift and wreck-wood, for 'the natives of the south end of Formosa are always hostile to strangers', their collecting of skulls 'well authenticated'. And this view of the Austronesian peoples of the island was wholly shared by Qing officials and the Han and Hakka settlers from Fujian who lived on this maritime frontier and whose relations with the native peoples were fraught with friction, conflict and fear.[2]

The international pressures on the Qing now forced it to confront the wildness of Taiwan's coasts as periphery moved centre-stage. After 1876 there were more Chinese ports open by treaty, more bases for traders and missionaries, and more scope for expeditions – the Chefoo Convention, for example, made provision for the entry of a British expedition into Tibet. The Qing found itself forced to revise or remodel its notions of its relations with states that had previously accepted it as overlord, such as the Ryukyus. And it had to attempt to strengthen its frontiers, accelerating processes of conquest and consolidation already long under way, and to demonstrate effective control in these outlying areas and over outlying peoples that were now often at the heart of its relations with Japan, Britain and Russia. What use were precise borders and claims of sovereignty if there was an alleged lack of control on the ground, a vacuum that foreigners could 'identify', and seek to fill, borders that they could redraw in their favour, slicing away the patrimony of the Qing? Translated extracts from textbooks of international law, which stressed the need for control to be substantive and effective, were presented to the Zongli Yamen by the Japanese as justifications for the 1874 venture, challenging Qing practices in Taiwan, and implicitly on all its borders.[3] Driven by this, and by the fact of the Japanese incursion, Governor General Shen Baozhen was instructed to direct a campaign to more systematically extend control over Taiwan's southern and eastern coasts and its peoples, and all the resources of the self-strengthening state were brought to bear on the island so as to leave no room for doubt that it was irrefutably part of the Qing domain even though it had not previously been thought to be of much discernable importance.

One of those involved was a young Welshman, John Reginald Harding, born in Monmouth, who built a lighthouse at South Cape as

one part of this enterprise. Europe came to the beautiful bay, purpose-
fully interrupting the view of the mountains. This was a feat of civil
engineering, but it was also a fortress with a stockade protected by a
new invention, barbed wire, which thereby got, Harding later claimed,
its first ever military use. As the Japanese withdrew from their proto-
settlement, leaving their litter behind, the Maritime Customs was sent
in. In January 1875 the engineer-in-chief of the Customs, David Marr
Henderson, trekked to Eluanbi Point, returning 'with my coat and shirt
torn off my back', but with sketches of the proposed site. His assistant
engineer, Michael Beazley, was part of a party sent in June of that
year to negotiate the purchase of land from the Paiwan aborigines in
the area.[4] The region they passed through was in turmoil, for Shen
Baozhen's forces were fighting to pacify the Paiwan and to bring
them under Qing control. South Cape would have been more easily
approached by sea, but in amongst the disarray Beazeley was able to
savour the rich vegetation, monkeys scampering off as they approached,
orchids growing in profusion among the trees. There was all this beauty
to enjoy and natural history to report, with unfamiliar plants and new
forestry resources to assess. The Chinese were constructing forts in the
area that the Japanese had occupied, but there was as yet nothing on
this eastern side of the peninsular. What sort of building do you want
to construct, asked some of the Paiwan, who alternately threatened
and protected them on the route through cliff-top forest and along
beaches towards the headland. So Beazeley roughly sketched it for
them, its simple outlines a premonition of a Taiwan locked securely
into a global circuit of science, technology and communications, and
into the realm of the Qing.

A lighthouse is an easy enough sketch, but will have been a weird
new sight for his Paiwan audience. Robert Hart had been outlining his
plans for a network of lights on the China coast for some years now,
for these new installations needed explaining to Zongli Yamen officials
and frontier aborigines alike. Lights were not new to China. In the
Pescadores (Penghu) island group Fisher Island light was built on the
site of an old, long-established beacon, but Hart's vision of a lit coast,
each light visibly different by day (in the colour and shape of its tower),
by night (in the colour and frequency of its light) and in poor visibility
(in the pattern of its fog warning), was grander by far than anything

seen before. He had been lobbying the Zongli Yamen for permissions, and husbanding funds. There was a clear logic to this new development. The Customs Service had already served politically to defuse that potential flashpoint at every port – the meeting of Qing officials with foreign traders emboldened by extraterritorial rights – and did so simply by recruiting foreign nationals to be those Qing officials. More widely, the Customs was making the business of landing and clearing goods rational and efficient on European terms. It was not that the old Customs system had not worked, for it was widely deemed more efficient and smooth-working than any other encountered – by British traders at least – but it was impaired by the swagger and sharp practices of the foreign traders after 1842, who felt themselves entitled to browbeat their way through the Qing bureaucracy. Lay and Hart's system, especially under Hart, curbed that vicious sense of entitlement, delivered more funds, and promised resource too for harbours, rivers, lighthouses: all that was needed to help a changing maritime world. Completing that process – making it more efficient, predictable and safer – involved following the ships back out of port along their routes thither, to deal with the dangers they faced as they approached: the craggy coasts and hidden rocks and reefs that hindered the smooth and predictable immersion of Chinese ports in international trade routes. There had long been murmurs in support of such a scheme, not least from those who had themselves survived wreck (and one can imagine the weary anger of one of those, Captain Percy Cracroft RN, shipwrecked on the Pratas shoals in 1851 as he went to rescue the already wrecked crew of another ship).[5] This was not a task a customs service usually undertook – it was a far cry from revenue assessment – but it showed the peculiar nature of Hart's Service as an agency undertaking foreign technology projects for the Zongli Yamen, and that, and the vision and ambition of Hart and many of his subordinates, transformed the Shanghai compromise into a vast and wide-ranging enterprise, one which lit the coast. The Customs Marine Department had also begun hydrographic surveys, and Royal Navy surveyors, too, had been sketching China's coastline, noting its sights and landmarks in the remark books that fed into the Admiralty's pilot manuals, fixing for navigators the contours of the shorelines, and the temperaments of their inhabitants. Would local people allow you to call for water

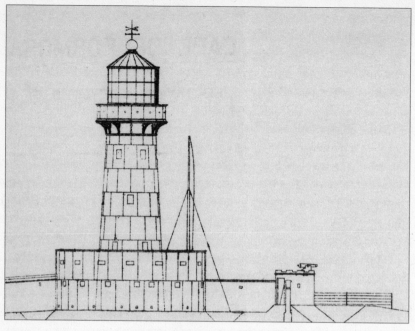

8. South Cape Lighthouse

and supplies? Would they help you? Would they try to kill you? The surveyors' remark books catalogue their findings: Hesan [Heishan] islands, inhabitants 'in all probability pirates'; Buffalo's Nose, 'water may be had in small quantities'; Gulangyu island supplied the best water, and the worst caulkers. When Hart launched his lights scheme he instructed James Campbell in London to call on the Admiralty surveyors, to seek their advice on where the lights were most needed. After all, what was good for the Admiralty must be good for China. Navy surveyors had already assessed the suitability of the Pratas islands as a site at his request in 1867.[6]

In November 1881 two ships landed Henderson, Harding, an interpreter, seventy-three Chinese workmen and a large supply of stores and materials through heavy surf at a beach a mile from the lighthouse site. Over the next 440 days Harding, who directed operations, had to contend with some sixteen earthquakes (as he termed them), one of which produced a tidal wave that destroyed their lighters; termites that ate away their wooden constructions; incessant rain; and the 'astonishing' rapidity with which the cleared jungle grew back. The party was protected by a troop of Chinese soldiers, but the Paiwan actually proved no problem. Their local chiefs were regularly given presents as the work progressed, in a bid to strengthen and personalize ties with them, and they were hired to fence the compound in. The soldiers proved troublesome, however, and one was eventually tried and ineptly beheaded after a fight with the workmen. Lightkeeper George Taylor arrived in April 1882 to tend a temporary light, and a year later the tower and lamp were properly installed and in operation.[7] South Cape was not one of the twenty sites identified in Hart's 1868 six-year scheme for lighthouse construction; but the international politics of Taiwan brought it forward, sending Henderson and Beazley into its thickets in 1875, although local Qing official suspicions about the venture still delayed its construction.[8]

Harding had in fact built a fortress, a 'fighting-lighting machine' he later called it. Inside the large compound was the fifty-foot-high cast-iron tower, holding a First Order white light that could be seen over nineteen miles out across Kwaliang Bay and beyond, flashing eight seconds on, two off, through the steamy nights. The lantern had bullet-proof steel shutters that could be closed to protect the glass. Around its base was a platform equipped with loop-holes for rifles, and a Gatling gun set on a metal track for all-round defence. There was emergency accommodation in the tower for the foreign staff, a great reservoir of water (enough for a siege), and at the base was a wrought iron forty-foot diameter 'refuge' for Chinese employees. Each of the houses in the compound was connected to the refuge by a covered passage. The square compound wall was also loop-holed, with two cannon set up at opposite corners, and it was further protected by a twenty-foot ditch and the barbed-wire fence beyond that. On the refuge roof a mortar was set up, and a second Gatling gun.[9] So much firepower – to what aim? The Paiwan generally were armed with matchlocks, tenderly oiled and polished, deadly enough to kill at close range, but matchlocks nonetheless. The Gatling gun fired hundreds of rounds a minute: there were fewer than 2,400 Paiwan men in the area in the 1870s.[10]

Lovers of lighthouses often talk dreamily of their humane functions, their disinterested service to those travelling by sea. It is difficult not to love them, if only for their stark beauty, contrasting stolid rock with the wildness of the water that often batters them. But set aesthetics aside: lights were important tools serving to help integrate colonized shores and browbeaten states into the Western ordering of global communications. Louis Napoleon's France cajoled the Ottoman Empire into establishing a lights system, financed by French loans and supplied by French manufacturers. Britain and the Netherlands lit their southeast Asian colonial shores. Japan was bullied into developing a lights system through British pressure (in the 1866 Tariff Treaty), and the personal attention to the subject of the Minister there, Harry Parkes. Alcock forwarded to the Navy Hart's request about surveying the Pratas 'with pleasure'.[11] Local officials were intensely suspicious of the South Cape project, seeing it as a foreign plan to control southeast Taiwan and suborn the Paiwan people. But the fortress-light was also shaped by fear: fear of placing potential hostages – lightkeepers – in insecure territory, and fear of failing to find staff to agree to man the light unless it was safer than safe. So they made a redoubt at South Cape. Suspicion of the Customs and of Robert Hart's grand schemes was ungrounded up to a point, for in Hart's eyes foreign interests were served by a strong Chinese state whose sovereignty was not impaired. But local Chinese officials charged with pacifying the Paiwan, who had also endured the Japanese encounter and the 1874 war-scare, reasonably feared that this was no light but a Trojan horse. They were right in a sense, for it was certainly that, although it served the Qing. While the light at South Cape was a part of the ordering of the maritime highways to China that served foreign shipping and commercial interests, that trade also brought increased revenue to the Qing state, and the lighthouse was also a base for the Qing, a new outpost in territory it had not previously fully occupied. Lights were, as they remain, markers of sovereignty and intent in territorial disputes over the South China Sea islands – the Pratas, the Spratleys – which lay at the heart of the Admiralty's undercharted and under-lit 'Dangerous Ground'.

Who, though, in their right mind, would volunteer to live at a place like South Cape, however beautiful? For, on top of the seeming dangers, the country in wild chaos, 'what occupation could be more doleful for a European than that of a lighthouse-keeper on a barren Chinese island'? Thus wrote Julia Hughes, wife of the Xiamen Customs Commissioner, of the predicament of the keeper on Fisher (Xiyu) Island in the Pescadores, visited on a cruise in late 1876 which had the ultimate aim of checking up on the South Cape site.[12] That light stood on a 'barren hill', an hour's hard walk from any neighbours. Her sentiments are echoed often enough in the Customs archives, in letters from dispirited men serving their time at the lights. Scores did so, dozens of men occupying the lighthouses and lightships established by the Service. Their presence in such out-of-the-way places is testament to this odd refashioning of China. For in some of the most inaccessible spots on Chinese soil, on coasts and islands mostly little noticed, inhabited by marginal communities often beyond the law and beyond the state, the Customs pitched up and built its stations, staffing them with Germans, deemed attentive to their gardens; Britons, thought more slovenly, Portuguese, Eurasians and others. The world visited these obscure Chinese stages. The keepers were lower-class men, some of the least-educated and lowest status foreigners who lived and worked in China. Former seafarers mostly, and they had to be men suited to the loneliness of lighthouse life and to its rigid routines. They were workers. A light is a machine that must shine, regularly, relentlessly, at full power, and so to its full expected visibility, as advertised in the Customs *List of Lighthouses* and the pilot manuals: lights brooked no slack. They were workers in a colonial culture, even though formally Chinese state employees, so they actually oversaw the labour of others – oversight, the records show, that was often delivered with a kick, a shove or a punch. Europeans were placed in charge of each light, with an ancillary Chinese staff, and they often brought to them families, or their 'house-keepers' – their Chinese or later Japanese wives and mistresses – or they brought prostitutes, hired for a few weeks from brothels in the treaty ports. Some they loved; some they paid; some both. To the building sites were brought – by sea – all the equipment, supplies and construction materials, and teams of workers too to build them. The refuge, tower and light at South Cape were all made in Birmingham, at Chance Brothers' works, where they were first lit and tested, and then shipped east. Hart portioned out the work also to France, as ever evenly balancing his patronage and forestalling too much pompous complaint from diplomats. The lights were linked together by a Customs supply network, a small fleet of light tenders, vessels which visited each at least twice a year, transporting staff, shipping in food for them and barrels of vegetable oil for the lights, taking away semi-literate letters of complaint, as well as the relieved, the sick, the mad, and sometimes the dead. The light at South Cape, and the lights along the coasts and on islands were enclaves, fragments of Europe in exile. European iron, glass, steel; European flesh, food, drink, made up these outposts of the treaty system grafted onto Chinese coasts. Their occupants mostly looked to the sea and the tenders, rather than inland, for a keeper was instructed to look to his lights, and seawards, not to get involved in local affairs; and a light was an interloper, not there to serve the land. Still, lights offered employment for local people, as menial staff (for Europeans did not polish the lenses and clean the wicks) and as servants. They engaged in some trade with their neighbours where they had them, and single lightkeepers often looked to these communities for sex. George Taylor's foray, when he bunked off from his post at Fisher Island one night in 1880 was a little more dramatic than most, for he somehow purloined the local Chinese administrator's official clothing as a disguise and went across to Magong town on Penghu island 'for the purpose of bringing a Chinese girl'. This so 'exasperated' local residents that they attacked the girl's house, believing her mother to be complicit in the affair.[13] Such was often enough the stuff of the staff files of the Customs: men champing at their self-assumed bit, events sometimes spiralling out of control.

But when some years later, in 1887, Taylor, having been transferred from Fisher Island to South Cape, ventured forth from his lighthouse on a route north along the east coast, he was driven by inquisitiveness and had permission from his superiors.[14] The headless corpse of an unlucky Chinese settler he encountered on the way would surely have dampened priapic ardour. Much to the surprise of his Paiwan companions, Taylor insisted that the poor man be buried, and they covered him with the shining coral sand, and then went their way along the shoreline. Taylor was on an anthropological 'ramble', as he put it, if a hike of a few days through a climate rather like that of a Turkish bath could be thought rambling. It was one of several he wrote about, this one apparently taking up the opportunity of an invitation to join in a hunting trip from a village north along the coast. He almost picked up a bride himself on the way, a chief's widowed daughter assigned him on an overnight stay. Such an alliance with a man who had so much firepower to call on seemed a good match to the woman's father. In most such accounts, and this is no exception, the European evades capture and treks on. Taylor and such companions wandered through a number of his articles in the pages of the *China Review* and the *Journal of the Royal Geographical Society*, which brought to vivid life the insecurity of frontier Taiwan, where men came from the mountains to wait the opportunity to seize a Chinese head and so demonstrate their manhood, and where these Austronesian peoples lived with the changes to their world brought about by the defensive state-building measures of the Qing. A Scot, the son of a retired harbour master, Taylor had joined the lights service in 1877, and came to South Cape in 1882. He quickly learned one of the Paiwan languages, and we might hazard a guess that a Paiwan mistress helped consolidate this.[15] The lighthouse was otherwise appropriated by the local people but not besieged by them – at least, not besieged with hostile intent, for they certainly turned up at it in person, or wrote to it an 'incessant stream' of supplications for quinine, 'fever medicine' they called it. They came for cures and not for heads. And Taylor got to know them, laying out his findings on Paiwan customs and beliefs, and the nature and hierarchies of the different groups he encountered, in his untutored writings. He even organized an archaeological dig, but mostly the lighthouse-keeper had turned amateur ethnographer, that way tying his light into the local communities, rendering the Gatling guns and mortar blessedly redundant. But if South Cape proved peaceful, the rest of Taiwan was not. Forty campaigns were fought by Qing troops to pacify the various tribes between 1884 and 1891.[16]

Robert Hart had hoped that the lights could serve science, as well as commerce and seafarers and the Qing. The keepers would be at least literate, 'fairly intelligent Europeans', who 'will only be too glad to have something given them to do, to occupy the lonely hours of their isolated lives'. Meteorology was the first additional project. Hart's London agent, James Duncan Campbell, was instructed in 1873 to consult the British Astronomer-Royal, Sir George Airey, then president of the Royal Society, about the instruments needed and then to ship them. But he was also instructed to consult other scientists, in any field at all, 'to find out if there is any special line in which such stations can be made useful'.[17] Reports like Taylor's added another dimension.

Hart encouraged the keeper's excursions and his accounts of the aborigines, and Taylor found himself promoted out of the lower ranks of the service to an 'indoor' position as a clerk in the more prosaic confines of the Shanghai Harbour Master's Office. He had also found himself reading a paper at the 1888 meeting of the British Association for the Advancement of Science at Bath, alongside other reports to the Geographical Section that same day on irrigation in Egypt, the US Geographical and Geological Survey, the Ordnance Survey's use of photography, and the Malay kingdom of Pahang, brought under effect-ive British control not long before. Genteel, sleepy Bath was a long way from Taylor's Formosa and his steamily rambunctious rambles, but British science sucked in even the self-taught reports of a lowly lighthouse-keeper in its omnivorous hunger for knowledge. And lighthouses themselves, we might note, had a special place in narratives of British engineering triumph. The President of the British Association, Frederick Bramwell, had concluded his opening address that year with a hymn of praise to lighthouse construction, for it showed that 'the work of the civil engineer . . . [was] consistent with true poetical feeling, and is worthy of the highest order of intellect'.[18]

Hart ultimately lacked true poetical feeling. That was his strength, just as a violent poetry marked men like Lindsay or Parkes, which was in turn both their strength and their weakness. But he had that keen eye for opportunity, and would never build a system if he could not make it serve a half-dozen purposes. The lights crept out of his diary and Zongli Yamen palavers, and out of survey reports and harbour mouths.[19] The island close by the mouth of the Yangzi long-before named for Gützlaff acquired a light in 1869, fuelled by imported vegetable oil, visible for twenty-four miles, and equipped with fog cannon. A telegraph station was built there too, to wire news of shipping arrivals to Shanghai, for the days of watching for the flags at Wusong from the church tower had long passed. The next two years saw seventeen light installations placed at points on the Yangzi, lighting the way to the open river ports, and then the first in a chain of lights along the southeastern seaboard, the uninhabited 'lonely and isolated' Chapel Island, connected only twice a month by sampan from its hazardous landing stage to Xiamen. There was Middle Dog on Mazu Island, notable for its large compound with 'beautiful turf', and for the incessant low-level conflicts with its neighbouring four villages and their 'independent and unruly' inhabitants. As South Cape was being finished, 200 islanders occupied the Middle Dog compound as a dispute with the station staff escalated, necessitating the arrival from Fuzhou of the Zhixian to 're-establish the moral position of the lighthouse as a Government station' and the keepers as 'Government officials, not lightly to be disregarded or interfered with'.[20] Shaweishan, in the middle of the Yangzi estuary, was also completed in 1872, with a cast-iron tower rising 229 feet above sea level, showing a light which took a prodigious annual toll on migrating birds. Many of the characteristics of the lights story are contained in these early stations: the feats of engineering which brought these structures and their machinery to isolated coasts and which would have impressed Frederick Bramwell, the lonely life of the keepers, or if not, then fraught with tension; and the arrival of the Qing state amidst formerly 'independent' communities. There was the blasting of the fog guns, and later haunting and powerful fog-horns, new sounds for China's ears. And there was the ecological disruption: Taylor hunting – and the toll of Western huntsmen on China's bird life was marked – and those powerful beams killing the disorientated flocks. The tops of hills were lopped off to make sites for the towers. The lights were hardly obscure, despite their locations, for Hart was not simply content to set this work going in China, but had to have it shown, known and appreciated, in Britain and internationally. At the 1883 International Fisheries Exhibition in London, the Customs-organized Chinese display included a model of the 120-foot iron tower for Breaker Point, south of Shantou, and 'a chart showing the Lights on the coast of China', which Prime Minister W. E. Gladstone 'seemed to be much struck with'. Campbell made the lights the key focus of his little discourses to visiting royalty and others about the work of the British-led Customs and the British presence in China, the display shining light on Hart's achievements so far away from South Kensington, yet so closely bound up with British interests. The Exhibition jury awarded the Customs a gold medal and a diploma of honour for the 'System of Lights on Chinese coast'.[21]

As the lights developed along the coasts so did Hart's plans for a meteorological service, the next layer in the shield to better protect shipping. The first steamer to sail through the newly opened Suez Canal

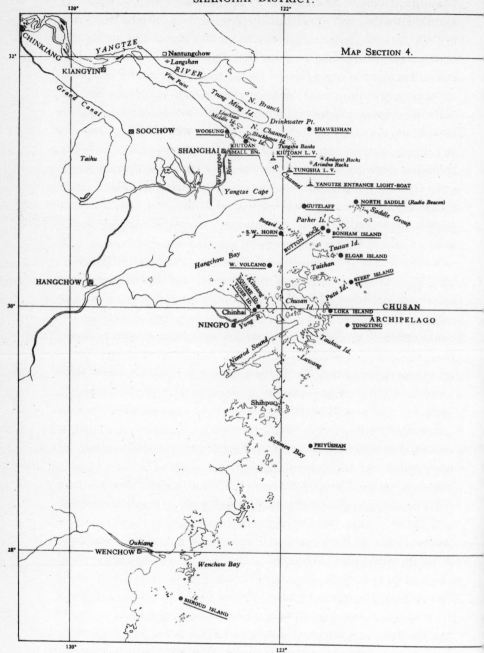

9. Lighthouses on the approaches to Shanghai

to China arrived in Shanghai on 19 March 1870; steamers waited at Hankow that season to sail direct from there to Europe, twenty-one of them that year, bypassing Shanghai where cargoes had traditionally been transhipped, taking a quarter of the tea crop with them on a route cut in length by about a third.[22] Lights such as Breaker Point helped captains shave about a day off the journey north from Hong Kong, by allowing them to sail more directly around that dangerous headland, rather than take a wide loop to be safe – one which in fact took some to ruin on Taiwan coasts. The hitching of key China coast cities to the spreading network of submarine and overland telegraph cables also proceeded apace. After much hesitation, British diplomatic intervention had secured Chinese agreement for the Danish Great Northern Company to begin laying a telegraph cable from Hong Kong to Shanghai. It came ashore at Wusong on the night of 8 December 1870. Four months later the line came into use. Chinese merchants crowded into the Hong Kong and Shanghai offices on the day the service was inaugurated, given an opportunity to communicate with branches in the other city. They leapt at this new technology, which tied Chinese communities together as much as it tied the China coast more swiftly into wider worlds of information and communication. By August, telegrams from Shanghai just three days old were being printed in London. A trans-Pacific line had to wait another thirty years, but a Siberian landline was operating to Vladivostok, and then undersea to Japan by 1871 and onto Shanghai that same year, beginning operations on 1 January 1872. People, goods and precious information could now travel more and more swiftly, though the latter at some cost, for a telegram was not cheap. Passenger rates, however, got cheaper, and so did freight rates. (Sail was superceded, for the Suez Canal benefited only the steamship, and by the end of the 1870s the clipper era was all but over.) But all this science and technology – the compound engine in the steamers and the tighter navigation of the masters, the clear bright shining lights and carefully surveyed charts – all of it proved to little avail on the night of 31 July 1879 in the face of the 'indescribable fury' of a typhoon that rampaged north along the coast across the mouth of the Yangzi, or on 26 August 1881 when a typhoon smashed Fuzhou and destroyed villages on Taiwan's west coast, wrecking ships and destroying buildings and lives.[23] The science and the new technology proved to little avail in these cases because it remained as yet un-connected. Now Hart set in motion dormant plans to make even more effective use of his 'fairly intelligent Europeans' and the telegraph to try to master yet more firmly the passages to China.

At South Cape then, at Middle Dog, Gutzlaff, Breaker Point, and a host of other Customs stations and lights, a new regime was instituted, with staff now required to keep daily observations of the weather, and with a number of stations linked to telegraph lines sending their data immediately onwards twice a day.[24] Although Hart had planned to establish a meteorological centre in Peking, heading it up with a scientist recruited from Europe, he had been unable to find a man prepared to risk his career on a post in Asia, and instead the Marine Department began a close working relationship with the Jesuit-run Zikawei Observatory, which had been established at Shanghai in 1872. Science had historically lain at the heart of Jesuit activity in China in the work at the Ming and Qing courts of men like Matteo Ricci and Ferdinand Verbiest, but more pertinently the observatory at Zikawei was part of an international network of scientific research institutes established by the Society. Led by Father Marc Dechevrens, who had formerly held the chair of physics at the Jesuit Collège Vaugirard in Paris, the Observatory both conducted scientific research into the meteorology of the region, and worked with the Customs to establish a weather forecasting service. Tracking the course of typhoons across the year, Zikawei's scientists could start to properly map their patterns over time, providing better understanding of their frequency and most travelled courses, the better to advise on the longer-term planning of routes and services. To do this they needed data, and the Customs provided it. Hart had published another of his grand schemes in 1873, this one set out in a circular letter to colonial governments in Asia. He outlined a plan for a network of stations in China and a telegraph-based weather forecasting system across Pacific Asia. The destructive-ness of the typhoons that so battered the China coast cities and took their toll on shipping, had also prompted the British to propose establishing an observatory in Hong Kong in 1879, an idea based on the success of recent developments in British India. But Hart evaded proposals to hitch his new initiative into that British-led enterprise, not least as the government there proposed that its observatory should become the centre of 'the meteorological service of China'. Hart preferred to work with the Jesuit centre in Shanghai, for working so closely to British colonial interests in Hong Kong would have been diplomatically difficult. Nor did he take to rivals. Data from the Customs stations was directed instead in the first instance to Zikawei, which coordinated a new forecasting system also prompted and part-funded by Shanghai's (foreign) General Chamber of Commerce, aghast at the havoc wreaked by successive typhoons in the late 1870s, and disseminated its data across the Pacific coasts.[25] Zikawei was to be closely tied into French colonial enterprise in China and east and southeast Asia, and was part-funded by the French navy and other interests, but it was not anybody's state enterprise. It provided a neat civilian solution to Hart's problem, which was that meteorology was an area where the scale of his ambition proved impractical, though the problem remained deadly. The annual toll of shipping, the devastating impact of storms on cities like Hong Kong, Shantou and Shanghai, was such that the new tools now available had to be fashioned together and coordinated.

The meteorological network grew and grew. Shanghai's Bund acquired a new landmark, a storm signal tower and time ball, at the eastern end of the French concession. The Customs acquired instruments from Britain. Dechevrens imported dozens more from France and had them installed on ships running regular routes in and out of Shanghai. And so, from the lighthouses and from Yokohama, Manila, Hong Kong and Cochin China – Zikawei's network of corresponding stations – weather telegrams flowed in twice-daily, were collated by the fathers and their Chinese assistants, and forecasts were then issued to the newspapers, and to the Bund tower, which semaphored the state of the weather and any storm warnings to shipping in Shanghai's harbour. At noon each day, too, the time ball dropped, allowing Shanghai's masters to calibrate their chronometers, and so navigate more accurately and more swiftly. Less dramatically, meteorological logs were deposited by ships and posted to Zikawei from sites beyond the telegraph lines, building up the corpus of data that Dechevrens and his successors pored over. There were wider connections too. When Hart first turned to meteorology he sent J. D. Campbell off from London to Vienna to the inaugural congress of the International

Meteorological Organization. This began a process of standardization and coordination which the Customs noted and wanted to be aligned with. The Zikawei Observatory came to assume a role first reporting on, then representing, 'China', at least informally, at the periodic world conferences that ensued, a feat of *lèse majesté* kept up into the twentieth century. The scientific research work of Dechrevens, and especially of his later successor Father Louis Marie Froc – director from 1897 to 1932 – garnered an international reputation for the Observatory. The Customs came to take a less active role, and Hart never returned to his own grand scheme for a Peking-based service, but in the practical meteorology which served maritime communications, French and Italian Jesuit scientists and Hart's mainly British directors of the Marine Department worked very closely together, a seemingly unlikely alliance of interests, but one which characterized the increasingly sophisticated and intertwined world of the treaty ports.

Customs meteorological data had first appeared in print in the series of *Medical Reports*, published from 1871 onwards. Here was another initiative that aimed to serve much wider interests than Robert Hart's Qing paymasters. Hart thought the publication a success that should in time become a 'first-class medical journal'. This work, he asserted, will 'give the West sets of facts concerning the East that must prove useful to scientific men'. And to further circulate its work he later subsidized the compilation of the reports by British Army Surgeon General Charles Gordon. It was, he claimed, 'a handsome monument to some of the doings of the Customs Service', and Hart liked monuments.[26] He ordered the creation of the series when yet again he found he had a resource – the medical officers on the Customs payroll at each treaty port – that could be called on to provide material that 'may prove highly useful to the medical profession both in China and at home, and to the public generally'. In this Hart's own ambitions also matched the metropolitan ambitions of some of the men employed, not least Patrick Manson, who had served at Dagou and Xiamen, and who would move on to Hong Kong, and Alexander Jamieson, who put the idea to him and edited the series.[27] Publication in the *Medical Reports* series was one way of securing visibility abroad, especially if, like Manson, you made a point of forwarding them onwards to better-established experts in Britain.[28] Meteorological data was contained in these reports because of the still widespread acceptance of a climate-based theory of disease: understanding the climate in each port would inform an understanding of its 'medical topography'. The reports throw much additional light on life in the open ports, on Shantou's apparent unhealthiness (399 cases of disease in six months in 1871 amongst a population of 500), of the contrasting wholesomeness of Niuzhuang, where 'frequent winds' blew away – it was asserted – 'unwholesome gases, noisome smells, and disease germs', although the slow pace of work grated on even the healthiest, leaving them prone to 'extreme nervous irritability' that only hard work and hard, healthy play could alleviate. There were descriptions and assessments too of Chinese practice. John Dudgeon claimed wryly in a note from Peking that the only treatment that the Chinese had found for extreme forms of dyspepsia was 'bread saturated with the blood of decapitated criminals'. At Shanghai Jamieson concluded that there was no perceptible health risk to foreign residence that was any greater than in Britain as long as a man was sensible. But many men were not sensible, and while doctors advised moderate consumption of alcohol, drink too much fuelled the world of work and play in the foreign communities and directly and indirectly took a great toll. It did not help that the drink, not least the drink the seaman could afford, was too often adulterated and just about guaranteed, Shanghai's Municipal pharmacist concluded in 1875, to knock a man out for a good and thorough robbing.[29]

Medical work in China provided a ready stream of patients, and new or unusual diseases and conditions, as well as a good supply of fees for private practice and for attending emigrant ships. Medicine had proved the most immediately successful field of missionary society work – though contentious, for many were treated but very few converted. One estimate noted twelve converts at Canton out of 409,000 patients seen between 1861 and 1872.[30] Science reaped a harvest even if Christendom did not. For an ambitious researcher like Manson, this volume of patients provided data and detail galore, and his work on the filaria worm, which causes elephantiasis, most spectacularly in the form of large scrotal tumours, made his reputation internationally. Manson, far removed from the libraries and resources of Europe, set about a series of careful observations of his patients and ad hoc experiments to identify the cause of this and related conditions, and to tie down the life cycle of the worm, following up the hypothesis proposed by other researchers that the intermediate host might be the mosquito. Not the least noteworthy of his experiments was that on a 48-year-old Chinese cook who was carrying the worm, 'Hin-Lo', who was 'persuaded' to spend a night served up as an easy feast for the insects. The sated and swollen mosquitoes were recovered from the man's room the following morning, and Manson confirmed this way that the worm's life cycle took it through the insect, for he found that it was not digested by the mosquito. How it got back into the human body was not to be apparent for some years more, but the discovery that an insect was the vector through which the filaria worm moved was to transform understandings of disease, and of public hygiene: eradication of potential breeding sites for mosquitoes was to become a key strategy in disease prevention. The new insight further prompted Manson to hypothesize that the mosquito was the likely vector for the transmission of malaria, a theory that was later confirmed by his collaborator Ronald Ross. The Customs medical officer was in time to be regarded as the 'father' of 'tropical medicine', for Manson was later to become medical adviser to the British Colonial Office, and proposed the establishment of what became the London School of Tropical Medicine. He made it abundantly clear how handicapped he had been in Xiamen, with the 'absence of a good library, of competent assistants, of friendly advice and criticism', as well as the 'depressing influence of a hot climate'. The *Medical Reports* were 'virtually inaccessible', Manson claimed, so his work needed wider circulation, but even so Xiamen made his career, that and the persuadable Hin-Lo.[31]

Another of the Customs surgeons who also published in this area was 'F. Wong', Wong Fun (Huang Kuan), Europe's first Chinese university graduate, who had been awarded his MD at Edinburgh University in 1857. Wong sailed back to China that year initially to work at the London Missionary Society Hospital in Canton, working in Hong Kong or that port until his death in 1878, which was recorded, with excessive attention paid to detailing his physical condition, by his successor as Customs surgeon: the data collection imperative devoured its own. Wong wrote fluently in English as a doctor of Western medicine practising in China – assessing, for example, the chances of Chinese adoption of Western treatments for fevers (very remote, he thought), or noting that quinine alone currently stood a chance of gaining acceptance, as indeed it had in south Taiwan. 'We,' he wrote, and note that pronoun, 'can do no more' than could be achieved in this area by Chinese physicians.[32] Wong had studied in a mission school in Macao and then in Hong Kong since 1840, had left to pursue study in English in America in 1847, then in 1849 embarked to study medicine in Scotland. He wrote 'we' when most Europeans would still find it difficult to accept treatment by a Chinese doctor, even a Christian trained at one of the world's finest medical schools, and would do so for some decades yet to come. Even his most positive colleagues in the LMS in China had difficulties in accepting him on a completely equal footing. But Wong still saw himself as 'we', as part of the Western and Customs medical establishment in China.

All these 'sets of facts' and Customs-related publications piled up on shelves, and were reprinted and excerpted in newspapers and periodicals globally, meat for others to work on as well. Scientific and technological advances seemed intertwined in the treaty port world of the 1870s and 1880s. Robert Hart helped establish sets of connections from his China stations out across east and southeast Asia, and internationally – bringing out into the treaty ports trained engineers and inquisitive doctors; facilitating and encouraging a range of scientific research by Jesuit meteorologists and Scottish-trained physicians, as well as George Taylor's affable but still-read ethnographic sketches. All the while he was building up the resources of his own administration to deliver funds to the Qing and facilities to the trader. Customs work was underpinned by the furious publication programme at Shanghai, and by the frantic publicity activities of the London Office, lobbying royalty at South Kensington, badgering scientists in Vienna – anything which could help advertise the utility of the Customs' capacity to deliver new data about 'such a comparatively unknown part of the world', as Hart put it: 'unknown', it might be remembered, at least in terms of Western scientific understanding.[33] The elder Medhurst's proposition that China's rich literary heritage might usefully be mined for understandings of its history, natural history, science and epidemiology, was at this time displaced by a confident, chauvinist belief in the primacy of Western scientific practice and understanding, a faith placed instead on the learning and research of the foreigner in China. The pages of the *China Review,* the *Chinese Recorder* and the *Journal of the Royal Asiatic Society,* as well as Customs' publications, all made clear this belief in the supremacy and mastery of foreign knowledge. And this was aided too by the growing ordinariness of China as a field of experience and study, for it was more and more the site of a respectable career, or at least a phase in one, for those not involved in commerce, war or diplomacy. An architect, a surgeon or a civil engineer might well spend time there – perhaps a life, more often still a good stretch, good enough to build a solid reputation. Men once sailed back from China to buy a political place, or settle amongst the landed wealthy in Boston or the English or Scottish shires. Now they found it useful for professional advancement too, and it was becoming far less an eccentric byway to success, and more an established mainstream route. It was not El Dorado, but it was not a backwater.

Hart always had other schemes and enthusiasms: the gas plant in his own backyard and the brass band, for example. Railways exercised him and others, turning up in his correspondence and journal from at least 1867 onwards, in notes from his lobbying at the Zongli Yamen. They were, he would stress, surely vital to China's development and for defence. 'It is not that we do not know the utility of Railways, or that we do not appreciate them,' responded Wenxiang in 1867, but there were issues of the cost, and control, and a concern about the wider strategic designs of what came to be termed railway imperialism.[34] Who else, for example, would be served by a railway from Burma to Yunnan but the British and British power and influence there, countering the French and infringing further on the Qing? Railways were part of the talk in treaty revision and in the Margary negotiations, but nothing came of that. Railways came, though, haltingly, and initially in a peculiar episode. In fifteen months from July 1876 over 190,000 tickets were sold for journeys on a little railway, built without permission, from Wusong to Shanghai. The British-managed firm had been given approval to build a road, but had always intended to install the railway, expecting that the fait accompli would be accepted in the end. But the sleight of hand was politically too gross to stand. The company, including its Chinese shareholders, was bought out by the local authorities who then had the plant and equipment shipped to Taiwan, where it rotted away, a British consular report in 1882 noting that it was by then 'very nearly useless'.[35] The affair was taken as symbolizing, again, the hopelessly obscurantist opposition of the Chinese to modernizing progress, but it was nothing of the kind. Before it was closed down people flocked to travel on it in their tens of thousands, and they came in droves simply to watch it. They crowd out the European staff in the photographs Williams Saunders took of its opening; they read about it and bought prints of it; and local entrepreneurs operated omnibus services from the walled city to the station in Hongkew, cannily copying the railroad livery for their vehicles and staff uniforms. The Chinese embraced the railway as they had the steamships and the telegraph. The problem was simple due process, the protection of sovereign rights, and the local and international politics of a capital construction project.[36] The authorities had no option but to close it, although they did so perfectly properly and carefully, and without haste; paid a good price for it, and packed it all off to Taiwan's much abused shores. But by October 1888 Hart could write to Campbell that 'rail is fact': a line had been built from the Kaiping coal mines at Tangshan to the nearest canal, and had started operating in 1881. This was then extended west to Dagu, and in 1888 was running the seven miles from the port to Tianjin. This venture was securely laid: the railway was staying. The fact established, Hart backed out of the fray, for he had 'worked hard in my time to get an opening for rail', and now left its next stage to the lobbying diplomats and commission hunters.[37]

This was something: 'fire wagons', as they were called in Chinese, running on Chinese soil; but it is telling of a wider change too, for centrally involved in financing and managing the Woosung Railroad Company from its inception in 1865 onwards, and in discussions about the Kaiping mines, was Jardine, Matheson & Co. The foreign commercial presence in China was changing. The object of all of this innovation by the Customs remained trade, although as we have seen a different and more static interest had also developed, not least at Shanghai, and flexed its muscles there – the property-owning clique, men such as Thomas Hanbury, who looked no further than the Settlement boundaries except when they hungered to extend these, and the interests of Chinese residents, their tenants. There were the wider interests too, those who had invested in treaty port infrastructure or who provided services that depended on the wider foreign presence: lawyers, provision merchants, tavern owners, dock owners and employees, staff of the foreign-run municipalities. But the China trade, the trade that needed those lights and charts and storm warnings, was evolving too. More giants of the Canton era became unsteady: pious Olyphant & Co. failed in 1878; the ever-shameless Russell & Co. lost out on the Yangzi, and were to fail completely in 1891. Most notable of all was the withdrawal of firms like Jardines from opium, for the largest of the British China companies had abandoned direct involvement in the trade by 1873. The ironic effect of legalization under the 1860 treaty was the erosion of advantages the firm had previously built over its competitors, and a shift in the market in China towards cheaper indigenous opium. For firms like Jardines the key element in the trade became costs in India, and although returns on the opium trade in the 1860s proved some of the (peace-time) highest, and volumes some of the largest, they were finally outflanked in India. British Indian firms moved centre-stage in the trade, not the Parsee firms which had long been an integral part of the entire machinery from the start, but Sephardi Jewish companies from Bombay like David Sassoon and Sons.[38]

Tea was changing too. Demand from Britain was in steady decline as British tastes switched to black teas from India and Sri Lanka, aided by aggressive marketing campaigns that lambasted the quality of Chinese green teas, insinuating or claiming that they were coloured with poisonous dyes and heavily adulterated.[39] From its business importing cotton piece goods and yarns, Jardines started to look to establish cotton mills in China as early as 1877, either as agent to Chinese interests or manager. As discussions meandered about such projects in the 1880s the issue provided another target for commercial lobbying of diplomats and politicians, for Qing officials rejected the notion that there was any right under any treaty for foreigners to establish manufacturing plants. The old business model, importing and exporting, proved unsustainable and unprofitable overall.[40] Firms like Jardines had to evolve. They accelerated a process of diversification, for the increasingly strong-rooted treaty world in China provided new opportunities. Jardines' investment in steamship operations was restructured as the China (later Indo-China) Steam Navigation Company in 1873, and it moved generally to focus on servicing trade through insurance and shipping rather than operating on its own account. Jardines also worked through Alexander Michie, now its agent in Tianjin, to secure commissions from the Qing for plant at the Kaiping mines, and for fortifications and armaments at Port Arthur (Dalian).[41] Michie also found himself administering loans from the company directly to the imperial household in Peking through the 1880s and 1890s. The motive was political, a vain (but harmless) attempt to curry favour, for far better and more reliable returns were available elsewhere and the business was fraught with difficulty, not least as Michie had never learned to speak Chinese. But what a different world it was for the former partner in Lindsay & Co., and for the Jardines, whose founders had been marked men in 1839 as war loomed, viewed as gangsters acting without the law, aggressively sending their opium fleet east and north in the contraband trade. Now they were funding the imperial household, investing in railways, and running a legitimate shipping fleet: princes serving emperors.

But Chinese firms were coming to dominate the distribution of imports and the processing of goods for export. Smaller traders like the Little brothers were defeated: driven out of Hankow, and beaten in Shanghai. Their operations collapsed in 1882. Bob Little was left with the International Settlement's new electricity company – 'I am a fixture here,' he wrote, and a fixture was secure.[42] His brother Archibald pursued potential openings way up the Yangzi in Sichuan. But there were important new interests starting up as well. In 1864 a prospectus for a new Hongkong and Shanghae Banking Company heralded the arrival of the firm in March 1865. From the start, although registered and headquartered in Hong Kong, the bank was a multinational, if not a transnational enterprise. Its controlling interests were British, German, American and Indian (Parsee and Sephardi). It was a bank for the treaty port world and its regional hinterland. Its operations were varied but the Taiwan crisis saw it arrange the first public loan to China (the 1874 Foochow loan), which was secured on Customs revenues and subscribed to in Hong Kong and Shanghai and, with less enthusiasm, on the London market. *The Economist* warned off investors: it was 'quite uncertain whether such a country can possess the kind of political stability which is essential for financial good faith', it wrote. But wariness should not detract from this striking development: the securing of capital in London for Qing needs. Originating in the bubble period at the end of the Taiping crisis, the new bank survived a rocky start, working across the major treaty ports and in Japan and Singapore, as a bank to private customers, businesses and governments, as well as through the London market.[43] The Foochow loan was a harbinger of many more to come, and the politics of loan-making would move to a more central place in the jockeying for interest and position amongst the foreign powers. Finance could make a very big player out of a small power like Belgium. Another new name entering the China fray was Butterfield & Swire, established in Shanghai and Yokohama in 1866–7 by John Samuel Swire, whose firm was already well established. The firm grew the routine China operations of such companies but also built on its Liverpool and shipping connections as agents for Alfred Holt's Blue Funnel Line (formally the Ocean Steamship Company), established in 1866 to chip a way into the steamship business between Europe and Asia. Swire's developed their own China Navigation Company in 1872 – the only entirely foreign-owned one – to attack the coastal and Yangzi trades, driving Russell's from the river and by 1894 building up the largest of the river fleets. It was a duller firm than its great rival Jardines, lacking its history and the taint of that history, and the merchant-prince splendour. It did not have a company stable at the Hong Kong or Shanghai racetracks, and it long kept out of local treaty port politics, for it deliberately based itself in Shanghai's French concession. But it secured a central position in the treaty port commercial world. All these firms were hit by a financial crisis in 1883–4 that bankrupted scores of Chinese banks and firms as fears of war came to impact on a market distorted by a pell-mell bout of 'company mania' and speculation in 1882. But they survived.[44]

All of this new and old activity remained dependent on Chinese partners, whether Michie's interpreters or the suppliers of finance, connections, information and local nous who worked with and for the foreign firms. The most prominent of these, because their rise altered the social balance in the Chinese cities they operated in and the localities they came from, were the compradors. The term was a catch-all, taking in the provisioner of a ship, the supervisor of Chinese labour at the treaty port municipalities, as well as the sometimes enormously wealthy and powerful businessmen whose world was intimately intertwined with that of the foreign businesses, yet at the same time carefully distinct from it, not least socially. The men allied to the big foreign firms are those most thought of when the world of the comprador – the *maiban* – is now invoked: the great traders of Hong Kong, Canton and Shanghai – powerful men, more than equal in splendour and pretensions to Dent's and Jardines' taipans; a new class in Chinese society. A foreign firm's fortunes depended in great measure on the comprador, and getting and keeping the right man was vital and worth cutting a good deal for, however symbiotic the relationship was. The comprador for a firm ran its active business operations, its engagement with Chinese dealers and with the Chinese market, and where necessary Chinese officialdom, through what was effectively a parallel organization. He worked to drum up business, negotiating the Chinese commercial and official world that monoglot foreigners even of longstanding and close connections with the Chinese, could find difficult. Russell & Co. had a run of good luck rooted in their Canton days – comparadors were still mostly Cantonese, that strong connection staying tight – and Jardines did well too. The association with firms like Jardines or Russell's brought prestige as well as profit, and conversely, foreign firms competed to establish formal relations with the most prominent merchants. Comprador funds were also channelled into foreign-managed business ventures, as well as into Chinese-initiated projects. Former Dent comprador Xu Run had investments across coastal China, from Hong Kong to Tianjin, in mining, insurance, shipping, a sugar refinery, a paper mill and more, with 50 per cent of his assets in International Settlement land at Shanghai.[45] The transforming state, notably in the guise of Li Hongzhang, secured comprador investment and involvement in a new breed of 'mandarin bureaucratic' enterprises, semi-state businesses, most famously of all the China Merchant's Steam Navigation Company in which Xu Run was heavily involved, and which challenged foreign domination of coastal shipping.

The comprador has come to be symbolic in many ways of the story of China's open century, for the comprador was cast by Chinese Communist historians and nationalistic politicians as a villain, a traitor to his country, a willing tool of foreign imperialism and the sclerotic and 'feudal' Qing state. The word is tainted. Merchant status certainly changed in the latter half of the nineteenth century, and the rise of the comprador and comprador wealth is a key part of that story.[46] Compradors bought office, rank and degrees, and they acted as gentry, being expected to act in public and cultural life. The way they lived had an impact too. Operating in two worlds, they lived across them, their dress, style of housing and furnishings, and their home's location in the foreign concessions, often testifying to a catholicity in taste and interests – wealth enabling them to pursue expensive connoisseurship of Chinese arts, as well as to purchase new foreign goods. But my catholicity is your tasteless, uninformed vulgarity. The successful merchant everywhere is the butt of caricature about conspicuous consumption, and no less so in Qing China. Some became Christians, others were converts whose language skills learnt at mission schools had helped them enter the world of treaty commerce. Several prominent men had also passed through the ranks of the Customs, such as the sometime Jardines compradors Tang Tingshu and Robert Hotung. Successful men proved dynastic in ambition, which was not always good for the foreign firms involved, since business competence is hardly hereditary. They hitched their family's future success to continued involvement in Sino-foreign trade, sending thier sons to foreign-run or foreign-style schools, to the detriment, it was routinely alleged, of their Chinese language skills and facility in their own culture. In fact the comprador was not only the target of sneers from his own country-men – he was illiterate, he fawned on the foreigner, he was vulgar – but also the subject of derision from foreign observers, who increasingly saw him as part-deracinated; not really Chinese. All this was long before he became a political villain.[47] But successful compradors were vital actors in the changing world of the late Qing state, in its self-strengthening projects, and also in the responses to the catastrophic drought and famine in the north of 1876–9 and the 1887 Yellow River floods. And they remained absolutely central to the foreign trading world, not least because while a few of Lindsay's generation of busi-nessmen had fancied themselves Sinologists, learning Chinese largely remained the province of the consul, the Customs officer and the missionary. Very few others bothered. Compradors interpreted the market for foreign traders quite literally. They also gate-kept: they rationed information, as rational actors would. Sometimes both foreign firm and comprador benefited from a market opportunity, sometimes perhaps the comprador himself moved alone: the functional illiteracy of the foreign trader was a handicap. So foreign firms did not sneer. They also did not for too long move away from this tried and tested system, which by the early twentieth century was to grow moribund and commercially unrealistic.

We must not always think in terms of opposites, of Chinese and foreign as separate, or locked in uneasy embrace (because each thought it unnatural) – outwardly smiling, inwardly queasy. Certainly the modes of interaction between business partners could often hardly be thought satisfactory. Young foreign businessmen asserted themselves forcefully, and in the long term settlement ingrained notions of superiority. The foreigner at his desk often never thought to ask his Chinese caller to sit; nobody did, not in Shanghai. But the logic of settlement also drove accommodation and close interaction. Thomas Hanbury's Chinese alliances long outlasted the years of the Small Sword Crisis at Shanghai where they were born. The canny Quaker realized that there was more profit in land than in silk, and in servicing this new rich Chinese community at Shanghai – with housing and with a Chinese newspaper (the *Shanghai xinbao*) that advertised property and shipping news to Chinese customers. A sense of justice, as well as sound ready reckoning, made Shanghai landowners like Hanbury or Edwin Smith protest at Shanghai Municipal Council treatment of Chinese residents. This was hardly restricted to the elite. At a meeting of the Council in July 1871, Smith railed against its treatment of Chinese taxpayers: notices to pay were 'presented by a policeman – a baton shook in the China-man's face – he was told he must pay'. 'There is no fairness towards the Chinese,' he claimed. Smith and others had tenants and rents to lose if they did not speak out for them (and the Chinese feared 'coming here', to the Council House, he claimed), but even if ultimately functional and crude, there was a community of interest, or at least a language of the same, developing in the settlement.[48] An entirely hybrid language and community of interest was represented by Britons Ernest and Frederick Major, and their great commercial publishing enterprise, the *Shenbao* newspaper, founded in 1872, and its related and various ventures. *Shenbao* was a British-owned Chinese newspaper published in the International Settlement, which rapidly achieved a wide circulation across China. In its first issue it called for contributions from its readers and in they poured, touching on the Wusong railroad, corruption, local news, occurrences abroad, steamships, on the functions of newspapers. In these pages a new form of editorial debate and discussion was fashioned, one deliberately designed to contribute ideas from the Chinese public to debates amongst officials. It was a 'new Censorate', it was claimed, a new forum for holding officials to account. In extraterritoriality's shadow (though often on bare consular sufferance) this Sino-foreign enterprise shaped a new world of discussion about Chinese society, culture and affairs. From the safety of colonial Hong Kong, an entirely Chinese-owned paper, the *Tsun-wan yat-po*, could much more explicitly criticize policy and propose reforms from 1874 onwards.[49]

But there was another world of compradors and interactions too. A Taiwan trade report sketched this in 1883 when it sought to explain why Qing officials routinely failed to respond with any alacrity to formal claims for settlement of disputes from British firms. It was like this, he explained: a British businessman moving to the port entered into a formal agreement with a comprador, who posted a $50,000 security, but was engaged on a nominal salary of only $50 a month. The entire business of the firm was placed in his hands, and all monies due were to be met by him: 'in other words, all goods are sold to him and the [foreign] merchant looks to him alone for payment.' The British trader had no ability to read or understand the comprador's books, and felt little need to, for if payment did not come, he had the bond to call on. So he could not lose, surely. Compradors took this responsibility on, it was explained, simply because it allowed them to carry on their own business as well, using the foreign firm's name, and chasing their own claims as foreign ones. They extraterritorialized their own business. That way, they aimed to secure swifter and easier settlements, for they had new routes to law and its enforcement, and they deluged the consulate with cases. The parallel with the behaviour of some convert communities is very clear, and so too the response: for knowing what the game was, Chinese authorities often looked suspiciously at all claims, and felt little need to rush decisions.[50] Fragile understandings on the part of foreign traders of the actual activities and commitments of their compradors could have dire results, for comprador use of the foreign name could be much more actively unethical, leading to contractual requirements that compradors (even of a firm of Jardines' standing) should not use the foreign firm's name. And when William Pickering was woken up one morning by his 'boy' in Takao with the news that the comprador had fled with all his staff, and that soldiers were sealing the American firm's warehouse, his seniors, he felt, had only themselves to blame, for they had ignored the whispers that he and others had relayed about the man. Pickering chased the man's trail all the way to the Pescadores, but it then went dead. The firm collapsed as a result in May 1867, its owners ruined.[51]

On top of this were the out-and-out 'lie *hongs*', where Europeans were merely passive remittance men, hiring out their name and nationality to Chinese interests. This was a new variation on the old theme, that of the foreign 'masters' of the *lorchas* – the *Arrow* and others. Charles Nail was one such, a drunk who had held and lost jobs in a trading firm, the Shanghai gasworks, and at Hall & Holtz, who was in 1885 the nominal owner of an opium shop in Shanghai's International Settlement. This became the subject of a legal and political dispute with the Chinese authorities, and it emerged that Nail had rented out his name and nationality for $50 a month, enough to keep his willing throat well-wetted. The Chinese owners of the business gained exemption from the internal transit taxes (*lijin*), and so had a cheaper product, as well as safety from the long arm of those enforcing the tax. There was more than enough of this collusion in smuggling to cause much complicated jurisdictional dispute with the Chinese authorities. Nail, as a drunk living on the edge of Shanghai's foreign world, was an easier target than Frank Edwards & Co. at Xiamen two decades on, for this firm had been a legitimate business for almost fifteen years. Frank Edwards had spent years working for other foreign firms locally as a clerk before setting up on his own as 'Auctioneer, Commission Agent, and Exporter of Narcissus Bulbs' in 1896. But the British consular correspondence registers relating to him are packed with references to claims he pressed dealing with illegal detention of staff or goods, seizure of property inland, debts owed, illegal taxes levied – all the bothersome stuff of business in extraterritoriality's protective shadow. Some of this is legitimate, but in other cases he was clearly renting his firm's name out to different Chinese interests. Letters questioned the use of the firm's registered business name by Chinese opium shops, asked him to explain and document with precision his ownership of properties, asked why he had two business names, reminded him that British subjects were not permitted to own godowns in the interior, and declined to act on his behalf. He was denounced by other more law-abiding British firms, and asked how he responded to allegations that he was 'protecting' lie *hongs*. And on top of this the consul was pestered by letters from the man's indigent father in Singapore. Edwards was not alone in all this. He was probably more embedded in local Chinese trading networks than other small British firms, through marriage to a Chinese woman, and as a Singapore-born Eurasian linked into firms trading across southeast Asian port cities. Consuls probably gave him shorter shrift as a result, and they routinely noted that he was a 'half-caste'. But he had also lodged himself in the small British world in Xiamen, was sometime secretary of the Masonic Corinthian Lodge, and later secretary of the (British) Amoy Club.[52] He faced both ways, and made the most of what he had. The treaty system had made nationality a commodity for hire. Nail and Edwards rented theirs out brazenly, but it was really a question of degree and fine detail. The single biggest asset of the foreign firm, and the foreigner, was nationality and treaty privilege. The second was the alienated concession area, both physically, in terms of land, and jurisdictionally, in the diminished and constrained sovereignty of the Qing over Chinese subjects and enterprises within them, guarded by consuls, Settlement police, courts and administrators, and by the efforts of Thomas Hanbury or E. M. Smith.

Stepping back into this changing world from a Japanese steamer on 6 September 1883 was one of the men who had shaped it, 55-year-old Sir Harry Smith Parkes, fresh from eighteen years as Minister to Japan. Wade had been recalled, for he had refused to reopen discussion on parts of the Chefoo Convention relating to opium duties which British traders and the British Indian government strongly objected to, instead pursuing his own initiatives to embed the principle of the equality of status of the Qing and foreign states in all forms of diplomatic and consular interaction. He later simply admitted that he was 'not equal to the effort' of getting the Convention ratified. In the treaty ports he was also widely believed to have spent most of his and his staff's time preparing dictionaries and translations. The chair in Chinese at the University of Cambridge which he later took up was a better fit for the scholar he was.[53] The Tongzhi emperor had died in 1874, and the Empress Dowager's nephew assumed the throne, aged four, as the Guangxu emperor, while she retained effective power. The return of Parkes promised 'progress' on stalled issues. He was met at Shanghai by a large and enthusiastic crowd, eager for the change of tone he represented. 'All the consulates are jubilant,' reported Robert Hart; they believed that Parkes would 'check the Mandarins and worry the Customs'. It was 'the dawn of a new era' reported one consular officer, Herbert Giles. We want 'practical common sense' wrote a Shanghai correspondent. The British Minister still retained the old title of 'Super-intendent of Trade', and he wanted Parkes to remember that and act on it. Diplomatic Peking under Alcock and Wade had become a land of 'lotus-eaters'.[54] British diplomats did not understand what foreign commerce, what British commerce, needed. Parkes, they felt, certainly did. And, oddly, he had arrived days before a riot in Canton led to destruction of property on Shamian, which he had so attentively laid out two decades earlier. The coincidence was noted by Chinese ob-servers, who thought it an augury, and were already nonplussed at the return of this bullying voice from the past. It certainly suggested there would be sticky demands for compensation, although the new Minister had bigger problems to contend with, for the Japanese now pressed the Qing with greater vigour in Korea, and the French likewise over Tonkin. Hart hoped Parkes had mellowed, and that Japan might have taught him more wisdom than the wildness of the early treaty world had allowed. Widowed, but with his children, he revisited the sites of his adventures – even, on the anniversary of his relief, the prison he had been held in with Loch. His Chinese, he said, was 'rusty'. It was, observed Giles, at least confident, if at times obscure, for he 'rattled gaily on, after the old school of Chinese speakers, with a very limited vocabulary and utter disregard of tones . . .'[55] It was precisely that limited vocabulary that British traders loved, but others now thumped the war drum that Parkes had once so gaily carried, for the French were coming to the fore, and when he banged the table at the Zongli Yamen over Shamian the officials there banged it right back and told him he was a warmonger.

Robert Hart was more sensitive to tone in general, and his vocabulary and thinking was very wide indeed. He was also an opportunist. One of his mottoes might be the telegraphed injunction to 'improve the opportunity' that he dispatched to James Duncan Campbell in January 1885, when he sent him to Paris to settle a little Customs contretemps with the French navy, and through such improving help resolve the wider, disastrous war being waged between the French and the Qing. The Customs light-tender *Fei Hoo* was one of three steamship light-tenders commissioned into service in 1868 which tied the still rapidly developing network together, shuttling back and forth from the southern lights, keeping the system oiled. On 2 November 1884 she was making her usual foray in Taiwanese coastal waters under Captain Booth with supplies for the Taiwan lights, when she was seized by the French navy outside Anping on the island's west coast. A blockade had been in force since 23 October, as the French brought a war to detach Indo-China from the Qing to the beautiful island. French troops had seized Jilong (Keelung) in the north, but had limited success in breaking further out, for there, as on the Yunnan–Annam border, the struggle had not gone entirely and easily their way. They had little sympathy from other foreign observers. The new blockade was to presage a new phase in the campaign, and Captain Booth had sailed straight into trouble on his way north from South Cape. Linguistic confusions may have been at fault, for Booth thought he had received permission to proceed as normal, but the shots fired across his bows needed no translation. The *Fei Hoo* was taken off to occupied Jilong, and then as supplies dried up the lights went out. South Cape was extinguished on 1 December, and the entire system in the south was endangered.[56] Hart thought he had safely arranged back in August for the lights system and its transports to be left alone, but it was a useful way for the French to put a little pressure on him, and his was, after all, a Chinese government service. The telegraph was already chattering briskly as Hart informally sought out official British attitudes towards the worsening conflict, and now he had a cause to send Campbell straight to Jules Ferry, the French President, 'in the interests of humanity', in the interests of getting his lights working again.[57] When Alcock had thundered over Margary, he had had to sail south to Shanghai to communicate swiftly with his Foreign Office superiors in London, which added a certain further physical theatre to his fulminations. In 1883 the telegraph reached Tongzhou outside Peking and the following year offices were opened in the capital itself, and from these Inspector-General Hart could send his precise and careful instructions directly to Campbell in Paris.

Such ease of communication was long a China dream, but was realized in the midst of nightmare. The first message ever sent from Peking contained the news that the French Legation had left the city on the eve of war.[58] The Qing empire was assailed in the north, and in the southwest. As the French moved to secure complete control in Indo-China the embattled Tu Duc emperor had called for assistance from his suzerain, the emperor of the Qing. There was no possible response but to try to protect the patrimony of the empire. Moreover, the French had moved in force to consolidate their hold in Tonkin and to better project power north across the border into China. So as with Taiwan the periphery was now at the centre. A fitful, undeclared war ensued from late 1883, which exposed the shortcomings of both the French and the new Qing armies, for neither side effectively vanquished the other in Tonkin. But the French took the war to the China coast, panicking the cities (people stampeded out of Shanghai and Canton) and shaking the markets. The French navy instituted its blockade, made its landing at Jilong, and occupied the Pescadores, the expedition's commander Admiral Courbet raising the tricolour there on 1 April 1885 while Campbell still parleyed at Paris. There are many things to note about this imperialist smash and grab. There was the way other powers rattled their sabres while the empire was preoccupied, and rattled the Qing; not least, but not only, the Japanese in Korea. There were the supranational pretensions of Hart's Customs, serving 'humanity', continuing to employ enemy nationals. There were the new difficulties of war: the French announced an interdiction of the rice trade, but this was mostly now carried in foreign shipping and the foreign firms wailed about neutrality. There was the nationalistic anger of Chinese dockworkers and others at Hong Kong who refused to work on French ships there, and who struck and rioted when Courbet sailed into the harbour. There was the fierce debate within the Qing elite about the merits of war – which many thought could be won – and appeasement, for others such as Northern Ports Commissioner Li Hongzhang thought war far too great a risk, certainly with the Japanese active in Korea.[59] Qing troops won the last battle of the war in Tonkin and thereby actually also toppled the French President (whose government fell when news of the defeat was received in Paris), leaving the field and Indo-China with some martial honour. But the most chilling note was struck in a matter of minutes – in 'practically seven minutes' according to one eyewitness report – and struck in Fuzhou's well-charted harbour on 23 August 1884. It was struck eleven times in those seven minutes as Courbet's ships shelled and torpedoed eleven ships of the Chinese Southern Navy and destroyed Prosper Griquel's arsenal. 'It cannot be called a battle,' reported the Customs commissioner: 'it was a butchery.' 'A good beginning has been made,' Courbet reported back to Paris. And as the ships floundered and their crews were massacred – no quarter given them, no chance of surrender as machine guns raked the decks – the hopes of twenty years of self-strengthening floundered with them and the southern fleet.[60]

Self-strengthening had been based on the belief that an otherwise unreformed Qing could harness foreign military technology and related useful learning, and restore itself that way. Arsenals, dockyards, steamers, rifles, Armstrong guns and telegraphs could all be harnessed, while foreign advisors could help deliver revenue and training; and then the empire could hold its own. In one sense it worked, for it held its own just about on the battlefields in 1884–5, and the war proved a stalemate, which was itself a kind of bitter victory. But the Qing lost Indo-China, were harried in Korea, and were humiliated as the fleet sank at Fuzhou. The dynasty emerged hyperactive: orders were placed liberally for new guns and fortifications, scores of new foreign advisors were recruited into the army and navy, and torpedo boats were secured. The war still gave the Chinese pause for thought. A key reason it did so was that it was so widely known – the new Chinese print media reporting and discussing it. *Shenbao* sent a correspondent, a Russian, to Tonkin; new titles were even established to capitalize on the hunger for detail. Ernest Major launched the *Dianshizhai huabao* ('Dianshizhai pictorial') in 1884, starting publication with an issue whose pages depicted the conflict in Tonkin. The war was replayed swiftly and re-envisioned in this monthly's pages, as no war had ever been before. And as a result of that, of the *Shenbao* and Hong Kong press debates, of discussion and reflection, perhaps younger thinkers started to conclude that the problem of China might be not that the Qing lacked Armstrong guns, or brave soldiers, or organizational competence, but that other reshaping was needed. One who later claimed to have been radicalized by the war and its outcome was Sun Yat-sen, who would lead a succession of revolutionary organizations, and who would briefly serve as China's first republican president in 1912. The Qing had long faced enemies – religious uprisings, minority revolts, anti-dynastic secret society activities – but the sinking of self-strengthening as its strategy for facing internal and external pressure caused others to pause and reconsider, people who had no truck with the normal sphere of revolt or rebellion. The new press generated new forms of discussion alongside those of the world of official memorials and debate, debates which developed a momentum and character all of their own. There were far, far greater shocks to come, and to come very soon, but already for some there had been humiliation enough. Some other route forward to survival must be found. It did not help that some of the funds available to rebuild and strengthen the navy were instead directed to a pet project of the imperial household, the renovation of the new Summer Palace.[61] It did not help at all that instead of extra officers or new and modern ships, the navy found itself paying for the construction of an exquisite marble pleasure boat, uselessly resplendent in Kunming Lake in the Summer Palace complex northwest of Peking. It was at least safe there from torpedoes.

10

Jubilees

'In what region of the earth is not Shanghai known.' Such was the motto printed on a banner strung across the flag and lantern-bestrewn mouth of Shanghai's Peking Road in November 1893, part of the florescence of bunting, lantern and gas-jet illuminations that marked the golden jubilee of the establishment of the international settlement. It was no question, you will note, but simple assertion, for those who inscribed this and over a dozen more such mottoes in English and Chinese above Shanghai's streets and on its buildings ostensibly lacked no confidence in the fact of their triumph. We are known, they claimed: we are strong; we have built; we look forward. They took as their date to mark the anniversary Balfour's formal opening of the port to British trade on 17 November 1843, and so gave their celebration of cosmopolitan amity a rigid British frame. This was entirely apt, as we have seen, for all the foreign powers had followed in the wake of the British in the secular drive into China. They had a choice of dates. They might have taken the anniversary of the Nanjing Treaty, or of Balfour's arrival six days earlier in 1843, or the establishment of the proto-Municipal Council. But these were too overtly tied to the war which created the treaty port, or else were obscured in the archive, so the date of Shanghai's 'opening' to British trade it was. And Shanghai, the banners claimed, was not just a jewel standing alone, but the jewel in their Chinese world, and they boasted too of its place in their wider Asian hinterland: 'Shanghai,' barked another banner, 'Queen of Eastern Settlements'; 'All Eastern ports rejoice in their Mother's Jubilee.' 'Omnia Juncta in Uno' ('All joined in one') was another – the Council's motto, writ also on their new flag, and on the silver and bronze jubilee medals they ordered cast in Britain. A steamer heading east, and tea and cotton plants also decorated the medals. The P&O steamers were still stocked with opium, of course, but it was a word missing from the jubilee. The banners and the flags had a good enough wind on the jubilee days and were easy to read. But it was as if the buildings and streets themselves did not speak eloquently enough, nor the statues or memorials that now lined the Bund. A sense of unease perhaps crept in, which had directed this inscribing of the urban landscape in words hoist above their streets under which they paraded or watched on the 17 and 18 November.

They assembled the Volunteers at the race course that morning, joined as ever by naval contingents from ships in harbour, for no late-nineteenth-century public ceremonial at home or abroad lacked its touch of martial splendour. The men paraded past the new municipal flag, saluting council, consuls and assorted regular military guests.[1] These included the officer commanding the Royal Navy's China Station, Admiral Sir Edmund Fremantle, who had first served at Shanghai in 1853. 'We are today commemorating the conclusion of fifty years of amicable relations with the natives in whose midst we dwell,' declared the chairman of the Municipal Council to those present with no sense of irony, despite his uniformed and rifle-bearing audience. And in return for the 'pretty free hand' we are given here, he continued, Shanghai's foreign community needed to show readiness to defend itself. Two hundred and fifty of them turned out on 17 November, one in eight male foreign residents demonstrating just such martial readiness. They were mustered on the site of that 1854 'Battle of the Muddy Flat', and after self-congratulatory speeches marched back down the way they had come that year, along the Nanjing Road, led by the Shanghai Light Horse, the unit of choice of Shanghai's foreign elite, all the way to the lawns on the banks of the Huangpu south of the Public Garden. There a 'jubilee oration' was delivered by the Revd William Muirhead, a voice from another age, for he had arrived in Shanghai in 1847 as a member of the London Mission. Muirhead sketched Shanghai's history, skipping lightly over the centuries before 1843 and conflating city and Settlement throughout. He drew the attention of his listeners again and again to what they saw about them: the park, the trees, the buildings, the busy harbour with its wharves and warehouses, the supreme court. Just north of them now stood a new memorial to join Margary's and the

Ever Victorious Army's – that statue of Sir Harry Parkes looking west into the heart of China. He had died in post in March 1885, and they now had to make do with his memory and spirit. This urban landscape exhibited these signal achievements, and spoke these five decades of history, though only the Russell *hong* survived from early days[2] – and so too, Muirhead claimed, did the establishment of English homes and family life, and the examples therein of 'our higher civilization', of a Christian civilization. And while 'Christ and Christianity' remained 'the great want of this country', Muirhead turned also on the Settlement and its toleration of 'evils and vices'. He might equally have meant the brothels and opium divans that peppered the settlement, and the opium hulks that were still moored off the Bund – at least three of them in the panorama photographs taken that year of the Settlement's front face. They let venerable Muirhead have his white-haired say, applauded heartily, and then got on with the usual stuff of communal celebration, firing salvoes from the warships in the harbour and the Volunteer artillery at noon, then volleys from the infantry and marines. They always liked playing this martial music, all cannon and rifle, but that day they fired an even more furious celebratory fusillade into the Shanghai air.

There had been no end of debate about what was a fitting way to mark the jubilee, and what was affordable. Bob Little, now editor of the *North China Herald*, lambasted through his editorials the final 'invertebrate' decision of a committee of ratepayers which had been convened to discuss various proposals.[3] A new park had been proposed, as were an isolation hospital, a new town hall, a public school for Chinese children, and a refuge for poor Chinese. Ranged on one side of the debate were those who wanted something permanent, something that might also elicit sympathy and interest from the Chinese literati who, remarked Little, 'are rather apt to look on us as an inferior race of mere money grubbers'. He lobbied for an educational initiative. Others concurred: Chinese in the Settlement were 'our people', Muirhead claimed during this debate; our subjects, and were taxed like the foreign residents, and so were owed the consideration owed the subjects of British colonies or children at 'home', by which he meant England, where recent education legislation had introduced free elementary education. Ranged on the other side were the more fiscally cautious, indisposed to allowing long-term calls on Council finances and rate-payer pockets, and still smarting from a stock market crash the previous year. They proposed instead that the Settlement hold a party, feed itself and its foreign children, and then get back to work, which is what they thought Shanghai did best. Impassioned speeches and letters to the press from missionaries and educators failed to swing the ratepayers, who settled decisively on the holding of a jubilee celebration. A token gesture to something more concrete was delivered in the form of a new fountain in the Public Garden (fully public only on that day when Chinese visitors for once were allowed in, before its gate was once more shut to them). It was sited in the garden precisely 'to prevent the Chinese from interfering with it'.[4] But, discrimination notwithstanding, tens of thousands of Chinese visitors came into the Settlement to watch the celebrations – upwards of half a million all told in the Council's final estimate. Although eager spectators, the Chinese partners in the Sino-foreign condominium at Shanghai were lukewarm about partici-pating. The 'leading Canton men don't seem to care about a public demonstration of any kind' reported the Council chairman in early October despite invitations to the guilds to contribute a procession.[5] While some of the Chinese-language mottoes lauded a claimed 'Fifty years of Treaty Amity' – a claim that the sight of the Volunteers might have tested – as well as the mutual benefits of commerce, others blandly and uncontroversially commented on the day's second big public event, a night-time procession, lauding in advance the brightness of the lanterns that would light up the city. But there was a great crowded confusion that evening: too many people jammed the streets, and the firemen had to roughly shove their way through helplessly compacted crowds, twenty deep, even to get started. They then made their way down the Nanjing Road, led by the town band and a large dragon constructed atop one of the fire trucks, with illuminated slogans or pictures on those following, and processed up and down the Bund, its buildings all lit up, passing through a great jubilee arch constructed for the event. The guilds processed too in the end, but out of step and to their own tune, for if foreign residents disagreed about what legacy their celebration should leave, many Chinese residents, though happy enough to watch it, were more sceptical still about the occasion of such display and resented the restrictions placed on them in Shanghai's streets.

The celebration has been discussed for the light its illuminations and confusions sheds on Shanghai in 1893 and the nature of the Sino-foreign condominium in the city, but two factors stand out: firstly, the assumption on the part of foreign organizers and participants that it was a commemoration of an enterprise that had been of wholly mutual benefit, and secondly the light it sheds on the new insecurities of the position at Shanghai, and more widely in the treaty ports in China; and of one stark face of that insecurity, namely the violence of the 'New Imperialism' of that decade as it unfolded in China.[6] The French grab in Tonkin was a sign of changing times, wholly integrated as no other China war had been before in a wider global pattern of systematic territorial aggrandizement. The 1880s saw a new and energetic phase in the European assault on Africa, sparked by the British occupation of Egypt in 1882, the Suez Canal and nationalist revolt having sucked them in, but marked most potently by the irruption into the colonial landscape of Bismarck's Germany. In 1884–5 a clutch of protectorates were declared by Germany over territories in Africa and the Pacific. Berlin also hosted the first of those map-making congresses, settling claim and counter-claim, and sketching out borders. The partition of Africa entered a new and dizzying phase. British traders and schemers had mostly given up their protectorate dreams for China by the 1880s. It was now 'too late', the real opportunity having sailed back west with Sherrard Osborn and H. N. Lay's doomed Anglo-Chinese fleet in the winter of 1863–4.[7] Short sharp shocks were the stuff of the policy they wanted and expected: sharp enough to deliver a change of Chinese minds when needed, short enough not to inconvenience. 'We don't want war with China,' Little had declared privately, for example: 'We want our prestige preserved'; it was 'the necessary assertion'.[8] But the new claims staked by new powers changed the atmosphere. For all the domestic wholesomeness that formed one key theme in the foreign fiesta at Shanghai, in its talk of children, and of their future fifty years on, others with a mind to China were in fact getting eager for yet more plunder.

They remained insecure at Shanghai. Even after the French war, force looked less and less a viable option for maintaining 'our hold on the country', as a *North China Herald* editorial had put it in 1888. So they must 'amalgamate' their interests closely with the Chinese, one commentator argued in reply: they must lobby at home and intertwine themselves so tightly in Shanghai that they would prove impossible to root out as China changed. Bob Little published a poetic rejoinder to this plea for amalgamation, which sketched out a future of Chinese dominance. In this routine topsy-turvy conceit the Public Garden was now reserved for Chinese, a 'native gave the orders' on a passing steamer, 'the chain-gang all were white, the stalwart warders / Yellow from head to heel'. In a zoo was preserved a 'Prehistoric man', this was 'the last Taipan'.[9] Such was 'amalgamation': it would in fact bring defeat, and worse, humiliation. 'Our hold on the country' would be lost. There was nothing unusual about these anxieties, for a sense of insecurity was a basic fact of colonial life; it was part of the equipment of the colonist, carried out in the mental baggage. It was best symbolized by the fact that British troops in India carried weapons into church services, a lesson in guardedness learnt the hard way in 1857. Watchfulness was the instruction given to the colonial administrator at his office and to the mistress in the colonial home. So there was nothing unusual in the Council chairman's remarks on 16 November 1893 about the Volunteers being needed to deal with 'those local risings which may from time to time occur in the best regulated places'.[10] What was more unusual was a hysterical fantasy published in the *North China Herald* in late September 1893, 'The Shanghai Exodus and the Capture of the Chinese Fleet' by 'S. B. R.' This was an invasion tale that was shaped by new insecurities stemming from European tensions rooted in the rise of Germany, and a new source of local disorder. In 1891 a series of evidently coordinated risings broke out, led by a central-China based network of criminal gangs who called themselves the *Gelaohui* – the Elder Brother Society – and whose political agenda was initially anti-foreign and eventually anti-Qing. Originating mainly in the now-disbanded forces which had suppressed the Taiping, *Gelaohui* members operated gambling houses and extortion rackets, and were willing participants in a series of riots against missionaries in Yangzi cities.[11] An orphanage was attacked at Yangzhou, churches were destroyed at Wuhu. A missionary and a Customs examiner were killed at Wuxue. There were fears of a rising against the settlements at Shanghai. British and German gunboats cruised the Huangpu. Council circulars issued defence instructions and signals: four guns fired quickly would announce the outbreak of a riot. (Cannon fire in the Huangpu served many purposes.) It is 'incipient rebellion rather than hostility to either foreigners or Christianity' claimed Robert Hart, and indeed although the now-usual anti-Christian propaganda had circulated widely, what added a new frisson to the events was the arrest in September that year of a young Customs assistant, Briton Charles Mason, for smuggling arms for the *Gelaohui*.[12] 'Anything like organization would enable a mob to wreck the settlement there in an hour or two,' continued Hart, a theme he and others would return to. Mason's involvement, and the thirty-five crates of revolvers and rifles that he was smuggling into Zhenjiang, seemed to suggest a new order of seriousness and organization in the threat made evident on the Yangzi.

These developments gave new shape to old fears. S. B. R.'s invasion tale was hardly original, borrowing its form from a new and popular Victorian genre, the most notabe example of which was George Chesney's wildy successful *Battle of Dorking* (1871), a tale of a successful German invasion of an unprepared Britain; more recent contributions being, *The Great War of 189*–, serialized in 1892, and *The Great War of 1897* by William Le Quex, serialized the following year. It was not even the first Shanghai version: a similar skit had been published in 1871, when events at Tianjin were still fresh in foreign minds, but this one was firmly rooted in current developments and fears.[13] As war breaks out in Europe, 100,000 foreign-trained Chinese troops march on the Shanghai settlements. They are all members of an anti-foreign secret society, claims the Zongli Yamen, and beyond their control. The skeleton foreign naval forces remaining in China coast waters suspend hostilities and combine to sail to rescue the foreign community, landing parties who assemble with the police and volunteers to attempt a defence (after a 'good substantial breakfast'), but they are too hard pressed, and the enemy too many, even after the Gatling guns have reaped their harvest. The urban landscape so praised by Muirhead is impossible to defend, lacks redoubts, and is too open. The bridges are held, but the Chinese force breaks into the International Settlement through the cemetery on its border with the French concession. The foreign force retires to the fleet in the river and withdraws as the Settlement is illuminated in a deadly glow, for Chinese soldiers and looters fire those buildings left standing after a barrage from the ships' guns, a sight 'magnificent as a spectacle'. Their solace is that their dead are far outnumbered by those of the enemy, and that before they assemble at one of Robert Hart's lightships to set sail south for the safety of Hong Kong, they manage to seize the Chinese fleet. The conceit ends mid-story, for while the European war continues no final resolution is possible, but undoubtedly, notes S. B. R., there will be punishment, and there will be an indemnity, 'secured from the Customs revenue'. This derivative and violent tale with its pedestrian detail (the breakfast, the financial vengeance) is notable for its timing, for it serves as a preamble to the nominal celebration of amity and commerce which was otherwise being prepared and which illuminated the Settlement with a less destructive glow. It also suggests how the routine militarization of foreign life in the settlements was inflected in the early 1890s by new fears, of secret anti-foreign societies, of the potentially bitter outcome of the foreign training of Chinese forces, and by wider *fin de siècle* fears of war. 'Shanghai guards her own' ran another one of those jubilee mottoes; but how competently, S. B. R. and others asked, when the forces of opposition could be so vast in number and if they were to be properly organized, and how dependent might the order of the China settlements now be on the growing caprice of European power-politics?

After fifty years then they were in fact still scared. Not scared to walk their settlement – Muirhead proudly noted that they could walk their streets 'without the slightest fear', so different from the early days and from the days of war he and Fremantle had experienced.[14] But they were concerned that Chinese strength and European competition could conflict in ways that would undermine their gains of fifty years. They need not have worried so, for Chinese military strength soon proved chimerical, and European and Japanese rivalry would presently go on to open up whole new theatres of action for them: new treaty ports, new opportunities for securing financial and other concessions, new rights to diversify the operations they could undertake in their model and other settlements. But there were other challenges nonetheless that they had to face soon. In fact, in the months running up to the festivities in Shanghai, a host of China coast personalities trooped into a committee room in the House of Lords in London, to be quizzed by the members of a Royal Commission on Opium. Some of these we are already familiar with: James Legge, James Hudson Taylor, Horatio Nelson Lay, Sir Thomas Wade, William Lockhart and Alexander Michie all had their say. The past was as much the focus of these early sessions as opium, as lessons in the history of Anglo-Chinese relations over the previous fifty-five years were delivered. Donald Matheson recounted his experiences of the Canton closure in 1830. Lay told the panel how he had learned from experience that 'the moment you prostrate yourself before a Chinese, his answer is the knife', and argued that the calumnies of the Anti-Opium Society, as he saw them – wild claims that opium was forced on China at the point of the bayonet – should equally be met with no kowtow but firm and principled rebuff. History showed that such charges were not true, Lay stated. But this, the anti-opiumists explained, was what the Chinese say, not us, for the history 'may be one way or the other', but Chinese interpretations damage all of us and impair trade's potential. Wade less heatedly delivered his version of that history: opium did not figure; conflict stemmed from the British desire to 'secure endurable relations'. Others were leading lights in a Society for the Suppression of the Opium Trade that had been lobbying for two decades for a proper discussion on Britain's role in the trade. Galvanized by the failure to ratify the Chefoo Convention precisely because of the proposed changes it would bring to the opium trade regime, they built up tremendous support which gained its day with the election of William Gladstone's fourth ministry in 1892, and the appointment of the commission charged with investigating the worlds of opium in India and the possibilities and costs of prohibition. For abolitionists the commission was a fizzle, for it concluded in 1895 that their concerns were more moral than practically grounded, and that the finances of India were dependent on the business of opium, a mostly harmless drug, for whose prohibition they found there was no popular support in India. It also delivered a lengthy historical appendix surveying the British record in China up to the Treaty of Nanjing, and while critical – it was 'not, it must be admitted, creditable to this country' – it judged that 'the war was not undertaken to force opium on China'.[15]

If the history of the British presence was being contested in Parliament, it was largely skated over at Shanghai two months later, at least in public utterances on the day. The press and pamphlets however delivered various surveys of fifty years 'of progress' as mementoes to join the batches of commemorative photographs rushed out by Chinese, Japanese and foreign-owned studios. Bob Little and others penned sketches of the 'early days', contrasting most commonly the physical changes wrought on the English Ground since the 1840s – the now common tale of the triumph of foreign enterprise over the 'wilderness of marshes', as Fremantle put it. For the first time someone browsed through the Council archives, a 'mass of recorded detail', plucking out gems and notes from the Council minute books to show how the 'our predecessors devoted themselves to the task of founding the Model Settlement'.[16] But in that mass of detail itself lay good cause for insecurity. For when one opponent of the scheme to mark the jubilee with a school for Chinese demanded that the Council seek a formal legal opinion as to its right under the Land Regulations to establish or run schools he was quickly persuaded to withdraw the proposal. As Little put it, 'It has never been the policy of our Councils to ask for a strict delineation of their powers', and they have deliberately avoided it, for 'nothing could be more inconvenient and possibly injurious than to have strictly defined what those regulations permit and what they forbid'. Precedents and contingent innovations underpinned the International Settlement, and 'we should be content with what we have got'.[17] This quickly stymied debate exposed a further fundamental insecurity, the fact that the very position at Shanghai was not on firm foundations. This was hardly a Shanghai problem. The tiny British concession at Xiamen, for example, rested on no firmer legal basis than arrogant assertion and defiantly protected custom.[18] The Europeans and their allies had made much more of the land set apart for them than had ever been envisaged by the Qing treaty makers or the local officials who had had to actually implement agreements in the chosen localities. This is hardly surprising, for empire was made by men who pushed at boundaries and staked claims, but it resulted in an insecurity which added a note of armed hysteria to treaty port life and politics, and potentially undermined efforts to defend the status quo or 'improve' the gains made at Shanghai.

There were of course other sites of jubilee. Hong Kong had marked its own two years earlier, in January 1891, on the anniversary of Elliot's proclamation of its cession to the British crown.[19] It was a more staid affair, for a more staid and more British outpost. There were thanksgiving services at both Anglican and Roman Catholic cathedrals, and a Parsee ceremony too. There was no need to mark out the streets with firm military tread, as Shanghai did, for Hong Kong was more solid British ground, and the guns fired a simple royal salute in the harbour rather than the wild salvoes that Shanghai let loose. The social highlights – balls at City Hall, at Jardine, Matheson's *hong*, and at the German Club Concordia – testified to the prevailing centres of power and influence in the colony. Jardines was powerful there, and the German community in the British colony was socially and commercially prominent. Anglo-German commercial collaboration across the treaty ports was to be a feature of the next two decades. But most importantly Hong Kong feasted no less on Sino-foreign amity than the city in the north was to, although with different import (and with no Chinese-focused strand to the celebration), for the governor's address to Queen Victoria stressed how the 'numerous races' in the colony received 'the same rights and equal justice'. Prominent Chinese figures were members of the organizing committee; none were at Shanghai because its committee was chosen from the list of foreign ratepayers. Here, however flawed in practice, was a different discourse about relations with the Chinese. Muirhead's claim for Shanghai was the fact at Hong Kong: Chinese residents in Hong Kong were British colonial subjects, and while subject to a punitive policing regime (which thwarted a massive 'clan fight' on the morning of the jubilee), and otherwise often discriminated against in regulation and practice, they were equal before the government in one sense, for Britons in Hong Kong were also unenfranchised.[20] Shanghai's foreign traders could shape their local politics, and in 1893 for the first time foreign women attended and cast votes at the meeting of ratepayers. The Crown Colony at Hong Kong, however, was formally part of a wider British colonial world, directed from a different branch of the British government – the Colonial Office – and staffed administratively by a different cadre of officials. Governors had considerable autonomy, but were also subject to formal policy directives and legal norms that were absent at the treaty ports. And British subjects there, like British subjects elsewhere in British possessions outside the settler colonies, had no political rights. Legal structures were often weighted towards them; 'white' solidarity meant colonial officials leaned towards them; the language of power was English: but they had no right to any say in their government.

What was signally different about the foreign world in China as it was celebrated in 1893 to what might have been noted twenty-five years earlier was its domesticity. If the Shanghai jubilee did not leave new schools in its wake, it gave the foreign children of the Settlement a party, and even a 'jubilee hymn' to sing, two hundred of them in choir: 'Our walls were raised by builders few / Shanghai's old founders, brave and true!'[21] Their future, and their future in Shanghai it might be noted, received much attention. The almost entirely adult, masculine world of the early decades had been steadily diluted. It was hardly gone for good, for it became standard practice for commercial firms, missions and municipal or other administrations to prohibit marriage of male employees for at least the first term of service before home leave.[22] Young men were left to their own devices, as long as these were discreet, and providing they avoided scandal. Not all of them succeeded, but companies no longer tolerated foreign staff ostentatiously keeping Asian mistresses, and while China long remained a site of foreign male opportunity, it also started steadily to fill up with foreign women and families. In 1870 there were 1,666 foreign residents in the Settlement at Shanghai, men outnumbering women six to one, and there were 167 children. By 1895 there were 1,389 children and 3,295 resident foreign adults, with a much more balanced ratio of men to women (1.7 to 1). And some of the women who started to arrive by the end of the century came to work, not least the nurses recruited by the Council after 1895, including those hired for the Victoria Nursing Home, which was to open in 1901. At the same time, there was an upsurge in numbers of European and North American women arriving in China to work in prostitution.[23] Still, most women came to marry, or came as wives.

The growth of foreign family life was shaped also by the spectacular rise in the size of the mission presence. When Taylor gave his evidence to the Royal Commission on Opium, the China Inland Mission had 580 workers, operating in fourteen out of China's eighteen provinces. An 1889 survey had identified nearly 1,300 foreign missionaries (including nearly 400 couples).[24] Housing so many families meant a reshaping of treaty port architecture, the separation of residence from workplace, and the need for family houses to be built as the traditional *hong* compound went into decline. The latter was also aided by rising land values, which meant that the old and conspicuously leisurely use of space proved uneconomic. Speculative building saw new foreign-style villas snake their way along the streets far from the old centre of Settlement life at Shanghai, not least because of a continuing desire on the part of foreign residents to live at a remove from Chinese neighbourhoods. In those new compounds different and at times emotionally highly complex fields of Sino-foreign interaction developed, with the European mistress of the home responsible for day-to-day supervision of the household staff, while children were placed in the hands of Chinese 'amahs', nannies and wet-nurses. The latter because, as it was widely understood and stated, climate prevented European women breastfeeding their own children. Female bodies could not cope: 'the European constitution must be altered in this respect before it could flourish here' reported one doctor at Xiamen in 1873.[25] Amahs were prominent figures in the home life of the Europeans. Shipping companies had special rates for their passage to Europe; correspondents to the press complained that they took all the seats in the parks while overseeing children. The photograph of the foreign child with the Chinese amah is a commonly surviving one, and often untold are the intense relationships that developed between servants and young foreign children, who, it is often attested, better spoke the language of their carers than that of their parents. More often noted, though, was the more bitter fact that the death rates for foreign children residing in the treaty ports and mission stations remained high, climate being blamed, and childbirth itself took its toll.[26] Bob Little's brother Louis and his wife lost two out of their four children in early infancy in Shanghai; in Peking Stephen Bushell and his wife lost five out of six. The foreign cemeteries had once been filled with soldiers, but now were commonly stocked with infants.

Memoirs make great play of relations with loyal and affectionate servants, or of the daily cheeky knavery and thievery of cooks and 'boys'. Very little of this was ever unique to China. Moreover, the imperatives placed on European women to police the domestic sphere were as strong there as elsewhere in European colonial and metropolitan worlds, and so too the contradictory fact of real relations with servants.[27] Homes, memoirs show, now became sites for the assertion of the supremacy of the European woman over her servants, a relationship often made more fraught by the fact that many of the foreign women concerned were new to China, coming out to marry, or married at home on men's long leaves. And it was 'not the custom among foreigners to speak Chinese to the servants in Shanghai', which further complicated things.[28] And Master/servant relationships that they would be familiar with were additionally and strongly infused with the notion of European dignity in relations with Chinese that for some made every concession a kowtow. Consuls and courts were expected to deal with some of the results, as servants charged employers with violence, or with refusing to pay money due, and employers attempted to enforce (usually hazily verbal) contracts and routinely charged servants with theft. Hart seems to have been a little unlucky, as three of his 'boys' over the years went mad: 'I fancy *their* life is too dull, and *I* don't rage and row enough!'[29] But if relations with servants could be problematic, and if like Hart's third, Li, some exceptionally might need restraining and disarming (having stolen his master's pistol), there was more usually much more compromise – memoirs routinely make play of excessive food bills, for servants often took commissions this way – and there was often simple loneliness that could prompt stronger bonds. It was a curious situation, for they shared and they did not share the physical and emotional spaces of European households. Then there were also concerns about health and cleanliness. Check your servants' hands, check their quarters, watch how they wash food, watch how they prepare it. Foreigners were assured that lives – yours, your children's – depended on it. The sanitation front line lay in the kitchen, and the European mistress of the home was tasked with guarding it. Health aside, there was another concern about the effects of growing up in this environment on foreign children, especially boys. Commentators worried that amahs 'spoilt' children, sycophantically indulging the every whim of the young 'master' and 'missee'. Boys would be unmanned by such indulgence. Children should be taken out of such environments as soon as possible, it was argued, but this was not always practical. The growing domestic complexity of the treaty port and missionary world was matched by a more fundamental social complexity, and the growth of a settled foreign lower-middle and middle class. These were the residents who could hardly afford to send children overseas to school, and for whom even at large settlements like Shanghai there was limited provision. There was, in addition to the cultural insecurities foisted on foreign mothers, a darker set of fears about the possibilities of transmission of disease by servants to children, or even the dangers of nurses or amahs using opiates to quiet their charges. Doctors as a result began more and more to caution against employing Chinese wet-nurses, and recommended bottle feeding instead.[30] Some, like Hart, could afford to bring foreign governesses or maids out to China, but most could not.

But if community was celebrated in the Hong Kong and Shanghai jubilees (and performed, as they dispatched sports teams to play each other), separation and dispersal still often lay at the heart of that community. Children were sent home, young mothers too were sometimes dispatched west or east for their health and that of their infants. Travel itself still meant real danger: the P&O steamer *Bokhara* sailed out of Shanghai on 14 October 1892 and two days later was driven onto the Pescadores in a typhoon, twenty-three surviving out of 146 passengers and crew. All but two members of the Hong Kong cricket team drowned. Customs Tidewaiter Cunnify's wife and child were sailing home on the ship, and did not survive. Her body was found, the infant still tied to her. Cunnify killed himself.[31] The tragedy echoed so loudly because it seemed anachronistic, the mechanics of transportation now so firmly embedded and family strategies so strongly relying on them. But the charts and the weather forecasting only reduced risk. They did not remove it. The long, convivial voyage home also provided an atmosphere of enclosed intimacy amongst passengers that broke marriages possibly as often as it served, mostly in reverse, as a venue where prospective partners met. Separation across continents certainly crippled marriages and engagements – it broke James Dow's, and it broke Bob Little's – but separation itself was a fact of colonial life, and of the life of the migrant. Its emotional cost was no less diminished for all its routine nature or easier and swifter communications. Sons and daughters left homes for good, or for long periods, when they sought out positions or joined husbands in China. Consular and employer files are often punctuated with letters from concerned parents, asking for news about their offspring who had failed to write, or send remittance, or to be told of change of circumstance or address.

Such letters and other files show how even modest China incomes supported parents or siblings in Europe, or were used to invest in property or business at home, or to pay for the emigration of other family members. The China coast was not separate from the other spheres of European colonialism and migration: letters and remittances, steamers and telegrams, love, loss and longing, weaved them tightly together.

The jubilees celebrated success but the archives also tell of failure, which was as common, if not more so. Most of the big early China firms went bankrupt eventually, as we have seen, for most failed to adapt and diversify as the trading world changed. Smaller businesses and partnerships were even less able to weather such storms as 1865 or 1883. James Dow never recovered financially from his bankruptcy in 1865, dying in Shanghai in 1875 leaving a small estate of under £300 to show for his own silver jubilee. But starker tales are told in the records of the intestate dead: Mathew Logan died in 1885, leaving a widow '(a China woman)', who had 'no money and no food', 'little furniture and that poor'; prostitute Ida Plumb left only her clothes and a few items of jewellery; Alex Stuart, watchman at the Kiangnan Acid Works, left 'no watch, no money, or jewellery . . . no letters or papers'; ex-lightkeeper Stanford, found in a 'shanty' with his Japanese partner, left 'property small – debts large'; Andrew Milligan had been 'out of employment. Intemperate habits. General break up.' They were police, ex-Customs, bar-owners, prostitutes, store assistants, seamen; and often no employment is given because none was had. They died in the Shanghai General Hospital, often in the free beds. They died of cholera, dysentery, typhoid, tuberculosis. They drowned; they slit their throats; they overdosed on opium. They were given pauper burials. Regularly they are listed as having no kin. There are no papers, and no effects. Quite often all that the men have is a watch, ticking on indifferently once the man was dead. They were otherwise invisible, melted into air, antecedents obscure, unplaceable and untraceable. All that remains is the consul's scrawl in the memo book. Their possessions were sold; the proceeds held against debts owing or some contact from a relative. Chinese or Japanese women living with them seem routinely to be discounted from this process, assumed not to have any call; they are never named, and sometimes their nationality is not clear, for they did not count and were not properly noticed unless they could prove marriage under British law, and few could. The indigent foreign world can be glimpsed through these files, as can lower-class attempts to make a living. William Wheeler kept the Hole in the Wall tavern, running it with his Japanese wife. An illiterate Black American and sometime prostitute, Mary Berry, pooled her savings with ex-policeman Robert Wright – and she pawned her jewellery – to make a go of a pub, the Boar's Head in 1879. 'Old woman,' she claimed he said, 'we'll see what we can make. We'll go partners.' He died the following year: pauper burial. Berry stayed on in Shanghai, surfacing again in 1887 when the mariner she had been living with for two years died, and his details were recorded in the same files.[32] We have few other records of these foreign lives in China, but they were there, and died there too.

'General break up' took enough of them, but more just about got by, for there were sound billets to be had for an upper working class of overseers, police sergeants, foremen and examiners. Such opportunities were fixed there, and so were they, for it worked because the living was easier, servants cheap enough for this class also. If some sank with little trace, others hung on for decades, their children, and grandchildren in some cases, finding employment or a husband. George Skinner, ex-seaman, joined the Shanghai police in 1866 and left to become custodian of the town hall, his three daughters marrying better – because they were rarer – than they would have done in England's Somerset from whence he came. George Crank followed the same route through the police in 1893, and then Customs: four of his daughters married policemen in Shanghai, and two sons joined the force. Frank Edwards lodged a son in the Customs lights service, another in a dockyard business in Amoy. His daughter married into the Customs. A job for a son was often found by the Service for its staff, a daughter too, George Taylor's securing a typist's post after her father's death. The reasons might be charitable, but they might be politic: Hart disbursed nominations for appointments to please foreign diplomats or politicians in Europe. Shanghai's Council recruited from London but likewise kept some jobs in the family, or within a small circle. 'I must stick to Shanghai,' wrote Bob Little when things seemed insecure, 'where I know & am known.'[33] He applied for a post at Singapore, but got back on his feet by lighting Shanghai for the first time with electricity in 1882, ten lamps burning on the Bund by October that year.[34] He died in Shanghai in 1906, forty-four years after arriving. Archibald Little, more restless, had headed west, following Harry Parkes' stony gaze all the way up the Yangzi. While Hong Kong served as a jumping-off point for some, for posts in China, especially from the military, Shanghai despatched men north to Tianjin, or west along the great river. An elite world of more successful Shanghailanders was layered above this lower and middling life. And as businesses developed, firms like Swire's, Jardines, the Hongkong and Shanghai Bank, customarily moved their staff from port to port, and sometimes over to Japan, and across to southeast Asian branches. A firm distinction became visible between the settled Shanghailander and Tientsiner, and the mobile expatriate. The former were 'poor whites' in expatriate eyes and on wagging expatriate tongues. At the jubilee in 1893 their place in the administration or Volunteers meant that they were given the bronze commemorative medals; their social betters received the silver ones. Even though they shared many interests with the local elite, the next fifty years would show an increasingly strong divergence in their politics, for the mobile expatriate interest proved more nimble and flexible politically, but the Shanghailander, elite or humble, was immobile politically too.

There was still room for pioneering attempts in the old mould, chasing El Dorado to the next port, and the next. Alexander Michie roved no more, but Archibald Little assumed the mantle. After he went west in February 1883, sending back letters earmarked for publication and for making his objective known, Little became an advocate for expansion into this ripe new frontier territory, unoccupied Sichuan – unoccupied that is, by foreign traders and entrepreneurs. Why should not the steamship go further west; why not all the way? The Chefoo Convention allowed trade, but only in Chinese vessels. But why lose six weeks to ship goods by junk the last 500 miles to Chongqing, he asked, when it took less time than that to travel from London to Shanghai? Because of the gorges and rapids, most assumed, but no, he thought, it could and should be done. The heroic mode could still be enacted. So Little lobbied; raised funds in London; ordered a steamship, to be prefabricated in Glasgow ready for assembly in Shanghai; and then sailed it to Yichang in February 1889, ready to strike west. But

British diplomats would not press the issue, and the Zongli Yamen and local officials prevaricated. Oh, thought Little and others, it is the same old story: evasive Chinese officials and spineless British ones. 'Although one cannot anticipate any fresh concessions,' mused a supportive observer, 'it is strange to find the Chinese withholding one already granted.' The Chinese were, J. O. P. Bland later remarked, 'highly trained passive resisters', and they resisted this initiative quite successfully.[35]

Pioneers did not always succeed. A more fruitful initiative took place further down the Yangzi when the (unrelated) Edward Selby Little secured for himself and others a slice of the Qing imperium. Little, a Dorset-born Methodist missionary working in Zhenjiang from 1886, acquired the title to a cool-aired mountain top south of summer-steamy Jiujiang in late 1895. He rechristened it Kuling – 'cooling', a feeble pun which stuck – and started selling parcels off to missionaries and other foreign residents. He developed an infrastructure, and had soon sold 130 lots, and this real estate development acquired the trappings of a formally alienated enclave: there was a Kuling Council, a hospital, a public library.[36] Each treaty port had its 'hill station', as we have seen, a bolt hole from the enervating iron heat of the plains and ports. These began as informally rented temples; some turned into mini treaty ports. Kuling became a major sanatorium and summer resort, with some 500 houses by 1921, attracting the Shanghai and Tianjin department stores to open summer branches, and the steamer firms to advertise their routes to it from Shanghai. Year-round settlement grew as well. It housed more foreigners than most of the Yangzi ports. It developed its own local segregation, not just between Chinese and Europeans, but between missionaries, heavily represented there, and the secular. Many from either camp would not countenance mingling, even though the young unmarried staff of the new women's missionary associations (some 300 by 1889) were one of the few cohorts of eligible foreign women living in China (the others being nurses, and daughters).[37] Accounts of sleepy Kuling are hazy with nostalgia, but these minor land grabs were to be as tenaciously held in time as the larger ones, and their legal foundations were even more murky. This hill-station purchase provoked violent confrontation with local people, the fallout from which was resolved at one stage by missionary Little threatening to use force to free his Chinese employees from official custody, and dragging in consuls and the Minister in Peking to confirm his rights and support his development.[38] Little was perhaps better cut out by temperament and talent for the secular life he opted for in 1900, when he became ICI-forerunner Brunner Mond's general manager in China, but the muscularity of his resort- and road-building enterprise was different only in degree to that of many of his missionary peers.

So missionaries built roads and mapped new settlements, and tea traders designed new types of steamer and harried officials. The course of events in China and the consequences of the predisposition of many there to strike when advantage offered, and never to retreat from any position gained or even demanded, meant at times a far greater involvement in Chinese affairs than was ever imagined. At Shanghai, for example, the landowners and merchants who ran the Municipal Council found themselves officially concerned with the content of and performers in Chinese plays, and the design of Chinese theatres. This seems bizarre. Other forms of intrusion into Chinese worlds and bodies made colonial sense. The regulation of prostitution – which had involved establishing in 1877 a system of invasive inspections of Chinese prostitutes – was driven by foreign military demands.[39] But theatres? Yet it was the ponderous logic of control that led them to this position, to sitting around their council table discussing the mores and locales of Chinese theatre, a world they knew little of and cared for less. The Taiping boom had brought theatres to Shanghai, and they became a fixed and famed part of its entertainment world. They had first drawn Council attention because they operated under foreign protection, glibly stated on their name-boards, to try to avoid Chinese tax levies. The local authorities thought them a 'trysting place of thieves', and wanted controls on opening hours, but the Council refused to accept that the Daotai or Zhixian had any authority in the Settlement.[40] Next they were assumed to be a fire risk, and licences demanded new safety conditions to be met, thereby proposing a redesign of the interiors. Courtesan performers in *shuchang* ('sing-song houses' foreigners called them), places of musical entertainment, were also a target for drives against immorality and licentiousness by local Qing officials, and female performers were routinely proscribed. That hardly stopped them, and certainly did not stop one enterprising Chinese manager in 1887 hiring a foreign prostitute to perform on his stage, adding a touch of the exotic to his normal fare.[41] At times the foreign councillors and officials rebuffed Qing attempts to enforce standards of public morality, usually on the grounds that they alone governed the Settlement, but eventually the councils themselves regulated the entertainment world, issuing licences, setting out conditions and policing the content of plays. The limits to their power were equally highlighted by their interaction with the entertainment world. Recurrent surveys of fire safety suggest that theatres resisted structural change for decades, and a police scandal in 1897 highlights how other factors helped them evade foreign interference. In December of that year one of the International Settlement's Chinese detectives testified to its Watch Committee about wholesale institutional corruption amongst his colleagues. Amongst other routine practices, each detective was said to have a financial interest in 'one or more theatres', and to 'make a profit from sing-song houses where indecent plays are performed'. They were all fired, but most of the damning detail of the scandal was expunged from the Council's annual report.[42] So there is another story behind the triumphs of jubilee, of a logical imperative which led to the creation of intrusive rules and regulations in ever wider spheres of Chinese life and culture within the Settlement, of passive or other resistance to this, of Shanghai's own resilience and liveliness, of sovereignty as the paramount issue for the foreign administration, and of the inadequacy of its tools for control fostering comprehensive corruption. None of the Council's foreign detectives spoke a word of Chinese. So settler ambition was tempered by the practical world, and by the darker consequences of jubilee.

Others, too, began to engage with Chinese society and culture more intimately. For much of this narrative the atmosphere has been resolutely male. The growing numbers of female residents in the treaty ports and at mission stations changed that, and amongst them were also pioneers. For twenty years Archibald Little's enterprises were assisted, photographed and publicized by his wife, who also carved out her own career as a commentator on China and an activist. Alicia Bewicke was a prominent and politically engaged novelist when she married Little and then moved to China with him in 1887. She partnered him as he lobbied for his steamer to be allowed to make its way to Chongqing, and she wrote novels, travel sketches and a stream of articles for the *North China Herald*. Bewicke's politics and radical views stood out awkwardly in Shanghai's small foreign society. 'She has queer ideas about the freedom with which men & women should talk together on certain subjects that are not particularly nice,' wrote her brother-in-law Bob Little, who was happiest when she lived up-river.[43] Bewicke ruffled treaty port society with her novel *A Marriage in China*, rich in treaty port detail and thinly disguised local characters, and set against a backdrop of anti-foreign riots on the Yangzi. It centred around a British consul, who took 'what he called to himself a Chinese wife', and his Eurasian children, and the consequences for his relationship with the British woman he loves and marries. This was the familiar colonial tale, rewritten many times over in many different settings, but it provided a fresh look at the inner dynamics of foreign society in the treaty ports.[44] Bewicke was also confident enough to comment on an even touchier subject: relations between foreign women and Chinese men. Foreign visions of Chinese revenge or triumph routinely coalesced around images of sexual rebellion, of Chinese men taking 'white' wives; or in crisis, of rape and spoliation. In this as in its other fears, the China coast world was wholly integrated into other colonial circuits and discussions. It had wanted to control the circulation of pornographic images of European women. It wanted to control the women themselves, for uncontrolled they exposed all to a new degradation. In Bob Little's poetic vision of 'amalgamation' at Shanghai 'Two fat Chinese drove by with English spouses; /A white man held the reins.' When Norwegian missionary Anna Sofie Jakobsen married her Chinese colleague Cheng Xiuqi in Shanxi province in 1898, she was disowned by the China Inland Mission and castigated by the treaty port press. She had 'imperilled scores of single ladies in the interior' claimed one writer. 'The faces of some of the native Christians have brightened considerably,' claimed another, nastily, 'as it puts it within the range of possibility, that they also may gain a similar prize.' The legal subordination of Chinese wives to their husbands was often the overt excuse for such dismay, but it cloaked a virulent racism as well as that instinct to control women's actions and choices. Jakobsen was widely thought reprehensible, even though she and Cheng had held back from marriage for five years, but Alicia Bewicke and others were more sympathetic to the situation of foreign women who had married Chinese students or diplomats overseas and returned to China with them. They still thought them 'British girls in peril', though, and that this was still a 'crime'. Chinese views were hardly positive either, and while behaviour would very slowly change, public opinion overall did not.[45]

Bewicke did not restrict her energies and opinions to print. She actively opposed the Municipal Council's policies on prostitution in the International Settlement, for example. Although the Contagious Diseases Acts that had inspired these had been repealed in Britain in 1886, the Council, in line with a wide range of formal colonial administrations, maintained its commitment to an interventionist regulatory system. Bewicke had no formal voice in the one public forum which could affect decisions, the annual Ratepayers' Meeting (which could reject or amend budgets, for example), but she was clearly involved with those who unsuccessfully challenged the Council's policy at the meeting in 1888.[46] Greater success came from an issue which seemed far less problematic in foreign eyes. In 1895 she founded what became an influential social reform movement, the Natural Foot Society (*Tianzu hui*), which campaigned against foot-binding. The set of varied and long-entrenched Chinese customs around binding women's feet was a fixture in foreign critiques and representations of the country and its culture (and had always had Chinese critics). William Milne once noted that foreigners newly arrived in China (who viewed the country, he said, as a 'monster curiosity shop'), looked out on arrival for their first sight of a woman's bound feet.[47] Photographers secured them for their stock of Chinese images; travellers gathered them for their stock of evidence of Chinese ills or evils. Attacking the practice in 1895 brought together voices which had opposed each other in 1888, for it was an issue that transgressed no foreign sensitivities. Bewicke had no Chinese, but she brought to bear on this initiative all her professional skills, connections and anger. The campaign used new technologies, not least lantern slides of X-rays of women's bound feet, to try to alter Chinese elite perceptions of the issue. And she was no cultural relativist. It was a 'nasty, dirty practice', she thought, and she marshalled medical opinion to show clearly and soberly how dangerous and damaging it was. The Society mobilized missionary networks and built on their own initiatives, but it was not a missionary movement, and in 1906 its leadership was transferred to its leading Chinese activists.[48] Based in China, Bewicke thought internationally, not least

as the jobbing journalist she remained, but as an activist too, seeking
to publicize the Society and raise funds overseas. This was a new type
of foreign intervention in Chinese society. It was secular and reformist,
as well as feminist. She was, nonetheless, still a believer in establishing
respect for the British in China, through force if necessary.[49] And her
chatty account of a summer's search for cool in the cauldron of Sichuan
in 1893 showed the still brittle state of Sino-foreign relations, even if
it proved for her that these 'China-men' were 'real men and women',
with 'simple wants and wishes not after all so unlike our own'. A thief
stole many of their belongings one night. The zeal of the local authorities'
efforts to identify a culprit was disquieting, and rumour told that it
threatened to provoke a violent backlash against the couple from local
people. Downriver two Swedish missionaries were killed that summer
near Hankou. So Mr and Mrs Little practised their revolver shooting.
Bewicke went armed in China with more than simple indignation.[50]
That, too, was the Shanghai jubilee year.

Western gains in China by 1893 were still tiny, however talked up,
however complex and difficult for the hundreds of thousands of Chinese
directly affected, and however vexatious for Qing officials. And many
foreigners still hungered for yet more. This is a tale of insatiability, of
appetites whetted and never wholly satisfied, as if those hungering were
addicted, ever sure that the next acquisition, the next venture forward,
would bring them the necessary relief: if not Hankou, then Yichang;
if not Yichang, then Chongqing. The plain cause of their distress was
that the Chinese actors in the game adapted too quickly, or pre-empted
change, or ploughed forward themselves – securing markets, capturing
back the gains of the foreign traders, cold-shouldering them successfully
out of this game and that one. Foreign traders sought new opportunities
as older ones faded, and as more foreigners started to arrive, and they
began to try to secure exclusive rights; tried as hard to do this as they
once had struggled against Chinese exclusivity and monopoly. A sullen
sort of stasis had been reached by 1893, but then the six years following
the jubilee pantomime saw an unprecedented expansion and deepening
of the foreign presence, and a tightening of the foreign grip. Individual
entrepreneurship and aggressive state intervention redrew the maps of
the Qing. Everything accelerated: all the pressures here and there, the
steady exertion of force; all turned cyclonic in reach and violence. The

ordered world of jubilee was smashed. By 1898 the Qing had lost provinces and ports, armies and fleets, riches, an emperor and a future.

Less than a year after a Japanese warship at Shanghai had poured benign fireworks into the sky after Muirhead's homily, Japanese warships and cannon poured shell after awful shell into Chinese forts. They bombarded Weihaiwei, Port Arthur and Dalian, the defences on the Pescadores and Taiwan, and Li Hongzhang's Northern Fleet. Japanese torpedo boats swept up to hammer home the barrage. And Chinese armies were smashed in Korea, the Liaodong peninsular and Manchuria. By March 1895 Peking lay at their feet, the roads open from the east and the south, no prospect of successful defence in sight.[51] The Qing could but capitulate, sending Li Hongzhang to Shimonoseki to negotiate, where he lost an eye to a Japanese would-be-assassin but gained thereby a little more sympathy for prostrate China's plight. But even though the Japanese demands were softened, the Qing lost. They lost Taiwan. They lost Korea. They lost Dalian and the Liaodong peninsula. They lost a fearful sum as an indemnity to Japan, and so also the use of those revenues thereby redirected. They lost the confidence and loyalty of a generation of their subjects, who howled with rage at this defeat and all it symbolized. The European powers had had the advantages of technology in 1842, in 1858 and 1860. The French had too, in 1884–5, though it was a harder fought war. Those defeats made a sort of sad sense. But Japan was an Asian neighbour, a former tributary state, itself still formally subject to the same style of foreign-serving treaty system as China's. It had only recently been as unprepared to deal with foreign aggression as the Qing, and like the Qing had set itself to restoration and to self-strengthening. But now the 'dwarf pirates' – as officials still routinely called the Japanese, even when they were defeated by them – had smashed China's forces, and shattered its pride.

Many had actually assumed that the Chinese would win. The conflict arose over competing claims for domination in Korea where the Qing had used all the tools of its tributary relationship, as well as the tools of informal empire practised on them, to keep the kingdom clear of the Europeans and of the Japanese. But the Japanese recognized no special Chinese position in their common neighbour.[52] When the Korean court called for aid to suppress an anti-foreign religious uprising in

1894, both the Qing and Japan sent forces, and these clashed, and the moment was seized for war. Well, thought Robert Hart, China 'will have many a defeat to put up with before stay and numbers begin to turn the scale in her favour'.[53] Informed opinion in Britain agreed with him. Chinese staying power, the strong new navy, and, more than anything, an 'awakening of China', a nationalist will to fight, would surely swing victory her way.[54] The forts were strong and ready. But everything went wrong. 'No shells for the Krupp's, and no powder for the Armstrong's!' wailed Hart, dispatching orders to Campbell for urgent shipments of rifles.[55] The forts were smashed and fell. The troops, brave but often lacking leadership and ammunition, were broken and fled. Some turned on their commanders. European and American observers were shocked, as the historian is shocked, by the vileness of the conflict, of the three-day slaughter by Japanese forces of the population of Port Arthur after it fell in November 1894, rigor mortis leaving many in the kowtow they had vainly made to plead mercy. A day's madness observers could just about understand; three days of murder was something else.[56] The port with its modern Krupp guns had fallen in a matter of hours. The spectre of defeat troubled foreign residents in China. Would the Chinese rise, adding outraged anti-Japanese sentiment to that latent 'xenophobia' so recently demonstrated on the Yangzi? They certainly thought so, believing that the mob would rage in Peking. Evacuation plans were drawn up for Shanghai (although the port was declared neutral territory), and new surveys made of key buildings which could serve as bulwarks of a defence against popular attack. Chinese popular prints portrayed it as a war against foreigners, the Japanese troops shown all physically European. (In the popular print, moreover, there was no defeat, only exemplary heroism.) In the aftermath of Shimonoseki some thought Chinese popular outrage had found some vent in attacks on foreigners, not least when eleven members of a missionary community, mostly women and children, were murdered in Fujian province on 1 August 1895 but, as ever, foreign residents only ever saw themselves centre Chinese stage. The beaten Qing and its injured peoples had greater worries.[57]

It was failure, too, for the defensive state-building project in Taiwan, and for decades of politicking in Korea. It was a defeat more shattering than any other. There was no limit to its awfulness. It could not be

ignored, as in 1842. It could not be evaded as in 1860 when the
Emperor went hunting, nor engaged with as self-strengtheners and the
cooperation policy diplomats had worked to preserve the shaken court
in the 1860s. It could not be spun as victory, as some had spun the war
with France. It was a crushing, humiliating defeat, shocking the empire.
Its consequences crippled the Qing. It was photographed, sketched and
reported in great detail. Cameras could now catch the fleets in action
and the torpedoes launching, the columns of Japanese troops pressing
ever forwards. The tales of the popular prints were disproved by the
photographs of shattered forts. And for a moment everything seemed
up for grabs. The balance of nations in China was knocked out of
kilter. The old European club had been piqued by Foreign Minister
Soejima's pre-emptive audience with the young Emperor in 1873, had
condescended to the Japanese expedition in 1874, tolerated samurai
swords in Shanghai streets, and taken Japanese women into its treaty
port bedrooms in great numbers. It had not taken Japan seriously
otherwise. Now it found itself outflanked and its cosy cosmopolis –
which in Shanghai symbolically excluded the Japanese flag from its
Council logo – was endangered.[58] The club of the 'Powers' now moved
swiftly to discipline the Japanese and strip them of some of their gains.
A 'triple intervention' – Paris, Moscow and Berlin combined – forced
them to relinquish the Liaodong peninsular, their coordinated 'friendly
advice' suggesting that this threatened Russia's strategic position.
Formal notes were underpinned by informal murmurings that Russia
saw a Japanese presence on the Asian mainland as a cause for war. So
the Japanese withdrew, and were furious. But they could not risk
such a war, not just yet. They kept Taiwan – a self-declared rearguard
republic and stubborn resistance notwithstanding – and it passed
into their new colonial empire.[59] Those Chinese who did not sell up
and leave within two years of the treaty became Japanese citizens.
A few thousand did, and some thousands also registered themselves
at Japanese consulates in Amoy or Fuzhou as Taiwanese residents
sojourning in China, and thereby savvily acquired extraterritorial
status. It suited the Japanese, who like all the powers, played a numbers
game in negotiations with the Qing or their foreign rivals, and it
certainly suited their new subjects.[60] The Treaty of Shimonoseki
delivered new open ports and concessions others had long sought, for

all benefited as ever from the spoils of war – most significantly for the treaty ports, there was a new right to establish manufacturing plants. Chongqing, notably, became a new treaty port with a new right of inland steam navigation all the way there. And that massive indemnity was levied, and the rewards of loaning the Qing the money to pay this off were well spread around European banks. It was, when all was said and done, and panic passed, a profitable affair, as long as you were not Chinese.

The chief impact of the Japanese victory was twofold. First it initiated a slow-burning and hysterical clamour for yet more concessions, which became a real scramble for advantage amongst all the foreign powers. They drew back at first in 1895, and drew Japan back, but two years later all restraint was let loose, and the powers moved dazzlingly swiftly. The European, and as a result the international scene, was changing rapidly in the 1890s. Germany was pushing for a more prominent global position. Russia was now growing stronger and more ambitious, and closer to France. This relationship worried Britain, their common rival, and threatened its position and perceived interests. So when new Chinese opportunity beckoned, all must needs leap. Germany found its pretext – the murder of two members of a politically aggressive mission, the Society of the Divine Word, in November 1897 – and pounced. It had already located and vainly proposed a site to the Zongli Yamen, but now seized its target, Jiaozhou Bay on Shandong province's southern coast, and proclaimed it a new colony, alienated in perpetuity and to be run by the German Navy.[61] Over the next 200 days the maps of China were redrawn, and the fate of the Qing seemed in the balance. Russia pounced next, arrogating to itself the Liaodong peninsular ports of Dalian and bruised Port Arthur. Britain grabbed Shandong's Weihaiwei to counter the Russian and German moves. In the south it pushed north of Kowloon to secure a 99-year lease over the rural 'New Territories'. The French had tabled their demands in March 1898, demanding a reply within eight days (the curt deadline being thought 'customary in dealings with China'), and leased coastal Guangzhouwan west of Canton.[62] Some thrusts the Qing beat back, slapping down the Italian lunge at Sanmen Bay, close to Ningbo, but most of the rapid, breathless theft they had to concede. Spheres of interest were marked out with bold lines: to Britain the 'Yangzi Valley', to Germany Shandong,

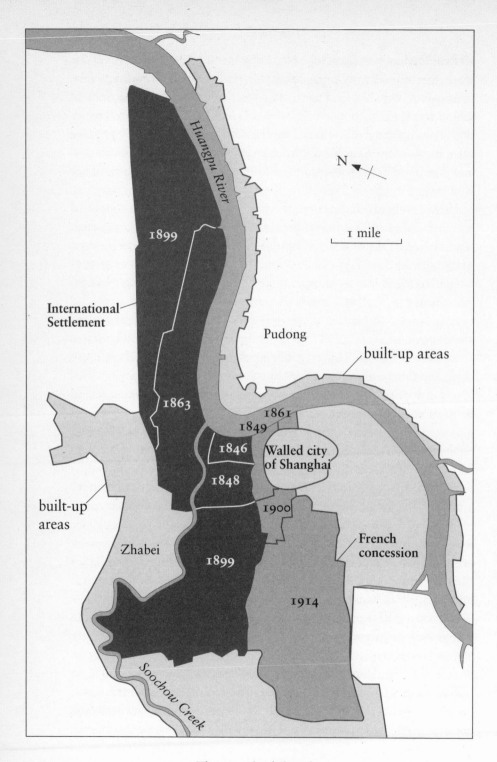

10. The growth of Shanghai

to Russia Manchuria, and the southwest to France. Chinese ministers were summoned to foreign ministries and ordered to convey firm messages to the Zongli Yamen. Foreign diplomats did so in Peking. China was the field of play in European chancelleries and secret meetings. Diplomats or their private envoys sounded each other out. If we were to —— what might be the attitude taken? If you were to ——, well, we might not look unfavourably. What would be the attitude of X, if Y were to do this, with our blessing? Dizzy panic clouded thinking; action was reflexive. Grab the Yangzi Valley, they demanded – but what was this 'Yangzi Valley' that tripped lightly off tongues? Nothing in fact but a dream of the map-bound; not a place, but contours and concept. Grab Sanmen Bay. Grab Guangzhouwan – grab what? Where precisely? Guangzhouwan: the most obscure and apparently pointless of concessions, a site of 'negligible strategic or commercial significance'.[63]

Lust-blind they prodded the maps, dispatched stiff telegrams instructing ministers to call at the Zongli Yamen, and sent in their naval squadrons. They demanded a concession here; rights to build a railway there; that other powers be blocked from this province, west of this line, south of that one. Guarantees were secured: a Frenchman would be head of the Postal Service, a Briton head of the Customs. Much of it seemed unreal, and was the stuff of waggery in the press: 'Weihaiwei': 'Where are we?' 'Why are we?' 'Why oh why?' they asked. It was real enough on the ground, ground that changed hands, home to people who changed hands. And it was real too in fact in those cabinet rooms and foreign ministries, as China-question tensions generated white heat in European diplomatic relations.[64] The powers held back, for now, from the Taiwan option – from wider and more formal colonial occupation – but it was a close-run thing. A general carve-up could set off a yet more destabilizing scramble, and what routinely became the 'China question' was now often intertwined with other 'questions' – with Africa and with other scrambles. A final feast would stoke up Anglo-French antagonisms, already dangerous because of competing claims in Africa; Anglo-Russian tension, already high; Franco-German bitterness – stoke it all up towards a European conflagration. China was not worth that, at least not now. The United States largely stood aloof, but brokered an 'Open Door' declaration to try to limit and counter the new exclusivity of colonial possession, and meanwhile got on with creating its own Asian empire in the Philippines. All must have prizes, after all.

To the villagers of Jiaozhou and Guangzhouwan, to the two and half million people of Taiwan, the 200-day carve-up was real enough. To Chinese students and officials it seemed real enough. To residents of Tianjin or Shanghai it seemed real enough, for the free-for-all emboldened the foreign municipalities to better secure their own futures, to expand to give more space for their growing populations and new factories. The International Settlement at Shanghai tripled in size in 1899 and its new borders were marked with sixty inscribed concrete blocks speaking plainly the fact that this was alienated territory, marked out as such by Qing officials. So there were another 10,000 houses in the International Settlement, and over 50,000 more Chinese now living under the 'cosmopolitan' flag, and its rules and regulations. Residents had not calmly accepted the growing propensity of the foreign administrations to order their worlds, and reshape their city. In July 1898 when the French authorities had dispatched marines to oversee the destruction of the Ningbo guild cemetery, partly in the interests of urban hygiene, partly to demonstrate their authority over affairs in the concession, they provoked resistance and a riot, and up to twenty-five Chinese were killed before the affair was settled.[65] At Tianjin they had been pushing to expand, British firms buying land neighbouring the concession, all of it brought formally inside it in 1897. Germany and Japan had secured settlements there in 1895 and 1896; development of the former was outsourced to the Deutsch Asiatische Bank. The state's grasp had exceeded its own capabilities. And thanks to the Japanese war, Archie Little got a steamer up the Yangzi to Chongqing. He commissioned a new vessel from a Shanghai shipyard, the *Leechuen*, and was received at Chongqing on 8 March 1898 by the Daotai, salutes from Chinese gunboats, and explosions of firecrackers. Officials lower down the river had still said no, but the time for taking no for an answer was now past, and Archie Little's sense of honour was finally vindicated as the *Leechuen* berthed at Chongqing.[66]

J. O. P. Bland himself took another course. After fourteen slow years in the Customs he cast an eye on his future, and took the position of assistant secretary to the Council at Shanghai in 1896, knowing he would soon succeed to the post of secretary. While waiting he

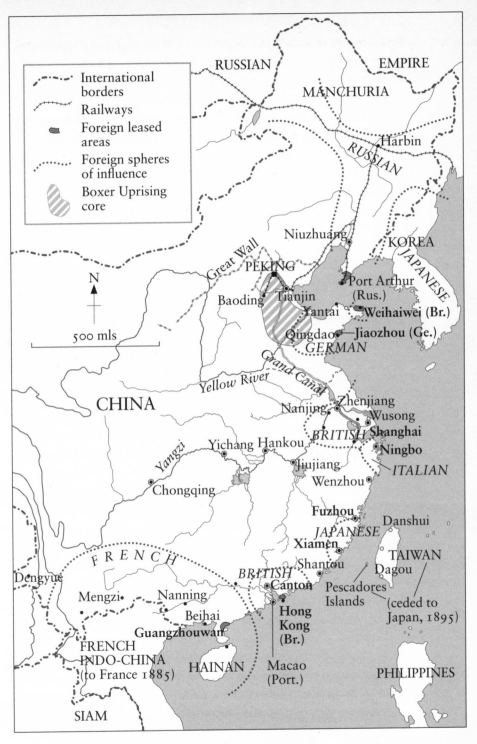

commenced working as correspondent at Shanghai for *The Times*. It was never going to be enough for the foreign enterprise merely to reach Chongqing or build its new concessions. It had to write itself steadily into the imagination of its domestic publics. China was always just off the imperial stage, even a formal colonial holding like Hong Kong was a minor point in a vast colonial treasure chest. So the China British and others had to shout to be heard. With every war they had their visiting 'special' correspondents, who got their copy, did their damage and left, and they had their celebrities – Gordon, Parkes, the Tianjin dead – but they needed to impress themselves more systematically and steadily on metropolitan minds. Therein lay security. Bland dabbled in treaty port journalism, but his work for the *The Times* which began in late 1896, was sustained and serious. The desire of the Chinese coast foreigners to be heard was now matched directly with the new strategic seriousness of the 'China question'. *The Times* appointed a special correspondent to Peking, Australian George Ernest Morrison, better to cover the frenetic clamour there for concessions. Morrison was already a canny celebrity, famous for tramping across Australia, and most recently for trekking from Hankou to Burma in 1894, part-following Margary's route, stopping in temples he had stayed in, noting the tree at whose foot the consul had allegedly been killed, but pointing out also in his account of the journey how much safer it really was for foreigners in China, than for Chinese in America. Bland's was a more orthodox line, and he set out a familiar stall in an early retrospect on British policy: if there was such a thing it was 'to decide every controversy in favour of the native', and maintain the 'political status quo in China'. The course of British engagement with this 'semi-barbarous' state was marked by 'alternate coercion and apology, menaces and pressure'. But the pair were united in their imperialism and in the seemingly unfettered opportunity offered by the great game in China after the Japanese victory: 'The heyday was in the blood, there were crowns to be broke, and Morrison, like myself, was over bent on stratagems and spoils for the glory of the Raj,' Bland recalled. 'The most England can claim out here is the Yangtse Valley,' wrote Morrison to his Shanghai conspirator. 'Do you think that sufficient? I do not.' 'Our true heritage in Asia,' he concluded, 'is all South Eastern Asia up to and including the Yangtse Valley' – not spoils, but a British birthright, a British heritage.[67]

The second result for the Qing of defeat and its consequences had two faces. When official attention was able to turn from managing the press of demands and ultimatums from the powers, there was a new impetus for reform; for the Qing administration had failed. It could not fight a modern war, for it could not organize itself: there was no centralized command. The reform movement culminated in an extraordinary 'one hundred days' of renovation and seeming political renaissance in June to September 1898, when the Guangxu emperor finally cast off the 'Old Buddha' – his Aunt, Cixi – and ruled in his own name, issuing decrees aimed at reviving the Qing from the centre.[68] Over 100 decrees were issued, reforming government, education, the military. New institutions were to be created to strengthen commerce and industry. Advocates of such change were promoted; opponents were dismissed. But this mournful romance of reform was cut abruptly short by *coup d'état*. Reform-minded officials were toppled and executed, and others fled. The Emperor was placed under house arrest, and Cixi moved back centre stage. The edicts were suppressed. The reform movement was rooted in the intense florescence of scholarly debates about the state of the nation and the path forward from defeat and through the turmoil of the concession scramble. The examination candidates of 1895 had petitioned en masse for a rejection of Shimonoseki. One leading figure in that movement and in the reform agitation was Kang Youwei, a scholar who had progressed through the orthodox rounds of civil service examination, but the thrust of whose thinking was seemingly unorthodox. Most dramatically, Kang charged himself with saving China. 'Saving' China was becoming a routine way of presenting problems and solutions. As ports and colonies were sliced away, a greater catastrophe was feared. Even though we know that European diplomatic tensions made it unlikely, we also know that foreign attitudes were hardening, that the scramble for concessions carried its own inexorable momentum towards greater and greater claims, and that there was much talk of partition, of pre-emptive declarations, of vital national interests. Kang used his orthodox scholarly expertise to support his claim that reform lay at the heart of Confucian ideology. China, he argued, needed a constitutional monarchy to bring the emperor and his subjects together to strengthen and protect the nation. His student Liang Qichao took the critique further, and was to turn against the idea of monarchy. Both lobbied and debated through clubs and newspapers, sparring with censorship and suppression, making use of the freedoms of the treaty port and Hong Kong publishing worlds, and of havens provided by sympathetic officials. Kang then became a key figure in the Guangxu emperor's reforms, appointed high into the Qing administration during the heady 'hundred days'. But the Emperor needed many more such officials, and most opposed his plans.

Defeat of reform gave greater impetus to those who had not countenanced success for it. One of those was a Hong Kong-trained doctor, Sun Yat-sen, whose seditious and rebellious activism had already gained him notoriety. Sun had circled the globe, rousing overseas Chinese support for his efforts to save China, and to save China by smashing the Qing. He launched a revolutionary society in Honolulu, set up a branch in Hong Kong, and planned a rising in Canton in October 1895 combining fellow revolutionaries with hired secret-society forces. This was the first of eleven failed risings that Sun launched or planned, but his reputation grew nonetheless, for persistence if nothing else. It did so not least when he blithely called at the Chinese Legation in London in 1896 assuming, it seems, that no one would recognize him. Seized, held captive, readied for secret dispatch out of London so that he could be dealt with, Sun gained his freedom by smuggling a note out via a British servant begging for help from a British friend, his former teacher in Hong Kong, Dr James Cantlie. 'Oh woe to me!' his missive concluded.[69] Cantlie and colleagues – including Patrick Manson – mobilized press opinion, and the British Foreign Office soon acted to demand Sun's release. The freed revolutionary published a breathless account of his seizure and gained great publicity for his cause internationally. It could hardly have been better scripted. It was one of those 'romantic episodes which rarely happen outside the realm of fiction' declared one excited newspaper, and it proved in turn a boon for Anglophone thriller writers seeking copy for tales of Chinese and 'oriental' duplicity, of anti-dynastic secret societies, and of the dramas of Chinese rebellion acted out globally, in Hawaii, Canada or London.[70] That revolutionary activity was no mere episodic romance. Sun spent another eight months in London, ploughing his way through books in the quiet of the British Library, developing new contacts with Russian anti-Tsarist exiles and

Japanese visitors, capitalizing on his celebrity, and publishing a call for 'British benevolent neutrality' towards Chinese opponents of the Manchus. In that article he made his analysis very sharp and clear: the Manchu Qing were 'foreigners'; they, not the Chinese people, were 'anti-foreign'; 'nothing short of the entire overthrow of the present utterly corrupt *régime*' and its replacement by initially European-advised 'native Chinese' would be in the interests of China, and of foreign powers. Do not protect the Qing, he pleaded, as you protected them from the Taiping.[71] Sun then moved to Japan, for – state aggression towards China notwithstanding – increasing numbers of Japanese thinkers shared Sun's own desire to strengthen Asia against the Western powers. 'Pan-Asian' thinking was diverse in its advocates and varied in its manifestations. And just as often as it served to mask Japan's own imperialist aggrandizement, it served also as a philosophy under-pinning anti-imperialist belief and action. Their politics divided Sun and Kang, the one an anti-Manchu revolutionary, the other a reforming royalist, but they both came to underpin their proposed programmes and analyses through reading, as much as through action. Kang studied the Chinese canon, interrogating and challenging it, reading translations from foreign-language texts. Sun drew directly from a different body of political economy, diplomacy, law and military subjects, and took another, competing, route in his thinking about change. Taiping leader Hong Xiuquan had offered a millenarian vision of another possible realm, drawn from the Bible. Kang and Sun offered a new practical politics and philosophy of reform, revolution and development.

Sun was lucky, sitting in the great round reading room in London, and so was Kang Youwei, who fled China, with sympathetic foreign assistance helping him evade arrest at Shanghai.[72] The villagers of Hanjiacun and Bailiancun outside the German leasehold were less lucky in April 1898, when a German 'police action' saw a column of marines march into and burn down their homes, as a 'punishment' for clashing with a German surveying party the previous month. This was part of a sustained programme of pacification of the new territory's borders, and of impressing on the minds of local officials and residents that German power was not to be contended with.[73] It sent a message also to potential European rivals. But the incident had arisen because German missionaries were demanding intervention to counter hostility towards them and their congregations. At Guangzhouwan Chinese officials resisted passively when the tricolour was raised in April 1898, but the inhabitants (there were 190,000 of them) proved 'unruly' and 'insulting', and needed a demonstration of force. And there was slaughter as British forces imposed control on the New Territories in a bloody campaign in 1899.[74]

The growing movement against the Qing was global in its reach and interconnections, as funds secured in Canadian Chinatowns financed arms and fighters against the dynasty, and as refugee reformers published newspapers in Japan that filtered back to China and across to other communities of émigrés and sojourners. At the same time the threats to the Qing from foreign power and the foreign powers had been internationalized and multiplied a thousandfold. The empire of the Qing was a subject for discussion globally, in press and parliament, in foreign office and legation. It was also a subject for discussion amongst reformers and would-be revolutionaries, emigrant or now refugee. And the threat within was internationalized. German, Russian and Japanese troops joined the British and the French. In 1893 foreign paranoia imagined vast Chinese armies marching on the settlements, and foreign commemoration countered these visions with its phalanxes of volunteers and marines, dressing it up with professions of amity. But by 1899 it was foreign armies and foreign marines that had disembarked from their troopships and gunboats and marched into dozens of Chinese cities, towns and villages: razing some, informing their new colonial subjects of the new order of things, fighting those who resisted, and raising their flags. At Weihaiwei when the British took over in May 1898 the Union Flag was raised alongside the Qing dragon standard (a creation of the Customs Service) as the naval band played 'God Save the Queen' at the handover site, one of those neutered Chinese forts. They followed this with a 'Chinese national anthem', although none yet formally existed, and listeners and players alike found the tune played 'rather difficult to follow'.[75] And then, that necessary but discordant piece of musical courtesy concluded, and after having given three cheers for the Queen and one for the Emperor of China, they set to work empire-building on Chinese soil.

16. Beautiful uselessness: the marble boat, Summer Palace, Peking, *c.* 1919–20

17. 'Great Japanese Naval Victory off Haiyang Island', 1894

18. 'Cha-see': John Charles Oswald in a tea-tasting room, Fuzhou, 1890s

19. R. F. C. Hedgeland, Customs officer, and his servants, Hoihow

20. Jesus on the cross: 'Shooting the pig and beheading the goats', puns on 'God' and 'foreigners' respectively

21. 'Pig sect gouging out eyes': foreign missionaries portrayed taking the eyes from a man; two others, blinded by them, kneel in the foreground

22. Slicing it up: 'The Royal Cake or The Western Empires sharing China between them'

23. Boxers on the march, 1900

24. Britain's Chinese soldiers: drummer boy, First Chinese (Weihaiwei) Regiment, c. 1901–2

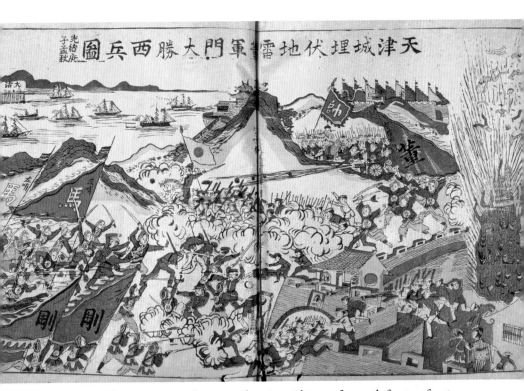

25. Fantasies of victory: popular print showing Chinese forces defeating foreign troops at Tianjin, 1900

26. Aftermath of battle: British officers on Chinese destroyer they have just seized at Dagu, 17 June 1900

27. Sitting pretty in Nanjing: Customs officers R. F. C. Hedgeland and P. P. P. M. Kremer, c. 1899–1903

Dec. 18. 1905.

28. Defenders of the Laozha police station, Mixed Court riot,
Shanghai, 18 December 1905

29. China Inland missionaries at play, *c.* 1900s

30. Young man at Confucius
Temple, Qufu, 14 June 1913

31. New Army soldier,
Shenyang, 1912

I I

Extinction

'Mission station' reads the sign across the gates. What purport to be Chinese characters presumably announce the same. A sword-carrying man, dressed in Chinese-style clothes approaches it, more follow in his wake, queues dangling down their necks (we see them only from behind), the gate is forced, they kneel and fire, then run forward. The scene cuts: a man and wife, missionaries presumably, walk in the garden in front of a house. The attackers are seen, he hustles her inside, so too their child and its nurse, and re-emerges with a revolver to fire at the intruders. One falls, but the missionary is overpowered and the assailants rush the house. The film cuts, reversing the view, now it looks back towards the gate as a party of British marines runs up, a mounted officer in the rear. In ranks four abreast they fire at the attackers, that is they fire directly at the camera, and they then storm forwards. The scene cuts again to the garden where the marines are shooting now at close quarters. Soon it is over: the women and child are rescued, the Chinese are killed or captured, but the missionary is dead. Four minutes long, the film, *Attack on a China Mission*, was first shown 'with appropriate music' – whatever that might have been – in a programme of musical turns on 17 November 1900 in Hove, on England's south coast. It was filmed there too.[1] The attackers are gaudily dressed Britons; the girl the director's daughter. Some of the events it re-enacted were still being played out across north China when a derelict house was mocked up as the film's mission station. Attacks on mission stations had ceased, but columns of foreign soldiers were still fanning out across the countryside and into Chinese villages and towns, firing as they did so volley after deadly volley. A new technological marvel, 'animated photography', the cinematograph, was being used to augment and illustrate the news from China, the troops firing round after round at the audience, a new source of those old thrills once experienced at the re-enactments so lavishly staged at Astley's Amphitheatre, now brought into every venue where the film was shown. *Attack on a China Mission* was a landmark in the history of film, for those cross-cuts were innovations. The attacks on missions across north China in 1899–1900 formed a landmark event in China's modern history. Refracted through cinema, telegraph and photograph they seemed rooted in fears and desires seemingly from another age, but were as modern as the technologies that reported and represented them.

It had all begun two years earlier with what must have seemed like the end of the world. The great Yellow River, China's wandering sorrow, had risen and risen, and on 8 August 1898 it broke its high banks and poured its silt-laden waters down the sides of the dykes over a seven-mile stretch and out onto the farmlands below. But even this deluge could not alleviate the pressure of water moving after heavy rains – the 'greatest rainfall on record,' reported the Customs at Yantai – had filled the river to overflowing. The banks failed further downstream, and then in November once again. Water flooded out, covering thousands of square miles of farmland, destroying or otherwise affecting thousands of villages in thirty-four counties, drowning people and their livestock, blocking wells with debris, washing away the autumn crops, supplies of food and seed, and winter clothes, and making refugees out of the survivors.[2] A million people were displaced and 'thousands' drowned, more dying later of dysentery and other diseases. Reports spoke of people standing for days in the water, holding their children out of it, or hanging from trees until they fell, exhausted, into the water.[3] The spring harvest had already been poor, and famine had begun to infect these regions. Now the great floods destroyed anything that had survived. The court at Peking was distracted with the hundred days and its aftermath, and foreign diplomats and observers were frantic with the politics of the scramble, interpreting everything in the light of that game; and for many, Chinese floods and other natural disasters had simply become part of the landscape. They were a part of the natural order of Chinese things. But no, some argued, this was politics, not nature. Sun Yat-sen had laid out his case a year earlier in London that a corrupt and decrepit administration proved its unfitness now to rule precisely because it could no longer manage the business of feeding and protecting the people. Natural disasters could be grappled with, he argued, and either prevented or alleviated, and the Qing state like its predecessors had long focused on managing flood prevention. Sun's diagnosis was that the 'foreign' state was moribund and corrupt. Politics aside, the state was certainly in crisis, its capacity, already stretched by rebellion and the intense effort of self-strengthening, was further shaken by the Japanese war, the indemnity, the 200-day foreign feast thereafter, and the days of abortive reform and reaction. The Qing had taken decisions at the beginning of the 1890s to reallocate central resources away from water control. Local resources would have to suffice and it was the provincial governor's job to maintain the dykes, but the incumbent had failed to attend to this, and had had his attention distracted not least by the German threat to his province, with punishment raids from Qingdao and aggressive provocations from Society of the Divine Word missionaries. With Shandong as its 'sphere of influence', German interests looked hungrily at possible railway and mining concessions far beyond Jiaozhou Bay, and German prospectors and concession hunters were routinely reported moving deep in to the Shandong interior. So when the rains came the dykes failed, and their remnants served instead as sites of refuge for the pitiful shanty encampments of hundreds of thousands of refugees.

But it got worse. Those heavy summer rains of 1898 were followed by drought. Significantly less rain fell in 1899 than in normal years, compounding distress and preventing a return even to fragile normality. Li Hongzhang was sent to investigate. The governor was censured and replaced. Private relief efforts aided tens of thousands, using refugee labour to reconstruct new river banks.[4] But most people fended for themselves as best they could. The effectiveness of the state in some of the regions affected had long been tenuous. From here the Nian had risen and taken their warfare across north central China. The Taiping had rampaged through on their great march north. Villages were used to defending themselves, and to competing with each other for resources in a fragile system. Violence was necessary, and endemic; and now people were idle. They talked, news spread, rumour spread. Increasing numbers of young men were attracted to a new set of martial arts and religious practices that was being popularized in northwest Shandong by groups who called themselves Spirit Boxers, and who gave new form to communal self-protection bands operating in this fragmented rural society.[5] Self-protection and banditry were often indistinguishable, and both challenged the state. Provincial and local authorities dealt with such groups where they could by seizing and executing their leaders, and dispersing the followers. To a limited extent these old policies were used to some effect, but two new factors were at play: the growth of anti-foreign feeling rooted in specific local confrontations with Chinese convert communities and their missionary protectors, and the infusion of invulnerability and spirit-possession rituals in the practices of the new bands. The powerless gained power. Not only did they have specific targets for their discontent, but they had a new tool to call upon, for they could summon the gods to possess them, make themselves invulnerable, and wage war without mercy against their enemies. And they had by 1899 nothing else to lose, no other option to them for salvation, for saving the world.

The origins and the course of what happened in 1900 are layered with myth and fictions, but dry fact can be teased out. Accurate scholarship might identify hydraulic mismanagement as an underlying fault, and contemporary report could call for inquiries and reforms, cashiering of officials, the institution of new and more effective control systems. Missionaries in conference lauded the private relief efforts of the Chinese gentry, and insisted that foreign advisors and assistance ought to be brought in to solve the problem. Baptist Timothy Richard had blazed such a trail with his relief work during the 1876–8 north China famine.[6] Observers could look more closely at the fragmented patterns of administration in the northwest Shandong countryside, rationalize it, re-garrison it, and send properly paid soldiers there, to suppress the banditry and to remove the need for self-protection bands. But many hungry and frightened residents of the now scarred region and its hinterland knew better; knew themselves that the world itself was out of balance; and knew too, increasingly, of a solution. Missionary scholarship had long pondered why the 'hordes of homeless, famishing, and desperate refugees' from China's incipient flood and drought had seemed so passive in their plight. American missionary Arthur Smith, an influential cataloguer of what he termed 'Chinese characteristics', who lived and worked in the Shandong countryside, concluded that this was due to the 'unlimited capacity of the Chinese for patient endurance'. But in fact people and officials had long taken what practical and proactive measures that they could to call for rain or prevent flood: propitiating the gods and protecting the cosmological landscape.[7] In dry June 1898 officials in Peking were said to have been asking about US army rainmaking experiments involving dynamite-primed balloons in Texas. Had they worked? Would firing into the air by soldiers work instead?[8] They were desperate for rain. But an equally entirely rational and practical view of the causes of the problem in 1898–9 was developed, and it forced a solution. For what had changed? What might have tipped the world out of balance? Was there an offence which had kept the skies dry? North China farmers knew that into their brittle world had come new forces, with alien ideas and practices backed up with foreign diplomatic power, perverting the course of local justice and government. The towers of churches, one anti-Christian ditty noted, blocked out the sky.

Christianity, as we have seen, was not abstract belief, but practical local politics and local change. It had given converts a type of invulnerability, a seeming freedom from orthodox control and licence to subvert the law. In property and resource disputes they had secured mission support and so through them diplomatic representations to the Zongli Yamen over this local dispute and that one. And every local victory in such disputes emboldened Christian communities, who like all others struggled for adequate resources in good times, let alone these bad ones. When would-be converts came forward en masse, missionaries knew to search for the reason, for villagers would often do so in the midst of law suits, angling for advantage, or to counter advantage. Would-be Protestants arrived to thwart Catholics.[9] Local process was being usurped. And these forces were foreign, so to rebalance the upside-down world of north China the foreign needed to be expunged. People little distinguished one set of foreigners from another, just as the prints that circulated little distinguished Japanese from European soldiers. They did not distinguish believers in foreign religion from foreigners, for Chinese converts had in their eyes deracinated themselves, set themselves outside communities and outside Chinese culture. They did not distinguish between the useful foreign things so wanted by the dynasty to which they remained wholly loyal – telegraphs, railways – and other foreign things. They wanted a land wiped clean of all of these pollutants. And the practices of the new combined bands of Boxers, the *Yihequan*, 'Boxers united in righteousness', gave them mastery over foreign things, not least mastery over foreign fire-arms. They were invulnerable, they believed, to foreign bullets. They demonstrated their new skills at rural fairs, shouted down Chinese or foreign preachers who also sought new supporters there, brandished their weapons, and drove them back into their compounds. Boxer rituals and performances were often derived straight from popular theatre, which gave them a vocabulary and the dramatis personae of spirit possession. But there was nothing theatrical about the threat they offered, and by June 1899 some mission stations had already undergone virtual sieges, guarded by bands of Christians, the men sitting up at nights, revolvers and prayer their protection.[10]

No missionaries had strolled Shandong gardens in 1899 unaware of the clamour outside their gates. They had their usual run of kidnapping scares (notably in 1897) and low-level abuse. But as the provincial authorities countered a growing series of violent outbreaks – attacks on Christian villages, reprisals, pre-emptive forays – fuel was thrown on the fire by German and French diplomatic intervention which condemned inaction and demanded redress. The new Shandong governor, Yuxian, was removed at foreign insistence, although he had countered various outbreaks bloodily and effectively, or at least had the heads of alleged leaders to show for his policies. A British missionary, Sidney Brooks, fell victim in December 1899 to a band that included some Boxer adherents. The usual diplomatic protests followed, and were followed up. But some Qing officials now struck a new note in memorials on the increasing disorder, urging the court not to strike hard against the militants, for fear equally of inflaming anti-Christian feeling, and emboldening Christian communities. A decree issued in January ordered officials to suppress those fomenting disorder, but it deliberately did not identify any particular sect or society, which some foreign observers thought effectively a public statement of support for the Boxers. In troubled times, was the retort, why could not loyal subjects organize for self-defence? Practical politics meant not alienating this spreading popular upsurge, even as it fought the Qing army, for it could easily turn anti-dynastic if mishandled. And there were other considerations: the British were bogged down in their South African war, their seeming impotence galvanizing their opponents globally. The Chinese say, old Robert Hart reported, that 'If these English can't fight the Boers, why need *we* fear them?' Officials, their critics, and commentators alike, in palace memorial and newspaper editorial, analysed the dilemmas of the British in the Transvaal, and American difficulties in the Philippines. For some it fed into new notions of a Chinese nationalism, for others it offered a strategic opportunity of the moment.[11] Some of this global sense of imperialism contested found its way through news-sheet and word of mouth into the countryside, but it was the local politics of the encounter with Christians and the new hope for cosmological rebalance that inspired the thousands of young men who took up the new boxing. That and simple boredom. Asked why he had joined the band which had captured and then later killed Brooks, one young man simply answered that he wanted to '*kan renao*', to watch the fun.[12]

Out of Shandong the Boxers and their ideas flowed, gaining followers and adherents, their power and spectacle intimidating others into silence or acquiescence. They poured north across Zhili province, which had been battered by a decade of flooding and economic insecurity, their slogan 'Revive the Qing, exterminate the foreign', and where they encountered the foreign, they duly exterminated it.[13] Long-fractured communities, mired in disputes with Catholic or Protestant converts in their midst found in Boxer beliefs a new weapon, and the tenor of the times gave their attacks on their neighbours new legitimacy, if not vital urgency. Boxer bands fought and defeated Qing troops sent to counter them in May 1900 at Baoding southwest of Peking, and thereafter they and their ideas spread north to the capital and the other cities of the north China plain. Now events spiralled. With the agreement of the Zongli Yamen the foreign legations called up small military detachments from the coast in May. More were then requested, as Boxers drilled in the capital and in Tianjin, attacked converts, and set fire to churches and other symbols of the foreign presence. Missionaries fled their stations, sometimes aided by equally fearful Qing officials and soldiers, sometimes abandoned by them to the popular clamour. This second draft of foreign troops for Peking was viewed by the Qing as an invasion force, for no approval was sought or given for this force which moved on the capital led by British Rear-Admiral Seymour. It found itself quickly bogged down: the railway cut, Boxers and Qing troops resisting it. To gain some control over the situation, the foreign forces at Dagu seized the forts there, and by way of response to this unambiguous act of aggression, and emboldened by the mass loyal uprising, the court at Peking declared the existence of a state of war 'in the ancestral shrines' on 21 June 1900.

It was, announced this eloquent and compelling edict, a war against foreign violence masquerading as civilized diplomacy. It was fought to 'vindicate the dignity of our country' after thirty years of insult and aggression. It was a fight for survival.[14] Others thought too of the survival of nations, for it was the language of the times. For some it was a new science, for others simple rhetorical shorthand. In May 1898, at the height of the scramble for concessions, the Marquis of Salisbury, British Prime Minister, had delivered a widely reported speech to the annual meeting of the Primrose League, a pro-empire, grass-roots Conservative Party organization. In the capacious setting of the Albert Hall, its stage garlanded with flowers, Salisbury surveyed the diplomatic turmoil of the past months, and then mused on the fates of nations, for, he declared, 'you may roughly divide the nations of the world as the living and the dying'. In an analysis infused with the language of Social Darwinism, he contrasted the 'great countries of enormous power growing in power every year, growing in wealth, growing in dominion, growing in the perfection of their organization'. The contrast was with 'a number of communities which I can only describe as dying', mostly non-Christian (mostly, for Spain was included), where 'disorganization and decay are advancing almost as fast as concentration and increasing power are advancing in the living nations', where 'decade after decade they are weaker, poorer', their administrations corrupt, no reform party in view. In time, inevitably, proposed Salisbury, 'the living nations will gradually encroach on the territory of the dying'. There were dangers: in such encroachments lay the 'seeds of conflict' amongst the living powers, but Britain would have its share whatever the danger, he complacently assured his audience, even if it could not have the 'profitable monopoly of curing or cutting up these unfortunate patients'.[15] At this the Primrose Leaguers chortled. For them the extinction of China was a fact in the natural order of things, and in the British order of things: China was a dying nation. 'Inane drivel,' thought the *North China Herald* when reporting Salisbury's speech, but only because his analysis was in its eyes far too passive. China was not a nation, but a 'geographical expression', and 'a boatswain and a dozen bluejackets could take any seaport in China without firing a shot.'[16] It wanted an active policy, wanted Britain to wield the knife and take cuts of its own choosing, not Russian or German leftovers: to be left with Weihaiwei when Russia took Port Arthur? Weihaiwei? Where-are-we?

Salisbury's view of the life and death of nations was echoed by anxious Chinese observers. For them the extinction of nations was a reality, one close to home and close to realization in Korea, and one with a glaring European precedent in Poland, partitioned and destroyed as an independent state in the late eighteenth and early nineteenth centuries. Liang Qichao had written about the destruction of that country; Kang Youwei had presented a study of Poland's extinction to the Guangxu emperor during the hundred days. 'Polandization' gained currency as a term, a stark warning of the fate of once great nations become sclerotic. Some feared the Boxer upsurge would hasten such an end, that by encouraging and then by coopting the Boxers, the court was bringing about final partition, since foreign armies would arrive and slice up the Chinese melon.[17] Many were aghast at Boxer superstition, at these heterodox and ignorant beliefs which stood in opposition to China's own cultural norms and dignity, and which were beneath contempt. But the court had calculated that national salvation lay now within its grasp, that the power of the loyal people could be harnessed to the power of the state, and that this fortuitous combination would defeat the foreign war against China launched by Admiral Seymour, and heralded by the seizure of the Dagu forts. Confirmation of its analysis was provided by an ultimatum from the foreign Powers discussed at the court on 17 June. The ultimatum effectively demanded the passing to foreign control of Qing finances and military affairs, and the reinstallation of the emperor: it was a simple demand for the extinction of Qing authority. But it was a forgery, designed to inflame, although it was probably by that point entirely unnecessary. Resistance to invasion needed no fictional rationale: Seymour had given reason enough.[18]

A congeries of wars was fought across north China that year and long into the next.[19] In the north only, for the officials in the south demurred, evaded the call for war, and negotiated a watchful truce with foreign diplomats and the foreign forces that were dispatched from Japan, Asian colonies and European heartlands. The south was not free of incident, and no less affected by the shock of despoliation after 1895, but it was not hungry. At Shanghai, however, just in case, the International Settlement Police raided incoming steamers and seized Buddhist priests, believing them to be agents spreading Boxer ideas.[20] Volunteer Corps officers were issued sealed secret orders giving them permission to open fire on rioters and looters, enjoining them not to fire in the air if they did so. They must be prepared to guard their own, and to hell with 'fifty years of treaty amity': 'shoot to kill', was the order the Council chairman proposed. His colleagues insisted that the final phrase be struck out, but it was the reflexive position.[21] War was fought across Manchuria, as Russian forces razed Amur river cities, and smashed their way south into Manchuria and north out of Port Arthur. It was fought in Tianjin, the foreign concessions besieged by Boxer bands and the Qing army. It was fought all the hot dusty way to Peking, as a multinational force of foreign troops slugged their way to the capital and relieved the besieged legations and Christian cathedrals. War was fought in Shanxi province, as German and British columns tramped to Taiyuan, slaughtering opposition on the way – every Chinese village deemed a Boxer 'nest'; thousands killed in passing.

War was fought between Boxers and Christians, between the Qing armies with Boxer allies, and the 'Eight Power' allied expeditionary force. It was fought by British marines and Japanese infantry, as well as by Sikhs, Bengalis, Black Americans, Annamese, Algerians and a British regiment of Chinese from Weihaiwei.[22] Colonial subjects fought this colonial war. It was fought as a 'police action', as German forces occupied and 'pacified' the north China countryside. It was a cruel war: a war between states, a civil war, a fight for personal survival. It was fought too in the press worldwide. Anti-imperialists castigated the foreign record which had borne such fruit, and they castigated the criminal cruelties of the armies, looting their way to Peking, raping and murdering as they went. They castigated the dynasty, and the Chinese, as vile, cruel and superstitious. 'Boxerism' was not a reflex of a people in crisis, some declared, it was the colour of the entire history of Chinese responses to foreigners. It was the old story of contempt. Foreign dignity must be upheld by total and undeniable victory. No 'rabble on the heights' should be left to claim the abandoned field as at Sanyuanli; there must be no swift withdrawal from the conquered capital as in 1860. Kaiser Wilhelm spoke the mood plainly. Give no quarter, he told departing troops on 27 July: remember the Huns, take no prisoners: '*Führt Eure Waffen so daß auf tausend Jahre hinaus kein Chinese mehr es wagt einen Deutschen scheel anzusehen.*' (Wield your weapons so that for a thousand years hereafter no Chinese will dare look askance at a German.) 'Pave the way once and for all for civilization,' he concluded. This firm and clear instruction for slaughter evaded his own Chancellor's censorship, for while a less explosive text was actually issued to journalists, the version as delivered escaped into the international press, and in Germany it appeared swiftly on postcards sailing through the mails. German soldiers occupying the triangle of countryside between Tianjin, Baoding and Peking clearly complied with the spirit, and often with the letter of this murderous instruction.[23]

It must have seemed like the end of the world. War came to the sleepy Tianjin concessions at about half past two on the afternoon of 17 June. News of the Dagu forts seizure had already come to some by telephone, and a reaction was expected, but the 'Boxer bubble', it was thought, would be easy to 'prick'. But then, tiffin just over, residents 'were appalled to find bursting above their streets and houses shells fired from the city'. 'Some of the best native soldiers in China were shelling us and at no distant range,' reported the Customs Commissioner; a hundred shells falling in the normally torpid streets of the second largest foreign settlement in China in the first thirty minutes alone.[24] The siege lasted a week. Sniping and cannon fire took a steady toll. People died in their houses; burial parties were killed in the cemetery. Chinese with allegedly pro-Boxer documents were executed on the Bund. By chance a large contingent of Russian troops was in place, in transit to Peking, and fought steadily to defend the concessions. Chinese corpses filled the river. In the aftermath of the relief of the siege, allied soldiers shot and bayoneted house servants as they searched for drink and loot. A fierce battle crushed the Chinese forces by 14 July and the city and its forts were captured. Photographer James Ricalton caught the carnage of the immediate aftermath in a series of photographs echoing Beato's four decades earlier: dead soldiers on the shattered walls, corpses in the fouled river.[25] War had come to Blagoveshchensk on the Amur river, the Sino-Russian frontier, on 2 July. That day firing broke out between Chinese and Russian forces across the river, the main communication route for Russian reinforcements to Pacific Siberia and north China. The following day thousands of Chinese and Manchu residents of the Russian city – servants, traders, labourers, men, women and children – were rounded up by police and volunteer militia, and on 4 July they were systematically herded into the river, and those who were not drowned were shot or hacked to death. Thousands were murdered on that and succeeding days. Similar pogroms happened elsewhere along the frontier.[26] The Amur river was reported still thick with 'a tangled and mangled mass of thousands of corpses' weeks after the massacre there.[27] Fear of foreign invasion, fear of communal uprising, racism, hatred and despair made enemies out of neighbours. Rage was the field order of the day in the campaigning armies. Colonial rebellion perhaps always sparked the fiercest of responses and foulest of retributions from the betrayed colonial overlord. And as China was a colony in the foreign mind, the uprising and war fell neatly into the category of rebellion in the eyes of many foreign participants, and to rebellion no quarter was given. Combine that with the viciousness of war fought against an enemy belittled in racist thought, and the countless cruelties of the Boxer war begin to make a little sense. And foreigners in China had long assumed that they were invulnerable, immune to Chinese threat and violence, their protecting spirits not gods, but consuls, courts and the fact of extraterritoriality – and its aura too. They acted to restore that invulnerability, which in fact ultimately rested most securely on recourse to terrible violence.

Foreign power won as its technology and the 'perfection' of its organization of violence and cruelty combined to subjugate opposition. It ignored its own new conventions on the conduct of warfare, agreed at The Hague the previous year. After all, these did not come into effect until 4 September 1900, and anyway, could they really apply to those who had already so transgressed civilized norms? The court fled a blasted and burned capital. The ageing Li Hongzhang negotiated yet another peace, a 'Boxer Protocol' that dealt with punishment, reparations and an indemnity, and extraterritorialized the legation quarter in Peking. New concessions were demanded in Chinese cities. Partition, the promised end, again in fact receded as a possibility, for the jealousies of hungry foreign nations proved too great, too dangerous, too capable of sparking war in Europe more widely. Russia failed to conform, though, and hung on in Manchuria with 200,000 troops.[28] So the British and the Japanese opened up a new world of international politics by entering into a formal alliance in 1902, breaking with decades of British practice, and in 1904–5 the Japanese smashed Russian forces in Manchuria and Siberia, shocking the European world, and offering new hope for the colonized and threatened.

But the view from Peking in August 1900 could not have been worse. Foreign officers lounged on the thrones in the imperial palace. Supply trains headed to the coast stuffed with treasure. Thousands lay dead and unburied in the capital's streets. Victory did bring pause for thought amongst some foreign participants and observers, and in the south and interior nothing much changed. Some panicked. Alicia Little thought 'the Chinese in Shanghai look at one with quite a new expression, and one I do not like at all.' Some foreigners packed and fled, sure that massacre was coming. Fearful too were Chinese residents and local authorities. Assuming the worst when the Volunteer Corps practised its drills in June, local Chinese military units prepared themselves for attack. Blagoveshchensk showed that there was rational cause for worry.[29] Other foreigners got ready to exploit the rebalancing of China. New opportunity presented itself. Thousands more soldiers were to be garrisoned in the north? Build a brewery for them in Qingdao: they will be thirsty and there are reliable supplies of water nearby. The Anglo-Germania Brauerie Company began operations in 1903 as a result. Thousands of soldiers were a market for prostitution: in flowed prostitutes to serve this new demand. Many came from Eastern Europe, others were American (and most said they were, for Shangai preferred 'American' girls in the brothels).[30] The impact on Chinese Christians and church workers in north China was huge. The missionary cause had lost scores of foreign workers: at least forty Catholics and 135 adult Protestants of all denominations were killed. Their martyrdom however had consecrated Chinese soil more richly than ever before, and their experiences and those of the survivors were vividly recorded in pamphlets, books and lectures. More workers were needed to replace those lost or too unsettled to return. They were called for, and came forward, some arriving even by the end of 1900. The numbers of missionaries greatly increased over the next two decades, doubling by 1920, their ordained Chinese staff growing in strength five times over.[31] Missionaries, soldiers and prostitutes, beer and bibles, all made their way to 'pacified' China.

Besieged foreigners and many of their relievers had kept copious notes, their diaries and journals flooding the pages of the press as the conflict passed through its different phases. Photographs taken in the minutes after the besieged legations were relieved show impromptu dancing for joy, as the tension of the six-week ordeal was lifted. The dancing turned wilder, turned to carnival, turned to a 'perfect carnival of looting', to 'riot, tumult, debauch'.[32] They looted at Tianjin; they looted at Peking; they looted everywhere in between, and far out into the northern provinces. They looted for days, for weeks, for months. They looted arsenals, granaries, mints and palaces. They looted the instruments from the old Jesuit Observatory. They looted salt stocks in Tianjin, and treasure from pawnshops. They looted houses and hovels. They looted tombs. They took furs, silks, paintings, jades and porcelains. They looted gold-plate from the roofs of temples. They took books and statues. What they did not like or could not take they trampled underfoot, tore, burned or wrecked. Military convoys were organized to ferry out the stocks of silver from treasuries; prowling private soldiers butchered householders and stole their possessions. In Tianjin those in the know – Chinese residents who remained, foreigners who had been besieged – rushed to the pawnshops and jade shops in the walled city, keeping ahead of the foreign troops who blundered their way about. For every graphic account of the looting spree that was published, indignant letters followed denying the charges, and lambasting the troops of other armies for their rapacious cruelty. The French were orderly, but the Russians! The British were disciplined, but the French! The armies in the field institutionalized the process, seizing the loot and auctioning it off, sharing the resulting prize fund amongst the troops. But such order masked anarchy on the streets. Better bombardment than such chaos, lamented one victim from re-lieved Tianjin – than the 'devastating deluge' of foreign soldiery which swept in and swept everything up.[33] While politically radical newspapers attacked the organized looting of the Japanese military, and censured British, French and American forces, some US missionaries published eloquent defences of the 'ethics of loot', and organized expeditions and forays to secure 'indemnities' for their convert survivors from their alleged persecutors.[34] It was easy to 'scoff', wrote Alicia Little, defending the besieged for pragmatically shifting for themselves in the aftermath, but 'What would *you* have done?' – your colleagues or converts dead, your possessions lost, home burned. Well, remarked Mark Twain, one of the pithiest public critics, here comes Christendom back from her 'pirate raids', her 'soul full of meanness, her pocket full of boodle and her mouth full of pious hypocrisies. Give her soap and a towel,' he concluded, 'but hide the looking-glass.'[35]

They hid the looking-glass, not least, because privately foreign diplomats readily accepted that it was the foreign action at the Dagu forts that had definitively turned the scales. And their long-lasting lack of enthusiasm for the mission enterprise remained firm, especially now that it had sparked a greater cataclysm than was ever seen at Tianjin, or at such much-protested sites as Yangzhou. 'Do you imagine that [Christians in China] are slaughtered simply because the Chinese dislike their religion?' asked Lord Salisbury at the bicentenary meeting in London in mid-June 1900 of the Society for the Propagation of the Gospel, Sidney Brooks' mission. No, it was because missions were viewed as instruments of secular powers. Be prudent, he cautioned, and don't run to the consul and demand a gunboat when trouble occurs. Still, 'who lets loose the hurricane is responsible for the wreckage', diplomats would also add, and the Qing let loose these terrible winds.[36]

While the north was wasted much remained unchanged – the level of anxiety excepted – in the south. The sensational news of the war filled up the pages of the foreign-language press in Shanghai, but those same pages reported the usual business of treaty port life as well. As shells fell on the Tianjin concessions the Shanghai Cricket Club defeated the Shanghai Public School Team in a desultory match.[37] The Shanghai Yacht Club held its usual race down the Huangpu and back. At the Mixed Court the Council prosecuted a carriage builder for running unlicensed carriages; a groom for running down a woman on the Nanjing Road; cases of house-theft; and some opium houses for breaking their licence conditions. A tea-shop owner was charged with allowing an 'improper play' to be performed (and yet more correspondence with the Daotai on the subject was published, the Council yet again denying his authority within the Settlement). Brief notes of routine foreign fatalities were recorded: accidental drownings, a suicide, two deaths from alcohol-related illnesses – the Shanghai usual. The International Settlement Council published the results of its latest census taken on 26 May 1900, recording details of the 6,774 foreign residents in the Settlement (over 500 of them Eurasians, 360 of those children), and the occupations of the 3,181 adult males: clerks, accountants, merchants, mercantile assistants and storekeepers were joined by police, journalists, Professors of Music, hairdressers and photographers. The soldiers who poured in and queued noisily in the streets outside the brothels, or brawled with each other and the police, went unrecorded. When the *Peking & Tientsin Times* resumed publication in Tianjin in late August it recorded the roll of damaged property, the continuing insecurities of life and property in the city, and the mission stations known to have been destroyed, and by the end of September was able to report that the municipal band was practising again. China's calamity was partial geographically, but total within the zones of combat and vengeance. The ordered business of its routine engagement with the world at the treaty ports elsewhere was able to continue, and provided a basis for a swift return to a sort of normality.

Normality cost. Urban and rural north China were already paying a high price for the disorder and the inflicted peace. The state was now subject to a massive indemnity, some of the legacies of which are still active in the early twenty-first century. The staggering scale of the imposition was to prove far in excess of the worth of actual claims for compensation from it. The US found 70 per cent of the reparations it received remained unclaimed. As one scholar noted, it was 'determined in anger and mitigated at leisure'.[38] Many payments ceased by the 1920s as world politics changed – as Germany was defeated and Russia imploded. Mitigation of the remainder took the form of educational programmes – funding schools and colleges in China, providing funds for Chinese students to study overseas – but the entanglements of the indemnity were not easily undone. Of course, the victorious powers had arranged to have the funds advanced to the Qing, and then they planned to dun it for four decades for repayment, securing the loans on the revenues collected by the Customs Service, which became nothing less than a debt servicing agency. Qing finances were hideously distorted, and so were those of their successors. Where once Hart's Service provided the funds for state-led restoration, now its ever-growing revenues were alienated to service the Boxer loans.

There were other impositions, now equally as routine in the ironing out of such creases in smooth Sino-foreign relations (smooth in foreign terms, though often, like this indemnity, they were excessive in scale and purported meaning). The German Minister, Baron von Ketteler, had been shot dead in Peking in June as events were unfolding towards open conflict. A Chinese memorial arch was ordered to be erected at the site, bestriding Hatamen Street by the Zongli Yamen. Unveiled in January 1903 it stood, the Guangxu emperor's brother announced, as a symbol of peace, of friendly Sino-German relations, and as 'a warning to the people'. German troops paraded through it, reinforcing that last point.[39] Other new monuments were erected across north China, and overseas too: memorials to the military and the missionary dead. A bullet-scarred wall at the British Legation in Peking was fashioned into a permanent memorial, its centrepiece that flexible phrase of Rudyard Kipling's: 'Lest we forget.' Lest they forget also motivated the drive to repair and reconstruct older memorials. Ernest Satow returned to Peking as British Minister in September 1900, after docking at Tianjin in a captured Chinese destroyer. The capital seemed a 'huge city of the dead,' he reflected in his diary, and a 'feeling of profound melancholy took possession of me, such as I have never experienced'. There was much to do for the new Minister: fighting still sometimes flared up, columns stood ready to move out, the elements of the Protocol needed to be discussed; but repairing the shattered monument to the captive dead of 1860 was on his list too. Satow had made his pilgrimage to it in 1862, now he visited it again and the British organized its reconstruction.[40] The worlds of 1862 and 1900 were intimately connected through men like the new Minister and Robert Hart, but they were also seamlessly joined by stone monument and the unchanging meanings accorded them: British sacrifice and Chinese perfidy, the men 'treacherously seized' and inhumanly treated; lest we forget.

The Boxer war was vicious, and its legacy long-lasting. It was a conflict whose first shots were reported by telephone, and whose

progress was monitored and discussed equally by chattering international telegraph and through word of mouth from village to village.
Photographers accompanied the columns or were themselves besieged
in Peking. Footage for the new cinemas was created by James Williamson in Hove, and by Mitchell and Kenyon in Blackburn.[41] In the United
States the Edison company mocked up a bombardment of the Dagu
forts: model ships floating in front of what looks more like London's
Tower Bridge than any Chinese city, the three-minute scene stuffed
with explosions, smoke rising from the model townscape. This was
topical entertainment, not fakery – a novel *bonne bouche* in an evening
of musical turns. The real action that could be documented was much
less dramatic, but no less novel as a record of the China enterprise or
response to it. Two weeks before the Edison film was copyrighted, and
fresh from hearing the Kaiser's instructions, German troops departing
from Bremerhaven on 31 July 1900 were filmed by Guido Seeber, a
pioneering German film-maker. British marines were filmed boarding
transport for China in late June.[42] Cameraman Joseph Rosenthal made
his way to China from South Africa in late 1900, missing any action,
but securing stock for later exhibition. The new film-making companies
were electrified by the Boer War, scenes from which dominated their
catalogues, and the China expeditions found their niche within these
new records of Europe's conflicts. Meanwhile, and just as close to any
truths of the realities of the conflict, 'gaudily coloured broadsheets'
had already appeared for sale on the streets of Shanghai's walled city,
showing battles between Chinese and foreign forces.[43] The Chinese are
always winning. But if an immense amount of material was circulated
in new as well as in older forms of visual and print media – much of
it sensationalist, inaccurate and serving a wide range of purposes – the
Boxer spasm passed. There was much worth forgetting, and new
opportunities and new horrors to face, not least the Russo-Japanese
conflict, which diverted world attention.

In all of this mass of material there was a notable absence. We have
very few photographs that we can confidently accept show Boxers,
aside from one taken in Tianjin. There are other photographs of
captured men, allegedly Boxers, and many of those executed as such,
or about to be killed. But in the summer of 1900 and for months
afterwards, every Chinese male was deemed a Boxer. The Boxers

themselves spoke in their actions and pamphlets, and some of these survive. But so vicious was the suppression, and so violent the reaction against them within China, that their own faces and voices were expunged until oral history projects in the early 1960s tried to capture some of their world of thought.[44] There are other photographs which purport to show Boxers, some genuinely taken in north China at the time, but in many other cases agencies or publishers keen for topical illustration grabbed any old likely photograph and labelled it 'Boxers'. There was a dearth of authenticity in this much-faked war, characterized and impelled as it was by forgery and wild rumour. False diplomatic demands were believed at the Qing court; the 'news' of the massacre of the foreign legations at Peking was so widely believed in mid-July that obituaries were published and invitations to memorial services issued. And all the accompanying detail was perfectly tuned and right out of the China-side versions of the *Battle of Dorking*: 'standing together, as the sun rose fully,' reported the *Daily Mail* correspondent of the last moments at Peking, 'the little remaining band, all Europeans, met death stubbornly.' Evolving mass news media meant that the demand for copy, for authentic accounts and photographs, was growing insatiable. 'Half the telegrams were deliberately "faked" in Fleet Street' claimed the managing editor of *The Times*.[45] Everything was known about the conflict; much of it was not true, but that hardly mattered.

A war of words was fought. China crises, like other crises, had seen experts rush to print, and publishers rush to resurrect old books. Moral urgency impelled some: Robert Hart, who had endured the siege in Peking, traded on his reputation, so nicely confirmed in his recent premature obituaries, to secure the publication of essays calling for calm moderation in responding to the crisis. It was a rational and patriotic national uprising against foreign imposition, he declared. British philosopher G. Lowes Dickinson pleaded the Chinese case in the anonymous *Letters from John Chinaman* (1901), which most assumed was the work of a Chinese writer (and some responded to as such). *The Chinese Crisis from Within* (1901) was an analysis by a truly Chinese critic living in Singapore. Much of what was published served to damn the behaviour of missionaries and converts, even pious Robert Hart's work; and his private correspondence is thick with letters to and from missionaries.[46] Arthur Smith provided analysis rooted in his own view from the Shandong countryside. An ex-employee of Hart's, Bertram Lenox-Simpson, chose the sensationalist route, exposing foreign incompetence and cowardice in his *Indiscreet Letters from Peking*, allegedly based on his journal of the siege there. Another, J. O. P. Bland, safe in Shanghai where he was busily interrogating arrested Buddhist priests in the Settlement town hall, was later gulled into publishing a book 'revealing' the inner deliberations of the Qing court in 1900. *China Under the Empress Dowager* was published in 1910 and hailed as a masterpiece exposing the real history of the Qing during the crisis. The core evidence it furnished was the purported diary of a minor Manchu official, Jing Shan. Here was definitive evidence of Manchu duplicity, of the guilty xenophobia of leading officials, as well as exoneration of others. Queried by a few at the time, despite the diary being long-exposed as a forgery, it still has a life of its own.[47] Fakery and rumour, meeting the needs of a sensationalist new-style press, and news of massacres at Peking fitted well the paranoia and anxieties of imperialism under threat. New 'insider evidence' best suited those who saw the Boxer outbreak as a Qing court conspiracy, years in the making. Never had there been such a clamour for work on China, and never such supply, and while some of it pleaded China's case, much of it served to damn the country, its cultures and its peoples yet further in foreign eyes and minds.

But looking at the weighty, stately pages of a 1908 survey, Wright and Cartwright's *Twentieth Century Impressions of Hongkong, Shanghai, and Other Treaty Ports of China*, the pomp and plenty of the China coast world seem unfettered by the calamities of that recent past or affected by the marching youths of Shandong and Zhili. The volume was one of a series that aimed to advertise to metropolitan readers the triumphs and opportunities of the British world beyond formal empire. The setting of this volume was a new China. Here was a yet-again resurgent Qing government in the midst of its last great reformist era, that of the 'New Policies', a return in all but name to the startling revolution of 1898. In January 1901 an edict called for reform proposals, a new route now being taken to restore dignity and strengthen China. Suggestions poured in to a new 'Bureau of Government Affairs', and by the end of that year, with the indemnity agreement still not yet agreed, the Qing moved forward, abolishing the old civil service examination syllabus based on mastery of the canon of Chinese classics, and introducing new foreign subjects. Western-style schools followed, and students were directed to study overseas. The military and the administration itself were reformed, and a 'New Army' developed. New ministries replaced the old. The Zongli Yamen was replaced by a more internationally orthodox Ministry of Foreign Affairs that restricted itself to diplomacy. This was a demand, too, of the 1901 Protocol. A Ministry of Commerce was established. Justice was reformed, and some punishments abolished – the cangue, corporal punishment and *lingchi*, 'death by a thousand cuts'. Preparations were put in place for a constitutional form of government, leading to a parliament that it was planned would sit for the first time in 1917. 'China has at last really reached the parting of the ways,' concluded Wright's introduction: a parting with the ways of its past.

Shipyards and schools, silk filatures and cotton mills, post offices and race clubs, the houses of the Chinese merchants, their new motor cars, the homes of foreign traders – all decorate the volume, verses of a hymn to the triumph of the China coast world. And this was now a world that after 1903 could be reached overland, via the Trans-Siberian railway, in about a fortnight from London – war, derailment and other inconveniences permitting.[48] The mails too could go swiftly to and fro this way, binding China coast residents more tightly yet to Europe. So vibrant was the world portrayed that some of the concessions secured after 1900 were as surplus to any conceivable demand or purpose as much of the indemnity was. Of course, developing a concession always took time, but the China coast landscape was so thickly settled that it proved problematic in many places to get foreign residents to live in the right place: to get Germans to uproot themselves from the British concession in Tianjin, or to negotiate the problem of British interests which found themselves in the new Russian concession at Hankou. The Austro-Hungarian concession at Tianjin never had any Austrian residents aside from the consul. Others failed in different ways. The British had long lobbied for an opening of West River ports into Guangxi province. The Chinese obliged, not least as this usefully brought British interests into an area long coveted by the French across the border in Indo-China. But despite the advantages foreign trade brought with it, existing commercial interests at places like Nanning, opened in early 1907, could not be shifted. Foreign Customs staff and the handful of representatives of the firms that set up shop there found themselves with little to do except drink and rot – waiting, hoping, begging for transfer. What was a treaty port: a bund, a zone marked out for foreign residence, a Customs house, a club, the offices of a handful of *hongs*. At Nanning the Customs house was decrepit, the bund collapsed not once, not twice, but at least four times in the first two years; and a theatre was built on the part of the still-unoccupied foreign Settlement that was not simply 'a network of large ponds'. What was a treaty port, mused Bland in 1906, 'a piece of mud, some miles from the city, being indicated for the residence of foreigners and situated so as to be useless for the purposes of trade.'[49]

There was momentous change in other spheres in the post-Boxer decade. Opium has perfumed this entire narrative. In 1900 the Shanghai census recorded twenty-six foreign men living on opium hulks, half of them British. These unsightly ships were shifted off the Bund in 1906 and moored instead at Pudong, but the trade still flowed through them, as it had at one anchorage or another for a century. Many firms with British-protected status from India were still heavily involved, and British China-coast finance and logistics still served the drug. That same year, however, momentum was building from a number of directions towards a comprehensive change in policy. The new Liberal government in Britain restated an old and often wryly spoken pledge, that if China could suppress opium use, it would start to wind down exports of opium from India. An anti-opium decree was issued by the Qing in 1906, and a comprehensive campaign of suppression began. It caught foreign observers, and many users and addicts, completely, and often very unpleasantly, by surprise: for the recalcitrant addict risked execution.[50] A formal commitment to whittle down the trade was made in a Sino-British convention in 1907, and the following year the British started reducing direct exports from India by 10 per cent a year. Municipalities in the concessions were under no less pressure to conform. At Shanghai there were over 1,000 public opium houses in the International Settlement alone, each one licensed, the revenues forming a small but noteworthy part of municipal revenues. Despite a rearguard action, the Council eventually put a prohibition proposal to its foreign ratepayers, who voted to suppress the houses, and by

1910 they had closed. Opium shops remained, however, but vigorous campaigning was to see these too closed down by 1917, although not before foreign merchants and Chinese traders had joined together in what they termed the 'Combine' to keep prices high, and joined with Chinese gangsters, based in the ever-troublesome Chinese detective branch of the Municipal Police, to stamp out competition.[51] Opium revenues continued to be important to the finances of the British Indian government into the 1920s, and that government was openly complicit in the indirect smuggling to China of the drug, but the visible landscape had been altered. Off the Shanghai Bund there were none of the hulks that lurked still in the panorama photographs, nor were they to be found across at Pudong or downriver at Wusong. On Shanghai streets there were no opium houses, and no shops openly selling the drug. Where once opium and Chinese were inextricably linked in foreign eyes, and opium and foreign trade in many eyes also, now the drug was seemingly displaced. What was a moral victory for some was a bore for others, for it had a disruptive effect on the finances of the International Settlement at Shanghai. It was also deemed unfair, for properly colonial Hong Kong and Singapore did not suppress legal trade in the drug. And it was also – its critics complained, with good reason – bound to stimulate an underground and illicit trade that could not effectively be combated, and which could inflame criminality and corruption. This is precisely what it did.

The international position of the Chinese also evolved, feeding into Chinese politics and those of other countries. A pragmatic solution to labour shortages affecting the reconstruction of the South African goldfields after the Boer War saw the recruitment of 64,000 indentured Chinese labourers, mainly from Shandong. The political outcry in Britain was huge: 'Are the Chinese serfs intended to keep British workmen out of South Africa?' demanded the title of one party pamphlet. The street theatre of the 1906 election saw 'Chinese' marching British streets in chains.[52] Anti-Chinese cartoons and posters appeared in great abundance, and found their way quite swiftly to China and a hostile reception there. The free migration of Chinese labour was obstructed by racist exclusionary immigration regimes in Canada, Australia and the United States. A powerful protest movement developed in China in 1905 in response to the renewal of this US legislation, its tactics coalescing around a boycott of American goods that took effect across a number of Chinese cities and communities overseas and had wide support across Chinese society. If you breach the boycott, activists cried, foreigners will laugh at you. This was a dignified protest, 'enlightened anti-foreignism' one leading figure called it. While the US consulate at Shanghai adopted a policy of 'passive contempt', American trade was significantly hit by this, the first of many more boycotts to come.[53] 'Enlightened anti-foreignism' was to prove a far stronger weapon than any previously deployed. It had a legitimacy and dignity that the despairing violence of the Boxers lacked, and it could not be so easily countered by foreign violence. 'Boxers' could be slaughtered by foreign troops, but nobody could be forced to smoke an American cigarette.

The pages of Wright's compendium sparkled with photographs of solid *hongs* and lavish private homes: China commerce beckoned investment and recruits. But they also showed the hard military wariness that underpinned the new peace. Volunteer Corps at the treaty ports were better armed and better trained. The garrisons in north China were large, the China station fleets bigger, and facilities greatly developed. Tensions evolved rather than faded. In December 1905 official conflict over court jurisdiction in Shanghai sparked protests, a general strike and a riot that saw crowds burn the Laozha station, and attack the International Settlement's town hall. Troops and volunteers fired on the crowds and cowed them. We have dramatic photographs of moments of tension on the streets: crowds circling Sikh policemen; the Volunteers grimly stalking past Chinese bodies; rifle-wielding police in the burnt ruins of their station. Why had not the police at Laozha fired on the mob, demanded critics in the post-mortem. Why had the police been ordered to disarm, as indeed they had? It was partly a misunderstanding of the scale of the disorder, but, the police countered, the damage was 'more than compensated for by the effect, on public opinion amongst the Chinese, of the restraint shown under severe provocation'. Well, this was all nicely put, but in the aftermath the Council plotted to greatly increase the Sikh police contingent, a 'fighting machine' in the police chief's eyes, by bringing hundreds of new recruits in for settlement defence. They were thwarted, not least by British officials, who decried a military occupation of the city.[54] Shanghai's foreigners remained ready to fight nonetheless, and celebrated their volunteering prowess by route-marching up and down their streets. They could march; they could shoot, killing rioters and – 'an unavoidable misfortune' – bystanders; but while a riot could be suppressed, the interlinked grievances and beliefs that fed the strike in 1905 could not be so simply struck down. The events of 18 December 1905 were fed by the growing nationalistic clamour across Chinese society, by specific local complaint about foreign actions, including the American boycott, and by the more opaque aspiration for Chinese dignity – all gaining a momentum that was beyond the capabilities of foreign violence to corral.

The flurry of Qing reform went hand in hand with a growth in expectations that the dynasty could hardly match, and a steady development in various forms of passive or active opposition. There were reformists – impatient with the pace of change – revolutionaries, and ethnic nationalists. Opposition found vent in newspapers, abortive uprisings, and shifting groupings and alliances which opposed the Qing. The new armies proved recruiting and training centres for new revolutionaries. A virulent strain of anti-Manchu thought grew stronger: racist in form, drawing the attention of Han Chinese to the slaughters of the mid-seventeenth-century invasion as backing for lurid calls for arms and revenge. Meanwhile the fine detail of constitutional reform developed an ethnic character, places being reserved for Manchus out of all proportion to their presence in the state administration, this protective favouritism causing disquiet, and seeming to contradict the new emphasis on efficient reform. Students studying overseas, especially in Japan, were radicalized there. Sun Yat-sen remained a prominent figure in the revolutionary world, but there were others. And outside the world of active revolutionaries was a far wider world of rapid reform and change, strengthening the position of women, changing the contours of public and private life, reshaping social and family relations. People experimented with new marriages (young people choosing their own partners), writers with new genres, all of them living and thinking China afresh. Some did so by breaking with the past, others by re-assessing it, reformulating it to serve a changing present. The pace of urban and rural change was different; coastal and interior urban change differed too, but all were interconnected as people moved, as books and periodicals spread through the mails, as railways were laid and new steamer routes opened up. All that had seemingly been fixed was shattered by the guns of 1900 and the state-driven reformation thereafter. Some sought to re-fix it, many sought other paths, promiscuously sampling opportunity and possibility. Everything seemed possible, everything seemed open to question.

All this tinder was ignited by a carelessly dropped match on 9 October 1911. Revolutionary conspirators in New Army units in Hankou used a house in the Russian concession there as a bomb factory, ahead of a planned uprising. Blowing themselves up, not through rough handling of the explosives, but through smoking (ever a recognizable danger to health), they drew the Russian police to them, and through that the Chinese authorities, who straight away took bloody action against the survivors. But China exploded with them, for their colleagues mutinied the following day to avoid arrest, and within days held the city. Within a month many major cities were in revolutionary hands, and Manchu residents in Xian, Nanjing and other cities had been massacred, the black smoke from their burning quarters caught in countless photographs. Province after province announced its independence from the Qing. Throughout this bloody autumn of fighting a careful balance was also sought between those who had military power, such as Qing commanders; those who now held moral sway, such as Sun and the revolutionaries; and those with increasingly nominal authority, namely the Qing court. The power of the gun prevailed. The Emperor abdicated, and the dynasty stood down, having been guaranteed personal security, a generous pension, and the Forbidden City to boot. Sun Yat-sen was proclaimed provisional president of a new Republic of China, and in turn stepped down in favour of Yuan Shikai, the most powerful of the Qing commanders. This was not simply a surrender to force, but came from a desire to re-establish unity and order as swiftly as possible, for at the backs of the revolutionaries could always be heard the chariots of foreign power, ready to hurry into any breach. 'You ought to be able to turn matters to your advantage,' wrote Bland to his successor as secretary at Shanghai – a good extension to the Settlement, for example.[55] There were some foreign gains: the Settlement police at Shanghai took over the courts there, and most importantly for national politics, the Customs Service took over the actual collection of revenue (rather than its assessment) as office holders in the treaty ports fled to safety. But the swift transition of power served its primary purpose. The Qing empire, with the exception of what became Mongolia, became the Chinese Republic, a staggering achievement, given the forces arrayed against it. The foreign concessions proved themselves vital alien ground during the months of revolution. Qing officials decamped into them when local revolt threatened. Revolutionaries too enjoyed their security. Sun had been overseas when Hankou exploded. He arrived in Shanghai on 25 December and was hosted in the palatial Settlement residence of a sometime opium trader and property tycoon, Silas Aaron Hardoon. The British concession at Hankou and the International Settlement's town hall were venues for negotiations between competing parties. China's fractures aided in these small ways its transitions to a republic, both as threat, and as useful foreign enclaves.

In the eyes of more belligerent foreign observers and residents all these opportunities to turn matters to their advantage were wasted. All the openings offered by two decades of war or revolution had ultimately not produced advantage enough. They had too much favoured new powers such as Japan, or Russia and Germany. Some argued that preserving stability and balance served foreign interests better, that any single advance in China would see the loss of all past gains, or war in Europe. The Boxer settlement surely had delivered the foreign goods: a reforming Qing, chastened by the punishment of 1900–1901, and a quiescent populace. What more could traders want? Think back to those belligerent pamphlets and memorials, and all of those demands made of the Chinese. Now they had commercial legislation, a ministry of commerce, republican government; the opium trade was being vigorously suppressed, and cruel punishment abolished. On top of this they still retained extraterritorial privilege and dozens of open ports. Their old images of China were surely redundant. They could surely want nothing more now. But in fact a new layer of foreign contempt was bedded in, and victory brought its own complacencies. And so entrenched were their notions of China and the Chinese, that they were given new life by the Boxer rising, and were twisted too by the unnerving rise of Japan, so much so that the first two decades of the twentieth century saw a great flowering of Sinophobic feeling. On election posters across the English-speaking world vicious caricatures of Chinese faces leered down at voters; Chinese villains such as Fu Manchu conquered the bookshelves of the young. Real Chinatowns became fictionalized nests of opium dens and sites of the despoliation of white girls by Chinese men. (Tourists took organized trips to enjoy the frisson of the forbidden offered in their local orients.)[56] *Attack on a China Mission* provided a long-lasting template for cinema, for it portrayed in its four grainy minutes Chinese male threats to European women, xenophobic violence and bloody white revenge: this remained the core of any film about China or the Chinese for decades to come. Layered on to this were anxieties about opium, and later about cocaine. China and the Chinese drugged Europeans and Americans. This evolving political and cultural contempt undoubtedly informed diplomatic relations. 'Young China', modern China, reforming anti-Manchu westernized China was treated with as much contempt as China unreformed. A 'Chinaman' in the straw boater now favoured as a mark of republican modernity was still in their eyes a 'Chinaman'.

What more did they really want at Shanghai, Hankou and even at dreary Nanning? Well, solving that question was simple. At one level they wanted imperial prestige preserved and furthered, something seemingly intangible but actually no less real to them than a bund (a bund which did not collapse). British free-traders also fretted about the monopolistic tendencies of the new powers in their new domains, about being squeezed out of opportunities in Shandong or Manchuria, or out of the Russian or German concessions they found themselves working in. They still wanted free trade, but if they could not have it they wanted privilege and advantage, and many wanted monopoly. At another level they wanted hard cash opportunities: they wanted more railways, more mining concessions, more access to more ports and markets, more land for the profitable settlements they already had. They lobbied for it. At Shanghai they lobbied unceasingly for an extension north, into an area known as Zhabei. Maps they drew up showed foreign-owned land dominating the suburb, and showed it in imperial red, as all maps should. Repeatedly rebuffed by the local authorities, the Council in 1903 started building roads into the district, and then acted on its assumed right to police the roads and tax house-holders along them. There was a hygienic imperative too, they claimed. Zhabei was a health threat to the Settlement, a corridor into the concessions for plague, a source of disorder of every kind. This was a routine excuse across the colonial world: aggrandizement masquerading as hygiene. The new opposition sparked by the American boycott and the Mixed Court incident opposed this 'normal development of Foreign administrative influence in the Settlement and its environs'.[57] The era of such 'normal' development was starting to pass. There was popular opposition now, and a Chinese municipality was formed, organizing a police force to contest this arrogation of sovereignty, which led to repeated minor clashes between officers on the ground. They build roads to spite us, claimed the advocates for extension; they establish utility companies to keep out our own. Their institutions are a sham, just a political ruse to deny us our rights, to deny us our 'normal development'.[58] Lectured for decades about how the model Settlement showed them how they should run their municipalities, Chinese urban reformers were damned for doing just that; were damned either way. Reformed China was to prove no less unacceptable to foreigners than unreformed China.

A new spasm of disorder in 1913 seemed to offer a solution of the old style, what the British minister to China termed 'one of those unexpected "opportunities of exercising pressure on the Chinese government"' that had proved so helpful over the decades, such as the death of Margary.[59] In July a revolt broke out at Shanghai against Yuan Shikai, who had proved himself a militarist dictator, not least by having the winner of China's 1912–13 elections assassinated at a Shanghai railway station. This was Song Jiaoren, and his party was Sun Yat-sen's, the new Guomindang (National People's Party). The Guomindang led the revolt. The rising was chaotic and bloody, and swept around the Settlement. Stray shells fell there, damaging property and gravestones, the *North China Herald* reported, and scaring bystanders witless. Residents flocked to get a view of the fighting from the roof gardens of the new Palace Hotel on the Bund, or from sampans in the river, continuing that long tradition of watching the China spectacle just outside their borders.[60] Journalists wandered in amongst the battling forces, dashing back to file their copy, seeing close up how bloody the spectacle actually was.[61] Other residents ignored it, listening as the orchestra played on in the Public Gardens, until a shell fell there too. As disorder spread into Zhabei, and the revolutionaries based themselves there for an attack on the government arsenal, property owners begged for protection, their petitions translated and neatly filed in Council and consular archives. Now, wrote the Council secretary, this was the moment: 'Said we', sotto voce, 'once in we'll never come out'. It would be the Settlement's reward for restoring order, and anyway, possession would not easily be undone. 'It is decided to go in insidiously, bobby by bobby', but the police commander, C. D. Bruce, a Briton, blundered (he must have been bribed, some thought), and he marched in a 'grand triumphal procession' of the Volunteer Corps, mustering its Chinese and Customs' companies, the Americans, and its elite Light Horse squadron, and with Council chairman Edward Pearce, a long-time resident, accompanying them.[62] They processed to the Zhabei police headquarters, expecting to meet there a Chinese deputation which would formally hand over to Pearce policing control of the suburb, but nobody turned up. It is difficult to not leave, if nobody officially recognizes that you have come in the first place. The colonizing dance always requires a partner.

The Settlement mobilized for the grand march on Zhabei was a cross-section of the China coast establishment.[63] Chairman Pearce, sportsman, and noted badger hunter, had already spent thirty years in Shanghai, working for Ilbert's – general importers, insurance agents and managers of a cotton spinning enterprise. By convention six Britons, one German and one American took Council seats and his fellow councillors included Shanghai-born Edward Isaac Ezra, legitimate opium merchant as well as land-owner and publisher, who was also busy – as part of his strategy to defeat the reform of the trade – papering the British consulate with reports on Chinese failures to eradicate opium. When that failed he took to smuggling instead. On the Council he spoke for the Combine and opium – 'Indian imports' his 1921 obituary termed the trade. Briton Henry Gulland managed the American International Banking Corporation; Heinz Figge managed the Deutsch Asiatische Bank. Lawyer Alfred White-Cooper had helped future US president Herbert Hoover retain illicit foreign control of the Kaiping coal mines in north China, which had been bundled over to nominal foreign ownership in 1900 to protect them from looting and confiscation and never returned, an egregious and wholly routine theft.[64] The business interests of these men and their fellow councillors crossed and crossed again. In various combinations they held directorships of many of the same companies, and were connected too through freemasonry, social clubs, and sometimes by marriage. This was a bankers' council, an opium traders' council, a rubber-boom speculators' council, if not simply just another company board, '7/9ths British in composition and wholly pro-Shanghai in policy' (according to the British minister), a pretty crew representing the intertwined worlds of legitimate commerce and huckster dealing that still marked the China coast establishment.[65] There was more than just a little huckster dealing. The most recent financial crisis in 1910 – which had crippled the Shanghai stock exchange – had been caused by a wild boom in rubber shares, which had at its heart market-rigging on a 'gigantic' scale by interests influential enough to distort any jury or trade committee's view of the affair.[66] It had been an unusually extreme crisis, but the shady practices at the heart of it were routine, and the coalitions of interests that had coalesced were a regular feature of the multinational scene at Shanghai. Even though British interests predominated at Shanghai, and on the Council, they were enmeshed in a web of ties that cut across nationalities throughout Settlement life. Anglo-German connections were particularly strong: Jardines had allowed the Germans to build a monument to shipwrecked naval dead on its Bund foreshore. The German Club Concordia hosted the British when their Shanghai Club was being rebuilt. German firms registered under British company law. *Social Shanghai*, a society journal, reported August 1913's festive life in this cosily intertwined cosmopolitan world: the twenty-fifth anniversary of the Kaiser's accession celebrated; Bastille Day; the Fourth of July. They strove to outshine each other with night-time illuminations and torch-lit parades, but all joined in together, for they were all in it together.[67]

The other chief actors in the Zhabei drama were Police Chief Bruce, 'ever so distinguished looking', who had come from the Army – from the British Chinese Regiment at Weihaiwei – as part of a strengthening of Settlement defence capability in 1906 after the Mixed Court riots. Council secretary William Leveson had taken over from Bland. Leading the Volunteer Corps was a regular British army officer, A. A. S. Barnes, who had also come from Weihaiwei. Arrayed behind them during the weeks of crisis were all the resources of the Settlement and its guardian angels. There were new volunteer companies of Chinese, Japanese, American and Portuguese regiments, again mostly formed in response to the Mixed Court crisis. The Boy Scouts did their bit, bicycling around the Settlement delivering messages. The American volunteers were always 'ready for trouble', and had sought like other SVC companies direct material support from their national government. Parties of sailors and marines from various warships deployed to the shore. But it was Shanghai that marched north, to the 'unfeigned satisfaction' of residents – foreign and, the *North China Herald* assured itself, Chinese as well.[68] Though the council was mostly British (and that Britishness itself was a complex matter, including as it did a Shanghai-born, Sephardi Jew of Baghdadi ancestry), the force mobilized to parade into Zhabei was also multinational, and as cosmopolitan as the China coast foreigners always described themselves. It was also, like the Council, 'wholly pro-Shanghai': their Shanghai; Settlement Shanghai.

You have the advantage of force right now, declared one of the Zhabei officials that weekend, but this was an 'act of piracy, a raid', and 'it is not possible to perpetrate Jameson raids in a country like China'. As we have seen, Chinese observers knew their history of British actions in South Africa, knew how 'restoring order' could cover an attempted land grab, as it had, unsuccesssfully, in late 1895 when British raiders from Cape Colony tried to provoke an uprising in the Boer Transvaal republic.[69] But piracy had of course been possible, if not routine in the later 1890s, for that was the Jiaozhou story. However, nationalistic 1913 was another China, even if Pearce, Bruce and Leveson did not yet appreciate it. Chinese feeling on the streets of Zhabei became 'hourly more hostile'. The stationing there of Sikh members of the International Settlement Police also outraged Chinese residents: insult was added to occupation in their eyes by the use of these 'Black slaves' to take over Chinese police functions.[70] As some of the foreign consuls angrily accused the Council of exceeding any defensive brief, Zhabei was evacuated by Settlement forces two days after the grand entry. The Volunteers snuck out at dawn, leaving small pickets of police that they had to return to rescue later in the day. Swaggering columns in the streets, and the attitude of the Council towards the Zhabei councillors at a meeting on 28 July, when they were told that their views could be 'freely expressed' but that orders were to come from the International

Settlement, confirmed local fears that this was exactly what most foreigners intended it to be: another incremental gain, a coup while Chinese concerns were diverted. Despite frantic appeals from the Council during the temporary occupation, Zhabei was never to come under Settlement control, even though President Yuan Shikai assured Pearce that summer that he had no objection, not least as the Council had been so helpful in the suppression of the rebellion against him. The government, remarked G. E. Morrison, now an adviser to the president, 'is well satisfied'.[71] But a satisfied state notwithstanding, popular nationalist sentiment, Chinese administrative innovation and the threat of violent resistance combined to hem the marching empire-builders at Shanghai back into their Settlement. Others would parade their troops in the future into bombed and rubble-strewn Zhabei indeed, but a China where it could confidently be expected that might was right and would easily triumph, was passing. A 'boatswain and a dozen bluejackets' could never have seized a Chinese seaport, though many long held this as a credo. In 1913 a much larger force could not take and hold a Shanghai suburb. The limits of this private-enterprise imperialism, of the sweaty plans of Bland and his ilk were reached on the early Sunday morning of 28 July 1913, when Bruce and his band blundered noisily into sleepy Zhabei, and nobody met them to play their scripted part in the local drama of Settlement extension.

Still, this second revolution had delivered into foreign hands more power over the Chinese state than they had ever had before. The revolution was beaten not least because the British pitched their support behind Yuan Shikai, departing from ostensible neutrality, but in fact aligning themselves, as was usually the pattern, behind the force best guaranteeing order and stability. This had a practical impact, for Yuan's ability to defeat the Guomindang was bolstered by his ability to pay his forces. And that ability lay in a new 'Reorganization Loan', so called after its ostensible purpose, the financing of the reorganization of the new state. This loan both inflamed Guomindang opposition to Yuan, for it was deemed unconstitutional of him to have agreed to it without parliamentary approval, and provided the resource with which he quashed that revolt. At the very least it freed up other funds for bribery, paying troops and purchasing munitions, more than one third of the loan becoming available during the period of the revolt. But at Shanghai, foreign staff of the Customs, the British consul, naval officials and bankers worked together to help release large sums for the Chinese navy which kept them on the government side.[72] This was a massive multinational loan predicated on new foreign supervision of the state salt monopoly, and the appointment of a team of foreign advisors. With the Customs now collecting revenue and controlling its disbursement to the central government – after servicing foreign debt obligations – the finances of the Chinese state had effectively passed into foreign hands. In October Yuan's government was formally recognized by the Treaty Powers. But at exactly the same time as the British and others secured apparent stability for their interests in China, a new worry had also emerged. As he reflected on the course of events in the immediate aftermath of the Guomindang's defeat, the acting British minister Beilby Alston (who saw bribery as having been Yuan's key weapon) raised a new worry. Many commentators had noted the involvement of Japanese individuals in the fighting around Shanghai, mainly it seemed working with republican troops. Alston filed a report outlining what he saw as 'intense' Japanese involvement in the revolt. Japanese interests in China were great, he noted; her gains in Manchuria after the war with Russia were a poor return for the investment made. They were more than ever now predisposed to direct intervention, and the British should note this and plan how to keep an open door should the Japanese act. London was much more sceptical, relying on the alliance signed with Japan in 1902 to reassure Alston that they saw no threat to British interests, nor danger of unilateral Japanese action.[73]

Confident, nonetheless, they memorialized now more steadily and readily. Two such monuments unveiled at Shanghai the year following the Second Revolution show the ambition and self-image of the China coast establishment, even as together they also marked the onset of fragmentation. The first was certainly cosmopolitan in speech. Sir Robert Hart died in 1911 just before the revolt broke out, and in May 1914 a statue of him was unveiled on the Bund at Shanghai. He was a 'trusted counsellor of the Chinese government', read one of the inscriptions, a 'true friend of the Chinese people'. With the Customs, the Post Office and the lights service Hart had 'accomplished a work of great beneficence for China and the world'. The foreign-directed Customs, at its moment of greatest autonomy, was recast as a disinterested and humanitarian enterprise. Hart's was no British-dominated venture in this light, even if they chose a sculptor, Henry Pegram, with an impeccable British empire pedigree, best known for his bust of Cecil Rhodes and work on the Imperial Institute in London. Hart, of course, really had little by way of any Shanghai connection, but this statue on the Bund offered a symbol that overrode the facts of war and treaty that had brought Balfour and his successors and their peers from the other treaty powers to the Huangpu. And where he was once seen as a traitor, his service interfering with trade, his sympathies and energies too much with the Chinese, now it was claimed that he had in fact made Shanghai – their Shanghai. The figure was unveiled with all the cosmopolitan ritual of settlement life, massed ranks of marines and consuls in attendance, and even though the new flag of the Chinese republic flew behind him on the day, and Chinese officials were there as well, it was a celebration of multinational foreign power, and Shanghai's central place within that. 'China and the world' were on equal footing, but at the cost of Chinese sovereignty.[74] And while Hart was uncovered moves were already afoot to bring to the city another monument, a rootless stone commemorating the first British envoy to China, Charles Cathcart. Hapless Colonel Cathcart had died at sea off Anjer Point in 1788, failing to get to China and so failing to stay out of the footnotes in histories of Sino-foreign relations to which he was then consigned. A wooden tablet was erected by his companions, later reworked in stone and built into a monument at Anjer on the orders of Stamford Raffles when the British controlled Java in 1811–16. So the Cathcart Monument had been part of the passage to China from the Indian Ocean throughout most of the nineteenth century, for it was easily visible there until in 1883 it was demolished by tidal waves caused by the eruption of Krakatoa.[75] The stone then languished in a shed until sought out in 1912 by a descendent of one of the envoy's party, the Shanghai Municipal Council's chief engineer. It was, he thought, really part of the fabric of the British world in China, and when the Legation and the Shanghai Consulate declined to house it (not wanting to turn their grounds into 'graveyards'), he had it shipped to Shanghai by Swire's, and fixed into the wall of Holy Trinity Cathedral in late 1914.[76] So Shanghai gathered to itself telling symbols of the foreign enterprise in China across its long history and far back into its prehistory. There was no ceremonial for Cathcart, and as the stone was fixed with concrete into the fabric of the city, hundreds and hundreds of foreign men made their way through nearby streets to the jetties, to sail to Europe to fight each other there. So the unveiling of Sir Robert Hart turned out to be the last of the cosmopolitan ceremonies, and national sagas and destinies came instead to the fore.

Spotting when the tide turns is always tricky. If you were J. O. P. Bland there never was advance resolute enough, all gains being frittered away by lotus-eating diplomats seduced by Peking's charms, happily conniving in their own lack of respect from the Chinese. Their 'apathy', Bland would complain, was the 'real burden of the white man' in China.[77] But the whining China coaster could not truly ignore the blasting violence of the 1890s which had carried so many foreign interests so much further into China, and so shattered Chinese certainties and Qing stability. The Boxer war had been a point zero for the Qing state, and it displayed nakedly as never before the realities and capacities of foreign violence – militarized, racist violence of foreign power given free rein at the high point of the new imperialism. No Hague Conventions applied to those deemed outside the sphere of civilization. It ushered in a new era of Qing reform and growth of foreign interests, the latter ever-seasoned with complaint, but profitable nonetheless in most places, and often cosily transnational despite the jingoist alarms of the imperialists. The revolution changed fundamentally the field of play in China. For even though it heralded years of disorder and the breakdown of central power, its great achievement lay in the fact that during the ultimate crisis China faced – the dissolution of empire – the land still held by the Qing in October 1911 was almost wholly passed on to the new republic. And thereafter a different era opened up. China would yet face dire emergency, would find its finances compromised, extreme pressure placed on its central and regional administrations, and in time would face full-scale invasion, but the seemingly routine piecemeal aggrandizement of the nineteenth century, the pulling together of the 'Asian heritage' of the European, was curtailed. No more could the empire-builders of Shanghai, Pearce and his gang, blithely march across their stone-marked frontier and annex a Chinese suburb. They did not stop planning and scheming such expansions, or memorializing their achievements, but mostly thereafter they were on the defensive. They were also divided.

After the summer of 1914 and the outbreak of the First World War, the European concert in China was broken, and the multinational nature of the foreign enterprise in China was sharply eroded. They kicked each other out of their clubs and off their boards of directors, though it was a difficult process that mostly went against the grain of their China coast practice. And they rightly worried what message this intra-imperial and intra-racial conflict sent to the Chinese. But Germany and Austria were knocked out of the great China game, and while Britain and France were distracted in Europe the Japanese did indeed pursue a game of their own, aiming to entrench their pre-eminence in Chinese affairs, and to do so at the expense of other foreign powers. Nonetheless, despite these changes and threats, the China coast settlements still lobbied for more and protected what they held with violent words, concessions to their critics overseas and in China, legal pleading and violent acts. But now the China game was also about-turned, and the scramble amongst the Europeans was to be overshadowed by Japanese militarism, and more importantly by a developing scramble for China from within, amongst Chinese republicans, Chinese militarists, Chinese imperialists (for there was even an attempted Manchu restoration in 1917), and more thereafter, all of them searching for, struggling and fighting for a steady, secure path to Chinese futures.

12

History

Whose history was this? Not, if the librarians at the Foreign Office in London had anything to do with it in 1935, Tingfu Tsiang's. 'It would be dangerous,' they concluded briskly in response to a request to discuss access to historic records, 'to have a Chinese grubbing about in our 1886–1895 archives.'[1] Tsiang, the leading young historian of his generation, a Columbia University PhD who would shortly join the Chinese government, was on sabbatical from his post as head of the history department at Peking's Tsinghua University. He had been working through documents in the Public Record Office in search of material on China's political history in the later nineteenth century. Having found the material that was open to researchers 'unexpectedly rich', he now requested to be able to read documents after the 1885 cut-off date for access to Foreign Office archives. Such permission was certainly given to some, but this was different; Tsiang was different. Presumably, it was noted, he will 'return to China with the material obtained and we shall have no check on the use he makes of it'. And as 'of course we cannot separate the harmless element in the correspondence', then what mischief might 'a Chinese' make with what he might find. There might be devil in amongst the diplomatic detail. Sensitivities about the obscure contents of the diplomatic archive were rooted in ongoing debates and disagreements about the publication of records of European pre-First World War politics, not least Anglo-Russian rivalries, but in these discussions the India Office had made a point accepted widely within the British establishment: 'In the east these problems go on forever; eastern memories are long, and eastern politicians read past policy into the present and the future.'[2] They meant Afghanistan and Persia, but China was 'the east' too: such fear held good there. And the British had by 1932 faced years of sustained nationalist assault on their position in China, and were in fact in steady retreat as a result, and Britain's Chinese history was on public trial too in the discourses of this triumphant nationalism. In London they thought the potential of the archive to further fuel nationalistic hostility to the British record and presence was real enough to prompt them swiftly to make no exception for Dr Tsiang.

Those documents had piled up in China itself. They rotted in Customs stations, company warehouses, municipal offices and consulate archives. They were tunnelled through by termites, and gathered thick layers of adhesive dust. Some were already obscurely lost; fire had culled others – at the Shanghai Consulate General in December 1870 most notably, a catastrophe that wiped out most of its holdings up to that point.[3] But there in China, on the whole, they were; stashed away in the overcrowded and by then generally antiquated consular buildings of the British establishment. Foreign Office archives practice was in theory quite clear. All records of missions, embassies and legations were to be kept in their entirety and in perpetuity, but routine consular archives, correspondence files in the main, were to be destroyed after twenty years. This was easily laid down by circular, but in the main staff in the offices across China were too harassed by the everyday work of the consulates, not least the mediation of domestic disputes which took up a disproportionate amount of their time, to get around to destroying anything.[4] They were also busy filing their required periodic reports to the Legation and dealing (depending on whether they were located – in the orbit of control of the National Government established by the Guomindang at Nanjing in 1928, or in the many parts of China now under autonomous warlord rule) with all the fallout from fielding nationalistic pressure against foreign privilege or the wayward happenstance of disorder and conflict. Dealing with the archives was a low priority. The Legation records were shipped back to Britain – in 1927 records up to 1890 were sent back – but when Tingfu Tsiang was busy in London at the Public Record Office in quiet Chancery Lane, the consular archives were all lodged more or less securely in China.

For a new generation of historians such records were an absolute priority. Tsiang was at the forefront in China of a new move to re-examine Chinese records. At least in Britain there was a Public Record Office, and in principle archives were transferred to public access, but nothing of that like existed in China. In many cases historians were reliant on the foreign-language record, on translations made by foreign officials in the nineteenth century, on all those documents presented in the *Chinese Repository* or the *North China Herald*. Yuan Shikai's government had established a historical bureau to prepare a history of the Qing dynasty, but the working records of the Manchu state had in some cases passed through various hands – including those of a paper-making firm, having been purchased by weight for re-cycling – before being secured. Many had been lost. By 1935 things were changing. An important Qing compilation of documents presented to the Xianfeng emperor in 1856, having survived in private hands, had been published in 1930 as *Chouban yiwu shimo* (A complete account of the management of barbarian affairs), and other series had commenced. Tsiang published various articles in English showing how readings of these and related documents undermined existing under-standings of Sino-foreign interaction in the 1830s and 1840s, which had hitherto been based very extensively on foreign diplomatic records published at the time or shortly afterwards, usually to justify turns of policy and recourse to conflict.[5] These were the British 'blue books', or French '*livres jaunes*'; they were useful, but they never told the whole story by any means, and what they lacked, notably, were discussion minutes – the stuff of debates and disagreements, uncensored talk. While Yuan's Qing history bureau had prepared an encyclopaedic account of the dynasty wholly in a traditional vein – for it was the task of each new dynasty to prepare the history of its predecessor – Tsiang and other thoroughly modern foreign-trained historians expected to write that history using the types of documents they had worked with at universities overseas, and that was how they trained their own students at colleges in China. So while the new compilations of Qing documents were, and are, vital (and a vast improvement on the forgeries that had caught out J. O. P. Bland), they were also as selective and partial as the blue books. More was needed, and there it was, in the archives in London, in unpublished letters and memoranda, minutes and maps, plaints and denunciations. Here was much blunt talk and detailed record; here was the fuller story of the scramble for China.

Another historian had petitioned the Foreign Office about its China records in 1932. John Fairbank, a Rhodes Scholar from Harvard studying at the University of Oxford had also been working through the Legation and Foreign Office records in London. His own programme was now taking him to China, to study Chinese, and to seek for materials there, if there were any. Fairbank arrived at the Foreign Office on 8 January 1932 and left a memo explaining his project, which was to be an exploration of the establishment of the Customs Inspectorate system in the 1850s. He asked the library staff if they had any idea if the old consulates had any records, for 'the mere knowledge of their existence or non-existence would be of considerable help'.[6] Harvard and Oxford opened doors for the young American that were kept firmly closed to Tsiang, but he was also researching material before the 1885 cut-off. In 1934–5, as Tsiang worked away in London, Fairbank made a grand tour of the old British China consulates – Shanghai, Ningbo, Fuzhou, Xiamen and Canton, as well as Hong Kong – looking at their records, the tedium of his work softened by the comforts and social pleasures of the treaty port world – tennis at the clubs, convivial evenings on the verandas. Afterwards he pestered the Foreign Office and Legation to get these files out of their stores and safely to London. It was not simply that they were long, long redundant as active consular files, but that there was a whole new level of detail about the everyday world of the early treaty ports revealed in them, material that only partially made its way to the Legation in Peking, and that was mostly missing from anything that could be found in the new Qing records. The treaty ports, Tsiang had pointed out, were 'too trivial' a subject for report to the emperor. Here Fairbank found 'the most detailed picture of the actual day-to-day conduct of Sino-foreign relations, the issues involved and the tactics used on either side'. The 'real story of Anglo-Chinese relations,' mused Victor Kiernan, a young British Marxist historian, is 'perhaps contained in these local chronicles'.[7] Diplomats and politicians debated the publication of this or that official minute, but Fairbank went where Kiernan mused, believing that understandings of the China story lay in uncovering these 'day-to-day' issues from the opaque frontier of Sino-foreign interaction. Back sailed the files as a result of this pleading. Back too in 1936 sailed 700 crates containing archives of Jardine, Matheson & Co. rescued, as a result of Fairbank's interest and prodding, from the white ants infesting the old tea chests that housed them in the company's Hong Kong warehouse. Found with them were the archives of Augustine Heard & Co., long defunct, which were shipped to the US.[8] Files of the post-1860 consulates, the officials in London also concluded, would also merit the same treatment, for historians were already nosing around them on site, digging out materials on Thomas Taylor Meadows or the early history of treaty port Shanghai.[9] Fairbank produced in time a still important history of the early treaty ports and the origin of the Customs compromise in 1854, and became one of the most prominent figures in the institutional growth of Chinese studies in the United States and in the public understanding of China there and more widely. (For his part Tingfu Tsiang became Chinese ambassador to the Soviet Union, to the United Nations in 1945 and later to the United States.)

Fairbank's mentor as he began this work was another figure from that old world. Hosea Ballou Morse had resigned from the Customs in 1909, after thirty-five years of service. Recruited from Harvard University, he had risen steadily through the ranks, and like many of its able employees had been loaned out to other Chinese enterprises, in his case the China Merchants' Steam Navigation Company; had risen to commissioner, being based at Danshui in Taiwan during the Sino-Japanese war, where George Mackay recalled decades later having seen him conveyed about in his sedan chair; and had served as statistical secretary at Shanghai. He had lived and worked through decades of change and conflict, and had felt its stresses – his wife too, who never quite recovered from the shock of the Mixed Court riots in Shanghai in 1905. The Chinese, she assured Fairbank, will poison you.[10] Even before leaving, Morse had been preparing accounts of China's foreign trade and history, using his access to the Customs archives and his connections with Hart and other senior officials to collect materials for a three-volume history of *The International Relations of the Chinese Empire* published between 1910 and 1920, that strongly shaped understandings of the course of events down to 1911. Before his death in 1911, Robert Hart had offered his private journals which, much to his professed chagrin, a junior employee had rescued from the burning Inspectorate in 1900. The old man's career spanned most of the course of Morse's volumes, for he only retired in 1908. As there was too much in the journals of Hart the introspective man, and father of Eurasian children, the family blocked their use by Morse, but nonetheless he located much new material to add to what he had from the archives. Later he worked steadily through the India Office archives, extracting the detail of the Canton history of the old Company and the China trade up to 1834. Add to this the similar work on French records of Henri Cordier, who also produced a massive bibliography of western-language works on China or printed in China, and the work of understanding was for the first time laid on the firmest, albeit entirely foreign-sourced, foundations. As Fairbank later wrote, it supplanted the amateur histories of Alexander Michie and others, and shaped the understanding of events from the 1830s onwards as documented history, not as justification or denunciation, myth or romance.[11]

This was important, not least as it was not simply history. For a start, the world outlined in these old records still thrived, though the political upheavals of the 1920s had reshaped it and put it on sufferance. The road from 1913 had been hard for China. Sun Yat-sen's party had reconstituted itself in Canton after the debacle that year, establishing a rival and at times singularly threadbare National Government recognized by none. Slowly, however, it built up a strong enough party machine and military force to launch, a year after Sun's death in 1925, a 'Northern Expedition' to unite China under its rule. After Yuan Shikai had died in 1916, a succession of military men had dominated the internationally recognized government in Peking, but their hands were tied by the foreign powers and their control of the Customs revenues as a result of the Reorganization Loan. Provincial militarists ran local and regional fiefdoms. The Northern Expedition knocked some out, and others pledged allegiance to the Guomindang's new government at Nanjing by 1928.[12] This 'National Revolution' changed the treaty port landscape too. Some of the concessions had already gone: Russian, German and Austrian holdings had been surrendered after the First World War and in the early 1920s. In early 1927 the British concessions at Hankou and Jiujiang had been seized, and were now Special Administrative Districts, 'SADs' the wags dubbed them. The new government's talented diplomats, heavy with PhDs and legal training, fluent in English, were more than a match for their undereducated foreign counterparts.[13] They ran circles around them, picked off smaller powers such as Belgium, which had staked a claim in Tianjin in 1902; shaved off the now insignificant possessions of the greater ones; and readied themselves to secure the most desired prizes, the return to full Chinese sovereignty of Shanghai and Tianjin, and the abolition of extra-territoriality. The British surrendered moribund Zhenjiang and affable but useless Jiujiang, and signed away little Weihaiwei and Kuling, but were not yet quite ready to lose their principal ports, the heart of their China prestige, the jewels in the east Asian crown. Even so, while the China coast world was in steady retreat, it was hardly dead and it had a century's history behind it, longer by far than many European states and most colonial territories. Fairbank noted how the treaty port cemeteries housed a good few of the men and women he met in the documents, and that at Jardines' grand headquarters in Hong Kong he dined off plate 'inherited from the East India Company's Canton factory back in the 1880s'. In the various ports were some very long-term foreign residents, and at others were descendants of early figures, with surnames that echoed loudly in memory's halls. In death, material and people there were multiple continuities in modern 1934 with the long century of the foreign presence in China since the early 1830s. For Fairbank, moreover, various characteristics of the treaty port life he experienced were entirely rooted in and familiar from the world he met in the early archives: its comfortable hospitality and generosity that so depended on its cheap servants; its interconnectedness; its nature as a single frontier zone; and the absolute reliance on Chinese partners of every sort in all its enterprises – commercial, educational, evangelical. So he found himself researching the connected roots of the world he moved through in 1934–5.

That world was more than ever concerned with its own history as well. History gave it credibility: it was always a tool of British and other foreign power in China. It was not simply that the record served to justify its defence of its own position – in particular to justify extraterritoriality and the continuation of settlement and concession, which in the eyes of its propagandists and of many residents it did – but that it gave depth to the foreign communities in China, and through that depth a greater legitimacy. If they had a longer history than Southern Rhodesia, which was granted responsible government in 1922, then ought that not be factored into debates about retrocession and reform, especially if it was not simply a superficial tale but one with layers of cultural richness and variety. If more recent settlers such as the white Rhodesians had rights, why did not they, with their longer history? This they believed, and these 'rights' some asserted, so uncovering that history was vital. In 1906 the Municipal Council at Shanghai commissioned a history of its own development. George Lanning spent fifteen years on the task before dying, and only reached 1854; for in his view, and in his title, this was a *History of Shanghai*. The International Settlement was the city: it had supplanted the thriving port which had sucked the British up the coast, and its history encompassed the long history of the city – more, even: 'Whence came the Chinese people?' were its opening words. The project was jinxed, for the editor of volume two died before it appeared and it was then pulped – deemed too old-fashioned, tedious and tendentious by the councillors of 1927, who lacked any interest in the origins of the Chinese people. The books made liberal use of Lanning's notes on his researches in the Council archives, and in the archives of the Legation at Peking. Foreign residents turned historians grubbed around the local archives, reminding officials, transient holders of their posts, precisely what some of the crumbling monuments were that littered the grounds of their establishments.[14] Most were well known, and were tended by works departments or visiting navy ships, their brass inscriptions polished all the better to allow them to speak their statements of Chinese 'perfidy' and violence to the streets of Tianjin and Shanghai, and in cemeteries in Peking and much further afield. Settlement police were told off to keep the indigent from kipping by them, or worse. Shanghai's foreign bookstores became well stocked with English-language histories of 'Shanghai'. Lanning's volume was supplanted by a pithier *Short History of Shanghai*, and was beaten to the shelves by Montalto de Jesus's *Historic Shanghai*. The Council's archivist, Anatol Kotenov, an emigré White Russian, worked through the records producing further surveys. Settlement Tianjin got a lengthy history as well; slimmer Shamian a slimmer account.[15] It did not really matter that Lanning's book sold so poorly, for all that history was learned anyway – informally, instinctively – from any foreign reading of the past: at least the crucial elements – confinement at Factory Canton, the fate of the gunner of the *Lady Hughes*, the years of dishonourable

Company subservience, the insufferable superiorities of Chinese officials, their whipping up of xenophobic hostility. This all foreign residents knew, for to them it explained the world they lived in the 1920s and 1930s and why it should be preserved.

It was important to tease out an empire romance in these tales, to stress, as the diplomats and others had also sometimes stressed, that this was not simply a tale of predatory commerce. George Lanning lamented that he could not tell a tale of great families in Shanghai: there was nothing of the 'romantic, the heroic, the idyllic or the dramatic'. It was a utilitarian 'Klondyke' rather than a great settler centre, a place of 'temporary abode'. 'Those who make the legends hereafter will have . . . to "pretend very much"', for the story was one of 'TRADE', and where was the glory in that?[16] Well, this is our peculiarity he concluded, and this is what I record; but others pretended, and this lament riled his sponsors on the Council, who already too often in their eyes encountered the snobbery of pukka empire – snotty naval officers who derided them as suburban shop-men; sniffy visitors who thought their world and achievements simply vulgar, the Bund fatuous and pompous. They and their predecessors had long tried to hitch themselves to the path of imperial 'glory': their Canton discomfort they had claimed as the matter of imperial dishonour; Gordon's forays against the Taiping gave them a link to empire's martial celebrity; their achievements on the Huangpu far excelled those of Singapore or Hong Kong. They did this partly as insurance, to make themselves useful to the wider empire, and so deserving of attention and support. They did it also because they could, or because they deliberately misunderstood or misrepresented their own place in those schemes of things. Yet they were men of commerce and outside what was formally recognized as British empire, and their enterprise was multinational and often makeshift. They had no imperial project. These peculiarities shaped the course of developments in China even after the high imperialism of the 1890s changed things utterly. So Lanning's detail was important, if his own undiplomatic snobbery misplaced. Victor Kiernan thought that 'accidents helped stave off conquest'; that China was only saved imperialism's full grasp because two of the China wars coincided with unprecedented imperial emergencies elsewhere: the Indian Mutiny and the Boer War; but the tale told by the 'local chronicles' suggests how important instead the internal dynamics and details of the China coast world themselves were in shaping the evolution and course of Sino-foreign relations.[17] China's fates were not decided overseas, but at home.

Not all history-making was pointedly political or diplomatically functional. Some was simply nostalgic, or typical diversionary activity, for a spot of local history, fossicking around in old cemeteries and registers, never did any harm, and kept many a man occupied when time hung heavy and days seemed long. Guidebooks for Shanghai, Peking and Tianjin all delivered detail of the history of the foreign presence and its sites of note. The rail system, coastal passenger lines and new roads from Shanghai to Hangzhou all made travel easier, tourism possible. A visitor might make a point of idling around the East India Company cemetery at Canton, might nose around this church or that chapel. Fairbank chatted with old residents, met Lester Little, then Canton commissioner of Customs, a man active in the difficult present, but always interested too in conversing about the past. It was also curiosity: who was this whose name was inscribed here? Why, for example, was a memorial stone (in fairly bad Latin) fixed into the Holy Trinity Cathedral wall for a man who died at sea in the Sunda Straits between Java and Sumatra in 1788? Who was this Charles Cathcart? Memories could be short.[18] The past could be unavoidable: the bore at the club bar droning on about the good old China, when privilege was not threatened, when the Chinese knew their place and men were hardier and life and politics simpler. Steadily increasing numbers of families had long connections now – two or three generations that had lived and worked in China – and had much to recount (and the Settlement administrations that employed many of them had grown complex and large, so that the bureaucrats' defence of their own livelihoods was a potent political factor). So not all self-consciousness about history was political. Curiosity had its place. There were stories enough, and no shortage of eccentrics. The human cost of the scramble for China had been great. And so we might pause at their sense of themselves as pioneers, as if they were 'settling' Kenya or Rhodesia: we have seen much in this tale of the ordinary workings of the globalizing world, and its impact through the new opportunities it provided ordinary men and women to make their way through it as best they could. The China tale is more than Harry Parkes and Robert Hart; it encompasses the intestate dead, those scraping by, James Dow, those trying. It had its share of braggart bullies, too, but it is mainly a tale – in the sheer weight of human numbers – of migration and enterprise in the frantically unfolding nineteenth-century world of speeding steamships and chattering telegraphs, and yes, too, of gunboats, Enfield rifles, 'wonderful' Armstrong and deadlier yet Maxim guns.

These were not the only stories, and other sides to them needed telling. Chinese scholars were anxious to set things right in the local contexts too, not just through nosing around Chancery Lane, although other treasures could be found in Britain. One scholar spent time transcribing the previously unknown Chinese documents relating to the *Lord Amherst* voyage brought back by Hugh Hamilton Lindsay from the coast, or collected at Canton by the East India Company, publishing them in Shanghai in 1931.[19] Other students collated new materials from the open Foreign Office archives for doctoral studies on this or that phase of the history of Sino-British relations; on Margary and others.[20] At Shanghai or Tianjin Chinese scholars did not have Lanning's privileged access to the archives, but like the students overseas, they worked to counter this Settlement and foreign-focused history with their own compilations of materials in a quiet war of words and detail. They needed fact to help them counter the dead weight of alleged precedent with which Settlement authorities justified their powers; powers which had so outgrown the original land regulations, let alone the intentions of those who had marked out the English Ground at Shanghai, and Settlements at other ports. They used old and new forms: those compiling a new gazetteer of Shanghai also published dozens of short historical essays in a Shanghai newspaper.[21] Their scholarship vied with that of the popular histories, sagas and romances of the British in China or the treaty ports, which delivered a coherent and justificatory narrative of Chinese exclusion and cruelty; of the reasonable desires of free trade thwarted; of the regretful recourse to just war; of British great men such as Parkes and Gordon; and of Chinese treachery. These writers sang of the marvels created from mud-flats by the Huangpu or the Beihe, of 'barren' Hong Kong island transformed, Asian ports built by the men from the West; and some like Lanning were frankly embarrassed by the paramountcy of trade, so told tales more rooted in the growth of empires, of international right and Chinese wrong. More scholarly works could not ignore the intemperance and violence they found in blue book and archive. Still, Oxford scholar W. C. Costin's account of the decades up to 1860, *Great Britain and China*, declared flatly that the world had shrunk, that 'no wall could shelter' the Chinese from the 'restless activity' of the European, who was likely as not a short-sighted money-grubber, but was part of a dynamic surge that 'was not in any proper sense "imperialistic"', and that was not 'representative of the highest of Western society'. And anyway, Chinese exclusion was the problem.[22] Was denying the archives to Tingfu Tsiang really going to make a difference? Certainly, without realizing it, they had him right as a scholar who would publish what he found in compilations of archival documents, but why could young Harvard be trusted and not Tsinghua University? It could hardly really make any difference, for the history of Sino-foreign relations in the Foreign Office archive and that history which lived in Chinese politics were diverging, and nothing the custodians of a respectable British past could do could rein back in the new understanding of the British and wider foreign record that was spreading.

The recasting of Chinese history by scholars like Tsiang was related to a wider political concern of Chinese nationalism. Rethinking the history of the Qing was a feature of late-imperial nationalism and revolutionary thought, as Chinese writers 'rediscovered' and published angry denunciations of the bloody years of the Manchu conquest of seventeenth-century China. Men like Sun Yat-sen had explained to the British, in their own language, and in terms calculated to secure a hearing (or so he thought), that a Chinese nationalism was entirely in accord with foreign interests. Han Chinese, unlike the 'decadent' Manchus, were on the side of history. Practical foreign support had been crucial to Sun's analysis of how China's problems might be solved: foreign support had saved the Qing from the Taiping disorder; now it should save China from warlord disorder. But the cynicism with which the foreign powers acquiesced in Yuan Shikai's destruction of the democratic republic in 1912–13 alienated the nationalists. The treachery of the 1919 Versailles Treaty, which handed to Japan the German possessions in China, a country which had joined the Allied side in 1917, convulsed Chinese society and politics.[23] Out of the nationalistic May Fourth Movement which resulted came many new social and political developments, not least a turn to Marxism amongst some; but a disenchantment with the Western world and its professed ideals was a profound, overriding consequence of the maltreatment of China's claims at the peace conference. Obtuse foreign diplomats further inflamed nationalists by their actions, for they felt that the ordered world of the treaty ports was threatened by the 'adventuring' of Sun Yat-sen and his Guomindang, and pledged their support to the militarist status quo and 'order'. This was partly pragmatism, but many also felt ever more strongly in the years after the revolution that the Chinese were only amenable to force, and that 'warlords' and strong-men gave them what they wanted and deserved. In 1923, when Sun's revolutionary government at Canton attempted to claim its share of the revenues raised by the Customs at ports it controlled, which were in fact being transmitted to its enemies at Peking, it was rebuffed, and told that foreign force would be used to prevent any interference. 'Imperialism' very shortly thereafter took a prominent and lasting place in Sun's analyses of China's problems. His party adopted an anti-imperialist agenda as a key part of its platform, and found new friends in Soviet advisors. The phrase 'unequal treaties' as a description of the body of Sino-foreign agreements from Nanjing onwards became common political parlance after 1923. It was unknown before then, all-pervasive afterwards.[24] Subsequent reflex actions of the foreign powers in China, the run-of-the-mill responses to 'incident' and 'dispute', the now long-habitual lashing out when a foreign national was inconvenienced by Chinese disorder or simply criminal activity, was reconceived and became evidence of 'imperialist' aggression, became a central part of China's woes and the target of those who would build a nation. Bloody incidents sealed treaty port China's fate in Chinese and many foreign eyes in 1925–6: at Shanghai the International Settlement Police shot to kill in a mêlée on the Nanjing Road on 30 May 1925; two weeks later the Volunteers at Hankou machine-gunned a protesting crowd; days later scores of marchers in Canton were killed by British and French bullets; at Wanxian a year later British navy ships bombarded the city. None of this was premeditated, but all of it was now anachronistic; there was impunity no longer. The Chinese bodies that lay in Settlement streets after the Mixed Court riots in 1905 had not been avenged. They were shot without much account by Volunteers and police. By 1925 no such immunity remained, as a nation responded to a policeman's bullet, and international protest was hurled at the foreign establishment. Shaken by the impact of the wayward, narrow-mindedness of their China coast charges, British and other diplomats worked to countermand their autonomy, forcing them to adapt and reform, and to acknowledge the new realities of a nationalist China.[25]

'Imperialism' became more than the analysis of one struggling revolutionary grouping. It evolved rapidly into a central issue in China's politics in the 1920s. All factions came to vie with each other to denounce imperialism and imperialists: it was impossible for any political figure in China not to. Chinese children in mission schools denounced their teachers and went on strike. Seamen, servants and factory hands all took part in protests; Chinese police in Settlement employ deserted. Consumers smoked 'patriotic' Chinese-made cigarettes and wore Chinese-made fabrics, their purchase of 'national products' a political statement, and a huge commercial fillip for Chinese producers and retailers.[26] Sustained popular anger at the incidents of 1925–6 was galvanized into nationwide mass movements. The power of anti-imperialism to mobilize hundreds and hundreds of thousands of people from all sectors of Chinese society became all too evident. The American boycott movement of 1905 was but a small taste of the boycotts and protest movements of the 1920s. The British bore the brunt – on the Yangzi, at Hong Kong – but the Japanese too found challenges, and all powers who retained privileges in China felt the heat. Chinese political legitimacy became more strongly rooted around the issue as Japan made plainer those intentions dismissed by the wise men of the British Foreign Office in 1913, then bucked the trend of withdrawal by strengthening its hold over Manchurian politics in the later 1920s. In September 1931 the Japanese Kwantung Army deliberately provoked conflict with Chinese troops as a pretext for launching what became a full-scale invasion of Manchuria, the province in which the Army was stationed. This plot led to the establishment of a puppet 'Manchukuo' state, overseen nominally by the last of the Manchu emperors, Puyi. Throughout the 1930s Sino-Japanese tension developed yet further, the failure of other powers to rein in the aggressors being denounced as evidence of their continued imperialist inclinations, until in July 1937 a full-scale Japanese invasion of China commenced. Such was the power of the issue that even Chinese collaborators with the invader pursued an anti-imperialist propaganda agenda. Japan, they claimed, would not only liberate China from the threat of Communism, but also from the stranglehold of Anglo-American imperialism and the unequal treaties. The Japanese surrendered the treaty ports in their occupation to the collaborators in 1943 to back up this claim. But in most eyes, of course, the invasion was located firmly in a prehistory of British, Russian and Japanese aggression in China since 1839, and was no solution to it. Defeating imperialism became China's most urgent political task, and finally a matter of absolute national survival. The fears of national extinction seemed on the verge of realization: Manchuria wrenched away; the great coastal cities wrecked and occupied; the national capital pillaged, its inhabitants butchered, raped and brutalized by Japanese soldiers. In the longer term how far did this really differ from 1842, from 1857–60, 1884–5, 1894–5 or 1900? Had not foreign soldiers been wreaking such cruel revenge on the Chinese people for a hundred years now, if not in Nanjing, then in Peking in 1900 or in the north China plain villages? Aerial bombing was surely simply the old *Nemesis* advantage updated.

But history got more important for those wishing to pillory the foreign record, or wishing to distance the British tale from the Japanese assault. Nationalism was winning anyway, whatever the short-term gains of Japanese militarism, and it was already rewriting history. When Fairbank visited Shanghai in 1934 he tried to access the archives of the Maritime Customs. The original records, save for those personal journals of the IG, had perished in the Peking siege in 1900, but the Inspectorate had called in from Customs stations all the nineteenth-century records and lodged them in a new Customs archive in Shanghai. Professional jealousies prevented Fairbank from getting far, for the archivist, Stanley Wright, was preparing his own study of Hart and the Customs, and moreover objected to a young American nosing around the material. Whose history was it? Not an American academic's, Wright thought; it was the Customs' own history.[27] The Customs Service was alive to the present perils of the past. Robert Hart's nephew,

Sir Frederick Maze, had assumed the post of Inspector-General in 1929, and expended much energy on sponsoring various historical projects which were published by the Customs: a history of Sino-foreign trade, of the lights' service, of Hart and the Customs itself. As Maze noted later, the aim was 'to place the deeds of the Administration . . . on the map for future historians', for 'otherwise the history of the great work performed by the Service for China and the world may not be kept alive by the chief beneficiary'. China was that 'chief beneficiary' and Maze feared that the triumph of nationalism would see the work of the foreign Customs expunged from any historic record, for that triumph would naturally place its own development and struggles at the heart of the story of the Customs.[28] And if there was anything worse than the denunciation of history, then surely it was going to be silence, a thankless silence for all that had been done 'for China' by men like his uncle and himself. And to make sure that the record was securely lodged overseas, copies of these publications were dispatched to foreign libraries and universities. Maze might lose access to the archive in time, but he wanted time to have access to the key story that he felt that archive ought to tell.

At the same time that their history was being incorporated into the very heart of Chinese political life, residents in the treaty ports like Maze felt themselves and their record not only traduced, but on the verge of being expunged, except when there were Chinese victims. The battle over history was also replayed as a battle over concrete symbolism. Having always set great store by their inscriptions on stone on Chinese soil – their monuments, memorials, cemeteries and statues – they could hardly have been surprised that Chinese nationalism affected the same interest, and sought to purge such symbols of their presence. The foreigners set the precedent more firmly, for Allied nationals vandalized German monuments in Tianjin and Shanghai in November 1918 in the heat of victory. And monuments to the foreign presence were easy targets each time a concession was surrendered. A quiet process began whereby cemeteries and such communal institutions as could be involved were often discreetly transferred to consular ownership in the expectation that as diplomatic property they would survive any depredations after eventual handover. The British cemeteries at Weihaiwei were leased back along with the naval base when the territory was returned in 1930s. The dead were to be protected, or at least rented back from nationalism. There was cause, for there was none of the fine distinction that Maze wanted made, between those who had performed great work 'for China', and those who might with more difficulty be defended. After the Japanese occupied the International Settlement at Shanghai at the onset of the Pacific War in December 1941, they lodged a request that symbols of British imperialism in the city's public spaces be removed, that the statues of Harry Parkes and Robert Hart, as well as monuments to the Ever Victorious Army and Margary be taken down. Neutral foreigners on the Council argued that memorials to those who had served China should stay, that Hart and the Ever Victorious Army were not symbolic of the British venture in China; but this was too fine a point for most. They were all British; they were all representative of a British lust for conquest and power; and so all were taken down in orderly fashion, the work costed and receipts issued. This was not simply the impatience of Japanese militarism with fine distinction, but the likely wider fate of the concrete statements of the China coast world as nationalism fully triumphed.

After 1945 the monuments were not rebuilt. More recent Japanese ones were blown up. Anti-imperialism was central in the politics of the Guomindang, and its enemy and successor after 1949, the Chinese Communist Party. Extraterritoriality, the concessions and settlements, the British claim on leadership of the Customs, had all been abolished by wartime 'friendship' treaties, and most foreign privilege had been removed by 1945 and the defeat of Japan.[29] The collapse of the European colonies in the face of the Japanese attack had dismayed and enraged the Guomindang. Chiang Kai-shek's regime had already been unimpressed by the appeasement policies that the British in particular had followed in the face of Japanese demands. The British had cut off supplies to unoccupied China along the Burma Road for three months in 1940, failed to counter Japanese campaigns against their Tianjin concession, or intense and violent Japanese pressure in Shanghai. They had attempted to negotiate agreements about Customs' revenues without consulting the Chinese government.[30] The fall of Hong Kong and Singapore in the winter of 1941–2 destroyed British Great Power credibility in Chinese eyes (and many others). The treaty ports remaining after the first years of the Nationalist revolution had actually been given an additional lease of life after the Japanese invasion of Manchuria, as Chiang sought allies to help China cope with the cold new threat in the northeast. Keeping foreign interests in China bound the foreign powers much more tightly into events. There had been little to be gained by alienating the British or French while Japan threatened, but there was now nothing to be lost in terminating their anachronistic rights after Pearl Harbor. And China was a United States theatre of operations during the 1941–5 Pacific War, so other foreign voices – and especially the old Shanghai and China coast ones – found it difficult to make themselves heard. Meanwhile, thousands of missionaries and treaty port foreign residents were moved into internment camps by the Japanese in early 1943, which were dreary, but more comfortable than most others in southeast Asia.[31] Their firms were placed under Japanese administration, and their homes requisitioned. The cosmopolitan world prattled on outside the camp fences without them: neutral or Axis nationals, for example, still living the internationalized Shanghai life. Foreign councillors still ran the International Settlement. Russians still policed the city, and Filipino bands played on in its night clubs. The number of Japanese residents increased markedly, as people fled the bombing of Japan, or leftists sought out the relatively freer political climate in Shanghai.[32] So the treaty port cities functioned as they always had; as safer havens than most others, even though their time was almost up.

Victory further emboldened the nationalism of the state, which had no reason to pussyfoot with British and French interests, for the United States now dominated and, initially at least, had no patience with European pretensions to empire. Foreign life in China was not uncomfortable after 1945, but it was a changed world that wartime internees and refugees alike returned to. Most Settlement foreign employees lost their jobs as the extraterritorial administrations were wound up, so their communities were sharply cut down in size. Recovering assets seized by the Japanese was a problem for foreign and Chinese businessmen alike, but the foreign presence was much more tightly corralled and controlled than it had been before, and its pretensions to influence and autonomy had to be abandoned. 'The Chinese,' remarked one inter-war British ambassador after a brief visit back in 1946, 'enjoy flaunting their newly won power over foreign nationals.' Adjusting to the changed power relationship was difficult for those who had blustered and bullied their way through the 1920s.[33] But at the same time the Guomindang state was defending itself against Communist insurrection, its economy was shattered, and its popular support ebbing away. The Communist government ran down the rump foreign presence after its victory in 1949, and most firms and institutions were closed. The *North China Daily News* lasted until 1951. The clubs were surrendered. And yes, their cemeteries were in time bulldozed, their remaining monuments removed, even inscriptions on buildings and tombstones erased. Archives were rifled through by scholars search- ing for detail to support the truth already adopted as policy, and also by those seeking details of the collaboration of those still living with the agents and agencies of the 'enemy' (for 'enemy archive' was routinely stamped on the cover of many such files). But even so, as the Communist government reshaped Chinese society in the 1950s, imperialism, while a fundamental category by which modern Chinese history was under- stood by the new regime – and by which history was itself understood and was periodized, for 'modern history' began with the Opium War – it was not the driver. Class struggle was the central feature of China's bitter 1950s and 1960s. Imperialism had been vanquished. There was little sign of it left in China at all. Hong Kong remained in British hands, functionally useful to the new regime as a gateway to inter- national markets, its future return barely mentioned for decades. But history as class struggle defined modern China.

So why then did the nine-year-old son of a Chinese friend surprise me and embarrass his father in 1997 by launching into an impassioned attack on the British record in China in the quiet of Tiantan Park in Peking? Why do young Chinese today routinely lecture me on British crimes in China when I tell them what I study? Why in the ruins of the old Yuanmingyuan did I come across in 2007 a corps of early teenage schoolchildren, standing to ranked attention as one of their number recounted its destruction by the Anglo-French expedition in 1860? It certainly is not the case that 'eastern memories' are long. Such memory is the product of hard state work. The Chinese govern- ment in response to the Tiananmen events of 1989 instituted a 'Patriotic Education Campaign' aimed at instilling in young Chinese as they traverse the educational system, from pre-school to university, a strong pride in being Chinese, contextualizing that in a sustained critique and description of what are routinely described as Western and Japanese imperialism's crimes in China. Textbooks were rewritten, museums and memorials revamped or constructed – sites for pilgrimage that highlighted the inequities of imperialist actions and China's century of 'national humiliation' at foreign hands.[34] What was once routinely made invisible as one part of the nationalist project, is now made hyper-visible by its successor. A rash of publications appeared in the early 1990s: dictionaries, atlases, surveys of national humiliation, a clutch of accounts of the concessions and settlements. Chinese memory has been constructed afresh this way. Routinely the ruins of the Yuanmingyuan figure in the illustrations, as do foreign police and soldiers on Chinese streets; a photograph of the regulations at the Public Gardens in Shanghai; and victims of Japanese soldiery. The count-down to the handover of Hong Kong in 1997 was accompanied by a massive public campaign: clocks counted down the days, hours and seconds. Pop singers yearned for reunion. A big-budget movie recreated the Opium War. Hong Kong, long all but ignored, was re-cast as an affront to Chinese dignity.[35] An emphasis on 'national humiliation' has a longer history nonetheless. The Chinese calendar of the 1920s and 1930s was peppered with 'humiliation days': commemorations aimed at keeping issues alive. May was a month full of history, full of potential to spark demonstration and confrontation. But as others have argued, the contemporary focus differs not in that it is embedded in school textbooks – for it was there and the British complained about it in the 1920s – but because it is divorced from China's current situation. It is history; it is a history that the young, indeed most Chinese, have never experienced. But they learn it and are taught too that the Chinese Communist Party alone delivered the nation from these crimes. The party's own legitimacy today is part-mortgaged to this strong nationalistic education programme. China is not unique in this, nor unique in its emphasis on victimhood and humiliation, but it is perhaps more evident in China than elsewhere, and it can be evident in everyday interaction between young Chinese and foreigners – that chat in the park, for example, with Little Wang. It is embedded in vocabularies, in ways of describing the past, and encoded in assumptions about that past and about any current events that seem to echo it today. Humiliation is always just around the Chinese corner.

Well, in that case might we not simply ignore it, or treat it with a circumspection that its political origins demand? Does it really matter? Yes, it all happened, of course. Hugh Hamilton Lindsay got his war; Harry Parkes got his, and his knighthood; Elgin ordered the Summer Palace burned. Foreign concessions and Settlements were laid out and grew; Hanbury made his rentier fortune; James Dow lost out. Lay and Hart ran the Customs Service; foreign ships sailed on China's rivers, bombarded this port or that; Sikhs policed parts of Hankou, Xiamen, Shanghai, Tianjin. German troops ravaged the 'Boxer' triangle. Light-houses were built, mission stations were opened. It all happened. And no, we cannot ignore it; not least, because we do not really know it. Chinese schoolchildren learn it, but we might reflect that European and American schoolchildren do not. The bafflement with which the Chinese charge is therefore received is telling. We do not really know this history, nor quite realize how it has been retold in China. It was not the only Chinese story, of course, and the national humiliation tale is as much a distortion as the prissy histories of Sino-British relations which concluded, conclusively, on their fair assessment of all the available evidence, that opium played no role in the conflict of 1839–42. But to understand contemporary China's view of the world, we need to understand both its vision of its modern history, and the source of this vision: this story of missionaries and gunboats, quick fortunes and bankruptcies, globalizing infrastructures and tiny cemeteries filled with foreign infants. That history needs adequate understanding if we are to find a happier medium between foreign bafflement, which is generally tempered by a vague notion that somewhere opium was an issue that prompted conflict – and that this was not a good thing even by the assumed different standards of the time – and the politicized presentation of history that now dominates in China itself.

The scramble for China took place. As a multinational enterprise it peaked in 1913 when the Yuan dictatorship sold its republican pre-tensions for the 'Reorganization Loan', and then the onward 'normal development' of Settlement 'influence' was halted in the confusion of Zhabei. It was not the only such scramble; it was not uniquely vicious or predatory. It was tempered more so than many other such pirate raids abroad by the resilience of Qing institutions and Chinese culture, by the flexible adaptability of Chinese merchants and officials, by foreign weaknesses and capacities, as well as through intra-imperial competition that kept each individual foreign power more in less in check. Sun Yat-sen argued however that China suffered much worse because it was not a colony, not the single province of one power. Its subjugation was multiplied because its oppressors were plural. But in fact however unacceptable politically or seemingly ethically, the fact remains that the foreign assault on China was until the 1930s tempered by the size of the crowd involved. Today's Chinese framework itself belittles the achievements and talents of the non-Communist past, of all those who worked adeptly within the reality they found, or who parried diplomatic thrust, thwarted foreign schemes and negotiated routes out of subordination for a changing China. The scramble was tempered too by the fact that China was after all not so very important for most of the time to the foreign powers involved as they were to it. Britain was more concerned with its formal empire, and with the European continent and North America. This is stark solace to the memory of those whose worlds were wrenched apart by marching troops and steamships. But the asymmetry between Britain's impact in China and China's importance to it is startling, even when the caution-ary note of the importance of opium revenues to the British Indian state is factored in. China did not really matter. It mattered to the China coast British and their allies of course, and they tried to make it matter more widely – and at times their frantic journalism and lobbying paid off, and their vision of China's needs and problems dominated. All that scribbling by J. O. P. Bland or his successors had an impact: 'Chinese characteristics' were widely 'known'; *What's Wrong With China* was debated; Bland's swansong *China: The Pity of It* was taken seriously. But for all their rhetoric and indignation, China was a minor issue in most ways most of the time. China did not really matter to France, either; or to Germany, Italy or Belgium. It mattered more to its neighbours – to Russia, and most of all to Japan. This further asymmetry, between how China questions are assumed to have mattered to those concerned, and how little they actually did matter, most of the time, has the potential to shock if not to offend. The Chinese themselves probably mattered more, and more visibly. They mattered as indentured labour in the Caribbean, Peru or South Africa. They mattered as opportunist migrants in California and Australia, and as the subjects of fierce political debate, pogrom, and exclusion acts. Their presence and their perceived threat galvanized their opponents to propose racially exclusive understandings of national identity, of being Australian, Canadian, American. Chinese were not, could never be, any of those. Canada was 'white', Australia was 'white', America's immigrant story excised and excluded the Chinese. This is a history not yet properly factored into histories of modern China, but diasporas generally get shorter shrift in the domestic histories of their homelands.

But even as this history of the scramble for China needs proper contextualization, its recurrent specific characteristics need recognizing: violence, honour, constraint, bafflement. All were as present in other contexts, of course, but the precise combination uniquely shaped the course of Sino-foreign interaction. The predisposition to violence never left the story, from first moment to last. If only the Mandarins are battered, or battered again, then they will get the message: a little violence or at least a little force, is never wasted and will do the trick. Things will change, entry will be effected, the people will acquiesce. Lindsay and Rees set the tone with their 'experiment'; Parkes gloried in it; many missionaries wanted it. Very few foreigners did not, at some point. Violence was a routine tool, a normal part of the repertoire. It was never the exception. And the ordinary violence of the everyday needs remembering: shoving, guiding the rickshaw with your stick, violence of speech, the violence of simple bad manners. It was also intimately tied to notions of honour, and the dignity of the individual and the dignity of the state were conflated explosively. We are not accustomed to taking honour seriously, but if we are to understand the course of the scramble we must. Lindsay set the tone as he parried with the officials in Shanghai, but it was even by 1832 a fixed issue for the British and their allies. Their position was degrading, and they were not a people who intended to suffer degradation. This was affected too by the rise of British power more widely and the new shapes this gave to Britishness and its manifestations, to individual comportment, and the necessary international theatre of the state. That is, the acts the agents of the state felt they must undertake to maintain national prestige in Chinese eyes, in other international eyes, or in their own eyes. Constraint is the theme against which the first two scraped and clashed. Foreigners felt imprisoned in the Canton factories, then confined in the five treaty ports. They felt constrained no matter how many open cities or rivers there were. The foreign traders only ever saw new restriction; never saw their horizons broadened but only new barriers to overcome. Partly this was because they were often swiftly out-manoeuvred by Chinese traders, and so had to move restlessly on to try to reshape the field of commercial play to try to regain advantage and initiative. Often, too, it was because the system, however intricately codified it got, always gave scope for evasion, gamesmanship and profitable innovation. This occurred not least because there was never simply one system, but as many systems as there were powers and nationalities (and categories of subjects). The frontier could never be tamed while that situation lasted. And there was no shortage of players, and shifting coalitions and partnerships among them. Power also far outstripped knowledge. Gods of ignorance and bafflement reigned over the China theatre. Understandings of China always lagged behind the pace of events and new capacities. There were never enough sinologists; lamentably few who could understand and communicate China, never even enough who could simply speak Chinese languages. The British in particular better ordered and used what they had, but it was skimpy still. The problem was entirely mutual, of course, certainly until the 1860s. But then the small programmes began which later accelerated Chinese thirst for and understanding of the West, of European and American thought, culture and technology, which eventually far outstripped the efforts of the foreign China experts. Robert Hart's publication programme was impressive, but pales into insignificance when compared to the scale of publication in Chinese of equivalent bodies of information. And the failure in 1919 at Versailles to treat China by the standards Woodrow Wilson set for the victors of the First World War, was then an even greater affront to Chinese honour and dignity. Variations on these themes lie at the heart of the discordant China coast symphony. Against all this was set the great empire of the Qing, with its own notions of dignity and the proper place of foreigners. Its own bafflement and incapacities have been the subject of recurrent critiques by modern Chinese historians. If the empire had opened the door when Lord Macartney visited; if Lin Zexu and others had had any conception of the capability of the British in 1839, then might not China have had a better journey through the nineteenth century?[36] But in fact nobody could predict or understand the ways in which European power and thinking evolved. Change was too rapid, and too destabilizing of existing orders – political orders, technological orders, economic orders. The Europeans themselves were working through these changes, and China and the wider world bore the brunt of their capricious global experiments with violence and power.

But at the same time, however, another school of Chinese historians has been quietly factoring this foreign story back into its own accounts of modern China in a different way. For decades the foreigners in Shanghai were villains, but now they are in a more neutral fashion reinserted into narratives of the development of such cities. It began with utilitarian projects that were designed to support economic development policies by outlining how treaty ports contributed to China's economic trajectory after the 1840s, and also what perils lay within them; what lessons might be learned from that past. They were intended to serve debate about the various 'special economic zones' started after 1980, and often established in former treaty ports. But scholarly curiosity went steadily beyond that remit, and the history of Shanghai, Tianjin or Hankou is incomplete if the foreign is factored out or simply pilloried. It helps also that China's re-emergence onto the global stage has encouraged a search for cosmopolitan precedents to underpin its new cosmopolitan present, or at least its cosmopolitan ambitions. Where it once boasted at anniversaries of 'liberation', how it had reclaimed such and such a city from imperialism, and had started afresh a 'New China', a 'New Shanghai', we now find the pre-1949 histories of institutions and companies reclaimed. The Shanghai Symphony Orchestra celebrated its 120th anniversary in 1999; Tsingtao Beer celebrated its centenary in 2003; Robert Hart's lighthouses appeared on Chinese stamps. Look, say such histories, we have always been cosmopolitan, we have always been modern. There is a contradiction here, for the sketching out of how the foreign was woven into the tapestry of modern China's growth in this way sits awkwardly with the shrill emphasis on humiliation and outrage. And the language of cosmopolitanism must remind us of the language of celebration in 1893, or 1891. We know that 'cosmopolitan' was no neutral term then, but a substitute for a description of the real event, a commemoration of Settler power on Chinese soil. And there is always a danger that the real inequities, sharp practices, and blunt actions of the treaty century might be downplayed in this lust for cosmopolitan authenticity. Patriotic Education redresses perhaps part of that imbalance, but the two approaches will tussle and conflict for years to come, for they cannot easily be reconciled when they live the political life.

There was nothing uniquely shameful or uniquely humiliating about China's treaty century. Events were wholly and always tied up with global trends – the rise of British predominance internationally not least, and then its contestation in the 1890s and after. Understanding this story alone is not the key to understanding modern China either, although China was also changed by it – its borders redrawn, its people dispersed globally, its culture and economy reshaped. There are equally vital stories in developments in China's nineteenth and twentieth centuries that call for at least equal attention and understanding. But to understand how modern China, how young China today understands the world, and its own history, we do need to understand the history of the encounter between Westerners and Chinese, Westerners and Manchus, in *yamen* and street, trading house and council chamber, on battlefields and inside chapels. We need to understand what the foreigners wanted, and how they got it; how they felt they were viewed and treated – by their own governments and representatives, by Qing officials, and by ordinary Chinese people, the rural and urban folk they encountered. We need to understand how intertwined and interconnected our histories are: that China and the Chinese were equally a part of the flows of people and ideas that marked the nineteenth century. A globalized China is not new; but a powerful global China is unprecedented. That provides new food for thought, especially as Chinese youth come out into the world equipped for instinctive indignation at China's past humiliations and what they feel to be contemporary echoes of those. The awkward confidence that such sensitivity engenders in them might make for all of us a very awkward world.

Acknowledgements

Firstly, I am grateful to my editor at Penguin, Simon Winder, for encouraging me in this venture, and to my agent David Miller for his support, and to both for their cheerful patience and tolerance. The book has been much longer in the making than was planned. I owe a great many thanks to Heather Bell, Rana Mitter and Christian Henriot, who took time out from other projects to read the manuscript and to help me improve it in many ways. For introducing me to the archives of the Chinese Maritime Customs Service I am indebted to Hans van de Ven, and for facilitating my access to it recently I am grateful to Ma Zhendu at the Second Historical Archives of China. For references, answers to queries and for supplying material, corrections or questions, I am grateful to Rob Allan, Chih-yun Chang, Songchuan Chen, Ines Eben von Racknitz, Cord Eberspächer, Doug Fix, Dan Hopper, Jon Howlett, Isabella Jackson, Hirata Koji, Cathy Ladds, Tom Layton, Regina Llamas, Tehyun Ma, Bridie Andrews Minehan, Sue Naquin, Emma Reisz, Annie Reinhardt, Michael Richardson, Gary Tiedemann, Sarah Vaughan, Rudolf Wagner, and Deidre Wildy. I must also especially thank Jamie Carstairs, Rosanne Jacks, Caroline Kimbell and Susannah Rayner for their support and assistance, as well as my copyeditor Jane Birdsell, and Caroline Elliker and Richard Duguid at Penguin. For practical and other support I remain especially grateful to Bob and Joan Bickers and to Carol Murphy.

For their assistance with the illustrations, for providing copies and permissions to reproduce photographs in their possession, I am very grateful to Terry Bennett, Pierre-Henri Biger, Patrick Conner and the Martyn Gregory Gallery, Penelope Fowler, Jane Hayward, Peter Lockhart-Smith, David Oakley, Dr William Sinton, Mary Tiffen,

Michael Towers, Sophie Couchman and the Chinese Museum of Melbourne, Matthew Edmondson and the Hongkong and Shanghai Banking Corporation, Maisie Shun Wah and John Swire & Sons, Ltd., the Wellcome Library London, Peabody Essex Museum, Fine Art Museum, Boston, and the Council for World Mission.

For allowing me to see and to quote from papers in their possession and copyright my thanks go to Shirley and Jim Brand (James Dow journal); Liz Boylan and family, and especially Elizabeth Shippee, and Liza Little (Lester Little diaries); and Ann Currie (Little family correspondence). Material quoted here from Sir Robert Hart's journals is copyright of Queen's University Belfast. Valuable materials, leads and information also came to me from Anthony Chalmers Bourne, Tita and Gerry Hayward, Joanna Helme, Peter Hibbard and David Mahoney. Many, many others in fact have also helped with information over the last few years about members of the foreign communities in the Chinese treaty ports, too many to mention, but I am grateful to them all.

The research and the writing of this book has been supported by a University of Bristol Research Fellowship, and though an Arts and Humanities and Research Council Research Leave award (AH/F015526/1). It was also thereby directly and greatly assisted by my colleagues at the University of Bristol. My research in the archives of the Chinese Maritime Customs was supported by an earlier award from the AHRC, and I have also received support for parts of this project from the Language Based Area Studies scheme through the British Inter-university China Centre, as well as the AHRC's Knowledge Catalyst Programme and the British Academy. As with all works of scholarship, this one is indebted to the published work of a large number of my fellow historians, to the work of archivists and librarians, and especially to those who, in the 1930s in particular, secured for posterity many of the records used here, rescuing them from decay and neglect in consulates and godowns across China.

Glossary of Place Names

In the text I have mostly used the modern Hanyu Pinyin transliteration system, with one or two exceptions (such as Canton and Peking, or where I could not find original characters for names). I have left quotations unchanged. I list here the older, Wade–Giles equivalents, which may be more familiar to many readers.

Pinyin	*Wade–Giles*
Beihe	Pei-ho
Chongqing	Chungking
Dagou (Gaoxiong)	Takow
Dagu	Taku
Dalian	Dairen, Dalny, or Port Arthur
Fuzhou	Foochow, Foochowfu
Guangdong	Canton Province, Kwangtung
Guangxi	Kwangsi province
Gulangyu	Kulangsu, Kulangyu, Koolangsu
Hankou	Hankow (often alone used to refer to the three cities – Hankou, Wuchang and Hanyang – which now from the conurbation of Wuhan)
Huangpu	Whangpoo
Jiangnan	Kiangnan region
Jilong	Keelung
Jiujiang	Kiukiang
Nanjing	Nanking
Ningbo	Ningpo
Niuzhuang	Newchwang

Eluanbi	Oulanpi, South Cape
Penghu islands	Pescadores
Pudong	Pootung
Qingdao	Tsingtao
Qiongzhou	Kiungchow
Shantou	Swatow
Suzhou	Soochow
Taibei	Taipeh, Taiwan-fu
Tianjin	Tientsin
Wusong	Woosung
Xiamen	Amoy
Xujiahui	Zikawei, Siccawei
Yangzhou	Yangchow
Yantai	Chefoo
Yichang	Ichang
Zhabei	Chapei
Zhenjiang	Chinkiang
Zhoushan	Chusan

Some Chinese names will be more familiar in longer-established non-Pinyin forms.

Cixi	Tz'u-Hsi, the Empress Dowager, Yehonala
Daoguang	Tao-kuang
Gong, Prince	Prince Kung
Guomindang	Kuomintang (KMT)
Hong Xiuquan	Hung Hsiu-ch'üan
Hong Rengan	Hung Jen-kan
Jiaqing	Chia-ch'ing
Li Hongzhang	Li Hungchang
Lin Zexu	Lin Tse-hsü (Commissioner Lin)
Qianlong	Ch'ien-lung
Qing	Ch'ing
Qiying	Kiying
Wenxiang	Wen-hsiang
Ye Mingchen	Yeh Ming-Ch'en (Viceroy Yeh)

Unpublished and Archival Sources

Admiralty Hydrographic Office Archives, Taunton

British Library

   Asia, Pacific and Africa Collections, India Office Records

      IOR/G/12   Factory Records: China and Japan

      IOR/R/10   Records of East India Company Factory at Canton

Harvard University Archives

   John King Fairbank papers

Hong Kong Public Records Office

   HKRS356   Royal Hong Kong Observatory records

Houghton Library, Harvard University

   Lester Knox Little papers

Lambeth Palace archives

   Holy Trinity Shanghai, Marriage and Baptism registers

National Archives of the United Kingdom, Kew

FO 228	Embassy and Consular Archives China, Correspondence Series 1
FO 232	Foreign Office: Consulates and Legation, China: Indexes to Correspondence
FO 369	Foreign Office: General Correspondence, Consular
FO 370	Foreign Office: Library and the Research Department: General Correspondence from 1906
FO 371	Foreign Office: General Correspondence, Political
FO 663	Foreign Office: Consulate, Amoy, China: General Correspondence
FO 670	Foreign Office: Consulate, Ningpo, China: General Correspondence and Various Registers

FO 671	Embassy and Consular Archives China, Shanghai Correspondence
FO 676	Embassy and Consular Archives China, Correspondence Series 2
FO 917	Embassy and Consular Archives China, Shanghai Supreme Court, Probate records
FO 1048	East India Company: Select Committee of Supercargoes, Chinese Secretary's Office: Chinese-language Correspondence and Papers
FO 1092	Shanghai Courts, China: Judges' and Magistrates' Notebooks
PRO 30/33	Sir Ernest Mason Satow: Papers

Queen's University Belfast, Library Special Collections

MS15	Sir Robert Hart collection

School of Oriental and African Studies Library and Archives, London
E. C. M. and C. A. V. Bowra papers PPMS 69
Overseas Missionary Fellowship, China Inland Mission archives
Council for World Mission, London Missionary Society archives
Horatio Nelson Lay papers, Add MS 72819, 72820
William Lockhart papers, MS 380645

Second Historical Archives of China, Nanjing
679(1–9) Archives of the Chinese Maritime Customs
This includes the formally separate archives of the Marine Department, the archive of nineteenth-century records created for the Customs' Reference Library (679(2)), and the records of the Inspectorate General and its secretariats, including the Central Registry.

Shanghai Municipal Archives

U1	Archives of the Shanghai Municipal Council

Staffordshire Records Office

D(W)1920	Antrobus papers (including papers of Hugh Hamilton Lindsay)

University of Toronto, Thomas Fisher Rare Books Library
J. O. P. Bland papers

Papers in Private Hands

James Dow journal

Little family letters (correspondence of Robert William Little, Archibald John Little, Alicia Little nee Bewicke, and other family members)

Lester K. Little diaries

Abbreviations

APAC, IOR	Asia, Pacific and African Collections, India Office Records
BL	British Library
C.	Parliamentary Papers
CIM	China Inland Mission
CWM/LMS	Council for World Mission, London Missionary Society archives
EIC	East India Company
FO	Foreign Office
IG	Inspector-General (of Chinese Maritime Customs)
LMS	London Missionary Society
NCH	*North China Herald*
PP	Parliamentary Papers
QUB	Queen's University Belfast, Library Special Collections
SHAC	Second Historical Archives of China (Nanjing), Chinese Maritime Customs Service Archives
SMA	Shanghai Municipal Archives
SMC	Shanghai Municipal Council; their annual reports, referred to here by year – SMC, *Annual Report 1874–5* or *1880* – were published as *Report for the Year Ended 31st March 1875* (Shanghai: 1875) or *Report for the Year Ended 31st December 1880* (Shanghai: 1881)
SMP	Shanghai Municipal Police
SOAS	School of Oriental and African Studies, London University
SRO	Staffordshire Records Office
SVC	Shanghai Volunteer Corps
TNA	The National Archives, Kew
UKHOA	UK Hydrographic Office Archives

Notes

INTRODUCTION

1. Confidential Despatch to Minister of Finance, no. 98, 5 December 1949, in Houghton Library, Harvard University, L. K. Little papers, Ms Am 1999.18; I. G. Circular no. 21 (Canton–Taibei series), 27 December 1949; L. K. Little diary, 5 December 1949 – 14 January 1950. The photograph is reproduced in *Zhonghua Minguo haiguan jianshi* [A Short History of the Customs Service of the Republic of China] (Taibei: Caizhengbu Guanshui zongju, 1995).

2. A good guide to the Bund past and present is Peter Hibbard, *The Bund Shanghai: China faces west* (Hong Kong: Odyssey, 2007).

3. A standard account of this process is Beverley Hooper, *China Stands Up: Ending the western presence, 1948–1950* (London: Allen & Unwin, 1986). The flavour of the deliberate confrontation of old with new was caught in publications marking the tenth anniversary of the revolution, such as *Shanghai jinxi* [Shanghai today and yesterday] (Shanghai: Shanghai renmin meishu chubanshe, 1958).

4. There are many such accounts, in the form of popular histories or memoirs. Some are referred to later in this book, for their writers were often also actors in events, but see also, for example, Carl Crow, *Foreign Devils in the Flowery Kingdom* (New York: Harper & Brothers, 1940); O. M. Green, *The Foreigner in China* (London: Hutchinson & Co., 1942), and J. V. Davidson-Huston, *Yellow Creek: The story of Shanghai* (London: Putnam, 1962).

5. A detailed early survey, and a deliberate attempt to steer between these two positions, is Hosea Ballou Morse, *The International Relations of the Chinese Empire*, 3 vols (London: Longmans, Green, 1910–18). Comprehensive, too, within a briefer time-span was Henri Cordier, *Histoire des relations de la Chine avec les puissances occidentales, 1860–1900* [History of China's relations with the Western Powers], 3 vols (Paris: Felix Alcan, 1901–2). One

of the few modern accounts of the socio-cultural life of the treaty port foreign communities is Frances Wood, *No Dogs and Not Many Chinese: Treaty port life in China 1843–1943* (London: John Murray, 1998), while James L. Hevia's survey, *English lessons: The pedagogy of imperialism in nineteenth-century China* (Durham, NC: Duke University Press, 2003), explores the currents of European and American diplomatic discourse and practice in China in its wider colonial contexts.

6. Robert Bickers and Jeffrey N. Wasserstrom, 'Shanghai's "Dogs and Chinese Not Admitted" Sign: Legend, history and contemporary symbol', *China Quarterly* 142 (1995), pp. 444–66; '"Gentlemen" and "Chinese",' *People's Tribune* (NS) 5, 16 August 1933, pp.68–9.

7. See Marek Kohn, *Dope Girls: The birth of the British drug underground* (2nd edn, London: Granta, 2001).

8. See, for example, Yin Shan and Ji Weihua (eds.), *Bainian Qingpi* [A century of Qingdao beer] (Beijing: Zhonghua shuju, 2003); Chen Xieyang (chief ed.), *Shanghai jiaoxiang yuetuan jiantuan 120 zhounian (1879–1999) jinian huace* [The 120th anniversary album of the Shanghai Symphony Orchestra] (1999).

9. Missionary influence is highlighted in the still stimulating account by Harold R. Isaacs, *Scratches on Our Minds: American views of China and India* [1958] (Armonk: M. E. Sharpe, 1980).

10. On this, and on the current life of 'National Humiliation' in China, see William A. Callahan, *China: The pessoptimist nation* (Oxford: Oxford University Press, 2009).

11. 'Conversazione' transcript, 16–17 December 1971, G. E. Bunker, K. F. Bruner, L. K. Little: Harvard University Archives, John King Fairbank papers, HUG (FP) 12.28, Box 4.

12. Danson family information: various Shanghai Municipal Police and related records; L. K. Little, 'To whom it may concern', 6 January 1950 in L. K. Little papers, Ms Am 1999.14; and courtesy of Joanna Helme.

13. Hanchao Lu, 'Nostalgia for the Future in China: The resurgence of an alienated culture in China', *Pacific Affairs*, 75:2 (2002), pp. 169–86.

14. Explored in Robert Bickers, *Britain in China: Community, culture and colonialism, 1900–49* (Manchester: Manchester University Press, 1999), chapter 2.

15. L. K. Little diary, 30 April 1949.

16. L. K. Little diary, 12, 13 September 1949.

17. L. K. Little papers, Ms Am 1999.18; Little to Evelyn W. Hippisley, 4 June 1949.

18. L. K. Little diary, 1 January 1950.

2 UNWELCOME GUESTS

1. *Report of Proceedings on a Voyage to the Northern Ports of China, in the Ship Lord Amherst* (London: B. Fellowes, 1833), p. 173. This is a republication of the official report to the East India Company by Lindsay (pp. 1–267), with Karl Gützlaff's journal appended (pp. 269–96). The report was printed as a Parliamentary Paper, *Ship Amherst* (House of Commons 410; London, 1833), with the Court's response. A manuscript of the Lindsay text, identical with that published except that Chinese characters have been inserted where Chinese names, ranks or places are mentioned in the first half of the report, is in the Canton committee records of the East India Company: 'Journal by Hugh Hamilton Lindsay of Voyage of the *Lord Amherst*', British Library, Asia, Pacific and Africa Collections, India Office Records [BL, APAC], IOR/R/10/70. Unless otherwise specified, all quotations are from Lindsay's account. A fuller version of Gützlaff's account was published in New York in 1833 (as *The Journal of Two Voyages Along the Coast of China in 1831 & 1832*) and in London in 1834 (as *The Journal of Three Voyages Along the Coast of China in 1831, 1832 & 1833*).

2. H. B. Morse, *The Chronicles of the East India Company Trading to China*, iv (Oxford: Clarendon Press, 1926), p. 332. On Lindsay, see Harriet Low: Nan P. Hodges and Arthur W. Hummel (eds.), *Lights and Shadows of a Macao Life: The Journal of Harriet Low, Travelling Spinster* (Woodinville, WA: History Bank, 2002), i, pp. 204, 589.

3. H. H. Lindsay to mother, draft, 'Amoy', April 1832, Staffordshire Record Office [SRO], D(W)1920/4/1.

4. Arthur Waley, *The Opium War through Chinese Eyes* (London: George Allen & Unwin, 1958), p. 228.

5. On Gützlaff, see Jessie G. Lutz, *Opening China: Karl F. A. Gützlaff and Sino-Western Relations, 1827–1852* (Grand Rapids: Wm B. Erdmans, 2008).

6. *Report of Proceedings on a Voyage to the Northern Ports of China*, p. 26.

7. Gützlaff, *Journal of Two Voyages Along the Coast*, p. 72.

8. Ibid., pp. 101, 113.

9. *Report of Proceedings on a Voyage to the Northern Ports of China*, p. 171.

10. On the Macartney embassy, see James L. Hevia, *Cherishing Men from Afar: Qing guest ritual and the Macartney embassy of 1793* (Durham, NC: Duke University Press, 1995), which also discusses Amherst.

11. *Report of Proceedings on a Voyage to the Northern Ports of China*, pp. 174, 26–7.

12. Hugh Lindsay, 'An adventure in China', in Lord Lindsay, *Lives of the Lindsays: Or, a memoir of the houses of Crawford and Balcarres* (London:

John Murray, 1849), iii, pp. 479–86. J. L. Cranmer-Byng was sceptical of
Lindsay senior's claims that this episode unpicked the 1810–11 *imbroglio*
but, setting aside inaccuracies rooted in imperfect memories of events almost
forty years earlier, there seems little reason to doubt that the episode itself
occurred: see his 'Incident between the Hong Merchants and the Supercargoes of the British East India Company in Canton, 1811', *Journal of the
Hong Kong Branch of the Royal Asiatic Society* 15 (1975), pp. 49–60.

13. Select Committee at Canton to Court of Directors, 10 January 1812,
extracted in *Appendix to Report on the Affairs of the East India Company,
II, China Papers* (London, 1831), p. 54. There is debate about the correctness
of these interpretations of the Qing code in this instance, but this is besides
the point; foreign traders acted on the understandings and suspicions that
they had developed.

14. *Lives of the Lindsays*, iii, pp. 482–3, 481.

15. Clarke Abel, *Narrative of a Journey in the Interior of China: And of a
voyage to and from that country, in the years 1816 and 1817* (London:
Hurst, Rees, Orme and Brown, 1818), pp. 107, 109.

16. The events are narrated in Morse, *Chronicles of the East India Company
Trading to China*, iv, pp. 278–92.

17. *Canton Register*, 6 June 1831, p. 52.

18. Morse, *East India Company Trading to China*, iv, pp. 199–222, 242–3.

19. H. H. Lindsay to mother, 15 November 1829, 10 December 1829, SRO,
D(W)1920/4/2.

20. This dispute is documented in various letters transcribed in BL, APAC,
IOR/G/12/249, 'Factory consultations'.

21. H. H. Lindsay to J. H. Davis, President, Select Committee, Canton,
5 February 1832, BL, APAC, IOR/R/10/30, 'Secret Consultations of Select
Committee of Supercargoes'.

22. William Jardine in Canton to James Matheson in Macao, 28 January 1832,
Alain Le Pichon (ed.), *China Trade and Empire: Jardine, Matheson & Co.
and the origins of British rule in Hong Kong, 1827–1843*. Records of Social
and Economic History, New Series, 38 (Oxford: Published for the British
Academy by Oxford University Press, 2006), p. 144.

23. BL, APAC, IOR/G/12/287, Secret Department, Select Committee to Court,
15 January 1832.

24. *Canton Register*, 16 February 1832, p. 21, 8 March 1832, p. 32.

25. BL, APAC, IOR/G/12/287, Secret Department, Select Committee to Court,
7 November 1831; TNA, FO 1048/32/8, 'Copy of a printed paper landed
by the *Lord Amherst* at Ningpo. Received at Macao, for translation, July
1832'.

26. *Canton Register*, 18 July 1832, pp. 68–9. The text is in all but a couple of instances identical with the English original, in BL, APAC, IOR/10/30, 'Secret Consultations of Select Committee of Supercargoes'. See a more recent transcription in: Ting Man Tsao, 'Representing "Great England" to Qing China in the Age of Free Trade Imperialism: The circulation of a tract by Charles Marjoribanks on the China coast', *Victorians Institute Journal* 33 (2005), pp. 179–96.

27. *Report of Proceedings on a Voyage to the Northern Ports of China*, pp. 157–8.

28. BL, APAC, IOR/G/12/249, *passim*.

29. Jardine on the pamphlet, writing to Thomas Williamson, Canton, 13 July 1832: quoted in Gerald S. Graham, *The China Station: War and diplomacy, 1830–1860* (Oxford: Clarendon Press, 1978), p. 70, n.13.

30. Michael Greenberg, *British Trade and the Opening of China 1800–1842* (Cambridge: Cambridge University Press, 1951), p. 3.

31. Lin Man-houng, *China Upside Down: Currency, society, and ideologies, 1808–1856* (Cambridge, MA: Harvard University Asia Center, 2006), p. 288.

32. Yangwen Zheng, *The Social Life of Opium in China* (Cambridge: Cambridge University Press, 2005).

33. David Anthony Bello, *Opium and the Limits of Empire: Drug prohibition in the Chinese interior, 1729–1850* (Cambridge, MA: Harvard University Asia Center, 2005), pp. 115–22.

34. Wm Jardine to H. P. Haddow, 10 March 1831, in Le Pichon, *China Trade and Empire*, p. 117. On the firm's Parsee partner, see Le Pichon, *China Trade and Empire* and Asiya Siddiqi, 'The business world of Jamsetjee Jeejeebhoy', *Indian Economic and Social History Review*, 19:3/4 (1982), pp. 301–24.

35. Quoted in Greenberg, *British Trade and the Opening of China*, p. 140; James Innes to James Matheson, 7 December 1832, in Le Pichon, *China Trade and Empire*, p. 167; Gützlaff, on the *John Biggar*, to Lindsay, 6 September 1833, SRO, D(W)1920/4/1.

36. Edward LeFervour, *Western Enterprise in Late Ching China: A selective survey of Jardine, Matheson & Company's operations, 1842–1895* (Cambridge, MA: East Asian Research Center, 1968), p. 13.

37. Hsin-pao Chang, *Commissioner Lin and the Opium War* (Cambridge, MA: Harvard University Press, 1964), pp. 23–7; Joyce A. Madancy, *The Troublesome Legacy of Commissioner Lin: The opium trade and opium suppression in Fujian province, 1820s to 1920s* (Cambridge, MA: Harvard University Asia Center, 2003), pp. 50–52.

38. Chang, *Commissioner Lin and the Opium War*, pp. 28, 30; William Jardine

to Captain John Rees, 19 August 1837, in Le Pichon, *China Trade and Empire*, p. 304.

39. Harriet Low, on 12 October 1833: Hodges and Hummel (eds.), *Lights and Shadows of a Macao Life*, ii, p. 639.

40. EIC, Canton, Public Consultations, 10 March 1832, BL, APAC, IOR/G/12/248. Studies of the practical workings of the Canton trade can be found in Paul A. Van Dyke, *The Canton Trade: Life and enterprise on the China coast, 1700–1845* (Hong Kong: Hong Kong University Press, 2005); Jacques Downs, *The Golden Ghetto: The American commercial community at Canton and the shaping of American China policy, 1784–1844* (Bethlehem, PA: Lehigh University Press, 1997); and Morse, *East India Company Trading to China*.

41. *Chinese Repository* 4:1 (May, 1835), p. 42.

42. The days allotted were those when Canton officials would not bump into them, for they were the days when the officials received petitions at their *yamens*: Morse, *East India Company Trading to China*, iv, pp. 153–4; see also Fa-ti Fan, *British Naturalists in Qing China: Science, empire and cultural encounter* (Cambridge, MA: Harvard University Press, 2004), pp. 29–31.

43. Peter Quennell (ed.), *Memoirs of William Hickey* (London: Routledge & Kegan Paul, 1975), p. 134.

44. Henry Ellis, *Journal of the Proceedings of the Late Embassy to China* (London: John Murray, 1817), p. 409.

45. *Chinese Repository* 4:1 (May, 1835), p. 45.

46. C. Toogood Downing, *The Fan-Qui in China in 1836–37* (London: Henry Colburn, 1836), ii, p. 229.

47. Quoted in Jonathan A. Farris, 'Thirteen Factories of Canton: An architecture of Sino-Western collaboration and confrontation', *Buildings and Landscapes* 14 (2007), p. 74.

48. Removed to Government House, Hong Kong in 1842 from Macao: E. J. Eitel, *Europe in China: The history of Hongkong from the beginning to the year 1882* (London: Luzac & Co., 1895), p. 17.

49. *Chinese Repository* 4:2 (June, 1835), p. 96.

50. Van Dyke, *Canton Trade*, chapter 4; Quennell (ed.), *Memoirs of William Hickey*, pp. 131–2.

51. Downing, *Fan-qui in China*, i, pp. 83–4.

52. Osmond Tiffany, *The Canton Chinese: Or, the American's sojourn in the celestial empire* (Boston: James Munroe and Company, 1849), p. 135.

53. Nan and Hummel (eds.), *Lights and Shadows of a Macao Life*, ii, 28 October to 21 November, pp. 453–65.

54. BL, APAC, IOR/G/12/247, 'Diary of Transactions 1831/32'; and IOR/G/12/248, Statement of Consumption Value of Indian Opium in China from 1st April 1831 to 31st March 1832'. American participation in the contraband trade brought additional stocks of 'Turkish' opium (although sometimes it was only nominally Turkish, and was in fact Indian).

55. See Fred W. Drake, 'Protestant Geography in China: E. C. Bridgman's portrayal of the West', in Suzanne Wilson Barnett and John King Fairbank (eds.), *Christianity in China: Early Protestant missionary writing* (Cambridge, MA: Harvard University Press, 1985), pp. 89–106; Michael C. Lazich, *E. C. Bridgman (1801–1861): America's first missionary to China* (Lampeter: Edwin Mellen Press, 2000). The world of opinion-making is explored in Song-Chuan Chen, 'The British Maritime Public Sphere in Canton, 1827–1839' (unpublished PhD dissertation, University of Cambridge, 2009), and Ulrike Hillemann, *Asian Empire and British Knowledge: China and networks of British imperial expansion* (Basingstoke: Palgrave Macmillan, 2009).

56. Matthew Liam Brockley, *Journey to the East: The Jesuit mission to China, 1579–1724* (Cambridge, MA: Belknap Press of Harvard University Press, 2007).

57. Colin Mackerras, *Western Images of China* (Hong Kong: Oxford University Press, 1989), pp. 28–42.

58. See Fan, *British Naturalists in Qing China*, for example.

59. J. L. Cranmer-Byng (ed.), *An Embassy to China: Being the journal kept by Lord Macartney during his embassy to the Emperor Ch'ien-lung, 1793–1794* (London: Longmans, 1962), p. 212. On the impact of the embassies, see Shunhong Zhang, 'British Views on China During the Time of the Embassies of Lord Macartney and Lord Amherst (1790–1820)' (unpublished PhD thesis, University of London, 1989).

60. *The Times*, 1 September 1835, p. 6. On Chinnery and Lam Qua, see Patrick Conner, *George Chinnery, 1774–1852: Artist of India and the China coast* (Woodbridge: Antique Collectors' Club, 1993).

61. Stephen Rachman, '*Memento mobi*: Lam Qua's paintings, Peter Parker's patients', *Literature and Medicine* 23:1 (2004), pp. 134–59; Edward V. Gulick, *Peter Parker and the Opening of China* (Cambridge, MA: Harvard University Press, 1973).

62. Robert Fortune, *Three Years' Wanderings in the Northern Provinces of China* (London: John Murray, 1847), p. 144.

63. Fan, *British Naturalists in Qing China*, pp. 19–26; Richard Drayton, *Nature's Government: Science, imperial Britain, and the 'improvement' of the world* (New Haven: Yale University Press, 2000), pp. 92–3; Georges Métailié, 'Sir Joseph Banks – an Asian Policy?', in R. E. R. Banks et al. (eds.),

Sir Joseph Banks: A global perspective (Kew: Royal Botanic Gardens, 1994), pp. 157–69.

64. Paragraph based on Jardine to Weeding, 7 December 1830, in Le Pichon, *China Trade and Empire*, pp. 104–6.

65. *Report of Proceedings on a Voyage to the Northern Ports of China*, p. 32.

66. Brian Harrison, *Waiting for China: The Anglo-Chinese College at Malacca, 1818–1843, and early nineteenth-century missions* (Hong Kong: Hong Kong University Press, 1979).

67. *Report of Proceedings on a Voyage to the Northern Ports of China*, pp. 173–87, quotation from p. 187.

68. Lydia H. Liu, *The Clash of Empires: The invention of China in modern world making* (Cambridge, MA: Harvard University Press, 2004).

69. *Report of Proceedings on a Voyage to the Northern Ports of China*, p. 202.

70. Contemporaries generally used 'Viceroy' when referring to the position now normally, as here, referred to as 'Governor General'.

71. *Report of Proceedings on a Voyage to the Northern Ports of China*, p. 207.

72. *Canton Register*, 17 September 1832, p. 99.

73. [Illegible], at Macao, to Lindsay, 16 December 1832, SRO, D(W)1920/4/1.

74. *Report of Proceedings on a Voyage to the Northern Ports of China*, p. 44.

75. Ibid., pp. 60–62.

76. Charles Marjoribanks to Lindsay, undated, but evidently winter 1831–2; Charles Marjoribanks, at St Helena, to Lindsay, 19 April 1832; Charles Marjoribanks, at London, to Lindsay, 11 June 1832, SRO, D(W)1920/4/1.

77. John Francis Davis, *The Chinese: A general description of the empire of China and its inhabitants* (London: Charles Knight & Co., 1836), i, pp. 117–18.

78. *Report of Proceedings on a Voyage to the Northern Ports of China*, pp. 148, 74.

79. Ibid., pp. 52, 61.

80. Ibid., p. 52.

81. H. H. Lindsay to mother, draft, 'Amoy', April 1832, SRO, D(W)1920/4/1.

82. Napier diary, 26 November 1833, quoted in Glen Melancon, *Britain's China Policy and the Opium Crisis: Balancing drugs, violence and national honour, 1833–1840* (Aldershot: Ashgate, 2003), p. 35.

83. Extract from the Royal Commission Appointing Lord Napier . . . Enclosure in Viscount Palmerston to Napier, 25 January 1834, in *Correspondence Relating to China* (London: T. R. Harrison, 1840), p. 3.

84. Napier to Viscount Palmerston, 14 August 1834; Napier to Earl Grey, 21 August 1834, *Correspondence Relating to China* (1840), pp. 13, 27.

85. Letter from Ling Ting Bay, 26 September 1834, *The Times*, 2 March 1835, p. 3.

86. *Canton Register,* 21 October 1834, quoted in *Chinese Repository* 3:6 (October, 1834), p. 282.

87. Extract from the private notes of T. R. Colledge, Surgeon to HM Super-intendent, *Chinese Repository* 3:6 (October, 1834), p. 284

88. James Matheson in Canton to John Purvis in Singapore, 25 September 1834, Le Pichon, *China Trade and Empire*, p. 224.

89. Alexander Mitchie, *The Englishman in China During the Victorian Era* (Edinburgh: William Blackwood & Sons, 1900), i, p. 40.

90. Gideon Nye, *The Morning of My Life in China* (Canton: [privately published], 1873) p. 48.

91. Duke of Wellington to Napier, 2 February 1835; Napier to Viscount Palmerston, 14 August 1834; *Correspondence Relating to China* (1840), pp. 26, 14.

92. Lindsay and May Ride (edited by Bernard Mellor), *An East India Company Cemetery: Protestant burials in Macao* (Hong Kong: Hong Kong University Press, 1996), p. 261.

93. James Matheson to Lady Napier, 25 June 1839, Le Pichon, *China Trade and Empire*, p. 369.

94. 'Passage to Europe Via the Red Sea, by a Late Resident of Canton', *Chinese Repository* 3:6 (October, 1834), pp. 252–5.

95. Daniel R. Headrick, *The Tools of Empire: Technology and European imperialism in the nineteenth century* (New York: Oxford University Press, 1981), pp. 23, 135–7.

96. Gerald S. Graham, *China Station: War and diplomacy 1830–1860* (Oxford: Clarendon Press, 1978), pp. 69–71.

97. *Canton Register*, 20 December 1832, pp. 140–41.

98. H. Hamilton Lindsay, *Letter to the Right Honourable Viscount Palmerston on British Relations with China* (London: Saunders and Otley, 1836), pp. 3, 4, 12–13, 16–17. Others noted the scale of the coasting trade as well: *Canton Register*, 3 September 1832, pp. 91–2.

99. P. P. T.[homs], review of Lindsay, *The Monthly Magazine, or British Register*, 21:125 (May 1836), p. 410.

100. *Memoirs of the Chief Incidents of the Public Life of Sir George Thomas Staunton* (London: L. Booth, 1856), pp. 84–5.

101. *Chinese Repository* 6:1 (May, 1837), pp. 44–7; various items of correspondence in SRO, D(W)1920/4/2.

102. Paragraph based on Matheson to White, 11 March 1832, in Le Pichon, *China Trade and Empire*, pp. 155–6.

3 ON A CHINESE STAGE

1. W. H. Medhurst, *China: Its state and prospects* (London: John Snow, 1838), pp. 460–62.

2. Ibid., p. 456. Stevens and Medhurst both published their accounts of this 1835 expedition, which have been drawn on for this section: Stevens, 'The Voyage of the *Huron*', *Chinese Repository* 4:7 (November, 1835), pp. 308–35 (he records the arrival at the temple on p. 329), and W. H. Medhurst, in 'Extract from the manuscript journal of the Reverend W. H. Medhurst', *Chinese Repository* 4:9 (January, 1836), pp. 406–11, and much more fully in *China*, pp. 451–63. A brief biography of Stevens is in Wylie, *Memorials of Protestant Missionaries*, pp. 84–5.

3. *Report of Proceedings on a Voyage to the Northern Ports of China, in the Ship Lord Amherst* (London: B. Fellowes, 1833), p. 172.

4. On the history of the Tianhou temple, see Gu Bingquan (ed.), *Shanghai fengsu guji kao* [Investigations of Shanghai folk customs] (Shanghai: Huadong shifan daxue chubanshe, 1993), pp. 167–70; Xue Liyong, *Shanghai zhanggu cidian* [Dictionary of old Shanghai tales] (Shanghai: Shanghai cishu chubanshe, 1999); *Shanghai chunqiu* [Annals of Shanghai] (Hong Kong: Xianggang nantian shuye, 1968), xi-a, pp. 32–3; Shanghai tongshe (eds.), *Shanghai yanjiu ziliao* [Shanghai research materials; 1935] (Shanghai: Shanghai shudian, 1984), pp. 517–23. There seem to be no surviving images of it, but it will have looked very much like the Tianhou temple at Ningbo; see illustration no. 3.

5. James L. Watson, 'Standardizing the Gods: The promotion of T'ien-hou ('Empress of Heaven') along the South China coast, 960–1960', in David Johnson, Andrew Nathan and Evelyn Rawski (eds.), *Popular Culture in Late Imperial China* (Berkeley: University of California Press, 1985), pp. 292–324; W. H. Medhurst, *General Description of Shanghae and its Environs Extracted from Native Authorities* (Shanghai: Printed at the Mission Press, 1850), pp. 163–4.

6. The emperors assumed reign titles, such as 'Daoguang', or 'Qianlong', by which they will be referred to here, usually either simply by the title, for example 'Daoguang', or as 'the Daoguang emperor'.

7. The key contributions to the debate include: Watson, 'Standardizing the Gods', and the papers collected in Donald Sutton (ed.), 'Ritual, Cultural Standardization, and Orthopraxy in China: Reconsidering James L. Watson's ideas', *Modern China* 33:3 (2007).

8. Bryna Goodman, *Native Place, City, and Nation: Regional networks and*

identities in Shanghai, 1853–1937 (Berkeley: University of California Press, 1995), pp. 103–6.

9. Wang Tao, quoted in Ye Xiaoqing, *The Dianshizhai Pictorial: Shanghai urban life, 1884–1898* (Ann Arbor: Center for Chinese Studies, University of Michigan, 2003), p. 199.

10. Jane Kate Leonard, 'W. H. Medhurst and the Missionary Message', in Suzanne Barnett Wilson and John King Fairbank, *Christianity in China: Early Protestant writings* (Cambridge, MA: Committee on American–East Asian Relations of the Dept of History in collaboration with the Council on East Asian Studies, 1985), p. 55, quoting an 1824 letter.

11. Revd Charles Gützlaff, *China Opened. Or a display of the topography, history, customs, manners, arts, manufactures, commerce, literature, religion, jurisprudence, etc, of the Chinese empire* (London: Smith, Elder & Co., 1838), i, p. 509.

12. Mark C. Elliott, *The Manchu Way: The Eight Banners and ethnic identity in late imperial China* (Stanford: Stanford University Press, 2001), pp. 287–8.

13. Goodman, *Native Place, City, and Nation*, pp. 103–6.

14. A good brief general survey is in Susan Naquin and Evelyn S. Rawski, *Chinese Society in the Eighteenth Century* (New Haven: Yale University Press, 1989), pp. 83–8. The account of the Shanghai year in this paragraph is based on Gu (ed.), *Shanghai fengsu guji kao*, pp. 336–401.

15. Revd Justus Doolittle, *Social Life of the Chinese* (London: Sampson, Low, Son & Marston, 1866), ii, pp. 55–60.

16. Ye, *Dianshizhai Pictorial*, pp. 200–202; Goodman, *Native Place, City, and Nation*, pp. 92–103.

17. A good survey is still Linda Cooke Johnson, 'Shanghai: An emerging Jiangnan port, 1683–1840' in Linda Cooke Johnson (ed.), *Cities of Jiangnan in Late Imperial China* (Albany: State University of New York Press, 1993), pp. 151–81.

18. For population estimates for Shanghai in 1840s, see Linda Cooke Johnson, *Shanghai: From market town to treaty port, 1074–1858* (Stanford: Stanford University Press, 1995), pp. 120–21; for Tianjin in 1842, see Gilbert Rozman, *Population and Marketing Settlements in Ch'ing China* (Cambridge: Cambridge University Press, 1982), p. 58; for Xiamen in 1847, see *Chinese Repository* 16:2 (February, 1847), p. 76; Fuzhou's population is routinely given as *c.* 600,000 in Western accounts, for example Doolittle, *Social Life of the Chinese*, i, p. 17.

19. Timothy Brook, *The Confusions of Pleasure: Commerce and culture in Ming China* (Berkeley: University of California Press, 1999).

20. William T. Rowe, *Hankow: Commerce and society in a Chinese city,*

1796–1895 (Stanford: Stanford University Press, 1984), pp. 180–81.

21. On the enmeshing of the literati and merchant worlds in Canton, for example, see Steven B. Miles, *The Sea of Learning: Mobility and identity in nineteenth-century Guangzhou* (Cambridge, MA: Harvard University Asia Center, 2006), chapter 2.

22. Rowe, *Hankow*, pp. 23–4; Antonia Finnane, *Speaking of Yangzhou: A Chinese city, 1550–1850* (Cambridge, MA: Harvard University Asia Centre, 2004); Jane Kate Leonard, *Controlling from Afar: The Daoguang emperor's management of the Grand Canal crisis, 1824–1826* (Ann Arbor: Center for Chinese Studies, University of Michigan, 1996), pp. 98–105.

23. Junks at Singapore: *Asiatic Journal* 7:4 (April 1832), pp. 185–6. Gützlaff himself estimated that eighty junks made their way to Bangkok each trading season: *Journal of Three Voyages*, pp. 53–4. Other estimates are outlined in Sarasin Viraphol, *Tribute and Profit: Sino–Siamese trade, 1652–1853* (Cambridge, MA: Council on East Asian Studies, Harvard University, 1977), pp. 195–200.

24. Lin Man-houng, *China Upside Down: Currency, society, and ideologies, 1808–1856* (Cambridge, MA: Harvard University Asia Center, 2006), pp. 44–7, 63–8; Naquin and Rawski, *Chinese Society*, pp. 102–6.

25. Weng Eang Cheong, *The Hong Merchants of Canton: Chinese merchants in Sino-Western trade* (London: Routledge, 1997), chapter 4.

26. Rowe, *Hankow*, pp. 45, 123–4. On the Russians in Peking, see Eric Widmer, *The Russian Ecclesiastical Mission in Peking During the Eighteenth Century* (Cambridge, MA: Harvard University Asia Center, 1976).

27. See, for example, Jennifer Cushman, *Fields from the Sea: Chinese junk trade with Siam during the late eighteenth and early nineteenth centuries* (Ithaca: Southeast Asian Program, Cornell University, 1999); Benito J. Lehgarda, Jr, *After the Galleons: Foreign trade, economic change and entrepreneurship in the nineteenth century Philippines* (Manila: Ateneo de Manila University Press, 1999); Ng Chin-keong, *Trade and Society: The Amoy network on the China coast, 1683–1735* (Singapore: National University of Singapore Press, 1983).

28. *Report of Proceedings on a Voyage to the Northern Ports of China*, pp. 13–14, 56, 101.

29. For the early nineteenth-century economy see the papers in Jane Kate Leonard (ed.) and John R. Watt, *To Achieve Security and Wealth: The Qing imperial state and the economy, 1644–1911* (Ithaca: Cornell East Asia Series, 1992), and Madeleine Zelin, 'The Structure of the Chinese Economy During the Qing Period: Some thoughts on the 150th anniversary of the opium war', in Kenneth Lieberthal et al. (eds.), *Perspectives on Modern China:*

Four anniversaries (Armonk: M. E. Sharpe, 1991), pp. 31–67.

30. Madeleine Zelin, *The Merchants of Zigong: Industrial entrepreneurship in early modern China* (New York: Columbia University Press, 2005).

31. Peter C. Perdue, *China Marches West: The Qing conquest of Central Eurasia* (Cambridge, MA: Harvard University Press, 2005).

32. Susan Naquin, *Millenarian Rebellion in China: The Eight Trigrams uprising of 1813* (New Haven: Yale University Press, 1976), pp. 179–83.

33. Revd Charles Gützlaff, *The Life of Taou-Kwang, Late Emperor of China* (London: Smith, Elder & Co., 1852); see Jessie G. Lutz, *Opening China: Karl F. A. Gützlaff and Sino-Western Relations, 1827–1852* (Grand Rapids: Wm B. Erdmans, 2008), pp. 146–8. The exception to this picture is Leonard, *Controlling from Afar*.

34. Evelyn S. Rawski, *The Last Emperors: A social history of Qing imperial institutions* (Berkeley: University of California Press, 2001), pp. 48–9, 118, 141–2, 134.

35. Pierre-Étienne Will, 'Views of the Realm in Crisis: Testimonies on imperial audiences in the nineteenth century', *Late Imperial China* 29:1 (Supplement) (2008), pp. 125–59.

36. On the complexities of Manchu identity, see also Pamela Kyle Crossley, *Orphan Warriors: Three Manchu generations and the end of the Qing world* (Princeton: Princeton University Press, 1991).

37. R. Kent Guy, *The Emperor's Four Treasuries: Scholars and the state in the late Ch'ien-lung era* (Cambridge, MA: Council on East Asian Studies, 1987). See also Jonathan Spence on Qianlong's father: *Treason by the Book* (London: Allen Lane, The Penguin Press, 2001).

38. Philip A. Kuhn has explored how the power of the emperor could be tempered: *Soulstealers: The Chinese sorcery scare of 1768* (Cambridge, MA: Harvard University Press, 1990).

39. Manchuria and the other Manchu realms were administered by different systems.

40. Leung Yuen-Sang, *The Shanghai Taotai: Linkage man in a changing society, 1843–90* (Singapore: National University of Singapore Press, 1990), pp. 14–15.

41. On religion: Tung-tsu Ch'u, *Local Government in China Under the Ch'ing* (Cambridge, MA: Harvard University Press, 1962), pp. 164–6.

42. Benjamin A. Elman, *A Cultural History of Civil Examinations in Late Imperial China* (Berkeley: University of California Press, 2000) (the estimate for the overall pool of candidates is on p. 143); Iona D. Man-cheong, *The Class of 1761: Examinations, state, and elites in eighteenth-century China* (Stanford: Stanford University Press, 2004).

43. Immanuel C. Y. Hsü, 'The Secret Mission of the *Lord Amherst* on the China Coast, 1832', *Harvard Journal of Asiatic Studies*, 17:1/2 (1954), pp. 231–52. Originals of this documentation were printed in Xu Dishan (ed.), *Dazhong ji* [Arriving at the inner truth] (Shanghai: Shangwu yinshuguan, 1931). On the memorial system, see Silas H. L. Wu, *Communication and Imperial Control in China: Evolution of the palace memorial system, 1693–1735* (Cambridge, MA: Harvard University Press, 1970) and his 'The Memorial Systems of The Ch'ing Dynasty (1644–1911)', *Harvard Journal of Asiatic Studies* 27:1 (1967); on the government post, see: J. K. Fairbank and S. Y. Teng, 'On the Transmission of Ch'ing Documents', *Harvard Journal of Asiatic Studies* 4:1 (1939), pp. 12–46, and Ying-wan Cheng, *Postal Communication in China and its Modernization 1860–1896* (Cambridge, MA: East Asian Research Center, 1970), pp. 8–36.

44. *Report of Proceedings on a Voyage to the Northern Ports of China*, pp. 202–5. Both Lindsay and Gützlaff state that Bao came especially to meet them, and while neither lacked a sense of their own importance, it seems possible that officials decided that the impasse could only be undone with a little more official weight.

45. Hsü, 'The Secret Mission of the *Lord Amherst*'.

46. Wei Yuan, quoted in Richard D. Cushman, 'Rebel Haunts and Lotus Huts: Problems in the ethnohistory of the Yao' (unpublished PhD dissertation, Cornell University, 1970), p. 235.

47. Cushman, 'Rebel Haunts and Lotus Huts', pp. 223–33, has a narrative of the rebellion, and in appendix XII (pp. 235–49), translates Wei Yuan's 1842 account.

48. A correspondent in China, 'Intercourse with China', *Asiatic Journal and Monthly Register* NS 13:50 (1834), p. 101.

49. 'John Crawfurd, 'Voyage of the Ship *Amherst*', *Westminster Review* (January, 1834), p. 47.

4 LINDSAY'S WAR AND PEACE

1. Lindsay, writing as 'A Resident in China', *Remarks on Occurrences in China Since the Opium Seizure in March 1839 to the Latest Date* (London: Sherwood, Gilbert and Piper, 1840), p. 101.

2. Lin Man-houng, *China Upside Down: Currency, society, and ideologies, 1808–1856* (Cambridge, MA: Harvard University Asia Center, 2006).

3. Peter Ward Fay, *The Opium War, 1840–1842: Barbarians in the Celestial Empire in the early part of the nineteenth century and the war by which*

they forced her gates ajar (New York: Norton, 1975), has its critics, and Fay had no Chinese, but it remains a fine account of the British side of events. Hsin-Pao Chang, *Commissioner Lin and the Opium War* (Cambridge, MA: Harvard University Press, 1964), presents a more integrated narrative and analysis.

4. *The Times*, 2 August 1842, p. 5.

5. James M. Polachek, *The Inner Opium War* (Cambridge, MA: Council on East Asian Studies, 1992), pp. 125–31.

6. One got to London, but the Foreign Office refused to meet its British bearer: Chang, *Commissioner Lin and the Opium War*, p. 138.

7. Quoted in Alain Le Pichon (ed.), *China Trade and Empire: Jardine, Matheson & Co. and the origins of British rule in Hong Kong, 1827–1843*. Records of Social and Economic History, New Series, 38 (Oxford: Published for the British Academy by Oxford University Press, 2006), p. 362, n. 26.

8. James Matheson to Wm Jardine, London, 1 May 1839 in Le Pichon, *China Trade and Empire*, p. 359.

9. Ibid.

10. W. C. Hunter, 'Journal of Occurrances [sic] at Canton During the Cessation of Trade, 1839', *Journal of the Hong Kong Branch of the Royal Asiatic Society*, iv (1964), p. 22; Gideon Nye, *Peking the Goal; – the Sole Hope of Peace* (Canton: 1873), pp. 18–22.

11. Glen Melancon, *Britain's China Policy and the Opium Crisis: Balancing drugs, violence and national honour, 1833–1840* (Aldershot: Ashgate, 2003) lays this out well.

12. Full text of the letter: H. B. Morse, *The International Relations of the Chinese Empire* (London: Longmans, Green & Co., 1910), i, appendix A, pp. 621–6.

13. W. D. Bernard and Commander W. H. Hall, *Narrative of the Voyages and Services of the Nemesis from 1840 to 1843*, 2 vols (London: H. Colburn, 1844).

14. Palmerston to Victoria, 10 April 1841, Victoria to King Leopold of Belgium, 13 April 1841, in A. C. Benson and Viscount Esher (eds.), *Letters of Queen Victoria: A selection from Her Majesty's correspondence between the years 1837 and 1861* (London: John Murray, 1908), i, pp. 260–62.

15. Lieutenant John Ouchterlony, *The Chinese War: An account of all the operations of the British forces from the commencement to the Treaty of Nanking* (London: Saunders and Otley, 1844), pp. 312–16; *The Times*, 22 November 1842, p. 4.

16. Granville G. Loch, *The Closing Events of the Campaign in China: The operations in the Yang-tze-kiang and Treaty of Nanking* (London: John

Murray, 1843), p.108; Sir John Francis Davis, *China, During the War and Since the Peace* (London: Longman, Brown, Green and Longmans, 1852), i, p. 282; Duncan MacPherson, *The War in China: Narrative of the Chinese expedition from its formation in April, 1840, to the treaty of peace in August, 1842* (London: Saunders and Otley, 1843), p. 270.

17. Letter from 'H. W.', *The Times*, 26 November 1842, p. 5.

18. *The Times*, 22 November 1842, p. 4.

19. Frederic Wakeman Jr, *Strangers at the Gate: Social disorder in south China, 1839–1861* (Berkeley: University of California Press, 1966); Polachek, *Inner Opium War*, pp. 137–75.

20. Minutes of evidence taken before the select committee, Captain George Balfour, 1 June 1847: *Report from the Select Committee on Commercial Relations with China; together with the minutes of evidence, appendix, and index* (PP 654) (1847), p. 333.

21. Robert Montgomery Martin, 'Report on the Island of Hong Kong', 24 July 1844, in *Report from the Select Committee on Commercial Relations with China* (1847), appendix 3, p. 450.

22. *The Times*, 12 May 1841, p. 5.

23. On Dunn, see Helen Saxbee, 'An Orient Exhibited: The exhibition of the Chinese collection in England in the 1840s' (unpublished PhD thesis, Royal College of Arts, 1990), and John Rogers Haddad, *The Romance of China: Excursions to China in US Culture, 1776–1876* (New York: Columbia University Press, 2005), chapter 4.

24. Saxbee, 'An Orient Exhibited', pp. 54–5; Charles Dickens and R. H. Horne, 'The Great Exhibition and the Little One', in Harry Stone (ed.), *Uncollected Writings of Charles Dickens*: Household Words *1850–1859* (London: Allen Lane, 1969), i, p. 324. Although a jointly written piece, the phrase is Dickens's. See also his essay, 'The Chinese Junk', originally published in *The Examiner*, 24 June 1848: Charles Dickens, *The Amusements of the People, and Other Papers: Reports, essays and reviews, 1834–51*, Michael Slater (ed.) (London: Dent, 1996), pp. 98–102; Jeffrey Auerbach, *The Great Exhibition of 1851: A nation on display* (New Haven: Yale University Press, 1999), p. 178; Haddad, *Romance of China*, chapter 5. A 'beautiful collection of China' was exhibited at the Great Exhibition courtesy of Hugh Hamilton Lindsay, who was also commended for the silks, and sea slugs, that he contributed: *Reports by the Juries* (London: W. Clowes, 1852), pp. 66, 163, 393. The junk had its admirers: see the original impressions of the *Illustrated London News* (1 April 1848, p. 220).

25. Lt F. E. Forbes, *Five Years in China: From 1842 to 1847* (London: Richard Bentley, 1848), p. 1.

26. American difficulties in this regard are laid out in Eldon Griffin, *Clippers and Consuls: American consular and commercial relations with Eastern Asia, 1845–1860* (Ann Arbor: Edwards Brothers, 1939).

27. W. H. Medhurst and William Lockart to Revd A. Tidman, 15 October 1844, SOAS, Council for World Mission, London Missionary Society archives [hereafter CWM/LMS], Central China Incoming, Box 1.

28. *The Maitland Mercury & Hunter River General Advertiser*, 9 June 1847, p.1. Report from pre-March 2nd Hong Kong papers; 'Victoria Town' was idly proposed for the new concession at Shanghai also: 'Description of Shánghái', *Chinese Repository* 16:11 (November, 1847), p. 542.

29. William Maxwell Wood, *Fankwei: Or, the San Jacinto in the seas of India, China, and Japan* (New York: Harper & Brothers, 1859), p. 267.

30. Minutes of evidence taken before the Select Committee from Robert Montgomery Martin, 18 May 1847 in *Report from the Select Committee on Commercial Relations with China* (1847), p. 289.

31. Ibid., p. 449.

32. Robert Fortune, *A Journey to the Tea Countries of China* (London: John Murray, 1852), p. 3.

33. See Virginia Berridge, *Opium and the People: Opiate use and drug control policy in nineteenth and early twentieth century England* (revised edn, London: Free Association, 1999).

34. Alexander Matheson to John Abel Smith, 3 July 1843, in Le Pichon, *China Trade and Empire*, p. 528.

35. Christopher Munn, *Anglo-China: Chinese people and British rule in Hong Kong, 1841–1880* (London: Routledge, 2001), pp. 75–8.

36. Edward LeFervour, *Western Enterprise in Late Ching China: A selective survey of Jardine, Matheson & Company's operations, 1842–1845* (Cambridge, MA: East Asia Research Center, 1968), pp. 15–17.

37. Alexander Matheson to John Abel Smith, 31 July 1843, in Le Pichon, *China Trade and Empire*, p. 531.

38. John King Fairbank, *Trade and Diplomacy on the China Coast: The opening of the treaty ports, 1842–1854* (Stanford: Stanford University Press, 1969 [1953]), chapter 9.

39. Balfour to Pottinger, 12 November 1843, 2 December 1843, TNA, FO 228/31.

40. *The Chinese Repository* 16:11 (November, 1847), pp. 242–5.

41. Ningbo no. 30, 19 June 1844, TNA, FO 228/31.

42. G. Tradescant Lay, *Trade with China: A letter addressed to the British public* (London: Bopyston & Brown, 1837), p. 6; G. Tradescant Lay, *The*

Chinese as They Are: Their moral, social, and literary character (London: William Ball, 1841), p. vii.

43. Despatches from Fuzhou, 1844–45, TNA, FO 228/52, quotation from Fuzhou no. 3, 15 February 1845. P. D. Coates, *The China Consuls: British consular officers in China* (Hong Kong: Oxford University Press, 1988), pp. 14–18.

44. Letter to William Lockhart, 1 March 1845, quoted in Stanley Lane-Poole, *The Life of Sir Harry Parkes* (London: Macmillan and Co., 1894), i, p. 82.

45. Balfour to Davis, Shanghai no. 38, 28 April 1846, TNA, FO 228/64; Minutes of evidence taken before the Select Committee, Captain George Balfour, 1 June 1847, in *Report from the Select Committee on Commercial Relations with China* (1847), p. 320.

46. Robertson to McCullock, 12 January 1847, TNA, FO 671/1; Balfour to Davis, Shanghai no. 19 July 1846, TNA, FO 228/64.

47. Balfour to Davis, Shanghai no. 19 July 1846, TNA, FO 228/64.

48. Robert Fortune, *Three Years' Wandering in the Northern Provinces of China* (London: John Murray, 1847), pp. 116–18.

49. Fortune, *Journey to the Tea Countries*, pp. 14–18

50. James Dow journal, 29 September, 28 October, 1851.

51. 'R. W. L[ittle]', introduction to *The Jubilee of Shanghai 1843–1893* (Shanghai: North China Daily News, 1893), p. 3.

52. Reproduced in Edward Denison and Guang Yu Ren, *Building Shanghai: The story of China's gateway* (Chichester: Wiley-Academy, 2006), pp. 36–7.

53. Fortune, *Three Years' Wandering*, p. 405.

54. Fortune, *Journey to the Tea Countries*, p. 18.

55. Ibid., p. 14; James Dow journal, 29 September 1851.

56. W. H. Medhurst and William Lockart to Revd A. Tidman, 15 October 1844, SOAS, CWM/LMS/Central China Incoming, Box 1; William Lockhart, *The Medical Missionary in China: A narrative of twenty years' experience* (London: Hurst and Blackett, 1861), p. 243.

57. James Dow journal, September–October 1851.

58. Stephen C. Lockwood, *Augustine Heard and Company, 1858–1862* (Cambridge, MA: East Asian Research Center, Harvard University, 1971), pp. 54–5.

59. Hoh-chueng Mui and Lorna H. Mui (eds.), *William Melrose in China 1845–1855: The letters of a Scottish tea merchant*, Scottish History Society, Fourth Series, 10 (1973), p. 271; James Dod to R. C. Antrobus, 23 December 1865, SRO D(W)1920/5/3.

60. Alcock to Shanghai no. 90, 6 September 1847, TNA, FO 228/77.

61. W. H. Medhurst, *A Glance at the Interior of China Obtained During a Journey Through the Silk and Green Tea Districts* (Shanghai: Mission Press, 1849), p. 14; Fortune, *Journey to the Tea Countries*, p. 42.

62. Van Dyke, *The Canton Trade*.

63. *Canton Repository*, XI (1842) pp. 687–9.

64. On the Cantonese sex trade see Christian Henriot, *Prostitution and Sexuality in China: A social history, 1849–1949* (Cambridge: Cambridge University Press, 2001), pp. 84–5.

65. Fuzhou no. 3, Lay to Davis, 15 February 1845, TNA, FO 228/52.

66. Fuzhou no. 30, Jackson to Davis, 10 May 1847, TNA, FO 228/74.

67. Alcock at Fuzhou in 1845: no. 65, 26 November 1845, FO 228/52.

68. Ningbo no. 37, 3 July 1844, TNA, FO 228/42.

69. Fairbank, *Trade and Diplomacy on the China Coast*, pp. 216–17.

70. Bowring to Malmesbury, 3 August 1852, in *China: Correspondence with the superintendent of British trade in China, upon the subject of emigration from that country* (PP 1686) (1853), p. 4. A sketch map of the Syme 'barracoon' is in Harvey to Bowring, 22 December 1852, Enclosure G, between pp. 74–5. It was clearly not designed for easy access or egress: it was meant to detain.

71. Bowring to Malmesbury, 17 May 1852, ibid., p. 2.

72. Enclosures 5 and 6 in item 17, ibid., pp. 92–3.

73. Shanghai no. 75, 9 August 1848, TNA, FO 228/104; *North China Herald* [*NCH*], 8 January 1853, p. 90.

74. Consular and Hong Kong government officials on leave held discussions with an agent of the British Guiana government in 1853: *Correspondence upon the Subject of Emigration from China (in continuation of papers presented August 20 1853* (1854), no. 1 and enclosures.

75. The Sassoons and allied families had originally come from Baghdad, and remained conscious of these roots: Chiara Betta, 'From Orientals to Imagined Britons: Baghdadi Jews in Shanghai', *Modern Asian Studies* 37:4 (2003), pp. 1001. For a partial survey of the Parsee story, see John R. Hinnells, *The Zoroastrian Diaspora: Religion and migration* (Oxford: Oxford University Press, 1995), pp. 145–88.

76. Shanghai no. 83, 4 August 1848, TNA, FO 228/89.

77. Shanghai no. 51, 11 July 1844, Balfour to Davis, TNA, FO 228/43; Shanghai no. 41, 10 June 1844, TNA, FO 228/31.

78. Shanghai no. 62, 14 June 1847, TNA, FO 228/77; Shanghai no. 10, 22 January 1848, TNA, FO 228/89. On comfort: James Dow journal, 28 September 1851; on monotony: the letters of receiving ship's mate Thomas Gerard in Sir Clement Wakefield Jones, *Chief Officer in China:*

1840–1853 (Liverpool: Charles Birchall and Sons, 1955), *passim.*

79. Shanghai no. 48, 10 January 1848, TNA, FO 228/89.

80. Sir Perceval Griffiths, *The History of the Indian Tea Industry* (London: Wiedenfeld and Nicolson, 1967), pp. 38–43; Fortune, *Journey to the Tea Countries,* pp. 363, 374, 393; Superintendent Botanical Gardens to Secretary to Government, North-Western Provinces (no. 285), Seharanpure, 12 May 1862, in *East India (Tea Plantations): Copy of reports made to the government on the extension of tea plantations in India* (PP 95) (1863), p. 17.

81. Fairbank, *Trade and Diplomacy,* pp. 335–46.

82. Fuzhou no. 3, 10 January 1848; no. 21, 17 April 1848; no. 22, 29 April 1848, TNA, FO 228/87.

83. Shanghai no. 21, 10 March 1848, TNA, FO 228/89; Wood, *Fankwei,* p. 323.

84. Shanghai no. 93, 11 September 1848, TNA, FO 228/91.

85. *NCH,* 3 August 1850, pp. 1–3.

86. On the dominance of free trade doctrine, see Frank Trentmann, *Free Trade Nation: Commerce, consumption, and civil society in modern Britain* (Oxford: Oxford University Press, 2008).

87. Edwin Lai, 'The Beginnings of Hong Kong Photography', in *Picturing Hong Kong: Photography 1855–1910* (New York: Asia Society Galleries, 1997) pp. 49–50; *NCH,* 7 August 1852, p. 1.

88. *NCH,* 8 January 1853, p. 90.

89. Revd J. Stronach to Revd A. Tidman, 25 July 1845, SOAS/CWM/LMS Fukien Incoming, Box 1.

90. Their statements are in the *Chinese Repository* 17:3 (March, 1848), pp. 151–7.

91. Harvey to Bowring, 22 December 1852, in *China: Correspondence with the superintendent of British trade* (1853), p. 44.

92. *Report of Proceedings on a Voyage to the Northern Ports of China,* p. 107. One unintended consequence of this Ningbo episode had been the introduction of the soyabean to the United States: T. Hymowitz and J. R. Harlan, 'Introduction of Soybean to North America by Samuel Bowen in 1765', *Economic Botany* 37:4 (1983), pp. 371–9.

93. Fortune, *Three Years' Wandering,* pp. 42–3; *NCH,* 25 June 1853, p. 188. See also Laurence Oliphant, *Narrative of the Earl of Elgin's Mission to China and Japan in the Years 1857, '58, '59* (London: William Blackwood and Sons, 1859), i, p.239.

5 MODEL SETTLEMENTS

1. Lewin R. Bowring (ed.), *Autobiographical Recollections of Sir John Bowring, with a Brief Memoir* (London: Henry S. King & Co., 1877), p. 218.

2. John King Fairbank, *Trade and Diplomacy on the China Coast: The opening of the treaty ports, 1842–1854* (Stanford: Stanford University Press, 1969 [1953]), p. 276; John J. Nolde, 'The "False Edict" of 1849', *Journal of Asian Studies* 20:3 (1961), pp. 302–3; Frederic Wakeman Jr, *Strangers at the Gate: Social disorder in South China, 1839–1861* (Berkeley: University of California Press, 1966), pp. 86–8.

3. Vice-Consul Robertson to Capt Wade, 6 July 1848; and to W. P. Watson, 8 December 1848, TNA, FO 671/1.

4. James Dow journal, 22 August 1851.

5. For Longfellow, see the *China Magazine*, March 1868, p. 16; and Charles G. Leland, *Pidgin-English Sing-song or Songs and Stories in the China-English Dialect* (London: Trübner & Co., 1876), pp. 114–16; on pidgin, see S. Wells Williams, *A Chinese Commercial Guide* (Canton: Chinese Repository, 1856), p. 225. Here it is termed 'Canton English'. For the Shanghai version, see Hong Kong Museum of History, *Modern Metropolis: Material culture of Shanghai and Hong Kong* (Hong Kong: Hong Kong Museum of History, 2009), p. 43; for the former see Anne and Stephen Selby, 'China Coast Pidgin English', *Journal of the Hong Kong Branch of the Royal Asiatic Society* 8 (1995), pp. 113–41.

6. *NCH*, 7 December 1850, p. 73.

7. 'Introduction', *Chinese Repository*, 1:1 (May, 1832), p. 3.

8. *General Description of Shanghae and Its Environs Extracted from Native Authorities* (Shanghai: Printed at the Mission Press, 1850), pp. 2–3.

9. 'Introduction', *Chinese Repository* 1:1 (May, 1832), p. 1.

10. *British Museum: Accounts, estimate, number of persons admitted, and progress of arrangement* (PP 139) (1848), p. 9. On the development of European libraries, see T. H. Barrett, *Singular Listlessness: A short history of Chinese books and British scholars* (London: Wellsweep, 1989).

11. Helen Saxbee, 'An Orient Exhibited: The exhibition of the Chinese collection in England in the 1840s' (unpublished PhD thesis, Royal College of Arts, 1990), pp. 51–5.

12. *NCH*, 15 January 1853, p. 95; 29 April 1854, p. 156.

13. James Dow journal, 13 February 1852.

14. Saxbee, 'An Orient Exhibited', pp. 49–50.

15. *NCH*, 3 August 1850, p. 1; 14 August 1852, p.5; *The China Directory for 1861* (Hong Kong: Printed by A. Shortrede & Co., 1861). These lists are

always subject to error, typographical slips, and mis-transcription of names, but the general pattern is clear. *NCH*, 24 August 1850, p. 2; *An Address by the Rev. Dr. Nelson read on the 20th June 1879, at a farewell gathering of his friends, on the occasion of his leaving the old mission house in Hongkew* (Shanghai: Shanghai Mercury Office, 1879), pp. 3–4.

16. P. Richard Bohr, 'Liang Fa's Quest for Moral Power', in Suzanne Wilson Barnett and John King Fairbank (eds.), *Christianity in China: Early Protestant missionary writing* (Cambridge, MA: Committee on American–East Asian Relations of the Dept of History in collaboration with the Council on East Asian Studies, 1985), pp. 40–46. The identification of Stevens is that of Jonathan D. Spence in *God's Chinese Son: The Taiping heavenly kingdom of Hong Xiuquan* (New York: W. W. Norton, 1996), p. 31.

17. I. J. Roberts, 'Tae Ping Wang: The Chinese revolutionist', *Putnam's Monthly* (October, 1856), pp. 380–83. See also, amongst others, Spence, *God's Chinese Son*.

18. Yuan Chung Teng, 'Reverend Issachar Jacox Roberts and the Taiping Rebellion', *Journal of Asian Studies* 23:1 (1963), p. 57.

19. On the Taiping, see Spence, *God's Chinese Son*, Wakeman, *Strangers at the Gate*, chapter 12; Jen Yu-wen, *The Taiping Revolutionary Movement* (New Haven: Yale University Press, 1973).

20. Gerald S. Graham, *The China Station: War and diplomacy 1830–1860* (Oxford: Oxford University Press, 1978), pp. 272–5.

21. Thomson Taylor Meadows, *The Chinese and their Rebellions . . .* (London: Smith, Elder & Co., 1856), pp. vii–viii.

22. Ibid., chapter 16.

23. Confidential, Alcock, 3 March 1853, TNA, FO 228/161.

24. Jen, *Taiping Revolutionary Movement*, pp. 274–5.

25. *NCH*, 7 May 1853, quoted in Prescott Clarke and J. S. Gregory (eds.), *Western Reports on the Taiping: A selection of documents* (Canberra: Australian National University Press, 1982), p. 54.

26. *The Times*, 30 August 1853, p. 6.

27. But a significant enough proportion of the agents who were nominally out in the closed provinces sat comfortably in Canton or Hong Kong, filed imaginative reports about their conversion successes, and sold back to Gützlaff the tracts they had supposedly distributed: Jessie G. Lutz and R. Ray Lutz, 'Karl Gützlaff's Approach to Indigenization: The Chinese Union', in Daniel H. Bays, *Christianity in China: From the eighteenth century to the present* (Stanford: Stanford University Press, 1999), pp. 269–91.

28. The fixing of a Chinese term for the Christian deity proved difficult, and

contentious: Irene Eber, 'The *Interminable Term Question*', in Irene Eber, Wan Sze-kar and Knut Walf (eds.), *Bible in Modern China: The Literary and Intellectual Impact* (Sankt Augustin: Institute Monumenta Serica, 1999), pp. 135–61; and as it affected Taiping thinking, see Thomas H. Reilly, *The Taiping Heavenly Kingdom: Rebellion and the Blasphemy of Empire* (Seattle: University of Washington Press, 2004), pp. 80–104.

29. Letter to *NCH*, 26 November 1853, reprinted in Clarke and Gregory, *Western Reports on the Taiping*, pp. 86–90. See also his summary, 'General Views of the Chinese Insurgents', May 1853, enclosure 10 in item 6, Bonham to the Earl of Clarendon, 11 May 1853, *Papers Respecting the Civil War in China* (PP 1667) (1853), pp. 41–4.

30. Meadows, *Chinese and their Rebellions*, pp. 265, 272.

31. Bonham to the Earl of Clarendon, 11 May 1853, no. 6 in *Papers Respecting the Civil War in China*, pp. 23–6.

32. See Capt. [E. G.] Fishbourne, *Impressions of China: And the present revolution; its progress and prospects* (London: Seeley, Jackson, and Halliday, 1855), see chapter 4; quotations from pp. 182, 184.

33. Meadows, *Chinese and their Rebellions*, p. 275.

34. Fairbank, *Trade and Diplomacy on the China Coast*, pp. 410–13; Commander, HMS *Rattler*, to Consul Blackburn, Amoy, 30 August 1853, TNA, FO 663/12.

35. His own description in his confession, translated in Franz Michael, *The Taiping Rebellion: History and documents* (Seattle and London: University of Washington Press, 1971), iii, p. 1511.

36. Quoted in Jessie G. Lutz and Rolland Ray Lutz, *Hakka Chinese Confront Protestant Christianity, 1850–1900: With the autobiographies of eight Hakka Christians, and commentary* (Armonk: M. E. Sharpe, 1998), p. 62; Theodore Hamberg, *The Visions of Hung-Siu-Tshuen, and Origin of the Kwang-si Insurrection* (Hongkong: The China Mail Office, 1854).

37. On Hong Rengan's Hong Kong sojourns, see Carl T. Smith, *Chinese Christians: Élites, middlemen, and the church in Hong Kong* (Hong Kong: Oxford University Press, 1985), pp. 77–84; and Lutz and Lutz, *Hakka Chinese*, pp. 62, 124–6.

38. Shanghai no. 61, 17 June 1852, TNA, FO 228/147. There is no doubting that this was his aim: Leung Yuen-Sang, *The Shanghai Taotai: Linkage man in a changing society, 1843–90* (Singapore: National University of Singapore Press, 1990), pp. 53–6.

39. Bryna Goodman, *Native Place, City, and Nation: Regional networks and identities in Shanghai, 1853–1937* (Berkeley: University of California Press, 1995), pp. 72–83; Fairbank, *Trade and Diplomacy*, pp. 406–9.

40. Shanghai no. 71, 21 September 1853; no. 82, 1 November 1853, TNA, FO 228/161.

41. Thomas Hanbury to his father, 4 April 1854, *Letters of Sir Thomas Hanbury* (London: West, Newman & Co., 1913), p. 43; *NCH*, 1 April 1854, p. 138.

42. The description comes from the *NCH* commentary, 15 April 1854, p. 146; on suspicions of Wu, see Shanghai no. 84, 1 November 1853, TNA, FO 228/162.

43. *Chinese Repository* 16:12 (December, 1847), p. 612.

44. Thomas Hanbury to his father, 4 April 1854, *Letters of Sir Thomas Hanbury*, p. 43; Shanghai no. 30, 5 April 1854, TNA, FO 228/176; *NCH*, 6 May 1854, p. 158; I. I. Kounin (comp.), *Eighty-five Years of the SVC* (Shanghai: Cosmopolitan Press, 1939), p. 1.

45. W. S. Wetmore, 'The Battle of Muddy Flat', *NCH*, 13 January 1890, pp. 13–15, quotations from p. 15.

46. Details of Municipal Council activities from Shanghai Municipal Archives (ed.), *Minutes of the Shanghai Municipal Council* (Shanghai: Shanghai guji chubanshe, 2001), *passim*; Wood, *Fankwei*, p. 324.

47. *NCH*, 22 July 1854, pp. 202–3; 24 March 1855, pp. 136–7; 3 June 1854, p. 174; *Minutes of the SMC*, i, 15 December 1856.

48. Wood, *Fankwei*, p. 325.

49. *NCH*, 24 March 1855, pp. 136–7; 30 June 1855, p. 192.

50. Memorandum by Mr Lay, Chinese Inspector of Customs, on the Complaints of the Hong Kong and Shanghae Chambers of Commerce, 11 January 1862, in *Further Papers Relating to the Rebellion in China* (PP 3104) (1863), pp.177–9; and Alex Perceval, chairman of the Hong Kong General Chamber of Commerce, to Lord John Russell, 26 August 1861, in ibid., pp. 161–3.

51. Fairbank, *Trade and Diplomacy*, p. 432.

52. Shanghai no. 3, 11 January 1855; no. 10, 20 January 1855, TNA, FO 228/195.

53. Shanghai no. 26, 20 February 1855; no. 31, 7 July 1855, TNA, FO 228/195.

54. Katherine F. Bruner, John K. Fairbank, Richard J. Smith (eds.), *Entering China's Service: Robert Hart's journals, 1854–1863* (Cambridge, MA: Harvard University Asia Center, 1986), entries of 7 May and 1 July 1855. Shanghai no. 32, 26 June 1855; no. 120 6 August 1855, TNA, FO 670/44. *NCH*, 21 July 1855, p. 205; 18 August 1855, p. 9.

55. Stanley Lane-Poole, *The Life of Sir Harry Parkes* (London: Macmillan and Co., 1894), i, pp. 150–53.

56. Shanghai, unnumbered, 3 May 1854, TNA, FO 228/176.

57. Circular, 30 May 1854, *Hong Kong Gazette*, 3 June 1854, p. 145.

58. *NCH*, 29 December 1855, p. 86.

59. *NCH*, 30 December 1854, p. 86; 24 February 1855, p. 120; 5 January 1856, p. 90.

60. Ibid., 29 December 1855, p. 86.

61. Lilian M. Li, *Fighting Famine in North China: State, market, and environmental decline, 1690s–1990s* (Stanford: Stanford University Press, 2007), p. 284. On the battle to control the river see Randall A. Dodgen, *Controlling the Dragon: Confucian engineers and the Yellow River in late imperial China* (Honolulu: University of Hawai'i Press, 2001).

62. Bowring, *Autobiographical Recollections*, p. 218.

63. H. Labouchere to Governor Sir J. Bowring, 12 December 1855, and Acting Attorney-General to the Colonial Secretary, 29 August 1855, in *China: Correspondence respecting the registration of colonial vessels at Hong Kong* (PP 2166) (1857), pp. 6, 8.

64. Lane-Poole, *Life of Sir Harry Parkes*, i, p. 51, which volume supplies the biographical information used in this paragraph.

65. Letter to J. C. Patteson, 27 October 1852, quoted in Lane-Poole, *Life of Sir Harry Parkes*, i, p. 169.

66. *NCH*, 11 April 1890, p. 440.

67. Letter dated 14 November 1856, Lane-Poole, *Life of Sir Harry Parkes*, i, p. 229.

68. On Ye: Fairbank, *Trade and Diplomacy on the China Coast*, p. 277. On the 1849 episode and its repercussions: Wakeman, *Strangers at the Gate*, pp. 90–105, and Polachek, *The Inner Opium War* (Cambridge, MA: Council on East Asian Studies, 1992), pp. 242–57. Ye is quoted in Wakeman, *Strangers at the Gate*, p. 102.

69. Unless otherwise noted, all details in this and the following paragraph come from *Papers Relating to the Proceedings of Her Majesty's Naval Forces at Canton* (PP 2163) (1857), and *Further Papers Relative to the Proceedings of Her Majesty's Naval Forces at Canton* (PP 2192) (1857).

70. Bowring to Parkes, 16, 21 October, quoted in Lane-Poole, *Life of Sir Harry Parkes*, i, p. 245; analysed in J. Y. Wong, *Deadly Dreams: Opium, imperialism, and the Arrow War (1856–1860) in China* (Cambridge: Cambridge University Press, 2002), pp. 87–91.

71. Parkes to Revd T. M'Clatchie, 9 May 1857, quoted in Lane-Poole, *Life of Sir Harry Parkes*, i, p. 262.

72. Mrs Parkes to Mrs M'Clatchie, 11 December 1856, ibid., i, p. 254.

73. Parkes to Revd T. M'Clatchie, 9 May 1857, ibid., i, p. 262.

74. Parkes to Mrs Lockhart, 15 December 1856, ibid., i, p. 254.

75. Ibid., i, p. 254; and letter to Revd T. M'Clatchie, 9 May 1857, p. 262.

76. Christopher Munn, *Anglo-China: Chinese people and British rule in Hong Kong, 1841–1880* (London: Routledge, 2001), pp. 276–83, p. 421; correspondent from Hong Kong quoted in *The Times*, 3 March 1857, p. 5. When tempers cooled remains of the bread became souvenirs, picked up by early globe-trotters: Albert Smith, *To China and Back: Being a diary kept, out and home* (London: privately published, 1859), p. 53.

77. Laurence Oliphant, *Narrative of the Earl of Elgin's Mission to China and Japan in the years 1857, '58, '59* (London: William Blackwood and Sons, 1859), i, p. 209.

78. *NCH*, 15 November 1856, p. 62; dissent is found in 'Old Cathay', 'The Canton War', 2 February, 1857, p. 110.

79. *Hansard's Parliamentary Debates*, cxliv, 1802 (3 March 1857); see Gladstone's annotations to his copy of *Papers Relating to the Proceedings of Her Majesty's Naval Forces at Canton* (1857), University of Bristol Library Special Collections, DM2237, p. 111.

80. *Hansard's Parliamentary Debates*, cxliv, 1812 (3 March 1857).

81. Miles Taylor, *The Decline of British Radicalism, 1847–1860* (Oxford: Clarendon Press, 1995), pp. 269–80.

82. Oliphant, *Narrative of the Earl of Elgin's Mission*, i, p. 212; Theodore Walrond (ed.), *Letters and Journals of James, Eighth Earl of Elgin* (London: John Murray, 1872), pp. 212, 214.

83. The cruel insecurity of 1858 in Canton is well caught in Robert Hart's journal.

84. *The Times*, 6 April 1858, p. 10; *Illustrated London News*, 10 April 1858, p. 362.

85. Oliphant, *Narrative of the Earl of Elgin's Mission*, i, pp. 158–9.

86. Parkes to Gideon Nye, 21 January 1858, quoted in Lane-Poole, *Life of Sir Harry Parkes*, i, p. 272; *The Times*, 26 February 1858, pp. 9–10, reprinted in George Wingrove Cooke, *China and Lower Bengal* (London: Routledge, Warne, & Routledge, 1861), pp. 340–43.

87. Shanghai no. 149, 23 November 1857, TNA, FO 228/243.

88. R. K. I. Quested, *The Expansion of Russia in East Asia, 1857–1860* (Kuala Lumpur: University of Malaya Press, 1968), pp. 115, 133. Russian weapons were eventually delivered: 10,000 rifles and 50 cannons in November 1862, S. Y. Teng, *The Taiping Rebellion and the Western Powers: A comprehensive survey* (Oxford: Clarendon Press, 1971), pp. 280–81.

89. This stage of the war is covered in Ines Eben v. Racknitz, 'Die Zerstörung des Yuanming yuan als "imperialistische Lektion"? Plünderung, Preis und Beute im britisch-französischen Chinafeldzug von 1860' (unpublished PhD thesis, Universität Konstanz, 2009).

90. The assessment comes from *The Times*, 27 April 1857, p.8. The new Hythe School of Musketry consolidated the effectiveness of the new fire-power.

91. Robert Swinhoe, *Narrative of the North China Campaign of 1860* (London: Smith, Elder and Co., 1861), p. 92; David Harris, *Of Battle and Beauty: Felice Beato's Photographs of China* (Santa Barbara, CA: Santa Barbara Museum of Art, 1999).

92. See his account of reconnoitring under feint of parley at Dagu, letter to Mrs Parkes, 21 August 1860, in Lane-Poole, *Life of Sir Harry Parkes*, i, pp. 362.

93. J.L. Cranmer-Byng (ed.), *An Embassy to China: Being the journal kept by Lord Macartney during his embassy to the Emperor Ch'ien-lung, 1793–1794* (London: Longmans, 1962), p. 95; Henry Brougham Loch, *Personal Narrative of Occurrences During Lord Elgin's Second Embassy to China in 1860* (London: John Murray, 1869), p. 274.

94. Revd R. J. M'Ghee, *How We Got into Pekin: A narrative of the campaign in China of 1860* (London: Richard Bentley, 1862), pp. 287–8.

95. Quoted in A. Egmont Hake, *The Story of Chinese Gordon* (New York: R. Worthington, 1884), p. 24.

96. Walrond (ed.), *Letters and Journals of James, Eighth Earl of Elgin*, p. 369.

6 CHINA EL DORADO

1. F. C. Jarrett (ed.), *Jottings from the Log of a New South Welshman: Or, six years in the opium trade* (Sydney: Gibbs, Shallard & Co., 1867), pp. 6–7; W. A. Pickering, *Pioneering in Formosa: Recollections of adventures among Mandarins, wreckers and head hunting savages* (London: Hurst & Blackett, 1898), pp. 176–7. The ship, the *Macto*, had been driven out of Dagou harbour by a typhoon in August 1859, then foundered on the shore: Peter-Michael Pawlik, *Von der Weser in die Welt: Die Geschichte der Segelschiffe von Weser und Lesum und ihrer Bauwerften 1770 bis 1893*, 2nd edition (Kabel Verlag: Hamburg, 1994), p. 44. I am grateful to Cord Eberspächer for this reference.

2. Rutherford Alcock, 'Memorandum on suggested Heads of a New Treaty', 31 December 1857, no. 49 in *Correspondence Relative to the Earl of Elgin's Special Missions to China and Japan 1857–1859* (PP 2571) (1859), pp. 54–61.

3. E. G. Ravenstein, *The Russians on the Amur: Its discovery, conquest and colonisation* (London: Trübner & Co., 1861), p. 154.

4. Stanley Lane-Poole, *The Life of Sir Harry Parkes* (London: Macmillan and Co., 1894), i, p. 433; 'The Yang-Tse-Kiang', *The Times*, 2 August 1861, p. 11.

5. James Dow journal, 12–15 March 1862.

6. R. W. Little to parents, 12 September, 30 September 1862, Little papers.

7. James Dow journal, 14 March 1862.

8. Alexander Michie, *The Siberian Overland Route from Peking to Petersburg* (London: John Murray, 1864), p. 2; Lt. Col. Sarel, 'Notes on the Yang-tsze-Kiang, from Han-kow to Ping-shan', *Journal of the Royal Geographical Society*, xxxii (1862), pp. 1–25; C. M. Grant, 'Journey from Pekin to St. Petersburg, Across the Desert of Gobi', ibid., xxxiii (1863), pp. 167–77; Alexander Michie, 'Narrative of a Journey from Tientsin to Moukden in Manchuria in July, 1861', ibid., xxxiii (1863), pp. 153–66; Clement Williams, *Through Burmah to Western China: Being notes of a journey in 1863 to establish the practicability of a trade-route between the Irawaddi and the Yang-Tse-Kiang* (London: William Blackwood and Sons, 1863).

9. Elgin's journal, 12 June 1858, quoted in Jack J. Gerson, *Horatio Nelson Lay and Sino-British Relations, 1854–1864* (Cambridge, MA: Harvard East Asian Monographs, 1972), p. 214.

10. George Wingrove Cooke, *China and Lower Bengal* (London: Routledge, Warne, & Routledge, 1861), p. 399.

11. Cooke, *China and Lower Bengal*, p. 411.

12. Christopher Munn, *Anglo-China: Chinese people and British rule in Hong Kong, 1841–1880* (London: Routledge, 2001), pp. 221–6; Chan Yue-shan, 'A Study of the Adoption and Enforcement of Transportation in Hong Kong 1844–1858' (unpublished PhD dissertation, University of Hong Kong, 2006).

13. Roger Daniels, *Asian America: Chinese and Japanese in the United States since 1850* (Seattle: University of Washington Press, 1988), p. 9.

14. John Fitzgerald, *Big White Lie: Chinese Australians in white Australia* (Sydney: University of New South Wales Press, 2007), p. 13.

15. On the paranoia and the realities of resistance and confrontation behind it, see Munn, *Anglo-China*, pp. 275–81.

16. On Ye's intelligence network: J. Y. Wong, *Yeh Ming-ch'en: Viceroy of Liang Kuang 1852–8* (Cambridge: Cambridge University Press, 1976), pp. 175–7.

17. Robert Swinhoe, *Narrative of the North China Campaign of 1860* (London: Smith, Elder and Co., 1861), p. 139.

18. Lt. Col. G. J. Wolseley, *Narrative of the War with China in 1860: To which is added the account of a short residence with the Tai-Ping rebels at Nankin and a voyage from thence to Hankow* (London: Longman, 1862), p. 97; Elgin to Clarendon, 9 February 1859, from *Furious*, off Canton, in *Correspondence relative to the Earl of Elgin's special missions* (1859), p.144.

19. Sir Perceval Griffiths, *The History of the Indian Tea Industry* (London: Weidenfeld and Nicolson, 1967), pp. 41–2, 55–8; Simon Naylor, 'Fieldwork

and the Geographical Career: T. Griffith Taylor and the exploration of Australia', in Simon Naylor and J. Ryan (eds.), *New Spaces of Discovery: Geographies of exploration in the twentieth century* (London: I. B. Tauris, 2009).

20. *NCH*, 25 October 1856, p. 49.

21. *Illustrated London News*, 5 June 1858, pp. 569–70; 27 June 1858, p. 637.

22. Henry Grant, *Incidents in the War in China* (Edinburgh: William Blackwood and Sons, 1875), pp. 29–30, 15.

23. Wolseley, *Narrative of the War with China*, pp. 112–13; Revd R. J. M'Ghee, *How We Got into Pekin: A narrative of the campaign in China of 1860* (London: Richard Bentley, 1862), pp. 103–4. 'A Romance Spoiled' is the heading of one review of D. F. Rennie's *Peking and the Pekingese*, which rebutted the story: *Manchester Times*, 2 December 1865, p. 380.

24. Elgin to Malmesbury, 26 October 1860, *The Times*, 29 December 1860, p. 5.

25. 'Discussion on the China Papers', 8 December 1862, *Proceedings of the Royal Geographical Society of London* 7:1 (1862–3), p. 30.

26. Daniel R. Headrick, *The Invisible Weapon: Telecommunications and international politics, 1851–1945* (New York: Oxford University Press, 1991), pp. 20–24, 40.

27. *Canton Register*, 5 August 1834, p. 121.

28. Freda Harcourt, *Flagships of Imperialism: The P & O Company and the politics of empire from its origins to 1867* (Manchester: Manchester University Press, 2006), pp. 86–113.

29. James Dow journal, 23 July 1851.

30. Thomas W. Blakiston, *Five Months on the Upper Yang-Tze* (London: John Murray, 1862), appendices.

31. Fa-ti Fan, *British Naturalists in Qing China: Science, empire and cultural encounter* (Cambridge, MA: Harvard University Press, 2004), outlines much of this.

32. *NCH*, 5 April 1862, p. 54; Linden Gillbank, 'The Origins of the Acclimatisation Society of Victoria: Practical science in the wake of the gold rush', *Historical Records of Australian Science* 6:3 (1986) pp. 359–73.

33. Blakiston, *Five Months on the Yang-Tze*, p. 355; D. F. Rennie, *The British Arms in North China and Japan: Peking 1860; Kagosima 1862* (London: John Murray, 1864), p. 32.

34. *Illustrated London News*, 20 March 1858, p. 293; see also 26 June 1858, p. 637.

35. He had accompanied Théodore de Lagrené in 1844: Gilbert Gimon, 'Jules Itier, Daguerreotypist', *History of Photography* 5:3 (1981), p. 232.

36. *NCH*, 10 October 1863, p. 631, which in turn amplifies and comments on Rodolphe Lindau, *Un Voyage autour du Japon* (Paris: Librairie de L. Hachette et Cie., 1864), p. 33. The medium was new, but not the content: see Patrick Conner, *George Chinnery, 1774–1852: Artist of India and the China coast* (Woodbridge: Antique Collectors' Club, 1993), p. 265, plate 106, for a copy of Ingres' *Grande Odalisque* painted in Lam Qua's studio at Canton.

37. Robert Fortune, *A Journey to the Tea Countries of China* (London: John Murray, 1852), pp. 1–2.

38. Anon., *The Englishman in China* (London: Saunders, Otley, and Co.), pp. 135–6.

39. R. W. Little to parents, 19 April 1865, Little papers.

40. D. R. MacGregor, *The Tea Clippers* (London: Conway Maritime Press, 1972), pp. 50–51, 61–2. The triumph of sail in the nineteenth century is outlined in Gerald S. Graham, 'The Ascendancy of the Sailing Ship 1850–85', *Economic History Review* NS 9:1 (1956), pp. 74–88.

41. Alexander Michie, *The Englishman in China During the Victorian Era* (Edinburgh: William Blackwood & Sons, 1900), i, p. 238.

42. H. Hamilton Lindsay, *Is the War with China a Just One?* (London: James Ridgway, 1840), p. 3.

43. Andrew S. Cook, 'Establishing the Sea Routes to India and China: Stages in the development of hydrographical knowledge', in Huw V. Bowen, Margarette Lincoln and Nigel Rigby (eds.), *The Worlds of the East India Company* (Woodbridge: Boydell & Brewer, 2002), pp. 119–36; Charles Rathbone Low, *History of the Indian Navy 1613–1863* (London: Richard Bentley & Son, 1877), i, pp. 394–6; L. S. Dawson (comp.), *Memoirs of Hydrography* (Eastbourne: Henry W. Kay, 1885), pp. 30–33, 36–7; *China Surveys* (PP 149) (1857); Sir Archibald Day, *The Admiralty Hydrographic Service 1795–1919* (London: HMSO, 1967), pp. 62–3, 68; Jim Burton, 'Nineteenth Century Meteorological Observatories of the British Army', in Joan M. Kenworthy and J. Malcolm Walker (eds.), *Colonial Observatories and Observations: Meteorology and geophysics* (Durham: Department of Geography, University of Durham Occasional papers 31, 1997), pp. 59–65. Rees is mentioned in James Horsburgh, *The India Directory: Or directions for sailing to and from the East Indies, China, Australia . . .* 6th edition (London: Wm H. Allen, 1852), ii, p. 488.

44. Lt. M. F. Maury, *Explanations and Sailing Directions to Accompany the Wind and Current Charts* (Washington, DC: C. Alexander, 1851). On Maury's work, see Steven J. Dick, *Sky and Ocean Joined: The US Naval Observatory, 1830–2000* (Cambridge: Cambridge University Press, 2002), pp. 60–117.

45. Horsburgh, *India Directory*, pp. 281–2.

46. Michie, *Englishman in China*, i, p. 258; Wm Fred. Mayers, N. B. Dennys and Chas. King, *The Treaty Ports of China and Japan* (London: Trübner & Co., 1867), appendix, p. v.; James Dow journal, 20 June 1851, 1 December 1851.

47. *NCH*, 3 May 1851, p. 159; 21 January 1860, p. 11; 1 April 1865, pp. 50–51.

48. Rennie, *British Arms in North China*, p. 4; W. A. P. Martin, *The Awakening of China* (New York: Doubleday, Page & Company, 1907), p. 167; 'The Disaster in China', *The Times*, 16 September 1859, p. 10.

49. Eldon Griffin, *Clippers and Consuls: American consular and commercial relations with Eastern Asia, 1845–1860* (Ann Arbor: Edwards Brothers, 1939), pp. 180–82.

50. Thomas Hanbury to Daniel Hanbury, 3 August 1865, *Letters of Sir Thomas Hanbury* (London: West, Newman & Co., 1913), p. 124.

51. Alasdair Moore, *La Mortola: In the footsteps of Thomas Hanbury* (London: Cadogan Guides, 2004).

52. Charles M. Dyce, *Personal Reminiscences of Thirty Years' Residence in the Model Settlement Shanghai, 1870–1900* (London: Chapman & Hall, 1906), p. 3.

53. *The Times*, 12 September 1864, p. 6; E. C. M. Bowra diary, *c*.7 May 1863, SOAS, PPMS 69, box 2.

54. Michie, *Englishman in China*, i., pp. 220–23.

55. TNA: Shanghai no. 118, 31 December 1855, FO 228/196; Shanghai no. 149, 23 November 1857, FO 228/243; Shanghai no. 103, 28 June 1856, FO 228/2200; Shanghai no. 78, 29 May 1857, FO 228/242; *Commercial Reports from Her Majesty's Consuls in China 1862–64* (PP 3489) (1865), p. 153.

56. *NCH*, 25 August 1860, p. 134; Charles Alexander Gordon, *China from a Medical Point of View in 1860 and 1861* (London: John Churchill, 1863), p. 83.

57. Extracted from *NCH*, 1 September, enclosure no. 5 in no. 72, *Correspondence Respecting Affairs in China 1859–60* (PP 2754), pp. 137–44.

58. T. P. Crawford, letter of 3 October 1861 quoted in John A. Rapp, 'Clashing Dilemmas: Hong Rengan, Issachar Roberts, and a Taiping "Murder" Mystery', *Journal of Historical Biography* 4 (2008), p. 40. Rapp also has an extended discussion on Roberts' poor Chinese.

59. Lin-le [Augustus F. Lindley], *Ti-ping Tien-kwoh: The history of the Ti-ping revolution* (London: Day & Son, 1866), p. viii.

60. *Correspondence Respecting the Opening of the Yang-Tse-Kiang River to Foreign Trade* (PP 2840) (1861), pp. 22, 28.

61. Ibid., pp. 32–3.

62. On these forces, see Richard J. Smith, *Mercenaries and Mandarins: The Ever-Victorious Army in nineteenth century China* (Millwood: KTO Press, 1978).

63. *The Times*, 5 August 1864, p. 6; see also 16 March 1865, p. 8.

64. The standard account of the episode is Gerson, *Horatio Nelson Lay.*

65. The Borneo solution seems in fact to have been Osborn's suggestion: 'Discussion on the China Papers', 8 December 1862, *Proceedings of the Royal Geographical Society of London* 7:1 (1862–3), pp. 32–5.

66. R. W. Little to parents, 24 November 1864; Frederick Bruce to Harry Parkes, 2 January 1864, quoted in Gerson, *Horatio Nelson Lay*, p. 207.

67. A. Michie to R. C. Antrobus, 2 September 1862, D(W) 1920/5, SRO; Stanley F. Wright, *Hart and the Chinese Customs* (Belfast: William Mullen and Son for Queen's University, Belfast, 1950), p. 249.

68. *NCH*, 19 July 1862, p. 108; 13 September 1862, unnumbered page.

69. *NCH*, 11 April 1863, p. 58; Burlingame to Secretary of State, 3 June 1864 and enclosures: *Papers Relating to Foreign Affairs Accompanying the Annual Message of the President to the Second Session Thirty-eighth Congress* (Washington, DC: US Government Printing Office, 1864), iii, pp. 400–419. The surname was also given as Berkeley; Williams and White: Burlingame to Secretary of State, 1 and 2 June 1864 and enclosures, ibid., pp. 392–9.

70. Shanghai no. 148, 19 December 1863, no. 30, FO 228; 2 April 1864, FO 367, TNA; 'Shanghae police sheets, 1863', TNA, FO 97/111.

71. Kerrie L. Macpherson, *A Wilderness of Marshes: The origins of public health in Shanghai, 1843–1893* (Hong Kong: Oxford University Press, 1987), p. 30.

72. Ibid., p.19.

73. E. S. Elliston, *Shantung Road Cemetery Shanghai 1846–1868* (Shanghai: Millington, 1946), pp. 44–5; Sir Rutherford Alcock, *The Capital of the Tycoon: A narrative of three years' residence in Japan* (London: Longman, Green, Longman, Roberts, & Green, 1863), i, p. 60.

74. John Ashton (Shanghai) to R. C. Antrobus, 21 June 1866, SRO, D(W)1920/5/6.

75. Thomas Gerard, letter of 15 November 1852, quoted in Sir Clement Wakefield Jones, *Chief Officer in China* (Liverpool: Charles Birchall and Sons, 1955), p. 110.

76. R. W. Little letters, 17 May 1865, 8 April 1865.

77. Customs recruit E. C. M. Bowra: diary, 23 March 1863, SOAS, PPMS 69, box 2.

78. On the firm's shipping, see Edward Kenneth Haviland, 'American Steam

Navigation in China, 1845–1878, Part VI', *American Neptune* 17: 4 (1957), pp. 302–4. On Antrobus: J. H. Haan, 'The Shanghai Municipal Council, 1854–1865: Some biographical notes', *Journal of the Hong Kong Branch of the Royal Asiatic Society*, 24 (1988), pp. 210–11.

79. Thomas Hanbury to Daniel Hanbury, 3 August 1865, *Letters of Sir Thomas Hanbury*, p. 124; see Bowra on Dents's in Tianjin: diary, 12 June 1863, SOAS, PPMS 69, box 2; H. H. Lindsay to Sir Edmund Antrobus, 24 September 1865, SRO, D(W)1920/5/4; Lindsay to R. C. Antrobus, 26 May 1865, D(W)1920/5/3.

80. W. H. M., 'Reminiscences of the Opening of Shanghae to Foreign Trade', *Chinese and Japanese Repository*, 2 (1864), pp. 85–7.

81. On this see, e.g., Thomas G. Rawski, 'Chinese Dominance of Treaty Port Commerce and Its Implications, 1860–1875', *Explorations in Economic History* 7:1–2 (1969), pp. 451–73; and Yen-p'ing Hao, *The Commercial Revolution in China: The rise of Sino-Western mercantile capitalism* (Berkeley: University of California Press, 1986), pp. 212–76.

82. H. H. Lindsay to mother, draft, 'Amoy', April 1832, SRO, D(W)1920/4/1; 'Contents of the Packages addressed to H. H. Lindsay, Esq.', SRO, D(W) 1920 4/3.

7 A THE HEART OF THE HEART OF EMPIRE

1. Gideon Nye, *Morning of My Life, in China* (Canton: [privately published] 1873), p. 71; and *'Peking the Goal; – The sole hope of peace* (Canton: 1873) pp. 3–4, 83–4.

2. *London and China Telegraph*, 13 February 1866, pp. 83–4; Wm Fred. Mayers, N. B. Dennys and Chas. King, *The Treaty Ports of China and Japan* (London: Trübner & Co., 1867) pp. 131–4; H. S. S. (comp.), *Diary of Events and the Progress on Shameen*, 1859–1938 (Hong Kong: Ye Old Printerie, 1938); Jonathan A. Farris, 'Thirteen Factories of Canton: An architecture of Sino-Western collaberation and confrontation', *Buildings and Landscapes* 14 (2007); Parkes to William Lockhart, 11 October 1859, to Mrs Parkes, 8 September 1861, in Stanley Lane-Poole, *The Life of Sir Harry Parkes* (London: Macmillan and Co., 1894), i, pp. 317–18, 445–6.

3. Mayers, *Treaty Ports of China and Japan*, pp. 390–91.

4. Shanghai Muncipal Archives (ed.), *Minutes of the Shanghai Municipal Council* (Shanghai: Shanghai guji chubanshe, 2001), ii, 10 October 1865.

5. Richard S. Horowitz, 'Central Power and State Making: The Zongli yamen

and self-strengthening in China, 1860–1880' (unpublished PhD thesis, Harvard University, 1998), p. 57.

6. For a full account of the establishing of the office and its activities, see Horowitz, 'Central Power and State Making', and Jennifer Rudolph, *Negotiated Power in late Imperial China: The Zongli yamen and the politics of reform* (Ithaca: Cornell University East Asia Program, 2008).

7. Masataka Banno, *China and the West, 1858–1861: The origins of the Tsungli yamen* (Cambridge, MA: Harvard University Press, 1964), p. 220.

8. Bowra diary, 11 June 1863, SOAS, PPMS 69, box 2.

9. Katherine F. Bruner, John K. Fairbank, Richard J. Smith (eds.), *Entering China's Service: Robert Hart's journals, 1854–1863* (Cambridge, MA: Harvard University Asia Center, 1986), entries of 9 May, 6 June, 1863, pp. 263–6; H. N. Lay, *Our Interests in China* (London: Robert Hardwicke, [1864]), pp. 19–20.

10. Hart's description, letter to C. Hannen, 9 August 1861, quoted in H. B. Morse, *The International Relations of the Chinese Empire: ii, The period of submission, 1861–1893* (London: Longmans, Green & Co., 1918), p. 58.

11. Lease in SOAS, Lay papers, vol. 2, dated 10 May 1864, for Deacons, Ewhurst, Surrey. His latter career is most notable for an attempted fraud on the Japanese government; Bowra diary, 25 November 1863, SOAS, PPMS 69, box 2.

12. D. F. Rennie, *Peking and the Pekingese During the First Year of the British Embassy at Peking* (London: John Murray, 1865), i, p. 264.

13. Bruner, Fairbank, Smith (eds.), *Entering China's Service*, entry of 6 June 1863, p. 264.

14. Ibid., entries of 18 July 1858, 3 July 1858.

15. See, for example, Matthew Brown, *Adventuring through Spanish Colonies: Simón Bolívar, foreign mercenaries and the birth of new nations* (Liverpool: Liverpool University Press, 2006).

16. Bruner, Fairbank, Smith (eds.), *Entering China's Service*, entry of 9 October 1854.

17. Ibid., entries of 7, 19, 29 October 1854; Richard J. Smith, John K. Fairbank, Katherine F. Bruner (eds.), *Robert Hart and China's Early Modernization: His journals, 1863–1866* (Cambridge, MA: Harvard University Asia Center, 1991), entry of 14 August 1864. There is no comprehensive modern biography of Hart. These two volumes contain much useful information, as does Stanley F. Wright, *Hart and the Chinese Customs* (Belfast: William Mullen and Son for Queen's University, Belfast, 1950). On Hart's Irish background and connections, see Richard O'Leary, 'Sir Robert Hart in

China: The significance of his Irish roots', *Modern Asian Studies*, 40:3 (2006), pp. 583–604.

18. Hart to Lay, 20 August 1868, SOAS, Add MS 72819, Lay papers, vol. 1; Wenxiang: Smith, Fairbank, Bruner (eds.), *Robert Hart and China's Early Modernization*, entry of 4 August 1866.

19. On Hart's 'Bystander's View' see Smith, Fairbank, Bruner (eds.), *Robert Hart and China's Early Modernization*, pp. 282–93.

20. Queen's University Belfast, Library Special Collections [QUB], Sir Robert Hart collection, MS 15/1/9, journal, 27 March 1867.

21. Richard S. Horowitz, 'Mandarins and Customs Inspectors: Western imperialism in nineteenth-century China reconsidered', *Papers on Chinese History* 7 (1998), pp. 41–57.

22. Horowitz, 'Central Power and State Making', p. 220.

23. Such as the judge at the British supreme court at Shanghai, Sir Edmund Hornby: *An Autobiography* (London: Constable & Co., 1929), pp. 238–9.

24. IG Circular no.8/64, 21 June 1864, in *Inspector-General's Circulars. First series: 1861–1875* (Shanghai: Statistical Department of the Inspectorate General, 1879), pp. 54–60.

25. For Martin's own, sketchy account of the college, see his *A Cycle of Cathay* 3rd edition (New York: Fleming H. Revell, 1900), pp. 293–327.

26. Knight Biggerstaff, *The Earliest Modern Government Schools in China* (Ithaca: Cornell University Press, 1961); Thomas L. Kennedy, 'The Establishment of Modern Military Industry in China 1860–1868', *Jindaishi yanjiusuo qikan* 4 (1974), pp. 779–823; Steven A. Leibo, *Transferring Technology to China: Prosper Giquel and the Self-strengthening movement* (Berkeley: Institute of East Asian Studies, Center for Chinese Studies, 1985); David Wright, 'Making Space for Science in China: John Fryer and the Shanghai Polytechnic', *British Journal for the History of Science* 29:1 (1996), pp. 1–16, and chapter 4 of his *Translating Science: The transmission of Western chemistry into late imperial China, 1840–1900* (Leiden: Brill, 2000).

27. Hart to Lay, 20 August 1868, SOAS, Add MS 72819, Lay papers, vol. 1.

28. Hart to Campbell, 14 March 1873, no. 49, in John King Fairbank, Katherine Frost Bruner, Elizabeth Macleod Matheson (eds.), *The IG in Peking: Letters of Robert Hart, Chinese Maritime Customs 1868–1907* (Cambridge, MA: The Belknap Press of Harvard University Press, 1975).

29. Hart to Marquess of Salisbury, 26 August 1885, in *Documents Illustrative of the Origin, Development, and Activities of the Chinese Customs Service* (Shanghai: Statistical Department of the Inspectorate General of Customs, 1938), vi, p. 544.

30. QUB, MS, 15/1/9, Hart journal, 10 January 1867.

31. Ibid., 17 January 1867.

32. Ibid., 12 July; 14 March, 3 March, 22 February 1867.

33. I. G. Circular, 2/75, 12 January 1875, *Inspector-General's Circulars*, p. 598.

34. *The Times*, 1 November 1873, p. 4.

35. Paul Greenhalgh, *Ephemeral Vistas: The* expositions universelles, *great exhibitions, and world's fairs, 1851–1939* (Manchester: Manchester University Press, 1988), p. 226 and *passim*; Peter H. Hoffenberg, *An Empire on Display: English, Indian, and Australian exhibitions from the Crystal Palace to the Great War* (Berkeley: University of California Press, 2001).

36. Robert Fortune, *Yedo and Peking: A narrative of a journey to the capitals of Japan and China* (London: John Murray, 1868), p. 353.

37. Rennie, *Peking and the Pekingese*, pp. 55–6; A. B. Freeman-Mitford, *The Attaché in Peking* (London: Macmillan & Co., 1900), pp. 66–7.

38. Rennie, *Peking and the Pekingese*, i, pp. 94–5; Satow diary, 2 May 1862, TNA, PRO 30/33/15/1; see also Mrs Hugh [Mary] Fraser, *A Diplomatist's Wife in Many Lands* (New York: Dodd Mead & Company, 1910), ii, p. 182.

39. 'A British Resident in Peking', *British Memorials in Peking* (Tianjin: Tientsin Press Ltd, 1927).

40. *The Times*, 14 October 1863, p. 9.

41. *Guide for Tourists to Peking and its Environs* (Tianjin: The Tientsin Press, 1897), p. 33.

42. Bruce on Peking, letter to Lord Elgin, 24 September 1862, quoted in Jack J. Gerson, *Horatio Nelson Lay and Sino-British Relations, 1854–1864* (Cambridge, MA: Harvard East Asian Monographs, 1972), p. 148; J. S. Gregory, *Great Britain and the Taipings* (New York: Praeger, 1969), pp. 111–16; Banno, *China and the West*, p. 243; Samuel S. Kim, 'Burlingame and the Inauguration of the Co-operative Policy', *Modern Asian Studies* 5:4 (1971), pp. 337–54.

43. Smith, Fairbank, Bruner (eds.), *Robert Hart and China's Early Modernization*, entry for 16 July 1864, and commentary, pp. 288–9.

44. For one take on the student view, see 'A Student Interpreter' [W. H. Wilkinson], *'Where Chineses Drive': English student life at Peking* (London: W. H. Allen & Co., 1885), chapter 3; P. D. Coates, *The China Consuls: British consular officers in China* (Hong Kong: Oxford University Press, 1988) pp. 336–7.

45. Hornby, *Autobiography*, p. 227; 'A Student Interpreter', *'Where Chineses Drive'*, pp. 154–69; N. B. Dennys, *Notes for Tourists in the North of China* (Hong Kong: A. Shortrede & Co., 1866), p. 36; Freeman-Mitford, *Attaché in Peking*, p. 119.

46. Burlingame to Secretary of State, 2 June 1864: *Papers Relating to Foreign Affairs Accompanying the Annual Message of the President to the Second Session Thirty-eighth Congress* (Washington, DC: Government Printing Office, 1864) iii, pp. 395–6.

47. Coates, *China Consuls*, pp. 292–7; QUB, MS 15/1/9 Hart journal 1867, *passim*, re Meadows and MacPherson.

48. Horowitz, 'Central Power and State Making', pp. 261–77.

49. Burlingame to Secretary of State, 14 November 1867 and enclosures: *Papers Relating to Foreign Affairs Accompanying the Annual Message of the President to the Second Session Fortieth Congress* (Washington, DC: Government Printing Office, 1868), i, pp. 512–15; Warren B. Walsh, 'A Visit to the Tsungli Yamen', *Pacific Historical Review* 14:4 (1945), pp. 452–4.

50. QUB, MS 15/1/9, Hart journal, 10 April 1867. The mission is discussed in Knight Biggerstaff, 'The Official Chinese Attitude Toward the Burlingame Mission', *American Historical Review* 41:4 (1936), pp. 682–702; Immanuel C. Y. Hsü, *China's Entrance into the Family of Nations: The diplomatic phase, 1858–1880* (Cambridge: Harvard East Asian Studies, 1960), pp. 167–71; Mary C. Wright, *The Last Stand of Chinese Conservatism: The T'ung-Chih restoration, 1862–1874* (New York: Atheneum, 1966 [1957]), pp. 277–9; useful contemporary material is also in Frederick Wells Williams, *Anson Burlingame and the First Chinese Mission to Foreign Powers* (New York: Charles Scribner's Sons, 1912).

51. QUB, MS 15/1/11, Hart journal, 14 November 1868, 17 September 1868, 26 October 1868.

52. Text is in Godfey E. P. Hertslet, *Treaties etc, Between Great Britain and China and Between China and Foreign Powers*, 3rd edition (London: HMSO, 1908), i, pp. 554–7; Williams to Seward, 12 April 1866 and enclosures, *Papers Relating to Foreign Affairs Accompanying the Annual Message of the President to the Second Session Thirty-ninth Congress* (Washington, DC: Government Printing Office, 1867), i, pp. 507–10.

53. For a sustained example, see Johannes von Gumpach, *The Burlingame Mission* (Shanghai: [no publisher], 1872). Gumpach was embroiled in litigation with Robert Hart over his dismissal from a post at the Tongwenguan, and this 900-page book was also part of his vituperative assault on Hart. The case went to the privy council in England, and there established the principle that a British subject in foreign employ was not answerable to the consular courts for his official acts: see Wright, *Hart and the Chinese Customs*, pp. 334–52.

54. Katherine F. Bruner, John K. Fairbank, Richard J. Smith (eds.), *Entering*

China's Service: Robert Hart's journals 1854–1863 (Cambridge, MA: Harvard University Asia Center, 1986), 5 April 1866; on the mission, see Knight Biggerstaff, 'The First Chinese Mission of Investigation Sent to Europe', *Pacific Historical Review*, 6:4 (1937), pp. 307–20; Smith, Fairbank, Bruner (eds.), *Robert Hart and China's Early Modernization*, pp. 348–61.

55. *The Times*, 28 September 1865, p. 6. Chang later performed in Australia and for P. T. Barnum in the United States. He married a Liverpool-born woman, eventually opening a tea and curio shop in Bournemouth, where he died in 1893.

56. *China Mail*, undated cutting in Bowra scrapbook, SOAS, PPMS 69, box 2.

57. Quoted in QUB, MS 15/1/11, Hart journal, 8 January 1869.

58. Rennie, *Peking and the Pekingese*, ii, pp. 226–8.

59. Angela Ki Che Leung, 'The Business of Vaccination in Nineteenth-Century Canton', *Late Imperial China* 29:1 (2008), pp. 7–39.

60. SOAS, MS 380645: Lockhart correspondence, letters of 24 September 1861, 3 January 1864; William Lockhart, *First Report of the London Missionary Society's Chinese Hospital, at Peking* [Peking: 1862]; *Second Report of the London Missionary Society's Chinese Hospital, at Peking Under the Care of W. Lockhart, F.R.C.S.* (Shanghai: London Mission Press, 1864); *The Fourth Report of the Peking Hospital, in Connexion with the London Missionary Society, Under the Care of John Dudgeon, M.D.C.M., for the year 1865* (Shanghai: Presbyterian Mission Press, 1865), pp. 1–2.

61. *Records of the General Conference of the Protestant Missionaries of China Held at Shanghai, May 7–20, 1890* (Shanghai: American Presbyterian Mission Press, 1890), p. xxiii.

62. Letters to Lockhart of 22 November 1861, 10 May 1862, quoted in Lane-Poole, *Life of Sir Harry Parkes* i, pp. 462–3, 471–2.

63. On the morphology of the city, see Susan Naquin's richly detailed *Peking: Temples and City Life: 1400–1900* (Berkeley: University of California Press, 2000).

64. More comfort was to be had by the more leisurely route along the river to Tongzhou: Alexander Michie, *The Siberian Overland Route from Peking to Petersburg* (London, John Murray, 1864), p. 23; Dennys, *Notes for Tourists*, pp. 10–11.

65. Ibid., p. 38.

66. J. L. Cranmer-Byng (ed.), *An Embassy to China: Being the journal kept by Lord Macartney during his embassy to the Emperor Ch'ien-lung 1793–1794* (London: Longmans, 1962), p. 156; Susan Legouix, *Image of China: William Alexander* (London: Jupiter Books, 1980), plate 30, 'Ping-tze

Muen', pp. 52–3; John Barrow, *Travels in China* (London: T. Cadell and W. Davies, 1804), i, pp. 92–3.

67. QUB, MS 15/1/9, Hart journal, 15 May 1867, 23 July 1867.

68. Regine Thiriez, *Barbarian Lens: Western photographers of the Qianlong emperor's European palaces* (Amsterdam: Gordon and Breach, 1998), pp. 75–83.

69. Dennys, *Notes for Tourists*, p. 13.

70. Thiriez, *Barbarian Lens*.

71. On Thomson, see Richard Ovenden, *John Thomson (1837–1921), Photographer* (Edinburgh: National Library of Scotland/The Stationary Office, 1997); Nick Pearce, *Photographs of Peking, China 1861–1908: An inventory and description of the Yetts Collection at the University of Durham. Through Peking with a camera* (Lewiston: The Edwin Mellen Press, 2005), pp. 36–42.

72. Caption to John Thomson, *Illustrations of China and Its People* (London: Sampson Low, Marston, Low, and Searle, 1873), ii, plate VIII; John Thomson, *Through China with a Camera* (Westminster: A. Constable & Co., 1898), p. 93.

73. [John Thomson], 'Three pictures in Wong-Nei-Chung', *The China Magazine* (September 1862), pp. 52–6, quotations pp. 53, 56.

74. Oliver Moore, 'Zu Boqi on Vision and Photography in Nineteenth-Century China', in Kenneth J. Hammond and Kristin Stapleton (eds.), *The Human Tradition in Modern China* (Lanham: Rowman & Littlefield, 2007), pp. 33–53. Chinese photographs: see those of Lai Afong in National Library of China and British Library (eds.), *Western Eyes: Historical photographs of China in British collections, 1860–1930*, i, (Peking: Guojia tushuguan chubanshe, 2008), pp. 200–298.

75. Captions to *Illustrations of China and Its People*, iv, plate XII.

76. Satow diary, 14 April 1862, TNA, PRO 30/33/15/1; Fraser, *Diplomatist's Wife*, pp. 111–12.

77. Rennie, *Peking and the Pekingese*, i, p. 292.

78. Pearce, *Photographs of Peking, China 1861–1908*, pp. 43–62.

79. Osbert Lancaster, *All Done from Memory* [1953] (London: John Murray, 1963), p. 105.

80. *Minutes of the SMC*, ii, 10 February 1866; 7 June 1865.

81. Ibid., 27 July 1864.

82. Ge Yuanxu, *Huyou zaji* [Miscellaneous notes on travelling in Shanghai] (1876) (reprinted Shanghai: Shanghai guji chubanshe, 1989) p. 3; *Shanghae Evening Courier*, 20 July 1869, p. 979; 30 September 1869, p. 1227.

83. *Minutes of the SMC*, ii, 11 November 1865; 10 January 1866; iii, 11 March 1867; Shanghai Municipal Archives [SMA], U1-1-683, 'General

1864', Consul Winchester to Secretary, 13 October 1865. A copy of the notification issued to residents is in vol. 67 of the J. O. P. Bland papers, Thomas Fisher Rare Books Library, University of Toronto (hereafter referred to as 'J. O. P. Bland papers').

84. Lan Li and Deidre Wildy, 'A New Discovery and Its Significance: The statutory declarations made by Sir Robert Hart concerning his secret domestic life in 19th century China', *Journal of the Hong Kong Branch of the Royal Asiatic Society* 43 (2003), pp. 63–87.

85. J. O. P. Bland papers, 'Memoirs', chapter 2, p. 6.

86. Edward Henderson, *A Report on Prostitution in Shanghai* (Shanghai: printed at the North China Herald Office, 1871), pp. 16–17, 11. Five years later the police calculated there were 312 Chinese women working as prostitutes receiving foreigners: *NCH*, 2 March 1888, p. 245.

87. Alasdair Moore, *La Mortola: In the footsteps of Thomas Hanbury* (London: Cadogan Guides, 2004), pp. 194–9; information on Hunter from Thomas N. Layton, 'China Mail: Commerce and conscience in an American family', ms. in preparation, 2010; Mrs Archibald Little [A. E. N. Bewicke], *A Marriage in China* (London: F. V. White & Co., 1896), p. 305.

88. *Minutes of the SMC*, ii, 18 January 1866.

89. Hornby, *Autobiography*, pp. 288–90; H. Lang, *Shanghai Considered Socially* (Shanghai: American Presbyterian Mission Press, 1875), p. 56.

90. W. A. P. Martin alludes to 'the son of an MP' ostracized for having married a low-class Chinese woman, *Cycle of Cathay*, p. 99.

91. He was also obsessed with dental hygiene, boasted he could extract a hundred teeth an hour, and had pulled some 21,000 by 1895: George Leslie Mackay, *From Far Formosa: The island, its people and missions* (Edinburgh and London: Oliphant Anderson and Ferrier, 1900), pp. 315–16; Alvyn J. Austin, *Saving China: Canadian missionaries in the Middle Kingdom, 1888–1959* (Toronto: University of Toronto Press, 1986), pp. 30–35.

92. Lambeth Palace archives: Holy Trinity Shanghai, marriage registers, vol. 2, Mss.1565, 24 April 1866, 21 June 1867; baptism registers, vol. 3, ms. 1576, 6 October 1889.

93. Moore, *La Mortola*, p. 189; F. L. Hawks-Pott, *A Short History of Shanghai* (Shanghai: Kelly & Walsh, Ltd., 1928), p. 119; [J. D. Clark], *Sketches In and Around Shanghai* (Shanghai: Shanghai Mercury, 1894), pp. 120–21; William T. Rowe, *Hankow: Commerce and society in a Chinese city, 1796–1895* (Stanford: Stanford University Press, 1984) p. 50.

94. Hanbury, letter to his father, 16 June 1871, *Letters of Sir Thomas Hanbury* (London: West, Newman & Co., 1913), p. 223.

95. Hart to Campbell, 29 October 1883, no. 442, *IG in Peking*, i; Bruner, Smith, Fairbank (eds.), *Entering China's Service*, pp. 230–31.

96. James Dow journal, 18 December 1851; *Hong Kong Government Gazette*, 27 May 1854, p. 143. They are digested for Shanghai in J. H. Haan, *The Sino-Western Miscellany: Being historical notes about foreign life in China. Vol.1, Thalia and Terpsichore on the Yangtze* [sic]: *Foreign Theatre and Music in Shanghai, 1850–1865; a survey and calendar of performances*, 2nd edition (Amsterdam: unnamed publisher, 1993).

97. Chen-zen Hung, 'Travelling Opera Troupes in Shanghai, 1842–1949' (unpublished PhD thesis, The Catholic University of America, 1997).

98. Han Kuo-huang, 'Zhongguo diyi ge Xiyang guanxian yuedui – Beijing Hede yuedui' [The first Chinese brass band – Hart's Chinese Band] *Yinyue Yanjiu*, 1990: 2, pp. 43–53; Hart to Campbell, 1 September 1889, no. 715, *IG in Peking*, i; Juliet Bredon, *Robert Hart: The romance of a great career* (London: Hutchinson, 1909), pp. 184–8. The inspectorate-general was relocated to a site in the Legation quarter, close by the French Legation, in 1879: 5 October 1879, no. 260, *IG in Peking*, i, pp. 305–6.

99. *Minutes of the SMC*, ii, 31 August 1863, 10 February 1866, 8 May 1866.

100. Ye Xiaoqing, *The Dianshizhai Pictorial: Shanghai urban life, 1844–1898* (Ann Arbor: Center for Chinese Studies, University of Michigan, 2003) p. 132.

101. *History of the Shanghai Recreation Fund, from 1860–1882 . . .* (Shanghai: Celestial Empire, 1882), pp. 192–5.

102. Henry Brougham Loch, *Personal Narrative of Occurrences During Lord Elgin's Second Embassy to China in 1860* (London: John Murray, 1869), p. 189; Hornby, *Autobiography*, pp. 227–8; *The Journey of Augustus Raymond Margary, from Shanghae, to Bhamo, and back to Manwyne* (London: Macmillan & Co., 1876), p. xvi.

8 INLAND DREAMS

1. The episode and Zhang's statement are recounted in correspondence between Wade and the Zongli Yamen, and Wade and the foreign secretary in TNA, FO 682/2049, and *China No.1: Papers relating to the massacre of Europeans at Tien-Tsin on the 21st June, 1870* (PP 248) (1871), pp. 154–6.

2. On the Tianjin massacre, see John K. Fairbank, 'Patterns Behind the Tientsin Massacre', *Harvard Journal of Asiatic Studies* 20:3/4, pp. 480–511; Paul A. Cohen, *China and Christianity: The missionary movement and the growth of Chinese antiforeignism, 1860–1870* (Cambridge, MA: Harvard University

Press, 1963), pp. 229–61. Much detail is also drawn from Tianjin despatch no. 52, 16 July 1870, in Second Historical Archives of China (Nanjing), Chinese Maritime Customs Service Archives [hereafter SHAC] 692(2), 1928; *China No. 1* (1871); Henri Cordier, *Histoire des relations de la Chine avec les puissances occidentales, 1860–1900* (Paris: Felix Alcan, 1901), i, pp. 347–90; Baron de Hübner, *A Ramble Round the World*, vol.ii, translated by Lady Herbert (London: MacMillan & Co., 1872), and *Notices et documents sur les Prêtres de la Mission et les Filles de la Charité de S. Vincente de Paul* (Paris: 1893). See also, notably, Henrietta Harrison, '"A Penny for the Little Chinese": The French Holy Childhood Association in China, 1843–1951', *American Historical Review* 113:1 (2008), pp. 72–92.

3. Description from No. 3. Dennys, *Notes for Tourists in the North of China* (Hong Kong: A. Shortrede & Co., 1866), p. 8.

4. Cohen, *China and Christianity*, p. 58.

5. Harrison, '"A Penny for the Little Chinese"', p. 86.

6. Daniel H. Bays, 'Christianity and the Chinese Sectarian Tradition', *Late Imperial China* 4:7 (1982), pp. 35–55.

7. Bishop of Victoria to Earl of Clarendon, 6 December 1869, in *China No.9: Correspondence respecting inland residence of English missionaries in China* (C.89) (1869), p. 43; J. Edkins letter, 22 August 1871, SOAS, CWM/LMS, North China letters, box 2.

8. Letter to Daniel Hanbury, 27 April 1854, *Letters of Sir Thomas Hanbury* (London: West, Newman & Co., 1913), p. 47.

9. There is a dearth of scholarship on the CIM that is uninflected by faith, but a useful survey is Alvyn Austin, *China's Millions: The China Inland Mission and late Qing society, 1832–1905* (Grand Rapids: William B. Eerdmans Publishing, 2007). More hagiographical but still informative work includes A. J. Broomhall's 7-volume biography, *Hudson Taylor and China's Open Century* (1981–89). Broomhall was Taylor's great-nephew.

10. My account of the Yangzhou episode comes from *China No.2: Correspondence respecting the attack on British Protestant missionaries at Yang-Chow-Foo, August 1868* (PP 4097-1) (1869), pp. 77–8, and Cohen, *China and Christianity*, pp. 180–99.

11. For a discussion on this controversial interpolation, see Cohen, *China and Christianity*, pp. 298–9, n. 13.

12. *The Times*: editorials, 3 December 1868, p. 9, 11 January 1869, p. 6; parliamentary intelligence, 10 March 1869, p. 6; editorial, 10 March 1869, p. 8.

13. Secretary, LMS to Clarendon, 5 February 1869; E. Hammond to secretary, LMS, 10 February 1869, *China No. 2* (1869), pp. 77–8.

14. J. Edkins letter, 2 July 1869, SOAS, CWM/LMS, North China letters, box 2.

15. S. Wells Williams, *List of Protestant Missionaries Sent to the Chinese* (Canton: 1 July 1855); *Directory of Protestant Missionaries in China, June 1st 1866* (Fuzhou: American Methodist Episcopal Press, 1866).

16. The exchanges are reproduced in *China No.9* (1869). The last phrase is from Hankou LMS missionary Griffith John, from 1868: R. Wardlaw Thomson, *Griffith John: The story of 50 years in China* (London: Religious Tract Society, 1906), p. 244.

17. Taylor to Alcock, 28 December 1869, in *China No.10: Further correspondence respecting the attack on British Protestant missionaries at Yang-Chow-Foo, August 1868* (PP 4097) (1869), p. 17. The same claim is made in an 18 November 1868 letter extracted in the *Occasional Papers of the China Inland Mission*, nos. 3–4, p. 240.

18. J. Edkins letter, 12 August 1870, SOAS, CWM/LMS, North China letters, box 2.

19. QUB, MS 15/1/11, Hart journal, 2 March 1869; Cohen, *China and Christianity*, pp. 177–8.

20. Letter no. 16, 21 July 1870, in John King Fairbank, Katherine Frost Bruner, Elizabeth Macleod Matheson (eds.), *The IG in Peking: Letters of Robert Hart, Chinese Maritime Customs 1868–1907* (Cambridge, MA: The Belknap Press of Harvard University Press, 1975) p. 57. The course of the diplomatic fallout is narrated in James C. Cooley, *T. F. Wade in China: Pioneer in global diplomacy 1842–1882* (Leiden: E. J. Brill, 1981), pp. 69–80.

21. Shanghai Municipal Archives (eds.), *Minutes of the Shanghai Municipal Council* (Shanghai: Shanghai guji chubanshe, 2001), iv, for 2, 11, 18, 25 July, 22 August, 26 September, 10 October 1870.

22. Contemporary references to this include Daniel Hanbury, *Notes on Chinese Materia Medica* (London: John E. Taylor, 1862), p. 3; J. Dudgeon, 'On the Disgusting Nature of Chinese Medicines', *Chinese Recorder*, March 1870, pp. 285–7; Frederick Porter Smith, *Contributions Towards the Material Medica and Natural History of China* (Shanghai: American Presbyterian Mission Press, 1871), p. vi.

23. In Zambia and Congo, for example: Luise White, *Speaking with Vampires: Rumour and history in colonial Africa* (Berkeley: University of California Press, 2000), pp. 181–207.

24. George Thin, *The Tientsin Massacre: The causes of the late disturbances in China and how to secure peace* (Edinburgh: William Blackwood and Sons, 1870), pp. 10–12. A doctor, Thin had formerly worked in Shanghai.

25. *Death Blow to Corrupt Doctrines: A plain statement of facts published*

by the gentry and people (Shanghai, 1870), preface, pp. iii, v, viii.

26. Letter to Acting Consul Lay, 6 July 1870, *China No.1* (1871), p. 110. On conspiracy, see, e.g. General Charles W. Le Gendre, *How to Deal with China* (Amoy, 1871). LeGendre was the US Consul in Xiamen.

27. This and the two succeeding paragraphs draw in particular from Daniel H. Bays (ed.), *Christianity in China: From the eighteenth century to the present* (Stanford: Stanford University Press, 1997); Cohen, *China and Christianity*; Ryan Dunch, *Fuzhou Protestants and the Making of a Modern China* (New Haven: Yale University Press, 2001); Joseph Tse-Hei Lee, *The Bible and the Gunboat: Christianity in south China, 1860–1900* (London: Routledge, 2003).

28. Revd M. T. Yates, 'Ancestral Worship and Fung-shuy', *Chinese Recorder*, July 1868, p. 39.

29. Liu Xihong, a diplomatic envoy, parts of whose journal are translated in J. D. Frodsham, *The First Chinese Embassy to the West: The journals of Kuo-Sung-T'ao, Liu Hsi-Hung and Chang Te-yi* (Oxford: Clarendon Press, 1974), quotation from p. 147.

30. S. Wells Williams, *The Middle Kingdom* . . . (New York & London: Wiley & Putnam, 1848), ii, pp. 343–4.

31. Dunch, *Fuzhou Protestants*, pp. 32–47.

32. Charles A. Litzinger, 'Rural Religion and Village Organisation in North China: The Catholic challenge in late nineteenth century China', in Bays (ed.), *Christianity in China*, pp. 41–52.

33. 'A Missionary', 'On Native Contributions', *Chinese Recorder*, January 1870, p. 213.

34. Forcing herself to confront this was why she was still in Tianjin on 21 June 1870, when she had received permission to leave China: Revd. Matthew Russell S. J., 'Alice O'Sullivan: The late Irish martyr', *Irish Monthly* 4 (1876), pp. 545–51.

35. 'Missionary Intelligence', *Chinese Recorder*, December 1868, p. 168.

36. H. B. Morse, *The International Relations of the Chinese Empire: ii, The period of submission, 1861–1893* (London: Longmans, Green & Co., 1918), pp. 253–60; Lloyd Eastman, *Throne and Mandarins: China's search for a policy during the Sino-French controversy, 1880–1885* (Cambridge, MA: Harvard University Press, 1967), pp. 23–5; Richard S. Horowitz, 'Central Power and State Making: The Zongli yamen and self-strengthening in China, 1860–1880' (unpublished PhD thesis, Harvard University, 1998), pp. 111–13, 181–2; Mary C. Wright, *The Last Stand of Chinese Conservatism; The T'ung-Chih restoration, 1862–1874* (New York: Atheneum, 1966 [1957]) pp. 295–9.

37. On the convention: ibid. pp. 279–95; Cooley, *T. F. Wade in China*, pp. 67–73.

38. Immanuel C. Y. Hsü, *The Ili Crisis: A study of sino-Russian diplomacy, 1871–1881* (Oxford: Clarendon Press, 1965); Hodong Kim, *Holy War in China: The Muslim rebellion and state in Chinese central Asia, 1864–1877* (Stanford: Stanford University Press, 2004).

39. Kirk W. Larsen, *Tradition, Treaties, and Trade: Qing imperialism and Chosŏn Korea, 1850–1910* (Cambridge, MA: Harvard University Asia Center, 2008).

40. Morse, *International Relations of the Chinese Empire*, ii, pp. 267–70; Tseng-tsai Wang, 'The Audience Question: Foreign representatives and the emperor of China, 1858–1873', *Historical Journal* 14:3 (1971), pp. 617–26.

41. Ian Nish (ed.), *The Iwakura Mission in America and Europe: A new assessment* (Richmond: Japan Library, 1998).

42. Wayne C. McWilliams, 'East Meets East: The Soejima Mission to China, 1873', *Monumenta Nipponica* 30:3 (1975), pp. 237–75.

43. On this voyage and the early Japanese community in Shanghai, see Joshua A. Fogel, *Articulating the Sinosphere: Sino-Japanese relations in space and time* (Cambridge, MA: Harvard University Press, 2009) chapters 2 and 3.

44. *Minutes of the SMC*, iv, 22 August 1870.

45. *The Times*, 11 August 1874, p. 10; Japan-based US journalist Edward H. House's pro-Japanese *The Japanese Expedition to Formosa* (Tokyo: 1875), is the only English-language narrative of the expedition. House accompanied the force, although some additional material is in James W. Davidson, *The Island of Formosa Past and Present* (London: Macmillan, 1903), pp. 123–69. For analysis, see also Robert Eskildsen, 'Of Civilization and Savages: The mimetic imperialism of Japan's 1874 expedition to Taiwan', *American Historical Review* 107:2 (2002), pp. 388–418; and his '"Leading the Natives to Civilization": The colonial dimension of the Taiwan Expedition', *Edwin O. Reischauer Institute for Japanese Studies, Occasional Papers* 2003-01 (2003). The extent of the impact on local society is explored in Douglas L. Fix, 'The Changing Contours of Lived Communities on the Hengchun Peninsula, 1850–1874', in *Guojia yu yuanzhumin: YaTai diqu zuqun lishi yanjiu* [Nations and aborigines: History of ethnic groups in the Asia Pacific Region] (Nankang: Institute of Taiwan History, 2009), pp. 233–82.

46. House, *Japanese Expedition*, pp. 25–6.

47. Hart to Campbell, 25 July 1874, no. 110, Fairbank, Bruner, Matheson (eds.), *The IG in Peking*; Robert Gardella, 'From Treaty Ports to Provincial Status, 1860–1894', in Murray A. Rubinstein (ed.), *Taiwan: A new history* (Armonk: M. E. Sharpe, 1999), pp. 183–6.

48. George Taylor, 'Tortoise Hill, Formosa', *China Review* 15:5 (1887), pp. 305–6.

49. Horowitz, 'Central Power and State-making', pp. 307–11; Cooley, *T. F. Wade in China*, pp. 101–15.

50. T. T. Cooper, *Travels of a Pioneer of Commerce in Pigtail and Petticoats* (London: John Murray, 1871), pp. 450–51.

51. Ibid., pp. 15–16. This paragraph draws on this, as well as David G. Atwill, *The Chinese Sultanate: Islam, ethnicity, and the Panthay rebellion in southwest China, 1856–1873* (Stanford: Stanford University Press, 2005); Brian L. Evans, 'The Panthay Mission of 1872 and its legacies', *Journal of Southeast Asian Studies* 16 (1985), pp. 117–28; *East India (British Burmah:. Further return. Official narrative of the expedition to explore the trade routes to China via Bhamo, under the guidance of Major E. B. Sladen* (PP 165) (1871); John Anderson, *A Report on the Expedition to Western Yunan via Bhamô* (Calcutta: Office of the Superintendent of Government Printing, 1871).

52. Cooper, *Travels of a Pioneer of Commerce*, pp. 28, 90, 106, 142, 198, 249–50, 328, 349.

53. Milton Osborne, *River Road to China: The Mekong river expedition 1866–1873* (New York: Liveright, 1975); Lt. Col. A. P. McMahon, 'On Our Prospects of Opening a Route to South-Western China, and Explorations of the French in Tonquin and Cambodia', *Proceedings of the Royal Geographical Society* 18:4 (1873–4), pp. 463–7.

54. R. Swinhoe, 'Special Mission up the Yang-tsze-Kiang', *Proceedings of the Royal Geographical Society* 14:3 (1870), pp. 235–43, and *Journal of the Royal Geographical Society* 40 (1870), pp. 268–85. See also *China No. 2: Reports by Consul Swinhoe of his Special Mission up the River Yang-tsze-Kiang, &c.* (1870).

55. Anderson, *Report*, p. 3.

56. Letter to parents, 15 August 1874, *The Journey of Augustus Raymond Margary, from Shanghae to Bhamo, and back to Manwyne* (London: Macmillan & Co., 1876), p. 101. Its complexity is explored in C. Patterson Giersch, *Asian Borderlands: The transformation of Qing China's Yunnan frontier* (Cambridge, MA: Harvard University Press, 2006).

57. *Journey of Augustus Raymond Margary*, pp. 104, 109.

58. Letter to his parents, 14 September 1874, *Journey of Augustus Raymond Margary*, p.131.

59. Rutherford Alcock, 'Concluding Chapter', ibid., pp. 371–2.

60. Letters to Campbell, 27 June 1876, 24 August 1876, *IG in Peking*, i, pp. 221–4.

61. Wade to Lord Derby, 5 August 1876, in *China No. 3: Further correspondence respecting the attack on the Indian expedition to Western China and the murder of Mr. Margary* (C.1832) (1877), pp. 51–2.

62. Section draws on S. T. Wang, *The Margary Affair and the Chefoo Agreement* (London: Oxford University Press, 1940); Cooley, *T. F. Wade in China*, pp.116–31.

63. R. W. Little to parents, 5 October 1876, Little papers.

64. Russell, 'Alice O'Sullivan', p. 551. The later Protestant debates in this vein have been explored in James L. Hevia, 'Leaving a Brand on China: Missionary discourse in the wake of the Boxer movement', *Modern China* 18:3 (1992), pp. 304–32.

65. *NCH*, 15 June 1880, pp. 513, 522–3; Susan Beattie, *The New Sculpture* (New Haven: Yale University Press, 1983), pp. 24–5; R. W. Little to parents, 22 June 1875, Little papers.

66. Immanuel C. Y. Hsü, 'Gordon in China, 1880', *Pacific Historical Review* 33:2 (1964), pp. 147–66; Smith, *Mercenaries and Mandarins*, pp. 172–6.

67. A historical survey of the Bund-side monuments is contained in Commissioner of Public Works to Secretary, SMC, 30 November 1942, SMA, U1-14, 6290; SMC, *Annual Report 1880*, pp. 115–16.

68. George Lanning and Samuel Couling, *The History of Shanghai* (Shanghai: Kelly & Walsh, 1923), ii, pp. 410–3.

9 COASTWISE

1. A mournful list of wrecks is in James W. Davidson, *The Island of Formosa past and present* (London: Macmillan, 1903), pp. 180–82, 216–18, 256. Head-hunting was certainly practised, but cannibalism was a myth: see Josiane Cauquelin, *The Aborigines of Taiwan: The Puyuma; from head hunting to the modern world* (London: RoutledgeCurzon, 2004), pp. 149–52, and Janet B. Montgomery McGovern, *Among the Head-hunters of Formosa* (London: T. Fisher Unwin, 1922), pp. 10, 115–16; on surveying, see Commander E. W. Brooker, 'Formosa', 1 November 1867, in UK Hydrographic Office Archives [UKHOA], OD 157. How far myths of Formosa were still influenced by the fancies of the 'Formosan imposter' George Psalmanazar, author of the entirely fictitious *An Historical and Geographical Description of Formosa* (1704), with its accounts of mass sacrifice of children and cannibalism, is a moot point, for there was enough of a contemporary record of danger. Kwaliang Bay is now known as Nanwan (South Bay), although the origins of the European term for

the bay remain obscure (personal communication, Doug Fix).

2. *China Sea Directory*, 2nd edition (London: Hydrographic Office, Admiralty, 1884), iii, p. 265; Emma Jinhua Teng, *Taiwan's Imagined Geography: Chinese colonial travel writing and pictures, 1683–1895* (Cambridge, MA: Harvard University Asia Center, 2004).

3. Sophia S. F. Yen, *Taiwan in China's Foreign Relations, 1836–1874* (Hamden: Shoe String Press, 1965), pp. 260–63.

4. D. M. Henderson to Commissioner, Amoy, 26 August 1884, SHAC, 679(2), 65; M. Beazeley, 'Notes of an Overland Journey Through the Southern Part of Formosa from Takow to the South Cape, in 1875', *Proceedings of the Royal Geographical Society* New Monthly Series, 7:1 (1885), pp. 1–23.

5. See 'The Loss of the *Reynard*', *The Times*, 2 September 1851, p. 8, and his own later letters to the paper: 30 December 1856, p. 10; 27 January 1857, p. 9.

6. 'Surveying and Chinese Names of the Islets Forming the Chusan Archipelago', in UKHOA, OD 153, 'Surveying Journal of Captain Richard Collinson, China 1840–42'; composite remark books, 1852 I-W: HMS *Salamander*, UKHOA; QUB, Hart journal, 21 July 1867; Commander E. W. Brooker, 'Report on the Pratas Reef and Proposed Light House', 8 November 1867, in UKHOA, OD 157.

7. The account of the building of South Cape draws on J. Reginald Harding, 'Report on the Construction of a First Order Light-house Station at S. Cape of Formosa', 17 July 1883, in SHAC 679(2), 62, and correspondence from the site preserved in SHAC 679(2), 60 and 61; J. R. Harding, 'Talk to Monmouth Working Men's Club', undated clipping from the *Monmouth News* (internal evidence suggests post-1902).

8. IG Circular no. 20, 22 June 1868, in *Inspector-General's Circulars. First Series: 1861–1875* (Shanghai: Statistical Department of the Inspectorate General, 1879); Glen Dudbridge, 'George Taylor and the Peoples of the South Cape', in his edition of Taylor's papers: *Aborigines of South Taiwan in the 1880s* (Taibei: Shung Ye Museum of Formosan Aborigines & Institute of Taiwan History, Academia sinica, 1999), pp. 6–12.

9. J. Reginald Harding, 'The Chinese Lighthouse Service' [1901], in *Origins, Development and Activities of the Chinese Customs Service*, vi, pp. 647–8; J. R. Harding, 'Talk to Monmouth Working Men's Club'; *The Times*, 1 September 1906, p. 10.

10. Population estimates for 1874 from Edward H. House, *The Japanese Expedition to Formosa* (Tokyo: 1875), p. 105. I am grateful to Doug Fix for this reference and for his discussion of Paiwan population figures.

11. Jacques Thobie, *L'Administration générale des phares de l'empire Ottoman*

et la Société Collas et Michel 1860–1960 (Paris: L'Harmattan, 2004); Eric Tagliacozzo, 'The Lit Archipelago: Coast Lighting and the Imperial Optic in Insular Southeast Asia, 1860–1910', *Technology and Culture* 46:2 (2005), pp. 306–28; Olive Checkland, 'Richard Henry Brunton and the Japan lights, 1868–1876: A brilliant and abrasive engineer'. *Transactions of the Newcomen Society*, 63 (1992), 217–28; *Building Japan 1868–1876* by Richard Henry Brunton with an introduction by Hugh Cortazzi (Folkestone: Japan Library, 1995); on Alcock, see QUB, MS 15/1/9, Hart journal, 21 July 1867.

12. Mrs Thomas Francis Hughes, *Among the Sons of Han: Notes of a six years' residence in various parts of China and Formosa* (London: Tinsley Brothers, 1881), p. 164; see also pp. 173–7.

13. Statement of R. A. Y. Santa Ana, Chief Lightkeeper, Fisher Island, 23 February 1881: 'Amoy Customs, Reports, Petitions etc. from staff', SHAC, 679(2), 80.

14. Taylor's papers are collected in Dudbridge, *Aborigines of South Taiwan in the 1880s*. See also George Taylor, 'Tortoise Hill, Formosa', *China Review* 15:5 (1887), pp. 305–6.

15. Harding reported in May 1883 that 'Mr Taylor can now speak a fair amount of savage dialect and his little savage boy can also interpret': Harding to Commissioner, Amoy, 17 May 1883, SHAC 679(2), 61.

16. Robert Gardella, 'From Treaty Ports to Provincial Status, 1860–1894', in Murray A. Rubinstein (ed.), *Taiwan: A new history* (Armonk: M. E. Sharpe, 1999), pp. 190–91.

17. Hart to Campbell, 14 March 1873, no. 49, in John King Fairbank, Katherine Frost Bruner, Elizabeth Macleod Matheson (eds.), *The IG in Peking: Letters of Robert Hart, Chinese Maritime Customs 1868–1907* (Cambridge, MA: The Belknap Press of Harvard University Press, 1975).

18. *The Times*, 6 September 1888, p. 4; 13 September, p. 4. Taylor resigned from the Customs in 1905, his health broken by recurrent bouts of fever probably traceable to his work at South Cape. He died the following year: Shanghai no. 8305, 30 January 1905, SHAC, 679(3) 1737; George Taylor, will and probate: TNA, FO 917/1228.

19. The two basic sources on the lights are Harding, 'Chinese Lighthouse Service', and T. Roger Banister, *The Coastwise Lights of China: An illustrated account of the Chinese maritime customs lights service* (Shanghai: Statistical Department of the Inspectorate General of Customs, 1932). Some additional material is in *Taiwan zhi dengta* [Lighthouses of Taiwan] (Taibei: Caizheng Bu Guanshui zongju, 2007).

20. Banister, *Coastwise Lights of China*, p. 115.

21. 'Record of Proceedings. Chinese Commission: International Fisheries

Exhibition, London, 1883', in *Documents Illustrative of the Origin, Development, and Activities of the Chinese Customs Service* (Shanghai: Statistical Department of the Inspectorate General of Customs, 1940), vii, p. 111; *Special Catalogue of the Chinese Collection of Exhibits for the International Fisheries Exhibition, London, 1883* (Shanghai: Statistical Department of the Inspectorate General, 1883); *The Times*, 15 May 1883, p. 6; Campbell to Hart, 18 May 1883, in Chen Xiafei and Han Rongfang (eds.), *Archives of China's Imperial Maritime Customs* (Beijing: Foreign Language Press, 1990) i, letter 1067, and various letters in April–June 1883.

22. Paragraph draws on: Erik Baark, *Lightning Wires: The telegraph and Chinese technological modernization, 1860–1890* (Westport, CT: Greenwood Press, 1997), pp. 72–5, 77–82; *The Times*, 22 August 1871, p. 5; *China No. 2: Commercial reports from Her Majesty's consuls in China, 1870* (C.567) (1872), pp. 10, 11, 15; Max Fletcher, 'The Suez Canal and World Shipping, 1869–1914', *Journal of Economic History* 18:4 (1958), pp. 556–73; Headrick, *Tentacles of Progress*, pp. 25–7; C. Knick Harley, 'Ocean Freight Rates and Productivity, 1740–1913: The primacy of mechanical invention reaffirmed', *The Journal of Economic History*, 48:4 (1988), pp. 851–76.

23. *NCH*, 5 August 1879, pp. 124–5; 16 September 1881, pp. 290–91.

24. Lewis Pyenson, *Civilizing Mission: Exact sciences and French overseas expansion, 1830–1940* (Baltimore: Johns Hopkins University Press, 1993), p. 158; Augustin Udias, *Searching the Heavens and the Earth: The history of Jesuit observatories* (Dordrecht: Kluwer Academic Publishers, 2003); *Documents Relating to 1. the Establishment of Meteorological Stations in China; and 2. proposals for co-operation in the publication of meteorological observations and exchange of weather news by telegraph along the Pacific coast of Asia* (1874); Le Père Marc Dechevrens, SJ, *Le Typhon du 31 juillet 1879* (Zikawei: Imprimerie de la Mission Catholique à l'Orphelinat de Tou-sè-wè, 1879).

25. Katherine Anderson, *Predicting the Weather: Victorians and the science of meteorology* (Chicago: University of Chicago Press, 2005), pp. 235–84; P. Kevin MacKeown, 'William Doberck: A stormy career', *Journal of Royal Asiatic Society, Hong Kong Branch* 44 (2004), pp. 5–39; 'Meteorological Service for the China Coast: Annual report of the director, 1882–1883', *Celestial Empire*, 10 October 1883, p. 274 (on Hong Kong's ambitions, see p. 2), on setting up at Hong Kong: W. Doberck, *Observations and Researches Made at the Hongkong Observatiory in the Year 1884* (Hong Kong: Noronha, 1885).

26. Hart to Campbell, 29 May 1873, no. 56, 14 September 1884, no. 494, *IG*

in Peking; C. A. Gordon (comp.), *An Epitome of the Reports of the Medical Officers to the Chinese Imperial Maritime Customs Service, from 1871–1882* (London: Baillière, Tindall, and Cox, 1884).

27. Circular no. 19 of 1870, 31 December 1870 in *Inspector-General's Circulars*; Hart to Campbell, 8 March 1884, no. 467, *IG in Peking*.

28. Douglas M. Haynes, *Imperial Medicine: Patrick Manson and the conquest of tropical disease* (Philadelphia: University of Pennsylvania Press, 2001), p. 49.

29. *Medical Reports*, April–June 1871, p. 18; July–Sept 1871, pp. 9, 79; Oct–March 1874–5, pp. 11–12; SMC, *Annual Report 1874–5*, pp. 12–13.

30. William Gauld, 'Medical Missions', *Chinese Recorder* 6:1 (1875), quoted in Theoron Kue-Hing Young, 'A Conflict of Professions: The medical missionary in China, 1835–1890', *Bulletin of the History of Medicine* 47:3 (1973), pp. 250–72, at p. 254.

31. Haynes, *Imperial Medicine*, pp. 30–55, 85–124; Patrick Manson, *The Filiaria Sanguinis Hominis and Certain New Forms of Parasitic Disease in India, China, and Warm Countries* (London: H. K. Lewis, 1883), p. vi; Patrick Manson, 'Further Observations on Filiaria Sanguinis Hominis', *Customs Medical Reports*, 14 (April–September 1877), pp. 10–11.

32. 'Dr F. Wong's Report on the Health of Canton . . .', *Customs Medical Reports* 4 (April–September 1872), p. 71. On Wong, see Bridie Andrews Minehan, 'Training Doctors *Versus* Building a Medical Profession: Illustrations of the difference from modern China,' paper prepared for conference on 'Intellectuals, Professions, and Knowledge Production in Twentieth-Century China', Center for Chinese Studies, University of California, Berkeley, 16–17 October 2009.

33. Hart to Campbell, 14 March 1873, no. 49, *IG in Peking*.

34. QUB, MS 15/1/9, Hart journal, 17 January 1867.

35. 'Taiwan Trade Report for 1881', 28 February 1882, TNA, FO 228/712.

36. Wusong railway: Richard C. Rapier, *Remunerative Railways for New Countries: With some account of the first railway in China* (London: E. & F. N. Spon, 1878), pp. 93–115; James Flath, 'The Chinese Railroad View: Transportation themes in popular print, 1873–1915', *Cultural Critique* 58 (2004) pp. 168–90.

37. Letters to Campbell, 7 October 1888, no. 669; 8 September 1889, no. 716: *IG in Peking*.

38. LeFervour, *Western Enterprise in Late Ch'ing China*, pp. 25–30 (I have drawn on the book more widely for this and the succeeding paragraph); Chiara Betta, 'Marginal Westerners in Shanghai: The Baghdadi Jewish community, 1845–1931', in Robert Bickers and Christian Henriot (eds.),

New Frontiers: Imperialism's new communities in east Asia, 1842–1953 (Manchester: Manchester University Press, 2000), pp. 38–54.

39. Erika Rappaport, 'Packaging China: Foreign articles and dangerous tastes in the mid-Victorian tea party', in Frank Trentmann (ed.), *The Making of the Consumer: Knowledge, power and identity in the modern world* (London: Berg, 2006), pp. 125–46.

40. Jerry S. L. Wang, 'The Profitability of Anglo-Chinese Trade, 1861–1913', *Business History* 35:3 (1993), pp. 39–65.

41. Named after Lt. William Arthur, the British naval officer who first drew its usefulness to foreign attention in 1858: Sir Edward H. Seymour, *My Naval Career and Travels* (London: Smith, Elder, 1911), p. 87.

42. Little papers, letters 1882 *passim*, and R. W. L. Little to father, 22 November 1882.

43. *The Economist*, 2 January 1875, p. 7; W. A. Thomas, *Western Capitalism in China: A history of the Shanghai stock exchange* (Aldershot: Ashgate, 2001), pp. 64–6; Frank H. H. King, *The History of the Hongkong and Shanghai Banking Coporation I: The Hongkong bank in late imperial China, 1864–1902; on an even keel* (Cambridge: Cambridge University Press, 1987). On the 1874 loan, see ibid., pp. 204–5, and more generally on financing of the Qing government, see chapter 14.

44. Thomas *Western Capitalism in China*, pp. 124–5; Yen-p'ing Hao, *The Commercial Revolution in China: The rise of Sino-Western mercantile capitalism* (Berkeley: University of California Press 1988), pp. 323–34.

45. Ibid., p. 332; Han-sheng Chuan, 'The Economic Crisis in 1883 as Seen in the Failure of Hsü Jun's Real Estate Business in Shanghai', in Chi-ming Hou and Tzong-shian Yu (eds.), *Modern Chinese Economic History* (Taibei: Academia Sinica, 1979), pp. 493–8.

46. Discussion drawn from Yen-p'ing Hao, *The Comprador in Nineteenth Century China: Bridge between East and West* (Cambridge, MA: Harvard University Press, 1970).

47. Ye Xiaoqing, *The Dianshizhai Pictorial: Shanghai urban life, 1884–1898* (Ann Arbor: Center for Chinese Studies, University of Michigan, 2003), p. 128.

48. Shanghai Municipal Archives (ed.), *Minutes of the Shanghai Municipal Council* (Shanghai: Shanghai guji chubanshe, 2001), iv, 17 June 1871. On Smith, see the sketch in George Lanning and Samuel Couling, *The History of Shanghai* (Shanghai: Kelly & Wash, 1923), ii, pp. 397–8.

49. Christopher A. Reed, *Gutenberg in Shanghai: Chinese print capitalism, 1876–1937* (New York: Columbia University Press, 2004), pp. 79–83, 104–15; Barbara Mittler, *A Newspaper for China? Power, identity, and*

change in Shanghai's news media, 1872–1912 (Cambridge, MA: Harvard University Press, 2004), pp. 334–6; Andrea Janku, 'Translating Genre: How the leading article became the *"shelun"'*, in Michael Lackner and Natascha Vittinghoff (eds.), *Mapping Meanings: The field of new learning in late Qing China* (Leiden: Brill, 2004), pp. 329–53; Rudolf G. Wagner, 'The *Shenbao* in Crisis: The international environment and the conflict between Guo Songtao and the Shenbao', *Late Imperial China* 20:1 (1999), pp. 107–38; Paul A. Cohen, *Between Tradition and Modernity: Wang T'ao and reform in late Ch'ing China* (Cambridge, MA: Council on East Asian Studies, 1974), pp. 76–81.

50. 'Taiwan Intelligence Report for the Three Months Ended 31st July 1883', TNA, FO 228/13.

51. W. A. Pickering, *Pioneering in Formosa: Recollections of adventures among Mandarins, wreckers and head hunting savages* (London: Hurst & Blackett, 1898), pp. 167–74.

52. Nail: Eiichi Motono, *Conflict and Cooperation in Sino-British Business, 1860–1911: The impact of the pro-British commercial network in Shanghai* (Basingstoke: Macmillan St Antony's, 2000), pp. 102–5; Edwards: see Amoy correspondence registers, TNA, FO 663/75–77. The actual letters no longer exist.

53. James C. Cooley, *T. F. Wade in China: Pioneer in global diplomacy, 1842–1882* (Leiden: E. J. Brill, 1981), 132–6; Wade, evidence 15 September 1892, para. 1337, *The Royal Commission on Opium, 1893–1895* (London: Ganesha Publishing, 2003) i, p. 97; *NCH*, 11 May 1883, p. 513.

54. *NCH*, 8 September 1883, pp. 287–8; Hart to Campbell, 8 June 1883, no. 420, *IG in Peking*; *The Times*, 11 October 1883, p. 3.

55. Hart to Campbell, 8 June 1883, no. 420, *IG in Peking*; Stanley Lane-Poole, *The Life of Sir Harry Parkes* (London: Macmillan and Co., 1894), ii, pp. 373, 369.

56. Amoy despatch no. 175, 13 December 1884, SHAC 679(2), 92; *NCH*, 3 December 1884, p. 636, 10 December 1884, pp. 657–8, 17 December 1884, p. 689.

57. As Campbell put it, letter to Hart, 9 January 1885, *Archives of China's Imperial Maritime Customs*, ii.

58. *The Times*, 23 August 1884, p. 5. The message was sent the previous day.

59. *NCH*, 29 August 1884, p. 237; Jung-fang Tsai, *Hong Kong in Chinese History: Community and social unrest in the British colony, 1842–1913* (New York: Columbia University Press, 1993), pp. 124–46; Lloyd E. Eastman, *Throne and Mandarins: China's search for a policy during the*

Sino-French controversy, 1880–1885 (Cambridge, MA: Harvard University Press, 1967).

60. John L. Rawlinson, *China's Struggle for Naval Development 1839–1895* (Cambridge, MA: Harvard University Press, 1967), pp. 109–28; *NCH*, 29 August 1884, pp. 239–42; *The Times*, 25 August 1884, p. 5 (full despatch 23 October 1884, p. 8); 28 August 1884, p. 5; Fuzhou despatch no. 115, 30 September 1884, SHAC, 679(2) 732.

61. The issue is debated in Rawlinson, *China's Struggle for Naval Development*, pp. 140–45.

10 JUBILEES

1. This account of the jubilee draws on *The Jubilee of Shanghai 1843–1893: Shanghai past and present and a full account of the proceedings on the 17th and 18th November, 1893* (Shanghai: North China Daily News, 1893), and additional reports in the *North China Herald* and *Celestial Empire*.

2. As it still does today, on the southern end of Fuzhou Road and its junction with the Bund.

3. Unsigned of course, but as he wrote the previous year, despatching a copy of the *Herald* to his father, it 'ought to represent me fully, for I put as much of myself into it every week as I can', letter 11 March 1892, Little papers; *NCH*, 19 May 1893, p. 709.

4. Little: *NCH*, 12 May 1893, p. 672; Muirhead: *NCH*, 2 June 1893, pp. 806–7; Shanghai Municipal Archives (ed.), *Minutes of the Shanghai Municipal Council* (Shanghai: Shanghai guji chubanshe, 2001), xi, 26 September 1893.

5. Ibid., 3 October 1893; 29 August 1893.

6. Jeffrey N. Wasserstrom, 'Imagining Community in the International Settlement: The Shanghai jubilee as an invented tradition' (unpublished paper, 1994); Bryna Goodman, 'Improvisations on a Semicolonial Theme: Or, how to read a celebration of transnational urban community', *Journal of Asian Studies* 59:4 (2000), pp. 889–926.

7. R. W. Little to father, 16 March 1881, Little papers.

8. R. W. Little to father, 14 November 1891, Little papers.

9. *NCH*, 26 October 1888, pp. 461, 474–6; reprinted in *Poems of Robert William Little* (Shanghai: North China Daily News & Herald, 1907), pp. 14–16. The poem apparently 'raised quite a sensation': see May Little to W. J. Little, 29 February 1891, and R. W. Little to W. J. Little, 26 October 1888, Little papers.

10. *NCH*, 24 November 1893, p. 827.

11. See: Edmund S. Wehrle, *Britain, China, and the Antimissionary Riots, 1891–1900* (Minneapolis: University of Minnesota Press, 1966); Cai Shaoqing, 'On the Origins of the Gelaohui', *Modern China*, 10:4 (1984), pp. 481–508).

12. S. B. R., 'The Shanghai Exodus and the Capture of the Chinese Fleet', *NCH*, 29 September 1893, pp. 505–8. Hart to Campbell, 4 June 1891, no. 400, in John King Fairbank, Katherine Frost Bruner, Elizabeth Macleod Matheson (eds.), *The IG in Peking: Letters of Robert Hart, Chinese Martitime Customs 1868–1907* (Cambridge, MA: The Belknap Press of Harvard University Press, 1975). On Mason, see Alan R. Sweeten, 'The Mason Gunrunning Case and the 1891 Yangtze Valley Antimissionary Disturbances: A diplomatic link', *Bulletin of the Institute of Modern History Academia Sinica* 4 (1974), pp. 843–80; and two chapters in Jean Chesneaux and Lucien Bianco (eds.), *Popular Movements and Secret Societies in China, 1840–1950* (Stanford: Stanford University Press, 1972): Charlton M. Lewis, 'Some Notes on the Gelaohui in Late Qing China', pp. 97–112, and Guy Puyraimond, 'The Ko-lao Hui and the Anti-foreign Incidents of 1891', pp. 113–24.

13. I. F. Clarke, *Voices Prophesying War*, 1763–1984 (London: Panther, 1970); Charles E. Gannon, *Rumors of War and Infernal Machines: Technomilitary agenda-setting in American and British speculative fiction* (Lanham: Rowman & Littlefield, 2005); 'The Battle at Sikawei', *NCH*, 15 September 1871, pp. 695–7. The original was published in the *Shanghae Courier*, and then as a pamphlet.

14. *NCH*, 24 November 1893, p. 828.

15. *The Royal Commission on Opium, 1893–1895* (London: Ganesha Publishing, 2003) i: on Lay, see paragraphs 1232, 1256–82; on Pease, paragraph 20; on Wade, paragraph 1292. Joyce A. Madancy, 'Money, Morality, and the Opium Trade: Re-examining the Royal Commission on Opium, 1893–1895', introduction to ibid., pp. v–xxix; John F. Richards, 'Opium and the British Indian Empire: The Royal Commission of 1895', *Modern Asian Studies* 36:2 (2002), pp. 375–420; R. M. Dane, 'A Narrative of the Circumstances That Preceded and the Causes That Produced the First Chinese War', appendix C, *Royal Commission on Opium*, vii, pp. 64–214, quote from p. 214. Dane later became chief inspector of the Chinese Salt Gabelle.

16. *NCH*, 24 November 1893, pp. 815–16.

17. *NCH*, 12 May 1893, pp. 672–3.

18. This was the conclusion of local British consular officers looking at their

own records in 1922: Amoy no. 30, 16 June 1922, and enclosure, TNA, FO 228/3182.

19. *Fifty Years of Progress: The jubilee of Hongkong as a British crown colony ... reprinted from Hongkong Daily Press* (Hong Kong: Daily Press office, 1891).

20. *Hong Kong Telegraph*, 21 January 1891, p. 1.

21. *The Jubilee of Shanghai 1843–1893*, pp. 41–2.

22. Home leave itself was gradually institutionalized as a concept: at Shanghai the Municipal Council introduced a scheme for its administrative officers for the first time in 1875. Three of its staff had not left Asia for seventeen years, the median was eleven years without return. Not all had any desire to go, but it became the practice to insist on staff taking leave of around nine months about once every seven years.

23. Census: SMC, *Annual Report 1876*, p. 14, *Annual Report 1895*, p. 30; On nurses, see Rosemary Wall and Anne Marie Rafferty, 'Emblems of Empire in the East: British nursing in China and Malaya, 1896–1966', in Ryan Johnson and Amna Khalid (eds.), *Intermediaries, Subordinates and the Practice of Public Health in the British Empire* (London: Routledge, forthcoming 2011); see also, for example, the memoir by Mrs de Burgh Daly, who arrived in 1888 to run a small hospital in Ningbo: *An Irishwoman in China* (London: T. Werner Laurie, 1916). On prostitution, see Eileen P. Scully, 'Prostitution as Privilege: The "American girl" of treaty port Shanghai, 1860–1937', *International History Review* 20:4 (1998), pp. 855–83.

24. *Royal Commission on Opium*, i, paragraph 383; *Records of the General Conference of the Protestant Missionaries of China, Held at Shanghai, May 7–20, 1890* (Shanghai: American Presbyterian Mission Press, 1890), p. 735.

25. C. A. Gordon (comp.), *An Epitome of the Reports of the Medical Officers to the Chinese Imperial Maritime Customs Service, from 1871–1882* (London: Baillière, Tindall, and Cox, 1884), pp. 220–21. See also E. M. Collingham, *Imperial Bodies: The physical experience of the Raj, c. 1800–1947* (Cambridge: Polity Press, 2001), pp. 94–7; Shang-jen Li, 'The Nurse of Parasites: Gender concepts in Patrick Manson's parasitological research', *Journal of the History of Biology* 37:1 (2004), pp. 103–30.

26. The *Medical Reports* are ambivalent overall, for while they often record a sorry toll of death, and judged the climate hostile to the health of European children, others judged the death rates on average no worse than European ones: Gordon, *Epitome of the Reports of the Medical Officers*, pp. 222–3.

27. Christopher Munn, 'Hong Kong, 1841–1870: All the servants in prison and no one to take care of the house', in Douglas Hay and Paul Craven

(eds.), *Masters, Servants, and Magistrates in Britain and the Empire, 1562–1955* (Chapel Hill: University of North Carolina Press, 2004), pp. 365–401.

28. May Little to Dr Little, 29 February 1891, Little papers.

29. Hart to Campbell, 27 May 1894, no. 930, *IG in Peking*.

30. Edward Henderson, *The Nurse in Hot Climates* (London: The Scientific Press, 1903), pp. 38–9.

31. *The Times*, 18 October 1892, p. 3, 19 October, p. 7, 18 November 1892, p. 11; Intestate estates, memo book, TNA, FO 1092/261; see also J. W. Bains (comp.), *Interport Cricket 1866–1908: A record of matches between Hong Kong, Singapore and Shanghai* (Shanghai: Shanghai Times, *c.* 1908), p. 2.

32. Intestate estates, memo books, TNA, FO 1092/260–61, 1885–1905; Scully, 'Prostitution as privilege', pp. 855–83, for Berry, see p. 861.

33. R. W. Little to father, 31 January 1883, Little papers.

34. R. W. Little to father, 18 October 1882, Little papers.

35. Archibald John Little, *Through the Yang-tse Gorges: Or, trade and travel in western China* (London: Sampson Low, Marston, Searle, & Rivington, 1888); 'The Navigation of the Upper Yangtsze: Its present position', *The Times*, 21 October 1889, p. 6, see also, 9 December 1889, p. 10; J. O. P. Bland papers, 'Memoirs', chapter 7, p. 7.

36. Albert H. Stone and J. Hammond Reed (eds.), *Historic Lushan: The Kuling Mountains* (Hankow: Arthington Press, 1921).

37. *Records of the General Conference of the Protestant Missionaries of China*, p. 735; Kenneth Scott Latourette, *A History of Christian Missions in China* (London: Society for Promoting Christian Knowledge, 1929), p. 395; Rhonda Anne Semple, *Missionary Women: Gender, professionalism and the Victorian idea of Christian mission* (London: Boydell & Brewer Ltd., 2003).

38. Maureen L. Rustichelli, 'Edward Selby Little: the Forgotten Victorian' (unpublished ms., 2003).

39. Kerrie L. MacPherson, *A Wilderness of Marshes: The origins of public health in Shanghai, 1843–1893* (Hong Kong: Oxford University Press, 1987), pp. 213–58; Christian Henriot, *Prostitution and Sexuality in China: A social history, 1849–1949* (Cambridge University Press, 2001) pp. 276–83. On the wider context, see Philippa Levine, *Prostitution, Race and Politics: Policing venereal disease in the British empire* (New York: Routledge, 2003).

40. *Minutes of the SMC*, ii, 1 and 8 February 1866.

41. Ye Xiaoqing, *The Dianshizhai Pictorial: Shanghai Urban Life, 1884–1898* (Ann Arbor: Center for Chinese Studies, 2003), p. 60.

42. George Lanning and Samuel Couling, *The History of Shanghai* (Shanghai: Kelly & Walsh, 1923), ii, pp. 444–9; SMC, *Annual Report 1877*, pp. 16–19;

'Watch Committee minutes 1897–1906', 9 December 1897, 19 January 1899, SMA U1-1-82.

43. R. W. Little to W. J. Little, 11 January 1888, Little papers, and *passim*. He also thought she would have secured the necessary permits to get to steamers into Chongqing much more quickly on her own.

44. Mrs Archibald Little [A. E. N. Bewicke], *A Marriage in China* (London: F. V. White & Co., 1896), p. 100–107.

45. *Poems of Robert William Little*, p. 16; on Jakobsen, see *NCH*, 15 August 1898, p. 304, 5 September 1898, p. 443, 12 September 1898, pp. 494–5; Alvin Austin, *China's Millions: The China Inland Mission and Late Qing Society, 1832–1905*, (Grand Rapids: William B. Eerdmans Publishing, 2007) pp. 289–91. The couple set up an independent mission. On 'British girls in peril', see *NCH*, 14 January 1898, pp. 37–8, 21 January 1898, p. 89; Mrs Archibald Little, *Intimate China: The Chinese as I have seen them* (London: Hutchinson & Co., 1899), p. 210; Frank Dikötter, *The Idea of Race in Modern China* (London: C. Hurst & Co., 1992), pp. 57–9. See also Levine, *Prostitution, Race and Politics*, pp. 231–56.

46. R. W. Little to W. J. Little, 18 January 1888, and to E. S. Little, 3 March 1888, Little papers; *NCH*, 2 March 1888, pp. 232–3, 245–7. On colonial opposition to repeal, see Levine, *Prostitution, Race and Politics*, pp. 91–119. The system remained in place in Shanghai for twelve further years.

47. James Dow did: 8 August 1850, James Dow journal; William C. Milne, *Life in China* (London: G. Routledge & Co., 1857), p. 8.

48. Little, *Intimate China*, pp. 134–63, and *In the Land of the Blue Gown* (London: T. Fisher Unwin, 1908), pp. 253–304; Letter to *The Times* on women's suffrage, 24 February 1908, p. 12; Elizabeth J. Croll, 'Like the Chinese Goddess of Mercy: Mrs Little and the Natural Foot Society', in David S. G. Goodman (ed.), *China and the West: Ideas and activists* (Manchester: Manchester University Press, 1990), pp. 41–56; Susan Schoenbauer Thurin, 'Travel Writing and the Humanitarian Impulse: Alicia Little in China', in Douglas Kerr and Julia Kuehn (eds.), *A Century of Travels in China: Critical essays on travel writing from the 1840s to the 1940s* (Hong Kong: Hong Kong University Press, 2007), pp. 91–103, and Susan Schoenbauer Thurin, *Victorian Travelers and the Opening of China, 1842–1907* (Athens, OH: Ohio University Press, 1999). On footbinding, see Dorothy Ko, *Cinderalla's Sisters: A revisionist history of footbinding* (Berkeley: University of California Press, 2005); on anti-footbinding campaigns and discourse, see, especially, pp. 9–49.

49. See her thoughts on E. S. Little's problems at Kuling: *In the Land of the Blue Gown*, pp. 108–10.

50. Mrs Archibald Little, *My Diary in a Chinese Farm* (Shanghai: Kelly & Walsh, Ltd, 1894), p. 94.

51. The war is covered in S. C. M. Paine, *The Sino-Japanese war of 1894–95: Perceptions, power, and primacy* (Cambridge: Cambridge University Press, 2003).

52. Kirk W. Larsen, *Tradition, Treaties and Trade: Qing imperialism and Chosün Korea, 1850–1910* (Cambridge, MA: Harvard University Asia Center, 2008).

53. Hart to Campbell, 8 July 1894, no. 933, *IG in Peking*.

54. Editorial, *The Times*, 24 July 1894, p. 9.

55. Hart to Campbell, 2 September 1894, no. 942, *IG in Peking*. On naval inadequacies, see John L. Rawlinson, *China's Struggle for Naval Development 1839–1895* (Cambridge, MA: Harvard University Press, 1967), pp. 167–97.

56. 'The Atrocities After the Fall of Port Arthur', and 'The Port Arthur Atrocities', *The Times*, 8 January 1895, p. 6, and 1 February 1895, p. 4; Frederic Villiers, 'The Truth about Port Arthur', *North American Review* 160 (March 1895), pp. 325–31. A balanced survey of these events is: Stewart Lone, *Japan's First Modern War: Army and society in the conflict with China, 1894–95* (London: St. Martin's Press in association with King's College, London, 1994), pp. 155–61.

57. James Flath, *The Cult of Happiness: Nianhua, art, and history in rural north China* (Vancouver: University of British Columbia Press, 2004); pp. 104–7; Mary Backus Rankin, 'The Ku-t'ien Incident (1895): Christians versus the Ts'ai-Hui', in *Papers on China* XV (1961), pp. 30–61.

58. To be fair, so was, for example, Norway's, to the irritation of its consul, see correspondence in SMA, U1-2-172; there were twenty-eight Norwegians in Shanghai in 1890, and over 300 Japanese.

59. On the republic, see Andrew Morris, 'The Taiwan Republic of 1895 and the Failure of the Qing Modernizing Project', in Stéphane Corcuff (ed.), *Memories of the Future: National identity issues and the search for a new Taiwan* (Armonk: M. E. Sharpe, 2002), pp. 3–24.

60. Barbara J. Brooks, 'Japanese Colonial Citizenship in Treaty Port China: The location of Koreans and Taiwanese in the imperial order', in Robert Bickers and Christian Henriot (eds.), *New Frontiers: Imperialism's new communities in east Asia, 1842–1953* (Manchester: Manchester University Press, 2000), pp. 110–14.

61. John E. Schrecker, *Imperialism and Chinese Nationalism: Germany in Shantung* (Cambridge, MA: Harvard University Press, 1971), pp. 19–42. On the German colony itself, see Klaus Mühlhahn, *Herrschaft und*

Widerstand in der 'Musterkolonie' Kiautschou: Interaktionen zwischen China und Deutschland 1897–1914 (München: Oldenbourg Wissenschaftsverlag, 2000).

62. The comment is G. E. Morrison's: *The Times*, 19 March 1898, p. 7.

63. Robert Lee, *France and the Exploitation of China: A study in economic imperialism* (Hong Kong: Oxford University Press, 1989), p. 303. Lee barely bothers to mention it.

64. T. G. Otte, *The China Question: Great power rivalry and British isolation 1894–1905* (Oxford: Oxford University Press, 2007).

65. SMC, *Annual Report 1899*, p. 212; *Annual Report 1900*, pp. 357, 361; Bryna Goodman, *Native Place, City and Nation: Regional networks and identities in Shanghai, 1853–1937* (Berkeley: University of California Press, 1995), pp. 164–9.

66. Little, *Through the Yang-tse Gorges*, pp. 283–300.

67. George Ernest Morrison, *An Australian in China* (London: Horace Cox, 1895), p. 268; 'British Policy in China: A retrospect and some conclusions, 1', *The Times*, 18 October 1897, p. 4; J. O. P. Bland papers, 'Memoirs', chapter 9, p. 12; G. E. Morrison to J. O. P. Bland, 17 January 1898 in Lo Hui-min (ed.), *The Correspondence of G. E. Morrison*, i, *1895–1912* (Cambridge: Cambridge University Press, 1976), pp. 60–62.

68. Luke S. K. Kwong, *A Mosaic of the Hundred Days: Personalities, politics and ideas of 1898* (Cambridge, MA: Council on East Asian Studies, Harvard University, 1984); Rebecca E. Karl and Peter Zarrow (eds.), *Rethinking the 1898 Reform Period: Political and cultural change in late Qing China* (Cambridge, MA: Harvard University Asia Center, 2002)

69. This paragraph is drawn from Marie-Claire Bergère, *Sun Yat-sen* (Stanford: Stanford University Press, 1998), especially pp. 49–59, 61–5; Sun Yat Sen, *Kidnapped in London: Being the story of my capture by, detention at, and release from the Chinese legation, London* (Bristol: J. Arrowsmith, 1897).

70. *Lloyd's Weekly*, 25 October 1896, pp. 10–11.

71. Sun Yat Sen, 'China's Present and Future: The Reform Party's plea for British benevolent neutrality', *Fortnightly Review*, 1 March 1897, pp. 424–40, quotations from pp. 424, 439.

72. Shanghai no. 59, 26 September 1898, TNA, FO 671/240; J. O. P. Bland papers, 'Memoirs', chapter 10, pp. 9–10.

73. Schrecker, *Imperialism and Nationalism*, pp. 96–7.

74. *NCH*, 16 May 1898, p. 856; 20 June 1898, p. 1084. Patrick H. Hase, *The Six-Day War of 1899: Hong Kong in the age of imperialism* (Hong Kong: Hong Kong University Press, 2008).

75. *Illustrated London News*, 16 July 1898, pp. 94–6; Ye Xiaoqing and Lance

Eccles, 'Anthem for a Dying Dynasty: The Qing national anthem through the eyes of a court musician', *T'oung-pao* 93:5–6 (2007), pp. 433–58.

II EXTINCTION

1. John Barnes, *The Beginnings of the Cinema in England, 1894–1901: Volume 5: 1900* (Exeter: University of Exeter Press, 1997), pp. 47–55; screening, p. 54. Remaining footage can be seen on the British Film Institute website, Screen Online, at www.screenonline.org.uk/film/id/520615/index.html

2. 'Report on the Health of Chefoo for the Year Ended 31st March 1899', *Medical Reports for the Half-year Ended 31st March 1899*, 57th Issue (Shanghai: Statistical Department of the Inspectorate General of Customs, 1899), p. 3; this section draws on Joseph W. Esherick, *The Origins of the Boxer Uprising* (Berkeley: University of California Press, 1987), pp. 173–81, and Kenneth Pomeranz, *The Making of a Hinterland: State, society, and economy in inland north China, 1853–1937* (Berkeley: University of California Press, 1993), pp. 153–212, and Iwo Amelung, *Der Gelbe Fluß in Shandong (1851–1911): Überschwemmungskatastrophen und ihre Bewältigung im China der späten Qing-Zeit* (Wiesbaden: Harrassowitz, 2000), pp. 134–45, 401–3.

3. *NCH*, 27 October 1898, p. 768, 19 December 1898, pp. 1156–7.

4. 'The Yellow River Floods: Relief committee's report', *NCH*, 12 September 1900, pp. 556–7.

5. On the roots and course of the Boxer movement, see Esherick, *Origins of the Boxer Uprising*, and Paul A. Cohen, *History in Three Keys: The Boxers as event, experience, and myth* (New York: Columbia University Press, 1997).

6. See Paul Richard Bohr, *Famine in China and the Missionary: Timothy Richard as relief administrator and advocate of national reform, 1876–79* (Cambridge, MA: Harvard University Press, 1972), and Kathryn Edgerton-Tarpley, *Tears from Iron: Cultural responses to famine in nineteenth-century China* (Berkeley: University of California Press, 2008).

7. Arthur H. Smith, *Chinese Characteristics*, 5th edition (Edinburgh and London: Oliphant Anderson and Ferrier, 1900), pp. 158–61, and his *Village Life in China: A study in sociology* (New York: Fleming H. Revell, 1899), pp. 169–73. On rainmaking, see Jeffrey Snyder-Reinke, *Dry Spells: State rainmaking and local governance in late imperial China* (Cambridge, MA: Harvard University Asia Center, 2009).

8. *NCH*, 6 June 1898, p. 976. The conclusion from the Texas experiments was

no: James Rodger Fleming, 'The Pathological History of Weather and Climate Modification: Three cycles of promise and hype', *Historical Studies in the Physical and Biological Sciences* 37:1 (2006) pp. 3–25.

9. Thomas Bryson, Report for 1899, 27 February 1900, CWM/LMS, North China Reports, box 2, SOAS.

10. Bruce Doar, 'The Boxers and Chinese Drama: Questions of interaction', *Papers on Far Eastern History* 29 (1984), pp. 91–118; for an example, see W. Hopkyns Rees letter, 8 June 1899, CWM/LMS, North China Correspondence, box 11, SOAS.

11. Hart to Campbell, 10 December 1898, no. 1153, in John King Fairbank, Katherine Frost Bruner, Elizabeth Macleod Matheson (eds.), *The IG in Peking: Letters of Robert Hart, Chinese Maritime Customs 1868–1907* (Cambridge, MA: The Belknap Press of Harvard University Press, 1975); Rebecca E. Karl, *Staging the World: Chinese nationalism at the turn of the twentieth century* (Durham, NC: Duke University Press, 2002), pp. 117–48.

12. *NCH*, 21 March 1900, p. 583.

13. Lilian M. Li, *Fighting Famine in North China: State, market, and environmental decline, 1690s–1990s* (Stanford: Stanford University Press, 2007), pp. 277–82.

14. Translations from *Peking Gazette*, quoted in W. Meyrick Hewlett, *The Siege of the Peking Legations* (supplement to *The Harrovian*, November 1900), pp. 84–5.

15. *The Times*, 5 May 1898, p. 7. On Salisbury and empire, see Michael Bentley, *Lord Salisbury's World: Conservative environments in late-Victorian Britain* (Cambridge: Cambridge University Press, 2001), pp. 220–50.

16. *NCH*, 23 May 1898, p. 878.

17. Mittler, *Newspaper for China*, pp. 363–7.

18. One recent analysis of the note is in Lanxin Xiang, *Origins of the Boxer War: A multinational study* (London: Routledge, 2003), pp. 293–6.

19. Bruce A. Elleman, *Modern Chinese Warfare, 1795–1989* (London: Routledge, 2001), pp. 116–37; George Alexander Lensen, *The Russo-Chinese War* (Tokyo: Sophia University Press, 1967); Roger R. Thompson, 'Military Dimensions of the Boxer Uprising in Shanxi, 1898–1901', in Hans van de Ven (ed.), *Warfare in Chinese History* (Leiden: Brill, 2000), pp. 288–320.

20. Police, semi-official correspondence, 1900: SMA: U1-1-741.

21. SVC Sealed orders, draft verbal instructions and correspondence, 11 July 1900, SMA, U1-1-721 General.

22. On the latter, see Captain A. A. S. Barnes, *On Active Service with the Chinese Regiment* (London: Grant Richards, 1902).

23. Reported in *The Times*, 28 July 1900, p. 7; 11 August 1900, p. 4; the story

of the official and unofficial versions of the speech is given in Bernd Sösemann, 'Die sog. Hunnenrede Wilhelms II. Textkritische und interpretatorische Bemerkungen zur Ansprache des Kaisers vom 27. Juli 1900 in Bremerhaven', *Historische Zeitschrift*, 222:2 (1976), pp. 342–58; Sabine Dabringhaus, 'An Army on Vacation? The German war in China, 1900–1901', in Manfred F. Boemeke, Roger Chickering and Stig Förster (eds.), *Anticipating Total War: The German and American experiences, 1871–1914* (Cambridge: Cambridge University Press, 1999), pp. 459–76.

24. Tianjin despatch no. 2380, 20 August 1900, SHAC, 679(2), 1938; *Tientsin Besieged and After the Siege: A daily record*, 2nd edition (Shanghai: North China Herald, 1901), p. 3.

25. Christopher J. Lucas, *James Ricalton's Photographs of China During the Boxer Rebellion* (Lampeter: Edwin Mellen Press, 1990).

26. S. C. M. Paine, *Imperial Rivals: China, Russia, and their Disputed Frontier* (Armonk, NY: M. E. Sharpe, 1996), pp. 213–14; Lensen, *Russo-Chinese War*, pp. 68–103.

27. *New York Times*, 14 November 1900, quoting a 6 September account.

28. Paine, *Imperial Rivals*, pp. 209–33.

29. Alicia Little to Ernest Little, 23 August 1900, Little papers; *NCH*, 27 June 1900, p. 1177.

30. Eileen P. Scully, *Bargaining with the State From Afar: American citizenship in treaty port China, 1844–1942* (New York: Columbia University Press, 2001), p. 94; Eileen P. Scully, 'Prostitution as Privilege: The "American girl" of treaty port Shanghai, 1860–1937', *International History Review* 20:4 (1998); Edward J. Bristow, *Prostitution and Prejudice: The Jewish fight against white slavery, 1870–1939* (Oxford: Oxford University Press, 1982), pp. 196–204.

31. Kenneth Scott Latourette, *A History of Christian Missions in China* (London: Society for Promoting Christian Knowledge, 1929), pp. 512–8; China Continuation Committee, *The Christian Occupation of China: A general survey of the numerical strength and geographical distribution of the Christian forces in China* (Shanghai: China Continuation Committee, 1922), p. civ.

32. Phrases from Laffan's agency reports in *Daily News*, 25 July 1900; *NCH*, 31 October 1900, pp. 946–7; *Tientsin Besieged and After the Siege*, p. 44.

33. Tianjin despatch no. 2541, 22 July 1901, SHAC, 679(2), 1938.

34. Gilbert Reid, 'The Ethics of Loot', *The Forum* 31 (1901), pp. 581–6, and 'The Ethics of the Last China War', *The Forum*, 32 (1902), pp. 446–55. James L. Hevia has explored this and the wider debate in *English Lessons: The pedagogy of imperialism in nineteenth-century China* (Durham, NC:

Duke University Press, 2003), pp. 231–40; on the Japanese, see Ben Middleton, 'Scandals of Empire: The looting of north China and the Japanese public sphere,' in Robert A. Bickers and R. G. Tiedemann (eds.), *The Boxers, China, and the World* (Lanham, MD: Rowman & Littlefield, 2007), pp. 115–32.

35. Mrs Archibald Little, 'Peking Revisited: Introductory. An anniversary study of August 1900', in *Round About My Peking Garden* (London: T. Fisher Unwin, 1905), pp. 27–8; 'A Salutation Speech from the Nineteenth Century to the Twentieth Taken Down in Shorthand by Mark Twain', 31 December 1900, in Jim Zwick (ed.), *Mark Twain's Weapons of Satire* (Syracuse, NY: Syracuse University Press, 1992), pp. 12–13.

36. 'Lord Salisbury and foreign missions', *The Times*, 20 June 1900, p. 10; entries for 29 October 1900, 11 February 1901 in Ruxton (ed.), *The Diaries of Sir Ernest Satow, British envoy in Peking (1900–1906)* (Morrisville: Lulu Press, 2006), vol. i.

37. Details drawn from *NCH*, 27 June 1900.

38. Frank H. H. King, 'The Boxer Indemnity – "Nothing but Bad"', *Modern Asian Studies*, 40:3 (2006), 663–89, quotation p. 665.

39. *New York Times*, 19 January 1903.

40. *Diaries of Sir Ernest Satow*, 13 and 20 October, 4 November 1900; file on 'Monument in Russian Cemetery', TNA, FO 676/17.

41. The Mitchell and Kenyon films are described in Barnes, *Beginnings of the Cinema in England*, 5, pp. 256–7.

42. Ibid., p. 255.

43. *NCH*, 29 August 1900, p. 429. On one of the artists and his work, see Flath, *The Cult of Happiness*, pp. 108–14.

44. Luke S. K. Kwong, 'Oral History in China: A preliminary review', *Oral History Review* 20:1/2 (1992), pp. 34–7.

45. 'The Massacre in Peking', *The Times*, 16 July 1900, p. 11, based on reports provided by the *Daily Mail*; C. F. Moberly Bell to G. E. Morrison, 10 August 1900 in Lo Hui-min (ed.), *The Correspondence of G. E. Morrison*, i, *1895–1912* (Cambridge: Cambridge University Press, 1976), pp. 141–4.

46. Hart's essays were collected in *These from the Land of Sinim* (London: Chapman and Hall, 1901); on missions and converts, pp. 4–5.

47. Lo Hui-min, 'The Ching-Shan Diary: A clue to its forgery', *East Asian History* 1 (1991), pp. 98–124 surveys the reception of book and diary; see especially also Hugh Trevor-Roper, *A Hidden Life: The enigma of Sir Edmund Backhouse* (London: Macmillan, 1976).

48. The necessary 'foraging for food' also broke up the monotony: 'A Journey Around the World', *The Times*, 19 July 1910, p. 68; Steven G. Marks, *Road*

to Power: The Trans-Siberian railroad and the colonization of Asian Russia, 1850–1917 (London: I. B.Tauris, 1991); Harmon Tupper, *To the Great Ocean: Siberia and the Trans-Siberian railway* (London: Secker & Warburg, 1965).

49. Nanning: see Customs files 'Nanning Semi-official Correspondence', SHAC 679(1), 32516; 'General Building Programme at Nanning', SHAC 679(9), 23700; J. O. P. Bland to E. T. C. Werner, 24 February 1906, J. O. P. Bland papers, box 4.

50. See, for example, Madancy, *Troublesome Legacy of Commissioner Lin*; and Judith Wyman, 'Opium and the State in late-Qing Sichuan', in Timothy Book and Bob Tadashi Wakabayashi (eds.), *Opium Regimes: China, Britain, and Japan, 1839–1952* (Berkeley: University of California Press, 2000), pp. 228–47.

51. Brian G. Martin, *The Shanghai Green Gang: Politics and organized crime, 1919–1937* (Berkeley: University of California Press, 1996), pp. 45–50.

52. Peter Richardson, *Chinese Mine Labour in the Transvaal* (Basingstoke: MacMillan, 1982).

53. See Police, semi-official correspondence, July–August 1905, SMA, U1-1-749; Karl Gerth, *China Made: Consumer culture and the creation of the nation* (Cambridge, MA: Harvard University Asia Center, 2004), pp. 127–31; Guanhua Wang, *In Search of Justice: The 1905–1906 Chinese anti-American boycott* (Cambridge: Harvard University Press, 2001).

54. Watch committee minutes, 21 December 1905, SMA, U1-1-82. Mixed court riots: Bryna Goodman, *Native Place, City and Nation: Regional networks and identities in Shanghai, 1853–1937* (Berkeley: University of California Press, 1995), pp. 187–95; SMC, *Annual Report 1905*, pp. 29–33. Sikhs: SMC, *Annual Report 1905*, p. 25, *Annual Report 1906*, pp. 129–34.

55. J. O. P. Bland to W. E. Leveson, 29 December 1911, J. O. P. Bland papers, box 6.

56. See, for example, Anne Veronica Witchard, *Thomas Burke's Dark Chinoiserie: Limehouse nights and the queer spell of Chinatown* (Aldershot: Ashgate, 2009), pp. 232–3.

57. These efforts are surveyed in 'Memorandum on Settlement Extension', in SMC, *Annual Report 1912*, pp. 101b–113b, quotation from p. 105b.

58. Quoted in Legation memorandum 'Chapei extension', August 1913, TNA, FO 228/2535. See also 'The Anti-Foreign Movement in China', *The Times*, 7 June 1906, p. 5. Chinese municipal reform is outlined in Mark Elvin, 'The Administration of Shanghai, 1905–1914', in Mark Elvin and G. William Skinner (eds.), *The Chinese City Between Two Worlds* (Stanford: Stanford

University Press, 1975), pp. 239–62; Christian Henriot, *Shanghai, 1927–1937: Municipal power, locality, and modernization* (Berkeley: University of California Press, 1993), pp. 8–15.

59. Peking no. 439, 21 November 1913, TNA, FO 228/2535.

60. *NCH*, 26 July 1913, pp. 290–91.

61. St Piero Rudinger, *The Second Revolution in China, 1913: My adventures of the fighting around Shanghai, the Arsenal, Woosung forts* (Shanghai: Shanghai Mercury, 1914).

62. W. E. Leveson, in a letter to his predecessor J. O. P. Bland, 4 November 1907, J. O. P. Bland papers, box 13; Bruce was, at the very least, conscious of not spoiling his chances of securing the position with the national government as advisor on police matters that was already under discussion when he marched into Zhabei: see Lo (ed.), *Correspondence of G. E. Morrison*, ii, pp. 180–83, 186–91.

63. My account of these events is drawn from SVC and SMP reports in SMA, U1-2-673; Shanghai no. 98, 3 August 1913, Peking no. 439, 21 November 1913, TNA FO 228/2535; Shanghai Municipal Archives (ed.), *Minutes of the Shanghai Municipal Council* (Shanghai: Shanghai guji chubanshe, 2001), xviii, 28 July 1913; W. E. Leveson to J. O. P. Bland, 30 August 1913, J. O. P. Bland papers, box 13; *Minutes of the SMC*, xviii, July–August 1913; *The Times*, 21 August 1913, p. 3.

64. Ian Phimister, 'Foreign Devils, Finance and Informal Empire: Britain and China c. 1900–1912', *Modern Asian Studies* 40:3 (2006), pp. 737–59. Hoover was later keen to suppress details of his connection to this case: Jeremy Mouat and Ian Phimister, 'The Engineering of Herbert Hoover', *Pacific Historical Review*, 77:4 (2008), p. 559, n. 17.

65. Peking no. 439, 21 November 1913, TNA, FO 228/2535.

66. On the boom, see W. A. Thomas, *Western Capitalism in China: A history of the Shanghai Stock Exchange* (Aldershot: Ashgate, 2001), chapter 8; on the fraud, see the well-documented report 'Shanghai Financial Crisis, 1910', Shanghai to FO, 15 November 1912, TNA, FO 228/2508.

67. *NCH*, 15 September 1926, p. 452; *NCH*, 17 December, p. 767; Arnold Wright and H. A. Cartwright (eds.), *Twentieth Century Impressions of Hongkong, Shanghai, and Other Treaty Ports of China* (London: Lloyd's Greater Britain Publishing Co., Ltd, 1908), p. 608; *The Times*, 10 September 1928, p. 17; Chiara Betta, 'From Orientals to Imagined Britons: Baghdadi Jews in Shanghai', *Modern Asian Studies* 37: 4 (2003); for interconnections amongst councillors, see H. E. Morriss and C. R. Maguire (comp.), *China Stock and Share Handbook, 1914* (Shanghai: North China Daily News and Herald, 1914); F. S. Gratton, *The History of Freemasonry in Shanghai and*

Northern China (revised by R. S. Ivy) (Tianjin: North China Printing and Publishing Co., 1913); *Social Shanghai, and Other Parts of China*, August 1913, *passim*.

68. W. E. Leveson to J. O. P. Bland, 4 November 1907, J. O. P. Bland papers, box 13; *New York Times*, 12 November 1911; *NCH*, 2 August 1913, p. 313.

69. *NCH*, 2 August 1913, p. 356.

70. See reports in US Consul-General to Pearce, 29 July 1913, SMA, U1-2-673.

71. Morrison to Bruce, 1 August 1913, in Lo (ed.), *Correspondence of G. E. Morrison*, ii, p. 207.

72. Chan Lau Kit-ching, *Anglo-Chinese Diplomacy in the Careers of Sir John Jordan and Yüan Shih-k'ai, 1906–1920* (Hong Kong: Hong Kong University Press, 1978), pp. 71–4.

73. Chan, *Anglo-Chinese Diplomacy*, p. 74; Alston no. 320, 15 August 1913, TNA, FO 371/1625, F400798/19283/10.

74. A. G. H. Carruthers to F. A. Aglen, semi-official no. 3, 10 March 1914, SHAC, 679(1), 31840; *NCH*, 4 April 1914, p. 71, 30 May 1914, pp. 671–3; *Social Shanghai*, June 1914, pp. 149–52.

75. The stone is noted in John Francis Davis, *The Chinese: A general description of the empire of China and its inhabitants* (London: Charles Knight & Co., 1836), i, p. 69, and Osmond Tiffany, *The Canton Chinese: Or, the American's sojourn in the celestial empire* (Boston: James Munroe and Company, 1849), p. 12. Krakatoa: *The Times*, 24 November 1883, p. 10.

76. *NCH*, 28 September 1912, pp. 885–7, 21 November 1914, pp. 570–71, 12 December 1914, p. 790; 'A Forgotten British Embassy: Colonel Charles Cathcart', *Oriental Affairs*, June 1938, pp. 303–7, and September 1938, pp. 161–3.

77. J. O. P. Bland to S. F. Mayers, 29 January 1905, J. O. P. Bland papers, box 4.

12 HISTORY

1. S. Gaselee minute, 13 May 1935, L2960/1240/402, TNA, FO 370/503. Tsiang retained this transliteration of his name in his subsequent career, and so I retain it here.

2. Lord Birkenhead, Secretary of State for India, letter to Sir Austen Chamberlain, Secretary of State for Foreign Affairs, 18 July 1928, quoted in 'The Publication of "British Documents on the Origins of the War"', 4 August 1928, paragraph 31, prepared by S. Gaselee, J. Headlam-Morley and

F. Hankey, reproduced in Keith Wilson, 'Imbalance in "British Documents on the Origins of the War"', in Wilson (ed.), *Forging the Collective Memory: Government and international historians through two world wars* (Providence: Berghahn Books, 1996), pp. 250–62.

3. Medhurst to Wade, 27 December 1870, TNA, FO 228/492.

4. 'Report by Inspector-General H. Philips upon his Inspection of His Majesty's Consulate-General at Shanghai', enclosed in Philips to FO, 25 March 1928, TNA, FO 369/2018.

5. Cyrus H. Peake, 'Documents Available for Research on the Modern History of China', *American Historical Review* 38:1 (1932), pp. 61–70; T. F. Tsiang, 'China After the Victory of Taku, June 25, 1859', *American Historical Review* 35:1 (1929), pp. 79–84, and 'New Light on Chinese Diplomacy, 1836–49', *Journal of Modern History*, 3:4 (1931), pp. 578–91.

6. J. K. Fairbank, 'Memo re Study in China', 8 January 1932, L118/118/402, TNA, FO 370/404.

7. Tsiang, 'New Light on Chinese Diplomacy', p. 588; J. K. Fairbank to S. Gaselee, 7 February 1935, and memo, L1280/1280/402, TNA, FO 370/583; V. G. Kiernan, *British Diplomacy in China, 1880 to 1885* (Cambridge: Cambridge University Press, 1939), p. x.

8. Jane Roth, 'The Jardine Matheson Archive', *Journal of Pacific History*, 2 (1967), pp. 172–4; John King Fairbank, *Chinabound: A fifty-year memoir* (New York: Harper & Row, 1982), pp. 114–24.

9. Some took decades longer to arrive: the Chinese-language files of the Legation were not sent back until 1959, and then amongst them were found the papers of Ye Mingchen's archive, captured in 1857; while the British Supreme Court records were rediscovered in 1981 lodged in the attic of the old consulate: David Pong, *A Critical Guide to the Kwangtung Provincial Archives, Deposited at the Public Record Office of London* (Cambridge, MA: Harvard University Asia Center, 1975). As I revised this text for publication a large collection of *c.* 1890s consular land registration records for Shanghai came to light in the recesses of the Foreign and Commonwealth Office.

10. Fairbank, *Chinabound*, p. 21.

11. H. B. Morse, 'Prefatory Note', *The International Relations of the Chinese Empire*, i (London: Longmans, Green & Co., 1910) pp. vii–viii; John King Fairbank, Martha Henderson Coolidge, Richard J. Smith, *H. B. Morse: Customs commissioner and historian of China* (Lexington: University Press of Kentucky, 1995), pp. 220–22.

12. C. Martin Wilbur, *The Nationalist Revolution in China, 1923–1928* (Cambridge: Cambridge University Press, 1984).

13. Dong Wang, *China's Unequal Treaties: Narrating national history* (Lanham, MD: Lexington Books, 2005), pp. 37–41; William C. Kirby, 'The Internationalisation of China: Foreign relations at home and abroad in the republican era', *China Quarterly*, no. 150 (1997), pp. 433–58.

14. See, for example, Lanning's memorandum enclosed in Shanghai no. 77, 5 June 1913, explaining the history of the de Norman monument in the grounds of the Shanghai Consulate General: TNA, FO 228/1875. On the books, see Robert Bickers, *Britain in China: Community, culture and colonialism, 1900–49* (Manchester: Manchester University Press, 1999), p. 39, and the file 'History of Shanghai', SMA, U1-3-164.

15. O. D. Rasmussen, *Tientsin: An illustrated outline history* (Tianjin: Tientsin Press, Ltd., 1925); H. S. S., *Diary of Events and the Progress on Shameen, 1859–1938* (Hong Kong: Ye Old Printerie, 1938).

16. George Lanning and Samuel Couling, *The History of Shanghai* (Shanghai: Kelly & Walsh, 1923), ii, pp. 1–2.

17. Kiernan, *British Diplomacy in China*, p. 314.

18. 'A Forgotten British Embassy: Colonel Charles Cathcart', *Oriental Affairs*, June 1938, pp. 303–7, and September 1938, pp. 161–3. The stone survives today.

19. Xu Dishan (ed.), *Dazhong ji* [Arriving at the inner truth] (Shanghai: Shangwu yinshuguan, 1931).

20. Such as S. T. Wang's *The Margary Affair and the Chefoo Agreement* (London: Oxford University Press, 1940).

21. Collected as Shanghai tongshe (eds.), *Shanghai yanjiu ziliao* [Shanghai research materials; 1936], and *Shanghai yanjiu ziliao xubian* [Further Shanghai research materials; 1937], both reprinted in facsimile by Shanghai shudian in 1984. Clarifying Settlement claims was an avowed intent of Xu Gongsu and Qiu Jinzhang's *Shanghai gonggong zujie zhidu* [The system of the Shanghai International Settlement] in 1933, reprinted as *Shanghai gonggong zujie shigao* [Draft history of the Shanghai International Settlement] (Shanghai: Shanghai renmin chubanshe, 1980).

22. W. C. Costin, *Great Britain and China*, *1833–1860* (Oxford: Oxford University Press, 1937), p. 344.

23. Rana Mitter, *A Bitter Revolution: China's struggle with the modern world* (Oxford: Oxford University Press, 2004).

24. Marie-Claire Bergère, *Sun Yat-sen* (Stanford: Stanford University Press, 1998), pp. 360–65; John Fitzgerald, *Awakening China: Politics, culture, and class in the nationalist revolution* (Stanford: Stanford University Press, 1998), pp. 169–70; Wang, *China's Unequal Treaties*, pp. 64–6.

25. This process is the subject of Bickers, *Britain in China*.

26. See Karl Gerth, *China Made: Consumer culture and the creation of the nation* (Cambridge, MA: Harvard University Asia Center, 2004).

27. It did not also help that Mrs Morse, without cause, accused him of stealing materials from her husband, who died in 1934; pursuing her case and forcing Fairbank to rebut the charge: Fairbank to Farrer & Co., 12 November 1934, enclosed in Fairbank to Maze, 13 November 1935, Maze papers, SOAS, PPMS2 Confidential Letters and Reports Volume 10.

28. 'IGS and Confidential Letters to N. R. S.', IGS no. 4, 24 September 1939 enclosing copy of Maze to Wright, 24 September 1939, SHAC, 679(1), 31476.

29. Chan Lau Kit-ching, 'The Abrogation of British Extraterritoriality in China 1942–43: A study in Anglo-American-Chinese relations', *Modern Asian Studies* 11:2 (1977), pp. 257–91.

30. On this, see Antony Best, *Britain, Japan and Pearl Harbor: Avoiding war in East Asia, 1936–41* (London: Routledge, 1995), and Nicholas R. Clifford, *Retreat from China: British policy in the Far East 1937–1941* (Seattle: University of Washington Press, 1967).

31. For an encyclopaedic study, see Greg Leck, *Captives of Empire: The Japanese internment of allied civilians in China, 1941–1945* (Philadelphia: Shandy Press, 2006). Some 300 men were arrested in November 1942 as political prisoners and imprisoned. A few prominent figures had been arrested as anti-Japanese activists almost immediately after Pearl Harbor, but although their experiences at the hands of the Japanese Kempeitai were unpleasant, in relative terms the communities overall had a reasonable war. For two accounts, see H. G. W. Woodhead, 'The Japanese Occupation of Shanghai: Some personal experiences', Chatham House lecture, 21 November 1942, TNA, WO 208/378a, and J. B. Powell, *My Twenty-five Years in China* (New York: The Macmillan Company, 1945).

32. On wartime, see e.g. Frederic Wakeman Jr, *The Shanghai Badlands: Wartime terrorism and urban crime* (Cambridge: Cambridge University Press, 1996); Bernard Wasserstein, *Secret War in Shanghai: Treachery, subversion and collaboration in the Second World War* (London: Profile Books, 1998).

33. Letter from Lord Killearn to Sir O. Sargent, 11 June 1946, F9715/25/10, reproduced in S. R. Ashton, G. Bennett and K. A. Hamilton (eds.), *Documents on British Policy Overseas, Series 1: viii, Britain and China, 1945–1950* (London: Whitehall History Publishing, 2002), p. 47. As Sir Miles Lampson, Killearn had been British Minister to China from 1926 to 1933.

34. On this phenomenon, see James L. Hevia, 'Remembering the Century of Humiliation: The Yuanmingyuan and Dagu museums', in Sheila Miyoshi Jager and Rana Mitter (eds.), *Ruptured Histories: War, memory, and post-Cold War Asia* (Cambridge, MA: Harvard University Press, 2007), pp. 192–208; Zheng Wang, 'National Humiliation, History Education, and the Politics of Historical Memory: Patriotic education campaign in China', *International Studies* 52:4 (2008), pp. 783–806; William A. Callahan, *China: The pessoptimist nation* (Oxford: Oxford University Press, 2009).

35. Chin-chuan Lee, *Global Media Spectacle: News war over Hong Kong* (Albany: State University of New York Press, 2002) outlines much of this, and also places it in useful wider contexts.

36. See, for example, Zhu Yong, *Buyuan dakai de Zhongguo damen: 18 shijie de waijiao yu Zhongguo mingyun* [China's closed door: the diplomacy of the eighteenth century and China's destiny] (Nanchang: Jiangxi renmin chubanshe, 1989); Mao Haijian, *Tianchao de bengkui: Yapian zhanzheng zai yanjiu* [Collapse of the Celestial Empire: A reanalysis of the Opium War] (Beijing: Sanlian shudian, 1995).

Index

Numbers in **bold** indicate maps or plates; numbers followed by 'n' indicate notes. Subheadings are arranged in chronological order.